THE PEOPLE'S CONSTITUTION

THE PEOPLE'S CONSTITUTION

200 Years, 27 Amendments, and the
Promise of a More Perfect Union

John F. Kowal
and
Wilfred U. Codrington III

NEW YORK
LONDON

Requests for permission to reproduce selections from this book should
be made through our website: https://thenewpress.com/contact.

Published in the United States by The New Press, New York, 2021
Distributed by Two Rivers Distribution

ISBN 978-1-62097-561-9 (hc)
ISBN 978-1-62097-562-6 (ebook)
CIP data is available.

The New Press publishes books that promote and enrich public discussion and
understanding of the issues vital to our democracy and to a more equitable world.
These books are made possible by the enthusiasm of our readers; the support of
a committed group of donors, large and small; the collaboration of our many
partners in the independent media and the not-for-profit sector; booksellers, who
often hand-sell New Press books; librarians; and above all by our authors.

www.thenewpress.com

Composition by dix!
This book was set in Fairfield LH

Printed in the United States of America

2   4   6   8   10   9   7   5   3   1

Contents

Notes to the Reader

First, a few notes on sources. This book has benefited greatly from the work of historians and legal scholars who blazed the trail before us. At the same time, we also rely heavily on original primary sources. In some instances, particularly in the early periods covered by this book, there is little or no primary source record. We try to indicate in the text where this is the case including, most notably, in early congressional records.

A special note is warranted concerning the records from the 1787 Philadelphia Convention, which produced the Constitution's original draft. While several delegates took notes, the most complete record by far is found in James Madison's *Notes of Debates in the Federal Convention of 1787*. Countless scholars have relied on his daily recordkeeping, which provides the best account of the delegates' speeches, debates, votes, and the proceedings in general. As the last surviving delegate from the convention, Madison revised his notes extensively prior to their publication in 1836, four years after his death. Some of those revisions appear to correspond with how he desired to be viewed by his contemporaries and in posterity, including his positions on controversial issues related to federalism and slavery. The reader should therefore be aware that his extraordinary record of the convention may not fully reflect his or others' contemporaneous thinking.

Relatedly, some historical sources—including Madison's notes—adhere to outmoded and non-uniform writing conventions. For example, they contain arcane words, inconsistent spelling, and the awkward use of capitalization, punctuation, abbreviations, and other grammatical departures. For the sake of clarity, we have taken the privilege of making small adjustments to modernize the prose while remaining loyal to the intent of the original authors.

Second, a note about our own conventions. Throughout the book, we have capitalized Framer when referring to those who drafted the original Constitution, but not those who were responsible for the various amendments that followed. This is not intended to diminish the successive generations of framers or to devalue the importance of their work that has improved our national charter. Rather, it is to make clear for the reader when we are referring to that first cohort versus the ones that followed. Also, we have decided to capitalize the word *Black* when describing persons of African ancestry. This is our small attempt to acknowledge both the dignity and respect due to those to whom dignity and respect were long denied. Some sources have recently begun to make changes to their own editorial style guides in adherence with this convention. We applaud this choice, and hope that others will emulate it.

Finally, this book uses the words *Black* and *African American* interchangeably with one caveat: we have opted to use the former exclusively in our account prior to the Reconstruction Era. This decision was made in acknowledgment of the fact that our early laws, institutions, and customs all too frequently withheld fundamental citizenship rights from this group. While the injustice persisted even after the Reconstruction Era, the significance of that period's amendments—particularly the Fourteenth Amendment—cannot be overstated for their long-overdue recognition of their citizenship and enshrining their rights permanently into our national charter. Similarly, we refer to those who resided on this continent prior to European settlement as Indigenous people, understanding (though not fully) the complexity of their relationship with the U.S. government that continues to this day. Chapter Three opens with a riff on the famous line in William Shakespeare's *Romeo and Juliet*: "What's in a name?" In truth, the answer is "a lot." Names, words, titles, and other identifiers are important; they can reflect pain and struggle, purpose and power, and so much more. To these subordinated groups and others who, like the Bard's "rose," would "by any other name . . . smell as sweet," we hope our that word choices will convey the respect that you deserve.

THE PEOPLE'S
CONSTITUTION

Introduction

Who wrote the United States Constitution?

The answer *seems* easy enough. One can visit the National Archives in Washington, DC, where the original parchment pages of America's national charter are preserved for posterity in argon gas–filled encasements of titanium and glass.[1] There Americans are invited to "meet the Framers of the Constitution"—the fifty-five men in powdered wigs who met in Philadelphia over the summer of 1787, representing twelve of the original thirteen states.[2] Some of the delegates to America's constitutional convention are known to every American: George Washington, the widely revered hero of the Revolution who left a comfortable retirement to preside over the deliberations and ultimately over the nation's affairs as its first chief executive; James Madison, the visionary scholar-politician whose energy and erudition made him the convention's driving force; and Benjamin Franklin, the ailing elder statesman who lent his unique prestige to soothe passions and cultivate a spirit of compromise. Other participants, like twenty-six-year-old Jonathan Dayton, described by a peer as a promising "young gentleman of talents" still mastering the fine points of public speaking, or William Houstoun, a nobleman's son with a "mind very little improved with useful or elegant knowledge," are little remembered today, except as the obscure namesakes of suburban high schools and city thoroughfares.[3]

These Framers traveled to Philadelphia to shore up a weak and dysfunctional political system established under the Articles of Confederation, America's first attempt at a national charter. Their mandate: "establishing in these states a firm national government."[4] Over four months, from the flowering of the chestnut trees in May to the first turning of the sugar maples in September, the debates at the Philadelphia Convention ranged from the finer points of comparative law and Enlightenment theory to the day's most divisive issues: taxation, voting, commerce, slavery. At every step, clashing interests pitted the large states against the small, the North against the South. Some delegates walked away from the deliberations in dismay, others for personal reasons. But those who remained, working in a room sealed shut to protect against eavesdroppers, forged a bold new plan of government. It was, fundamentally, a document based on compromise. Compromises between champions of a strong centralized government and those committed to robust state sovereignty. Compromises between defenders of slavery and those who professed to abhor it. Compromises between idealists who imagined a government elected "by the people" and skeptical elitists eager to counter the "excesses of democracy."

The Constitution they crafted was a remarkable achievement for its time. By providing the national government with powers it lacked under the Articles of Confederation, the Framers made sure the American people could act collectively to address pressing national problems. In a notable innovation, they divided these powers among three branches of government—legislative, executive, and judicial—with distinct roles and overlapping responsibilities. This carefully calibrated structure, based on the principle of separation of powers, was designed to prevent dangerous concentrations of power through "the proper checks and balances between the different departments."[5] At the same time, the new federal government would share power with the pre-existing state governments. Leaving a strong role for the states through the principle of federalism, America's distinctive system of dual sovereignty was intended as yet another check on the undue accretion of power—"a double security" for the people, as James Madison put it.[6]

It's the world's most enduring written national constitution. But though Americans in every generation have mythologized the story of the Philadelphia Convention—Thomas Jefferson memorably called it an "assembly of demigods"[7]—the drafters of the Constitution were fallible men, steeped in the values and worldview of a time long past. Though they subscribed to the creed that "all men are created equal," nearly half of them owned slaves. Most took it as a given that only men of property, like themselves, could possess the civic virtue necessary for self-governance. None could imagine a world in which women were truly equal, with rights independent of their husbands and fathers. So it should come as no surprise that the plan they crafted had its shortcomings.

For starters, the Framers' plan of government was antidemocratic in key respects, designed to shield politicians from popular pressure.[8] They delegated the power to choose our presidents to a small group of intermediaries we know as the Electoral College. In similar fashion, they left it to state legislatures to choose senators. In the Framers' republic, only members of the House of Representatives would be chosen by the people themselves. But which people? In their wisdom, the Framers failed to recognize a right to vote, leaving it to each state to determine voter qualifications. Through our entire history, even *today*, states have exercised this power to exclude women, African Americans, Indigenous people, immigrants, religious minorities, and others from equal participation in our democracy. As originally written, the Constitution also provided scant protection for individual rights and liberties against government abuse—a deficiency many saw as dangerous. Most appallingly, the Framers' Constitution scrupulously accommodated slavery, enabling the brutal subjugation of millions of Black people to flourish in America for another three quarters of a century.

The Framers never imagined their new plan of government would be perfect. Just two weeks into the proceedings in Philadelphia, George Mason, one of the project's leading skeptics, predicted that the new plan of government "will certainly be defective," just as the Articles of Confederation had proved to be. "Amendments therefore will be necessary," he posited, "and it will be better to provide for them in an easy, regular and Constitutional way than to trust to chance and violence."[9] Mason's point was well taken: to avoid the dysfunction and gridlock that hobbled governance under the Articles, the new governing charter would need a viable method of revision.

The process they devised, the amending "two-step," is set forth in a provision of the Constitution called Article V. The first step in the process is *proposing* an amendment. Article V specifies two means of doing this. The most familiar option, the method used to advance every amendment to date, requires Congress to propose an amendment by a two-thirds vote in each house. As an alternative, two-thirds of the state legislatures can petition Congress to call a convention for the purpose of proposing amendments. This latter method has been the subject of furious controversy throughout our history. Despite a few close calls, there has never been an Article V constitutional convention.

In a second step, once Congress or a convention has proposed one, it is up to the states to *ratify* the amendment. Again, Article V lays out two alternative paths. Congress may ask the state legislatures to approve the measure, the most commonly used method by far, or it may call on each state to organize a convention for this purpose—a process used only once, when Congress fast-tracked the repeal of Prohibition via the Twenty-First Amendment. When three-fourths of the states (currently, thirty-eight of fifty) lend their assent by one of these two methods, the amendment becomes part of our Constitution.

Through this process, much of the Constitution was written *after* 1787 in a series of twenty-seven amendments adopted over the course of two centuries. Of course, it would be a stretch to describe this complicated procedure—one that sets the high bar of winning supermajority support *twice*—as "easy" or "regular," as Mason urged. Out of more than twelve thousand additions and revisions put forward since the Constitution was adopted, Congress has managed to send just thirty-three amendments to the states for their consideration.[10] Of these, only twenty-seven secured the three-fourths support among the states needed to be ratified and incorporated into our national charter. Throughout our history, this meager success rate has bred a sense of futility. As far back as 1888, the *Washington Post* informed its readers that the Constitution was "virtually unchangeable," leaving the nation "under the control of unamendable fundamental laws made by a few men whose dust has long since been 'mingled with the elements.'"[11] A half century later, President Franklin Roosevelt cited the "impossibility" of resolving by constitutional amendment his fight with the "nine old men" of the Supreme Court over the legality of his New Deal programs. "It is, of course, clear," Roosevelt said, "that any determined minority group in the nation could, without great difficulty, block ratification by one means or another in at least thirteen states for a long period of time."[12]

This pessimistic view prevails among experts today. "The U.S. Constitution is best understood as *constructively* unamendable," argues University of Texas law professor Richard Albert, because its text "gives the mistaken impression that everything is freely amendable, but really nothing today is amendable."[13] His colleague Sanford Levinson, another leading expert on the topic, says that "as a practical matter, though, Article V makes it next to impossible to amend the Constitution with regard to genuinely controversial issues, even if substantial—and intense—majorities advocate amendment."[14]

This raises an important question: If the drafters of Article V were pragmatists who understood that America needed a national charter that could adapt to the needs and values of future generations, why did they make the process so difficult? As we will see, the Framers appear to have spent little time discussing the pros and cons of the amending procedure. To ensure that the Constitution would endure through changing times, they intended that it be amendable. But to lock in the political compromises that made the Constitution possible, they made sure it would not be *too* amendable. As James Madison put it, the two-step procedure of Article V was meant to strike a balance. It would guard against "that extreme facility, which would render the Constitution too mutable," while avoiding "that extreme difficulty, which might perpetuate its discovered faults."[15]

Did they get this balance right? It's hard to disagree with the blunt assessment offered by University of Chicago legal scholar Eric Posner. "The founders blundered," Posner says. "They made passing an amendment too hard."[16] Compared with state constitutions and those of other democratic nations, the U.S. Constitution is considered to be among the most difficult in the world to amend.[17] And yet, Harvard law professor Vicki Jackson offers a more optimistic view. "There is no question that the US amendment procedures are difficult," she concedes. But difficult does not mean impossible. A "myth of impossibility of amendment," Jackson argues, can be "self-reinforcing," making us "too reluctant to resort to popular democratic processes" to fix the Constitution and "too reliant on seeking constitutional change through other means," such as the courts. This disempowered view can only result, over time, in "a diminution in the Constitution's democratic legitimacy."[18] As it happens, previous generations of Americans have overcome this sense of resignation to put their imprint on our national charter through the amending procedure of Article V.

The People's Constitution tells the story of how the American people took an imperfect Constitution—the product of compromises and an artifact of its time—and, despite all obstacles, made it more democratic, more inclusive, and more responsive to the needs of a changing country through the constitutional amendment process. Some of these additions to the Framers' original Constitution have wrought profound changes to America's fundamental law: safeguarding individual liberties, ending slavery, expanding access to the ballot, upholding equality. Others are best described as technical fixes. But when we consider the twenty-seven amendments to the Constitution as a whole, it is no exaggeration to say that much of what we consider the very heart of our national charter—from its protections for free speech and religion to its guarantees of due process and equal protection of the laws—derive not from the 4,543 words in the Framers' beta version of our national charter, but rather from the 3,000 words added in periodic upgrades. It's the story of how We the People have improved our government's structure and expanded our democracy during eras of transformational social change.

In this book, you will meet the Constitution's original Framers—but also its many *other* framers: the visionaries and gadflies whose passion and perseverance helped ensure that our national charter could change with the times through periodic infusions of popular input. They include George Mason, the "forgotten founder" and modern conservative icon, whose refusal to sign a Constitution that lacked protections for individual liberties—a cover to extract changes to the new government's design—prodded a reluctant James Madison to champion the Bill of Rights.[19] John Bingham, the "Father of the Fourteenth Amendment," whose enduring achievement was rooted in a deeply held belief in a Constitution "based upon the equality of the human race."[20] Susan B. Anthony, the indefatigable feminist pioneer whose lifetime of campaigning to win women the right to vote, "60 years of hard struggle for a little liberty" as she put it, was vindicated after her death by adoption of the Nineteenth Amendment—the only words in our national charter not written by men.[21] And Birch Bayh, the "one-man constitutional reform machine" who earned the distinction of being the only lawmaker since Madison to author more than a single amendment.[22]

A close look at this history reveals an intriguing pattern. In recurring cycles, bursts of energy that add several new amendments in the span of a few years are followed by decades-long dry spells. During these periods of stasis, when the nation seems to lose its appetite for Article V solutions, the battle over the meaning and promise of the Constitution continues to be waged in the judicial arena and in the push and pull of politics. Over time, as the pressure builds, the tectonic plates eventually shift to produce the next seismic burst of amending activity.[23] In this way, our national charter has been revitalized—and its promise renewed—in four distinct waves of constitutional change.

The first ten amendments, the Bill of Rights, adopted in one bundle in

1791, united Americans in support of our fledgling Constitution by reassuring skeptics that a robust national government could be tempered by respect for individual rights. After the cataclysm of the Civil War, three transformative Reconstruction Amendments adopted between 1865 and 1870 promised a "second founding" that guaranteed equal citizenship and voting rights to newly freed African Americans while imposing significant new limits on the states. From 1909 to 1920, amid the heady modernizing zeal of the Progressive Era, Americans made four bold additions to the national charter: authorizing the federal income tax, providing for the popular election of senators, extending the franchise to women, and launching the idealistic (if ultimately disastrous) experiment of Prohibition. Finally, as the Civil Rights Era crested between 1960 and 1971, Americans added four amendments, decidedly less ambitious, to expand voting rights and modernize presidential succession for the nuclear age.

As this book reveals, the history of how Americans have gradually improved an imperfect Constitution through the Article V amending process has been, for the most part, an inspiring story of progressive legal change, driven by powerful social movements and an evolving array of civil society organizations. But ever since the 1970s, when the Equal Rights Amendment was thwarted by a demagogic campaign that presaged a sharp swing to the right in the nation's politics, progressives have pulled back. For nearly four decades, they have been unwilling to invest much energy into constitutional fixes. Faced with the myriad ailments plaguing our democracy today—from the democratic deficiencies of the Electoral College system of picking our presidents to the corrupting role of campaign cash in the age of *Citizens United*—only a few hardy reformers see much value in cranking up the unwieldy mechanism of Article V to repair a Constitution that too often fails to meet today's needs.

In the meantime, over that same period the right has seized the mantle of constitutional reform in a manner that has no precedent in American history. In Congress, conservative Republicans have pressed for a dizzying array of amendments to advance the right's policy goals in areas that include budget policy, term limits, flag desecration, marriage, and more. In the state capitals, activists have waged campaigns to trigger the first constitutional convention since 1787, opening the door to potentially drastic changes in the Constitution. Despite some close calls, those efforts have all fallen short for now.

Does this prove that our Constitution is no longer amendable? Or will this period of remission give way, as others have in the past, to a new period of ferment? In today's contentious and fractured politics, it may seem impossible to imagine the forging of the broad consensus needed to pass a constitutional amendment under the rules of Article V anytime soon. But we have been here before. If past is prologue, we are due for a new wave of constitutional change in the coming years.

1

An Imperfect Constitution

Today many Americans credit, even revere, the Framers of the Constitution as men of great wisdom and foresight. A bestselling history of the Constitutional Convention of 1787 went so far as to hail their handiwork as the "Miracle at Philadelphia."[1] It's true that the Framers bequeathed us a Constitution that has endured for more than 230 years. It's also true that, despite many serious shortcomings and omissions, our founding document has allowed a great democracy to grow and flourish and evolve with the times. But what most people overlook is that many Americans at the time saw the Constitution as a great betrayal. Crafted in what outraged opponents derided as a "secret conclave," the new charter divided the country.[2]

To be sure, countless Americans welcomed the formation of a new national government that could serve as the foundation for a "more perfect Union": one nation, strong, prosperous, and free. Others, however, with long memories of the abuses of King George III, worried that a powerful national government, ruling from a distant capital, would endanger their hard-won liberties. For them, decentralized governance was the surest defense against tyranny. Patrick Henry, the revolutionary patriot who would emerge as the Constitution's most implacable foe, spoke for many when he excoriated the Framers for their audacity. "Who authorized them to speak the language of, *We, the People*, instead of *We, the States*?" he demanded.[3] This fight over the Constitution's meaning and purpose persists to this day.

Why did the Framers create a plan of government that so many Americans viewed as dangerous? To answer this question, we need to understand the crisis of governance that enveloped thirteen loosely bonded states in the late 1780s.

America's First National Charter

By 1787, the Articles of Confederation, America's first national charter, was collapsing under the weight of its many faults. Forged in the crucible of revolution, more an alliance among independent states than a real constitution, the Articles established a weak national government that by its own terms aspired to be nothing more than "a firm league of friendship."[4] In the highly unrepresentative Confederation Congress, each state had an equal vote no matter its size.[5] And on the most important questions, which required amending the Articles, each state wielded a veto.[6] It soon proved to be a recipe for gridlock.

In the summer of 1776, just weeks after severing their ties to the most formidable military power in the world, a committee of luminaries went to work to devise a suitable form of government for what the signers of the Declaration of Independence pointedly referred to as thirteen "free and independent States."[7] From the start, a contentious debate over representation in the new national legislature paralyzed the drafting process, presaging a fight that would consume negotiations over a new Constitution eleven years later: how to divide power in a confederation comprised of states of varying size and population.

Representatives of the most populous states stood for the principle of proportional representation. "We stand here as the representatives of the people," declared Massachusetts delegate (and future president) John Adams. "In some states the people are many, in others they are few; . . . therefore their vote here should be proportioned to the numbers from whom it comes."[8] But delegates from states with smaller populations objected, demanding that each state be represented equally. "If an equal vote be refused," cried John Knox Witherspoon, representing New Jersey, "the smaller states will become vassals to the larger."[9] The impasse delayed the drafting process for over a year.

Finally, in November 1777, after advancing British troops forced the evacuation of Philadelphia, one of a series of temporary capitals, the negotiators acceded to the demands of the smaller states. Each state would have an equal vote in the new Confederation Congress. Elbridge Gerry, the Massachusetts politician famous today as the namesake of the word *gerrymander,* blamed "the obstinacy of the lesser states" for a result he never stopped resenting.[10] And yet, despite this concession, it would still take more than three years to secure the approval of all thirteen states. The Articles of Confederation did not go into effect until March 1781—six years into the war—when Maryland, the last holdout, signed on.[11]

In thirteen numbered sections, the Articles provided a bare framework for governance. The national government's few powers were "expressly delegated" in the document, largely confined to the arenas of war and foreign policy.[12] While the Confederation Congress had the responsibility for paying the national government's debts, it had no independent power to raise revenue through taxes. Instead it had to ask the states to supply funds through an unworkable system of "requisitions," with no means of compelling delinquent states to pay.[13] The national government similarly lacked the power to regulate domestic and foreign commerce. There was no independent chief executive to enforce the laws, and no national judiciary to resolve disputes over them. It was minimalist government, threatening America's very existence as a united and viable nation. Each state jealously retained its "sovereignty, freedom, and independence, and every power, jurisdiction, and right."[14] That included a state's right to print its own money, charge its own import duties, and conduct its own foreign policy.

An onerous amendment process only compounded the problem. Under its terms, "any alteration" to the Articles had to be "confirmed by the legislatures of every state."[15] It soon became clear that giving each state a veto over proposed changes was a fatal mistake, rendering the Articles effectively unamendable. Not that it stopped lawmakers from trying. Recognizing that the weakness of the national government threatened the fledgling republic's security, the Confederation Congress recommended numerous amendments to expand its powers, yet not one of these sorely needed fixes could win the unanimous support of all thirteen states.[16] In 1781, for instance, with the conflict with Britain in its sixth year, lawmakers sought the "indispensably necessary" power to levy a tax on imports to pay the nation's ballooning war debt.[17] Though twelve states supported this sensible measure, tiny Rhode Island refused, unwilling to give up the income it enjoyed from customs duties imposed at its ports. A prominent Virginian expressed astonishment "that one little state can stop so important an object, against the opinion of all the others."[18] Lawmakers revived the measure in 1783. With the fighting now over, a plan to pay down the war debt grew ever more urgent, but the proposal fell short again. While Rhode Island was persuaded this time around, New York—which had a lucrative port of its own—blocked the measure.[19] In this way, time and again, one state's self-interest stood in the way of changes the nation required.

As James Madison contemplated the unfolding crisis of governance, he felt a sense of alarm. The scion of a large Virginia plantation that thrived on the labor of more than a hundred slaves, the thirty-six-year-old Madison "retained the air of a perennial student."[20] Though he had a keen intellect and a passion for political theory, he was shy and soft-spoken with "a small and delicate form"[21]—more policy wonk than politico.[22] After three years representing Virginia in the Confederation Congress, Madison believed that the Confederation was doomed to failure. Writing to his friend George Washington, he complained of the "caprice, jealousy and diversity of situations" among the states. With new states already seeking to join the fractious original thirteen, Madison worried that "the difficulty now found in obtaining a unanimous concurrence of the states in any measure whatever, must continually increase."[23] The esteemed former general, who in retirement had hoped to remain aloof from politics, had concerns of his own. Monitoring developments from his plantation at Mount Vernon, he cringed at the sight of "a half starved, limping government, that appears to be always moving upon crutches, and tottering at every step."[24]

"Adequate to the Exigencies of the Union"

Something had to be done. The Virginia legislature proposed that the states meet in Annapolis, Maryland, in September 1786 to consider amendments giving the national government greater power over interstate commerce.[25] It proved to be another disappointment: after only twelve men representing five states showed up, the participants abruptly terminated the gathering.[26] But in one of history's great turning points, they used the occasion to express their "urgent and unanimous wish" for a new convention to meet in Philadelphia in May 1787.[27] In a joint communique, the delegates to the Annapolis Convention warned that "important defects in the system of the federal government" were "of a nature so serious, as . . . to render the situation of the United States delicate and critical." With "unanimous conviction," they urged the states to send delegates to Philadelphia "to devise such further provisions as shall appear to them necessary to render the constitution of the federal government adequate to the exigencies of the Union."[28]

In the ensuing months, Madison conducted an energetic campaign to make the Philadelphia Convention a success. He persuaded Washington to come out of retirement to lend his uniquely influential presence to the proceedings.[29] To inform the deliberations, he delved into a dizzying array of research topics—from Enlightenment political theory to the history of confederations in antiquity—poring over crates of books shipped to him from Paris by his friend Thomas Jefferson.[30] Determined to avoid another poor showing, Madison prodded each state to send a delegation. Twelve states would ultimately do so; only obstinate Rhode Island refused.[31] The state's parochial political leaders had no interest in ceding powers over trade, taxation, the printing of money, or much of anything to the national government. "Nothing can exceed the wickedness and folly which continue to reign there,"[32] Madison believed. Later, though, he would see a bright side to Rhode Island's absence. "If her deputies should bring with them the complexion of the state," he reckoned, "their company will not add much to our pleasure, or to the progress of the business."[33]

One potential obstacle was the Confederation Congress. When Madison sought its blessing for the planned gathering in Philadelphia, he encountered opposition. As the Confederation's secretary of war recounted in a letter to Washington, some members protested that the Articles did not explicitly provide for this "irregular assembly."[34] They had a point. The Articles authorized only one mode of revision: the Confederation Congress proposed amendments and the states confirmed them by a unanimous vote.[35] In the end, however, the lawmakers assented to a convention "for the sole and express purpose of revising the Articles of Confederation," moved by a growing sense that the national government would not last much longer without significant reform. Putting aside their doubts, they recognized that a convention, however irregular, appeared to be "the most probable mean[s] of establishing in these states a firm national government." When its work was done, the convention was instructed to report back to Congress and the state legislatures.[36]

All the while, Madison had a more radical plan in mind. In February 1787, as Congress lent its grudging approval, he confided in a missive to Washington that he intended to press for "a thorough reform of the existing system."[37] Washington liked Madison's bold way of thinking. He too was ready to "probe the defects of the Constitution to the bottom, and provide radical cures, whether they are agreed to or not."[38]

In his eagerness, Madison was the first delegate to arrive, reaching

Philadelphia on May 5.[39] As others converged on the city, he eagerly sought out kindred spirits. George Mason was one potential ally. At sixty-one, the slave-owning tobacco planter was one of the oldest delegates.[40] Though he had "little formal education," Mason was well versed in history, law, and philosophy.[41] In May 1776, he earned renown as the principal author of Virginia's pathbreaking Declaration of Rights, an accomplishment that inspired Thomas Jefferson as he composed the Declaration of Independence just a few weeks later.[42] Still, Mason had little interest in public life. Afflicted for years with painful attacks of gout, he rarely ventured far from his home at Gunston Hall, bordering the Washington family plantation. Not long after his arrival in Philadelphia, he penned a letter to his son noting that "the most prevalent idea" among the delegates from the big states was the "total alteration of the present federal system."[43]

Once the proceedings started, it was clear that the fifty-five men representing twelve states who would attend at least some part of the Philadelphia Convention brought diverging views and biases. (As the delegates came and went, there were never more than eleven states represented at any given time). It did not take long for tensions to rise. On May 29, Virginia proposed a set of fifteen resolutions calling for the Articles of Confederation to be "corrected and enlarged."[44] Madison had sketched out the framework in the weeks leading up to the convention. But it was Edmund Randolph, Virginia's energetic young governor, who had the honor of unveiling it. The son of Loyalist parents who fled to England at the start of the war, Randolph advanced quickly in the elite world of Virginia politics as heir to a well-connected family. By the age of thirty-four, his résumé included stints as mayor of Williamsburg, state attorney general, and delegate to the Confederation Congress.[45]

The Virginia Plan, as it came to be known, provided a completely revamped framework for government organized in three distinct branches: a legislature with two houses, one "elected by the people" and the other appointed; a chief executive appointed by the legislature, hewing to the practice in most states at the time; and an independent judiciary.[46] Lawmakers in the national legislature would have broad powers, including the ability to veto state laws.[47] Most controversially, "the rights of suffrage" in the legislature would be apportioned according to population, replacing the equal vote enjoyed by small states in the Confederation Congress.[48]

The plan signaled a decisive turn away from the "firm league of friendship" established by the Articles, wherein the states retained their independence and sovereignty, toward a federal system in which the na-tional government is supreme. As the delegates absorbed its many novel details, one "expressed a doubt" as to whether the Confederation Con-gress's limited mandate "could authorize a discussion of a system founded on different principles."[49] But thanks to the delegates' agreement to keep the convention's deliberations a secret, the American people would learn of the decision to scrap the Articles only months later when the new Con-stitution was unveiled for their consideration.

Over the next three and a half months, the delegates worked through seemingly irreconcilable conflicts under rules of procedure that gave each state's delegation a single vote on all contested questions, replicating the disadvantage large states faced in the Confederation Congress. Advocates of a strong national government tussled with those who wanted to preserve the power of the states. Proponents of popular democracy contended with those skeptical of giving too much power to the people. Delegates from the South, determined to prevent any interference with slavery, fought with Northerners, who opposed concessions that might strengthen the insti-tution. As a result, the Constitution they constructed was the product of compromises that left none of the delegates completely satisfied.

The first big fight pitted the larger states, which embraced the Virginia Plan's scheme of proportional representation, against the smaller states, determined to preserve their equal suffrage in the national legislature. The impasse over these competing visions—a government *of the people* versus a government *of the states*—dominated the first two months of the conven-tion, kindling animosities that nearly scuttled the entire enterprise.

"We the People" or "We the States"?

Virginia had an obvious interest in allocating seats in the national legisla-ture on the basis of population. The Old Dominion was by far the largest of the thirteen original states with a populace approaching 750,000, in-cluding nearly 300,000 slaves. That was nearly a fifth of the entire nation's population. By contrast, Delaware, the smallest state, had only 59,000 inhabitants, nearly 9,000 of whom were held in bondage.[50] Today we un-derstand proportional representation as a core democratic ideal grounded in the principle of "one person, one vote."[51] Back in 1787, however, the delegates from the smaller states were not about to give up the benefits of the "one state, one vote" system that enhanced their influence in the

Confederation Congress. "What, pray, is intended by a proportional representation?" asked William Paterson, a delegate from New Jersey. "Upon the whole, every sovereign state according to a confederation must have an equal vote, or there is an end to liberty."[52] George Read agreed, announcing that Delaware's delegates were "restrained by their commission from assenting to any change of the rule of suffrage."[53]

On behalf of the more populous states, Madison framed the matter as a simple question of fairness: "departing from justice in order to conciliate the smaller states and the minority of the people of the United States" or "justly gratifying the larger states and the majority of the people."[54] Given the short, unhappy history of the Confederation, delegates from the large states were determined to be "justly gratified" this time. Considerations of equity aside, the battle would also settle a crucial question: Would the United States be forged into a single nation, or would it continue as one (or more) confederations of sovereign and independent states?[55]

On June 15, two weeks after Randolph introduced the Virginia Plan, the small states countered with a proposal of their own, offering only modest revisions to the Articles of Confederation. The New Jersey Plan would grant the national legislature added powers to raise revenue and regulate trade. It would create a multimember executive elected by Congress along with a federal judiciary. And it would recognize the acts and treaties of Congress as "the supreme law." But the plan's key feature was conspicuous by its absence. Under the New Jersey Plan, the formula for representation in the Confederation Congress would remain just as it was. Large states and small would continue to have one vote each.[56]

The convention deadlocked for six weeks over the two competing plans. To gain an edge, the large-state backers of proportional representation entered into a cynical bargain with delegations from the slave states. As originally proposed, the Virginia Plan offered two formulas for apportioning legislative seats: according to "the number of free inhabitants" in each state or according to states' "quotas of contribution" to the federal government.[57] Delegates from the South, who wanted slaves to count the same as free persons, were drawn to the latter approach.[58] "Money is power," said South Carolina delegate Pierce Butler. "States ought to have weight in the government in proportion to their wealth."[59] Northerners, for their part, wanted to avoid the counting of slaves entirely. Out of these competing positions came a deal. Under the "three-fifths compromise," introduced on June 11, representation in the legislature would be based on "the whole number of white and other free Citizens and inhabitants of every age, sex and condition," *plus* "three fifths of all other persons." The representation formula excluded "Indians not taxed," living under the jurisdiction of a tribe.[60]

Representing Massachusetts, a state whose 1780 constitution declared that "all men are born free and equal,"[61] was Elbridge Gerry, who historian Richard Beeman describes as "instinctively opposed to an excessively strong central government." The Boston-area politician who would emerge as one of the Constitution's "most persistent and caustic critics"[62] greeted the proposal with scorn. "Why then should the blacks, who were property in the South, be in the rule of representation more than the cattle and horses of the North?" he demanded.[63] Over Gerry's objection, the measure passed by a vote of nine state delegations to two.[64] For the next seven decades, the controversial three-fifths rule, the first of several provisions in the Constitution legitimizing slavery, would give states with large slave populations enhanced political power even as they denied enslaved people any political rights and considered them chattel rather than citizens.[65]

That same day, Roger Sherman of Connecticut offered a third plan of representation, seeking a middle ground between the polarized positions of the large and small states. In what would come to be known as the Connecticut Compromise, Sherman offered to split the difference: one house of the legislature would be elected by the people through a system of proportional representation, the other would be chosen by the state legislatures with equal representation for each state.[66] While delegates from the small states quickly embraced this solution, representatives of the larger states refused to budge for an additional month. Finally, on July 16, nearing the brink of dissolution, the convention rallied around the Connecticut Compromise by the narrowest of votes, five states to four.[67] The deal sealed the creation of the House of Representatives and the Senate as we know them today.

Once again, the smaller states held firm to win the one concession that mattered most to them, unmoved by the larger states' claim of unfairness. "It became necessary . . . to compromise," recalled Alexander Hamilton as New Yorkers debated whether to ratify the Constitution, "or the convention must have dissolved without effecting anything."[68]

It was a consequential decision that reverberates to this day. No one could foresee back in 1787, when Virginia was twelve times larger than Delaware, the smallest state, how unequal representation in the upper house would become over time. Today the ratio of population between California and Wyoming is an astounding sixty-eight to one. The twelve smallest states, with about five percent of the population, now elect about a quarter of the chamber's members.[69] By 2040 it is estimated that half of all Americans will live in eight states with only sixteen senators to represent them.[70] It's a disturbing disparity that law professor Sanford Levinson rightly calls "a travesty of the democratic ideal."[71]

Compromises over Federalism

Another fault line dividing the convention was the proper scope of the national government's powers. To one degree or another, the delegates all understood that the country needed more effective governance than it had under the Articles of Confederation. Some believed this could be accomplished through minor tweaks to the Articles to expand Congress's powers. But Madison wanted none of that. He envisioned a strong national government with greatly reduced autonomy for the states.

Alexander Hamilton, one of Madison's principal allies, was willing to go even further. In a lengthy oration, the charismatic New Yorker proposed an extreme solution. Displaying great erudition, drawing on the experience of federations from classical Greece to eighteenth-century Europe, he argued that "all federal governments are weak and distracted." There could be only one course of action, he said: "To avoid the evils deducible from these observations, we must establish a general and national government, completely sovereign, and annihilate the state distinctions and state operations."[72]

For the accomplished orator, the speech was a rare flop.[73] Most of the delegates saw the states as "absolutely necessary for certain purposes."[74] Others, less attached to the states' prerogatives, still saw the practical need to craft a charter the states would accept. Given these constraints, the delegates struggled to create a workable system that would establish a more robust central government while preserving a vital role for the states.[75] It was a vexing problem, but Madison, the shrewd political theorist, saw a way forward. Even before the delegates convened, he shared his early thinking on the matter in a letter to George Washington:

> Conceiving that an individual independence of the states is utterly irreconcilable with their aggregate sovereignty; and that a consolidation of the whole into one simple republic would be as inexpedient

as it is unattainable, I have sought for some middle ground, which may at once support a due supremacy of the national authority, and not exclude the local authorities wherever they can be subordinately useful.[76]

Grounded in this basic insight, the delegates forged our distinctively American version of federalism—Madison's "middle ground"—rooted in a system of dual sovereignty. Federal authority would be robust within an array of clearly defined powers, from coining money to regulating interstate commerce to raising armies. States would retain control over law and policy on a much broader set of issues that touch people's lives every day, from criminal justice to contracts to family law. When these powers conflicted, federal law would be supreme. At the same time, states would help shape the composition of the national government through provisions giving state legislatures the power to choose senators and presidential electors (although, over time, this last part of the bargain slowly unraveled as the people demanded the right to make those choices themselves at the ballot box).

In forging these compromises, delegates favoring a vigorous national government had the upper hand at every stage of the deliberations. To quote the memorable refrain from Lin-Manuel Miranda's hit musical, *Hamilton*, this was largely due to who was "in the room where it happened." Some of the country's most renowned champions of states' rights, including Samuel Adams of Massachusetts and Patrick Henry of Virginia, declined to attend the convention. Later, as the summer wore on, delegates dismayed by the push for greater national power left before the proceedings concluded. Some, like Maryland's Luther Martin and New York's Robert Yates, would emerge as the Constitution's fiercest opponents in the state ratification contests to come. But their absence at key decision points made it easier for the nationalists to mold a Constitution more to their liking.[77]

That said, proponents of a strong national government did not get everything they wanted. Throughout the convention, Madison aggressively pushed for a provision giving Congress the power to veto (or "negative") state laws, as previewed in the Virginia Plan. To his great frustration, the delegates repeatedly rejected the idea. While sympathetic, George Mason wondered how such a veto would work. Would the national legislature have to spend all its time reviewing state laws? Would every bridge and road be subject to review?[78] To others, the idea smacked too much of the arbitrary edicts of King George III.[79]

In deciding how much power to give to Congress, the delegates initially approved a resolution giving the national legislature broad power to legislate "in all cases for the general interests of the Union."[80] But a specially designated Committee of Detail, working to weave a multitude of preliminary decisions into a coherent first draft, opted to limit Congress to "enumerated" powers instead. These powers included specific authorizations to levy taxes, coin money, regulate commerce, and raise armies and navies, among many others.[81] Notably, the committee also gave Congress the accompanying power to make all laws "necessary and proper" to execute any of its enumerated ones.[82] This "sweeping clause," as it was also known, was a clear repudiation of the stingy delegation of "expressly delegated" powers under the Articles of Confederation.[83] While there was no recorded debate over the Necessary and Proper Clause at the convention, its broad scope would elicit fierce criticism in the ratification contest that followed.[84]

As we will see throughout this book, shifting understandings of America's unique system of federalism, rooted in the interplay of national and state governments, has been a long-running leitmotif in the American story. From the early tug-of-war over the drafting and ratification of the Constitution, to the divisions over race and slavery that propelled eleven states to form their own purported confederacy, to the fateful showdown between Franklin Delano Roosevelt and a retrograde Supreme Court over the nation's power to fix a broken economy, to today's calls for a "Convention of States" to limit federal power, Americans have always searched for the "correct" balance.

Compromises over Democracy

In the decade following independence, newly constituted state legislatures were stirring up controversy. Responding to a severe economic depression that followed the war, a generation of neophyte citizen lawmakers enacted legislation to protect hard-hit citizens by stopping foreclosures and relieving private debt burdens through the issuance of paper money.[85] All eyes were on Rhode Island, where lawmakers running on a platform "to relieve the distressed" passed laws requiring creditors to accept the state's devalued currency, then worth less than a quarter of its face value. If a creditor refused to accept it, the debt was extinguished.[86] The objectionable acts didn't stop there. As noted earlier, states were often delinquent when asked to requisition the funds Congress needed to pay down a massive war debt.

To the Framers, an assemblage of wealthy landholders and members of the economic elite,[87] these popularly elected legislatures seemed *too* responsive to the public will, threatening private property rights they considered to be sacred.[88] In the safe space of their meeting room, sealed from public scrutiny, they didn't mince words. "The people should have as little to do as may be about the government," said Roger Sherman. "They want [lack] information and are constantly liable to be misled."[89] Elbridge Gerry agreed: "The evils we experience flow from the excess of democracy," he said. "The people do not want virtue; but are the dupes of pretended patriots."[90]

To guard against an "excess of democracy," the Framers devised a plan of government that sought to temper majority rule with protections against populist overreach.[91] It was a feature, not a bug. In the Framers' original design, only the House of Representatives would be chosen directly "by the people of the several states."[92] Madison believed strongly that it was "essential to every plan of free government" that *one* house of the national government be chosen through popular election. Otherwise, he argued, "the people would be lost sight of altogether; and the necessary sympathy between them and their rulers and officers, too little felt."[93] A majority but by no means all of the delegates concurred.

But what did the Framers mean when they spoke of choosing representatives "by the people"? In most of the thirteen original states, the franchise was limited to male owners of property.[94] In more liberal jurisdictions, taxpayers in good standing could also cast a ballot.[95] Typically, elections for the lower house in state legislatures had more inclusive electorates. Elections for the upper house were more likely to be restricted to men of significant wealth.[96]

Most of the delegates saw property requirements as a salutary practice. "Give the votes to people who have no property, and they will sell them to the rich who will be able to buy them," warned Gouverneur Morris, a delegate representing Pennsylvania.[97] Delaware's John Dickinson agreed that limiting the franchise to owners of land was "a necessary defense against the dangerous influence of those multitudes without property and without principle."[98] But some delegates pointed to the practical difficulty of imposing a uniform voter qualification standard over a patchwork of state rules. "It would be very hard and disagreeable," said Pennsylvania delegate James Wilson, the convention's principled champion of popular democracy, "for the same persons, at the same time, to vote for representatives in the state legislature and to be excluded from a vote for those in the national legislature."[99] Oliver Ellsworth of Connecticut concurred: "The people will not readily subscribe to the national Constitution, if it should subject them to be disenfranchised."[100]

In the end, the delegates left it to each state to determine who qualifies as a voter.[101] Simply put, if you are eligible to vote in elections for your state assembly, you can also vote for your representative in Congress.[102] It was a decision laden with consequences for the long and continuing fight to expand American democracy. As the historian Alexander Keyssar reminds us, "Although the Constitution was promulgated in the name of 'We the People of the United States,' the individual states retained the power to define just who 'the people' were."[103] In the years that followed, the various constituencies disenfranchised by the states would have to rely on the constitutional amendment process to secure this most fundamental of democratic rights, spurring the adoption of no fewer than five voting rights amendments to the Constitution.

Having decided to elect representatives "by the people," the Framers made sure that other key officeholders in the federal government—senators, president, and vice president—would be chosen by intermediaries. Madison called it "the policy of refining the popular appointments by successive filtrations."[104] Less dependent on the people's will, these indirectly chosen officials would in theory have more latitude to resist the intemperate demands of fleeting popular majorities.

Take the Senate. In their original design, the Framers gave state legislatures the responsibility for choosing members of the upper house. This method of selection would have two chief benefits, argued Dickinson. First, it would "more intimately connect the state governments with the national legislature." Second, it would "draw forth the first characters either as to family or talent."[105] The proposal met with broad acceptance, but it wasn't long before the American people insisted on more of a say in the selection of their senators. In time, this demand fueled a remarkable popular campaign to democratize the Senate, culminating in the ratification of the Seventeenth Amendment in 1913. The measure established our current method of electing senators by a vote of the people.

When it came to selection of the nation's chief executive, the delegates considered a wide variety of options before settling on the jerry-rigged invention we know as the Electoral College.[106] The Virginia Plan had envisioned a "national executive" chosen by the legislature for a single fixed term.[107] This was consistent with the way most state governors were chosen at the time.[108] But some delegates worried that selection by the legislature was inconsistent with the core principle of separation of powers, leading inevitably to "intrigues and contentions" among lawmakers and candidates.[109] Wilson argued that selecting the chief executive by popular vote would "produce more confidence among the people."[110] Madison said he agreed, at least in theory. Election by "the people at large," he reckoned, was the "fittest" way to "produce an executive magistrate of distinguished character." The only "difficulty," he admitted, was that the South would "have no influence in the election on the score of the Negroes."[111] In the end, there was little support among the delegates for Wilson's unabashedly democratic proposal. "The people are uninformed," sniffed Gerry, "and would be misled by a few designing men."[112] Twice, on July 17 and August 24, the delegates roundly rejected Wilson's motions to select the chief executive through an election "by the people."[113]

The idea of giving this power to an intermediary group of electors attracted support in the final weeks of the convention. In this novel mode of selection, each state would appoint a slate of electors equal to the number of its senators and representatives combined. The method of appointment would be left to each state's legislature, with no requirement that the people have a say at all. The idea appealed to those who wanted the states to play a meaningful role in the national government. It also benefited the slave states, boosting their electoral strength by leveraging the padded representation in Congress they obtained through the counting of slaves as three-fifths of a person for the purpose of apportioning seats.[114]

With time running out, the Framers gave only cursory attention to this untested and controversial feature of our democratic system. As it happened, it took only twelve years for the plan to fall apart, necessitating a rescue via the Twelfth Amendment. Since its inception, the Electoral College has on five occasions awarded the presidency to a candidate who failed to win the most votes, sparking numerous efforts over the years to abolish it by constitutional amendment.

Compromises over Race and Slavery

Nearly half of the fifty-five men who attended the Philadelphia Convention owned slaves.[115] Not all of them hailed from the South. Benjamin Franklin, for instance, a late-in-life convert to the abolitionist cause, owned slaves for much of his life.[116] But the delegates hailing from states south of the Mason-Dixon line made their dependence on the institution abundantly clear. James Madison, whose family's fortune was built on slavery,[117] saw clearly that the issue had the potential to divide the convention. As he observed in his notes, "the great division of interests in the United States . . . lay between the Northern and Southern," stemming "principally from the effects of their having or not having slaves."[118]

During the convention's early weeks, the delegates were content to tiptoe around their differences. By June, when the sponsors of the Virginia Plan brokered the three-fifths compromise, tensions started to simmer. But it was only in the fierce heat of July and August that contentions came to a boil. Delegates representing states in the South made clear they were determined to defend their interests. Citing a "duty to his state," General Charles Cotesworth Pinckney of South Carolina insisted on "some security to the Southern States against an emancipation of slaves," threatening to reject the Constitution if the demand was not met.[119] This was a misleading argument, since no one at the convention ever suggested that Congress should have the power to interfere with slavery in the states. Nonetheless, John Rutledge, Pinckney's fellow South Carolinian, drew a similar line in the sand, vowing that Southerners "will never be such fools as to give up so important an interest."[120]

Some, but by no means all, delegates from the North viewed slavery as antithetical to the nation's professed ideals of liberty and equality. Gouverneur Morris, perhaps the convention's most impassioned foe of slavery, inveighed against the "nefarious institution," condemning it as "the curse of heaven on the states where it prevailed." Morris piously insisted he "never would concur in upholding domestic slavery," but it's a promise he wouldn't keep.[121] In the interests of forging a permanent union, delegates from the North proved all too willing to accede to the South's demands, negotiating at least four distinct provisions that promoted and even privileged slavery in our fundamental law. Tellingly, the drafters relied on tortured euphemisms to avoid what one disaffected delegate called "the admission of expressions which might be odious in the ears of Americans."[122] As Madison put it, it just seemed "wrong to admit in the Constitution the idea that there could be property in men."[123] But it accepted slavery all the same.

The Three-Fifths Clause in Article I provided that "three fifths of all other Persons"—that is, *slaves*—would be counted in the apportionment of seats in the House of Representatives and, correspondingly, in the allocation of electoral votes.[124] Though slavery existed in every state, everyone understood that the arrangement would mostly benefit the Southern and border states with large slave populations. In the six states where the institution was widespread, enslaved people constituted more than a third of the population.[125] Counting them through the three-fifths rule boosted their owners' political clout. It's no coincidence that four of the first five presidents were slave-owners from Virginia.

The Slave Trade Clause, also found in Article I, barred Congress from outlawing the importation of slaves for at least twenty years.[126] This prohibition, which was also inserted in Article V as a limitation on amendment power, was added at the insistence of Pinckney, who maintained that "South Carolina and Georgia cannot do without slaves."[127] Madison preferred there be no mention of the slave trade in the Constitution, calling it "dishonorable to the national character."[128] But Pinckney pointed out that Virginia, which possessed the largest population of slaves, would actually benefit by a ban on importations. "Her slaves will rise in value, and she has more than she wants," he argued.[129] Pinckney was right. When Congress finally imposed a ban in 1808, Richmond became a leading center of the newly profitable *domestic* slave trade—a sophisticated commercial operation that gave rise to the state's own Wall Street.[130] In the decades to follow, trafficking in Black bodies, primarily to states in the Deep South, became Virginia's largest industry.[131]

Finally, the Fugitive Slave Clause in Article IV, the section of the Constitution that governs the rights and duties of the states, forbade states from passing "any law or regulation" to emancipate runaway slaves within their jurisdiction.[132] Antithetical to the principle of states' rights, the provision stripped Northern states of the power to enforce their own emancipation laws and purported to commandeer their participation in the roundup of slaves who absconded. Pinckney claimed it as a triumph. Addressing the South Carolina legislature, he boasted, "We have obtained a right to recover our slaves in whatever part of America they may take refuge, which is a right we had not before."[133]

Taken together, these clauses entrenched slavery in the Constitution, deepening its hold on America for three quarters of a century. In forging these odious compromises, the South had strength in numbers when it counted. The New York and New Hampshire delegations were frequently absent from the proceedings, and Rhode Island refused to attend. As a result, the Northern states were outvoted at key moments by the pro-slavery contingent. Some delegates from the North, where slavery was beginning to die out, consoled themselves with the naïve hope that the South would eventually follow their lead. "Slavery in time will not be a speck in our country," said one.[134] But that optimism was grievously misplaced. A Constitution that abetted slavery only strengthened it. In a slowly escalating series of crises, the fateful compromises of 1787 led inexorably to disunion and war.

Errors, Oversights, and Poor Drafting

After the long fight between the small states and large ones over representation in the national legislature, which consumed the first two months of the convention, the delegates had to make up for lost time. In their push to complete a draft, they introduced errors, oversights, and unclear language into the Constitution's text, with serious consequences. A misalignment in the government's start dates delayed the swearing in of a new Congress until thirteen months after the election, a problem later fixed by constitutional amendment.[135] A provision in the list of Congress's enumerated powers, authorizing the creation of a national capital district on land ten miles square, failed to provide for the political rights of American citizens living there—a glaring omission that leaves the citizens of the District of Columbia without voting representation in Congress to this day.[136] And a lack of clear and thoughtful drafting in Article II, the section of the Constitution establishing the Executive Branch, required no fewer than three amendments to clarify the rules of presidential selection and succession.

As a practical matter, the Framers' most serious mistake was their failure to add a bill of rights. While eight early state charters included declarations of basic rights and core democratic principles, the convention decided against incorporating one. The question arose only during the final week of deliberations. As the delegates wearily made their way down a long checklist of proposed changes to the draft, George Mason expressed the wish that the delegates add a bill of rights. "It would give great quiet to the people," he said, "and with the aid of the state declarations, a bill might be prepared in a few hours."[137] Gerry proposed that a committee be formed to draft one, but with little recorded discussion the convention rejected the suggestion by a vote of ten state delegations to none.[138]

Mason would later complain of "the precipitate and intemperate, not to say indecent manner in which the business was conducted during the last week of the convention, after the patrons of this new plan found they had a decided majority in their favor." [139] But as the long summer turned to fall, many of the men in the room grew tired of Mason's frequent and idiosyncratic objections, reflecting his strongly held views on topics ranging from the president's pardoning power to the collection of duties for harbor improvements. At one point, in a fit of peevishness, he announced that he would "sooner chop off his right hand" than sign the Constitution as it stood. [140]

During the delegates' brief but consequential debate over Mason's request for a bill of rights, Madison was unusually silent. It seems difficult to account for his reticence. Legal historian Paul Finkelman describes him as "uncharacteristically ambivalent" over the need to include such protections: at once "a firm supporter of individual rights and personal freedom" and, "for a variety of theoretical, practical, and political reasons, . . . uncertain if the new American Constitution ought to have a bill of rights." [141] The convention's casual rejection of Mason's eleventh-hour request would prove costly, making it far more difficult to win support for the new national charter. [142]

A New Amendment Process

As the Framers pieced together their new plan of government, one detail that merited particularly close consideration was the amending provision. After all, the decision to jettison the Articles of Confederation was motivated in large part by the great difficulty of making needed changes. The Framers knew their new charter would have to be more flexible. As Elbridge Gerry recognized, "The novelty and difficulty of the experiment requires periodical revision." [143] And yet, over four months of debate and deliberation, they spent remarkably little time pondering the ideal method of amendment.

From the outset, the drafters of the Virginia Plan signaled a more liberal approach, stipulating that "provision ought to be made for the amendment of the articles of Union whensoever it shall seem necessary." [144] The plan was short on specifics, except to note that "the assent of the national legislature ought not be required." [145] It was a curious stipulation. The Virginia Plan aimed to establish a strong national government. By what logic, then, should the national legislature have no role in crafting amendments?

When the delegates first discussed the amending process in early June,

George Mason framed its importance in starkly pragmatic terms. "The plan now to be formed will certainly be defective," he said, "as the Confederation has been found on trial to be. Amendments therefore will be necessary, and it will be better to provide for them, in an easy, regular and Constitutional way than to trust to chance and violence."[146] Though several delegates questioned the "propriety of making the consent of the national legislature unnecessary,"[147] Mason was quick to defend the choice. "It would be improper to require the consent of the national legislature," he insisted, "because they may abuse their power, and refuse their consent on that very account."[148]

It would be two months before the Committee of Detail unveiled the first draft of an amending clause. The August 6 proposal gave the initiating role to the states. Whenever two-thirds of them petitioned for amendments to the Constitution, the national legislature would be required "to call a convention for that purpose."[149] The plan deviated from existing practice in two significant ways: Congress would no longer have a role in crafting amendments, and the states would no longer provide consent.[150] And yet, with no recorded debate apart from the suggestion that Congress "should be left at liberty to call a convention, whenever they please," the convention adopted this formulation by a unanimous vote of the state delegations on August 30.[151]

The most serious and detailed discussion of the amending power did not occur until the convention's final week, when three influential delegates asked to revisit the question. Speaking first on September 10, Elbridge Gerry questioned the propriety of allowing a convention obtained by two-thirds of the states to impose changes on an unwilling minority. He warned that a convention, once assembled, could act by a simple majority to "bind the Union to innovations that may subvert the state constitutions altogether."[152] Reiterating a concern previously raised by others, Alexander Hamilton insisted that Congress should have its own power to call a convention. The national legislature would be "most sensible to the necessity of amendments," he argued. The states, by contrast, would seek only self-serving changes "with a view to increase their own powers."[153] For his part, James Madison worried about the "vagueness" of relying on conventions to craft amendments. "How was a convention to be formed?" he asked. "By what rule [would it] decide? What [would be] the force of its acts?"[154]

Seeing his opportunity, Madison suggested a completely revised process. Instead of investing conventions with this responsibility, his new plan would give Congress the power to draft amendments by a two-thirds vote of each house, or whenever two-thirds of the states ask Congress to do so. In a second step, amendments would become valid only when three-quarters of the states ratified them.[155] But before the convention could vote on these changes, a delegate from South Carolina raised another objection. Earlier in the proceedings, the Southern states had secured a commitment to protect the slave trade for two decades. Now John Rutledge rose to say he "never could agree" to allow this bargain to be "altered by the states not interested in that property and prejudiced against it."[156] To appease this last-minute demand, the delegates agreed to append language making clear that the Constitution could not be amended to affect the unfettered importation of slaves before 1808.[157]

With the addition of Rutledge's cruel proviso, Madison's proposal passed with the support of nine of eleven state delegations.[158] Notably, his language giving Congress the power to propose amendments made it into the final version of Article V. It's the method by which all twenty-seven amendments to the Constitution have been adopted.[159] The special protection for the slave trade also survived. It was the first of two limitations placed on the American people's power to alter the original 1787 Constitution.[160] Though moot today, this shameful carve-out still remains in the document's text, an enduring reminder of the Framers' callous acceptance of slavery.

There was still one more round of changes to come. On September 15, a rare Saturday session after a grueling final week, new criticisms emerged as the delegates were asked to approve the final text of the amending clause—styled for the first time as Article V.[161] Reopening the rift between the large states and small states that had nearly derailed the convention early in the summer, Roger Sherman expressed concern that a majority of states "might be brought to do things fatal to particular states," including undoing the deal sealed by the Connecticut Compromise.[162] After a brief but contentious debate, on a motion "dictated by the circulating murmurs of the small states," the convention agreed without opposition to add a second limitation on the amending power, stipulating that "no state, without its consent shall be deprived of its equal suffrage in the Senate."[163]

To no one's surprise, George Mason offered an objection of his own. The method of amending the Constitution was "exceptionable and dangerous," he said. As long as revisions proposed by the states depended on good-faith action by Congress, Mason predicted that "no amendments of the proper kind would ever be obtained by the people, if the government should become oppressive," as he believed it would.[164] In response, Morris and Gerry moved to require that an amendment-proposing convention be called on the application of two-thirds of the states.[165] Inexplicably, Madison indicated he "saw no objection" to the change. Just a week earlier, he had succeeded in eliminating such conventions.[166] But now, nearing the finish line, he was reduced to pointing out once again that "difficulties might arise" as to their form and procedures.[167] The change was approved unanimously, making it into the final version of Article V.[168]

If Madison hoped this one last concession would appease his fellow Virginian, he was wrong. Once, in the convention's early days, Mason had pledged that he "would bury his bones in this city rather than expose his country to the consequences of a dissolution of the convention without anything being done."[169] But by the end of August, his disaffection was evident. And now, minutes after the adoption of his momentous final edit to Article V, Mason declared he would refuse to sign the Constitution or to support its ratification unless the delegates agreed to call a second convention. "This Constitution had been formed without the knowledge or idea of the people," he said. "A second convention will know more of the sense of the people, and be able to provide a system more consonant to it."[170] It was a blow, to be sure. Mason's opposition would make it far more difficult to secure Virginia's crucial vote in the ratification contest to follow.[171] And yet the delegates simply ignored his one final demand, approving the new Constitution by a unanimous vote of the state delegations.[172]

"A More Perfect Union"

In the convention's final days, Gouverneur Morris took the pen, refashioning a jumble of provisions into seven coherent sections called articles. Providing an added flourish, he prefaced the document with an introductory Preamble articulating the Constitution's purpose and meaning in fifty-two elegant and stirring words:

> We the People of the United States, in Order to form a more perfect Union, establish Justice, insure domestic Tranquility, provide for the common defense, promote the general Welfare, and secure the

blessings of Liberty to ourselves and our Posterity, do ordain and establish this Constitution for the United States of America.[173]

Morris had discarded an earlier draft, which began, "We the people of the states of New Hampshire, Massachusetts, Rhode Island," and so on. In so doing, he made clear that this was a nationalist Constitution, forever closing the door on the old confederation of sovereign and independent states. Historian Joseph Ellis reckons it was "probably the most consequential editorial act in American history."[174]

To fully realize the Preamble's promise that "we the people" would "ordain and establish" their new national charter, the Framers gave the power to ratify the Constitution to specially elected conventions in each state—bypassing the politicians in the Continental Congress and the thirteen state legislatures.[175] As James Madison noted, it was "indispensable" that the new plan "be ratified . . . by the supreme authority of the people themselves."[176] In a controversial departure from the rule governing amendments to the Articles of Confederation, the approval of nine state conventions would be sufficient to set the new Constitution in motion, putting an end to the veto power enjoyed by any one state.[177]

As the gathering concluded on September 17, Ben Franklin rose to salute the delegates' great accomplishment. Ailing from kidney stones and gout, he was borne to the session in a chair held aloft by prisoners from a local jail. Struggling to speak, Franklin tapped fellow Pennsylvanian James Wilson to read his prepared statement aloud. Franklin appealed to the delegates to "make manifest our unanimity." Acknowledging that "there are several parts of this constitution which I do not at present approve," Franklin nevertheless pledged his full support. "I agree to this Constitution with all its faults," he said, "because I think a general government necessary for us." He continued:

I doubt too whether any other convention we can obtain may be able to make a better Constitution. For when you assemble a number of men to have the advantage of their joint wisdom, you inevitably assemble with those men, all their prejudices, their passions, their errors of opinion, their local interests, and their selfish views. From such an assembly, can a perfect production be expected? It therefore astonishes me, Sir, to find this system approaching so near to perfection as it does.[178]

In the end, only thirty-nine of the forty-two men still remaining were willing to affix their names to the parchment that was carefully laid out on the table. The Framers' Constitution, the initial version of our national charter, was just over 4,500 words in length—about three-fifths the length of today's Constitution with its twenty-seven amendments added over the years. It was, as Madison would later recall, "the work of many heads and many hands." [179] Like Franklin, none of the signatories was perfectly satisfied with the final product. In a letter to Thomas Jefferson, Madison despaired that the new charter would "neither effectually answer its national object nor prevent the local mischiefs which everywhere excite disgusts against the state governments." [180] Soon, however, they would have to put their disappointment aside to rally the Constitution's supporters to win the support of thirteen state ratifying conventions.

Standing on the sidelines in glum silence, refusing to sign, were George Mason, Elbridge Gerry, and Edmund Randolph. The last was a surprise. At the convention's start, Randolph had helped lead the charge, introducing the Virginia Plan that served as the early blueprint for the new government. Unlike the other disaffected delegates who drifted away during the course of the proceedings, these three dissenters remained until the end to shape the document as best they could. Returning home, they would be counted among the large army of opponents of the Constitution, who would mobilize a fierce campaign to stop it. Indeed, the fight had already begun: before the ink on the new Constitution was dry, there were already calls to undo the Framers' great achievement.

Ratification and the Rise of the Anti-Federalist Opposition

Within weeks, the Constitution was in wide circulation, reprinted in newspapers from New Hampshire to Georgia. In coffeehouses, taverns, and town squares, Americans argued over its merits.[181] As Madison marveled in a dispatch to Thomas Jefferson, the new charter of government "engrosses almost the whole political attention of America." [182] A Massachusetts newspaper described the scene more colorfully, reporting that "there are persons who appear to be *raving mad*, both for and against the plan." [183]

Those supporting the plan were quick out of the blocks, scoring an early coup in the public messaging battle. Calling themselves Federalists, they promised "a more perfect Union." Deftly, they branded those opposing ratification as Anti-Federalist, an unflattering label that tended to obscure what they were actually *for*. One frustrated foe of the Constitution demanded that the framing be reversed, insisting that "the friends to the new plan of CONSOLIDATION, are Anti-Federal, and its opposers are firm, Federal patriots."[184] Though few Anti-Federalists were willing to embrace the term, the moniker stuck.[185]

While the Anti-Federalists had many different reasons for opposing the new plan of government, they did agree on a few things. They believed the Constitution gave too much power to the federal government at the expense of the states. With memories of oppressive British rule still fresh, skeptics shuddered at Congress's sweeping new powers to tax and raise armies in peacetime. They feared that a distant "consolidated" government, unrestrained by a bill of rights, would overwhelm or even "annihilate" the states. Furthermore, they doubted as a matter of political philosophy that republican government could ever work in a nation as large as the United States. In the Anti-Federalists' estimation, only a "confederation of smaller republics" ruling over homogeneous populations could preserve democratic rule and secure the nation's hard-won freedoms.[186]

The Federalists argued that the nation's security and prosperity hinged on the adoption of a new system, based on "a principle of strength and stability in the organization of our government, and vigor in its operations."[187] To Washington, it was the key to realizing America's promise as a great nation. "The establishment of an energetic general government," he imagined, "will disappoint the hopes and expectations of those who are unfriendly to this country, give us a national respectability, and enable us to improve those commercial and political advantages which nature and situation have placed within our reach."[188] Parrying their opponents' criticisms, the Federalists pointed to the Constitution's careful design, rooted in limited government, separation of powers, checks and balances, and a meaningful role for the states, as reliable protection against the abuse of power.

"No group in American political history was more heterogeneous than the Anti-Federalists," notes legal scholar Saul Cornell.[189] While some were men of privilege, many more came from the ranks of striving "middling men" and backwoods farmers in every state who represented America's future as an increasingly egalitarian nation.[190] The Anti-Federalists' coalition was split between die-hard opponents of the Constitution, who wanted America to remain "thirteen confederated republics, under . . . [a]

federal head," [191] and those who would be willing to accept the new plan of government if certain changes were made. Though he famously refused to sign the Constitution in Philadelphia, Elbridge Gerry signaled that he leaned toward the latter camp. In an influential letter laying out his principal objections to the plan, he admitted, "In many respects, I think it has great merit, and by proper amendments may be adapted to the 'exigencies of government' and preservation of liberty." [192]

With a few exceptions, the Anti-Federalists' desired fixes fell within two broad categories: amendments guaranteeing fundamental rights and privileges, drawing on the practice in some state constitutions, and structural amendments altering the government's powers and design to protect the prerogatives of the states. While Anti-Federalists never agreed on a single slate of recommended amendments, they generally believed it was essential to engraft them into the Constitution *before* it took effect. For instance, the Anti-Federalist leader Richard Henry Lee, representing Virginia in the Confederation Congress, hoped that state conventions would propose "indispensable amendments" so that "a new general convention may so weave them into the proffered system." [193]

The Federalists countered that it was unrealistic to expect that a subsequent convention could ever reach consensus on an appropriate set of revisions. "Nothing but confusion and contrariety could spring from the experiment," warned South Carolina's Charles Pinckney, second cousin to Charles Cotesworth Pinckney. "The states will never agree in their plans. And the deputies to a second convention coming together under the discordant impressions of their constituents will never agree." [194] To avoid this unproductive path, supporters of the Constitution insisted that the ratifying conventions be limited to a simple choice: approve or reject the charter, with no amendments allowed. [195]

Each side understood the importance of shaping public sentiment. [196] Throughout the ratification contest, leaders of the two competing camps furiously penned letters and essays for and against the Constitution. Deploying high-minded argument and shameless invective, these works were printed in newspapers and circulated as pamphlets to reach a wide audience. It was, as historian Pauline Maier notes, an extraordinary "war of printed words" that produced "one of the greatest outpourings of political writings in American history." [197] In the most famous of these writings, known to later generations as the Federalist Papers, Alexander Hamilton, James Madison, and John Jay mounted a comprehensive defense of the new system. Writing under the shared alias Publius, a reference to a heroic defender of the Roman Republic, the three prominent spokesmen hoped to "vindicate and recommend the new Constitution." [198] The Anti-Federalist writers, by contrast, were far less organized. Writing under an assortment of pseudonyms, they criticized the Constitution from a bewildering variety of viewpoints. Most famously, Brutus published an influential set of sixteen essays warning of the new regime's "absolute and uncontrollable power." [199] Mercy Otis Warren, one of the only women to have participated in this great public debate, warned in her *Observations on the New Constitution* that the new plan of government was "a subversion of the union of confederated states," and "may be a means of involving the whole country in blood." [200]

In this fevered media climate, the stage was set for the great ratifying contest, waged in a series of thirteen elected state conventions. They constituted what one participant called "the fullest representation of the people ever known." [201] In New York, for example, the usual suffrage rules were relaxed to allow every male citizen over the age of twenty-one to have a vote. [202]

Delaware won the race to be "the First State" when its convention voted unanimously to approve the Constitution on December 7, 1787. [203] Just a few months earlier, its delegates had threatened to walk away from the Philadelphia Convention if their demand for an equal vote in the Senate was not met. But now, having secured the concession that mattered most, the state's convention approved the Constitution unconditionally after just four days of deliberation. For the same reason, Federalists rolled to easy victories in New Jersey, Georgia, and Connecticut. [204]

It was a different story at the ratifying convention in Pennsylvania, the first big state to organize a contest. Though pro-Constitution forces won a two-thirds majority in the delegate election, a determined faction of Anti-Federalists came prepared to fight. "We are going to examine the foundations of the building," announced Robert Whitehill, a lawmaker from the central part of the state. Despite Whitehall's insistence on the right to propose amendments, the Federalist majority limited the convention to an up-or-down vote. As one of their number framed the choice, "We are come to stamp the system with the authority of the people, or to refuse it that stamp." [205]

Over almost three weeks of debate, the Anti-Federalists dissected the Constitution and highlighted its chief deficiencies. Whitehill led the

charge, warning that the new plan of government was "designed to abolish the independence and sovereignty of the states."[206] He exhorted the
delegates to insist on "such restrictions as are best calculated to protect us
from oppression and slavery." Other Anti-Federalists echoed Whitehill's
demand for protections against government abuse. "There is no *security*
for our rights in this Constitution," cried one. "Why did they omit a bill
of rights?"[207]

The Constitution's chief defender at the Pennsylvania convention was
James Wilson, one of the document's primary drafters. Though Wilson
freely admitted that the Framers gave little thought to the need for a bill of
rights, he insisted that including one would have been "absurd." Since the
national government was authorized to act only within a set of enumerated
powers, imposing limits on them was "not only unnecessary, but prepos-
terous and dangerous."[208] But the Anti-Federalists were unpersuaded. On
December 12, the convention's final day, they defiantly introduced a set of
fifteen amendments and asked for an adjournment to give the people of
Pennsylvania a chance to consider them. The Federalists easily fended off
the motion and proceeded to a vote. With a high-handedness that would
come back to haunt them, they refused to print the proposals in the official
record.[209]

As news spread that Pennsylvania ratified the Constitution that day,
the streets of Philadelphia resounded with "shouts and huzzahs."[210] But a
week later, a group of disaffected delegates published their amendments in
the *Pennsylvania Packet*, along with a scorching rebuke of the convention's
actions.[211] Just over half of the recommended amendments were aimed at
protecting individual rights and liberties. They included guarantees for
freedom of speech and conscience, the right to a jury trial, and the right
to bear arms, along with limitations on general warrants and excessive
punishments—all of which would find their way into the Bill of Rights.
The list also contained several structural amendments, including one that
would reserve to the states all powers not "expressly delegated" to Congress, a provision lifted from the Articles of Confederation.[212] If added to
the Constitution, it would have precluded Congress's exercise of implied
powers. The minority's dissent was disseminated widely throughout the
state and beyond, stoking the Anti-Federalist demand for amendments.

In Massachusetts, where skepticism of the new plan of government ran
deep, the Federalists were determined to keep the door to amendments
firmly shut. In the state's delegate elections, however, the Anti-Federalists

had their strongest showing yet. Once the convention was gaveled into session in January 1788, they hammered away at the threat to rights and liberties posed by the new plan of government. The scope of congressional power was "big with mischiefs," warned General Samuel Thompson, a delegate from the separatist region of Maine. "But where is the bill of rights which shall check the power of this Congress, which shall say, *thus far shall ye come and no farther?*"[213]

For the first time, the Federalists were on the defensive. To deflect their opponents' criticisms, they opted for a change in strategy. In a concession to Anti-Federalist sentiment, they would soften their hard line on amendments by agreeing to ratify the Constitution with the promise of "recommendatory" amendments to follow.[214] It was left to John Hancock, the state's popular governor, to make the offer. Hancock had done his best to stay neutral in the debate, absenting himself for most of the convention with a serendipitously timed case of gout.[215] Now, in a blow to the opposition, he announced his support for the proposed plan of government.[216] But in recognition of the "diversity of sentiment" among the delegates, he asked "whether the introduction of some general amendments would not be attended with the happiest consequences."[217] Samuel Adams, Hancock's fellow hero of the Revolution, rose in support of the idea. Acknowledging that he and others have had their doubts about the Constitution, Adams volunteered that the "conciliatory proposition . . . will have a tendency to remove such doubts, and to conciliate the minds of the convention."[218]

With Hancock's "conciliatory proposition," the Federalists eked out a crucial win in the Bay State. In the end, the convention recommended nine amendments to the Constitution, calling on the state's representatives in the 1st Congress to make every effort to obtain their passage. It is noteworthy that only two of the proposals related to rights, an indication that Anti-Federalists in the Bay State were far more intent on obtaining structural amendments. One proposal would have clipped Congress's taxing power. Another sought to curtail its ability to regulate elections. And a third echoed the Pennsylvania minority's demand that "all powers not expressly delegated" to the federal government would be reserved to the states. As envisioned, the convention submitted the proposals as recommendations only, rejecting hard-line Anti-Federalist demands to make the state's approval of the Constitution contingent on their adoption.

Adams imagined that the convention's friendly compromise on amendments "must have weight" in the remaining contests.[219] And sure enough, every state but one followed the precedent set by Massachusetts.[220] When South Carolina's convention met in May, a pro-Constitution majority sought to appease the Anti-Federalist sentiment in the state's backcountry by recommending four structural amendments in its formal instrument of ratification.[221] A similar spirit of conciliation inspired a more closely divided convention in New Hampshire to endorse a dozen amendments to "remove the fears and quiet the apprehensions of many."[222]

New Hampshire's vote to ratify the Constitution on June 21, 1788, added the decisive "ninth pillar of the federal edifice,"[223] setting the gears of the new government in motion under the terms of Article VII. But there were important contests still to be decided, most notably in Virginia and New York, where Anti-Federalists remained determined to obtain modifications as a condition to any ratification. Each state would be an uphill fight. A loss in either could lead to the fledgling Union's premature demise.

At Virginia's ratifying convention, the opposition was led by Patrick Henry, the renowned orator and champion of the Revolution. Henry ridiculed the Massachusetts compromise on amendments. "Do you enter into a compact of government first, and afterwards settle the terms of government?" he asked. "Previous amendments, in my opinion, are necessary to procure peace and tranquility."[224] Sparring with James Madison, who defended the Constitution against his relentless (and often demagogic) criticisms, Henry attacked the very legitimacy of the Framers' enterprise.[225] "Who authorized them to speak the language of, *We, the People,* instead of *We, the States?*" he railed. "The people gave them no power to use their name."[226] From the convention's first day to the last, Henry did his best to stoke apprehensions about America's future under the proposed Constitution.

After three and a half weeks of contentious debate, the convention rejected Henry's demand for prior amendments, agreeing instead to ratify the Constitution with amendments "recommended to the consideration of the Congress."[227] To avoid the bad feeling that marred the vote in Pennsylvania, the Federalists agreed to join their opponents in endorsing a list of forty constitutional fixes. Half of the recommended amendments related to the protection of rights, based largely on George Mason's 1776 Declaration of Rights. Half were structural in nature, including measures to roll back Congress's powers in the areas of taxation, commerce, military affairs, and voting. The convention urged the state's representatives in the new Congress to seek their adoption in accord with the method set forth in Article V and to "conform to the spirit" of the proposed amendments in the meantime.[228]

With their June 26 victory in Virginia, the largest and most important state, supporters of the Constitution had cause for jubilation. (Little did they know that New Hampshire had beaten them by four days.) But it was cold comfort for Madison. In a letter to Alexander Hamilton written shortly after the vote, he complained that many of the proposals the Federalists agreed to recommend were "highly objectionable."[229] Moreover, he worried that there would be no end to the Anti-Federalists' schemes to "disgrace and destroy" the newly ratified Constitution by hastily invoking the amending process of Article V. "I suspect," he confided to Washington, that "the plan will be to engage two-thirds of the legislatures in the task of undoing the work; or to get a Congress appointed in the first instance that will commit suicide on their own authority."[230]

In New York, meanwhile, Anti-Federalists won an overwhelming majority in the state's delegate elections. But after Virginia's vote to ratify the Constitution without condition, their options dwindled. "The circumstances of the country are greatly altered," said a leader of the Federalist caucus. "The Confederation is now *dissolved*."[231] With little hope of revising the Constitution as long as New York remained outside the Union, the convention reluctantly voted to ratify on July 26. In a complicated ratification instrument rife with stipulations and explanations, the delegates recommended the addition of a twenty-five-point declaration of rights and thirty-two structural amendments.[232] However, in contrast to their confederates in other states, New York's Anti-Federalists were not about to entrust their "anxiously desired" amendments to Congress. Seeking "early and mature consideration" of their proposals, they announced their intention to obtain a general convention under the provisions of Article V. As the price of victory, the Federalists agreed to assist in the drafting of a circular letter calling on the state legislatures to act.[233] Madison saw the deal as more harmful than an outright rejection.[234] "It is a signal of concord and hope to the enemies of the Constitution everywhere," he lamented, "and will I fear prove extremely dangerous."[235]

With the contest in the Empire State concluded, adding an eleventh star to the flag, the ratification process paused for a time. North Carolina's convention, dominated by Anti-Federalists, made clear it would not approve the Constitution until Congress proposed suitable amendments, including a declaration of rights.[236] And the intransigent faction leading that "petty

State of Rhode Island"[237] was still refusing to even organize a convention. But though the completion of the Union would have to wait, the nation experienced a collective sense of relief. After the Federalists' triumph in the great ratification contest, most Americans seemed ready to give the new system of government a chance. For a brief moment, the rancor and sharp divisions were swept aside. Americans celebrated a moment of unparalleled national unity.

Well, almost.

New York's governor wasted little time in transmitting the circular letter to the state legislatures.[238] It quickly found a receptive audience in Virginia. At Patrick Henry's prompting, the state's lawmakers approved the first-ever application for a constitutional convention under Article V in November 1788, months before the new government had even launched.[239] In an urgent dispatch to Madison, a Virginia Federalist fretted that "the triumph of Anti-Federalism is complete."[240] Meanwhile, in New York City a group of unrepentant foes of the Constitution gathered at Fraunces Tavern to form "a society, for the purpose of procuring a general convention."[241] In an appeal to all kindred spirits, they called on Anti-Federalists in every state to elect members of Congress committed to supporting New York's call for a convention—urging them to "unite their utmost exertions to procure the amendments, in the only mode that is now left."[242]

2

The Founding Era Amendments
(1789–1804)

The ratification contest revealed that a great many Americans believed that the stronger national government promised by the new Constitution posed a threat to their hard-won liberties. Nevertheless, in an extraordinary expression of good faith, eleven state conventions assented to it by the summer of 1788 with only the promise of future changes. Only North Carolina and Rhode Island held back, refusing to enter the Union until Congress answered the people's call for amendments. But which amendments?

Accounting for duplicates, conventions in six states and minority reports in two crowdsourced approximately eighty-three separate amendment proposals for consideration before the 1st Congress was scheduled to convene.[1] Most were structural amendments aimed at reducing the government's powers and altering its design. Six conventions called for restrictions on Congress's ability to tax, a power James Madison deemed "essential to the salvation of the Union."[2] Six sought restrictions on Congress's power to regulate elections in the states. Five wanted limits on the reach of the federal courts. And five urged a cap on the size of House districts to prevent them from growing too large. The ratifying conventions also urged the adoption of numerous rights-related amendments. Topping the list were proposals relating to juries. Five conventions asked to guarantee the right to trial by jury in civil cases, while three wanted greater protections for criminal juries. Other frequent concerns raised included the free exercise of religion, the right to keep and bear arms, and protection against the quartering of soldiers in homes—guarantees identified as fundamental by four state conventions.

In response to the growing public sentiment in favor of amendments,

Madison's views on the subject evolved. In the early weeks of the ratification contest, he resisted any talk of amendments. Then, when faced with the Anti-Federalists' strong challenge in Massachusetts, he supported the pairing of unconditional ratification with "recommendatory" amendments, a compromise he tolerated as a "a blemish . . . in the least offensive form."[3] Later, to eke out a victory in his home state of Virginia, he acceded to the recommendation of a long list of structural amendments he considered damaging.[4] Now, with the Constitution safely ratified and elections looming, he pondered the way forward.

The biggest threat was New York's circular letter to the states. "It has a most pestilent tendency," thought Madison. "If an early general convention cannot be parried, it is seriously to be feared that the system which has resisted so many direct attacks may be at last successfully undermined by its enemies."[5] Anti-Federalists also organized to advance their objectives in Congress. In Pennsylvania, they nominated a list of candidates committed to securing amendments. Legislatures in four states instructed their congressional delegations to do the same.[6] George Washington worried that the Anti-Federalists were plotting to gain control of the new government to "impede or frustrate its operation."[7] For the man who would soon steer the ship of state, it was a painful prospect: "To be shipwrecked in sight of the port would be the severest of all possible aggravations to our misery."[8]

But how to head off the push for crippling structural amendments before the new government had the chance to prove it could work? Madison's inspired solution was to stop fighting. Instead of resisting amendments, he would embrace them. But only the right kind.

The Origins of the Bill of Rights

In June 1776, just weeks before the American colonies severed their ties with Great Britain, Virginia replaced its colonial charter with a new state constitution. In a first, the document was prefaced by a statement of fundamental rights that began with the proclamation "that all men are by nature equally free and independent and have certain inherent rights." (To prevent Black slaves from gaining their freedom, the drafters were careful to limit this principle to those who "enter into a state of society.")[9] With roots in Enlightenment theory and natural law, the Virginia Declaration of Rights restrained government from infringing on a sphere of individual rights, including the right to vote, the free exercise of religion, and the right to a jury trial.[10] Thomas Jefferson borrowed liberally from it when he wrote the Declaration of Independence a few weeks later. So did the drafters of six early state constitutions. In an evolution spanning two decades, they would gradually expand the canon of core rights to include many not mentioned in the Virginia Declaration, including the freedoms of speech, assembly, and petition and the separation of church and state.[11] These early bills of rights were, as legal historian Alan Grimes observed, "a distinctive American innovation in politics."[12]

Although the Framers rejected a request to incorporate a comprehensive bill of rights in the style of the Virginia Declaration, they did include some basic legal safeguards in the Constitution's text. They prohibited governments from enacting two kinds of abusive laws: bills of attainder, which impose criminal convictions without trial, and ex post facto laws, which retroactively punish conduct that was previously lawful.[13] They limited the power to suspend the writ of habeas corpus, a centuries-old protection against unlawful detention.[14] And they preserved an individual's right to be tried by a jury in criminal cases, ensuring that trials are held in the state where the crime was committed.[15]

When forced to account for their failure to include more comprehensive protection for individual rights, the Federalists offered several different explanations. A bill of rights was unnecessary, they said, because the federal government was already limited to a set of defined powers, and in any event, the people's rights were sufficiently protected by state constitutions and principles of natural law.[16] The omission was of no consequence, they added, because a bill of rights was little more than a collection of "parchment barriers" easily ignored by "overbearing majorities."[17] Moreover, they contended that a bill of rights was possibly even dangerous, because the decision to elevate some rights for special protection risked diminishing those not explicitly mentioned.[18] But few skeptics were reassured by these explanations.

As the historian Leonard Levy observes, the omission of a bill of rights was "the single issue that united Anti-Federalists throughout the country."[19] Through impassioned and often demagogic appeals they exploited the Framers' lapse as a powerful wedge issue. From Patrick Henry's lurid portrayals of the roving tax collectors who would invade homes to "search, ransack, and measure, everything you eat, drink and wear,"[20] to George Mason's warning that federal lawmakers could "lay a dangerous restriction on the press,"[21] the Anti-Federalists conjured up the specter of a despotic

Congress abusing its powers through its broad authorization to enact "necessary and proper" legislation to promote the "general welfare." Without the Federalists' promise to consider future amendments, the controversy might very well have led to the Constitution's rejection.

With ratification secured and elections to the new government under way, Madison was ready to unveil his strategy. In a December 1788 letter to Thomas Jefferson, he signaled that "the friends of the Constitution . . . are generally agreed that the system should be revised." But the revisions, he insisted, should "be carried no farther than to supply additional guards for liberty, without abridging the sum of power transferred from the states to the general government." Madison understood that while the Anti-Federalists remained "zealous for a second convention," the adoption of amendments safeguarding individual rights could help separate "well meaning" critics of the Constitution from those "designing opponents" who harbored the "insidious hope of throwing all things into confusion, and of subverting the fabric just established, if not the Union itself." [22]

Determined to lead this effort, Madison decided to run for a seat in Congress. To win, he would have to overcome the opposition of Patrick Henry, who schemed unrelentingly to sink his candidacy. "No person who wishes the Constitution to be amended should vote for Mr. Madison," Henry insisted. [23] After Anti-Federalists spread the word that Madison opposed amendments because he believed the Constitution to be "perfect," the candidate revealed his change of heart. [24] In a letter to a constituent, widely circulated in the district, Madison explained that he had opposed amendments prior to ratification because he saw them as "calculated to throw the states into dangerous contentions, and to furnish the secret enemies of the Union with an opportunity of promoting its dissolution." But now, with the new plan of government established, he declared that "it is my sincere opinion that the Constitution ought to be revised." The revisions, he pledged, would include "all essential rights, particularly the rights of Conscience in the fullest latitude, the freedom of the press, trials by jury, security against general warrants" and "sundry other alterations." [25]

With this assurance, Madison won a comfortable victory. He entered a Congress dominated by like-minded friends of the Constitution. In America's first landslide election, Federalist candidates took forty-eight of fifty-nine seats in the House of Representatives and all but two of the twenty-two seats in the Senate. Washington's fear of a Congress dominated by the enemies of the Constitution never came to pass. Despite the

Anti-Federalists' efforts to sow doubt, the American people were willing to give the new government a chance.[26]

Congress Proposes the Bill of Rights

The first Congress was scheduled to convene on March 4, 1789. In a letter written to his wife that very morning, a newly appointed senator grandly predicted that the date "which no doubt will hereafter be celebrated as a new era in the annals of the world."[27] But when the freshly minted crop of lawmakers filed into the ornate legislative chambers in New York's Federal Hall, to the accompaniment of booming cannons and cheering crowds, they were mortified to learn that they lacked the needed number of members to form a quorum and get to work.[28] The new national legislature would only gavel into session on the first day of April after four weeks of waiting.[29]

There were many pressing matters on the government's agenda. For a start, Congress had to raise revenue, create executive departments, and organize a federal judiciary. For the triumphant Federalists, amending the Constitution was low on the list of priorities. Indeed, some questioned the need to address the matter at all.[30] "The advocates for amendments will be but few," predicted one lawmaker.[31] But Madison intended to honor his campaign promise to secure amendments protecting rights. Though his fellow lawmakers were apathetic, he had the support of one important ally. In his April 30 inaugural address, written with Madison's assistance, President Washington announced his support for amendments reflecting "a reverence for the characteristic rights of freemen, and a regard for the public harmony." At the same time, he cautioned against alterations "which might endanger the benefits of a united and effective government, or which ought to await the future lessons of experience."[32]

Madison promised to unveil a set of proposed amendments on June 8, declaring he was "bound in honor and in duty" to bring them forward.[33] But before he could even present them, several members objected. "It must appear extremely impolitic to go into the consideration of amending the government, before it is organized, before it has begun to operate," said one.[34] Madison replied that a delay would "occasion suspicions." Though the Constitution was now adopted, "still there is a great number of our constituents who are dissatisfied with it," he said, people "respectable for the jealousy they have for their liberty."[35] Invoking "principles of amity and moderation," he pleaded with his colleagues to "conform to their wishes, and expressly declare the great rights of mankind secured under this constitution."[36] The prospect of enticing North Carolina and Rhode Island back into the Union, he added, provided an even "stronger motive" to act.[37]

His original set of proposals were drawn from provisions in state constitutions and the recommendations of the state ratifying conventions.[38] While familiar in content, they looked very different from the Bill of Rights we know today. Rather than place amendments at the end of the Constitution, the way we read them now, Madison envisioned them as edits to the original text, interlaced throughout the document. For example, his original proposal for what became the Fifth Amendment read:

> **Fifthly.** That in article 1st, section 10, between clauses 1 and 2, be inserted this clause, to wit: No State shall violate the equal rights of conscience, or the freedom of the press, or the trial by jury in criminal cases.[39]

Madison believed that there was "a neatness and propriety" to this approach. Appended amendments were more likely to be misunderstood.[40] But Roger Sherman offered a wiser alternative. Now a congressman from Connecticut, Madison's fellow Framer suggested it would be improper to tamper with the version of the Constitution signed in Philadelphia and ratified by the people. "We ought not to interweave our propositions into the work itself," he argued, "because it will be destructive of the whole fabric."[41]

In nine numbered amendments, Madison's original bill of rights introduced nineteen substantive changes to the Constitution. Among other things, it would have added protections for freedom of religion, speech, and assembly, as well as prohibitions against arbitrary searches, excessive fines, and double jeopardy.[42] The package of proposals focused primarily on the protection of rights, but it also included four minor structural revisions in the form of measures regulating the size of the House of Representatives, limiting lawmakers' ability to increase their salaries, setting a minimum monetary threshold for Supreme Court appeals, and clarifying that powers not delegated to Congress were reserved to the states.[43]

Amid the long list of proposals, one stood out. In a bill of rights intended to restrain the new national government, Madison wanted to include an amendment to limit certain *state* actions as well. His proposed Fourteenth

Amendment read: "No State shall violate the equal rights of conscience, or the freedom of the press, or the trial by jury in criminal cases."[44] It was one more attempt by the tenacious Virginian to leverage the Constitution as a check on the abuses of state governments, after his failure to secure a federal veto of state laws. "It must be admitted on all hands," said Madison, "that the state governments are as liable to attack these invaluable privileges as the general government is and therefore ought to be as cautiously guarded against."[45] For this reason, he considered this proposal to be the "most valuable amendment on the whole list."[46]

Madison's speech to the House lasted several hours. After the many months he'd spent on planning and research, he was surely dismayed by his colleagues' reactions. "I am against inserting a declaration of rights in the constitution," said a Federalist member from Georgia. "If such an addition is not dangerous or improper, it is at least unnecessary: that is a sufficient reason for not entering into the subject at a time when there are urgent calls for our attention to *important* business."[47] Even Elbridge Gerry, who had refused to sign the Constitution, displayed a lack of enthusiasm, asking when all the amendments proposed by the state conventions would be considered.[48] In the ensuing debate, not a single member saw much urgency in taking up Madison's proposals. Reluctantly, he agreed to defer them to a later time.[49]

By mid-July, the record shows that Madison "begged the House to indulge him in the further consideration of amendments."[50] After some debate, the members agreed to empanel a committee of eleven members, one from each state, to review the proposals.[51] Included in the group were Madison and four fellow veterans of the Philadelphia Convention.[52] (An Anti-Federalist member grumbled that they were "improper agents to bring forward amendments" given their likely views on "the perfection of the work.")[53] Over the course of a week, the committee made the first significant round of edits, tightening and sharpening Madison's wordy first draft.[54] After further prodding by Madison, the full membership of the House took up the committee's report in mid-August.[55] During ten days of extended debate on the merits of each amendment, the lawmakers made many additional edits to the committee's draft. Though most of Madison's proposals survived, two critical decisions made at this stage of the legislative process shaped the Bill of Rights we know today.[56]

First, a majority of the committee agreed with Sherman's view that the Bill of Rights should be attached as an appendix, overriding Madison's plan to incorporate them into the Constitution's text.[57] "The Constitution is the act of the people and ought to remain entire," Sherman explained.[58] As a result, the Constitution we read today is the same document Americans received in 1787, with all its strengths and shortcomings intact. It was a consequential decision that has also allowed every generation of Americans to appreciate the Bill of Rights as a coherent and powerful articulation of rights.

Second, the Federalist majority rebuffed the Anti-Federalists' attempts to include their desired structural amendments in the package of constitutional fixes. Chief among them was a measure restricting Congress's power to tax.[59] One dissenting member called the tax amendment "of more importance than any yet obtained."[60] But the House rejected it, along with other measures introduced by the outflanked Anti-Federalists, including a proposal to limit Congress's power to overrule state election laws,[61] and one that would give constituents the power to "instruct their representatives" in Congress.[62] Brushing off criticisms that he was going back on his pledge to bring forward the "solid and substantial" amendments recommended by the ratifying conventions, Madison explained he was simply being "a friend to what is attainable." By his reckoning, there was "little prospect of obtaining" the support needed to ratify amendments "likely to change the principles of government" or any other "dubious" proposals.[63]

The Anti-Federalists chafed at the majority's heavy-handed approach. In a moment of exasperation, Aedanus Burke, an Anti-Federalist congressman from South Carolina, brandished a document compiling the amendment ideas advanced by the states, complaining that "all the important amendments were omitted."[64] He disparaged Madison's proposals as "little better than whip-syllabub," a popular summer refreshment, "frothy and full of wind, formed only to please the palate."[65] But his complaints fell on deaf ears. On August 24, the House voted to send seventeen amendment proposals to the Senate, styled for the first time as discrete add-ons meant to be listed at the end of the Constitution.[66] Each bore Madison's fingerprint; not one of the Anti-Federalists' structural amendments was included in the package.

There is little record of the Senate debate, which lasted three weeks. Notes from the first day of their secret deliberation reveal that the senators were no more enthusiastic to take up amendments than their counterparts in the House. Several sought to postpone consideration until the following session.[67] When the Senate completed its work, it reshaped the House's draft into twelve amendments, modifying the language throughout. To Madison's dismay, the senators axed his "most valuable" amendment preventing the states from infringing certain fundamental rights.[68] With minor tweaks, the House voted to approve the changes on September 24. The Senate followed suit the next day, their last day of the session.

Two Unsuccessful Amendments

After three and a half months of intermittent debate and behind-the-scenes wrangling, Congress proposed a dozen amendments for the states' consideration. While largely focused on rights, the set of proposals included two structural fixes—Congress's intended First and Second Amendments— that failed to achieve ratification in a sufficient number of states to be included in the Bill of Rights.

The Representation Amendment

Congress's original First Amendment was meant to regulate the size of districts in the House of Representatives, answering one of the Anti-Federalists' chief complaints about the new plan of government.[69] While the Constitution provides in Article I that the number of representatives "shall not exceed" one for every thirty thousand constituents,[70] critics worried that the formula would yield districts too large to provide meaningful representation.[71] Patrick Henry lampooned it as "the strangest language that I can conceive," maintaining that the maximum size rule "may be satisfied by one representative from each state."[72] Five ratifying conventions recommended setting a *minimum* size of the chamber, pegged at one member for every thirty thousand constituents, to ensure that House districts remain suitably small.[73] The final version, sliced and diced by a drafting committee, imposed a complicated formula tying the size of the House to changes in the nation's population. It was sloppily drafted, to say the least.[74]

The measure proposed by Congress would have required at least one representative for every thirty thousand people until the House grew to one hundred members (representing a population of 3 million Americans).[75] Then the ratio would change to one representative for every forty thousand people until the House reached two hundred members (representing 8 million people). Afterward, Congress would have discretion to fix the size of districts, with two important constraints: there could never be fewer than two hundred members of Congress, nor could there be *more* than one representative for every fifty thousand people (reimposing a cap).[76]

In the end, the proposal fell one state short of the number needed to ratify, making it the first of six unratified amendments to the Constitution.[77] Had it been adopted, the Representation Amendment would have required Congress to expand the size of its membership over a few decades as its drafters intended. But thanks to poor drafting and faulty arithmetic, it would have eventually produced an absurd result. After the 1820 census, when the U.S. population passed the 9 million mark, the House of Representatives grew to 213 members, or one member for every 42,000 constituents. Had the amendment been in effect, the House would have been required to set its membership at no less than 200 . . . and *no more than 180!*[78]

Over time, as the nation's population continued to grow, so did the House of Representatives. By 1911, when the chamber froze its size at 435 members, each district represented an average of 210,000 constituents.[79] Today, thanks to population growth, the typical member of Congress represents over 750,000 Americans, a result the founding generation could have scarcely conceived.[80]

The Congressional Pay Amendment

The original Second Amendment addressed a concern relating to government ethics. Though each state paid the salaries of its delegates to the Confederation Congress, the Framers decided that Congress should determine its own compensation in a manner "to be ascertained by law."[81] The rule was intended to protect lawmakers' independence from state governments, but critics worried about the wisdom of allowing public servants to set their own pay. In response, Madison suggested an amendment providing that changes in compensation cannot take effect "until an election of representatives shall have intervened."[82] The measure was intended as a check on legislative self-dealing, giving the voters a chance to register their disapproval at the next election.[83] (The popular concern that lawmakers might abuse their office to enrich themselves was also evident in the Constitution's two Emoluments Clauses.)[84]

While three state ratifying conventions recommended this revision, Madison doubted it was necessary.[85] "I do not believe this is a power which, in the ordinary course of government, is likely to be abused," he told lawmakers. That said, he acknowledged "a seeming impropriety" in allowing his colleagues in Congress "to put their hand into the public coffers."[86] When only six states ratified the amendment by 1792, it was deemed to be rejected.[87] Why did this seemingly benign measure receive less support than any other amendment in the package? Perhaps the state legislators responsible for ratifying it were less keen on limiting lawmakers' salaries than the ordinary citizens who participated in the state conventions.[88] Before long, the amendment was all but forgotten—until it staged an improbable comeback two centuries later.

Had these first two measures been ratified with the rest, our present First Amendment would be known the Third Amendment (ironic, given how often people attach significance to its status as "the first"). The National Rifle Association would be the nation's most powerful Fourth Amendment lobbying organization. And suspects in criminal matters would avoid self-incrimination by invoking their right to "plead the Seventh."

Our Bill of Rights

The surviving ten amendments—items three through twelve on Congress's list—ultimately became *our* Bill of Rights. The First Amendment bundles six core democratic principles with a focus on constraining Congress. The Second and Third Amendments arise out of late eighteenth-century concerns about the military. The Fourth through Eighth Amendments safeguard the rights of individuals as they interact with law enforcement and the courts. And the Ninth and Tenth Amendments clarify the position of the states and the people in the Constitution's overall balance of power.[89]

The First Amendment: From Ideas to Action
In *Madison's Music*, his ode to the First Amendment, NYU legal scholar Burt Neuborne explains how one short paragraph elegantly combines six ideas—no establishment of religion, free exercise of religion, free speech, free press, free assembly, and the right to petition government for redress of grievances—to create "a rigorous chronological narrative of free citizens governing themselves in an ideal democracy," from the inner sphere of private belief and thought to its public expression through speech and action.[90] How did so many essential freedoms find themselves packed into a single amendment?

When the House of Representatives sent its draft amendments to the Senate in August 1789, it proposed one amendment aimed at religion and another dealing with the political rights of speech, press, assembly, and petition.[91] A few weeks later, after the Senate honed the House's seventeen amendment proposals to a tight dozen, the two provisions were merged and prefaced with the admonition "Congress shall make no law." The decision to unite these concepts in a single amendment, a combination not found in any state constitution at the time, was intended to make a point: this particular set of fundamental rights was off limits to the federal government.[92]

The First Amendment begins with religion, forbidding Congress from passing legislation "respecting an establishment of religion, or prohibiting the free exercise thereof."[93] Read together, these twin provisions protect freedom of individual conscience: the Establishment Clause says the state cannot force people to support or endorse religious beliefs they do not hold, while the Free Exercise Clause bars government from interfering with private religious practices and beliefs.[94] Madison's original wording was broader in scope, seeking to protect "the full and equal rights of conscience" as well, but the Senate struck out that language without explanation.[95] Today, however, the Supreme Court has vindicated Madison's vision by holding that First Amendment protections apply to all sincerely held beliefs, whether they be religious or secular.[96]

Throughout our history, these seemingly straightforward concepts have sparked furious disagreement. What does the ban on "establishment of religion" mean? Does it, as religious conservatives often argue, merely prohibit the recognition of an official state church like the Church of England?[97] Or does it create "a wall of separation between church and state" as Thomas Jefferson famously put it?[98] These disputes have intensified since the 1960s, when the Supreme Court struck down mandatory prayer and Bible reading in schools as the unlawful establishment of religion, violating the rights of nonbelievers and religious minorities alike.[99] Anger over judicially enforced secularism kindled an unprecedented surge of activism among religious conservatives, sparking a decades-long fixation on judicial appointments and spurring the introduction of *several hundred* failed amendment proposals.[100] In recent years, an increasingly conservative judiciary has shown less interest in shoring up Jefferson's wall of separation, seeking greater "accommodation" of religion instead.[101]

Similar questions arise regarding the "free exercise of religion." What happens when this freedom clashes with other important interests? Amid the patriotic fervor of World War II, the Supreme Court held that

Jehovah's Witnesses could not be compelled to recite the Pledge of Allegiance in school.[102] But in a 1990 ruling, in a case involving two men who were denied unemployment benefits over their use of peyote in a Native American Church religious ceremony, the justices ruled that their individual religious beliefs did not excuse them from complying with generally applicable laws prohibiting the use of hallucinogens. The controversial case sparked calls for a constitutional amendment to protect religion.[103] This debate continues to animate today's culture warriors, who demand religious freedom exemptions from laws relating to contraception or the rights and equality of lesbian, gay, and transgender people.[104]

Next, the First Amendment turns to freedom of speech and the press. The Free Speech Clause protects both private thought and public communication, rights essential to an open society.[105] Courts have interpreted "speech" to include a wide array of expression, from writing a newspaper article criticizing government officials to wearing a black armband in silent protest.[106] A high-profile 1989 case holding that flag burning was a form of protected speech fueled a long campaign to win a constitutional fix. Between 1990 and 2005, the House of Representatives approved a flag-desecration amendment no fewer than six times, only to see it fail narrowly in the Senate each time.[107]

Despite the First Amendment's clear command that "Congress shall make no law . . . abridging the freedom of speech," judges have long held that this freedom is not absolute. Lawmakers can place reasonable restrictions on the time, place, and manner of speech, such as rules regulating the use of loudspeakers in public, as long as they are not aimed at disfavored speech. They can regulate or even ban obscenity. And they can outlaw speech that causes particular harm, including incitements to imminent violence.[108] Neuborne reminds us that "the First Amendment as we know it today didn't exist before Justice William Brennan Jr. and the rest of the Warren Court invented it in the 1960s."[109] Before then, politically disfavored groups—labor activists, antiwar protestors, political radicals—found little protection from persecution and censorship.

In recent years, conservative legal advocates have looked to the First Amendment's guarantee of free speech to advance the right's jurisprudential goals. On the frontlines of the culture wars, lawyers for a Colorado baker argued that making a wedding cake for a gay couple would force him to express a view of marriage that conflicts with his religious beliefs.[110] In a series of cases, including the controversial *Citizens United v. Federal*

Election Commission, advocates have successfully equated electoral spending with speech, eviscerating dozens of laws that protected the integrity
of our elections.[111] Some reformers concerned about the corrupting role
of money in politics are looking to the amendment process to push back,
hoping to clarify in the Constitution that governments have the power to
regulate spending in political contests, particularly by corporations.

Freedom of the press, which James Madison called among the "great
rights of mankind," allows a speaker to reach a wide audience.[112] Without free and robust media, meaningful elections and accountable government would be impossible. At its root, freedom of the press consists of
"the right to criticize the government, its officers, and its policies," explains
historian Leonard Levy, including the right to "engage in rasping, corro-
sive, and offensive discussions on all topics of public interest."[113] And yet,
while three state conventions called for an amendment to protect it,[114] the
contemporaneous understanding of "freedom of the press" was "far from
self-evident."[115] There is little to be gleaned from the debates in Congress
or in the ratifying conventions, but the concept was widely understood at
a minimum to include freedom from prior censorship. At the same time,
governments could—and did—subject the press to criminal prosecution
after publication under laws punishing seditious libel, as they had under
the English common law.[116] Like many other liberties in the Bill of Rights,
our understanding of press freedom has become more expansive over
time. Since the 1960s, in particular, courts have afforded journalists more
robust protections against civil and criminal retribution.[117]

Finally, the First Amendment extends its protective umbrella to the
activities that put ideas into action: political organizing and demanding
change, rights inherent in a republican form of government.[118] In recent
years, courts have interpreted this right to include a broader freedom of
association.[119]

The Second and Third Amendments: Common Defense

The Second and Third Amendments are rooted in military institutions
and practices of a bygone era. For most of our history, they languished as
vestigial oddities and were largely ignored. But in recent years, the well-
funded efforts of the National Rifle Association (NRA) and a passionate
gun-rights constituency have moved the Second Amendment's history and
meaning to the center of a fierce public debate.

Like the failed Representation Amendment, the Second Amendment suffers from unclear wording: "A well regulated militia, being necessary to the security of a free state, the right of the people to keep and bear arms, shall not be infringed." [120] With its reference to a militia and a haphazard use of commas, it's hard to say for certain what Congress really meant. But we do know that Americans in the late eighteenth century were concerned over the future of the military.

The Anti-Federalists had a strong attachment to state militias, the thirteen disparate defense brigades manned by gun-owning citizen-soldiers. They worried that the new government would replace them with a standing army of professional soldiers or, worse, hired mercenaries like the hated Hessians who fought for the British during the Revolution. [121] When New York ratified the Constitution, it recommended an amendment clarifying that a militia was "the proper, natural and safe defense of a free State," declaring that standing armies in peacetime were "dangerous to liberty." [122] Three other states did the same. [123] At the time, no one foresaw how the dreaded standing army would evolve into today's modern military, drawn from the ranks of the citizenry. Within a few decades, the ragtag militias went the way of powder horns and flintlock muskets. [124]

When they crafted the Second Amendment, did lawmakers in the 1st Congress intend to confer on everyone a right to own a firearm? Or did they mean to tie that right to participation in state militias? In 1789, the term "bear arms" had a clear military connotation. [125] Consistent with that understanding, the Supreme Court declined on four occasions, between 1876 and 1939, to extend the amendment's protection beyond membership in a militia. [126] But starting in the 1970s, the NRA and its allies pressed for an interpretation rooted in the *individual's* right to bear arms. At first, few took the campaign seriously. Former chief justice Warren Burger, a conservative Republican, summed up the response of the legal establishment in memorable fashion. The NRA's position, he said, was "one of the greatest pieces of fraud, I repeat the word *fraud*, on the American public." [127]

Even so, the gun lobby's perseverance paid off. The NRA promoted constitutional scholarship to bolster its novel legal theories. Most important, it appealed to the court of public opinion, persuading millions of Americans that the Second Amendment guaranteed their right to own a gun. [128] By 2008, the group orchestrated a stunning jurisprudential volte-face. In the case of *District of Columbia v. Heller*, a narrow majority of five justices parsed evidence of the amendment's origins to find that its "central component" was the right "to use arms in defense of hearth and home," wholly divorcing it from the textual reference to a militia. Critically, in a concession to public safety, the justices also conceded that "longstanding prohibitions" on the use of guns were presumptively still valid.[129]

The opinion's controversial "originalist" dive into the amendment's origins has drawn criticism from all along the ideological spectrum. Richard Posner, an influential conservative federal appeals court judge, criticizes the justices' reasoning as an exercise in "freewheeling discretion strongly flavored with ideology."[130] But in the years since *Heller*, those "longstanding prohibitions" have held. To the gun lobby's dismay, judges in hundreds of cases have upheld gun safety laws that limit people's ability to obtain or carry firearms.[131]

While the Second Amendment emerged from obscurity to the white-hot center of public debate, the Third Amendment ban on quartering soldiers in private homes has little relevance for Americans today. The measure addresses a searing abuse of the colonial period. In 1765 and 1774, Parliament passed two Quartering Acts requiring local governments to house British soldiers in barns, inns, and "uninhabited houses."[132] The practice caused such resentment among the colonists that "quartering large bodies of armed troops among us" appeared in the Declaration of Independence's list of grievances against King George III.[133]

The memory still rankled a decade later when Americans debated the new Constitution. At the Virginia ratifying convention, Patrick Henry warned of the abuses that might arise from Congress's "very alarming power" to raise armies. "Here we may have troops in time of peace," he warned. "They may be billeted in any manner—to tyrannize, oppress, and crush us."[134] Four state ratifying conventions called for an amendment to abolish the practice.[135] The Third Amendment made it into the Constitution with little debate in Congress, and there has been little in the way of case law since. It would be cited many years later, in a landmark Supreme Court case striking down Connecticut's ban on contraceptives, as one of several constitutional amendments with "penumbras" and "emanations" that imply a fundamental right to privacy.[136]

The Fourth Through Eighth Amendments: Crime and Punishment

The next five amendments are best understood as a cluster of protections for those interacting with law enforcement and the courts. Burt Neuborne perceptively draws our attention to their numerical progression, which tracks the sequence of the legal process through investigation and arrest (Fourth Amendment), accusation and custodial interrogation (Fifth Amendment), adjudication (Sixth and Seventh Amendments), and punishment (Eighth Amendment).[137]

Like the two military-themed amendments, the Fourth Amendment was a response to British colonial abuses. To collect taxes (also known as excises), British officials often used general warrants providing broad license to search homes and seize goods without specific cause. For the Anti-Federalist essayist A Farmer and Planter, the memory of their depredations was still palpable. "The excise-officers have power to enter your houses at all times, by night or day," he recounted, "and if you refuse them entrance, they can, under pretense of searching for excisable goods, that the duty has not been paid on, break open your doors, chests, trunks, desks, boxes, and rummage your houses from bottom to top."[138] Three ratifying conventions proposed a ban on this abusive practice.[139]

The text of the Fourth Amendment goes even further, protecting "the right of the people to be secure in their persons, houses, papers and effects"—protections far more robust than those found in state constitutions of the time.[140] The amendment makes clear that warrants may be granted only when a neutral judge or magistrate finds there is "probable cause."[141] Furthermore, warrants must be "particular" (and not "general"). But warrants are not always required. In a nod to the practical realities of law enforcement, courts have long sanctioned warrantless searches and seizures in defined circumstances. For instance, police officers in hot pursuit of a subject are not required to call off the chase to obtain an arrest warrant. Upon reasonable suspicion, police may also perform precautionary "stop and frisk" searches. Likewise, they may seize evidence found in "plain view" or when there is an imminent risk of its destruction.[142] Civil libertarians rightly note that these commonsense exceptions can be easily abused. Just ask the over half million New Yorkers, mostly Black and Latino, stopped by the police annually from 2006 to 2012. Nearly nine in ten were completely innocent.[143]

There are five basic guarantees embedded in the Fifth Amendment, making it the longest of the ten amendments in the Bill of Rights. The amendment's first three sections relate to criminal prosecutions. The Grand Jury Clause requires that anyone accused of a serious crime may be indicted only by a grand jury comprised of ordinary citizens. Americans in the eighteenth century saw the grand jury as a crucial check on overzealous and corrupt prosecutors, helping to ensure that the evidence presented is sufficient to justify an indictment.[144] (By the amendment's terms, the protection is not available to military personnel during time of war or emergency.)[145] The Double Jeopardy Clause offers further protection against abusive prosecutions, guaranteeing that criminal defendants, once acquitted, cannot be prosecuted again for the same offense.[146] And the Self-Incrimination Clause, more commonly known as "the right to remain silent," is familiar to anyone who has ever watched a crime drama on television.[147] It upholds the principle that criminal defendants have no obligation to assist their own prosecution.

The remaining two provisions of the Fifth Amendment ensure procedural fairness, starting with "due process." The guarantee that no person may "be deprived of life, liberty, or property, without due process of law" ranks among the Constitution's most fundamental precepts. Along with a parallel provision in the Fourteenth Amendment, which applies the rule to state governments, the Fifth Amendment's Due Process Clause demands that government actors adhere to the law and abide by fair procedures.[148]

Rounding out the list, the Fifth Amendment's Takings Clause provides that government may not confiscate private property without fairly compensating its owners. Like the Second through Fourth Amendments, the clause harks back to abuses of the colonial period, most notably the British practice of impressing goods and property for military purposes.[149] The Takings Clause is the only provision in the Bill of Rights not recommended by any state ratifying convention, although three early state constitutions offered comparable protection.[150] Madison's decision to add it reflected his abiding belief in "the inviolability of property."[151] While the Takings Clause requires the government to adhere to a fair procedure, it also confers on individuals a substantive right: their property may only be taken for "public use," say to build a highway or a school. In a controversial 2005 decision, the Supreme Court held that this principle of "eminent domain" may be broadly construed. Government may take private property for a "public purpose," like redeveloping a blighted neighborhood or making harbor improvements, even if the land is not actually used by the public.[152]

The next two amendments, the Sixth and Seventh, cover criminal and civil procedure with a focus on the ancient common-law tradition of the jury trial. Eighteenth-century Americans cared deeply about juries. The Declaration of Independence condemned King George III "for depriving us, in many cases, of the benefits of trial by jury."[153] To this day, Americans have relied on juries as an essential part of democratic self-government in which citizens protect their peers from governmental overreach.[154] In total, five ratifying conventions proposed jury-related amendments.[155]

The Sixth Amendment guarantees the right to a jury trial in criminal cases, along with other protections to ensure fairness. The Framers had already provided for jury trials in their 1787 Constitution, requiring that all crimes be tried by jury in the state where the offense was committed.[156] But the Anti-Federalists complained that the provision could be read to deny the common-law right to be tried *locally*, where the crime took place. The Sixth Amendment addressed this technicality by specifying that trials must take place in the federal judicial district where the crime was committed.[157]

The rest of the amendment focuses on what is needed to ensure a fair trial. It provides that criminal trials must be both "speedy and public" and guarantees that the accused receive fair notice of the charges leveled against them. At trial, defendants have the right to confront and cross-examine witnesses who testify against them and to call witnesses of their own. They also have the right to be represented by a lawyer. For much of our history, this last protection meant little more than the right to retain an attorney. Those without the money to hire one had to fend for themselves. In 1932, a conservative Supreme Court ruled in *Powell v. Alabama* that the state must provide free and adequate counsel in all capital cases. Then, in 1963, in the celebrated case of *Gideon v. Wainwright*, the liberal Warren Court held that defendants in all felony cases have the right to a court-appointed lawyer if they cannot afford one.[158] Half a century later, this promise remains largely unfulfilled. State and local governments rarely commit the resources necessary to ensure that indigent people, who disproportionately swell the ranks of the criminal justice system, are guaranteed their constitutional right to competent and effective legal representation.[159]

The Seventh Amendment addresses the right to a jury trial in civil lawsuits in federal courts between private citizens. During the Philadelphia Convention's final week, the Framers considered, and quickly rejected, a motion to guarantee the right to a jury trial in civil cases. (The discussion prompted George Mason to make his last-minute plea for a declaration of rights.)[160] Americans were outraged by the omission. A group of concerned citizens from the small town of Preston, Connecticut, wrote to the state's ratifying convention to express their indignation. "This is repugnant to the custom handed down from our ancestors," they wrote, "and always set easy on the people and esteemed as a privilege."[161] Five ratifying conventions joined in the call for an amendment to preserve the civil jury.[162]

Despite acting to preserve this right, however, Congress sought to limit the provision's reach, requiring at least $20 to be at stake in the lawsuit, comparable to nearly $600 today.[163] The amendment also preserves the jury's traditional role as the trier of fact in private disputes. In recent years, conservative legal groups allied with business interests have vilified civil juries, seeking to curb them under the banner of "tort reform."[164] In an effort to rein in "frivolous lawsuits" and "out-of-control verdicts," they have successfully persuaded legislatures throughout the country to cap jury damage awards and restrict people's ability to bring their claims before juries in state courts.

Last, the Eighth Amendment limits the severity of punishments. Specifically, it bars excessive bail, excessive fines, and cruel and unusual punishments. These prohibitions were taken from the English Bill of Rights of 1689.[165] Americans in the colonial period embraced these core human rights principles, which found their way into nine early state charters.[166] And yet, that didn't stop them from meting out horrifically inhumane punishments, including branding, flogging, pillorying, and public hanging.[167]

The Anti-Federalists warned that the new national government would usher in a regime of torture and brutality. "They are nowhere restrained from inventing the most cruel and unheard-of punishments," inveighed one overwrought delegate at the Massachusetts ratifying convention, "and there is no constitutional check on them, but that racks and gibbets may be amongst the most mild instruments of their discipline."[168] Three state ratifying conventions proposed an amendment outlawing the most barbaric punishments.[169]

When it came time for Congress to consider the provision, however, two lawmakers balked. The term "cruel and unusual" was "too indefinite," said William Loughton Smith, a member from South Carolina.[170] New Hampshire's Samuel Livermore agreed: "It seems to have no meaning in it," he added. Livermore insisted that "it is sometimes necessary to hang a man, villains often deserve whipping, and perhaps having their ears cut off." Turning to his colleagues, he asked, "Are we in [the] future to be prevented from inflicting these punishments because they are cruel?"[171]

Livermore's musings proved prescient. Over time, judges began to consider whether long-accepted forms of punishment are compatible with our "evolving standards of decency."[172] Under that standard, once-common penal practices have been abolished. In recent years, for example, the Supreme Court ruled that the execution of children and mentally handicapped people, along with sentences of life without parole for people who have committed crimes when they were minors, all violate the Constitution's ban on cruel and unusual punishment.[173]

The Ninth and Tenth Amendments: Residual Power

Of the twenty-seven amendments to the Constitution, the Ninth and Tenth Amendments may have the least direct impact on people's lives. Until recently, they were rarely invoked in constitutional jurisprudence, and were debated mainly by legal theorists who scrutinize shreds of historical evidence and come to wildly different conclusions as to what they mean. They are best understood as explanatory arguments, offering general statements of principle.

The Ninth Amendment addresses a concern raised by the Federalists as they tried to justify their decision to forgo a declaration of rights. Would the guarantee of some rights in the Constitution imply that other rights were not protected? During the ratification debate, Madison argued it would be "dangerous" to even try, because "an enumeration which is not complete, is not safe."[174] Once he changed his mind on the desirability of a bill of rights, he included an amendment to guard against the implication that rights "not singled out . . . were consequently insecure."[175] In its final form, the Ninth Amendment provides: "The enumeration in the Constitution, of certain rights, shall not be construed to deny or disparage others retained by the people."

While the amendment's language suggests that Americans have constitutionally protected rights beyond those listed in the Bill of Rights, its text and history offer few clues as to what they are. Judges have rarely cited the Ninth Amendment.[176] In a lecture published in 1955, Justice Robert Jackson confessed that the exact rights it protected were "still a mystery."[177] Testifying in his ill-fated 1987 Supreme Court confirmation hearing, Judge Robert Bork memorably likened the amendment to an inscrutable "ink blot."[178]

Then how should we understand the Ninth Amendment's meaning and purpose? The experts are all over the map. Georgetown law professor Randy Barnett, a libertarian, insists that the Ninth Amendment "means what it says," guaranteeing that "all individual natural rights" are enforceable under the Constitution.[179] Russell Caplan, a conservative legal scholar, makes the minimalist case that the amendment merely ensures that rights guaranteed under state law will continue to be recognized.[180] Looking for a middle ground that renders the Ninth Amendment more than an ink blot but less than a "hopelessly subjective" invitation to decide cases on the basis of natural law, Burt Neuborne urges us to accept it as an invitation to interpret constitutional rights "generously" and to "expand the literal text in favor of freedom."[181] Take your pick.

Last in the Bill of Rights, the Tenth Amendment answered a question first posed at the Philadelphia Convention: What is the limit of Congress's powers under the Constitution? The Framers delegated a set of enumerated powers to the legislative branch—from levying taxes to regulating commerce to declaring war—along with broad implied powers stemming from its authority "to make all laws . . . necessary and proper" to carry out its responsibilities.[182] It was their antidote to the feebleness of the Confederation. But the Anti-Federalists preferred the stricter language in the Articles of Confederation, which confined the national legislature to the exercise of "expressly delegated" powers.[183]

This concern motivated six state ratifying conventions to recommend an amendment clarifying the respective rights of the state and federal governments under the new system.[184] As approved by the 1st Congress, the Tenth Amendment provides: "The powers not delegated to the United States by the Constitution, nor prohibited by it to the States, are reserved to the States respectively, or to the people." Madison frankly considered the measure "superfluous." But with a rhetorical shrug, he assured his fellow lawmakers that "there can be no harm in making such a declaration."[185] But as the lawmakers worked their way through a round of revisions, South Carolina Anti-Federalist Thomas Tudor Tucker proposed restoring the understanding that all "powers not expressly delegated" to the federal government would be reserved to the states.[186] It would be the Anti-Federalists' last stand in their campaign to roll back the Constitution's promise of a strong national government. Madison objected to the motion, arguing that it was "impossible to confine a government to the exercise of express powers."[187] In a highly consequential vote, the proposal was firmly rejected.[188]

Today most scholars view the Tenth Amendment as a simple reaffirmation of the Framers' vision: Congress can act only when it has the express or implied power to do so.[189] Only a few court decisions have ever cited it, most notably in the Supreme Court's notorious Lochner-era rulings curtailing Congress's powers to regulate the economy as infringements on state authority. In a recent line of cases, though, the conservatives on the Supreme Court have relied on the Tenth Amendment to invalidate laws that contemplate state enforcement of federal policies and to impose limits on federal spending power, including part of the Affordable Care Act.[190] Modern self-proclaimed "constitutionalists" on the far right have latched onto it as a battle cry in a modern-day campaign to diminish the federal government's power in the name of states' rights.[191]

Ratification by the States

After President Washington transmitted the package of amendments to the states on October 2, 1789, lawmakers in Congress could fairly claim to have heeded the popular call for amendments.[192] However, while some Anti-Federalists welcomed these added protections for basic rights, many more were disappointed by the lack of structural amendments. Their dissatisfaction made the task of winning the support of three-quarters of the state legislatures more difficult than anyone imagined. Despite the strong public backing, the ten amendments we know today as the Bill of Rights nearly failed to secure the support needed for ratification.

When Congress voted to approve the amendments, the consent of nine of eleven states would have been sufficient to ratify them. But as new states joined the Union the approval threshold ratcheted upward, keeping ratification just out of reach. When North Carolina and Rhode Island returned to the fold, as Madison hoped, they each acted quickly to take up the pending amendments.[193] By June 1790, after the vote in Rhode Island, nine states had ratified our first ten amendments—but in a Union of thirteen states, *ten* were now needed to ratify. In November 1791, the newly admitted state of Vermont followed suit, upping the tally to ten states—but in a Union now consisting of fourteen states, *eleven* were needed to ratify.

The fate of the amendments hinged on four holdout states: Connecticut, Massachusetts, Georgia, and Virginia. Through legislative ineptitude or principled opposition, none seemed to be in a hurry to act. In Connecticut, the proposals Ping-Ponged between the two chambers of the legislature without resolution.[194] In Massachusetts, lawmakers provisionally approved our First through Seventh and Ninth Amendments, but neglected to pass a final bill.[195] And in Georgia, lawmakers refused to take up the proposals on the ground that amendments were unnecessary.[196] These three states would get around to ratifying the Bill of Rights only in 1939, as Americans commemorated the 150th anniversary of its adoption by Congress.[197]

In the end, it came down to Virginia. Once again, Patrick Henry stood in the way. At the state's ratifying convention, Henry upbraided the Federalists for their failure to protect rights in the Constitution. "My mind will not be quieted till I see something substantial come forth in the shape of a bill of rights," the irascible Virginian declared.[198] But now, outmaneuvered by Madison and angry over "impediments" to the structural alterations he desired, Henry changed his tune. He complained that Congress's proposed amendments did not adequately safeguard the rights of the states. Their adoption, he thought, would "tend to injure rather than to serve the cause of liberty" by harming the Anti-Federalists' chances of obtaining a second convention.[199]

Henry delayed consideration of the amendments in the hope that North Carolina and Rhode Island would hold out for structural amendments as the price of ratifying the Constitution. But while the two states did endorse a raft of revisions, raising the total of amendments recommended by the state ratifying conventions to 232, they disappointed Henry by joining the Union without further conditions.[200] By the fall of 1791, after two years of delay, Henry's campaign of obstruction came to an anticlimactic end.[201] With the vote in Virginia on December 15, 1791, ten of the twelve amendments proposed by Congress obtained the support of eleven states, making them the first addition to the Constitution of 1787.[202] In time, the amendments would come to be known as the Bill of Rights, a charter of freedom standing alongside the Constitution and Declaration of Independence as one of our nation's founding documents.[203]

Madison must surely have savored this triumph. Through tireless effort and sheer force of will, this "small man with a quiet voice" helped to lead thirteen fractious states onto a new path: from the foundering "firm league of friendship" to the "more perfect Union" rooted in respect for individual liberty and the rule of law. To quote historian Richard Labunski, "It is fair to say that no other person in the nation's history did so much for which he is appreciated so little."[204] While it is justly celebrated as one of the great milestones in the advancement of human rights, the adoption of the Bill of Rights elicited remarkably little fanfare at the time. Few newspapers even took note of it. The honor of announcing their adoption fell to Thomas Jefferson, now the nation's secretary of state. In a circular letter to the nation's governors, he tepidly noted the ratification of "certain articles in addition to and amendment of the Constitution"—buried amid legislative updates on post offices and fisheries.[205]

Following on the heels of a ratification process designed to appeal to "the supreme authority of the people themselves,"[206] the addition of the Bill of Rights marked a second great infusion of democratic legitimacy to the Framers' Constitution. In contrast to the secrecy that marked the drafting of the original plan, this first set of amendments came on the recommendation of citizens elected to the state ratifying conventions. They were then drafted and ratified by lawmakers in Congress and the state legislatures, elected by the people.[207] To be sure, representation in these assemblies was grossly deficient. A majority of the population—women, Black people, and other minorities—were almost entirely excluded from the deliberation.[208] Still, the process was more participatory than ever before. With this demonstration that Article V was capable of remedying defects in our Constitution, the American experiment could slowly begin to move beyond its test phase.

Having fought a war to win them, a sizable number of Americans were unwilling to trust tacit assurances that their liberties were secure. The Anti-Federalists better understood the American people's passionate attachment to this birthright. As George Mason foresaw, adding protections for rights would indeed "give great quiet to the people."[209] The Federalists, invested in their philosophical stance against the enumeration of rights and understandably determined to give the new government a chance to prove itself, refused to change course until it was almost too late.

As Madison hoped, the adoption of the Bill of Rights marked the end of the Anti-Federalist campaign to undo the new system of government. While they lost no opportunity to castigate the Framers for their failure to include protections for rights, the real goal of the most ardent Anti-Federalists was the adoption of structural alterations to the new government's design. As Madison came to see, the adoption of amendments protecting rights would "kill the opposition everywhere."[210] And sure enough, as Jefferson reported in an April 1790 note to the Marquis de Lafayette, "The opposition to our new constitution has almost totally disappeared."[211]

Although the Anti-Federalists reconciled themselves to the new Constitution, their strain of political thought hardly went away. Instead, it helped to frame the worldview of a new political party, committed to states' rights and limits on the federal government, working within the system the Federalists created. As the historian Gordon Wood observes, "the Anti-Federalists may have lost the contest over the Constitution, but by 1800 they and their Jeffersonian-Republican successors eventually won the larger struggle over what kind of society and culture America was to have, at least for a good part of the nineteenth century."[212] Before long, states' rights would become the rallying cry of the South in its defense of slavery.

Two centuries later, Americans would come to revere the first ten amendments as "fundamental safeguards of liberty" that belong to all Americans.[213] But in one of history's great ironies, few people at the time foresaw the central role the Bill of Rights would play in the development of American law. The Federalists in Congress who agreed to support Madison's proposals considered them "harmless" at best. In time, however, these protections devised to constrain the power of the new national government would be invoked to limit state power as well.[214] It's a revolution the Anti-Federalists never saw coming.

In the meantime, it would not be long before the founding generation added two more amendments to the Constitution.

The Eleventh Amendment: Suing States

During the ratification contest, the Anti-Federalists voiced concerns about the scope and reach of the judicial power. While Alexander Hamilton argued that the judiciary's limited role of deciding cases would make it the "weakest" and "least dangerous" of the three branches of government,[215] the Anti-Federalists worried that independent life-tenured judges would wield unaccountable power. "The Supreme Court under this Constitution would be exalted above all other power in the government," said the Anti-Federalist essayist writing as Brutus. "There is no power above them that can correct their errors or control their decisions."[216]

One notable source of controversy was a provision in Article III extending the judicial power to lawsuits "between a state and citizens of another state."[217] Critics argued that this grant of jurisdiction would undermine the states' pre-existing sovereign immunity from suit, exposing them to the risk of financially ruinous litigation by wartime creditors and speculators.[218] The Federalists replied that the provision was only meant to establish jurisdiction in suits involving states as plaintiffs.[219] As James Madison assured Virginia's ratifying convention, "It is not in the power of individuals to call any state into court."[220] Delegates to New York's state ratifying convention recommended amending the Constitution to make clear that the states' sovereign immunity remained intact.[221] Madison insisted that there was no ambiguity. But just five years later, a ruling by the Supreme Court "triggered . . . a sense of betrayal."[222]

In the case of *Chisholm v. Georgia*, decided in February 1793, the justices heard a claim brought by the estate of a South Carolina businessman. The decedent had contracted with the state of Georgia to supply wartime provisions, but died before he could recover the sum due to him. When his executor filed a lawsuit seeking payment, Georgia refused to appear in the case, asserting it could not be sued without its consent. Four of the five justices ruled in the plaintiff's favor, citing the "strict and appropriated language" of Article III as a basis for jurisdiction.[223] Only one justice voted to uphold the state's traditional immunity from suit.[224] Georgia angrily defied the judgment, passing a law subjecting anyone trying to enforce the debt to death by hanging.[225]

In the meantime, Massachusetts was sued in a dispute over seized property by a British loyalist who fled to London. In a message to lawmakers, called to a special session to consider the matter, Governor John Hancock expressed his amazement at this turn of affairs. "I cannot conceive that the people of this Commonwealth . . . expected that each state should be held liable to answer on *compulsory civil process*, to every individual resident in another state or in a foreign kingdom," he declared.[226] To resolve the matter once and for all, the legislature instructed the state's congressional delegation to seek an amendment to "remove any clause or article . . . which can be construed to imply or justify a decision that a state is compellable to answer in any suit by an individual."[227]

When Congress reconvened, two Bay State lawmakers raced to introduce amendment resolutions in their respective chambers. Congressman Theodore Sedgwick's proposal struck a maximal blow for states' rights, preventing the federal courts from hearing any suit against a state.[228] Senator Caleb Strong's version took a more measured approach, trimming the courts' power to hear cases against states brought by individuals from other states or countries.[229] Though there is no recorded debate in either house to provide insights into the lawmakers' deliberation, there was broad consensus in favor of a constitutional fix. The Senate moved first, voting in January 1794 to adopt the Strong proposal by a vote of 23–2. Two months later, on March 4, the House approved the measure by the similarly lopsided vote of 81–9, sending it to the states for their approval.[230] It took only eleven months to gain the support of the twelve states needed to ratify the Eleventh Amendment. Though it took effect on February 7, 1795, when North Carolina lent its assent, the official announcement of its ratification was delayed for three years due to uncertainty over which states had ratified it.[231]

On its face, the Eleventh Amendment addressed a fairly narrow issue related to suing states in federal court, restoring the understanding that the Article III judicial power would be construed narrowly to preserve the sovereignty of the states.[232] But the amendment's significance is far broader. By invoking the constitutional amendment process to overturn a controversial judicial ruling, the Eleventh Amendment set an important precedent that would inspire no fewer than five amendments to the Constitution over the years (along with many unsuccessful efforts). Its quick adoption demonstrated that Article V provided a means of correcting the Court's errors, rebutting the Anti-Federalists' contention that there was no check on the Supreme Court's power to decide cases.[233] Finally, while the amendment's adoption resolved a potential impasse between the federal courts and state governments, the controversy that led to the Eleventh Amendment's adoption signaled that the young nation had yet to fully calibrate the balance of powers between the federal government and the states.[234]

For much of its history, courts read the Eleventh Amendment narrowly to permit broad categories of lawsuits against states, including suits against officers or subdivisions of a state.[235] But starting in the 1990s, the conservative Rehnquist Court relied on the amendment to justify an expanded view of state sovereignty found nowhere in its text or history. Under this doctrine, built on the notion that "the states entered the federal system with their sovereignty intact," courts have restricted Congress's power to subject states to suit when it legislates under its Article I powers. As a result, states—and state-owned entities like public universities and businesses— have been held to be immune from liability from federal labor and anti-discrimination laws in any court.[236] John Noonan, a respected conservative federal appeals judge appointed by Ronald Reagan, criticizes this push to "narrow the nation's power," calling the claim that the Eleventh Amendment permits states to flout federal laws "imaginary."[237]

The Twelfth Amendment: The Electoral College, Take Two

Called upon to defend the Electoral College system of presidential selection, Alexander Hamilton offered this Panglossian take: "If the manner of it be not perfect, it is at least excellent." [238] And yet, within just twelve years of its creation, this not quite perfect system required an overhaul.

As noted in chapter one, the Framers considered other, more obvious methods for selecting a "first magistrate" before settling on the Electoral College. The Virginia Plan recommended that Congress elevate an executive from its own ranks, as many state governors were chosen at the time. [239] Delegates protested that this would render the president too dependent on the legislature. [240] James Wilson advocated election by popular vote, believing it would "produce more confidence among the people." [241] The convention shot this idea down twice. [242] George Mason argued that "the extent of the country renders it impossible that the people can have the requisite capacity to judge" the candidates. [243] Hugh Williamson, a delegate from North Carolina, argued that candidates from the most populous states would have an advantage, with the pointed exception of Virginia as "her slaves will have no suffrage." [244] As the debate dragged on, the delegates pondered leaving the choice to state legislatures [245]—and even governors. [246] But each method of selection left something to be desired, prompting Wilson to lament that the subject was "the most difficult of all on which we have had to decide." [247]

Struggling to find a solution as their time in Philadelphia neared its end, the convention adopted an indirect system of election inspired by the method used by Maryland to select its governor. A panel of four political theorists who studied the origins of the Electoral College concluded that, though "no coherent theory supported" the Framers' elaborate scheme, they managed to check off the right boxes. Their system comported with "the broader constitutional principles of federalism, separation of powers, and checks and balances." [248] It was also consistent with the Framers' wariness of popular democracy and political factions, along with their casual accommodation of slavery. [249]

The Framers laid out the process in a densely written section of Article II. First, each state would be allocated electors based on its total number of senators and representatives. While the large states would receive more electors under this system, the smallest states were guaranteed at least three: giving them greater clout than they would have had in a system based purely on a vote of the people. (Currently, the ten least populated states, with about 3 percent of the nation's population, control over 6 percent of the total electoral vote.)[250] The Southern states also reaped an electoral advantage by virtue of their inflated representation in Congress under the Three-Fifths Clause.[251] By way of example, South Carolina and New Hampshire had virtually the same population of free people in 1790, just under 142,000. But South Carolina's 107,000 slaves—held as chattel with no political rights—ensured the state seven electoral votes to New Hampshire's five.[252]

Second, states would choose their electors "in such manner as the legislature thereof may direct."[253] In the early years of the republic, many state legislatures simply appointed them, but over time, the people demanded a say. By 1832, every state but South Carolina had adopted laws allowing the voters to choose presidential electors on Election Day.[254] It remains the practice in every state today but, incredibly, this is not required. Indeed, the Supreme Court has made clear that "the individual citizen has no federal constitutional right to vote for electors . . . unless and until the state legislature chooses a statewide election as the means to implement its power to appoint members of the electoral college."[255] In theory at least, legislatures can revise their laws to take back this power at any time (although some scholars argue that principles of due process would require states to respect the people's fundamental right to vote for president).[256]

Finally, electors would have only one job: meeting to cast votes for president and vice president. The Framers believed that the electors, whom they expected would be men of judgment and intellect, would decide among a broad field of candidates, much as presidential primary caucuses do today. To shield the process from undue "heats and ferments," they required electors to meet in their respective state capitals—not all together as a "college"—to reduce the risk of intrigue and corrupt deal-making.[257]

The 1787 Constitution established a voting procedure that differs in significant ways from the method used today. In the original design, created for what the Framers imagined would be nonpartisan elections with many candidates, each elector cast *two* votes. (To limit voting for "favorite son" candidates, electors could cast only one vote for a candidate from their home state.) From this field of contenders, the person receiving the most votes would be elected president so long as he won a majority of the total number of electors. The second-highest vote getter would become vice president.[258] If no candidate commanded a majority, the election would move to the House of Representatives, which would choose a winner from the top five contenders in a "contingent election" in which each state delegation casts a single vote, no matter its size.[259] In the rare instance that two candidates tied for the majority, the House would choose among them. Finally, if there was a tie for second place, the Senate would decide the election for vice president.

Confused? The Framers were too. Their convoluted process suffered from defects that became apparent from the very first election. When George Washington was selected as the country's consensus choice for president, sweeping every state that voted, the result surprised no one. But a deadlocked legislature failed to cast New York's eight electoral votes.[260] By the election of 1796, when Washington stepped aside after serving two terms, the system had to adapt to the emergence of two political parties, even though the Framers feared factions and hoped to avoid them. In a rancorous campaign, the Federalist leader John Adams faced off against Thomas Jefferson, the standard bearer of the emerging Democratic-Republican Party. Each man had a preferred candidate for vice president, but when the electors narrowly chose Adams as president, Jefferson was the runner-up. In their optimism, the Framers created a system that assumed the victor and the runner-up would govern together wisely and without partisanship, but these embittered opponents could barely stand each other.

By the fourth presidential contest in 1800, the system sparked a great national crisis. In a rematch between Adams and Jefferson, this time as the heads of rival political parties, Jefferson narrowly defeated Adams, boosted by the South's enhanced strength in the Electoral College. But in a twist the Framers never anticipated, every elector who voted for Jefferson also cast a vote for his purported running mate, producing a tie. It fell to the Federalist-controlled "lame duck" House to pick the winner. In an astonishing turn of events, Jefferson's would-be vice president, New York senator Aaron Burr, campaigned for the top job himself. Jefferson eventually prevailed, but only after thirty-six rounds of balloting over seven tumultuous days.[261]

The spectacle in the House was sobering. The young nation could ill afford to repeat the chaos of the 1800 election. If presidential elections could be so easily thrown to Congress, the system might devolve into a de facto legislative appointment system, inviting corruption and undermining the separation of powers.[262] Even Hamilton, a man not known for admitting error, acknowledged that the system posed "a danger of convulsion and disorder."[263] And yet, Congress dithered for nearly three years before taking action. Finally, in December 1803 lawmakers approved by the narrowest of margins an amendment to revise the Electoral College system.[264] A switched vote in either chamber would have scuttled it.[265] With the next election approaching, the proposal advanced rapidly through the states, achieving ratification in less than eight months.

The Twelfth Amendment regulates the presidential election system in use today, making three important changes to the original version. First, the amendment requires that electors cast their votes for president and vice president on separate ballots. In making this change, Congress recognized that presidential campaigns would be waged between political party tickets comprised of presidential and vice-presidential running mates. Second, the contingent election procedure in the House was modified to cap the number of finalists from five to three.[266] Finally, as they pondered the possibility of deadlocked votes in the House, the amendment's drafters provided that the vice president would step into the role of president if the body failed to choose a president by Inauguration Day (a change undone by a later constitutional amendment).[267]

With the new voting system in place, Jefferson was comfortably re-elected in 1804, winning the electoral votes of fifteen of the seventeen states then in the Union.[268] His running mate, New York governor George Clinton, won the first election for vice president.[269] But the Twelfth Amendment failed to cure the Electoral College's many shortcomings. In five of the fifty-five presidential elections conducted after its adoption—nearly one out of eleven—this relic of antebellum America has elevated a president who failed to win the popular vote. At times, the process has invited controversy and even chaos. In 1824, when the House once again decided a presidential contest, supporters of popular-vote winner Andrew Jackson charged that a "corrupt bargain" with a third candidate gave John Quincy Adams the presidency.[270] In 1877, Democrats in Congress ceded the election to Rutherford B. Hayes, who trailed in the disputed vote count, in exchange for an end to Reconstruction.[271] In 2000, George W. Bush landed in the White House after five Republican justices on the Supreme Court intervened to stop a recount of votes in the disputed state of Florida.[272] Most recently, Donald Trump prevailed in the 2016 presidential race despite running nearly 3 million votes behind his opponent. For these reasons and more, the Electoral College remains one of the Constitution's most undemocratic features.

Following the adoption of the Twelfth Amendment, it would be another sixty-one years before Americans made any additional changes to the Constitution—but not for a lack of trying. Congress proposed an amendment in 1810 on the unusual subject of foreign titles of nobility. It is the second of six failed amendments, approved by Congress only to fall short in the ratification process.

The Foreign Titles of Nobility Amendment: The Missing Thirteenth

Americans in the early nineteenth century worried a great deal about foreign interference in our politics. The young republic was encircled by territories ruled by emperors and kings who frequently waged war with one another. Unnerved by a steady drumbeat of international conflict and intrigue, from the French Revolution to the Napoleonic Wars to the rising tensions with Britain that would spark the War of 1812, newspapers and politicians fanned the flames of paranoia over foreign treachery and subversion.[273] The 1803 marriage of Jérôme Bonaparte, the youngest brother of the French emperor, to an American woman fueled almost comical speculation that Napoléon's nephew could rise to the presidency and consummate a merger between the United States and France.[274]

The Framers understood that the machinations of foreign powers could pose a danger to America's independence.[275] They included a Title of Nobility Clause in Article I specifying that no person holding an office of profit or trust may accept any "present, emolument, office, or title, of any kind whatever, from any king, prince, or foreign state," without the consent of Congress.[276] Also known as the Foreign Emoluments Clause, it was written to prevent federal officeholders from being corrupted by foreign entities. Six state ratifying conventions wanted the prohibition to be even stronger, recommending an absolute ban on these insidious foreign entanglements.[277]

By 1810, Congress was ready to revisit the matter when Senator Philip Reed, a Democratic-Republican lawmaker representing Maryland, proposed amending the Constitution to impose a categorical ban on the acceptance of honorific titles and honors from foreign powers. This would-be Thirteenth Amendment was the Title of Nobility Clause on steroids, expanding the Framers' narrowly tailored prohibition to apply to all U.S. citizens. The measure would have also barred the acceptance of any other form of emolument or gift from foreign powers without Congress's consent. By its terms, violators would "cease to be a citizen of the United States."

Reed's proposal was approved by overwhelming majorities in both chambers.[278] There was no recorded debate in Congress and almost no press coverage, so it's not entirely clear why lawmakers felt the need to propose such a draconian policy.[279] A few prominent theories have emerged.[280] Some believe the proposal was rooted in a longstanding wariness of foreigners that predates our country's founding.[281] Others attribute it to destabilizing pressure from European powers, notably France and Britain, in the years leading up to the War of 1812.[282] Still others credit *l'affaire Bonaparte*.[283]

The measure was very nearly adopted, winning ratification in twelve of the fourteen states needed. In an odd twist, many people believed it actually *did* become the Thirteenth Amendment, thanks to an editor's decision to include it the 1815 edition of the *Statutes at Large*, the official compilation of federal laws.[284] Textbook publishers followed suit, creating confusion that persisted for decades. Today, the "Missing Thirteenth" is fodder for a handful of conspiracy theorists who allege that the amendment was lawfully ratified in 1819, only to be suppressed by a conspiracy of lawyers, bankers, and foreign interests.[285] In 2010, the Iowa Republican Party called for reintroducing the amendment as a way to "make a statement" about President Barack Obama's acceptance of the 2009 Nobel Peace Prize.[286]

The Amendment Window Closes

The demise of the Titles of Nobility Amendment marked the end of America's first wave of constitutional change. In the twenty-one years from 1789 to 1810, twelve amendments were added to the Constitution. Congress also approved three additional measures that failed to achieve ratification at the time. To this day, this first amending period was the most productive. Congress would propose no new amendments until the advent of the Civil War. Even during this long dry spell, however, the Constitution continued to evolve. Over the first half of the nineteenth century, Americans revisited some of the big questions that divided the Framers at the Philadelphia Convention—this time in the courts. In three landmark rulings, the

Supreme Court addressed enduring controversies arising under the Constitution, clarifying its meaning.

The first of these three decisions, *Marbury v. Madison*,[287] was handed down in February 1803. The dispute arose out of the eleventh-hour creation of judicial positions by the lame-duck Federalist majority in Congress following the hotly contested election of 1800.[288] With the clock ticking, President John Adams moved quickly to fill the newly created positions and the Senate promptly confirmed them. John Marshall, the outgoing secretary of state, prepared the official paperwork on his last day in office—signed, sealed, and *mostly* delivered. But when the new administration took office, there were four justices of the peace still waiting to receive commissions formalizing their appointment. Irate over Adams's "midnight judges," incoming president Thomas Jefferson stopped the transmission of the commissions.[289] And so, William Marbury, eager to assume the office of justice of the peace, found himself in limbo. He brought suit in the Supreme Court to compel the delivery of his commission.[290]

The case suffered from two significant irregularities. First, sitting in judgment was none other than Chief Justice John Marshall, the very man who failed to deliver Marbury's commission in time. Adams had appointed him to the Court in January 1801 but asked him to wrap up his business as secretary of state before stepping into the new position.[291] Second, the justices concluded that the Constitution did not give them jurisdiction to hear the case at all, dismissing the underlying dispute. And yet Marshall seized the opportunity to make a far-reaching pronouncement that has reverberated through two centuries of constitutional law. Speaking for a unanimous Court, the chief justice declared, "It is emphatically the province and duty of the judicial department to say what the law is."[292] Put another way, it is the judiciary's role to interpret the Constitution in cases that came before it.[293]

The first Supreme Court ruling to overturn an act of Congress, *Marbury v. Madison* articulated the principle of judicial review, the distinctly American doctrine that allows unelected judges to declare acts of Congress and the executive branch unconstitutional.[294] Since then, Americans have mostly accepted that the power to interpret the meaning of the Constitution rests largely with the courts.[295] As a result, the branch of government Hamilton called "the weakest of the three departments of power"[296] would become powerful indeed, defining and at times reshaping the Constitution's meaning over many generations.

Sixteen years after *Marbury*, the Court issued another landmark ruling in the case of *McCulloch v. Maryland*.[297] The controversy was the third round in a dispute first litigated in the ratification contest of 1787–88 and then again during the drafting of the Tenth Amendment in 1789: What are the limits of Congress's power under the Constitution? The dispute centered on the Second Bank of the United States, the nation's central bank. In 1790, in his capacity as secretary of the treasury, Alexander Hamilton first proposed the idea of chartering a national bank to stabilize and improve the nation's credit. James Madison emerged as the chief opponent of the plan in Congress, breaking with his former ally to argue that it exceeded Congress's powers.[298]

Three years earlier, writing as Publius, Madison had passionately championed an expansive vision of national power. "No axiom," he declared, "is more clearly established in law, or in reason than that wherever the end is required, the means are authorized; wherever a general power to do a thing is given, every particular power necessary for doing it is included."[299] But now, in a jaw-dropping reversal, he channeled his inner Anti-Federalist.[300] Addressing his fellow lawmakers, Madison insisted that the Constitution's grant of power to Congress is "a grant of particular powers only." Therefore, he contended, it was "not possible to discover in it the power to incorporate a bank."[301]

Hamilton countered that Congress had power aplenty. Under the Constitution, it had the explicit authority to collect taxes, borrow money, regulate trade, and support armies and navies. To execute these powers it was surely "necessary and proper" to charter a national bank.[302] Who was right? At this defining moment, President Washington seemed to waver. Ultimately he sided with Hamilton, signing legislation to charter the first Bank of the United States for a twenty-year term. It remained a subject of political controversy for years to come.[303] After letting the initial charter lapse, Congress chartered a Second Bank of the United States in 1816, rekindling the dispute over its legality. The measure was signed by none other than President James Madison, who changed his mind yet again.

Not long after, Maryland passed a law imposing a tax on banks not chartered by the state's legislature. When the Second Bank refused to pay, the state sued cashier James McCulloch in a Maryland court. After the state courts ruled for Maryland, the Bank appealed to the Supreme Court. At long last, the justices had the chance to decide: Did Congress have the authority under the Constitution to establish a national bank?[304] The

Court's unanimous opinion was a resounding yes, vindicating Hamilton's expansive vision of federal power.[305]

Writing for the Court, Chief Justice Marshall noted that while the Constitution did not specifically authorize the creation of a bank there is no requirement that "everything granted shall be expressly and minutely described."[306] The decision by the drafters of the Tenth Amendment to reject language limiting Congress to "expressly" delegated powers only bolstered this conclusion. "The men who drew and adopted this amendment," the chief justice recalled, "had experienced the embarrassments resulting from the insertion of this word in the Articles of Confederation, and probably omitted it to avoid those embarrassments."[307] Marshall's elegant reasoning would be invoked by later generations of jurists to justify a robust vision of national authority. "Let the end be legitimate," Marshall declared, "let it be within the scope of the constitution, and all means which are appropriate, which are plainly adapted to that end, which are not prohibited, but consist with the letter and spirit of the constitution, are constitutional."[308]

The third major case that shaped the Constitution in the years before the Civil War justly ranks as the Court's most abhorrent decision. In 1857, the justices heard the plea of Dred Scott, a slave petitioning for his freedom. Their stunning ruling would propel a divided nation to the brink of war—and the next wave of constitutional change.

3

The Reconstruction Era
Amendments (1865–1870)

What's in a name? *Slavery,* by any other name, would still smell of *rot.* The Framers of the Constitution understood this all too well. Though nearly half of them possessed human chattel during their lives, enshrining the word slavery in the founding charter of the world's most democratic country made many of them uncomfortable. At the Philadelphia Convention, James Madison called "it wrong to *admit* in the Constitution the idea that there could be property in men."[1] Decades later, Frederick Douglass, the self-described "learned fugitive slave, smarting under the wrongs inflicted by this unholy union," wrote that the document was "so cunningly . . . framed, that no one would have imagined that it recognized or sanctioned slavery."[2] Of course, the Constitution did more than sanction slavery. It *incentivized* it.[3]

In at least four separate provisions, the Framers embedded slavery deep into our foundational law. The Three-Fifths Clause in Article I allowed the South to count three out of every five slaves ("three fifths of *all other persons,*" as they put it) toward the allocation of seats in the House of Representatives.[4] Over seven decades, this rule enhanced "the Slave Power's" grip on Congress. And because more seats in Congress meant more votes in the Electoral College, this hold extended to the presidency as well.[5] Seventy-four years separated the country's founding from Abraham Lincoln's inauguration. Within that period, ten men who owned slaves during their lifetime occupied the office for a combined fifty-three years. Control of the political branches gave the South control over Supreme Court appointments as well. It too became a "peculiar institution."

The Slave Trade Clause in Article I forbade Congress from outlawing the transatlantic traffic in enslaved Africans ("the migration or importation of *such persons* as any of the states now existing shall think proper to admit") before 1808.[6] A related provision, a restriction on the amendment procedure in Article V, prohibited any tampering with this pro-slavery concession in the meantime.[7] By 1787, ten of the thirteen states had already imposed a ban on the importation of foreign slaves. But Charles Cotesworth Pinckney, a South Carolinian, resisted any attempt to institute a nationwide prohibition, declaring "candidly" that his state was unlikely to "stop her importations of slaves in any short time."[8] In the deal the Framers struck, states were given at least twenty additional years to stockpile human cargo from across the seas. Thus from 1789 to 1808, traders made 393 slave voyages to North America, delivering 69,524 Africans to its ports. Nearly one-third of this trafficking occurred in 1807, the year before Congress was finally permitted to end the slave trade.[9] The Slave Trade Clause also subsidized the South's economy by capping the tax on each human purchase at ten dollars.

Finally, the Fugitive Slave Clause was inserted in Article IV, the section of the Constitution devoted to the rights and obligations of the states.[10] It mandated that any slave (that is, any *"person held to service or labor* in one state") escaping into another state "be delivered up on claim of the party to whom such service or labor may be due." It pre-empted any state law or regulation purporting to emancipate slaves fleeing from another jurisdiction, and it authorized Congress to enact legislation ensuring that, for Black people, no soil was free soil. Congress used this authority in 1793 to enact the first Fugitive Slave Act. That law was strengthened in the Compromise of 1850, at a time of heightened regional tensions, to counter the proliferation of "personal liberty laws" in the North that protected free people of color from kidnapping and enslavement.[11] The Fugitive Slave Act prohibited runaway slaves from testifying in court; it subjected law enforcement officials to prosecution for intentional or even negligent failure to comply with slave arrest warrants; and it authorized federal judges, their appointed "commissioners," and anyone they deputized to conscript bystanders—the *posse comitatus*—to enforce the hunt for fugitives.[12]

At the Philadelphia Convention, Connecticut's Oliver Ellsworth and Roger Sherman shared the sanguine view that "slavery in time will not be a speck in our country."[13] Soothed by this naïve expectation of gradual emancipation, they and other Northern delegates acceded to the South's demands. Northern elites thus allowed slavery to be enshrined in our foundational law. In exchange, they established a stronger centralized government, with greater national defense powers and authority to regulate the economy. The parties brokered a deal "to form a more perfect Union." But as long as slavery was entrenched in the Constitution—and rooted in American life—that "more perfect Union" would remain far out of reach. Meanwhile, the economic value of American slavery steadily grew, resulting in boom times for the South, which fueled the region's political aggression. By 1860, just before the onset of the Civil War, the total revenue taken in by the federal government peaked at $56 *million*. By contrast, the nation's stock of slaves was valued somewhere between $1.4 and $3.6 *billion*.[14] Nonetheless, slavery, the greatest source of capital in the United States, would also bring about the nation's ruin.

The "Great Division of Interests"

As the delegates at the Philadelphia Convention dickered over the rules for representation in Congress, Madison came to see that "the states were divided into different interests not by their difference of size, but by other circumstances, . . . principally from the effects of their having or not having slaves." That "great division of interests," which "lay between the Northern and Southern" states would define our nation's politics for the next seven decades, setting the country on a slow but inexorable path to war.[15]

The North and South clashed first over the admission of new states, which threatened to disrupt the balance of power between free states and slave states in Congress. When Missouri applied to join the Union as a slave state in 1819, Northerners objected. Rancorous debate raged for a year until Maine, a breakaway region of Massachusetts, submitted its own application for statehood. At the urging of the "Great Compromiser," House Speaker Henry Clay, Congress resolved the impasse with the Missouri Compromise. Signed into law on March 6, 1820, the plan admitted Maine as a free state, Missouri as a slave state, and prohibited slavery in the Louisiana Territory north of the 36° 30′ line of latitude (running along Missouri's southern border).[16] It set a precedent for the next thirty years, as Congress mostly admitted states in pairs—one slave state for every free state.

Anxieties continued to run high into the 1840s, as the admission of Texas as a slave state and the prospect of taking vast lands from Mexico rekindled the controversy over slavery's expansion. In 1846, when President James Polk, a slaveholder, sought funds to negotiate an armistice with Mexico, Congressman David Wilmot of Pennsylvania proposed an amendment to the bill to ban slavery in any territory gained from the war.[17] The slave states killed the measure, deepening Northern fears that additional slave states would be carved out of the newly acquired territory. "If any event in American history can be singled out as the beginning of a path which led almost inevitably to sectional controversy and civil war," argues historian Eric Foner, "it was the introduction of the Wilmot Proviso."[18]

Amid the recurring controversies over the expansion of slavery, a national abolitionist movement began to emerge. It built on the early successes of state-level movements, which by 1804 had prodded every state north of the Mason-Dixon line except Delaware to enact laws outlawing slavery or providing for gradual emancipation.[19] In 1833, famed New England journalist William Lloyd Garrison founded the American Anti-Slavery Society, the largest and most influential abolitionist organization.[20] By 1840, the group had two thousand chapters and over 250,000 members. Tapping into "moral outrage and religious conviction,"[21] the Society worked for "the entire abolition of slavery in the United States,"[22] organizing lectures, circulating petitions, and distributing pamphlets to advance the cause.

While often omitted from the historical narrative, the early and ongoing efforts of Black activists inspired and sustained the movement to eradicate slavery. Much of their activism predated the launch of larger abolitionist organizations, as Black leaders "formed Negro antislavery societies in the 1820s and early 1830s in many Northern states."[23] Indeed, it was the thinking of Black abolitionists in Baltimore and elsewhere, like Philadelphia's James Forten and Boston's David Walker, that had radicalized Garrison. Black abolitionists served alongside their white counterparts as members and leaders of antislavery societies. But they also advanced the movement in ways less well chronicled, because their activism frequently occurred in nonwhite spheres, particularly in the Baptist and Methodist churches where most of the free population worshiped.[24] Historian George Levesque credits the understated but integral role of Black activists in the 1830s and 1840s as "catalysts behind the radicalization of American abolitionism,"[25] responsible for the wider movement's embrace of "immediatism," as opposed to gradual emancipation. Of course, Black people had much less to lose—and far more to gain—from their antislavery activism than their white counterparts.

There were no corresponding successes for abolitionists in the South. Slavery was too tightly entwined in the region's agrarian economy and culture. Thanks to breakthrough innovations like the cotton gin, the need for field hands in the Deep South increased dramatically in the early decades of the nineteenth century. Meanwhile, the end of the international slave trade only stimulated a domestic slave trade. This expansion of a slave-based economy bred hostility to the antislavery position, forcing the few Southern activists underground and preventing them from making inroads.

In the years before the Civil War, the abolitionist position had few champions in Congress. Even Charles Sumner, the Massachusetts senator described by a Bay State colleague as a "one-idead abolitionist agitator,"[26] was not counted among the movement's radicals. Instead, the *antislavery* sentiment in the nation's capital was directed largely toward incremental measures—stopping slavery's spread into the territories, ending the slave trade in the capital, and weakening enforcement of the Fugitive Slave Law. In the words of one historian, "political antislavery effectively pushed abolitionists to the wings of the stage."[27] In such a political climate, amending the Constitution, a document that Frederick Douglass excoriated as "radically and essentially pro-slavery, in fact as well as in its tendency," was not on the political agenda.[28]

By the 1850s, it was clear that the problem of slavery could no longer be contained. Wisconsin entered the Union as a free state in 1848, restoring the equilibrium between free states and slave states that the admission of Texas had disrupted. But when California applied for statehood the following year, with a constitution that prohibited slavery, Southerners objected. An aging Henry Clay, now a senator, appealed for another compromise to "once more restore the blessings of concord, harmony and peace."[29] Clay's five-point plan, enacted in 1850, provided for territorial governments for New Mexico and Utah, a permanent boundary between New Mexico and Texas, and statehood for California. It also called for strengthening the Fugitive Slave Act and ending the slave trade in the District of Columbia.

President Millard Fillmore naïvely hailed the Compromise of 1850 as "a final settlement" of the slavery question.[30] But the question wasn't settled. In May 1854, Congress passed the Kansas-Nebraska Act, organizing two new territories.[31] In what Northerners called "a naked grab by proslavery forces,"[32] the measure repealed an essential part of the Missouri

Compromise. Under the new law, "the people" of territories were left "perfectly free to form and regulate their *domestic institutions* in their own way."[33] Since few slaves were held in Nebraska, most anticipated that it would enter the Union as a free state. The fate of Kansas, however, was less certain. Supporters and opponents of slavery descended upon the territory in a battle to influence its decision. The violence in "Bleeding Kansas" left scores dead as rival factions claimed control of the territory's government.[34]

As the warring in Kansas raged on, Charles Sumner took to the Senate floor. In a fiery address, delivered over the course of two days in May 1856, he decried "the rape of a virgin territory" being forced into "the hateful embrace of slavery." The Massachusetts senator then laid the blame on two Democratic colleagues, South Carolina's Andrew Butler and Stephen Douglas of Illinois, portraying them as slavery's "Don Quixote and Sancho Panza." Sumner had particularly harsh words for Butler, charging him with taking "a mistress," both "ugly" and "polluted in the sight of the world," though "chaste in his sight—I mean, the harlot, Slavery." Days later, Representative Preston Brooks—Butler's cousin—strode into the Senate chamber to exact vengeance. Wielding a gutta-percha walking cane, the young congressman beat Sumner mercilessly, continuing even after fragments of it began to rain onto the Senate floor.[35] The caning of Sumner soon became the new political rallying call for antislavery forces in Congress and throughout the nation.

In the wake of these events, a growing number of Americans came to see the truth in Frederick Douglass's earlier assessment that the Constitution "was made in view of the existence of slavery, and in a manner well calculated to aid and strengthen that heaven-daring crime."[36] The Massachusetts Anti-Slavery Society held an Independence Day rally in Framingham featuring speeches by some of the leading abolitionists of the day: Sojourner Truth, Henry David Thoreau, and William Lloyd Garrison. Emotions were raw in the sweltering heat. Seared in everyone's memory was the recent spectacle of Anthony Burns, a runaway slave marched in manacles through the streets of Boston toward a Virginia-bound ship. Upon taking the stage, Garrison brandished a copy of the Constitution, denouncing it as "a covenant with death, and an agreement with Hell." To the roar of the crowd he set the document ablaze, crying, "So perish all compromises with tyranny!"[37]

Bleeding Kansas, the Massachusetts rally, and the caning of Sumner were defining moments in an escalating crisis over the Constitution's meaning and promise. The breaking point came in 1856, when the Supreme Court heard the case of *Dred Scott v. Sandford*, an appeal from the Missouri Supreme Court. Scott, a Black man, had lived as the slave of a doctor, traveling extensively with his owner. At times they resided in slave states; at others, in free states. When the doctor died, Scott sued to be released from bondage, arguing that he and his family were entitled to their freedom because they had lived in states where slavery was outlawed. Scott won his case at trial, but the state supreme court reversed the decision.

In a 7–2 ruling, issued on March 6, 1857, the Supreme Court held that Scott "could not be a citizen . . . within the meaning of the Constitution of the United States, and, consequently, was not entitled to sue in its courts."[38] Black people, "whether . . . free or not" could not be "acknowledged as a part of *the people*," said Chief Justice Roger Taney. Far from being citizens with rights under the law, persons of African descent had long

> been regarded as beings of an inferior order, and altogether unfit to associate with the white race, either in social or political relations; and so far inferior, that they had no rights which the white man was bound to respect; and that the negro might justly and lawfully be reduced to slavery for his benefit.[39]

The Court also seized the opportunity to rebuke Congress, striking down the "very aggressive" Missouri Compromise and prohibiting lawmakers from legislating against slavery in the territories.[40] *Dred Scott* was the first decision since *Marbury v. Madison* to invalidate an act of Congress. Sumner rightly called the ruling "more thoroughly abominable than anything of the kind in the history of the courts."[41]

A Constitutional Alternative to War

Thirty-two million souls in 1860 inhabited a sprawling nation of thirty-three states and several territories stretching from the Atlantic to the Pacific. There were nascent plans for the construction of a railway to span the vast continent, connecting the rail network along the Eastern seaboard to the frontier and beyond the Rockies to gold-rich California. Waves of new arrivals had doubled the country's foreign-born population within a decade.[42] These newest Americans, mainly German and Irish, were most heavily concentrated in the urban centers of the Northeast and Midwest, though many made their way farther west.[43] They contributed to the nation's economy as laborers, farmers, mechanics, and merchants.[44] Meanwhile, of some 12 million people living in the states where slavery was legal one-third were held in bondage.[45] The fault line of America's peculiar institution had widened during the 1850s, but the complexion of the nation it was destined to engulf had changed dramatically.

Politics was no exception. An upstart political party gained millions of new adherents in the North. Founded in 1854 by former Whigs and Democrats in response to the Kansas-Nebraska Act, the Republican Party was firmly opposed to the spread of slavery into the Western territories. The party's first presidential candidate, John C. Frémont, won a third of the vote in the 1856 election. Buoyed by a wave of popular outrage over the *Dred Scott* ruling, its ranks began to swell. As the election of 1860 approached, the "fire eaters"—the South's most intransigent advocates of secession—threatened to break away if the Republican Party's new standard bearer, a little-known former congressman named Abraham Lincoln, won the White House.[46]

South Carolina's fire eaters were the first to make good on that threat, declaring the state's withdrawal from the Union on December 20, 1860. In short order, six other states in the Deep South—Mississippi, Florida, Alabama, Georgia, Louisiana, and Texas—followed suit. Operating in the political vacuum created by the four-month interlude between Lincoln's election and his March 1861 inauguration, lawmakers from the Northern and border states insisted that the rift could still be mended. In their scramble to keep the Union intact, they looked to the Article V amendment process. For the first time in five decades, constitutional change was on the agenda. During the final months of the 36th Congress, lawmakers introduced more than two hundred amendment resolutions offering nearly five dozen different solutions to the problem.[47] Remarkably, none of these measures would have abolished slavery outright. To the contrary, they sought to preserve the Union by mollifying the South, entrenching slavery more deeply where it already existed.

On the day South Carolina seceded, the Senate charged a special Committee of Thirteen with resolving the crisis. Its members endorsed a peace plan crafted by veteran Kentucky senator John Crittenden, recommending a package of six constitutional amendments to appease the Southern states. Among them were proposals to restore and extend the Missouri Compromise, curb Congress's power to limit slavery in the capital and territories, enhance the Fugitive Slave Clause to compensate owners of escaped slaves, and permanently bar future amendments on slavery.[48] Announced with great fanfare, the "Crittenden Compromise" died in the Senate.[49]

The House of Representatives assembled its own panel, composed of one member from each state.[50] Under the leadership of Ohio's Thomas Corwin, the Committee of Thirty-Three labored for weeks, unable to muster a majority in support of any plan.[51] In its January 14, 1861, report to Congress, the committee called for six "propositions," including a constitutional amendment protecting slavery where it already existed.[52] The release of seven minority reports only underscored the committee's inefficacy.[53] In a letter to president-elect Abraham Lincoln written two days later, Corwin despaired over the lack of a solution. "If the states are no more harmonious in their feelings and opinions than these thirty-three representative men," he wrote, "then, appalling as the idea is, we must dissolve, and a long and bloody war must follow."[54]

Following the failure of the two congressional committees, the Virginia legislature invited the states to an ad hoc "Peace Conference" to be convened in Washington on February 4, 1861. With the inauguration just a month away, 131 "highly distinguished but somewhat superannuated"[55] delegates from twenty-one of the thirty-four states assembled at the Willard Hotel, a block from the White House.[56] John Tyler, the seventy-year-old former president, chaired the gathering. In his opening remarks, Tyler recalled Virginia's role in summoning the Philadelphia Convention, proclaiming that theirs was "a task equally grand, equally sublime." He exhorted the delegates "to snatch from ruin a great and glorious confederation, to preserve the government, and to renew and invigorate the Constitution. If you reach the height of this great occasion your children's children will rise up and call you blessed."[57]

While Northern newspapers snickered at the assemblage of "political fossils" and the "tottering ashen ruin" who presided,[58] not everyone viewed "the Old Gentlemen's Convention"[59] as a joke. Some feared that the conference, "a body unknown to the Constitution and the laws," might try to impose a provisional government.[60] But after twenty days of deliberation, memorable only for its long-winded orations and the death of one infirm delegate, the Peace Conference ended with a whimper and dispersed "without accomplishing anything."[61] The delegates did produce a would-be Thirteenth Amendment—a warmed-over restatement of the Crittenden Compromise, preserving slavery in perpetuity.[62] But on March 2, when senators took up the plan, they rejected it resoundingly.[63] The House didn't even bother to consider it. Tyler, for his part, denounced the compromise as a "miserable rickety affair." Upon his return to Virginia, he joined the rebel cause, winning election to the Confederate Congress but dying before taking his traitorous oath of office.[64]

Meanwhile, on the day the Peace Conference convened, delegates from six of the seven seceding states had gathered some eight hundred miles away in Montgomery, Alabama, to lay the foundation for a new, sovereign nation in the American South.[65] After quickly approving a provisional constitution, they elected Mississippi's Jefferson Davis as the first president of the Confederate States.[66] Weeks later, on March 11, they unveiled a "permanent" Confederate constitution. Organized in seven articles, the Confederate charter mirrored the U.S. Constitution, copying most of its features.[67] While a reverence for state sovereignty permeated the document, it nevertheless recognized acts of its Congress as the supreme law of the land. It unapologetically sanctioned slavery, however, pointedly avoiding the tortured euphemisms of the U.S. Constitution's pro-slavery clauses. It borrowed the Three-Fifths and Fugitive Slave Clauses. And though the Confederate constitution did ban the "importation of negroes of the African race," it forbade any "law denying or impairing the right of property in negro slaves."[68]

Whereas the Preamble of the U.S. Constitution invokes the authority of "We the People of the United States," as one united nation, its Confederate counterpart made a point of rooting sovereignty in "We, the people of the Confederate States, each state acting in its sovereign and independent character." Uninterested in "a more perfect Union," it was meant only "to form a permanent federal government." This distinction was reinforced in Article VI of the Confederate charter, which reserved "certain rights" to "the people of the several States." Finally, its amending provision, also called Article V, made a "convention of all the States" the sole means of proposing changes, subject to ratification by an easier-to-reach threshold of two-thirds of the states.[69] A year later, upon the ratification of five states, the Confederate constitution formally took effect.[70]

The Corwin Amendment

Congress received the Peace Conference report on February 27, but it failed to placate the dwindling Southern caucus. One Southern member called it a "wishy-washy settlement."[71] Another saw "a miserable abortion."[72] As lawmakers looked for a way forward, Thomas Corwin saw an opportunity to seize the moment.

Though just a freshman congressman, Corwin had the air of an elder statesman. The sixty-six-year-old Whig-turned-Republican was born into an Ohio political family and spent half of his life climbing the rungs of political office: county prosecutor, state legislator, congressman, governor, senator. Now, after a stint as secretary of the Treasury, he found himself back in the familiar halls of Congress. Black Tom Corwin, as he was called, for his "mild, roguish black eye" and "*very* dark complexion," was no fire-brand.[73] In a city full of grandstanders, he preferred a quieter approach to statecraft.

As chair of the Committee of Thirty-Three, Corwin had championed an amendment to ingrain slavery even more deeply into the Constitution. The complicated measure would have barred free states from proposing any change to the Constitution affecting slavery in the states where it existed. Such amendments could be initiated only by slave states and would be sub-ject to ratification by *every* state.[74] Republican critics deplored the measure as "a constitutional decree of perpetual bondage" that would consign "mil-lions yet unborn" to captivity.[75]

On the evening of February 24, Corwin met privately with the president-elect to discuss the state of affairs. Lincoln had arrived furtively in the capital the day before, taking rooms at the Willard Hotel, where the Peace Conference was wrapping up its deliberations. At their meeting, the two men hatched a plan to introduce an amendment consistent with Lincoln's campaign vow to not interfere with slavery where it already existed. Cor-win would take the lead; Lincoln would provide help behind the scenes.[76]

Two days after the meeting, Corwin was ready to debut the "new" plan. In fact, Senator William Seward, the incoming secretary of state, had in-troduced it back in December.[77] The measure read: "No amendment shall be made to the Constitution which will authorize or give to Congress the power to abolish or interfere, within any State, with *the domestic institu-tions* thereof, including that of persons held to labor or service by the laws of said State."[78] In the two months since proposing it, Seward had moved on, advocating for a national constitutional convention to address the cri-sis.[79] He was content to let it be Corwin's amendment.

Insisting it was of "utmost importance," Corwin moved to substitute the new language in place of the pending proposal from the Committee of Thirty-Three.[80] A "wild scene of confusion and filibustering" ensued as antislavery Republicans fought to block the move. After a night of frantic arm-twisting, the House finally agreed to take up the revised amendment.[81] In a chaotic vote (the official record noted that "great confusion prevailed in the hall"), the measure passed by a narrow margin. The vote was greeted with "loud and prolonged applause, both on the floor and in the galleries."[82] That evening, after a serenade by a marine band, Corwin addressed a cheering crowd outside his home. With serene satisfaction, he declared that each state could "mold its own domestic institutions according to its own ideas of policy and propriety."[83]

But the Senate needed to approve it first. That chamber took up the measure on March 2, a Saturday, with just two days remaining in the legislative session. After a long day of debate that stretched past midnight, the senators returned the following evening, braced for yet another overnight talkathon. A reporter from *Harper's Weekly* published an eyewitness account, "Two Nights in the Senate."[84] The Corwin proposal, he ventured, was the "utmost that could be extorted" after the failure of all other options. In the reporter's analysis, "at least three-fourths of the Senate were anxious to see it defeated—the Republicans because it smacked of compromise, the Southern Secessionists because it had a tendency to strengthen the Union sentiment in their states."[85] By dawn, senators "were asleep on the sofas" and "the galleries had thinned out." With precious little time left, the Senate passed the Corwin Amendment with exactly the two-thirds majority required.[86] Eight reluctant Republicans were persuaded to support the measure, assuring its passage. Senator Seward, the man who first conceived it, was notably absent.[87]

President Lincoln broke the news in his inaugural address a few hours later. "I understand," he said, "a proposed amendment to the Constitution— which amendment, however, I have not seen—has passed Congress." Like many of his contemporaries, Lincoln considered it to be "implied constitutional law" that Congress lacked power to abolish slavery in the states. Accordingly, he had "no objection to its being made express and irrevocable."[88] Frederick Douglass condemned Lincoln's tacit endorsement of the Corwin Amendment as "a weak and inappropriate utterance," denouncing his willingness to prostrate "himself before the foul and withering curse of slavery."[89]

Press reaction to the proposed amendment was mixed. "Not one slaveholding state will be satisfied with so paltry a sop," said the *New York*

Herald.[90] But the *New York Times* had a more positive take, suggesting that the amendment might "soothe the excited public feeling of the South." The newspaper called the measure "eminently proper in itself." It would "add no new principle to the Constitution, but simply . . . render it unchangeable, in one important particular." The editors could not "imagine a solid objection to it."[91]

The proposal notably failed to address the core dispute between North and South: the spread of slavery outside the states where it existed. Four states did ratify the Corwin Amendment between May 1861 and January 1862.[92] But it failed to avert the crisis. On April 12, Confederate troops fired on the garrison at Fort Sumter. Virginia joined the Confederacy five days later, followed by Arkansas, North Carolina, and Tennessee. Four border states that recognized slavery under their states' laws—Delaware, Kentucky, Maryland, and Missouri—were persuaded through a combination of political and military pressure to remain in the Union. They were joined by West Virginia, a breakaway region admitted as a state in June 1863. As for Tom Corwin, he followed news of the war from his new post as U.S. minister to Mexico.

The Thirteenth Amendment: The Problem of Slavery

As the war ground on, abolition of slavery was not guaranteed. Secession rid Congress of slavery's most ardent defenders, but the new Republican majority was by no means committed to its eradication. After all, the party's platform had accepted the existence of slavery in the states where it existed. To end the bloodshed, some urged the negotiation of a truce—even on terms that perpetuated slavery. As late as August 1862, President Lincoln confessed some sympathy with this approach in a letter to Horace Greeley, the abolitionist editor of the *New-York Tribune.* "My paramount object in this struggle," wrote the president, "is to save the Union, and is not either to save or to destroy slavery." He would save the Union "without freeing any slave" or "by freeing all the slaves."[93]

However, as a wartime necessity, the federal government was already taking steps to weaken slavery. In August 1861, Congress passed a measure "to confiscate property used for insurrectionary purposes"—including slaves compelled "to take up arms against the United States"—effecting some limited emancipation. A March 1862 law prohibited the army from returning fugitive slaves.[94] Statutes ending slavery in the District of

Columbia and the U.S. territories, passed in April and June, were the first emancipatory acts of Congress not drawing on its war powers but on its general legislative jurisdiction.[95] Then, in September, President Lincoln invoked his power as commander in chief to announce that slaves in rebel states would be freed at year's end.[96] The Emancipation Proclamation, issued on January 1, 1863, made good on this promise.[97]

Despite these actions, Lincoln took a far more cautious approach toward emancipation in the five slave states remaining in the Union, consistent with his belief that the Constitution limited him from interfering with slavery except where justified by war. In his Second Annual Address to Congress, submitted on December 1, 1862, he proposed a constitutional amendment requiring each state to abolish slavery by the year 1900. Under its terms, the states would be entitled to compensation for their losses. The measure further authorized Congress to appropriate money "for colonizing free colored persons with their own consent at any place or places without the United States."[98]

In the latter half of 1863, after the Union Army's victory at Gettysburg, the war began to break for the North. As regiments advanced deep into the South, slaves fled the plantations to join the Union cause.[99] By the end of the conflict, approximately 180,000 Black men had served as soldiers in the Union Army. Hundreds of thousands more, men and women, served in noncombatant roles.[100] Though paid less than their white counterparts, they were willing to take on more dangerous missions, bravely facing risk of being sold into slavery upon capture.[101] It was the valor of Black fighters, Eric Foner argues, that finally "forced the question of slavery onto the national agenda."[102]

Congressman James Ashley, whom Frederick Douglass later praised as "among the foremost of that brilliant galaxy of statesmen who reconstructed the Union on a basis of liberty,"[103] had the distinction of introducing the first constitutional amendment to abolish slavery, on December 14, 1863.[104] The Ohio Republican would be a leading champion of the Thirteenth Amendment, playing a pivotal role in its passage. A month after Ashley introduced his amendment, Missouri Republican John Henderson introduced the first Senate resolution to outlaw slavery.[105] Notably, the Henderson plan included a proposal to liberalize the Article V amendment process to allow Congress to propose amendments by simple majority vote. The assent of only two-thirds of the states would be needed to ratify. Though destined to fail, the proposal evidenced a concern over the difficulties ahead in amassing supermajority support in Congress and the states to protect the rights of the 4 million emancipated slaves.

The final version of the Thirteenth Amendment, forged from competing proposals in the House and Senate, has two parts. Section One proclaims: "Neither slavery nor involuntary servitude . . . shall exist within the United States, or any place subject to their jurisdiction." This comprehensive ban encompasses a broad array of arrangements in which a person is forced to work by means of physical or legal coercion, including indentured servitude and peonage. It explicitly exempts forced labor imposed as punishment for a crime, a loophole that has permitted a wide range of exploitative prison labor practices—from chain gangs to license plate factories—that have been especially harmful for people of color. Filmmaker Ava DuVernay explores its troubling implications for racial justice in her Academy Award–nominated documentary, *13th*.[106]

The amendment's second section gives Congress the "power to enforce this article by appropriate legislation." This constitutional innovation was inspired by Chief Justice John Marshall's characterization, in *McCulloch v. Maryland*, of the broad grant of power given to Congress under Article I's Necessary and Proper Clause.[107] Seven later amendments include a similar enabling provision. By giving Congress the "power to enforce" their provisions through "appropriate legislation,"[108] they have added to Congress's original set of enumerated powers.

The Senate took up the Thirteenth Amendment on March 29, 1864. Lyman Trumbull, an Illinois Republican who chaired the Senate Judiciary Committee, was the resolution's sponsor. "Without stopping to inquire into all the causes of our troubles," Trumbull said, "and of the distress, desolation, and death which have grown out of this atrocious rebellion, I suppose it will be generally admitted that they sprung from slavery."[109] The senator noted that some Framers of the Constitution had naïvely anticipated the "early extinction" of slavery. Instead, the peculiar institution "had so strengthened itself that in 1860 its advocates demanded control of the nation."[110] Recounting the incremental steps already taken by Congress to curb it, the senator concluded that "the only effectual way of ridding the country of slavery, . . . so that it cannot be resuscitated, is by an amendment of the Constitution forever prohibiting it within the jurisdiction of the United States."[111]

The debate in the upper house spanned eleven days. Opponents were on the defensive from the start as the amendment's backers laid the blame for the war on the Slave Power. "Civil war now holds its carnival and reaps its bloody harvests," said Henry Wilson, a Republican from Massachusetts and future vice president. "The nation is grappling with a gigantic conspiracy, struggling for existence, for the preservation of its menaced life, against a rebellion that finds no parallel in the annals of the world."[112] In this great struggle, Wilson noted, the U.S. Army had "a hundred and twenty regiments of eighty thousand black men, who are bearing upon their flashing bayonets the unity of the Republic, and the destinies of their race."[113]

James Harlan, a Republican representing Iowa, identified the dehumanizing "necessary incidents" of slavery that undermined divine law. Slaves were denied the freedom to marry. They were deprived of natural guardianship rights over their own children. They were barred from owning property or seeking redress for grievances in court. They were denied the freedom of speech and the right to an education.[114] Given that "none of these necessary incidents of slavery are desirable," Harlan asked, "how can an American Senator cast a vote to justify its continuance for a single hour?"[115]

Willard Saulsbury, a Democrat from the slave state of Delaware, emerged as one of the amendment's leading opponents. A habitual drinker who was famously censured for drawing a pistol on the Senate sergeant-at-arms during a tirade against the "imbecile" President Lincoln,[116] Saulsbury held a fairly sanguine view of slavery. "It exists in this country, and has existed from the beginning," he said.[117] His reverence for states' rights was so extreme that he pined for a return to the old Articles of Confederation.[118] In a long oration, Saulsbury challenged Congress's authority to "invade the rights of the states" through the constitutional amendment process. "Property," he insisted, "is not regulated and was not intended to be regulated by the Constitution of the United States. Property is the creature of the law of the state."[119] An amendment destroying property in slaves, he alleged, "would not be binding" on any state that refused to accept it.[120] But a Northern senator pointed out the illogic in Saulsbury's argument. As the Framers drafted Article V, they had slavery "directly under their thought" when they added a provision barring amendments relating to the slave trade for twenty years. Since they imposed no similar restriction regarding slavery itself, it followed that abolition could be accomplished "whenever two thirds of both Houses of Congress see fit to propose the amendment and three fourths of the States to accept it."[121]

Like many foes of the amendment, Saulsbury blamed the nation's crisis on agitators—Northern abolitionists and the "fire-eaters of the South" alike—whom the senator condemned as "cooperators and coworkers in the same damnable cause." While decrying the "wrong on *both sides* of this question," Saulsbury saved his purest venom for the North: "Had political abolitionists refrained from intermeddling with the just rights of the South in respect to slavery, there would have been no secessionists. *Abolitionists*, therefore, are the real disunionists, and primarily responsible for our present troubles."[122]

Other members framed their opposition in more overtly racist terms. Thomas Hendricks, a Democratic senator from Indiana and future vice president, asked what would become of the 4 million freed slaves. "Are they to remain among us?" he asked, incredulously. "I can say . . . that they never will associate with the white people of this country upon terms of equality. It may be preached; it may be legislated for; it may be prayed for; but there is that difference between the two races that renders it impossible. If they are among us as a free people, they are among us as an inferior people."[123] Kentucky Democrat Lazarus Powell saw the measure as a threat to white supremacy. "The negro absorbs your every thought," he groused. "For him you will destroy the country; for him you will allow the liberties of the white man to be stricken down."[124]

Throughout the debate, Democrats offered alternative proposals crafted to enforce racial hierarchy in the Constitution. "No negro, or person whose mother or grandmother is or was a negro, shall be a citizen of the United States," read one offering.[125] Another called for Congress to resettle "all the population of African descent in the United States" among the states "in proportion to the white population."[126] These measures were voted down handily.

On April 8, the last day of debate, the old abolitionist Charles Sumner rose to speak. "The time, then, has come," he said, "when the Constitution, which has been so long interpreted for slavery, may be interpreted for freedom."[127] Earlier, Sumner had introduced an amendment of his own, a more expansive measure that would have declared that "all persons are equal before the law,"[128] but his colleagues ignored it. When the roll was called, the senators voted 38–6 to approve the Thirteenth Amendment.[129]

Defiant to the end, Saulsbury announced, "I now bid farewell to any hope of the reconstruction of the American Union.[130]

The proposal's speedy approval in the Senate contrasted with a far slower pace in the House. When the measure was introduced in that chamber on March 19, James "Tama Jim" Wilson, an Iowa Republican, made a fiery opening case. "We were slaves of the slave power," he declared. "It touched everything, defiled everything. And we submitted quietly, tamely, cowardly, while the work of destruction and death was carried on by this insatiable enemy of all that is lovely, desirable, just, and sacred."[131] But it was to no avail. When the lawmakers finally voted after two months' delay, the tally was 93–65; the amendment failed to clear the two-thirds bar.[132] With the presidential contest looming, the vote split largely along party lines. Undeterred, supporters pledged to bring the amendment up again after the election.[133]

Ohio's George Pendleton, who would join the Democratic Party ticket that year as its vice-presidential nominee, conveyed the sentiments of many in his party in a discursive speech. It was unwise to adopt a constitutional amendment "in the excitements of war," he argued.[134] It would be "impossible" to ratify the amendment "without a fraudulent use of the power to admit new states, or a fraudulent use of the military power of the federal government in the seceded States."[135] Furthermore, it would encroach on the proper domain of states, frustrating federalism's careful balance. "There is in three fourths of the states neither the power to establish nor to abolish slavery in all the States," he said. The Constitution grants "the power . . . to amend, not to revolutionize, not to subvert the form and spirit and theory of government."[136]

Lincoln's sweeping victory in the 1864 election marked a turning point. Now running on a platform that denounced slavery as "hostile to the principles of Republican Government,"[137] he won all but three states, bringing fifty-two new Republican congressmen to Washington on his coattails.[138] The party claimed a "popular verdict" in favor of the amendment. Taking advantage of the brief postelection session before the newly elected members would be seated, James Ashley led an effort to call another vote in the House.[139] If his motion to reconsider failed, lawmakers in both houses would have to start the process again in the new Congress.

Ashley scoured the chamber for votes. With the quiet support of President Lincoln, he promised patronage jobs and other favors—what critics described as bribery—to wrangle support.[140] On January 6, 1865, the congressman reintroduced the amendment on the House floor. "The eyes of the wise and good in all civilized nations are upon us," Ashley declared.[141] And so they would remain for the next three weeks. Finally, on January 31, the House adopted the Thirteenth Amendment by a vote of 119–56, with 8 members abstaining.[142] Among those who supported the measure were 24 members who changed their position from the vote a few months earlier. At least 2 more were conveniently indisposed due to illness.[143] According to the official record, there was "an outburst of enthusiasm" among jubilant lawmakers and onlookers following the vote.[144] "Male spectators in the galleries, which were crowded to excess, . . . waved their hats and cheered loud and long, while the ladies, hundreds of whom were present, rose in their seats and waved their handkerchiefs."[145] As the *Chicago Tribune* noted, the "whirlwind of applause" was "wholly unprecedented in Congressional annals."[146]

The Thirteenth Amendment was ratified eleven months later, on December 6, 1865, when Georgia became the twenty-seventh state to lend its approval. Included in that count were eight states of the ex-Confederacy, then under military control. An exuberant headline in the *New York Times* exclaimed, "THE CONSUMMATION! Slavery Forever Dead in the United States." It was a rare banner headline to celebrate a rare occasion: the Thirteenth Amendment was the first addition to the Constitution in sixty-one years.[147] "IT IS DONE!" said the editors. "Let us rejoice."[148]

In that same edition, on page four, the paper published a brief dispatch announcing the death of Thomas Corwin. He suffered a seizure at a dinner party, "surrounded by various circles, composed of United States Senators and Representatives, Judges of the Supreme Court, and other distinguished personages, whom he kept in an almost continual roar of laughter at his sallies of wit and humorous stories of adventure in Mexico."[149] There was no mention of the proposed amendment which, just four years earlier, the paper had predicted would "go far to soothe the excited public feeling of the South." Despite his personal opposition to slavery, Corwin's name continues to be associated with the ill-fated amendment.

In addressing America's original sin, the Thirteenth Amendment wrought the most profound change of any amendment to the Constitution. When the Framers met in Philadelphia, slavery had been practiced in the British colonies for over 150 years. Then, for almost eight decades, slavery infected our national charter even as the Framers recoiled from explicitly naming it. It took the amendment's ban on "slavery or involuntary servitude" to sweep away the fog of constitutional circumlocution meant to conceal a manifest injustice. In omitting the word, the 1787 Constitution exposed the country's failure to acknowledge the humanity of millions of enslaved Black people, leaving them without any means of self-determination or avenue for redress. Only upon ratification of the amendment could this peculiar atrocity begin to change.

The Thirteenth Amendment ranks with the Bill of Rights as a powerful guarantee of individual liberty and human dignity, changing forever the fate of 4 million enslaved persons and the generations that followed them. But it also represented something entirely new in constitutional law. For the first time, the Article V amendment process was used to expand the power of the national government, augmenting the list of Congress's enumerated powers in Article I. In another innovation, the amendment restricted the private acts of individuals, sweeping away the purported "rights" of slave-owners and all others who would subordinate people to involuntary labor. The Bill of Rights, by comparison, provided protection only against government abuse.

As its opponents foresaw, the Thirteenth Amendment revolutionized the American system of federalism. It was the first time the Constitution was amended to restrict the power of the states.[150] Seventy-six years earlier, as he crafted his set of amendments to constrain the powers of the new national government, James Madison hoped to include an amendment safeguarding certain individual rights from infringement by the states. The 1st Congress rejected the proposal. Now, going forward, future constitutional amendments would build on the precedent of the Thirteenth, setting a national standard for federal protection of individual rights and liberties and giving Congress the power to enforce them by "appropriate legislation" against state encroachment. Lawmakers invoked this authority to pass the first federal civil rights law a year after the Thirteenth Amendment was adopted.[151] Even so, establishing the rights of Black people would require two additional amendments in the space of five years.

The Fourteenth Amendment: The Problem of Citizenship

The ratification of the Thirteenth Amendment in December 1865 removed the stain of slavery from the Constitution and permanently released 4 million people from bondage. But what would become of them? How could the nation guarantee life's essentials—work, land, community, political, and civil rights—to a large Black population living amid their hostile former owners? As the fog of war dissipated, a few things became clear: the former slaves needed to be recognized, the states needed to be reunified, and the nation needed reconstruction.[152]

For the abolitionist movement, the Thirteenth Amendment marked a turning point after a decades-long struggle. With victory won, William Lloyd Garrison called for the American Anti-Slavery Society to dissolve. The Constitution was no longer a "covenant with death," he proclaimed, but rather a "covenant with life." But other movement leaders, including Frederick Douglass (who had also "modified" his views about the Constitution)[153] and Wendell Phillips, rightly saw abolition as just the first step. They stepped in to make sure the Society would continue the fight for equality.[154] "No emancipation can be effectual and no freedom real," declared radical activist Henry Clarke Wright, "unless the Negro has the ballot and the states are prohibited from enacting laws making any distinction among their citizens on the basis of race or color."[155]

Leaders in the Black community agreed that the Thirteenth Amendment could not be the end of the movement. For them, it was just beginning. As the amendment neared ratification, members of the National Equal Rights League, a Black activist organization founded in 1864, met in Cleveland. According to William Forten, a founding member and son of famed abolitionist James Forten, the new organization's mission was to promote equal citizenship and "the support of the people, without distinction of sex or color."[156] Forten addressed the League's first annual meeting in October 1865: "We have been deserted by those whom we faithfully supported," he said, "and insolently informed that this is a white man's country, though it required the strong arms of over 200,000 black men to save it." Forten urged his compatriots to "rally, and forge a chain of consanguinity and interest," for there was no alternative to full citizenship "upon terms of equality." "And to accomplish this much-desired end," he argued, "we must be a unit."[157]

Abolitionists were wise to continue their struggle because, even in the ashes of defeat, white Southerners were intent on rebuilding society as it existed prior to the war. In 1865, all-white legislatures in Mississippi and South Carolina, quickly reconstituted after the Confederacy's surrender, enacted laws to circumscribe the rights of the newly freed, compelling them to work for white employers in a situation akin to slavery. Other states quickly followed suit. The Black Codes, as these laws came to be known, regulated Black lives in countless ways: barring them from certain lines of work, limiting them from entering into contracts or testifying in court, and even restricting their physical movement.[158] Under a North Carolina law, a contract signed by a Black person, "whatever may be the value," was unenforceable unless "witnessed by a white person."[159] In Texas, Black people could testify in court, but only against another "person of color."[160] And in Florida, "leading an idle, immoral or profligate course of life"—if Black—was a crime punishable by imprisonment, hard labor, or "whipping not exceeding thirty-nine stripes."[161] Under the Black Codes, the freedom promised by the Thirteenth Amendment was tenuous at best. "The Codes spoke for themselves," said prominent Black sociologist W.E.B. Du Bois. "They meant nothing more nor less than slavery in daily toil."[162]

By its terms, the Thirteenth Amendment was meant to be self-enforcing, ending slavery entirely and immediately, but as the Old South fought to restore the antebellum order, the amendment's Republican sponsors insisted that Congress had an obligation to enforce it.[163] "With the destruction of slavery necessarily follows the destruction of the incidents to slavery," argued Lyman Trumbull, the Illinois senator, as well as "the badges of servitude which have been enacted for its maintenance and support."[164] James F. Wilson, the congressman from Iowa, concurred.[165] The Thirteenth Amendment authorized Congress to protect "the great fundamental civil rights" of the freedmen, he explained. "Whatever these great fundamental rights are, we must be invested with the power to legislate for their protection or our Constitution fails in the first and most important office of government."[166] Together, the two men pressed for the adoption of the nation's first civil rights law.

The Civil Rights Act of 1866, enacted under the Thirteenth Amendment's enforcement authority, was Congress's forceful response to the Black Codes. Repudiating the holding of the *Dred Scott* opinion, which denied the possibility of citizenship for Black people, the law declared that all persons born in the United States were citizens without regard to race, color, or previous condition of servitude. (The measure excepted subjects of a foreign power and "Indians not taxed," living under the jurisdiction of a tribe.)[167] It was the first act of Congress to recognize the principle of birthright citizenship, which later made its way into the Fourteenth

Amendment. The law also recognized a set of civil and economic rights—the right "to make and enforce contracts, to sue, . . . give evidence in court, to inherit, purchase, lease, sell, hold, and convey . . . property."[168]

The law's enforcement mechanisms were modeled on the Fugitive Slave Act of 1850, giving the federal courts jurisdiction to adjudicate claims against anyone who interfered with the civil rights of Black people.[169] The irony was not lost on its author. "Surely we have the authority to enact a law as efficient in the interests of freedom . . . as we had in the interest of slavery," said Trumbull.[170] Predictably, Willard Saulsbury objected. The Delaware Democrat, who had led the fight to defeat the Thirteenth Amendment in the Senate, now offered the cramped view that the measure banned slavery and nothing more. It could not be construed "to confer civil rights which are wholly distinct and unconnected with the status or condition of slavery," he argued.[171]

President Andrew Johnson, successor to the martyred President Lincoln, promptly vetoed the Civil Rights Act. In his message to Congress, he denounced the law's promise of citizenship—for "the Chinese of the Pacific States, Indians subject to taxation, the people called gypsies, as well as the entire race designated as blacks, people of color"—particularly since Republican lawmakers had refused to seat representatives from the former Confederate states.[172] Escalating the battle between the branches, Congress overrode the veto. When the law was challenged, a federal court in Kentucky upheld it, declaring that there was "no doubt of the constitutionality of the act in all its provisions."[173] "It would be a remarkable anomaly," wrote the Supreme Court Justice presiding over cases for that circuit, if Congress, "with the help of the amendment," could not bestow citizenship on "those of the African race who have been born and always lived within the United States."[174]

Soon after the 39th Congress was gaveled into session in December 1865, with its large new class of Republican lawmakers, it established a committee of nine representatives and six senators.[175] The Joint Committee on Reconstruction, as it was formally called, was charged with investigating "the condition of the States which formed the so-called Confederate States of America" and establishing terms for their readmission to the Union.[176] While ostensibly bipartisan, twelve of the committee's fifteen members were Republicans. Over the next fifteen months, it would lead the Reconstruction project, overriding President Johnson's conciliatory approach to the former Confederates.[177] Central to its work was the formulation of two new constitutional amendments.

Congressman Thaddeus Stevens of Pennsylvania chaired the committee. A leader of the Radical Republican faction in Congress, Stevens was distinctive for his "commanding appearance," says a chronicler, a firmly set expression of "severity and resolution" that evoked "an angry eagle."[178] To his peers, the senator's personal commitment to equal rights for all—including Black and Indigenous people, and Chinese immigrants—marked him as "a revolutionary, or at least the closest thing to one imaginable in American politics."[179] A brilliant political strategist, he was unafraid to use "daring and even outrageous means" to stake out a position, confident the country would catch up.[180] And though he rivaled Charles Sumner in passion, he understood that compromise was sometimes necessary. Said another biographer, "Stevens would take what he could get and try for more."[181]

The committee's other great leader was John Bingham. According to a biographer, politics was "always a serious business" for the Republican representative from Ohio.[182] His long and furrowed visage gave the sense of "an austere, thoughtful man." Though "quiet and inclined to reserve his manners," his facial expressions conveyed "a strong will inclined to extreme convictions," complementing a "temperament . . . inclined to antagonize . . . all or any, who do not think precisely in the same channel."[183] Bingham found himself "at the center of almost every dramatic event that shook the Capitol in the 1860s." In 1865, he served on the team that prosecuted John Wilkes Booth's accomplices. Three years later, he delivered the closing argument at the Senate impeachment trial of Andrew Johnson.[184] In the highly charged politics of the postwar years, defined by Johnson's obstinacy on the one hand and Stevens's radicalism on the other, Bingham reliably "steered the nation on a middle course."[185]

By the committee's second day in session, Stevens proposed four amendments to the Constitution. Among them was a measure to apportion congressional seats according to the number of "legal voters" in a state, one to reduce the representation of states that refuse to enfranchise their Black population, and another to make federal and state laws "equally applicable to every citizen" without regard to "race and color."[186] Many other ideas followed. By January 1866, lawmakers served up a bewildering array of amendment proposals for the Joint Committee's consideration.[187] From this collection, members hammered out the language of what would become the Fourteenth Amendment.

The first draft dealt solely with the question of how the former Confederate states should be represented in Congress. Now that the Thirteenth Amendment was ratified, there were no longer any slaves to be counted as three-fifths of a person. Going forward, Black people would count as whole persons for the purposes of apportionment. As a consequence, Southern states stood to gain as many as twelve additional seats in the House of Representatives after the 1870 census (with a corresponding gain in electoral votes), even as they took steps to disenfranchise Black voters.[188] One congressman complained that it would "give to the late slave States an undue and unjust amount of political power in the government."[189]

As proposed by Stevens, the representation amendment would rectify this perverse outcome by penalizing states that abridge the elective franchise "on account of race and color," excluding them from the basis of representation.[190] In other words, the measure would reduce the allocation of seats to transgressing states. Although the House approved the measure by the requisite two-thirds vote in January 1866,[191] it encountered opposition in the Senate. Charles Sumner slammed the proposal for its tacit recognition that states could deny the franchise to Black people for reasons indirectly related to race or color.[192] The American Anti-Slavery Society agreed, contending that the amendment's gaping loophole "leaves the Negro to his fate."[193] In a vote that March, Sumner joined with Senate Democrats to sink the Stevens amendment.[194] Later, however, this penalty provision would be included in the final version of the Fourteenth Amendment.

Despite the enactment of the Civil Rights Act that April, Bingham and Stevens believed that additional protections were needed. At their prodding, the two men persuaded the Joint Committee to endorse an alternative amendment, drafted by Bingham, giving Congress the power to enact legislation securing the "privileges and immunities of citizens in the several States" and "equal protection in the rights of life, liberty and property."[195] Conservative Democrats and some Republicans predictably opposed these new powers, claiming they would "utterly obliterate state rights and state authority over their own internal affairs."[196] Reformers raised a different concern, arguing it was dangerous to guarantee fundamental rights in legislation subject to repeal. "We may pass laws here today," said one congressman, "and the next Congress may wipe them out."[197] Bingham's plan died in committee. But with modifications, these two crucial concepts— guarantees of the privileges and immunities of citizens and the equal protection of the law—would form the core of the Fourteenth Amendment.

Along the way, the Joint Committee decided to combine several discrete proposals in a single amendment. A retired congressman suggested the strategy in a letter to Stevens. By the end of April 1866, the Joint Committee unveiled an omnibus Fourteenth Amendment comprising five sections.[198] As the *New York Times* observed, the disparate provisions were consolidated "not because they have any connection with each other, but in order to force Congress to swallow the whole or none!"[199]

As lawmakers in both chambers considered the measure, they made additional changes. Notably, the Senate added a provision to settle "the great question of citizenship."[200] At the end of a lengthy legislative process, Congress approved a final version of the Fourteenth Amendment reflecting the input of many authors. Section One is its heart, guaranteeing the citizenship of all persons born or naturalized in the United States. It also imposes important limits on state governments—prohibiting them from passing laws abridging the privileges or immunities of citizens of the United States, depriving any person of life, liberty, or property without due process of law, and denying to any person the equal protection of the law.

Section One's Citizenship Clause declares that all persons born or naturalized in the United States are free and equal citizens of the United States and of the state where they reside. This simple declaration repudiated the infamous holding of *Dred Scott* that Black people could not be citizens.[201] Though Congress had already affirmed the principle of birthright citizenship in the Civil Rights Act of 1866, the Citizenship Clause placed it on a firmer foundation.[202] Some lawmakers, including supporters of the concept like John Bingham, had questioned whether the Thirteenth Amendment empowered Congress to pass such a law.[203] John Martin Broomall, a Pennsylvania Republican, presciently insisted that citizenship protections needed to be "unmistakably in the Constitution," so as to "prevent a mere majority from repealing the law" in the future.[204]

The original Constitution lacked a clear definition of national citizenship. The Fourteenth Amendment changed that.[205] The Citizenship Clause extends the guarantee of citizenship to "all persons" born or naturalized in the United States and subject to the jurisdiction of the federal government. The few exceptions to this rule include "Indians not taxed," living under the jurisdiction of a tribe (no longer an issue today) and those who owe their allegiance to a foreign power (say, the children of diplomats born on American soil). The Supreme Court would later read the clause expansively, even at the peak of the "Yellow Peril" hysteria of the late nineteenth century, to affirm the citizenship of Asian Americans.[206] But today, right-wing pundits and politicians raising the inflammatory specter of "anchor babies" have called for the end of this protection, confirming the wise choice of the framers of the Fourteenth Amendment to prevent future generations from changing citizenship policy on a whim.[207]

The Privileges or Immunities Clause in Section One is the Constitution's "lost clause."[208] It provides: "No State shall make or enforce any law which shall abridge the privileges or immunities of citizens of the United States."[209] There was little debate in Congress over its meaning—and some confusion about the scope of its protection. When Jacob Howard, a member of the Joint Committee, presented the amendment to the Senate, he said that the privileges and immunities of United States citizens, "cannot be fully defined in their entire extent and precise nature." Among them, said the Michigan Republican, were fundamental rights that belong to citizens of free governments and "the personal rights guaranteed and secured by the first eight amendments of the Constitution."[210] Bingham also understood the clause to be a grant of power "to secure the enforcement of these provisions of the bill of rights in every state."[211] Nevertheless, just five years later the Supreme Court ignored this clear intent, reducing the Privileges or Immunities Clause to jurisprudential irrelevance. Half a century later, the justices would turn instead to the Due Process Clause to achieve the same purpose—enforcing individual provisions of the Bill of Rights against the states through a process known as "incorporation."[212]

The Due Process Clause, Section One's second great limitation on the states, was borrowed from the Fifth Amendment. It provides: "No State shall . . . deprive any person of life, liberty, or property, without due process of law." Though the provision was barely discussed in the congressional debate, Bingham made clear it was meant to protect "all persons, whether citizens or strangers, within this land."[213] Along with its parallel provision in the Fifth Amendment, the guarantee of due process demands that government actors adhere to the law and abide by fair procedures before depriving anyone of life, liberty, or property. Lawyers call this "procedural due process."[214]

In a series of controversial cases, the justices have also applied the guarantee of due process to vindicate rights not expressly mentioned in the Constitution under a doctrine known as "substantive due process." In the early twentieth century, the Court routinely struck down business and labor regulations interfering with the liberty of contract.[215] Then, beginning in the 1960s, the Court invalidated laws criminalizing contraception and abortion as encroaching on the right to privacy.[216] Legal scholars Kenji Yoshino and Nathan Chapman argue that the Privileges or Immunities Clause, not the Due Process Clause, is "the most natural textual source for those rights."[217]

The third and final constraint on the states bundled into Section One of the Fourteenth Amendment is the Equal Protection Clause. It provides: "No State shall . . . deny to any person within its jurisdiction the equal protection of the laws." Though the Declaration of Independence proclaimed that "all men are created equal," this core principle was omitted from the original Constitution and the Bill of Rights. Notably, while its original purpose was to provide Black people a remedy for discrimination, the Fourteenth Amendment's guarantee of equal protection of the laws applies to everyone.

Since the adoption of the amendment, the country has flagrantly disregarded this equality mandate in crucial ways. During World War II, for example, the Supreme Court sanctioned one of the government's most egregious violations of equal protection. Despite acknowledging that laws curtailing "the civil rights of a single racial group are immediately suspect" and subject "to the most rigid scrutiny," the justices ruled 6–3 that the president had the constitutional authority to order the relocation of more than one hundred thousand Americans of Japanese ancestry to internment camps based on "evidence of disloyalty on the part of some."[218] The ruling in *Korematsu v. United States* was finally overruled in 2018, nearly three-quarters of a century later, in a case upholding the Trump administration's "Muslim ban." Justice Sonia Sotomayor remarked on the irony in her dissenting opinion. "In the name of a superficial claim of national security," she wrote, "the Court redeploys the same dangerous logic underlying *Korematsu* and merely replaces one 'gravely wrong' decision with another."[219]

The drafters of the Fourteenth Amendment gave Congress the power to enforce its protections in Section Five. Following the precedent set by the Thirteenth Amendment, it authorizes Congress to effectuate its terms through "appropriate legislation." As Howard explained, Section Five "enables Congress, in case the States shall enact laws in conflict with the principles of the amendment, to correct that legislation by a formal congressional enactment."[220] When the Supreme Court upheld the Voting Rights Act a century later, it noted that the Fourteenth Amendment's "draftsmen sought to grant to Congress . . . the same broad powers expressed in the Necessary and Proper Clause."[221] In recent years, however, a more conservative Court has construed this power more narrowly.[222]

The remaining three sections of the Fourteenth Amendment have less relevance today. Section Two repealed the Three-Fifths Clause's formula for allocating seats in Congress, making clear that representation in the House of Representatives is determined by a count of "the whole number of persons in each state."[223] It also contains a penalty clause inspired by Thaddeus Stevens's failed representation amendment. The provision was meant to prevent states from obtaining greater political power by counting former slaves as persons while systematically denying them the right to vote. Far from guaranteeing the right to vote or even prohibiting states from denying it, Section Two left decisions about voter qualifications squarely in their hands.[224] Under its terms, whenever adult "male inhabitants" are denied the vote for any reason apart from "rebellion, or other crime," the state's "basis for representation" may be correspondingly reduced. If a state denied the franchise to half its male population, the drafters reasoned, it should lose half of its seats in the House of Representatives. Ultimately, however, the penalty proved to be an idle threat. Over the long era of Jim Crow, Congress never once used this power to punish even the most flagrant voter suppression.

Section Three was intended to ban former officials who supported the rebellion from holding high civil or military office. It was crafted, in part, as a rebuke to President Johnson. Throughout his term, the embattled president freely granted pardons to members of the ex-Confederacy, even allowing them to return to government posts. In its 1866 report to Congress, the Joint Committee insisted that those who had perpetrated the "treasonable withdrawal from Congress, and . . . flagrant rebellion and war," had "forfeited all civil and political rights and privileges under the federal Constitution."[225] Section Three's prohibition on office holding advances this aim. Its drafters hoped the ban would foster the establishment of loyal governments in the South by elevating "a different class of politicians."[226]

Under its terms, the disability imposed by Section Three may be waived by a two-thirds vote of both houses of Congress. In an 1872 amnesty law, enacted under this section, Congress removed it from all but a few hundred of the highest-ranking ex-Confederate officials. For all others subject to the provision, with the exception of the rebellion's two most prominent leaders, Robert E. Lee and Jefferson Davis, Congress restored all civil and political rights in 1898.[227] Ultimately, the Confederacy's top military and political officials had their rights restored posthumously under laws signed by Presidents Gerald Ford and Jimmy Carter.[228]

Notably, the ban was not limited to former Confederates. Section Three may be applied to anyone who engages in "insurrection or rebellion" against the United States, including those who provide "aid and comfort" to its "enemies." In 1919, Congress invoked this provision to bar Victor Berger, a socialist who opposed the nation's entry into World War I, from taking his seat in the House of Representatives. After the violent insurrection at the U.S. Capitol in January 2021, experts and commentators argued that the ban could be invoked to disqualify Donald Trump and any other officeholders who encouraged the siege from holding future office.[229]

Finally, in Section Four, the United States government disavowed any responsibility for Confederate war debt, including "any claim for the loss or emancipation of any slave."[230] State governments were also barred from making good on these debts. At the same time, Section Four ensures that the "validity" of the federal debt, including all government borrowing to this day, "shall not be questioned." (Somewhere, Alexander Hamilton was smiling!)

On May 10, 1866, the House of Representatives approved the Fourteenth Amendment after only a few days of debate. But the process of shaping the amendment was still not over. When the Senate began its deliberation, it added the crucial Citizenship Clause to Section One.[231] As the measure steamed toward final approval in the upper house, one senator hoped to sink it by limiting states to an abbreviated ratification period: no sooner than the next election and no later than three years after the vote in Congress.[232] On June 8, after senators rejected the time limit, they approved a modified version of the amendment with the Citizenship Clause added by a vote of 33–11.[233] Five days later, on June 13, the House accepted the Senate's changes by a vote of 120–32.[234]

Democrats opposed the amendment to the end, objecting to the extension of citizenship to "the Negroes, the coolies, and the Indians." The government, they insisted, "was made for white men."[235] There were many Republicans, on the other hand, who felt the measure didn't go far enough. "It falls far short of my wishes," said Stevens, "but . . . I believe it is all that can be obtained in the present state of public opinion."[236] Some activists were less forgiving. Wendell Phillips, the newly installed leader of the American Anti-Slavery Society, urged states to reject the Fourteenth Amendment, calling its failure to secure Black male suffrage "a fatal and total surrender."[237]

In a message to Congress, President Johnson argued it was unfair to advance the amendment when eleven Southern states were still not represented in Congress. "Grave doubts, therefore, may naturally and justly arise as to whether the action of Congress is in harmony with the sentiments of the people," he argued.[238] Breaking with tradition, the president campaigned that fall for candidates who opposed the Fourteenth Amendment.[239]

The 1866 election, says Eric Foner, "became the closest thing American politics has seen to a referendum on a constitutional amendment."[240] Republicans won a commanding victory in the Northern states that fall, winning control of many statehouses. By June 1867, a year after the vote in Congress, supporters had twenty-two of the twenty-eight states needed to ratify. But then the momentum stalled. Every Southern state rejected the measure except Tennessee.[241] The three border states of Maryland, Delaware, and Kentucky also withheld their support.[242] Then, in a further setback, Ohio and New Jersey acted to withdraw their support after Democrats retook their statehouses in the 1867 election.[243] Though Iowa was added to the yes column in March 1868, the prospects for ratification seemed to be slipping away.

To win ratification, the measure's backers embarked on a new strategy to secure the support of Southern states. The First Reconstruction Act of 1867, enacted over Johnson's veto, provided the cudgel. Among its many provisions, the law made ratification of the Fourteenth Amendment a condition for their readmission into the Union. In a transformational reform, the act also required the states of the former Confederacy to enfranchise their Black male populations.[244] In the face of this intensified political pressure, newly elected legislatures in seven Southern states, chosen by biracial electorates, ratified the measure between April and July 1868. Without the crucial support of Black voters in those states, the amendment would have surely failed. On July 20, Secretary of State William Seward proceeded to certify the Fourteenth Amendment as ratified by the requisite twenty-eight states, including Ohio and New Jersey in the tally.

Were these two states' ratifications still valid? Seward left the decision to Congress. In a concurrent resolution adopted the next day, Congress proclaimed the Fourteenth Amendment "to be part of the Constitution," disregarding the purported rescissions.[245] By July 28, however, when Seward issued a final certification, the controversy was mooted after South Carolina and Louisiana joined the list of ratifying states.[246] In contrast to the celebrations that accompanied the constitutional abolition of slavery, the adoption of the Fourteenth Amendment elicited little in the way of fanfare.

At 425 words, the Fourteenth Amendment is the longest of the Constitution's twenty-seven amendments. Americans today rightly focus on Section One—the amendment's core—and its guarantees of equal citizenship and fundamental rights against the federal and state governments alike. These transcendent concepts would lay the cornerstone for the nation's second founding.

Congress invoked Section One to enact the great civil rights statutes of the twentieth century, including the Civil Rights Act of 1964, the Voting Rights Act of 1965, and the Americans with Disabilities Act of 1991. In a way few anticipated, Section One also enshrines the Constitution's most litigated provisions: the guarantees of equal protection and due process of law that have fundamentally changed the relationship of the American people to their government. The Fourteenth Amendment's guarantee of equal protection was used to strike down the "separate but equal" doctrine in *Brown v. Board of Education*.[247] It undergirded the rule of "one person, one vote" in *Reynolds v. Sims*.[248] The Supreme Court invoked the amendment in *Gideon v. Wainwright* to ensure a defendant's right to counsel, and then again in *Batson v. Kentucky* to outlaw race-based dismissal of jurors by prosecutors.[249] Its guarantee of due process of law protects a woman's right to reproductive freedom and family planning. For interracial and same-sex relationships, once prohibited by discriminatory state laws, the promise of equal protection safeguards "the freedom to marry, or not marry," the person you choose.[250]

Today, many Americans revere the Fourteenth Amendment as the Constitution's "crown jewel."[251] And in many ways, it is. By affirming the citizenship for Black people, it allowed millions who helped build America to finally become Americans. In its promise to safeguard their rights, the Fourteenth Amendment established a framework for the humane treatment of the nation's longest held captives. Yet for much of our history, its promise was thwarted. The South persisted in its obstinance, and the country remained divided. It took another century (and counting) for

African Americans—the amendment's intended beneficiaries—to be afforded basic recognition of their human and civil rights.

The framers of the Fourteenth Amendment were aware of its shortcomings. While it was an important advance in the protection of civil rights, it offered inadequate protection for Black people's political rights. This crucial omission inspired a third Reconstruction Amendment.

The Fifteenth Amendment: The Problem of Suffrage

Back in the spring of 1866, as the Senate was making the final set of changes to the Fourteenth Amendment, Charles Sumner proposed adding a provision to outlaw racial discrimination in all "civil or political" rights "whether in the courtroom or at the ballot-box."[252] The proposal was voted down overwhelmingly. As Jacob Howard later explained on behalf of the Joint Committee on Reconstruction: "It was our opinion that three-fourths of the States of this Union could not be induced to vote to grant the right of suffrage . . . to the colored race."[253] Apart from Sumner, few political leaders were willing to champion Black suffrage publicly. In an 1865 letter to the governor of Louisiana, published after his death, President Lincoln indicated that he would support voting rights for "some of the colored people" in the state, "for instance, the very intelligent, and especially those who have fought gallantly in our ranks."[254] Even President Johnson privately conceded that literate, property-owning African Americans should be enfranchised.[255] But when the suffrage question arose during the debate over the Civil Rights Act of 1866, its drafters made sure the bill had "nothing to do with the political rights or status of parties."[256]

The Republicans' resounding victory in the 1866 midterm election spurred a new willingness to confront the suffrage issue. In the brief legislative session that followed the election, before the new class of lawmakers was seated, emboldened Republicans passed a measure to extend voting rights to African American men living in the District of Columbia. The law took effect in January 1867, after Congress voted to override yet another of President Johnson's vetoes.[257] That same month, lawmakers introduced Black male suffrage in the United States territories.[258] Then, in February 1867, they admitted Nebraska to the Union "upon the fundamental condition" that its eligible Black residents not be denied the right to vote.[259]

Once the 40th Congress assembled in March 1867, the expanded

Republican majority launched its project of Radical Reconstruction in the South. Its first order of business was to supplant the all-white state governments reconstituted from the wreckage of the Confederacy. Three Reconstruction Acts, enacted in 1867 over Johnson's vetoes, divided the South into temporary military districts administered by army generals and set new terms for the readmission of the former Confederate states. First, the rebel states were required to grant the franchise to "the male citizens of said State, twenty-one years old and upward, of whatever race, color, or previous condition." Second, they would have to hold conventions to draft new state constitutions guaranteeing universal male suffrage, subject to approval by Congress and the states' voters in a referendum. And third, as noted earlier, they had to ratify the Fourteenth Amendment.

The Reconstruction Acts also laid out procedures for registering voters and organizing state constitutional conventions. Taken together, these measures dramatically expanded the electorate in the ten covered states (Tennessee was exempted). Within a year, more than seven hundred thousand African Americans were added to the voter rolls[260] and, by 1868, they were voting in large numbers throughout the South.[261] In five Southern states—Alabama, Florida, Louisiana, Mississippi, and South Carolina—African Americans made up the majority of the electorate.[262] The Reconstruction Acts resulted in the broadest expansion of the franchise in a generation, since the Jacksonian Era push to expand the electorate to include all white men.[263] One local Tennessee newspaper criticized the new policy for its tendency to "degrade and disgrace our form of government." The Republican plan, the paper claimed, would "cheapen the right to suffrage, by bestowing it upon ignorant, besotted masses, excluding therefrom the brightest intelligence and political experience."[264]

This striking expansion of the franchise in the South stood in stark contrast to what was occurring in the rest of the country. By 1868, only seven states outside of the region permitted Black people to vote.[265] Most of the others had enacted laws decades earlier to exclude Black people from the rolls, even as they moved toward universal suffrage for white men. When voters in eight Northern states considered measures to repeal these race restrictions between 1865 and 1869, the ideal of equal suffrage crashed into a rock of white resistance.[266] Voters in Iowa and Minnesota agreed to liberalize their laws.[267] Elsewhere, though, Northern Democrats rode a wave of backlash, making big gains in the state elections of 1867. A San Francisco newspaper prayed that "the common sense and latent prejudice of the country may be relied upon . . . to preserve us from the monstrous folly of erecting unqualified negro suffrage into a national 'institution.' "[268] The Republican Speaker of the House, Schuyler Colfax, spoke for many in his party when he wondered if the Republicans had gotten "ahead of the people."[269]

As the presidential election of 1868 loomed, Democrats assailed the Republicans for their "unparalleled oppression and tyranny" in subjecting the South "to military despotism and negro supremacy." Their party platform pledged to return "the privilege and trust of suffrage" to the states.[270] Republicans, on the other hand, attempted to straddle the sectional divide, endorsing the Reconstruction policy of "equal suffrage to all loyal men" in the South while reassuring Northerners that "the question of suffrage in all the loyal states properly belongs to the people of those states."[271] This two-track approach drew fierce criticism. The New England Anti-Slavery Society denounced the position as "a practical surrender of the whole question."[272] Sumner called the platform plank "foolish and contemptible," while Stevens lambasted his "skulking" party for its "cowardly and mean" approach to the question.[273]

The election results shocked the Republicans. The party's nominee, the former Union general Ulysses S. Grant, won the popular vote by an unexpectedly narrow margin—about three hundred thousand votes out of nearly 6 million cast. During the campaign, Grant barely mentioned Black suffrage, hoping to sidestep a divisive issue. But now Republicans came to see that their interests lay in enfranchising this new and potentially loyal constituency.[274] They recognized too that the former Confederate states would act to suppress the Black vote at the earliest opportunity. With a sense of urgency, Republicans began work on a voting rights amendment. They had to get it done before the start of the next Congress, when Democrats would be returning in force.[275] Over two months of debate, lawmakers put forward more than sixty proposals.[276] One measure offered by a Pennsylvania congressman would have instituted universal suffrage with "no distinction of wealth, intelligence, race, family, or sex."[277] But for the most part, the proposals focused on *male* suffrage. The decision led to a rift with woman suffragists who had supported the abolitionist cause.

There was considerable disagreement on what the amendment should say. Should it affirmatively recognize a fundamental right to vote? Or should it merely prohibit discrimination in voting? Should the amendment outlaw only abridgments based on race, color, and previous condition of servitude? Or should it extend more broadly to discrimination based on religion, education, national origin, and property ownership?

Congressman George Boutwell, a Massachusetts Republican, was an early supporter of securing "universal suffrage to all adult male citizens of this country."[278] Willard Warner, a "carpet-bagging" Ohio Republican representing Alabama in the Senate, concurred, proclaiming "it is the duty of the hour to put into the Constitution a grand affirmative proposition which shall protect every citizen of this Republic in the enjoyment of political power."[279] Such an amendment would have the virtue of making the right to vote explicit in the Constitution for the first time. But most members of Congress were not ready to embrace such a radical break with the tradition, dating back to the decision of the Framers, of leaving voting rules in the hands of the states.[280] Their "dodge" has been to "our collective peril," says law professor Lani Guinier, leaving "one of the fundamental elements of democratic citizenship tethered to the whims of local officials,"[281] freeing them "to enact restrictive voting policies that would block millions of citizens from the ballot box."[282]

Nativism also figured into the lawmakers' hesitancy. Members of Congress from Pacific Coast states feared the amendment would enfranchise the region's Chinese American population. "They are a people who do not or will not learn our language," said a senator from Oregon. "They cannot or will not adopt our manners or customs and modes of life."[283] Lawmakers from the East had anti-immigrant prejudices of their own. Warning of an influx of Catholics from Europe, Senator James Patterson of New Hampshire asked, "Why should we throw open this portal of political power and let into the strongholds of our Government the emissaries of arbitrary power, the minions of despotism?"[284]

For these reasons, the lawmakers coalesced around a more tightly crafted amendment to prevent discrimination based on race. Massachusetts senator Henry Wilson argued for a broader ban on discrimination "on account of race, color, nativity, property, education, or creed."[285] But Nevada Senator William Stewart spoke for most when he argued that an amendment addressing race was the "logical" next step. "It is the only measure that will really abolish slavery," he said. "Let it be made the immutable law of the land; let it be fixed; and then we shall have peace."[286]

After agreeing to limit the amendment's protection to African American men, some in Congress wanted the measure to protect the right to hold office as well. Advocates of this approach cited an incident in Georgia, in which the legislature ousted more than two dozen duly elected Black members.[287] Some lawmakers worried that the added provision would complicate the prospects for ratification. Others, like Massachusetts congressman Benjamin Butler, rejected the premise that such a right needed to be spelled out.[288] "The right to elect to office carries with it the inalienable and indissoluble and indefeasible right to be elected to office," said Butler.[289]

As the session clock ticked down, Democrats raised familiar objections grounded in states' rights and white supremacy. They were joined by a handful of conservative Republicans. One decried a "revolution . . . striking at the life of republican institutions within the States themselves."[290] Echoing Willard Saulsbury's objection to the Thirteenth Amendment, another lawmaker maintained that the proposal exceeded implicit "limitations" on the constitutional amendment power, enabling Congress to undermine "the institutions of the State" to put "their local frames of government, their sovereignty, and their powers altogether within the control of three fourths of the other States."[291]

Democrats further charged that Republicans only supported the amendment for their own partisan advantage: "to maintain the dominance" of the Republican Party "by means of the degradation of the suffrage" as one lawmaker put it.[292] At the same time, they looked for ways to put this controversial question before the people in state ratifying conventions. Charles Sumner chastised the Democrats for their demagoguery, likening them to "the witches in Macbeth"—presiding over "a political caldron, into which will be dropped all the poisoned ingredients of prejudice and hate," wielding the amendment as "the pudding-stick with which to stir the bubbling mass."[293]

In the session's final days, the choice came down to two competing measures. The Senate passed a narrowly drafted amendment to ensure that the right to vote and hold office could not be denied or abridged on the grounds of "race, color, or previous condition of servitude."[294] The language approved by the House would protect more broadly against discrimination based on "race, color, nativity, property, creed, or previous condition of servitude."[295] It was left to a conference committee to reconcile the differences. What emerged is the language of the Fifteenth Amendment we know today: "The right of citizens of the United States to vote shall not be denied or abridged by the United States or by any state on account of race, color, or previous condition of servitude." While drafts from both houses

included protections for the right to hold office, that provision was myste-
riously dropped in the final measure.[296]

The redraft frustrated many members. But with adjournment approaching, there was little time left to make further changes. On February 25,
1869, the House adopted the conference committee's measure by a vote of
144–44.[297] The next day, senators who had hoped for more offered their reluctant support. "I am prepared to believe that we must accept the report of
this committee or abandon all hope of any amendment of the Constitution
being proposed by this Congress," said Vermont's Justin Morrill, reflecting the view of many Republicans. It was, he conceded, the "best that we
can obtain."[298] Senators approved the measure on February 26 by a vote of
39–13. Charles Sumner cast a principled vote of "absent," complaining that
the amendment did not go far enough.[299] Willard Warner called it "unwor-
thy of the grand opportunity that is presented to us."[300] He predicted that
his adoptive home state of Alabama would disenfranchise 90 percent of
the Black electorate through the use of literacy tests and property requirements not specifically based on race.[301]

Despite the controversy, the Fifteenth Amendment achieved ratification
in less than a year. A February 3, 1870, vote by Iowa's legislature put the
measure over the top. The border states of Delaware, Kentucky, Maryland,
and Tennessee rejected the measure, as did the Pacific Coast states of California and Oregon, where anti-Chinese sentiment was strong. In the end,
the amendment's adoption depended on the vote of four Southern states
still under military rule. Virginia, Mississippi, Georgia, and Texas all voted
to ratify the amendment as a condition to having their statehood restored.
Without them, the amendment would not have obtained the support of the
twenty-eight legislatures needed for ratification. The measure's adoption
was clouded by another controversy over rescission. In January 1870, New
York's legislature sought to revoke its ratification following an election giving control to the Democrats. Once again, when Congress certified the
amendment, it refused to recognize the action, including New York in the
list of ratifying states.[302]

On April 11, 1870, two months after the amendment's adoption, Mississippi senator Hiram Revels, the first African American to serve in Congress, delivered an address to mark the joyous occasion.

The final result of our triumph, the cap-stone of the temple of Liberty, the crowning glory of the edifice raised to Freedom, was the

ratification of the Fifteenth Amendment, which we now celebrate.
This sacred Amendment, now welded in and become part and parcel
of our glorious Constitution—bone of its bone, flesh of its flesh—
which strikes down the last hope of the rebellion; which abolishes, so
far as statutes can abolish, the last civil and political distinction between different classes of our citizens, uniting the entire nation into
one harmonious whole. "E pluribus Unum" is the glory of the hour.
This Amendment, which firmly places the ballot in the hands of the
male adult members of a race numbering from four to five millions,
had become a political necessity as imperious as was the military
necessity which placed the bayonet in the same loyal hands.[303]

Civil rights leaders also reveled in the amendment's ratification. The Philadelphia Female Anti-Slavery Society proclaimed: "Beneath that broad
banner of civil and political liberty, the white man and black man stand,
side by side."[304] William Lloyd Garrison celebrated "this wonderful, quiet,
sudden transformation of four millions of human beings from the auction
block to the ballot-box."[305] Over the protest of some of its members, the
leaders of the American Anti-Slavery Society, the organization Garrison
founded, declared that "the work for which the society had been organized
was complete."[306]

Since its adoption, scholars have debated the motives behind the last-
minute push to add a third Reconstruction Amendment. Some believe that
the Republicans were, first and foremost, concerned with their own political power. According to this view, adopting the Fifteenth Amendment was
aimed primarily at bringing Black voters into the party fold—"a conver-
sion of expediency rather than one of conviction."[307] Others see Radical
Reconstruction as "the last great crusade of the nineteenth-century ro-
mantic reformers."[308] In this analysis, the moral imperative that drove the
abolitionist cause also motivated the lawmakers' determination to secure
African American citizenship and political rights.

Ultimately, even principled politicians are politicians. Charles Sumner,
the great abolitionist champion, was well aware that the enfranchisement
of African Americans would be a boon to the Republican Party. "Wherever you most need them, there they are," he said, "and be assured they will
all vote for those who stand by them in the assertion of equal rights."[309]
But the claim that the party got behind Black suffrage out of calculating

self-interest obscures some essential history. Lawmakers who supported the Fifteenth Amendment were, for the most part, principled supporters of rights for African Americans who demonstrated this commitment by consistent votes on issues affecting the Black population.[310] Given the pervasiveness of racism in the country, Republicans took these positions at great political risk. In the North, where the party was strongest, there were relatively few African Americans to swing elections. Moreover, in states where the suffrage question was put before voters, the party paid a political price.[311]

In the end, the party of Lincoln was hardly "radical" when it came to voting rights.[312] Republicans pressed for the adoption of the Fifteenth Amendment while they still held a supermajority in Congress to advance it. Even so, despite constant prodding by idealists, the party coalesced around a conservative solution.[313] Hesitant to disrupt a core feature of the original Constitution, the drafters of the Fifteenth Amendment left states in charge of their own voting rules, with consequences that reverberate to this day.

For decades, segregationists and their enablers sought to discredit the "so-called Fifteenth Amendment," insisting that it was adopted under "duress."[314] It is clear that the South's recalcitrance justified the Radical Republicans' exercise in "constitutional hardball." The question is, was the product of all that effort enough? The recent proliferation of vote-suppression measures in the states—from voter ID laws to the suspicious purges of voter rolls, all sanctioned by the courts—suggests the answer is no.[315]

Redemption, Restoration, and the Corporate Fourteenth Amendment

In March 1876, Mississippian Blanche K. Bruce stood to address his Senate colleagues. He was the chamber's second ever African American member, and the only one serving at the time. Elected to the seat once held by Jefferson Davis, Bruce was generally inclined to hold his tongue in the belief that the docility he learned during his slave upbringing would benefit him as he learned the ways of Washington. But the senator also knew that "silence at this time would be infidelity to my senatorial trust and unjust to both the people and State I have the honor in part to represent." Bruce was desperate. There had been a drastic retreat in the federal government's enforcement of Reconstruction in the South. An "exceptional and peculiar" violence had filled the void. It was "an attack by an aggressive, intelligent, white political organization upon inoffensive, law-abiding fellow citizens," the senator explained, "a violent method for political supremacy, that seeks not the protection of the rights of the aggressors, but the destruction of the rights of the party assailed."

In his most important speech as a senator, Bruce called for a federal investigation into the violence that "put in question and jeopardy the sacred rights of the citizen." He implored his colleagues:

> We simply demand the practical recognition of the rights given us in the Constitution and laws, and ask from our white fellow-citizens only the consideration and fairness that we so willingly extend to them. Let them generally realize and concede that citizenship imports to us what it does to them, no more and no less. . . . We do not ask the enactment of new laws, but only the enforcement of those that already exist.[316]

Bruce's plea that Congress uphold the three new amendments to the Constitution, and the laws passed to enforce them, came at a perilous time. Just four days earlier, the Supreme Court ruled that Congress had no power under the Fifteenth Amendment to combat the Ku Klux Klan's brutal campaign of terror to keep African Americans from voting. Bruce's appeal for an increased federal presence in the region went unheeded. Reconstruction was coming to an end.

In theory, the Reconstruction Amendments should have settled any lingering questions about African Americans' place in the political and social order. Congress adopted the Thirteenth, Fourteenth, and Fifteenth Amendments to make full citizens out of former slaves, investing them with the full array of civil and political rights. The amendments also recalibrated the balance of power between the federal government and the states, giving Congress the lead role in enforcing the Constitution's new guarantees of liberty and equality. In 1870 and 1871, lawmakers exercised this power to pass Enforcement Acts to address the breakdown of law and order in the South. For a time, the Grant administration applied these measures vigorously, bringing over 2,500 prosecutions under the new laws and centralizing the federal government's prosecutorial power in a new Department of Justice to ensure compliance.[317]

Nevertheless, within a few short years, federal law enforcement was on the wane, undermined by a combination of scandal, poor funding, and Southern resistance. As President Grant sought re-election in 1872, his vice president was implicated in a bribery scheme. Later, the beleaguered president's personal secretary was indicted in a tax fraud conspiracy.[318] As the administration's political capital ebbed, the Justice Department deprioritized the prosecution of civil rights cases. A devastating financial panic in 1873 accelerated the withdrawal as Congress slashed funding for the courts and troops charged with maintaining the peace in the South. Amid these setbacks, the 1874 midterm election produced a Democratic House majority intent on eviscerating the Reconstruction regime.

Emboldened Southern vigilantes quickly filled the vacuum. Throughout the region, they assaulted—and even assassinated—Republican elected officials with impunity. In Mississippi, a carpetbagging state senator reported that "the Republicans were as helpless as babes." Most, he said, had simply fled the state.[319] As W.E.B. Du Bois later reflected, "The white South believed it to be of vital interest to its welfare that the experiment of negro suffrage should fail ignominiously, and that almost to a man the whites were willing to insure this failure either by active force or passive acquiescence."[320] In the face of this widespread violence and lawlessness, the North lost its will to resist. "In the final analysis," notes one historian, "Southern intransigence and Northern apathy together brought about the collapse of the enforcement program; white supremacy proved to be a more vital principle than Republican supremacy."[321]

The judiciary might have been expected to provide a strong line of defense, but in 1873 the Supreme Court signaled that it too was retreating from the promise of the Reconstruction Amendments, imposing a narrow interpretation of one of its key provisions. In the *Slaughterhouse Cases*, a set of lawsuits raising claims under the Thirteenth and Fourteenth Amendments, a group of white butchers challenged a Louisiana public health law establishing a regional monopoly over the slaughterhouse trade. The butchers alleged that requiring them to use a specially designated facility constituted involuntary servitude in violation of the Thirteenth Amendment, a claim the justices readily dispatched. The butchers also contended the law infringed "the right to exercise their trade," which they claimed was a "privilege and immunity" of U.S. citizenship protected by the Fourteenth Amendment.

In a 5–4 decision, the Court upheld Louisiana's law under its broad powers to regulate business in the state. Not content to stop there, the justices said they were "called upon for the first time to give construction" to the Reconstruction Amendments.[322] In its review of the amendments' history, which they acknowledged was "fresh within the memory of us all," the majority conceded that the "one pervading purpose found in them all" was "the freedom of the slave race" and the protection of their rights.[323] But they insisted that the Privileges or Immunities Clause was neither meant to make the Court a "perpetual censor" of state-enacted policies,[324] nor to "degrade the state governments by subjecting them to the control of Congress."[325] The privileges and immunities of U.S. citizens, said the justices, amounted to a circumscribed set of rights relating to *national* citizenship, from the right to access courts and government agencies to the free use of seaports and navigable waters. All other rights were "left to state governments for security and protection."[326]

The Court's sweeping "construction," in a case brought by white litigants wholly unrelated to race, effectively nullified the Privileges or Immunities Clause only five years after the Fourteenth Amendment's adoption. In a stinging dissent, Justice Stephen Field complained that the majority's opinion rendered the amendment "a vain and idle enactment, which accomplished nothing."[327] Indeed, the clause would not appear in another Supreme Court opinion for decades.[328]

Then, in the 1876 case of *United States v. Cruikshank*, the Supreme Court significantly limited Congress's enforcement powers under Section Five of the Fourteenth Amendment. The case arose out of the infamous Colfax Massacre. On Easter Sunday 1873, using "rifles, shotguns, six-shooters, hunting knives—even a small cannon," a paramilitary gang of ex-Confederate soldiers and members of the Ku Klux Klan and White League slaughtered as many as two hundred African Americans in Colfax, Louisiana, following a disputed election.[329] Ninety-seven white men were charged under the Enforcement Act of 1870 (also known as the Ku Klux Klan Act), a law enacted to punish violence intended to deprive Americans of constitutionally protected rights.[330] Only three were found guilty at trial, and on appeal, the Supreme Court allowed the killers to walk free. In its holding, the Court drew a sharp line between state action and private action. "The Fourteenth Amendment prohibits *a state* from depriving any person of life, liberty, or property without due process of law," the Court explained, "but this adds nothing to the rights of one citizen as against another."[331] Simply put, the Fourteenth Amendment did not authorize

Congress to legislate against private individuals who deprive African Americans of their constitutional rights.

That same day, the Court also narrowed Congress's enforcement powers under the Fifteenth Amendment. The dispute in *United States v. Reese*, the era's first voting rights case, arose from what the *New-York Tribune* called "A Peaceful Election Farce in Kentucky."[332] The city of Lexington, where the Black population outnumbered whites, instituted a tax as a prerequisite to voting. A local paper reported that "nearly all the colored voters have tendered their taxes to the Collector, who refused to receive them, evidently for the purpose of disfranchising the voters."[333] William Garner, an eligible voter turned away in the voter suppression scheme, filed suit under the Enforcement Act alleging a conspiracy to prevent Black people from voting. The Supreme Court ruled he had no claim. "The Fifteenth Amendment does not confer the right of suffrage upon any one," the Court declared; it merely prohibits its denial or abridgment "on account of race, color, or previous condition of servitude."[334] Because two key provisions of the Enforcement Act outlawed *all* interference with voting—and not just infringements based on racial discrimination—it exceeded Congress's "limited powers," said the Court. The Court's crabbed logic opened the door to creative state laws that disenfranchised Black voters on supposedly neutral grounds, from poll taxes to literacy tests, for decades.

These three cases, and many others that followed, betrayed the "second founding" promised by the Reconstruction Amendments—vitiating the new powers given to the federal government and instead resurrecting an antebellum conception of states' rights to perpetuate a regime of brutal racial oppression.

The election of 1876 marked the end of America's first experiment with biracial democracy. In a closely fought presidential race marred by pervasive violence and fraud, Democratic Party standard bearer Samuel Tilden of New York edged out Ohio Republican Rutherford B. Hayes in the popular vote. But the outcome hung on disputed electoral votes in three Southern states: Florida, Louisiana, and South Carolina.[335] To break the deadlock, Congress empaneled a commission that decided to award the contested electoral votes to Hayes in a party line vote. In a backroom deal, Southern Democrats agreed to support Hayes's claim to the presidency in exchange for the end of Reconstruction and a withdrawal of the federal troops that remained in the South. The "Compromise of 1877" gave white Southerners free rein. Twelve years after Lee's surrender at Appomattox, the spirit of the old Confederacy was ascendant.

In his first year as president, Hayes nominated John Marshall Harlan to the Supreme Court. This was arguably the Compromise's most positive externality. By some accounts, Harlan was deeply conflicted about race and slavery. He was raised in a Kentucky household that owned slaves, including his own brother, Robert. Yet he married Malvina "Mallie" Shanklin, who came from a Northern abolitionist family.[336] By other accounts, Harlan was a political animal—and a political opportunist. As his home state's attorney general in the early 1860s, he opposed the Thirteenth Amendment for "undercutting the right of each state to determine its own policies" and for abolition's potential to "stimulate racial unrest."[337] When seeking a post in Grant's administration later that decade, however, he came to support the Thirteenth and Fourteenth Amendments "just as vigorously as he had previously condemned them."[338]

In 1883, the Supreme Court heard a set of cases brought by Black plaintiffs from around the country. In New York City, William Davis was refused entry to a show at the Grand Opera House. In Grand Junction, Tennessee, a railroad company prevented Sallie Robinson from boarding "the ladies' car."[339] At inns in Topeka, Kansas, and Jefferson City, Missouri, Bird Gee and W.H.R. Agee were refused meal service and lodging. And in San Francisco, George Tyler was denied "a seat in the dress circle of McGuire's theater."[340] The essential facts were not in dispute. In each case, people had been turned away from places of public accommodation because of their race. The owners of these varied establishments were charged with violating the Civil Rights Act of 1875, which prohibited racial discrimination in public places. But was this law constitutional?[341]

The *Civil Rights Cases* quickly became a source of anguish for Harlan. Deep inside he knew the right outcome, but he struggled to put the right words to paper. During this bout with writer's block, Harlan's wife retrieved a historical trinket that he had come into possession of some years earlier.[342] It was former chief justice Roger Taney's inkstand. Mallie believed that this reminder of the man who authored the *Dred Scott* decision might prompt a flash of inspiration. Gauging from Harlan's opinion, her plan worked. If the justices curtailed Congress's power under the Thirteenth and Fourteenth Amendment, he wrote, the country would descend into "an era of constitutional law when the rights of freedom and American citizenship cannot receive from the nation that efficient protection which heretofore was unhesitatingly accorded to slavery and the rights of the master."[343]

However, Harlan's was the dissenting opinion. Rejecting this view, a majority of the justices invalidated the civil rights law, holding that the "badges of slavery" did not include mere discrimination.[344] "When a man has emerged from slavery," said the justices, "there must be some stage in the progress of his elevation when he takes the rank of a mere citizen and ceases to be the special favorite of the laws." The Court's message to African Americans was transparent and direct: slavery was a thing of the past.[345] Though the decision was "a surprise to the country," a Kansas newspaper cheerfully noted that "it agrees with the prejudices of almost every white man, woman and child in the United States."[346]

The disinclination of Congress and the courts to enforce the Reconstruction Amendments paved the way for the era of Jim Crow. The nation, said African American journalist T. Thomas Fortune in an 1884 speech, was "drifting back to the view of the States Rights doctrines where Calhoun and Webster left off, . . . ignoring the power of the national government as expressed in the Fourteenth and Fifteenth Amendment to the Constitution—the essence of our four years of bloody internecine conflict."[347] By the 1890s, the South's "redemption" was complete. Southern whites reconstituted their states' governments and laws, blotting out the achievements of their "black and tan" counterparts in the years following the Civil War and extinguishing Black liberty.[348] New constitutions in six Southern states legitimized the tools of voter suppression, including poll taxes, literacy tests, and grandfather clauses, to enforce white supremacy.[349] In the remaining five, lawmakers amended their states' constitutions to achieve the same result.[350]

"The white people of the State," said a delegate to Mississippi's 1890 convention, "want to feel and know that they are protected not only against the probability but the possibility of negro rule and negro domination."[351] In a state where Black people constituted 58 percent of the population, all but one delegate was white. "There is no use to equivocate or lie about the matter," said James Vardaman, a future governor and senator. "Mississippi's constitutional convention of 1890 was held for no other purpose than to eliminate the nigger from politics; not the 'ignorant and vicious,' as some of those apologists would have you believe, but the nigger."[352] The state's new poll tax and literacy test for voters did not specifically discriminate "against the negro race," the Supreme Court would later rule. They merely discriminated "*against its characteristics*, and the offenses to which its criminal members are prone."[353] That year, there remained only 3,573 Black people on Mississippi's voter rolls, down from more than 50,000 two decades earlier.[354]

With the Supreme Court's blessing, other states in the region were eager to emulate the "Mississippi Plan." In 1902, white Virginians met to draft a new constitution of their own. Delegate Carter Glass, a future senator and treasury secretary, boasted that the charter's new "plan of suffrage" would "not necessarily deprive a single white man of the ballot, but will inevitably cut from the existing electorate four-fifths of the negro voters." Asked how, he replied: "By fraud, no; by discrimination, yes. But it will be discrimination within the letter of the law, and not in violation of the law." Whites could suppress the votes of African Americans, he said, "strictly within the limitations of the Federal Constitution by legislating against the characteristics of the black race, and not against the 'race, color or previous condition' of the people themselves."[355]

The triumph of Jim Crow came in 1896, when the Supreme Court upheld the conviction of Homer Plessy, a New Orleans shoemaker, for riding in a whites-only railroad car. In the parlance of the day, Plessy was an octoroon: "seven eighths Caucasian and one eighth African blood." But under the "one-drop rule," he was Black.[356] The local Creole community formed a citizens' group to challenge the ban, selecting the light-skinned Plessy to test the law. When instructed to go to the colored car, he refused. (This test case would inspire the NAACP's legal strategy and the courageous activism of civil rights hero Rosa Parks half a century later.) Plessy was convicted under a state law requiring railroad companies to provide "equal but separate accommodations." In his appeal to the justices, Plessy argued the law relegated Black people to an inferior status, thereby violating their Fourteenth Amendment right to equal protection of the laws. The Court, by a vote of 7–1, disagreed. "If the two races are to meet upon terms of social equality, it must be the result of natural affinities, a mutual appreciation of each other's merits, and a voluntary consent of individuals," said the majority. "If one race be inferior to the other socially, the Constitution of the United States cannot put them upon the same plane."[357]

As he had done in the *Civil Rights Cases*, Justice Harlan penned a lonely dissent. He argued that the Fourteenth and Fifteenth Amendments "removed the race line from our governmental systems. They had . . . a common purpose, namely to secure 'to a race recently emancipated, a race that through many generations have been held in slavery, all the civil rights that the superior race enjoy.'"[358] Though he casually assumed that the "white race" would be "the dominant race . . . for all time," Harlan rebuked the majority in words that would prove prophetic: "In my opinion, the judgment this day rendered will, in time, prove to be quite as pernicious as the decision made by this tribunal in the *Dred Scott Case*."[359] The holding in *Plessy* remained the law of the land for more than a half a century, until it was overturned in 1954 in the case of *Brown v. Board of Education*.[360]

In his famous address at the 1895 Cotton States and International Exposition in Atlanta, Booker T. Washington expressed a willingness to accept the reality of racial segregation, arguing that African Americans could still improve their lot. "In all things that are purely social," Washington said, "we can be as separate as the fingers, yet one as the hand in all things essential to mutual progress."[361] But progress was not mutual. For the next six decades, African Americans remained mired in circumstances grossly inferior to their white counterparts: denied participation in commerce and labor markets, prevented from voting and standing for office, and all but excluded from civic life. By the dawn of the twentieth century, the Fourteenth and Fifteenth Amendments no longer had force as a weapon against racial injustice. A Georgia congressman spoke for many when he dismissed the two amendments as "adopted, if adopted at all, against the will of a majority of all the people in the Union, by trickery and treachery in the North and by force and violence in the South."[362]

Back in 1883, just six days before the Supreme Court issued its ruling in the *Civil Rights Cases*, the *Boston Daily Journal* predicted that the Court was "soon to hand down a decision on one of the most important questions of constitutional law that has been before it for years."[363] The paper was not referring to the *Civil Rights Cases* but rather to the case of *Santa Clara County v. Southern Pacific Railroad Company*, an obscure dispute involving a special California tax on railroads. The Southern Pacific Railway, one of the nation's most powerful corporations, claimed that the tax violated its Fourteenth Amendment right to equal protection of the laws. But was this guarantee, defined in the amendment's text as extending to "any person" under a state's jurisdiction, meant to protect corporations? The railway's lawyer, former Congressman Roscoe Conkling, was in a unique position to know. As a member of the Joint Committee on Reconstruction, Conkling participated in the drafting of the Fourteenth Amendment. As the last surviving member of the committee, he represented to the justices that the drafters of the amendment settled on the word "person," instead of "citizen," to ensure that corporations would also be covered. This was surely a lie.

In an 1886 opinion by Justice Harlan, the Court sidestepped the constitutional question, ruling for the railroad on other grounds.[364] However, a court reporter responsible for writing headnotes, the brief summaries published alongside judicial decisions in the official court volumes, erroneously stated that the *Santa Clara* decision held that "corporations are persons within the meaning of the Fourteenth Amendment." In what constitutional scholar Adam Winkler calls "a feat of deceitful legal alchemy,"[365] lawyers representing corporations cited the *Santa Clara* "precedent" in legal arguments until courts started to rely on it. As the next chapter explores further, a conservative Supreme Court would build on that hollow foundation as it embarked on a project unimagined by the drafters of the Fourteenth Amendment—to protect unfettered capitalism against state regulation.[366] Winkler calculates that from the adoption of the Fourteenth Amendment in 1868 until 1912, the Supreme Court decided 312 claims involving the rights of corporations. During that same period, it heard only 28 cases concerning the rights of African Americans.[367] "Both the Fourteenth and Fifteenth Amendments were thus made innocuous as far as the Negro was concerned," observed W.E.B. Du Bois, "and the Fourteenth Amendment in particular became the chief refuge and bulwark of corporations."[368]

The courts' newfound solicitude for the titans of industry helped spur a powerful new current of political activism—and a renewed push for constitutional change.

4

The Progressive Era
Amendments (1909–1920)

As the twentieth century dawned, America was changing, but our Constitution was not. "It is true," said the *Washington Post*, "that there is some dissatisfaction with the Constitution as it is." But efforts to adopt amendments on woman suffrage and the election of senators by popular vote were unlikely to succeed. Since the three "war amendments" were "shot into the Constitution" after the Civil War, "we may properly regard the Constitution as unamendable," the editors concluded.[1]

It was the peak of the Gilded Age. Then, as now, a transforming economy produced great disparities of wealth. Moneyed interests dominated politics and policy making. Immigration was transforming the country in ways that alarmed traditionalists. And a conservative Supreme Court stood as a barrier to progressive reform. (These uncanny parallels to our own time have led many people to speak of a "second Gilded Age.")[2]

The politics of the era were extremely polarized, exposing sharp regional and partisan divides. The North and West were Republican strongholds, the South solidly Democratic. Elections were decided by the narrowest of margins, leading to frequent swings in the balance of political power. In five straight presidential elections, from 1876 to 1892, the popular vote margin was three percentage points or less. Twice, in 1876 and 1888, the Republican candidate took the White House while losing the national popular vote. Control of Congress was also closely contested during this time. From 1877 to 1901, Democrats controlled the House of Representatives for fourteen years while Republicans held it for ten, trading the Speaker's gavel five times. In the Senate, the GOP had a stronger hold, thanks to a calculated strategy of awarding statehood to sparsely populated, reliably

Republican states in the West. As a result, they controlled the chamber for eighteen of twenty-four years.[3]

Out of this ferment, America transitioned from an agrarian to an industrial economy as its people migrated from the countryside to the cities. And new social movements emerged to harness the power of government to improve the individual and transform society. First came the Populists. Born of agrarian unrest, the People's Party crashed onto the political scene in the early 1890s, seeking to reform politics, liberalize monetary policy, and curb the influence of corporations and the wealthy.[4] "We meet in the midst of a nation brought to the verge of moral, political, and material ruin," declared the party's 1892 platform. "The fruits of the toil of millions are boldly stolen to build up colossal fortunes for a few, unprecedented in the history of mankind; and the possessors of these, in turn, despise the Republic and endanger liberty. From the same prolific womb of governmental injustice we breed two great classes—tramps and millionaires."[5] Though the Populists' heyday as a political force was brief, they had a profound influence on American politics in the first two decades of the twentieth century. Their agenda lived on, embraced by an emerging populist wing of the Democratic Party led by William Jennings Bryan, the "Great Commoner," who championed the rights of farmers and laborers.[6]

Next came the Progressives. With roots in the urban middle and upper classes, the Progressive movement demanded that government play a more active role in supporting the people's welfare.[7] Progressives could be found in both major parties, scrambling the distinctions between them. In the era that came to bear their name, they launched many great crusades, seeking to fight government corruption, rein in big corporations, and purify society. They stood for an ambitious agenda of social and economic reform: public health, workers' rights, progressive taxation, and votes for women, to name just a few. Theirs was also a time of resurgent racism and xenophobia, amid America's early forays as a global power. It was the era of Jim Crow, the Palmer raids, and the colonization of Puerto Rico and the Philippines.

Standing in the way of the reform movements was an activist Supreme Court, "employing the power of judicial review to an extent unprecedented in American constitutional history."[8] In the decades following its 1857 decision in *Dred Scott v. Sandford*, the Court came to embrace an extraordinarily cramped view of Congress's powers under the Constitution, invalidating scores of federal laws as intrusions on the reserved power of the states.[9] At the same time, based on their faulty reasoning in the *Santa Clara* decision, the justices perversely found a new purpose for the Fourteenth Amendment's protection of "due process of law," wielding it as a shield to protect businesses and corporations against regulation by the federal and state governments alike. This now discredited jurisprudence, rooted in laissez-faire economics and vague notions of "natural law," had no foundation in the amendment's text or history. Over four decades, it was a powerful brake on the people's ability to address new and unprecedented social harms through democratic means. All the while, the justices abandoned the Fourteenth Amendment's true purpose of protecting the equal rights and citizenship of African Americans and other oppressed minorities.

The era was epitomized by the notorious case of *Lochner v. New York*.[10] The dispute began with the passage of a typical Progressive reform. In 1895, the New York legislature enacted the Bakeshop Act, a measure regulating working conditions in the state's bakeries. The appalling conditions in these establishments were well known. As Ian Millhiser recounts in his colorful history of the Supreme Court, "New York's bakers worked fourteen-hour shifts in roach-infested basements, slept on their work tables, and then woke up the next day to do it again."[11] Besides the law's provisions requiring basic sanitation in all bakeries, it limited employment to sixty hours per week and ten hours in any one day."[12]

Six years later, the state fined Joseph Lochner, a bakery owner in Utica, for allowing an employee to work more than sixty hours per week. In his defense, Lochner claimed that the law interfered with his right to make a living. Though he lost his case at trial, he found a receptive audience at the Supreme Court. In a 5–4 ruling, the justices held that the Bakeshop Act interfered with the "general right to make a contract," a liberty protected by the Fourteenth Amendment. While they acknowledged that states may regulate dangerous industries like mining, they dismissed the idea that the baking trade was particularly hazardous. "There must be more than the mere fact of the possible existence of some small amount of unhealthiness to warrant legislative interference with liberty," they sniffed. Otherwise, we would all be "at the mercy of legislative majorities."[13]

In this manner, between 1895 and 1937, the Supreme Court struck down dozens of laws enacted by the people's representatives in Congress and the state legislatures. Minimum wage provisions, labor laws, banking reform, and business regulations were all swept aside in a period of unbridled judicial intervention—many hanging on the slender reed of the *Santa Clara* decision. In time, rising popular anger over an out-of-touch judiciary would arouse a popular clamor for constitutional change.

In the span of a decade, from 1909 to 1920, Americans added four new amendments to the Constitution. Like the Reconstruction Amendments, these reforms were the product of social movements that had striven for decades to achieve their aims. The Populists' demands for economic justice and democratic accountability were realized through amendments authorizing a fairer tax system and the direct election of senators. Temperance activists achieved their long-sought goal of banning alcohol nationwide, for a time at least. And woman suffragists ushered in the largest expansion of the franchise in American history. Taken together, these movements channeled the people's demand for reform through a new generation of civil-society organizations deploying an ever more sophisticated toolbox of strategies—organizing, research, lobbying, and communications—that would transform the way Americans campaign for legal change to this day.

The Sixteenth Amendment: The Power to Tax

The November 1889 edition of *The Forum* published an essay entitled, "The Owners of the United States." The author of the piece, Thomas Shearman, was a reform-minded leader of the New York bar. From data he painstakingly collected, Shearman calculated that fifty thousand families (out of 13 million) possessed half of the nation's wealth.[14] "No one can entertain a reasonable doubt," he said, "that there has been an accumulation of wealth in a few individual hands in the United States, during the last 25 years, vastly in excess of any which has taken place in other parts of the world. In no other country have railroad-managers, manufacturers, oil-refiners, mine-owners, bankers, and land speculators accumulated fortunes so rapidly as they have in this."[15]

Shearman observed that this new millionaire class—the Astors, Vanderbilts, Rockefellers, Morgans, and their ilk—amassed great wealth while managing to avoid taxes. The burden of federal taxation, raised mainly in the form of tariffs and excises, was cast "exclusively upon the working class," consuming 75 to 90 percent of their earnings. "Within 30 years," he concluded, "the present methods of taxation being continued, the United States of America will be substantially owned by less than 50,000 persons, constituting less than one in 500 of the adult male population."[16]

Of all the authorities granted to Congress by the Constitution, perhaps none was more important to the Framers than the power to tax. Article I gives Congress broad power "to lay and collect taxes, duties, imposts and excises, to pay the debts and provide for the common defense and general Welfare of the United States."[17] As Alexander Hamilton explained, this power is "plenary, and indefinite."[18] But the Constitution placed a special condition on one category of revenue—"capitation, or other direct" taxes—requiring they be apportioned among the states based on their relative population, just as seats in the House of Representatives are allocated.[19]

But what did the Framers mean by "direct taxes"? We know they understood them to include taxes on land or persons. But there is no evidence that they ever agreed on a definition.[20] When one delegate asked late in the convention, "What is the precise meaning of *direct* taxation?" the record shows that "no one answered."[21] In a legal brief prepared just eight years after the Constitution was written, Alexander Hamilton concluded that the term had no clear meaning: "What is the distinction between *direct* and *indirect* taxes? It is a matter of regret that terms so uncertain and vague in so important a point are to be found in the Constitution."[22] During the country's first century, the question rarely came up. The federal government raised most of its revenue from tariffs and excise fees, consumption taxes "drawn from the weary hands of labor."[23] On a few occasions, Congress did impose direct taxes in the form of excises on real estate or slaves.[24] But these assessments were unpopular and proved difficult to administer.[25]

Congress first considered a national income tax during the Civil War as it searched for ways to meet its staggeringly high cost.[26] It was a simple yet radical idea. "Why should we not impose the burdens which are to fall upon the people of this country equally, in proportion to their ability to bear them?" asked the congressman who proposed it.[27] The wartime measure set a 3 percent flat tax on incomes over $800,[28] supplanted the following year by a graduated tax rising from 3 percent on incomes over $600 to 5 percent on incomes over $10,000.[29] This brief experiment in progressive taxation lasted only a decade, however. After the war, when the wealthy called for an end to the tax, Congress let the measure lapse.[30]

For the next four decades, Congress relied primarily on regressive consumption taxes to fund government operations, leaving wage earners and farmers largely footing the bill.[31] Amid rising public anger over the failure of the wealthy to contribute their fair share, the People's Party called for a "graduated income tax" in its 1892 platform.[32] After the Democrats took

Congress and the White House that year for the first time since before the Civil War, party leaders adopted the issue as their own, proposing a flat 2 percent tax on incomes over $4,000.[33] Lawmakers representing the more prosperous, industrializing states of the East and Midwest were quick to oppose the measure. "By this legislation," thundered New York City congressman Bourke Cockran, "you place the Government in an attitude of hostility to the true patriots of this country, to the men by whose industry land is made valuable, by whose intelligence capital is made fruitful."[34] Cockran breathlessly warned that the tax would lead to a "rising tide of socialism."[35] But in August 1894, the measure passed comfortably.[36]

Opponents promptly challenged the law in court. It seemed like a frivolous case: just fourteen years earlier the Supreme Court ruled that the Civil War income tax was a legitimate exercise of Congress's taxing power.[37] But in *Pollock v. Farmers' Loan & Trust Co.*, the justices stunned the nation, declaring the 1894 law to be an unconstitutional application of a direct tax.[38] A dissenting justice called the decision "nothing less than a surrender of the taxing power to the moneyed class."[39] An outraged public agreed.[40] "The millionaire influence and power of the corporation capital of the country is more apparent in the decision than old-fashioned political principles of any kind," complained the *Pittsburgh Post*.[41]

The widely reviled decision presaged the hard-right turn of the *Lochner* era, which would stifle progressive reform for the next four decades. In the years following the decision, lawmakers introduced income tax bills in each new Congress, looking to defy the Court. But those efforts went nowhere.[42] Finally, in 1908, the winds began to shift. Led by William Jennings Bryan in his third run for the presidency, the Democrats that year endorsed a constitutional amendment to overturn *Pollock*.[43] Aware of its enduring popularity, Bryan's opponent, the conservative Republican William Howard Taft, let it be known that he too favored an income tax.[44]

The issue came to a head the following year. In April 1909, Senator Joseph Bailey, a Texas Democrat, offered an amendment to a tariff bill imposing a tax of 3 percent on all incomes above $5,000—a measure strikingly similar to the flat tax struck down in *Pollock*. Upping the ante, a group of progressive Republicans proposed a graduated tax, starting at 2 percent on incomes over $5,000 and rising to 6 percent on those making over $100,000.[45] As he monitored these developments, Nelson Aldrich, the powerful chairman of the Senate Finance Committee, began to worry that the income-tax measure might pass.[46]

According to one historian, "No one in the entire history of the Senate has ever dominated it more autocratically through sheer will power than Nelson W. Aldrich."[47] An imposing presence, with a "penetrating" and "disturbing" gaze,[48] the Rhode Island Republican rose from humble origins to amass great power over three decades in politics.[49] With "a lofty contempt for the masses, upon whom he looked as inferior folk,"[50] Aldrich preferred to lavish his attention on the privileged, who welcomed him into their ranks. In return, he advanced a pro-business agenda in Congress.[51] "Everybody knows," wrote Lincoln Steffens, a pioneering investigative journalist, "that Senator Aldrich, a very rich man and father-in-law of young Mr. Rockefeller, is supposed to represent 'Sugar,' 'Standard Oil,' 'New York,' and, more broadly, 'Wall Street.'"[52]

On May 24, Aldrich pleaded for President Taft's help in blocking the Bailey proposal.[53] Though the new president continued to favor an income tax, he worried that enacting one by statute would lead to a damaging showdown over the *Pollock* ruling. "Nothing has ever injured the prestige of the Supreme Court more than that last decision," Taft thought.[54] The chairman's public posture was resolute: "no income tax, no inheritance tax, no stamp tax, no corporation tax."[55] But by June 8, the *New York Times* reported that a "very nervous" Senator Aldrich had held "a number of mysterious conferences" at the Capitol following a furtive visit to the White House.[56] After lengthy negotiations, the senator announced that he'd struck a deal with the president: the two men would support a 2 percent excise tax on corporate income while scheduling a vote on a constitutional amendment to overturn *Pollock*.[57] Aldrich admitted that he had swallowed the tax on corporations "as a means to defeat the income tax."[58] He wasn't too worried about the constitutional amendment, however. What chance did it have to win the support of three-fourths of the state legislatures, a feat last accomplished in 1870?[59] The senator's confidence blinded him to the measure's expansive language, giving Congress "power to lay and collect taxes on incomes, from whatever source derived."[60]

With Aldrich's influential endorsement, the Senate approved the income tax amendment on July 5 after less than a day of debate. The vote, improbably enough, was unanimous.[61] After the measure breezed through the House the following week,[62] a progressive supporter of the tax marveled at "the unexpected spectacle of certain so-called 'old-line conservative' Republican leaders in Congress suddenly reversing their attitude of a lifetime and seemingly espousing, though with ill-concealed reluctance, the proposed income-tax amendment to the Constitution."[63]

The task of persuading thirty-five state legislatures to ratify the measure got off to a slow start. By the end of 1910, only nine states had lent their approval.[64] But the measure gained steam after the midterm election that year, when a feud between Taft and his disaffected predecessor, Teddy Roosevelt, divided the Republican Party, allowing pro–income tax Democrats to capture many statehouses. In the first seven months of 1911, another twenty-three states ratified the amendment. Resistance remained strong in the Northeast, the region with the highest concentration of wealth.[65] But the income tax also provoked suspicions in the South. Channeling Patrick Henry's warnings about the "dreadful oppression" of the federal "excisemen,"[66] a Virginia lawmaker questioned the wisdom of allowing the federal government to "invade its territory" to reach its citizens. "The adoption of this amendment will be such a surrender to imperialism that has not been since the Northern states in their blindness forced the Fourteenth and Fifteenth Amendments upon the entire sisterhood of the Commonwealth," he warned.[67]

A progressive tsunami in the election of 1912 swept away the final barriers to ratification as pro–income tax candidates won races from coast to coast.[68] By this time, the threshold of support ticked up to thirty-six, after Arizona and New Mexico achieved statehood. On February 3, 1913, Delaware, Wyoming, and New Mexico voted to push the Sixteenth Amendment over the top, three and half years after Congress proposed it.[69] Ultimately, forty-two states ratified the measure.[70] It was the first addition to the national charter in forty-three years. "Its adoption," noted the *Washington Post*, "marks the first change in the Constitution that gives warrant for the deduction that the government will not go on precisely as it did before. . . . The change is radical, as will be observed, and adds substantially to the powers of the national government."[71] Just a decade earlier, the paper had declared the Constitution "practically unamendable."[72]

Nelson Aldrich, the man who had vowed "no income tax," followed the events from his stately home in Warwick Neck, Rhode Island. A year after his fateful gamble, the "suave and steel-spined boss of the United States Senate"[73] announced he would retire, "tired of the great burden his position in the Senate had laid upon him."[74] Back in the nation's capital, lawmakers moved quickly to pass the Revenue Act of 1913. The measure established a 1 percent tax on incomes over $3,000 a year, rising to 7 percent on incomes over $500,000. At the time, only 4 percent of Americans earned enough income to be subject to the tax.[75]

The Sixteenth Amendment ranks among the most significant progressive achievements in American history. The income tax made modern government possible, repudiating the idea of a "limited" national government. A century later, about half of all federal revenue comes from the income tax. It is consistently the government's largest source of funding.[76] Those revenues support vital government programs, from the interstate highway system to the national parks to Medicare.[77] But even today, there are conservatives who dream of repealing the Sixteenth Amendment. In 2013, Tea Party types rallied around a proposal that would strip Congress's power to levy taxes on incomes, except in wartime.[78]

The enactment of the first constitutional amendment in four decades— and the fourth to correct an objectionable Supreme Court ruling[79]— renewed Americans' faith in the possibility of putting their own generation's stamp on the national charter. "The supreme significance of the amendment," wrote a leading constitutional scholar of the time, "is that its adoption proved that the constitution could be peaceably amended if the people really so desired."[80]

The Seventeenth Amendment: Electing the Senate

In the Constitution's original design, state legislatures elected members of the U.S. Senate. The Framers offered two reasons for choosing this indirect system of selection. First, they generally agreed that state lawmakers could be better trusted than the people to fill the Senate with "fit men" who could operate "with more coolness, with more system, and with more wisdom, than the popular branch."[81] Second, they believed the system would give the states a say in the composition of the federal government.[82] Still, amid a broader push to expand democracy in the early nineteenth century, Americans demanded the right to make the choice themselves. While the earliest proposed amendment to the Constitution dates all the way back to 1826,[83] the movement that culminated in the adoption of the Seventeenth Amendment gained steam toward the end of nineteenth century, driven by public outrage over corruption in "the world's greatest deliberative body."[84]

In a 1906 series of investigative reports published in *Cosmopolitan*, the popular novelist–turned–muckraking journalist David Graham Phillips exposed how a "sedate and decorous body" became a "Rich Man's Club" catering to the interests of large corporations and the wealthiest Americans. "Treason is a strong word," he said, "but not too strong, rather too weak, to characterize the situation in which the Senate is the eager, resourceful, indefatigable agent of interests as hostile to the American people as any invading army could be." As Phillips saw it, the senators' fealty to the rich and powerful was the product of a corrupt and undemocratic selection system. "The senators are not elected by the people," he said. "They are elected by the 'interests.'"[85] And no one embodied this corruption more than Rhode Island's Nelson Aldrich, "the intimate of Wall Street's great robber barons."[86]

Phillips had a point. "Once moneyed interests had a significant stake in who was elected to the Senate, the process became easily corruptible," say political scientists Wendy Schiller and Charles Stewart, the authors of a study of Senate elections before the Seventeenth Amendment.[87] Senate seats were bartered for patronage or special favors to the powerful. In some instances, the corruption took the form of outright bribery. In a notorious case, a Senate investigation in 1900 uncovered that William Clark, "an opulent mine owner, possessing $50,000,000 and upwards," spent more than $2 million dollars over the course of a decade in a successful scheme to purchase a Senate seat.[88] The investigators detailed a lengthy list of payments to Montana lawmakers, ranging from paid mortgages to the negotiated purchase of votes at $5,000 to $10,000 apiece.[89]

Corruption aside, state legislatures proved to be strikingly inept in discharging this important responsibility. Disagreements over the selection of senators often led to delays in the filling of seats—and sometimes to a failure to send anyone at all. As far back as the 1st Congress, bickering factions in New York's legislature failed to appoint the state's two senators.[90] From 1891 to 1905, there were nearly fifty deadlocked elections for senators.[91] Prolonged vacancies, lasting from ten months to several years, deprived states of representation.[92] In perhaps the most remarkable case, warring camps in Delaware's dysfunctional legislature left one of its two Senate seats unfilled for four years. The stalemate continued even after the second seat became vacant. With almost comic irony, the state that threatened to walk away from the Philadelphia Convention to defend the principle of "equal suffrage" of the states was not represented in the Senate at all from 1901 to 1903.[93]

The demand for greater democratic accountability moved to the center of the public debate in the last decade of the nineteenth century as part of a broader Populist reform agenda. In its 1892 platform, the People's Party approved a plank calling for the direct election of senators. By the next year, William Jennings Bryan had claimed the issue as his own. In his debut on the national stage, the little-known congressman from Nebraska framed the issue with simple, homespun logic. "If the people of a state have enough intelligence to choose their representatives in the state legislature," he supposed, "they have enough intelligence to choose the men who shall represent them in the United States Senate."[94] The measure passed in the House of Representatives.[95] In the Senate, though, lawmakers beholden to state legislatures for their appointments simply ignored it. Over the next decade, the House approved the amendment on four more occasions.[96] Each time, senators refused to take a vote.[97]

With the path to a constitutional amendment blocked by the Senate's intransigence, states looked for other ways to democratize the process.[98] Nebraska introduced preference primaries in 1875, a reform that allowed voters in each political party to nominate candidates for consideration by the state legislature.[99] After South Carolina adopted a similar law in 1888, the practice spread widely among the states of the one-party South.[100] Later, under the innovative "Oregon System," voters were given the opportunity to express their preference in a referendum meant to guide the legislature's choice.[101] In this manner, more than half the states had adopted some kind of workaround by 1912.[102]

To put additional pressure on the Senate, the state legislatures took a more drastic step—launching the first organized campaign to obtain an amendment by means of an Article V convention.[103] While Nebraska sent the first petition to Congress in 1893, the effort didn't kick into high gear until 1901, when Pennsylvania's legislature developed a model application for use by other states.[104] By February 1911, thirty-one state legislatures joined in the call for a convention—barely crossing the threshold required to summon a convention.[105] Despite Article V's command that Congress "shall call a convention for proposing amendments" on the application of two-thirds of the states, no action was taken.[106] It is not entirely clear why the lawmakers failed to act, but it appears there was uncertainty over the number of applications received and whether they were sufficiently alike to be counted together.[107] One concerned observer, journalist Henry Litchfield West, had warned that a convention "would open Pandora's box" of "a thousand proposed amendments," subjecting the country to "a period of uncertainty that would be almost disastrous."[108] But he need not have worried. The threat of an Article V convention helped to break the Senate's resistance after two decades of obstruction.

When Congress started its new session in March 1911, the amendment was back on the agenda for the first time in a decade. There was reason for optimism as the wave election of 1910 thinned the ranks of amendment opponents. Ten Republican senators who opposed the measure went down to defeat that year.[109] But there were some in the chamber who continued to defend the old system, even shifting the blame for its problems to their constituents. "There has been no claim," said Elihu Root, a New York Republican, "that the wise men who framed our Constitution were mistaken in their belief that wise and intelligent and faithful State legislatures would make the best possible choice for Senators of the United States."[110] If some were "unfaithful to their trust," it was the fault of the voters who "proved incompetent to select honest and faithful legislators."[111]

Just as victory seemed in reach, however, the amendment became ensnared in the politics of race when Southern Democrats in the House added a provision giving states exclusive control over the "times, places and manner" of holding Senate elections and stripping Congress of its power to preempt state laws.[112] The race rider, as it came to be known, was designed to give Southern states free rein to disenfranchise African Americans and, as one proponent bluntly put it, defend "the supremacy of the white race in those States."[113] It elicited fierce criticism from Northern Republicans. "If this passes," said one, "we have a Constitution presenting the ridiculous spectacle of guaranteeing the right of franchise to the negro in one section and effectually taking it away in another."[114] Another argued that the injection of this divisive new issue "will be responsible for the defeat of the legislation that is so universally demanded by the people."[115] But the House voted to approve the controversial measure on April 13 by a vote of 296–16, with 77 not voting.[116]

In a debate that stretched over two months, the Senate was also divided on this topic. The measure's sponsor, a progressive Republican senator from Idaho named William Borah, incorporated a provision similar to the race rider, insisting that the conduct of elections should be purely a local matter.[117] In a moment of candor, Borah distanced himself from the Republican Party's historic support for voting rights. Congress acted "eminently unwisely," he argued, when it sought to protect the voting rights of African Americans during Reconstruction.[118] As in the House, critics charged that the provision was a poison pill designed to sabotage the amendment. In a close vote, the chamber voted on June 12 to support a clean proposal.[119] That same day, it approved the amendment by the comfortable margin of 64–24, with 3 senators not voting.[120]

The Senate resolution had to be reconciled with the version adopted by the House. For nearly a year, House Democrats refused to budge, insisting on the inclusion of the race rider. Finally, in May 1912, they relented.[121] As the *New York Times* reported, the House leadership concluded that "it would be better to accept what they could get than sacrifice the whole movement." [122] Over the bitter objection of Southern members, the House approved the amendment, stripped of the race rider, by a vote of 238–39. The vote, a milestone in the long fight for democracy, was greeted by what news reports described as "thunderous applause" on both sides of the aisle.[123]

DIRECT ELECTION OF SENATORS IN SIGHT, cheered the headline in the *New York Sun*. But the paper predicted a difficult fight ahead: "Southern Democrats declared to-night that their States will never ratify the amendment in its present form." [124] Nevertheless, the Seventeenth Amendment achieved ratification in less than a year, propelled by the same progressive tailwind that lifted the Income Tax Amendment after a slow start. As the *Sun* predicted, support for the measure was weakest in the Southern and border states. On May 31, 1913, less than four months after the adoption of the Sixteenth Amendment, now Secretary of State William Jennings Bryan had the satisfaction of announcing the realization of yet another of his great causes.[125] In the first few decades after its ratification, the Seventeenth Amendment shifted the partisan balance in the chamber toward the Democrats, as malapportioned state legislatures lost the power to choose.[126] Without this reform, Democratic strength in the Senate would have been far weaker from the Progressive Era through at least the New Deal.[127]

The supporters of the Seventeenth Amendment believed it would cure the corrupting influence of big money in politics. "Wealth, plutocracy, and subserviency to the interests will no longer be the qualifications necessary for a Senator," was one lawmaker's sunny prognosis.[128] But did the measure fulfill the most idealistic hopes of its backers? Not entirely. The reform effectively ended the practice of securing Senate seats through outright bribery and influence peddling, but it has not insulated senators from the influence of special interests. Far from it. As Schiller and Stewart point out, "Before the Seventeenth Amendment, Senate candidates tended to be elite party members who could call on wealthy and influential friends to support their campaigns for office. After the Seventeenth Amendment, the same types of candidates continued to rely on the support of the same wealthy and influential people."[129] Today's Senate is still by and large a "Rich Man's Club."

The Seventeenth Amendment was the most significant change to our federalist system since the Reconstruction Amendments, moving the nation closer to "a government by the people."[130] Today, some conservative politicians and legal commentators lament the loss of an "essential" part of the Framers' original vision.[131] "Why would the state legislatures surrender their most important constitutional function?" asks legal scholar (now federal judge) Jay Bybee.[132] Senator Ted Cruz has criticized the Seventeenth Amendment as "a major step toward the explosion of federal power and the undermining of the authority of the states."[133] But the nostalgia of those who yearn for a return to the Framers' original design tends to gloss over the pervasive corruption and ineptitude that prompted a demand for change.[134] It also bears repeating that it was the states themselves that demanded this reform.[135] Repeal is not likely to happen anytime soon: a 2013 poll showed that only 16 percent of Americans would favor such a move.[136]

The Eighteenth Amendment: National Prohibition

The Prohibition Amendment was the capstone of a century-long drive to end the consumption of alcoholic beverages in the United States. The movement emerged in the early nineteenth century as a response to a pressing social problem. At a time when safe drinking sources were hard to come by, alcoholic beverages—in the form of beer, hard cider, whiskey, and gin—were the drink of choice for many Americans, at mealtime and throughout the day. In 1830, Americans on average drank seven gallons of pure alcohol a year, equal to seventy gallons of beer or fifteen quarts of distilled spirits. That's nearly three times the amount consumed today.[137] But what worked for the farmer, who kept a jug of cider out by the barn, didn't fit the faster pace of work in factories and mills. Reformers also blamed excessive drinking for a wide array of social problems, from crime to poverty to domestic violence.[138]

The Temperance Movement, as its name suggests, began as a plea for moderation. Before long, however, the call for "temperate" drinking morphed into a crusade for total abstinence, stoked by the zeal of evangelical Protestants.[139] Like today's war on drugs, the movement was buoyed by powerful racist undercurrents. "Better whiskey and more of it is the rallying cry of great dark faced mobs," said Frances Willard, the founder of the Woman's Christian Temperance Union.[140] The cause also appealed to nativists, who associated drinking with the alien habits of immigrant communities—a group Willard disparaged as "the scum of the Old World."[141]

The drive to banish "demon rum"[142] from American life made modest gains in the mid to late nineteenth century. In 1846, Maine enacted the first state prohibition law.[143] But although the movement attracted hundreds of thousands of adherents, forging strong ties with abolitionists and woman suffragists, it lacked strategic focus.[144] That would change with the founding of the Anti-Saloon League. Founded in Ohio in 1893, the League modeled a new and highly effective brand of advocacy, lending new energy to prohibition campaigns throughout the country. The group's mastermind was Wayne Wheeler, an unimposing man with the presence of a Sunday School teacher. With single-minded focus (a classmate called him a "locomotive in trousers"), he transformed a small startup into what historian Daniel Okrent calls "the most effective political pressure group the country had yet known."[145] It was a term Wheeler coined. He ran his organization like a business: strictly nonpartisan and focused on a single goal.[146] In a tactical innovation, the group worked for the defeat of lawmakers who opposed its agenda.[147] Politicians of all stripes quickly learned to fear the League and its millions of dues-paying, single-issue voters, much as they fear the National Rifle Association today.[148]

Initially, the League and its allies concentrated on winning state liquor bans.[149] At their prodding, twenty-six states banned the manufacture, sale, and consumption of at least some alcoholic beverages between 1907 and 1917, along with many localities. The "dry" states were clustered primarily in the South, West, and Plains regions. In addition, many of the remaining "wet" states had dry counties and towns under local-option laws.[150] For the surging prohibitionists, however, these successes paled as long as booze could be easily found across a state or county line.[151] As one temperance activist put it, "This nation cannot exist half license and half prohibition."[152] So in November 1913, the League announced the movement's "next and final step," an all-out push to impose national prohibition by constitutional amendment.[153] The following month, an "anti-rum army" of more than two thousand men and women marched on the Capitol singing hymns and brandishing petitions.[154]

In its first test, the House of Representatives scheduled a vote on the amendment in December 1914. That same month, Congress passed the Harrison Narcotics Act, a ban on nonmedical opiates and cocaine that laid the foundation for the federal government's war on drugs.[155] Indeed, the Prohibition Amendment's sponsors made an impassioned argument reminiscent of the rhetoric of today's drug warriors. Alcohol, they said, was "a narcotic poison, destructive and degenerating to the human organism." Its consumption "lays a staggering economic burden." Its social costs, including "crime, pauperism, and insanity," threatened "the future integrity and the very life of the nation."[156] To the surprise of many, the measure won a narrow majority.[157] In an encouraging sign for the prohibitionists, the vote revealed support from both parties and every region of the country.

Congress was ready to consider the amendment once again in the summer of 1917, shortly after America's entry into World War I. The transition to a war footing helped change people's views about the role of alcohol in American life. For the first time, citizens were asked to make sacrifices to support a modern war effort. There was also a "patriotic" push to expunge German influences from American culture, starting with beer.[158] "We have German enemies across the water," said a dry politician from Wisconsin. "We have German enemies in this country, too. And the worst of all our German enemies, the most treacherous, the most menacing, are Pabst, Schlitz, Blatz and Miller."[159]

The amendment's most enthusiastic champion in the Senate was Morris Sheppard, a reform-minded Democrat from Texas.[160] Over nearly two decades in Congress he was a reliable supporter of progressive causes, from the income tax to woman suffrage. He also earned renown as a scholar of Shakespeare.[161] But Sheppard is best remembered for his dedication to ending the liquor traffic.[162] As the "Father of the Eighteenth Amendment" (he delighted in the sobriquet), Sheppard delivered an annual oration on the Senate floor to celebrate the anniversary of the day the ban took effect.[163] His case for the amendment was suffused with moral judgment. "Alcohol is a liquid poison," he preached. "It impairs the highest functions of the brain, the sense of right, of moral conduct, of proper obligation to society and to God. It thus imperils virtue, integrity, respect for law and order— all that is sacred and pure in civilization. It is a chief source of immorality and crime."[164]

Offering a very different argument, Henry Myers, a Democrat from Montana, hailed the ban as a milestone in the march of human progress. He likened the measure to a litany of Progressive reforms, from pure food laws to child labor regulations, which moved the country toward "the bright sunlight of a better day." Myers's case for the amendment was rooted in a characteristically Progressive belief in science and expertise as the foundation of sound public policy. "It is the sense of an enlightened public," he explained, "sustained by the best professional and scientific authorities, that the use of liquor has no merit in it, neither as food nor medicine."[165]

Opponents argued that imposing a national ban violated the rights of wet states. "The proposition is intrinsically and radically vicious and intolerable," fumed Boies Penrose, a Pennsylvania Republican. "Legislation of this character, in my opinion, ought to be preeminently and primarily of strictly state concern."[166] Penrose also raised up the "gross inequality" inherent in an amendment process that gives large states and small an equal say in the ratification process. "By referring this joint resolution to the State legislatures, it is possible that it should be ratified by 36 States, with 46,000,000 population, against the wishes of 12 States, with 56,000,000 population, thus subjecting the country to the rule of the minority."[167]

Critics complained that a Protestant, native-born majority was imposing its standard of morality on a rapidly diversifying country. Others decried the injustice of obliterating the fifth-largest industry in the nation without compensation to owners and shareholders.[168] But those arguments were of little avail. Congress approved the measure with surprising ease, sending the Eighteenth Amendment to the states for ratification on December 17, 1917.[169] In a striking display of bipartisanship, Democrats and Republicans supported the amendment in nearly equal numbers.[170]

The amendment banned "the manufacture, sale, or transportation of intoxicating liquors . . . *for beverage purposes.*" Notably, the measure did not prohibit the use of alcohol for medicinal or religious purposes, nor did it forbid an individual's purchase or consumption of alcohol. These crucial loopholes would complicate enforcement efforts as pharmacies and religious institutions dispensed wine and liquor in prodigious quantities.[171] The amendment also gave the federal and state governments "concurrent power to enforce" its terms. And, in an innovation that would be imitated in most amendment proposals to follow, it imposed a seven-year deadline for ratification.[172]

Warren G. Harding, the Ohio senator and future president, proposed the time limit, saying he wanted "to see the question settled."[173] Cynics assumed his real goal was to kill the amendment without angering the measure's proponents. It proved to be unnecessary. The Eighteenth Amendment sprinted to ratification in a mere thirteen months. "It is as if a sailing ship on a windless ocean were sweeping ahead, propelled by some invisible force," said the editors of the *New-York Tribune*.[174] That force, of course, was the Anti-Saloon League, which helped to orchestrate congressional hearings into the activities of the National German-American Alliance, a leading opponent of Prohibition. When the investigation revealed that the Alliance was secretly funded by the beer lobby, the pace of ratification accelerated.[175] In the end, forty-six states ratified the amendment. Rhode Island and Connecticut were the only ones to reject it.[176]

By its terms, the Eighteenth Amendment took effect one year after ratification, on January 16, 1920. In the meantime, Congress passed the National Prohibition Act, better known as the Volstead Act, to enforce the nationwide ban. Drafted by the Anti-Saloon League's general counsel, the law took an aggressive approach, defining the amendment's prohibition on "intoxicating liquors" to include beer and wine.[177] The harsh law surprised some supporters who expected only hard liquors would be banned.[178] Passed over President Woodrow Wilson's veto, the Volstead Act remained in effect until the amendment's repeal in 1933.

The alcoholic beverage industry—brewers, distillers, and liquor distributors—launched a spate of lawsuits, arguing that the amendment exceeded implicit limits on the constitutional amendment process.[179] Cases from five states advanced quickly to the Supreme Court, where they were heard together as the *National Prohibition Cases*.[180] Elihu Root, now retired from the Senate after refusing on principle to seek election from the voters he so publicly scorned,[181] represented a New Jersey brewer. In the oral argument, Root argued that the Eighteenth Amendment improperly embedded a legislative policy in the Constitution in a manner that would allow a minority to block any future revision. A proper amendment, he insisted, would have given Congress the authority to pass and repeal prohibition laws by a simple majority.[182] But the Court dashed the embattled industry's hopes, ruling unanimously that the amendment had been legally adopted.[183]

Delivering on its promised public health benefits, Prohibition led to a significant decline in drinking and a reduction in alcohol-related illnesses.[184] By one estimate, total alcohol consumption in the United States declined by around 60 percent.[185] But while the measure found acceptance in the rural South and West, it was widely flouted in the former wet states of the North and Midwest.[186] With the new black market in illicit booze came organized crime. Soon enough, the specter of the saloon would be replaced by lurid accounts of gangland killings and raids on gin joints. Before long, the Eighteenth Amendment's unintended consequences would prompt a rethinking.

The Nineteenth Amendment: "Votes for Women!"

The Nineteenth Amendment was the second constitutional fix to limit the states' authority to decide who qualifies as a voter, following the path blazed by the Fifteenth Amendment. Through many decades of fruitless campaigning, woman suffragists imagined they were working toward the adoption of a Sixteenth Amendment to the Constitution. Instead, it would be the fourth (and last) of the four Progressive Era amendments.

With one exception, the new state charters adopted in the early years of the republic limited the elective franchise to men. Only New Jersey, which adopted a new constitution in 1776, opted to extend the vote to "free inhabitants," without specifying gender.[187] Lest anyone think it was an oversight, a 1790 state election law used the phrase "he or she."[188] For three decades, unmarried women who met the state's property and residency requirements cast ballots alongside men. (Married women could not vote because they had no separate legal existence from their husbands under coverture laws.) After it was reported that women cast nearly a quarter of all votes in the election of 1802, a Trenton newspaper worried that female turnout had reached "alarming heights."[189] The brief experiment with New Jersey's "petticoat electors" came to an end in 1807. A voter fraud scandal in a local referendum—amid allegations of men dressing as women to cast ballots, no less—provided the pretext to tighten voter qualifications. With little opposition, the state's legislature passed a statute limiting the franchise to "free white men, qualified according to the law."[190] It came amid a raft of laws across the Northern states rolling back the voting rights of free Black people and immigrants.[191]

Women's activism emerged in the early nineteenth century as women embraced the era's two great causes: abolition and temperance. "It was in the abolition movement that women first learned to organize, to hold public meetings, to conduct petition campaigns," notes historian Eleanor Flexner.[192] Female activists also found a natural home in the temperance movement, where they organized to protect women and children from the social ills associated with male "saloon culture." This early phase of the women's rights movement accelerated in July 1848 when a group of feminist trailblazers, led by Lucretia Mott and Elizabeth Cady Stanton, called for "a convention to discuss the social, civil and religious rights of women" in the small upstate New York town of Seneca Falls.[193]

Mott, the elder of the two, was a prominent abolitionist and pacifist whose sometimes radical views were animated by the values of her Quaker faith. Raised to view women and men as equals, her vision of equality would inspire a new generation of activists.[194] Stanton came to abolitionism through her marriage to Henry Stanton, a prominent member of antislavery societies.[195] She would apply its lessons to an entirely new crusade. As a biographer notes, "for her, the story of slavery and the emancipation of the slaves would serve primarily as a lesson in women's own status, degradation, and rights."[196]

The conference produced a Declaration of Sentiments signed by a hundred of the three hundred delegates who attended. It contained a controversial plank, approved by the narrowest of margins: "Resolved, That it is the duty of the women of this country to secure to themselves their sacred right to the elective franchise."[197] Stanton insisted on including it, convinced that "the power to make laws was the right through which all other rights could be secured."[198] Mott feared it was too radical. "We must go slowly," she warned.[199]

The notion that women had a "sacred right to the elective franchise" elicited reactions ranging from disbelief to outright derision.[200] Indeed, the very idea of votes for women was deeply disruptive.[201] That said, even as modern women's rights activism took shape in the decade following Seneca Falls, the right to vote remained low on the list of the movement's priorities. Reformers focused their energies instead on issues more closely tied to the daily lives of women and girls: access to education, women's legal status in marriage, and the right of women to their own wages and property. As Stanton grasped, however, women had little leverage to advance their interests when only men had "the power to make laws."[202]

Susan B. Anthony joined the cause during this formative period. Like Mott, Anthony was raised in a Quaker family steeped in liberal values.[203] And like Stanton, she came to women's activism through earlier work in the temperance and abolition movements.[204] Once found, it became her life's unwavering calling. Anthony brought "a prodigious talent for organizational detail, strategic planning, and plain old hard work," says a biographer.[205] She deployed those gifts on behalf of the cause in the decades following the Civil War, when the fight to gain the franchise for women was inexorably joined. For the duration of the war, Anthony and Stanton put their women's rights advocacy aside, focusing their considerable talents on the abolitionist cause.

In the Civil War's aftermath, "feminists of both races were convinced that suffrage was the key to the legal position of women as well" as the freedmen.[206] As Congress began to define the legal and political rights of formerly enslaved people, Anthony and Stanton launched a nationwide petition drive, urging an amendment to "prohibit the several States from disfranchising any of their citizens on the ground of sex."[207] In the early months of 1866, petitions flooded into congressional offices by the hundreds. "Remember," wrote a woman from New York, "the right of petition is our only right in the government."[208] But few in Congress took the demand for universal suffrage seriously. When lawmakers unveiled the first draft of the Fourteenth Amendment in the summer of 1866, guaranteeing birthright citizenship and equal protection under the law to all but identifying voters as "male," they sent an unmistakable signal.[209] Until then, the word "male" had never appeared in the Constitution.[210]

Some in the movement, heeding the dictum that "this hour belongs to the Negro,"[211] were content to wait their turn and support voting rights for Black men first. "I will be thankful in my soul if *any* body can get out of the terrible pit," said suffragist leader Lucy Stone.[212] Others, including Anthony and Stanton, saw it as reason to part ways with their abolitionist allies. Anthony vowed, "I will cut off this right arm of mine before I will ever work for or demand the ballot for the Negro and not the woman."[213] Stanton questioned why women "had better stand aside and see 'Sambo' walk into the kingdom first."[214] Her position, curdled with ugly racial animus, contrasted the "pauperism, ignorance and degradation" of the freedmen with the "wealth, education, and refinement of the women of the republic."[215]

Black women found themselves unwilling—and unable—to choose. In the early years of the women's suffrage movement, there was no cohesive organization among Black women, most of whom were enslaved. At the Seneca Falls Convention, free Black women were conspicuously absent. (Frederick Douglass, the only Black person in attendance, gave a rousing address in support of a suffrage plank in the Declaration of Sentiments.) But in the decade before the war, historian Rosalyn Terborg-Penn points out that "a growing number of Black female abolitionists joined the small circle of suffragists."[216] Among them was author Frances Ellen Watkins Harper, who was born free in the slave state of Maryland. Speaking at the National Women's Rights Convention in 1866, Harper, the self-styled "novice upon this platform" who went on to become a leader of the National Association of Colored Women, disabused the audience of any inherent tension in the quest for equality. "You white women speak here of rights. I speak of wrongs," she declared. Harper saw no need for division because, as she saw it, the struggles for racial equality and suffrage rights were inextricably intertwined. "We are all bound up together in one great bundle of humanity, and society cannot trample on the weakest and feeblest of its members without receiving the curse in its own soul."[217]

That 1866 Convention led to the creation of the American Equal Rights Association, with Anthony, Harper, Stanton, Stone, and Douglass among its founding members.[218] But the rift over the Reconstruction Amendments soon divided the movement into competing factions. On the one side, the National Woman Suffrage Association, led by Anthony and Stanton, welcomed partnerships with Southern Democrats and white supremacists to advance an agenda focused on federal reform. In contrast, the more inclusive American Woman Suffrage Association, led by Stone, welcomed men and women of color like Harper into its ranks to wage voting rights campaigns in the states.[219] (At the AWSA convention in 1873, Harper "delivered the closing speech," in which she "declared that as 'much as white women need the ballot, colored women need it more.'")[220]

After their fruitless advocacy in Congress, suffragists devised a litigation strategy based on civil disobedience. In the election of 1872, women arrived at polling places demanding the right to vote, insisting it was one of the "privileges and immunities of citizenship" guaranteed by the new Fourteenth Amendment. Anthony was famously tried and convicted on the charge of illegal voting the following year.[221] But it was the case of Virginia Louisa Minor, a Missouri suffragist, that made legal history. Minor sued the election official who refused to register her as a voter. In *Minor v. Happersett*,[222] an 1875 ruling, the Supreme Court unanimously rejected the claim, holding that citizenship alone "does not confer the right of suffrage upon anyone."[223]

With a judicial remedy closed off, suffragists had only one path forward: winning the right to vote through the political process. But in Congress, there were few men willing to champion the suffragists' cause. Senator

Aaron Sargent, the husband of suffragist Ellen Clark Sargent and intimate of Susan Anthony, was a rare exception.[224] In 1878, the California Republican introduced the proposal that would one day become the Nineteenth Amendment.[225] The language was drafted by Anthony and Stanton. Patterned after the Fifteenth Amendment, it provided: "The right of citizens of the United States to vote shall not be denied or abridged by the United States or by any State on account of sex."[226] The text would make it into the Constitution unchanged, forty-two years later.[227] To this day, they are the only words in our national charter written by women.

It would take almost a decade to get the Susan B. Anthony Amendment, as it came to be known, to the Senate floor. On January 25, 1887, senators debated the measure for the first time. One of the few to rise in support of the amendment, Oregon Republican Joseph Dolph, declared, "No one will contend but that women have sufficient capacity to vote intelligently."[228] But Joseph Brown, a conservative Georgia Democrat, spoke for many in the chamber when he expressed doubt that "the pure, cultivated, and pious ladies of this country" would have any interest in "the affairs of state and the corruptions of party politics."[229] The senator also warned that the amendment would enfranchise Black women, whom he dismissed as "grossly ignorant, with very few exceptions."[230] After a brief debate, the measure was soundly defeated. Though it was reintroduced in subsequent Congresses, lawmakers wouldn't vote on the measure again until 1913.[231]

In a development unforeseen by the movement's leaders, the first victories in the fight for equal suffrage came on the Western frontier. In 1869, the legislature of the Wyoming territory, a sparsely populated region where men outnumbered women six to one, voted to grant women the right to vote and hold public office.[232] Utah territory followed suit the next year.[233] Neither victory was the product of suffragist organizing. The sponsor of the Wyoming law saw it as a way to "attract attention to the . . . territory more effectually than anything else," while proponents of the Utah law sought to strengthen the voting power of Mormons in the state.[234]

Eager to replicate those successes, suffragists poured a great deal of energy into state-based campaigns. They waged ballot-measure campaigns in thirty-three states between 1870 and 1910—a prodigious effort that yielded just two additional wins and a string of dispiriting defeats.[235] By 1910, only four sparsely populated Western states granted full voting rights to women.[236] Among the many explanations for the movement's halting progress was the sustained opposition of the liquor lobby. A brewers' association sized up the threat: "When woman has the ballot, she will vote solid for Prohibition." In their fight for economic survival, the beer and liquor lobby committed millions of dollars to oppose woman suffrage "everywhere and always."[237]

The "doldrums," as suffragists described the period,[238] came to an end in 1910 when voters in Washington approved a referendum on woman suffrage. Californians passed a similar measure the following year.[239] But the state strategy quickly reverted to a depressing pattern. Over the next three years, suffragists won only five state ballot measures while losing twelve.[240] Around the same time, the moribund effort to win a federal constitutional amendment received a boost from the creative activism of Alice Paul, a young, thoroughly modern, and highly educated Quaker social worker who apprenticed in the militant tactics of radical suffragists during a three-year stay in England.[241] Described by a biographer as "a fast talker and faster thinker," Paul would devote the rest of her long life to the fight for women's equality under the Constitution.[242]

In March 1913, on the day before Woodrow Wilson's inauguration, Paul upstaged the new president (who opposed woman suffrage) with an attention-getting suffrage parade in the nation's capital. It quickly devolved into mayhem as rowdy crowds of men mistreated the marchers. While traumatic for many, the parade proved to be a public relations masterstroke. CAPITAL MOBS MADE CONVERTS TO SUFFRAGE, said the *New-York Tribune*.[243] The racial animus that bedeviled the movement resurfaced when Paul acceded to demands that Black activists march at the back of the parade.[244] Ida Wells-Barnett, the anti-lynching crusader and founder of the Alpha Suffrage Club, one of the first African American suffrage organizations, drew national attention when she defied the segregation order, marching proudly with her state's delegation "under the Illinois banner."[245]

The following month, Paul helped to form the Congressional Union, a new organization committed to passage of a suffrage amendment.[246] Movement leaders worried that the move was premature.[247] Within a year, however, sustained pressure through petition drives, rallies, and marches helped secure the first vote in Congress since 1887.[248] A slim majority of senators approved the measure in the March 1914 vote—progress, but nowhere near the two-thirds vote needed to advance.[249] In January 1915, supporters fell short of a majority in the House.[250] Many opponents of the measure rooted their objections in traditional religious values. "The Word of God inveighs against woman suffrage," thundered one congressman.[251] Establishment Republicans from the Northeast objected on federalism grounds, insisting that the issue was best left to the states.[252] But the fiercest resistance came from Southerners who saw the amendment as a threat to white supremacy, one of whom going so far as to propose pairing woman suffrage with repeal of the Fifteenth Amendment. As the ugly racial politics of the era often dominated the debate, any meaningful discussion of women's political equality was often crowded out.[253]

The suffragists understood they had to up their game to better combat the "unholy alliance" of Southern Democrats and Northeast Republicans who were blocking the measure.[254] Under the leadership of Carrie Chapman Catt, Anthony's anointed heir, a coalition of suffrage groups adopted "the Winning Plan": a closely held strategy to coordinate advocacy efforts at the state and federal levels. Approved in 1916, the plan signaled a move away from the unproductive effort to eke out wins in the states. Instead, the field would marshal its energies in an all-out campaign to persuade Congress to pass a constitutional amendment. The plan pragmatically emphasized top-down organization, a sophisticated approach to lobbying, and a communications operation aimed at swaying public opinion.[255] Lawmakers bristled at the intensified pressure. "Nagging!" barked one senator at a lobbyist waiting outside his office. "If you women would only stop nagging!"[256]

Paul's group, reconstituted in 1916 as the National Woman's Party—a splinter party dedicated solely to the adoption of the Susan B. Anthony Amendment—called for even more aggressive measures.[257] Their primary target was President Wilson, whose evolving support for the cause was lukewarm at best. In January 1917, they set up pickets outside the White House. Standing motionlessly for hours on end, "Silent Sentinels" held signs. One read, MR. PRESIDENT, HOW LONG MUST WOMEN WAIT FOR LIBERTY?[258] At first the protests were treated as a curiosity, but after the country entered World War I, public reaction took a menacing turn. Hostile onlookers assaulted the women. Arrests followed—of the protesters, not their attackers. But when the jailed suffragists went on a hunger strike, the movement gained new martyrs whose story was splashed on the front pages of newspapers nationwide.[259]

By 1918 public opinion began to shift in favor of the amendment. The country's entry into the war played a role. As women surged into the workforce to support the war effort, government propaganda campaigns extolled their crucial role on the home front.[260] On January 10, a new vote was scheduled in the House. When it looked to be close, four supporters were brought in from their sickbeds, including one on a stretcher. Another lawmaker left his dying wife's bedside to honor her final wish.[261] Those extraordinary efforts allowed supporters to claim a bare two-thirds majority, 274–136.[262] The first female member of Congress, Jeannette Rankin of Montana, proudly voted for the measure, having led the successful fight to bring woman suffrage to her state.[263] Jubilation was short-lived, however, as the measure stalled in the Senate. In an unusual appeal, President Wilson—now a convert to the cause—delivered an address imploring senators to approve the amendment as "vital to the winning of the war."[264]

After the start of a new session of Congress, supporters in the House had to start the process over. On May 21, 1919, representatives approved the amendment for a second time, by a far more decisive vote of 304–90.[265] Back in the Senate, however, Southerners filibustered, warning that the amendment posed a threat to Jim Crow laws.[266] Ellison "Cotton Ed" Smith of South Carolina, a notorious white supremacist with views so extreme that *Time* magazine later called him "a conscientious objector to the 20th Century,"[267] argued that the amendment threatened to undo his state's successful effort to minimize the "evil effects" of Black suffrage. "The southern man who votes for the Susan B. Anthony amendment votes to ratify the Fifteenth Amendment," he railed. "I warn every man here today that when the test comes, as it will come, when the clamor for Negro rights shall have come, that you Senators of the South voting for it have started it here this day."[268]

Amid "deafening applause," the Senate finally approved the measure on June 4, 1919, after voting down a motion to limit its guarantee to white citizens.[269] Catt predicted there was "no doubt" the amendment would secure the support needed for ratification. Three states raced to ratify within a week. But though the ratification process continued at a brisk pace, eight states—all from the South or border region—voted the amendment down, threatening its prospects for adoption. In March 1920, the measure was stalled just one state short of the thirty-six needed for ratification.[270] Supporters pinned their hopes on Tennessee, where the measure came up for consideration in August of that year.

Lobbyists and activists descended on Nashville for the final showdown. Opponents set up shop in a local hotel, plying the lawmakers with back-room bribes and illegal booze from their "Jack Daniels Suite."[271] It all came down to twenty-four-year-old Harry Burn, the youngest member of the Tennessee General Assembly. Though he was assumed to be a sure vote against ratification, he switched at the last minute, swayed by a note from his mother asking him to "be a good boy" and vote for ratification. "Hurrah and vote for suffrage and don't keep them in doubt," she wrote.[272] With Tennessee's pivotal vote on August 18, 1920, the Nineteenth Amendment achieved ratification: less than fourteen months after it was proposed by Congress and less than three months before the 1920 presidential election.

The pool of eligible voters doubled overnight, but there was no corresponding increase in participation that year. Nearly 27 million Americans voted in 1920, up from 18.5 million in 1916.[273] Because many women chose not to exercise their newly won right, the turnout rate dropped to 49 percent, an historic low.[274] While many opponents of the Nineteenth Amendment feared that the influx of women at the polls would lead to progressive domination of our politics, the opposite happened (at least initially). When the votes were counted, conservative Republicans swept to power under the banner of Senator Warren G. Harding, who promised "a return to normalcy" after a decade of progressive exuberance (not to mention a war and a pandemic). Research into voting patterns reveals that, as late as the 1980s, there was no discernable "women's vote."[275] Today, of course, women comprise a majority of eligible voters, and their votes are indispensable to progressive victories at the polls. That's one reason the idea of repealing the Nineteenth Amendment is floated from time to time in the sillier corners of the right-wing media. "If we took away women's right to vote," says Ann Coulter, "we'd never have to worry about another Democrat president."[276]

As legal scholar Akhil Amar notes, the Nineteenth Amendment "marked the single biggest democratizing event in American history."[277] It's a remarkable story of perseverance, stamina, and optimism over many decades. "To get the word male in effect out of the Constitution cost the women of the country 52 years of pauseless campaign," Carrie Chapman Catt later reflected.[278] Millions of American women were engaged in this inspiring struggle. For many Black women, though, the fight was far from over. As historian Martha S. Jones explains, the amendment "cracked open a door" for Black women living in the North and West, allowing some to vote and hold office for the first time.[279] But because the overwhelming number of Black women lived in the South, most had to wait another four decades, until the civil rights revolution of the 1960s, to be brought more fully into American democracy. Indeed, to win support in the South, Catt conceded that the right to vote would still be "subject to whatever restrictions may be imposed by state constitutions." Going even further, she reassured her audiences that "White supremacy will be strengthened, not weakened, by women's suffrage."[280]

This sentiment added to the barriers that women of color across the country encountered, something that historian Cathleen D. Cahill explores in a recent book. The contributions of untold activists within Indigenous, Latina, and Asian American communities working towards suffrage for all women helped to fulfill the promise of the Nineteenth Amendment years after its adoption.[281]

After a forty-year dry spell, the American people had added four new amendments to the Constitution in the space of a decade, but by 1920 the energy of the Progressive Era was spent as voters grew weary of the reformers' great crusades. At the same time, the pro-business fundamentalism of the *Lochner*-era Supreme Court severely limited the power of Congress and the state legislatures to solve pressing problems in a rapidly transforming economy. Frustration over the Court's activism fueled an unsuccessful effort to amend the Constitution to give Congress power to ban child labor. It was the fourth of six amendments proposed by Congress but never ratified.

The Child Labor Amendment

In the early twentieth century, child labor ranked as one of the nation's gravest social ills. For most of human history, children worked in the home or on farms alongside their families as a normal part of their upbringing, but industrialization ushered in the widespread commercial exploitation of the nation's youth.[282] Children as young as six worked long hours in sweatshops and mines for low wages, in appalling and often dangerous conditions. By 1900, as many as 2 million American children toiled outside the home—including a staggering one out of every six minors between the ages of ten and fifteen.[283]

Progressive reformers demanded an end to this pernicious practice. In 1904, activists founded the National Child Labor Committee. With a mission of serving as "a great moral force for the protection of children," the group deployed the tools of research, organizing, lobbying, and "quickening the public conscience."[284] Like earlier reform movements, its agenda focused initially on winning legal change in the states. The group made remarkable progress toward that goal, persuading thirty-nine states to enact some form of child labor legislation by 1912. But these protections were not uniform across the country.[285] In the South especially, where a booming textile industry thrived on the systematic exploitation of children, laws were notoriously lax.[286] This disparity gave the region a competitive advantage: sweatshop operators eagerly relocated their businesses there for the opportunity to extract the labor of children for meager pay.[287]

Reformers concluded that the only way to end child labor was to pressure Congress for a nationwide solution.[288] In 1916 the lawmakers responded by passing the Keating-Owen Act, a modest measure to restrict the shipment of goods produced through some of the worst child labor practices.[289] Congress justified the legislation under its constitutional authority to regulate interstate commerce. Upon signing the measure into law, President Wilson hailed "the emancipation of the children of the country by releasing them from hurtful labor."[290]

Alas, two years later, in the case of *Hammer v. Dagenhart*, the Supreme Court struck down the law as "repugnant to the Constitution."[291] The regulation of labor conditions in factories and mines was "a purely state authority," said a narrow majority of five justices.[292] A century earlier, Chief Justice John Marshall had declared that Congress's power under the Commerce Clause, "like all others vested in Congress, may be exercised to its utmost extent."[293] Now, however, to protect the powers reserved to the states under the Tenth Amendment, the justices placed a new and arbitrary limit on the federal government's freedom of action.[294] The ruling in *Dagenhart* was another shameful episode in the Court's history, impeding efforts to regulate child labor for two long decades. "Greedy, dollar-chasing mill owners alone will rejoice," said the *Washington Herald*.[295]

When Congress passed a new law under its broad taxing power, imposing a punitive tax on companies that employed child labor, it met a similar fate.[296] With a national solution to the problem of child labor choked off by a reactionary Court, reformers crafted an amendment to overrule the *Dagenhart* decision. By its terms, the Child Labor Amendment would have given Congress "power to limit, regulate, and prohibit the labor of persons under eighteen years of age."[297] Unlike the Prohibition Amendment, the measure did not attempt to inscribe a specific policy solution into the Constitution. It was simply meant to establish Congress's power to pass child labor legislation as it saw fit. Even so, the measure elicited fierce opposition from the anti-government conservatives of the day. South Carolina Democrat Nathaniel Dial slammed the proposal as "the most radical piece of legislation that has been proposed in the United States since the adoption of the Constitution." The senator, representing a state where nearly a quarter of ten- to fifteen-year-olds toiled in the textile mills, claimed the amendment "takes away from the states practically all the rights left."[298] Conservative groups called it "communism," tapping into anxieties unleashed by the period's Red Scare, the wave of fearmongering and repression precipitated by the Bolshevik Revolution in Russia.[299]

The rhetorical onslaught did little to dampen the resolve of lawmakers in Washington. When the measure came up for a vote in the House of Representatives in April 1924, it passed by a vote of 297–69.[300] A month later, it cleared the Senate, 61–23.[301] Opposition came, predictably, from pro-business Republicans in the East and conservative Democrats in the Southern and border states.[302] After the lopsided vote in Congress, the prospects for ratification seemed promising. The measure garnered the support of all three major candidates in the 1924 presidential contest— Republican Calvin Coolidge, Democrat John W. Davis, and Progressive Robert M. La Follette.[303]

But the path to ratification proved more onerous than anyone imagined. Amendment fatigue had set in as Americans grew tired of progressive policy reforms. "They have taken our women away from us by constitutional amendment; they have taken our liquor away from us; and now they want to take our children," complained an exasperated state legislator.[304] A sophisticated opposition campaign bankrolled by big business also took its toll.[305] Opponents lobbed misleading and demagogic attacks against the Child Labor Amendment and its supporters. A petition by the *Woman Patriot*, a far-right newspaper that had opposed woman suffrage, maligned it as "a straight Socialist measure . . . promoted under direct orders from Moscow."[306] Catholic clergy told parishioners that the measure would interfere with the rights of parents to educate and discipline their children.[307] A farm magazine warned parents that it "probably would be made illegal for sister Susie to wash a dish or sew on a button until after her eighteenth birthday."[308]

The torrent of misinformation did the trick. By the end of 1927, only five states had ratified the Child Labor Amendment. Another twenty-six had rejected it—enough to tank it.[309] Though supporters refused to concede defeat, most observers considered the amendment dormant, if not dead.[310] As the number of children working outside the home began to decline due to reform efforts in the states, some even wondered if there was still a need for the measure. But interest quickly revived after the onset of the Great Depression, when desperate children swarmed back into the job market to compete with the jobless adults.[311] In the first seven months of 1933, after a four-year lull, nine state legislatures ratified the measure. The new president, Franklin Delano Roosevelt, urged other states to follow suit.[312] In the end, twenty-eight states ratified the Child Labor Amendment.

The headwinds it faced was a sign that the window for amendments was closing once again. The grand coalition that propelled the adoption of the four amendments in the space of a decade had splintered.[313] Meanwhile, the tactics pioneered by its determined, well-funded opponents modeled a new brand of hardball politics that would reshape ratification contests to come, including what one scholar called "an instructive, almost eerie, parallel" with the campaign to stop the Equal Rights Amendment in the 1970s.[314]

This time, however, there was no pause in amending activity to rival the nearly six decades' gap that followed the unratified Titles of Nobility Amendment or the four decades following the adoption of the Reconstruction Amendments. Within just a few years, as the Roaring Twenties gave way to the Great Depression, Americans added two new amendments to the Constitution: one to modernize the government's calendar and another to end the failed experiment of Prohibition. These two constitutional fixes were made possible by a profound realignment in American politics, as Democrats came surging back under the banner of Franklin Delano Roosevelt's New Deal. The reform energies unloosed by the new Roosevelt coalition also fostered a recommitment to a robust Constitution—restoring its vitality as the Framers' had intended—without recourse to the formal mechanisms of Article V.

The New Deal—and the Amending Wave That Wasn't

On November 4, 1930, in the first midterm election following the onset of the Great Depression, Democrats won a sweeping victory that put them on track to take the House of Representatives for the first time since 1918. It was "a general and crushing defeat" for the Republican Party, said the *New York Times*.[1] The result was widely interpreted as a referendum on President Herbert Hoover's feckless response to the economic crisis—and the nation's desire to see an end to Prohibition.

Unfortunately, the 11 million Americans who voted for change could not expect action anytime soon. Due to the Constitution's odd timing, it would be another thirteen months before the new Democratic majority would be sworn in.[2]

The Twentieth Amendment: "Lame Duck" Governance

The Twentieth Amendment shortened the length of time between elections and the swearing in of a new Congress and president. It was meant to address the problem of "lame duck" governance. Prior to its enactment, each new government was inaugurated on March 4—four months after Election Day. This date was not mandated by the Constitution. It was simply an accident of history. When a ninth state ratified the Constitution, bringing it into operation, the outgoing Confederation Congress decided the new government would begin on March 4, 1789, providing time for each state to hold its first elections. For the next century and a half, the date just stuck. Because the Constitution dictates precise durations in office for the president, senators and representatives, their successors' terms began and ended on the same date.[3]

The four-month delay between the election and the start of a new government may have made sense at the end of the eighteenth century, when travel to and from the capital could take weeks. Prior to the adoption of the Seventeenth Amendment, it also gave state legislatures time to select new senators.[4] But at key junctures in our history, from the secession crisis that ignited the Civil War to the Great Depression, the long transition produced paralysis when decisive action was needed.[5] By 1932, lawmakers had introduced over ninety amendment proposals to fix the problem.[6]

A separate provision of the Constitution confused matters even more. Article I provided that Congress "shall assemble . . . on the first Monday in December," even though their terms began in March.[7] The Framers chose a December date to minimize interruptions to the spring planting season and fall harvest.[8] But it meant that a Congress elected in November of an even-numbered year would not take office until December of the following year—*thirteen* months later![9] As a workaround, the president had the authority to convene Congress earlier in an "extraordinary" session.[10] Absent such a step, however, a new president began his term in March while the incoming Congress was required to wait until December.

Given the long delay, outgoing Congresses often scheduled a three-month session after the election, running from December through the expiration of members' terms in March.[11] But allowing outgoing lawmakers to legislate after they were no longer accountable to the voters raised an important question of democratic legitimacy.[12] "Now, it seems to me inconceivable," said Emanuel Celler, an up-and-coming congressman from Brooklyn, "that for these many years lame ducks defeated by their constituents have been able to come back to this House and vote on any proposition. . . . It is inconceivable that we should allow something as illogical as that to adhere as a barnacle to our Constitution, and give these lame Members, repudiated at the polls, the right, for example, to vote for a President or a Vice President, as was the case on three distinct occasions in this Chamber."[13]

Celler was referring to one of the Constitution's most indefensible anomalies. When no candidate wins a majority of the electoral vote, it is left to the House of Representatives to choose the president by means of a special contingent election.[14] But due to the thirteen-month delay in seating new members, the two presidents elected in this manner—Thomas Jefferson (1800) and John Quincy Adams (1824)—were all chosen by a lame-duck House, elected two years prior.[15] (While not selected in a contingent election, a third president, Rutherford B. Hayes, also owed his victory to lame-duck Congress.) The authors of the Twentieth Amendment wanted to remedy this flaw by ensuring that contingency elections are "conducted by new Congressmen coming directly from the people, who have the interest of the people at heart when they come to cast their votes in that election."[16]

Leading the push for a constitutional fix was Senator George Norris. The Nebraska Republican was a renowned champion of reform over his three decades in the Senate, the leader of a group of "articulate and irreverent" progressive senators known as Sons of the Wild Jackass.[17] Described by a biographer as "a man with humility and a basic belief in the goodness of man,"[18] he believed in amending the Constitution "wherever and whenever it is necessary to meet changing conditions of civilization."[19] This conviction inspired a decade-long quest to enact the Twentieth Amendment. "In a government 'by the people,' the wishes of a majority should be crystallized into legislation as soon as possible after those wishes have been made known," he said.[20] In 1922, he introduced the first of many proposals to move the government's start date to January.

Norris encountered opposition from conservatives in both chambers, including the powerful Speaker of the House, Nicholas Longworth, who contended there were benefits to a lengthy cooling-off period before transferring the reins of power.[21] "Political campaigns and especially national campaigns are oftentimes heated and bitter," said one representative. Giving power to a new Congress too soon could be a "dangerous and perhaps expensive experience."[22] Some lawmakers even lionized the maligned lame duck. As one congressman saw it, the lame-duck session "is the one time in the life of a member of Congress when he can vote his real convictions without the hope of reward or the fear of punishment."[23]

Between 1923 and 1929, the Senate approved the amendment on five occasions, with Norris leading the charge. For years, Speaker Longworth prevented action in the House.[24] Progress was possible only after Democrats retook the House following the election of 1930.[25] Lawmakers approved the Twentieth Amendment in March 1932, three months after their long wait to be sworn in.[26] Under its terms, Congress begins its term at noon on January 3. The president is sworn in later, on January 20, to allow time for the formal counting of electoral votes and the possibility of a contingent election in the House. While the measure included a seven-year time limit, following the precedent set by the Eighteenth Amendment, it was ratified by the requisite thirty-six states in less than a year. By May 1933, all forty-eight states then in the Union had ratified the Twentieth Amendment.

In addition to its lame-duck provision, the Twentieth Amendment tweaked the rules of presidential succession to resolve ambiguities related to the period between an election and the start of the new term. If a president-elect dies before taking office, the vice president–elect is sworn in as president on January 20. If no president is lawfully chosen, the vice president–elect acts as president until one is qualified. And if both positions are vacant, Congress may determine who will act as president in the interim. The amendment also gives Congress the power to pass legislation establishing a chain of presidential succession.[27] Similarly, it authorizes Congress to establish a process to go into effect if one of the candidates in a contingent election dies.[28] But the Twentieth Amendment left other important "what ifs" unanswered. It would take another amendment, adopted more than three decades later, to provide a more comprehensive answer to the questions of presidential disability and vice-presidential vacancies.

The new political calendar took effect in January 1937, when Franklin Delano Roosevelt was sworn in for a second term with overwhelming majorities in both houses of Congress.[29] But while the Twentieth Amendment successfully shortened the transition period following an election, it did not realize its supporters' dream of extinguishing lame-duck governance. Presidents and members of Congress continue to wield power for many weeks after an election: issuing pardons, passing legislation, and confirming judges to lifetime appointments even after the voters have repudiated them. For this reason, constitutional-law scholar Sanford Levinson argues that the amendment "simply didn't go far enough."[30] No other country allows politicians rejected by the voters to remain in power for so long. But as law professor Akhil Amar reminds us, the "awkwardly long period of political limbo" is a concession to the multiple stages of the Electoral College system of choosing the president.[31]

The Twenty-First Amendment: Repealing National Prohibition

On December 12, 1928, a Michigan court condemned Etta Mae Miller to a mandatory life sentence for selling two pints of moonshine whiskey. Miller was prosecuted under the state's cruel "life for a pint" law, passed under a provision of the Eighteenth Amendment giving states "concurrent power" to enforce the nationwide ban on intoxicating liquors. It was her fourth infraction. "Never sold enough liquor in my life to get rich," said the impoverished mother of ten. Nevertheless, in her sentencing trial, described in news accounts as "a mere formality," it took the jury only thirteen minutes to render a verdict.[32] "Our only regret is that the woman was not sentenced to life imprisonment before her ten children were born," said Dr. Clarence True Wilson, a leading Prohibition advocate known as America's Number One Dry. "When one has violated the Constitution four times, he or she is proved to be an habitual criminal and should be segregated from society to prevent the production of subnormal offsprings."[33] After a public outcry, Miller's sentence was later commuted. But the law remained in force.

When Congress voted in 1917 to approve the Eighteenth Amendment, Senator Henry Myers conjured up a shimmering vision of the day when Prohibition would finally become the law of the land. "It will be a greater day than the day that witnessed the abolition of human slavery," the progressive Montanan gushed. "It will be a second Declaration of Independence."[34] Even a decade later, in his 1928 run for the presidency, Herbert Hoover memorably praised Prohibition as "a great social and economic experiment, noble in motive and far-reaching in purpose."[35] But by then, it was obvious to more and more people that the "noble experiment" was a failure by most any measure.

While the Eighteenth Amendment's ban on the "manufacture, sale, or transportation of intoxicating liquors" did reduce alcohol consumption significantly, it fell far short of its supporters' dream of eradicating alcohol from American life.[36] Millions of Americans disregarded the ban, obtaining alcohol on the black market even as lawmakers increased enforcement budgets and stiffened penalties. One metric is illuminating: in just five years, illegal imports of liquor from Canada surged more than a hundredfold, from 8,600 gallons in 1921 to over a million gallons in 1926.[37] As the Anti-Saloon League pushed for greater enforcement, they tolerated (and in some instances worked alongside) the vigilante violence of the Ku Klux Klan, which wielded its opposition to drinking as part of its broad hostility to immigrants.[38] According to historian Thomas Pegram, this controversial relationship "damaged the public standing" of the Anti-Saloon League and "weakened its potency as a dry public policy agency."[39]

All the while, America's unquenchable thirst for illicit booze lined the pockets of smugglers, bootleggers, and corrupt officials, fostering widespread disrespect for the law and a surge of violent crime.[40] "Somehow, it doesn't seem right," mused the author of a "Bartender's Guide to Washington," published in a 1929 edition of *Collier's Weekly*. "Of all cities, Washington, where all the prohibition laws are passed and millions of dollars appropriated to exterminate the liquor traffic—well, Washington ought to be dry. But shucks. The city's so wet that it squishes."[41]

Amid this epidemic of hypocrisy and lawlessness, President Hoover promised in his March 1929 inaugural address to appoint a national commission to conduct a "searching investigation" of law enforcement in the United States, including "the method of enforcement of the Eighteenth Amendment and the causes of abuse under it."[42] In January 1931, after twenty months of work, the Wickersham Commission released its findings to an awaiting nation.[43] In recommendations crafted to avoid embarrassing the president, the panel rejected growing calls for the amendment's repeal. Instead, the commission proposed that resources for enforcement be "substantially increased." But a deeper dive into the report's findings painted a damning picture of flagrant lawbreaking, widespread corruption, and overburdened law enforcement. In a set of individual statements, a majority of the commissioners concluded that the Eighteenth Amendment was unenforceable, calling for its revision or repeal.[44] Die-hard prohibitionists hailed the report as a vindication.[45] But Emanuel Celler, representing a community eager for repeal, savvily spun it as a win for the wets. "All the charges made against prohibition by the wets in the House for the past ten year[s] are now approved by the report," said the congressman. "The handwriting is on the wall."[46]

Yet the path to rolling back the Eighteenth Amendment was daunting at best. After all, no constitutional amendment had ever been repealed. Moreover, as an Anti-Saloon League leader pointed out, any attempt at repeal would fail as long as thirteen states stood firm.[47] Confident that his crowning legislative achievement was safe, Morris Sheppard, the unapologetic Father of the Eighteenth Amendment, practically taunted the wets. "There is as much of a chance of repealing the Eighteenth Amendment as there is for a hummingbird to fly to the planet Mars with the Washington Monument tied to its tail," he said.[48] But that didn't stop lawmakers from introducing measures to repeal the amendment or reduce the severity of the ban.[49]

A critical factor that would tip the balance toward repeal was the rapid growth of America's urban population, fueled by immigration and the

Great Migration. Dry leaders understood that demographic trends were not on their side. On the eve of Congress's 1917 vote to approve the Prohibition Amendment, Wayne Wheeler, the movement's "avenging angel," had exhorted delegates to the Anti-Saloon League's annual convention to seize the moment. "We have got to win it now," Wheeler said, "because when 1920 comes and reapportionment is here, forty new wet Congressmen will come from the great wet centers with their rapidly increasing population."[50] To forestall the consequences of this momentous demographic shift, a Republican-led Congress simply ignored the Constitution's mandate to reallocate House seats after the 1920 census, rejecting 42 separate apportionment plans between 1921 and 1928. Daniel Okrent calls it "one of those political maneuvers in American history so audacious it's hard to believe it happened."[51] When Congress finally fulfilled its obligation in 1929, only a year before the next census, the resulting tilt in the regional balance of power lifted the repeal cause just as Wheeler had predicted. States in the West and South lost nearly twenty seats, mostly to urban centers, assuring fairer representation from districts where Prohibition was most unpopular.[52]

In the meantime, shrewd organizing by a single-issue advocacy group helped turned the tide. From the moment it was founded in 1918, the Association Against the Prohibition Amendment conspicuously copied the successful tactics of the Anti-Saloon League.[53] With seed money from a small core of well-heeled donors, including three scions of the du Pont family, the Association quickly attracted hundreds of thousands of members, all pledging to vote for candidates who supported repeal of the Eighteenth Amendment.[54] The group's core message—that the Eighteenth Amendment was an improper expansion of federal power inconsistent with the Constitution—was crafted to ensure the widest possible appeal.[55] The group also touted the return of the alcoholic beverage industry as a source of jobs and tax revenues for Depression-battered state and local treasuries.[56]

In a notable innovation, the Association published meticulously researched studies to shape public awareness of Prohibition's hidden costs. A 1930 report documented how the enhanced enforcement of liquor laws overburdened courts and prisons, diverting attention from more serious crimes.[57] Another estimated that tax revenue from renewed alcohol sales could wipe out the federal deficit.[58] The Association's model, melding strategic advocacy with credible research, proved to be a powerful means of shaping public sentiment, an approach embraced by social movements working to advance legal change ever since.[59]

As the movement for repeal gained strength, the Anti-Saloon League fell on hard times. After Wheeler died suddenly in 1927, the organization was beset with infighting. One camp demanded ever more punitive enforcement to win the war on alcohol while the other called for a greater emphasis on public education and persuasion.[60] For the first time, the drys were on the defensive. In the 1930 midterm elections, wet candidates made major gains in every region of the country outside the South.[61] By 1932, it became even clearer that Prohibition was losing its popularity—and its bipartisan appeal.[62] As a pivotal presidential election loomed, the Democrats "went as wet as the seven seas," according to a news report.[63] The party's nominee for president, Franklin Delano Roosevelt, denounced Prohibition as a "stupendous blunder," shrewdly framing the case for repeal in the language of states' rights. "The experience of nearly one hundred and fifty years under the Constitution has shown us that the proper means of regulation is through the States," said the candidate who would soon lead an unprecedented expansion of federal power through the New Deal.[64] The Republicans proposed a mushy alternative: an amendment giving states more leeway while preserving "the gains already made in dealing with the evils inherent in the liquor traffic."[65]

When the Democrats won in one of history's greatest landslides that November, most Americans took it as a mandate for repeal.[66] That same day, wet forces prevailed in eleven state ballot-measure campaigns. In nine states, voters overturned local dry laws; in two others, they called on Congress to repeal the Eighteenth Amendment.[67] Calculating the scope of the "anti-prohibition sweep," the New York Times estimated that the new Congress would for the first time have a solid wet majority: 343 representatives and 61 senators committed to repeal.[68] Seizing the initiative, proponents introduced a repeal amendment in the postelection lame-duck session, months before the new Congress would be sworn in. The measure tersely provided, "The eighteenth article of amendment to the Constitution of the United States is hereby repealed."[69]

In two additional clauses, the amendment prohibited the transportation of intoxicating liquors into states with dry laws (a provision construed by the courts over the years to give states broad authority to regulate alcoholic beverages)[70] and set a seven-year time limit for ratification, following the precedent set by the Eighteenth Amendment.[71] Rather than run the gauntlet of state legislatures, many of which were malapportioned to overrepresent rural interests, Congress stipulated that delegates to state conventions, elected by the people, would be charged with ratifying the measure. It is the only time this alternative method of ratification in Article V has ever been used.[72] The idea appealed to dry politicians prepared to accept the inevitable but eager to avoid the wrath of the temperance lobby.[73]

As his metaphorical hummingbird took off for Mars, Morris Sheppard mounted a filibuster to stop the repeal amendment. Though the nation had clearly soured on Prohibition, Morris never ceased to be a true believer. In a January 1932 speech commemorating the ban's anniversary, he offered the serene assurance that "general liquor drinking among the American people is a thing of the past."[74] Now, just a year later, he was mounting a lonely last stand. Tenaciously, he held the floor for eight and a half hours, reading tedious transcripts of proceedings from the League of Nations to a mostly empty chamber.[75] "Tourists in the gallery gaped down at the spectacle of one little Dry defying the U.S. electorate," said one observer.[76] When no one stepped forth to support his filibuster, the Father of the Eighteenth Amendment reluctantly conceded defeat.[77]

Debate on the repeal amendment commenced the next day. Confident they had the votes, backers of repeal were content to allow dry lawmakers to dominate the discussion. "Any one voting for the adoption of this resolution votes for the return of the American saloon with all its evils," said one senator. "It is not safe to tinker with the Constitution. In 144 years of glorious history we have never yet repealed an amendment which went into the Constitution after the people had sanctioned it, and I submit that it is dangerous to tamper with the basic law."[78]

Once the diehard drys had their say, the repeal amendment cruised to an easy victory in the Senate on February 16, 1933.[79] Twenty-one members voting that day had also cast a vote on the Eighteenth Amendment in 1917. Of these, only one stayed true to the dry cause, while fifteen supporters of Prohibition reversed course, joining the call for repeal.[80] Their votes evinced a change of heart experienced by millions of Americans as the "noble experiment" went awry. On February 20, the House approved the measure after a brief debate, sending it to the states.[81] In taking this action, the 72nd Congress earned the distinction of being the first since 1789 to propose more than one amendment to the Constitution.[82]

James Beck, a wet Republican congressman from Pennsylvania, served up a fitting eulogy. "The American people," he declared, "after a practical trial of the Eighteenth Amendment of over ten years, are now convinced that it was a fatal error to write into the Constitution an amendment which was not only subversive of the fundamental principle of local self-government but also offended the greater and even more basic ideal of American individualism in vainly attempting, by governmental edict, to dictate to the citizen a narrow moral code of conduct in a matter of personal habit. This ill-fated experiment, which may have been 'noble in motive,' was doomed to failure from the beginning. It was alien to the individualistic spirit of America."[83]

Ulysses Samuel Guyer, a Kansas congressman, insisted that the fight was not over. "Let no one imagine that submitting this to the States is going to settle it," he said. "It is only the opening gun in a battle that will rock your district from center to circumference."[84] But America was ready to move on. By December 1933, ten months after the vote in Congress, thirty-eight states had organized ratifying conventions, while another ten, mostly in the Southern and Plains states, where dry sentiment ran deepest, declined. In the delegate elections, which offered a clear choice between wet and dry slates, the will of the people was clear: voters in thirty-seven of the thirty-eight state contests favored repeal.[85] In most of the contests, it wasn't even close. Of the 21 million Americans who cast a vote in the 1933 delegate elections, nearly three in four chose repeal.[86] The choice of ratification by convention proved to be a masterstroke. It provided for a quick and orderly ratification process while imparting unmistakable democratic legitimacy to the result.[87]

In just thirteen years, wet forces engineered a stunning reversal of the Temperance Movement's great triumph, undoing the work of nearly a century.[88] With Prohibition's end, corks popped from coast to coast. Even as the nation moved on, however, Morris Sheppard was unwilling to do so. Until his death in 1941, he introduced a resolution in each successive Congress calling for a new Prohibition Amendment.[89]

In *The Age of Reform*, his classic history of the Progressive Era, Richard Hofstadter dismissed Sheppard's crusade as a "pseudo-reform," memorably describing it as "a means by which the reforming energies of the country were transmuted into mere peevishness."[90] But was the Eighteenth Amendment just a constitutional blip? Arguably, the amendment set a precedent for direct intervention by the federal government into the lives of citizens, with consequences that last to this day. The futile effort to enforce

Prohibition laid the foundation for a vast expansion of the federal government's law enforcement powers, much as the misguided war on drugs has fueled mass incarceration today. With the blessing of the courts, law enforcement whittled away at Fourth Amendment protections, claiming new powers to wiretap and search suspected bootleggers and smugglers. Our Fourth Amendment protections remain weaker a century later.[91]

In perhaps its most enduring lesson, the nation's experience with Prohibition helped to seal a lasting consensus that it is unwise to invoke the constitutional amendment process of Article V to advance policy goals more appropriately by lawmaking.[92]

The Revolution of 1937

From the brief heyday of the Populists through the Progressive Era and New Deal, a powerful current of reform and modernization produced six new amendments to the Constitution. But during that same period of time, from 1895 to 1936, the jurisprudence of a reactionary Supreme Court sapped the Constitution of the "firmness and vigor in the national operations" its Framers intended.[93] Time and again, when the people's representatives in Congress passed laws through the democratic process to address the pressing economic and social problems of the day—advancing economic justice, protecting workers from exploitation and the hazards of industrialization—the justices audaciously blocked them on the basis of contrived legal theories.

This unprecedented display of judicial intervention was rooted in two distinct strands of legal doctrine. In one line of cases, the Court used the principle of federalism to construe Congress's powers under the Constitution narrowly. Relying on a turbocharged reading of the Tenth Amendment, the Court's conservative members were inordinately solicitous of the states' sphere of authority, checking Congress even when it had clear textual authority to act. The other line of cases, exemplified by the discredited case of *Lochner v. New York* discussed at the beginning of chapter 4, advanced the theory that the principle of due process of law in the Fifth and Fourteenth Amendments protected the "liberty of contract," a guarantee found nowhere in the Constitution's text. For decades, this wholly fabricated doctrine prevented the federal *and* state governments from enacting economic regulations, from minimum wage laws to maximum hour rules to child labor protections.[94]

After the onset of the Great Depression in 1929, the Court's stance became intolerable. In the 1932 election, Franklin Roosevelt won a massive popular mandate, defeating Herbert Hoover by 7 million votes and winning all but six states. The victorious candidate pledged "a new deal for the American people,"[95] promising "action, and action now"[96] to engage the entire nation in an unprecedented collective effort to overcome the economic crisis. Even at this moment of grave peril for the nation, the Court remained reflexively hostile to government action. In the first hundred days of his presidency, Roosevelt worked with Congress to enact an ambitious package of reforms to stabilize a foundering economy and provide relief to millions of struggling American workers and farmers. The justices consistently pushed back, blocking the president's New Deal programs in a series of controversial cases.

In *A.L.A. Schechter Poultry Corporation v. United States*,[97] a May 1935 ruling, the Court invalidated a key provision of the National Industrial Recovery Act. The 1933 statute was the centerpiece of the president's New Deal agenda, authorizing the creation of "codes of fair competition" in hundreds of business sectors.[98] Congress enacted the law under its power to regulate interstate commerce. But in a case involving a Brooklyn-based distributor of kosher chickens, prosecuted for violating a live poultry code established under the Act's regulatory regime, the Court ruled that Congress exceeded its authority to interfere with purely intrastate activity.[99] Though no one disputed that the company acquired its chickens from out of state, the justices contended that its business had only an "indirect" bearing on interstate commerce. Permitting Congress to use its commerce authority to regulate business operations within a state's boundaries, they insisted, would lead to "a completely centralized government."[100]

Roosevelt called a press conference to denounce the ruling, calling it "more important than any decision probably since the *Dred Scott* case." He warned that the logic of *Schechter* would create a country of "forty-eight nations," leaving the federal government powerless to address the nation's needs. He then asked, "Is the United States going to decide . . . that their Federal Government shall in the future have no right under any implied power or any court-approved power to enter into a solution of a national economic problem, but that the economic problem must be decided only by the states?"[101] The conservative *Wall Street Journal* hailed the ruling as confirmation that Roosevelt's New Deal "cannot be encompassed within the limits of the American Constitution."[102]

As an initial response, administration officials briefly considered whether they could devise "a 'quick' method of amending the Constitution by what would be the equivalent of a popular referendum." [103] A few months later, the president floated the idea of a more conventional Article V solution in a *Collier's* magazine profile:

> It is the deep conviction of Franklin D. Roosevelt that the Constitution of the United States was never meant to be a "dead hand," chilling human aspiration and blocking humanity's advance, but that the founding fathers conceived it as a living force for the expression of the national will with respect to national needs.

If the Court continued to strike down New Deal programs, the report suggested, the president would "have no other alternative than to go to the country with a Constitutional amendment that will lift the Dead Hand, giving the people of today the right to deal with today's vital issues." [104]

But the path to a constitutional solution was less than clear. For a start, there was no agreement on the amendment's language. Once drafted, the campaign to secure ratification would confront an army of powerful interests determined to stop it, just as the Child Labor Amendment faced. As Roosevelt often said, thirteen states comprising only 5 percent of the population had the power to kill any amendment. Finally, even after an amendment was adopted, it would still be subject to interpretation by the same hostile courts. [105]

When the justices struck down New York's minimum wage law for women in June 1936, Roosevelt complained that the Court was creating a " 'no-man's-land' where no government—state or federal—can function." [106] Allies in Congress said it was time to propose an amendment to the Constitution. Others counseled the president to bide his time until one of the Court's "nine old men" retired. Concerned that the country's economic emergency did not afford him the privilege of waiting, the president decided the "only practical solution" was to fight for his own vision of the Constitution, even if it meant changing the composition of the Court. In the 1936 campaign, he carefully avoided discussing his conflict with the justices. But when he won re-election in a landslide, Roosevelt treated it as a mandate for a bold response. [107] In his January 1937 State of the Union Address to Congress, he delivered an unmistakable message to the Court.

The Constitution, he said, "can be used as an instrument of progress and not as a device for prevention of action."[108]

In his inaugural address later that month, the first held on the political calendar reset by the Twentieth Amendment, Roosevelt reflected on the Constitution's meaning and purpose:

> This year marks the one hundred and fiftieth anniversary of the Constitutional Convention which made us a nation. At that Convention our forefathers found the way out of the chaos which followed the Revolutionary War; they created a strong government with powers of united action sufficient then and now to solve problems utterly beyond individual or local solution.[109]

In other words: no amendment was necessary. Though Roosevelt started his second term with overwhelming Democratic majorities in Congress, he would not urge revisions to the national charter. Instead, he would apply his considerable political capital to vindicate the Framers' vision of a robust national government. "The Constitution of 1787," the president insisted, "did not make our democracy impotent."[110]

Two weeks into his new term, Roosevelt unveiled a controversial bill to reorganize the federal judiciary.[111] Among other reforms, the measure would allow the president to add as many as six new justices to the Supreme Court, one for each jurist who reached the age of seventy. Roosevelt framed the proposal as a plea for "a constant and systematic addition of younger blood" on the federal bench, but everyone understood that the "court packing plan" would permit Roosevelt to shift the Court's ideological balance.[112] The *New York Times* reported that the carefully guarded plan "fell today like a bombshell."[113] Republicans, and more than a few Democrats, reacted with outrage. "If the President desires complete dictatorial powers, patterned after the Fascist or Communist dictatorships of the Old World, he could take no more direct step to bring it about," complained one GOP lawmaker.[114]

As Roosevelt's bill awaited consideration by Congress, his continued pressure on the Court may have spurred an unexpected change of heart. In March 1937, less than two months after the president unveiled his plan, the justices upheld a minimum wage law in Washington strikingly similar to the New York statute they had struck down a year earlier.[115] That decision was followed in short order by rulings upholding Congress's authority to regulate labor organizing under the National Labor Relations Act and to implement a system of unemployment insurance under the Social Security Act.[116] The justices' about-face—"the switch in time that saved nine"— was a jurisprudential watershed that brought down an entire edifice of case law that had stymied progressive legislation for decades, even though Congress ultimately rejected the court-packing plan.[117] "These New Deal opinions have operated as the functional equivalent of formal constitutional amendments," says constitutional scholar Bruce Ackerman, "providing a solid foundation for activist intervention in national social and economic life."[118] Over the next few years, as retirements gave Roosevelt the opportunity to appoint new justices, a transformed judiciary relegated the flawed jurisprudence of the *Lochner* era to "a symbol of an entire constitutional order that had been thoroughly repudiated by the American people."[119]

The Court's 1937 course correction provides the basis for much of modern government, from Medicare to the Clean Water Act, along with the federal agencies that enforce these essential laws. For some legal scholars on the right, then and now, it was the moment the Constitution of limited government went into "exile."[120] Some, like conservative jurist Janice Rogers Brown, have openly scorned the Revolution of 1937. She called it "the triumph of our socialist revolution."[121] In actuality, Roosevelt's "revolution" was a restoration of the Framers' vision of a muscular federal government, creating a new and enduring judicial consensus in favor of democratic action.

Elected to the presidency four times, Roosevelt was able to cement these gains over the course of a long and consequential presidency. Over a fourteen-year span, from 1933 to 1947, Democrats controlled all the levers of power in Washington as Republicans bided their time in the political wilderness. Only after Roosevelt's death in 1945 did Republicans return to power. They used the opportunity to settle an old score.

The Twenty-Second Amendment: Presidential Term Limits

In March 1937, as his showdown with the Supreme Court reached its climax, Franklin Roosevelt was already anticipating the retirement that awaited him at the end of his second term. "My great ambition on January 20, 1941," he told a gathering of Democratic Party stalwarts, "is to turn over this desk and chair in the White House to my successor, whoever he may be, with the assurance that I am at the same time turning over to him as President a nation intact, a nation at peace, a nation prosperous."[122]

But his dreams for a life after the presidency would never be realized. As war engulfed Europe in the latter half of 1939, Roosevelt pondered a run for a third term, worried that no one else could lead the country at a moment of supreme peril. For months, he kept those musings to himself, prompting political cartoonists to portray him as a sphinx.[123] Roosevelt had good reason to avoid appearing too eager. No president had ever violated the tradition of stepping down after two terms in office.

Finally, as delegates converged on Chicago for the 1940 Democratic National Convention, the president sought counsel from Felix Frankfurter, one of eight men he would appoint to the Supreme Court. Frankfurter assured the president that a third term was justified by the "unprecedented conditions" facing the country.[124] Days later, on July 18, the convention nominated Roosevelt by acclamation in what was pointedly styled a "draft." The *New York Times* noted that the move was "in contravention of one of the oldest and best established traditions in American politics."[125]

The president's Republican opponent, businessman Wendell Willkie, assailed the move as an unprincipled power grab. "The third term is one of the great issues of the campaign," Willkie insisted. "I'm afraid that, if President Roosevelt is re-elected for a third term, it will be impossible to return to our two-party system."[126] Herbert Hoover offered an even sharper rebuke. "This Republic has since the beginning held this tradition that there should be no third term for presidents," said the former president. "That is not just a tradition, like a silk hat for funerals. It has been an unwritten provision in our Constitution."[127]

To draw more attention to the issue, Willkie pledged to support a constitutional amendment limiting presidents to a term of eight years or less.[128] But the voters rendered their own verdict, re-electing Roosevelt by a wide margin. Four years later, when Roosevelt made a fourth run for the White House, he faced renewed criticism. "Four terms, or sixteen years, is the most dangerous threat to our freedom ever proposed," said the Republican nominee for president, New York governor Thomas E. Dewey.[129] Once again, the voters sent Roosevelt back to the White House with a comfortable, through somewhat smaller, margin of victory.

At the Philadelphia Convention, the Framers considered and rejected the idea of capping the number of terms a president could serve. At the time, six state charters limited the tenure of their governors through a practice called rotation in office,[130] based in the belief that "a long continuance in the first executive departments of power or trust is dangerous to liberty."[131] George Mason urged the adoption of this practice, arguing that "the great officers of state, and particularly the executive should at fixed periods return to that mass from which they were at first taken."[132] But after debating a variety of options, from a three-year term with the possibility of renewal to a single term of seven years to an unlimited term of service "during good behavior" (what Mason called an "elective monarchy"),[133] the delegates settled in the end on a four-year term with no limit on renewal.

The two-term tradition is often attributed to the wisdom of George Washington, who stepped down voluntarily after eight years in office. But the first president had no desire to bind his successors. He actually opposed term limits in principle. "I can see no propriety in precluding ourselves from the services of any man, who on some great emergency, shall be deemed, universally, most capable of serving the public," he said.[134] On the other hand, Thomas Jefferson made clear that "the perpetual re-eligibility of the President" was a feature of the Constitution he "strongly dislike[d]."[135] As he neared the expiration of his own second term in office, he cited "the sound precedent set by an illustrious predecessor" as a reason to "lay down my charge."[136] Over the next few decades, a succession of presidents—James Madison, James Monroe, and Andrew Jackson—abided by the two-term tradition. In this way, it became a constitutional norm.

The first controversy over the two-term tradition arose during the presidency of Ulysses S. Grant. In the heady days after his re-election in 1872, Republican newspapers urged Grant to seek a third term. The president did little to dampen speculations about his ambitions, even after his popularity sank due to an economic depression and swirling corruption scandals. The lingering third-term question contributed to his party's sweeping losses in the 1874 midterm election.[137] "It was very generally believed," said the *New York Daily Tribune*, "that the President's reticence on this subject was ruining the Republican prospects of success."[138] As Grant continued to flirt with another run, coyly leaving the door open should circumstances make it "*an imperative duty*,"[139] the House of Representatives passed a bipartisan resolution declaring that the two-term tradition "has become, by universal concurrence, a part of our republican system of government."[140]

Once he left the White House, the idea of a third Grant term refused to die. After his successor made civil service reform a signature issue, angering the Republican "spoilsmen" in Congress who thrived on corrupt patronage schemes during "the good old days under General Grant," allies orchestrated a comeback campaign for the retired president.[141] The "Grant boom" was surprisingly effective. At the 1880 Republican convention, he led his rivals through thirty-five rounds of balloting. But in the end, anti-Grant forces coalesced around the candidacy of Ohio congressman James Garfield, who went on to win the presidency.[142] *Harper's Weekly* wrote Grant's political epitaph: "The feeling of hostility to a third term is not a chimera. It is deeply founded, and upon cogent reasons."[143]

Theodore Roosevelt also tried to buck the two-term tradition. He assumed the presidency in 1901 upon the assassination of William McKinley. After serving the remaining three and half years of his slain predecessor's term, Roosevelt went on to win a term in his own right in 1904. Celebrating his victory, Roosevelt cited the "wise custom which limits the President to two terms," announcing, "under no circumstances will I be a candidate for or accept another nomination."[144] As the term neared its end, he made good on his promise, throwing his support to William Howard Taft in the election of 1908. But Roosevelt soon became disenchanted with his successor. In February 1912, amid a growing schism between the progressive and conservative factions in the Republican Party, Roosevelt declared, "My hat's in the ring! The fight is on and I'm stripped to the buff!"[145] In response, one journal gibed:

> *Washington Wouldn't,*
> *Grant Couldn't,*
> *Roosevelt Shan't.*[146]

Roosevelt defended his reversal, arguing that the two-term custom applied only to *consecutive* terms. After Taft won the nomination, Roosevelt continued his campaign under the banner of the newly formed Bull Moose Party. The GOP rift all but guaranteed victory for New Jersey governor Woodrow Wilson, the Democrat in the race. In the end, says one historian, Roosevelt's "flouting of tradition cost him very few votes."[147] He came in second, carrying six states. Taft won only two.

The idea of limiting presidential tenure by constitutional amendment dates back to the early days of the republic. The first such measure was introduced in 1803.[148] In all, lawmakers introduced some 270 presidential term limit resolutions in Congress, with increased frequency after the turn of the twentieth century.[149] But they went nowhere until Republicans regained control of Congress in the 1946 midterm election after sixteen years in the minority. It was a convincing victory: the GOP gained fifty-five seats in the House and twelve in the Senate.[150]

The new governing majority made term limits the first order of business. In January 1947, on the very first day of the 80th Congress, Michigan representative Earl Michener introduced an amendment to limit the president to two elected terms. The new Speaker of the House, Joseph Martin of Massachusetts, predicted it would be the "first important measure" passed by the new Republican majority.[151] Intent on securing its quick passage, the Republican leadership dispensed with public hearings and brought the measure to the House floor on February 6, allotting just two hours for debate.

As he introduced the amendment, Republican congressman Leo Allen of Illinois invoked the legacy of the first president with a shamelessly fabricated history lesson. "When he refused nomination for a third term," Allen said, "George Washington warned the people that they might again be subjected to the tyranny of monarchy if they permitted any individual to become too firmly entrenched as the chief executive." The congressman urged that the amendment be put to the people for their consideration "to protect them from the oppression of dictatorships that have arisen in other countries."[152]

The debate was fought largely along party lines as Democrats lined up to oppose the measure. Adolph J. Sabath, then the longest-serving member of the House, characterized the amendment as "insulting to the memory of our greatest president." The Illinois congressman admonished the Republicans for their "unseemly haste" in passing an amendment that would restrict the rights of the people. "We have frequently amended our Constitution, as the need arose, to extend and strengthen the democratic processes on which our Government is solidly built," he said. "This amendment goes backward, and limits the right of the majority to choose the president."[153]

Boston Democrat John McCormack, a future Speaker of the House, complained that the amendment "ties the hands of future generations of Americans."[154] Inevitably, he warned, there would be "some occasion when a grave emergency confronts them, when . . . they might be engaged in war, with a President coming to the end of his second term but possessing the confidence of the American people of that day."[155] He exhorted his colleagues: "Let us not put them into a strait-jacket, a strait-jacket that might be the factor resulting in the destruction of our country at some time in the future."

Republicans denied that the measure was driven by partisan revenge. Their only aim, said majority leader Charles Halleck, was to place "an unwritten law of the country firmly into the Constitution."[156] But an author of the measure admitted otherwise. "It grows directly out of the unfortunate experience we had in this country in 1940 and again in 1944, when a President who had entrenched himself in power by use of patronage and the public purse refused to vacate the office at the conclusion of two terms," said Karl Earl Mundt, a member from South Dakota.[157] Like many of his Republican colleagues, Mundt warned of a slippery slope to dictatorship:

> Almost all the rest of the world has slipped away from the foundations of freedom and skidded dangerously close to the shoals of executive domination, one-man rule, dictatorship, and ruthless tyranny. Let us consolidate our gains in self-government by passing this resolution to prevent any president hereafter—Republican or Democratic— from perpetuating himself in office.[158]

After the lawmakers rejected an alternative plan to limit the president to a single six-year term, the measure was put to a vote. The final tally was 285–121.[159] While Republicans voted unanimously to support the measure, the two-thirds majority was secured with the help of Southern Democrats, many of whom feared that a strong president might be emboldened to pursue a civil rights agenda.[160] Three future presidents cast a vote in the chamber that day. John Kennedy and Richard Nixon voted for the amendment. Lyndon Johnson voted against it. As circumstances would have it, the constraint imposed by the amendment would have no impact on any of their presidencies.

Senators debated the amendment over four days in early March. Following the House's lead, the Republican majority declined to hold public hearings. The arguments raised both for and against the measure were by now quite familiar, they explained. And they were right. Supporters warned that unlimited presidential tenure posed a risk to liberty. "To grant extended power to any one man would be a definite step in the direction of autocracy," said William Chapman Revercomb, a Republican from West

Virginia.[161] Opponents condemned the sponsors' partisan motives. "Perhaps it is feared," said Illinois senator Scott Lucas, "that the Democratic Party, the party of Jefferson, of Jackson, of Wilson, of Roosevelt, may suddenly bring forth another great giant among men, and that the American people, if they have the right to do so, may wish to continue him in office for more than the customary two terms."[162]

The Senate passed the measure by a vote of 59–23, with 13 not voting.[163] Once again, every Republican in the chamber voted for the measure, bolstered by a bloc of Southern Democrats who furnished the winning margin. The Senate modified the House proposal in one crucial respect, clarifying that a person who fills more than two years of a predecessor's term (as Theodore Roosevelt did) may stand for election only once. The change was proposed by Robert A. Taft, the Ohio Republican and son of the former president, who gained national fame as an implacable foe of the New Deal, which he excoriated as "a system tending inevitably to socialism."[164] Taft's modification extended the maximum length of a chief executive's tenure to ten years.[165] The House promptly voted to adopt the Senate's version.[166] On March 24, the proposal was transmitted to the states for their consideration.[167] By its terms, the incumbent president, Harry Truman, was exempt from the two-term limitation.[168]

Thirty-six states were needed to ratify the Twenty-Second Amendment. Within a year, twenty-one legislatures lent their assent. Many had fresh Republican majorities elected in the party's 1946 wave. But then the pace of ratification slowed. When only three additional states ratified in all of 1949 and 1950, the measure seemed destined for failure.[169] Then, in 1951, the *New York Times* reported on a "sudden spurt" of support, particularly in states controlled by Democrats. In the span of three months, seventeen additional states voted to ratify, surpassing the three-fourths threshold needed to put the amendment over the top. Citing "factional differences with President Truman," the *Times* reported that Democrats flocked to the amendment in the hope that ratification would "discourage him from standing for another term."[170] Only two states—Massachusetts and Oklahoma—voted to reject the measure. Five states took no action on it.

The Twenty-Second Amendment made good on Wendell Willkie's campaign pledge, offered in the final days of the 1940 election. It sailed through Congress, without any organized movement to support it beyond the pent-up resentment of Republican politicians. As historian David Kyvig notes, "No appreciable public interest in the measure ever surfaced in congressional mail, newspaper editorials, or opinion polls."[171] Shortly after its adoption, the *Times* contrasted the story of the Twenty-Second Amendment with that of the Eighteenth and Twenty-First Amendments. While the two preceding amendments were each buoyed by campaigns driven by "one bipartisan organization," the Twenty-Second Amendment followed "a different and curious path." It was "an instance where unorganized bipartisan public pressure added an article to the Constitution."[172]

A year after the amendment's adoption, Dwight Eisenhower became the first Republican to win the presidency in two decades. It didn't take long for GOP lawmakers to wonder if they made a rash decision. By Eisenhower's second term, some of them introduced measures to repeal it.[173] Eisenhower let it be known that he disapproved of the two-term policy as a philosophical matter, arguing that "the United States ought to be able to choose for its President anybody that it wants, regardless of the number of terms he has served."[174] But in the seventy years since the two-term limit became binding law, the nation has never faced the kind of crisis that might make an incumbent president "indispensable." With the exception of the three consecutive terms served by Ronald Reagan and George H. W. Bush, no party has occupied the White House for more than eight consecutive years since the limit on presidential terms took effect.

The Twenty-Second Amendment may be best understood as codifying a longstanding political norm. When Franklin Roosevelt shattered the two-term tradition after others tried, a constitutional amendment was the only way to ensure that future presidents would be bound to a precedent many Americans considered important. At a time when the nation faced down the threat of totalitarian regimes around the world, the amendment seemed to offer protection against the "greater danger that one man or one party might freeze a hold upon the Republic," as the *Wall Street Journal* put it.[175] On the day the amendment was ratified, the former speaker Joseph Martin, now thrust back in the role of minority leader, claimed vindication, hailing the measure as "a cause for rejoicing by every good American" and "a defeat for totalitarianism and the enemies of freedom."[176] But there were also reminders of the partisan pettiness behind the measure. Noah Mason, an Illinois Republican, argued that a litany of challenges facing the nation would not have happened if Roosevelt had been limited to two terms. "A sick President would not have gone to Yalta and surrendered to Stalin," he charged. "We would not be in Korea today, and World War III would not be threatening." To these charges, Congressman Eugene McCarthy, an up-and-coming Minnesota Democrat, replied that Americans "will not like jackals gather to feast on the flesh of the fallen lion." [177]

It was the first amendment—and the last—to embody the priorities of a conservative Republican majority in Congress.[178] By the onset of the 1960s, a mere decade later, a Democrat-controlled Congress would bring forth a new surge of amending activity reflecting the priorities of a rapidly changing America.

The opening page of James Madison's notes from the Philadelphia Convention. While they are considered the most detailed and authoritative record of the Framers' secret deliberations, Madison "corrected" and revised this day-by-day summary many times before his death in 1836.

Courtesy of James Madison Papers, Library of Congress

Elbridge Gerry (left) and George Mason (right) made significant contributions to the drafting of the Constitution, but in the end they refused, along with Virginia governor Edmund Randolph, to sign the document. In the ratification debate, the two men were among the most prominent Anti-Federalist critics of the Constitution.

Both images courtesy of New York Public Library

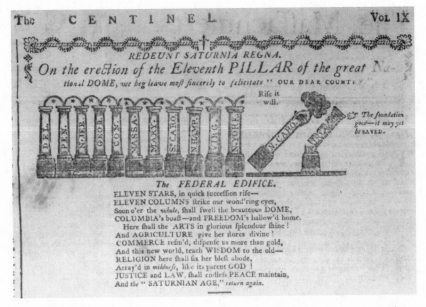

A widely circulated cartoon from the *Massachusetts Centinel* depicting the ratifying states as pillars of the "federal edifice." It was updated as each new state joined the Union.

Massachusetts Centinel, August 2, 1788, courtesy of Library of Congress

James Madison (left), celebrated as the Father of the Constitution, was also the key figure behind the adoption of the Bill of Rights. Patrick Henry (right), the Revolutionary patriot, emerged as Madison's chief rival and one of the country's most determined foes of the new Constitution.

Left image courtesy of Library of Congress; right image courtesy of New York Public Library

ARTICLE the FIFTH.

A well regulated militia, composed of the body of the People, being the best security of a free State, the right of the People to keep and bear arms, shall not be infringed, but no one religiously scrupulous of bearing arms, shall be compelled to render military service in person.

ARTICLE the SIXTH.

No soldier shall, in time of peace, be quartered in any house without the consent of the owner, nor in time of war, but in a manner to be prescribed by law.

ARTICLE the SEVENTH.

The right of the People to be secure in their persons, houses, papers and effects, against unreasonable searches and seizures, shall not be violated, and no warrants shall issue, but upon probable cause supported by oath or affirmation, and particularly describing the place to be searched, and the persons or things to be seized.

ARTICLE the EIGHTH.

No person shall be subject, ~~except in case of impeachment, to more than one trial or one punishment~~ for the same offense, nor shall be compelled in any criminal case, to be a witness against himself, nor be deprived of life, liberty or property, without due process of law; nor shall private property be taken for public use without just compensation.

ARTICLE the NINTH.

In all criminal prosecutions, the accused shall enjoy the right to a speedy and public trial, to be informed of the nature and cause of the accusation, to be confronted with the witnesses against him, to have compulsory process for obtaining witnesses in his favor, and to have the assistance of counsel for his defence.

ARTICLE the TENTH.

The trial of all crimes (except in cases of impeachment, and in cases arising in the land or naval forces, or in the militia when in actual service in time of War or public danger) shall be by an Impartial Jury of the Vicinage, with the requisite of unanimity for conviction, the right of challenge, and other accustomed requisites; and no person shall be held to answer for a capital, or otherways infamous crime, unless on a presentment or indictment by a Grand Jury; ~~but if a crime be committed in a place in the possession of an enemy, or in which an insurrection may prevail, the indictment and trial may by law be authorised in some other place within the same State.~~

A page from a draft of the Bill of Rights as marked up by the Senate in 1789. Senators reduced the seventeen amendments sent to them to a total of twelve, ten of which were ratified in 1791.

Courtesy of National Archives

SOUTHERN CHIVALRY — ARGUMENT versus CLUB'S.

The Supreme Court's infamous ruling in the 1857 case brought by Dred Scott (above) and the brutal caning of Republican senator Charles Sumner on the Senate floor (below) attracted new converts to the abolitionist cause.

Top image c. 1857, Wikimedia Commons; bottom image John L. Magee, 1856, courtesy of Digital Commonwealth Massachusetts Collection Online

On the eve of the Civil War, Representative Thomas Corwin (left) sponsored an amendment to enshrine slavery as a permanent institution in the South. Four years later, Representative James Ashley (right), an ardent abolitionist, worked closely with President Lincoln to adopt a constitutional ban on slavery.

Left image, J.A.J. Wilcox, 1882, Wikimedia Commons; right image courtesy of Brady-Handy Photograph Collection, Library of Congress, Prints and Photographs Division

A scene of jubilation on the House floor upon the passage of the Thirteenth Amendment in 1865. The amendment abolished slavery, ensuring that 4 million Black people would be forever free from bondage.

Frank Leslie's Illustrated Newspaper, *February 18, 1865*

Representatives Thaddeus Stevens (left) and John Bingham (right) were key figures in the framing of the Reconstruction Amendments.

Both images courtesy of Brady-Handy Photograph Collection, Library of Congress, Prints and Photographs Division

The ratification of the Fourteenth and Fifteenth Amendments brought the first class of Black lawmakers, all from the South, including Hiram Revels (far left), the nation's first Black senator.

Currier & Ives, 1872, Courtesy of Library of Congress

Senator Nelson Aldrich (left), the embodiment of Gilded Age corruption, sponsored the Sixteenth Amendment in the hope that it would kill efforts to introduce an income tax. William Jennings Bryan (right), known as "the Great Commoner," led the Democratic Party's populist wing. Though he lost three separate presidential elections, he helped push the Sixteenth and Seventeenth Amendments to adoption.

Left image Anders Leonard Zorn, 1913, Courtesy of National Portrait Gallery, Smithsonian Institution: gift of Stephanie Edgell in memory of Elsie Aldrich Campbell; right image c. 1900, Courtesy of Library of Congress

A 1918 poster (left) urging Ohioans to vote for Prohibition as state legislatures considered an amendment to impose a nationwide ban. The Eighteenth Amendment was adopted in 1919, driven by lobbying from the Anti-Saloon League and their crusading leader, Wayne B. Wheeler (right).

Left image Ohio Dry Federation, 1918, Courtesy of Ohio History Connection Archive; right image Harris & Ewing, 1920, Courtesy of Library of Congress

Elizabeth Cady Stanton and Susan B. Anthony (left) were two leading activists for woman suffrage in the late nineteenth century. Alice Paul (right) brought more-militant tactics to the final struggle to adopt the Nineteenth Amendment.

Left image c. 1880–1902, Courtesy of Library of Congress; right image Harris & Ewing, 1920, Courtesy of Library of Congress

Like the temperance movement, the women's suffrage drive was also linked to the war in Europe.
Nina Allender, 1917, Courtesy of Library of Congress

Racism infected the fight for women's suffrage. During the 1913 Women's March on Washington, Ida B. Wells (center right), a prominent Black journalist and anti-lynching activist, proudly marched with her state's delegation, ignoring the rules of the segregated parade, in which Black women were to march in the back.

Chicago Daily Tribune, *March 5, 1913*

Representative Emanuel Celler (left) and Senator James Eastland (right) ran their chamber's judiciary committees for decades, controlling and obstructing the flow of constitutional amendments.

Left image 1951, Courtesy of Library of Congress; right image 1956, Associated Press

Birch Bayh, a first-term Senator from Indiana, took over the Subcommittee on Constitutional Amendments in 1963. He was the driving force behind the Twenty-Fifth and Twenty-Sixth Amendments and led a failed effort to abolish the Electoral College.

c. 1970s, Senatorial Papers of Birch Bayh, via Wikimedia Commons

Days after his predecessor's assassination, President Lyndon Johnson speaks before a joint session of Congress. Behind Johnson were the two elderly men next in line for the presidency: Speaker John McCormack and Senate president pro tempore Carl Hayden.

1963, Wikimedia Commons

The Civil Rights Movement inspired three voting rights amendments to the Constitution.

Warren K. Leffler, 1965, Courtesy of Library of Congress

Walter Fauntroy was the first delegate to the House of Representatives from the District of Columbia. He attempted to secure full congressional representation for the citizens of the nation's capital via constitutional amendment but the states failed to ratify the measure.

1975, Courtesy of Washington Star Photograph Collection, People's Archive, District of Columbia Public Library

Representatives Martha Griffiths (left) and Shirley Chisholm (right) were two prominent leaders in the fight to persuade Congress to pass the Equal Rights Amendment in 1972.

Left image John Rous, 1963, Associated Press; right image Warren K. Leffler, 1973, Courtesy of Library of Congress

Conservative activist Phyllis Schlafly, the "sweetheart of the silent majority" who founded the STOP ERA campaign. The coalition led the successful effort to derail the Equal Rights Amendment.

Warren K. Leffler, 1977, Courtesy of Library of Congress

6

The Civil Rights Era
Amendments (1960–1971)

The 1950s were the first decade of the twentieth century in which Congress did not send a new constitutional amendment out to the states. Yet during that time, two issues of constitutional significance were on the minds of every American. The first was the emerging campaign to end Jim Crow segregation and uphold the civil rights of African Americans, invigorated by the Supreme Court's 1954 ruling in *Brown v. Board of Education*. The second was the Cold War, the geopolitical standoff that bred fear of a Soviet Union nuclear attack capable of killing tens of millions of Americans.[1] Taken together, these two great challenges raised new questions about the resilience of American democracy.

By 1959, however, a new crop of amendments was vying for the attention of lawmakers on Capitol Hill. After a series of health scares raised questions about President Dwight Eisenhower's fitness to serve, George Smathers of Florida proposed clarifying the rules of succession in the event of a president's death or inability to serve.[2] Kenneth Keating, a Republican from New York, introduced two measures to expand democracy—one that would give the District of Columbia representation in the House of Representatives and the Electoral College,[3] and another to lower the national voting age to eighteen.[4] The bipartisan duo of William Langer, a North Dakota Republican in the twilight of his career, and Thomas Dodd, newly elected Democrat from Connecticut, reintroduced the Equal Rights Amendment, a measure to bar sex discrimination first introduced in 1923.[5] And Spessard Holland, a Florida Democrat, continued his perennial campaign to secure an amendment to abolish the poll tax and other wealth-based restrictions on voting.[6]

Unknown to anyone at the time, these five proposals were the first green shoots of a new season of amendment activity. Over the next two decades, each would move in turn to the center of the political debate. Some would surmount the high bar of support set by Article V, while others would fall short, but first, each would have to make its way past two formidable committee chairmen.

"Big Jim" Eastland, a moon-faced, cigar-chomping Democrat from Mississippi, ruled the Senate Judiciary Committee with a firm hand. He was a master of the art of letting legislation he opposed "die a natural death on the judiciary vine."[7] Though he seemed to relish his reputation as an "ogre and bete noire," Eastland managed to maintain good relationships with liberal lawmakers.[8] Outside the halls of Congress, however, he was best known as a leader of his party's Southern bloc, a powerful faction committed to using every means at their disposal to hamstring civil rights legislation and defend white supremacy. "Among most American liberals and civil rights champions," said a 1965 Los Angeles Times profile, "few if any members of Congress are viewed with more aversion or mistrust than James Oliver Eastland."[9]

Eastland's counterpart in the House leadership was Emanuel "Manny" Celler, a brash New York Democrat from the party's liberal Northern wing. Celler first came to Washington in 1923, during the presidency of Warren G. Harding. By 1949 he had risen to the chairmanship of the influential House Judiciary Committee, a position that allowed him to wield great power for the next quarter century. "Emanuel Celler's capacity for righteous indignation knows no bounds," said a March 1960 "Man in the News" profile. "He is forever at war against monopoly, invasion of civil liberties, bias in all forms. The vigor of his attacks against conditions that to him are undemocratic belies his 71 years."[10] Bald, bespectacled, and blunt, the congressman from Brooklyn exhibited a "deadly earnestness." And yet he earned his colleagues' respect as "a genial companion, with an excellent sense of humor that he often turns on himself."[11]

The story of this era's wave of amendments began with a largely forgotten proposal, sponsored by Senator Estes Kefauver, a Tennessee Democrat who chaired a subcommittee on constitutional amendments. In January 1959, Kefauver introduced a measure to guarantee the continuous operation of the House of Representatives following a mass casualty event. The fix was needed, he argued, "to erase a defect in our Constitution which could not have been contemplated at the time of its adoption."[12] While the

Seventeenth Amendment sets forth an efficient procedure to fill vacancies in the Senate, and a 1947 law adopted under the Twentieth Amendment lays out an order of succession to the presidency,[13] vacancies in the House may only be filled by special elections taking sixty days or more. "This inability to provide for continuity of representation offers no insurmountable difficulty in ordinary times," said Kefauver. "But in periods of national emergency or disaster, it could well paralyze the functioning of representative government."[14]

Under Kefauver's continuity of Congress proposal, governors would be empowered to make temporary appointments to fill empty House seats whenever more than half of the chamber's seats were vacant. It was a sensible plan for an era in which "whole cities may be obliterated in a split second,"[15] one of more than thirty similar resolutions introduced since the advent of the atomic bomb. In July 1959, Eastland's committee cleared the proposal for consideration by the full Senate.[16] But as Kefauver awaited a vote on the measure, it collided fatefully with two voting rights measures still caught in Eastland's tight grip: an amendment to prohibit poll taxes and property ownership requirements as a precondition for voting and another to provide voting representation for the residents of the nation's capital. To break past Eastland's blockade, Kefauver allowed the two measures to be attached to his own. Though the original continuity of Congress proposal was destined to die in the House, a three-in-one amendment approved by Senate on February 2, 1960, served as the launching pad for two new additions to the Constitution.

The Twenty-Third Amendment: Presidential Electors for the District of Columbia

The Twenty-Third Amendment gave residents of the nation's capital the right to choose presidential electors, providing a partial remedy to one of the Framers' most glaring lapses—rooted in their decision to establish the seat of government in a specially created district.

During the first dozen years after independence, the Confederation Congress met in a succession of temporary capitals. The constant moving about, recalled one delegate to the Philadelphia Convention, "had dishonored the federal government, and would require as strong a cure as we could devise."[17] Unable to agree on a specific location for a capital, the delegates inserted a clause in the Constitution authorizing Congress to establish one later—in a district not exceeding ten miles square, on land to be ceded by one or more states, to be governed under the exclusive jurisdiction of Congress.[18] Yet with the capital's unique status as a district came a grave omission: the Framers failed to provide a means of representation for the district's residents. In their design, seats in Congress and votes in the Electoral College were all to be allocated among the states. But the district was not a state. While the record of the convention's debate over the District Clause is limited and contains no mention of this significant oversight,[19] it did not go completely unnoticed. One delegate to New York's ratifying convention protested that the plan for the capital "departs from every principle of freedom," warning that subjecting American citizens "to the exclusive legislation of Congress, in whose appointment they have no share or vote," would pave the way for "tyranny."[20]

When the 1st Congress convened in New York, the fight over the future capital emerged as the nation's first great sectional dispute. Members from the North wanted the capital to remain in New York or Philadelphia. Southerners demanded a more central location, worried that a Northern capital would be a breeding ground for abolitionism. Lawmakers debated the merits of over a dozen potential locations, but consensus proved elusive. The resolution came in 1790 as part of a larger political compromise. To win support for Alexander Hamilton's plan to stabilize the nation's credit and repay state war debts, Congress voted to establish a permanent seat of government along the banks of the Potomac River in the ten square miles of land ceded by Maryland and Virginia.[21]

For a decade, as surveyors and developers busily laid the foundations of the new capital, the fourteen thousand Americans living in the District of Columbia continued to be governed by the laws of Maryland and Virginia, where they possessed the right to vote and stand for federal office. Once Congress relocated to the District in 1800, however, it placed the area under federal control. Going forward, its inhabitants would no longer be residents of a state, forfeiting their voting representation in Congress and the Electoral College, along with any say in the constitutional amendment process. Pennsylvania congressman John Smilie decried the move. "Not a man in the District would be represented in the government," he warned. "Every man who contributed to the support of a government ought to be represented in it, otherwise his natural rights were subverted, and he left, not a citizen, but a subject."[22]

The other fundamental issue facing the residents of the new capital was the right to govern their own local affairs. Though the Constitution gave Congress the exclusive power to pass laws governing the District,[23] James Madison promised during the ratification debate that there would be "a municipal legislature for local purposes."[24] In response to organizing by residents, Congress authorized a charter in 1802 giving Washingtonians the right to elect a city council and later, a mayor.[25] But in 1874, Congress implemented a new form of municipal government, vesting power in three presidentially appointed commissioners.[26] For the next century, the arrangement deprived Washingtonians of the ability to govern themselves.[27]

The first proposed constitutional fix dates back to 1888, when New Hampshire Republican senator Henry Blair introduced an amendment to provide the District representation in Congress.[28] For the next half century, the cause would be championed by Theodore Noyes, the scion of a local newspaper dynasty, who had earlier fought for the sparsely populated Dakota Territory to be admitted as two separate states. In 1914, Noyes helped to organize the Citizens' Joint Committee on National Representation for the District of Columbia, an alliance of thirty local organizations working with the white business community to channel grievance into action. The Joint Committee deployed the tools of organizing and coalition building—grasstops advocacy to persuade trade unions, professional organizations, and community groups to support a constitutional amendment, and grassroots work to secure "favorable public opinion . . . in each state." Upon his death in 1946, Noyes made a generous bequest to keep the Committee going.[29] But success remained out of reach.

There was little progress until February 1960, when Kenneth Keating managed to bring a constitutional amendment proposal to the Senate floor hitched to Estes Kefauver's continuity of Congress measure.[30] The senator from Rochester, who had gained national stature as a leader of the GOP's moderate wing, said the measure was "as important as any other proposal which could come before Congress to enlarge the exercise of the franchise."[31] But the proposal fell short of the goal of full voting representation for the District. Instead, it would have given District residents the right to "elect delegates to the House of Representatives," who could become full voting members upon the approval of Congress, along with the right to choose presidential electors.[32] The measure did not provide for representation in the Senate.

Addressing his fellow senators, Keating offered three main arguments in support of the proposal. First, he noted that the District's population exceeded that of twelve states—with more residents than the three smallest states combined.[33] (Today, the District surpasses only Vermont and Wyoming in population.) Second, he reminded them that Washingtonians contributed more to the federal treasury than taxpayers in twenty-five states. "Taxation without representation is still the lot of our local citizens," the senator declared, a reference to the revolutionary era rallying cry that adorns license plates in the District today. Finally, he invoked the recent wartime service of more than one hundred thousand District residents who fulfilled the "obligations of citizenship," only to be "denied one of its most sacred privileges."[34]

Not a single senator spoke in opposition to Keating's resolution. The debate that day focused almost entirely on Spessard Holland's poll tax measure, which aroused the ire of Southern senators determined to suppress the Black vote. The chamber voted 63–25 (with 12 not voting) to append Keating's proposal to the final measure. The no votes came largely from Southern Democrats, who saw the proposal as a "slippery slope" toward increased demands for home rule. Moments later, the chamber adopted the tripartite Kefauver-Holland-Keating Amendment by a margin of 70–12.[35]

The three-part resolution was then referred to the House Judiciary Committee, chaired by Manny Celler, the Brooklyn Democrat who by now had a long history in the trenches of amendment politics. Celler supported the twin goals of outlawing the poll tax and remedying the District's unequal political status. But he also considered himself a realist. The poll tax measure would go nowhere, he thought. He had similar misgivings over the prospect of securing representation for the District in Congress. So he took it upon himself to pare down the measure to provide only for presidential electors for the District of Columbia. Howard Smith, the segregationist chairman of the Rules Committee, praised Celler for stripping the measure "down to the one, as I regard it, noncontroversial question."[36] But an ally of Keating complained that "the base of the amendment . . . has been almost whittled away."[37]

Celler's revamped resolution provided that the District's presidential electors would be appointed "in such manner as the Congress may direct."[38] It also ensured that the District could never have more electors than the least populous state, effectively limiting its allotment of electoral votes to three. John Lindsay, a liberal Republican congressman from Manhattan's "silk stocking" district, took issue with this imposition of a "permanent inferior status upon the District's participation in the electoral college."[39] In the 1964 and 1968 elections, the cap made a difference, costing the District one electoral vote.[40] Based on its population today, the District would be entitled to no more than three electoral votes even without the constitutional limitation.

Expecting opposition from Southern lawmakers, Celler brought the measure up on a special rule limiting debate to two hours.[41] As he kicked off the discussion on June 14, 1960, the veteran congressman explained it was "not the intention" of the Framers to deny District residents the right to vote in presidential elections. The denial, he said, stemmed merely from "an oversight or omission on their part."[42] But Basil Whitener, a North Carolina Democrat known for his harangues against "this radical organization, the NAACP,"[43] insisted it was purposeful. Making clear his opposition to enfranchising those "fictional characters who, some would say, are being taxed without representation," Whitener offered a bizarre take on the Framers' intent, suggesting it was "contemplated that this territory . . . would be sort of a no-man's land."[44]

Liberal members also criticized the measure, focusing on its lack of ambition. "There is no doubt that this resolution is a step in the right direction, but I must emphasize that it is only one step," said Abraham Multer, a New York Democrat. "I hope that no one who supports this bill will pretend that by so doing he has done all that needs be done for the citizens of the District of Columbia."[45]

The *Detroit News* reported that the resolution passed the House "with only two hours of desultory debate and without a roll call."[46] With an adjournment looming, Keating conceded he had no choice but to accept Celler's revisions to his amendment, but in doing so, he made his displeasure clear: "I can only voice my sorrow because of the fact that we have missed this opportunity to bestow full citizenship rights on our fellow Americans, the residents of the District of Columbia."[47] Over the protest of two Southern Democrats, including Chairman James Eastland, the Senate approved the stripped-down House version of the amendment on a voice vote.[48] With little fanfare, the measure went to the state legislatures for ratification on June 16, 1960.

It took just over nine months to ratify the Twenty-Third Amendment— the swiftest pace of adoption since the Twelfth Amendment in 1804.[49] Hawaii, the newly admitted state with a majority nonwhite population, was the first to ratify, in solidarity with the increasingly diversifying District.[50] On March 29, 1961, lawmakers in Ohio, Kansas, and New Hampshire competed for the distinction of putting the measure over the top.[51] But the *Washington Post* noted that "close calls" in some legislative chambers made "clear that an Amendment broader than the presidential voting proposal would have met with possibly fatal opposition."[52] Indeed, the ratification campaign revealed a depressingly familiar sectional divide. Of the eleven states that failed to ratify the Twenty-Third Amendment, ten were former members of the Confederacy.[53] The *New York Times* noted the "heavy Southern opposition to enfranchising the District of Columbia because of its large Negro population."[54]

President John F. Kennedy hailed the amendment's speedy adoption as proof of the nation's belief that "all American citizens" deserve "the right to share in the election of those who govern us."[55] Later that year, the Joint Committee declared victory and shut down its operations after forty-seven years.[56] But the work of bringing democracy to the District was far from over.

On November 3, 1964, eager Washingtonians waited in long lines to cast ballots in the District's first presidential election in 164 years. The Democratic candidate, Lyndon Johnson, earned 85 percent of the vote that day, sweeping every election precinct in one of history's biggest landslides.[57] Since then, the District has invariably awarded its electoral votes to Democrats, even when Republicans have won the national vote by large margins.[58] Given this strong partisan bent, it seems remarkable that the Twenty-Third Amendment garnered the strong bipartisan support it did. However, Republicans were hardly elevating principle over party. When Congress proposed the measure in 1960, few foresaw that the District would become an impregnable Democratic stronghold. Indeed, as late as 1956, when District residents gained the right to vote in party conventions, turnout was almost evenly divided between the parties.[59] The GOP platform that year championed the District's right to "self-government, national suffrage and representation in the Congress," reflecting confidence that the party could compete for votes there.[60]

Two factors explain why Washington, DC, is bluer than any blue state today. First came a dramatic demographic shift. In 1950, whites outnumbered African Americans in the District by nearly two to one,[61] and made up an even greater share of its voting age population.[62] By 1960, however, the District's population was majority Black.[63] Second, the 1964 election marked the beginning of a party realignment that would transform national politics. Senator Barry Goldwater, the GOP's ultraconservative presidential nominee, alienated African Americans by his vote against the Civil Rights Act of 1964 and his criticism of the Warren Court's civil rights rulings. Over the following decades, as Republicans courted Southern white Democrats, African Americans and urban voters flocked to the Democrats.

But to focus solely on the racial and partisan politics misses the moral issue. The District of Columbia, a place that more than seven hundred thousand Americans call home, remains an outsider looking in on the American experiment. No other democracy excludes the citizens of its capital from representation in the national legislature.[64] On the day Washingtonians celebrated the ratification of the Twenty-Third Amendment, the *Washington Post* aptly called it "a beginning rather than an end."[65] The fight to advance democracy in the nation's capital would continue. Many political battles lay ahead—including yet another constitutional crusade—to bring the District more fully into the flawed governmental structure the Framers devised over two centuries ago.

The Twenty-Fourth Amendment: Abolishing the Poll Tax

The Twenty-Fourth Amendment was the second voting rights amendment of the 1960s, coming as the Civil Rights Movement tugged ever more insistently at the nation's conscience. On February 1, 1960, North Carolina A&T students Ezell Blair Jr., Franklin McCain, Joseph McNeil, and David Richmond sparked a nationwide sit-in movement after refusing to leave the segregated lunch counter at Woolworth's in downtown Greensboro.[66] Six-year-old Ruby Bridges endured hostile crowds screaming racial slurs that November, as she bravely climbed the steps of an all-white elementary school in New Orleans, escorted by federal marshals.[67] And on Mother's Day in 1961, the Freedom Riders—young activists, Black and white, traveling through the South to challenge segregated bus stations—were savagely attacked by violent mobs.[68]

The nation was on the cusp of a transformational moment: a Second Reconstruction. And yet despite the building force of a powerful social movement behind them, the framers of the Twenty-Fourth Amendment resisted the opportunity to achieve a more far-reaching reform. Instead, they settled on the decidedly narrow aim of banning the poll tax—a fee on the franchise that represented just one of many tactics employed to suppress the Black vote in the Jim Crow South. At the time, only five Southern states still imposed it, in amounts ranging from one to two dollars.[69]

The poll tax had a long history in American politics. Its debut, surprisingly enough, was tied to the *expansion* of voting rights. When the Constitution was adopted, most states allowed only male freeholders to vote. This property ownership requirement was rooted in the belief that voters should have an economic stake in their communities—and, of course, a warped conception of who actually contributed to the economy. It was a conviction shared by most of the Constitution's drafters. "Give the votes to people who have no property," warned Gouveneur Morris, "and they will sell them to the rich who will be able to buy them."[70] As a growing class of merchants and manufacturers fueled the prosperity of burgeoning cities and towns, states began to relax their rules for voting. New Hampshire's 1784 constitution led the way, permitting any man who paid a poll tax to vote. Derived from an old English word meaning tax per head or "capitation tax," it was not, as one might assume, a fee assessed at a polling place. Instead, a would-be voter had to pay the levy before casting his vote. Other states followed the Granite State's lead in tying voting rights to the payment of a poll tax. But by the mid-nineteenth century, amid the Jacksonian Era expansion of the franchise to all white men, most states eliminated these requirements altogether. By the end of the Civil War, only three states—all in the North—still maintained a poll tax.[71]

Within the next few decades, however, Southern states resurrected the poll tax as they looked for ways to disenfranchise African Americans without violating the Fifteenth Amendment. The delegates to Alabama's 1901 constitutional convention were transparent about their aims. "What [it is] that we do want to do," explained John Knox, the presiding officer, "is, within the limits imposed by the federal Constitution, to establish white supremacy in this State."[72] On their face, most of these new restrictions— poll taxes, literacy tests, laws disenfranchising persons convicted of crimes involving moral turpitude—were race-neutral. But in legislative records replete with racist language, the laws' sponsors made their intentions abundantly clear. By 1908, the constitutions of the eleven states of the old Confederacy all authorized a poll tax.[73] The income it generated was typically earmarked for public schools, veiling its true intent. As expected, the tax depressed the participation of Black voters, who were disproportionately poor. After Florida imposed a two-dollar fee in 1889 (the equivalent of fifty-seven dollars in 2021),[74] voter turnout plummeted from 78.2 percent in the 1888 presidential election to 35.5 percent four years later.[75]

For decades, the Supreme Court was complicit in maintaining the Jim Crow regime, upholding discriminatory voting measures as constitutional if it could be argued, however implausibly, that they did not target a person's "race, color or previous condition of servitude." Time and again, the justices ignored the true intent and impact of these laws, callously indifferent to the systematic violence and intimidation that accompanied them. Only in the first half of the twentieth century did the Court begin to apply greater scrutiny to the most flagrantly discriminatory practices, such as grandfather clauses and white primaries.[76] But in *Breedlove v. Suttles*, a 1937 challenge brought by a white litigant, the justices upheld Georgia's poll tax as a proper exercise of its powers.[77] "The payment of poll taxes as a prerequisite for voting is a familiar and reasonable regulation long enforced in many states," said a unanimous Court. And since the "privilege of voting" is not derived from the Constitution, "the state may condition suffrage as it deems appropriate."[78]

A decade later, President Harry Truman's Committee on Civil Rights took a less sanguine view of the poll tax. In an October 1947 report, it identified the poll tax as an "important legal obstacle to full suffrage in some southern states." While the tax "limits white as well as Negro suffrage," the report noted, it "frequently had an unequal racial effect." Calling the poll "very effective as an anti-Negro device,"[79] the committee concluded it would be "appropriate and encouraging" for the remaining poll tax states to outlaw the practice. Should they fail to repeal their laws, the committee urged Congress to address the problem by statute or constitutional amendment.[80]

One senator was ready to heed the committee's call to remove "this final barrier to universal suffrage."[81] He was an unlikely champion, to say the least. Spessard Holland came to Washington in 1946, appointed to fill a vacant Senate seat. That same year, the Florida Democrat won election to a full term in his own right. For the former scholar-athlete who was scouted to play professional baseball, it was the crowning accomplishment in a storied career that included stints as county prosecutor, judge, state senator, and governor.[82]

Early in his political career, Holland embraced the elimination of the poll tax as a signature issue. In 1937, in only his second term in the Florida legislature, he led a campaign to repeal the state's half-century old law.

Then in 1949, not long after he arrived on Capitol Hill, Holland introduced a constitutional amendment to abolish the poll tax nationwide. The measure was opposed by a clique of powerful Southern Democrats who gained their clout through voter suppression devices like the poll tax. In those days, lawmakers from the region were elected and reliably re-elected by just a fraction of their voting-age constituencies. The average voter turnout in poll tax states was a paltry 3 percent.[83] With increased seniority came the coveted committee chairmanships, offering control of the legislative process and the power to squash reforms that might threaten their primacy.[84] In this way, the poll tax proved self-reinforcing.

After he failed to get a hearing, Holland dutifully reintroduced his poll tax amendment in every Congress.[85] From his sheer doggedness, one might imagine that he was a civil rights trailblazer. In reality, it was just the opposite. Throughout his long career, Spessard Holland was an avowed segregationist. In 1956, he signed the Southern Manifesto, the racist screed endorsed by a hundred federal lawmakers urging "all lawful means" to resist the desegregation mandate of *Brown v. Board of Education*. Poll tax aside, Holland was a reliable vote against every civil rights measure to come before Congress.[86]

Publicly, Holland offered two explanations for his stance on the poll tax. First, he believed a fee tied to voting allowed corrupt machine politicians to gain office through vote buying.[87] Second, he maintained that repeal would promote "sound democracy" by increasing voter participation.[88] "I realized that many good people were deprived of their privilege of voting by reason of the existence and enforcement of the poll tax provision," he explained.[89] Of course, by "good people" he meant white people.[90] By 1942, due to demographic changes, for every *three* African Americans the poll tax kept from the ballot, *five* white Americans were also disenfranchised.[91]

Between 1942 and 1949, the House passed legislation to ban the poll tax in federal elections on five occasions, only to see the bills die in the Senate.[92] For his part, Holland insisted that a constitutional amendment was necessary to eliminate the practice. Was he right? The answer hangs on a fine point of constitutional interpretation. While the Constitution empowers the states to determine voter "qualifications," subject to limits imposed later by constitutional amendment,[93] it gives Congress broad authority to override state laws regulating the "times, places and manner" of holding federal elections.[94] The question for lawmakers was whether payment of a poll tax was a qualification left to the states' discretion, or a regulation subject to congressional review.

Holland thought it "so completely clear" that the Framers understood "qualifications" to include requirements like the payment of a poll tax or ownership of property.[95] But the senator also wanted to avoid what he perceived to be a dangerous precedent. If a simple majority in Congress could override state poll tax laws through passage of a statute, it would surely invite further federal interference through "unconstitutional and coercive means."[96] The National Association for the Advancement of Colored People criticized Holland's amendment as "an unnecessarily cumbersome approach to the problem." Clarence Mitchell Jr., the group's Washington bureau director, testified that resorting to the Article V process would set a "bad precedent," because it might appear to concede "that a law passed by Congress would be unconstitutional."[97] Calling Holland's amendment "a travesty," the NAACP and six other civil rights organizations insisted on the "immediate abolition of the tax through federal legislation."[98]

Holland also faced an unyielding foe in his fellow Southerner James Eastland, who used his power as chairman to bottle the measure up. As far back as his first Senate campaign in 1942, Eastland lauded the poll tax as the "surest safeguard of white Democratic supremacy."[99] Finally, in February 1960, Holland found a means of bypassing Eastland by attaching his proposal to the Kefauver continuity of Congress amendment.[100] Despite warnings from segregationists that the poll tax amendment would "enable the federal government to completely control all elections in the United States,"[101] the measure gained the approval of seventy-two senators. But just four months later, Holland saw his victory slip away in the House when Manny Celler pared down the proposal to the measure later adopted as the Twenty-Third Amendment. Holland took the setback in stride, however. "I am willing to wait another year," he told his colleagues. "I would rather do that than defeat another good effort in its chance to be submitted to the 50 states."[102]

In the next Congress, Holland came armed with sixty-seven cosponsors, enough to guarantee passage in the upper house.[103] But once again, he would have to do battle with Eastland and other Southern senators who benefited from the mass disenfranchisement of Black people. At the time, the ten states with the lowest voter participation were all located in the South, and Mississippi was at the very bottom.[104] Still, John Stennis, the state's junior senator, insisted that "voting should be *further* restricted instead of being enlarged." [105]

Knowing his proposal would never get fair consideration in Eastland's committee, Holland struck a deal with the sponsors of a new legislative host: an uncontroversial bill to designate Alexander Hamilton's Harlem estate as a national monument.[106] The extraordinary maneuver provoked heated argument on the Senate floor. Richard Russell, the Georgia segregationist whose name adorns a Senate office building to this day, claimed he could not fathom how "the oldest tax known to mankind" got caught up in the civil rights struggle.[107] "I realize that a little matter like the Constitution is worthy of very short shrift when we become involved in one of the so-called civil rights bills," he sniped.[108] Not to be outdone, Eastland condemned the proposal as "a Hitler-type measure" that threatened to "destroy the rights of the people in their own community to determine their own affairs, which is the very basis of American liberty." [109]

In what onlookers called the "friendly filibuster," fifteen Southern senators held the chamber captive for eleven days.[110] In an era known for its bitter obstructionist tactics, this one seemed different, however.[111] A reporter described "a passionless struggle, suggesting a match between leaden-footed boxers with pillows over their fists instead of boxing gloves." [112] After a week and a half of complaints about the process—the use of the Hamilton bill amounted to a "wholly unconstitutional" procedure, the chamber had engineered "a third method of amending the Constitution"—the tepid talkathon ran out of steam. Holland's resolution survived.[113]

President Kennedy announced his support for the amendment, extolling it as "an important contribution to good government." [114] But Holland still had to overcome opposition from liberals who questioned the wisdom of pursuing the more arduous path of securing a constitutional amendment. Jacob Javits, a Republican senator from New York, reminded his allies that the Twenty-Third Amendment had only barely won ratification the year before. "A provision outlawing the poll tax is more likely to be enacted this time as a statute than as a constitutional amendment," he advised.[115] But on this question of strategy the Senate majority leader sided with Holland. A statute, said Senator Mike Mansfield of Montana, would face legal challenges "certain to delay" the final abolition of the poll tax.[116] With Mansfield's influential endorsement, the Senate approved Holland's poll tax amendment on March 27 by a vote of 77–16. Notably, 8 senators from the South broke ranks to support the measure.[117]

As Holland's measure moved back to the House, he faced a new antag-onist in Virginia's Howard Smith, the powerful chair of the Rules Com-mittee.[118] A *New York Times* profile called him "the second most powerful man in the House," after the speaker. "A dedicated conservative, Smith has killed, watered down or postponed more progressive legislation than any other Congressman in modern times."[119] True to form, the Virginian blocked the amendment for six months. To pry it free, Manny Celler forced the poll tax measure to the floor under a suspension of the normal rules.[120] In a truncated debate, each side was limited to twenty minutes.

Southern members condemned the measure as an undue intrusion on the prerogatives of the states. Said one Georgia Democrat: "I cannot believe any good will be accomplished by striking down the rights of the States to levy a poll tax for the purpose of trying to cure an imaginary ill nurtured by minority groups."[121] While proponents hailed the elimination of an un-warranted burden on the right to vote,[122] liberal Manhattan Republican John Lindsay dismissed the "sugar-coated proposition" as a meaningless exercise.[123] "This is using a sledge hammer, a giant cannon, in order to kill a gnat," Lindsay fumed. "If we are going to amend the Constitution, the amendment ought to be meaningful." In his estimation, it should "do away with *all* obstructions to the right to vote."[124] But on August 27, Lindsay voted for the measure "with a heavy heart,"[125] and the House approved the amendment in a bipartisan vote of 294–86.[126] Voting no were 71 Southern Democrats.

It took seventeen months to ratify the Twenty-Fourth Amendment. Florida and Tennessee were the only Southern states to approve it. At a February 1964 signing ceremony to celebrate its adoption, President Lyn-don Johnson declared, "There can now be no one too poor to vote."[127] But defiant officials in Mississippi and Alabama had already begun the compli-cated process of setting up two voter registration systems, one for federal contests and one for state and local elections not covered by the amend-ment.[128] Virginia also sought to circumvent the amendment through a revised poll tax law. But for the most part, the nation greeted the Twenty-Fourth Amendment with a yawn as events rapidly outpaced its modest ambitions.

In August 1963, some 250,000 Americans came together before the Lin-coln Memorial to protest the unequal treatment of African Americans a full century after emancipation. The event highlighted the need for more muscular civil rights protections. The assassination of President Kennedy later that year created an opportunity. While Kennedy had moved cautiously to avoid antagonizing the Southern wing of his party, Johnson—a Southerner himself—felt free to take bolder action. During his first months in office, the new president successfully pushed for the passage of the Civil Rights Act of 1964, overcoming the longest filibuster in Senate history. The Act's constitutionality emerged as a major campaign issue that fall. The GOP standard bearer, Arizona senator Barry Goldwater, voted against the measure, charging that its prohibitions against racial discrimination in employment and public accommodations "fly in the face of the Constitution." [129] When Johnson prevailed, winning a new term in a rout, he took it as a mandate for a racial equality agenda. [130]

After the election, the Johnson administration considered pushing for a constitutional amendment guaranteeing the right to vote. But like Franklin Roosevelt before him, Johnson decided against this course, pressing instead for the adoption of a robust statute, the Voting Rights Act of 1965. [131] Signing the measure into law, Johnson hailed it as "a triumph for freedom as huge as any victory that has ever been won on any battlefield." [132] As civil rights leaders predicted, the measure's opponents cited the "precedent" of the Twenty-Fourth Amendment as proof that a constitutional amendment was the only "proper course" to protect African American voting rights. [133] An ornery James Eastland insisted that the adoption of the Twenty-Fourth Amendment "had forever laid to rest the theory that these state qualifications could be abolished by any another method." [134] Back in the segregationist fold, Spessard Holland joined in denouncing the Act as the "suspension of constitutional rights of sovereign states." [135]

Because Congress limited the amendment's reach to federal elections, it fell to the Supreme Court to take the final step. In *Harper v. Virginia State Board of Elections*, a 1966 decision, the Court repudiated its holding in *Breedlove* to outlaw the poll tax in state and local elections. "A State violates the Equal Protection Clause of the Fourteenth Amendment whenever it makes the affluence of the voter or payment of any fee an electoral standard," the justices proclaimed. "To introduce wealth or payment of a fee as a measure of a voter's qualifications is to introduce a capricious or irrelevant factor." [136] Not once did they mention the newly adopted amendment.

The Twenty-Fourth Amendment lacked the ambition that characterized its Reconstruction era counterparts and the Voting Rights Act that followed it. To be sure, the amendment removed an unjustified barrier to the ballot. To that end, it advanced our Constitution's trajectory toward a more inclusive democracy. Some argue that the amendment has new relevance today as states devise ever more creative ways to link voting to the payment of a fee, from voter ID laws to requirements that formerly incarcerated people pay off fines before they can have their voting rights restored.[137] ACLU president and law professor Deborah Archer argues that the amendment can be "a tool to ensure voting fairness," urging the development of "a Twenty-Fourth Amendment jurisprudence that protects the right to vote of low-income citizens."[138]

The Twenty-Fifth Amendment: Presidential Succession and Incapacity

The assassination of President Kennedy on November 22, 1963, was the eighth time a president died in office. A famous photo captured a pivotal moment in the shooting's aftermath. In a solemn scene, Lyndon Johnson took the presidential oath of office aboard *Air Force One*, flanked by the slain president's grief-stricken widow, still wearing her bloodstained pink Chanel suit. The photo assured a country in mourning that a peaceful and lawful transfer of power had occurred. And yet, the events of that awful day, and the many what-ifs surrounding it, forced the nation to confront important, unresolved questions about presidential succession and inability. Though few doubted Johnson's legitimacy as president, legal scholars knew that a close reading of the Constitution raised some unnerving questions. What if Kennedy had lingered in a coma instead of dying, with an uncertain prognosis, unable to function as president for the remainder of his term? Or what if Johnson, who was following Kennedy in the Dallas motorcade, had also been wounded? Like many crucial choices the Framers made regarding the leader of the executive branch, the answer to these questions revealed a troubling lack of forethought.

The Framers addressed the topic of presidential succession and incapacity in Article II of the Constitution. With ambiguously placed commas, the 1787 Constitution provided: "In case of the removal of the President from office, or of his death, resignation, or inability to discharge the powers and duties of the said office, the same shall devolve on the Vice President."[139] But what did they mean by "the same?" Did the vice president inherit the office of the president? Or did he merely assume its powers and duties? Because the vice presidency was something of an afterthought at the Philadelphia Convention, invented only in the gathering's final weeks, the historical record offers little guidance.[140]

Americans had little reason to ponder these questions until 1841, when William Henry Harrison died a month into the job, leaving the office vacant for the first time. Harrison's vice president, John Tyler, rushed back to the capital to take the reins of government. When the late president's cabinet proposed that Tyler assume the title "Vice-President, acting president," Tyler boldly rejected the offer. "I shall be pleased to avail myself of your counsel and advice," he told them. "But I can never consent to being dictated to as to what I shall or shall not do."[141] Tyler took the presidential oath of office in their presence and delivered an inaugural address three days later.[142] "For the first time in our history," he declared, "the person elected to the Vice-Presidency of the United States, by happening of a contingency provided for in the Constitution, has had devolved upon him the Presidential office."[143]

John Quincy Adams took umbrage at the man's audacity. "Mr. Tyler . . . styles himself President of the United States, and not Vice-President, acting as President, which would be the correct style," said the former president."[144] Though both houses of Congress passed resolutions affirming his status as president, Tyler's opponents mocked him as "His Accidency."[145] Upon his death in 1862, after his defection to the Confederate cause, an obituary remembered Tyler as "the most unpopular public man that had ever held any office in the United States."[146] But the Tyler Precedent took hold. Over the next 125 years, seven other vice presidents—Millard Fillmore (1850), Andrew Johnson (1865), Chester Arthur (1881), Theodore Roosevelt (1901), Calvin Coolidge (1923), Harry Truman (1945), and Lyndon Johnson (1963)—succeeded to the office without controversy following the death of a duly elected president.

It was widely accepted that Johnson was now in command, yet the hypotheticals kept swirling. What if President Kennedy had not died that day but remained in an unresponsive state: unable to resign, much less govern? And what if doctors disagreed over the likelihood of his recovery? The original Constitution specified that the vice president takes over when the president is unable "to discharge the powers and duties of the said office." It also gave Congress authority to pass laws governing succession in cases of presidential "inability."[147] Yet in those very situations, history reveals an alarming pattern of indecision and uncertainty.

In 1881, President James Garfield was shot in the back by a mentally unbalanced political aspirant. The wounded president declined slowly over eighty long days, unable to perform his duties.[148] Some urged Vice President Chester Arthur to take the helm, but he hesitated for fear of being labeled a usurper (an understandable concern, given that the deranged assailant proclaimed "Arthur will be president!" upon his arrest).[149] Rebuffed in his attempts to learn more about Garfield's condition, Arthur traveled to New York City, where he remained isolated in his Lexington Avenue home until the president died.[150]

After Woodrow Wilson suffered two debilitating strokes in 1919,[151] the partially paralyzed president remained in isolation for seventeen months of convalescence. During that time, First Lady Edith Wilson informally assumed responsibility for running the government. Though she humbly referred to it as mere "stewardship,"[152] others warned of "petticoat government."[153] When Wilson's secretary of state assembled the cabinet to discuss the president's condition, he was abruptly terminated.[154] All the while, Vice President Thomas Marshall was kept from learning about Wilson's condition. Cowed by a president who dismissed him privately as a "small-caliber man," Marshall later confessed, "I was afraid to ask about it for fear some censorious soul would accuse me to a longing for his place."[155]

Garfield and Wilson disliked their vice presidents and preferred to keep them at arm's length. But in the Nuclear Age, that was no longer an option. America needed a fully functioning president at all times. So while Dwight Eisenhower had no great fondness for his own second in command, a series of health scares—including a stroke that left him briefly unable to speak or move his hand[156]—convinced him to make "specific arrangements" with his vice president, Richard Nixon.[157] In a letter, the men memorialized a "clear understanding" that Nixon would serve temporarily as acting president in such cases. But was their agreement constitutional? Nixon believed the letter constituted nothing more than "mere expressions of a President's desires," lacking "the force of law."[158] Nevertheless, their informal arrangement established another key precedent, one that helped shape what would become the Twenty-Fifth Amendment.

Once Lyndon Johnson was sworn in as president, he faced a more pressing concern: the absence of a vice president ready to step in should something happen to him. In their lack of foresight, the Framers failed to provide a means of replacing the vice president when the office becomes unoccupied. Remarkably, there were sixteen vice-presidential vacancies between 1789 and 1963. Eight ascended to the presidency, seven died in office, and one resigned to become a senator. Altogether, the position was left unoccupied for 37 years—an astounding one-fifth of the period since John Adams took the first vice-presidential oath.[159] For more than one-third of that time, the person next in the line of succession was of a different party than the president.[160]

For much of American history, the vice presidency mattered little. John Adams famously bemoaned it as "the most insignificant office that ever the invention of man contrived or his imagination conceived."[161] A century and a half later, John Nance Garner, who served under Franklin Roosevelt, more crassly complained that the office was "not worth a warm bucket of piss."[162] Experts considered it an "electoral expedient," a "useless appendage," or even a "constitutional mistake."[163] But over time, an office long perceived as irrelevant became ever more consequential. With the vast expansion of the federal bureaucracy in the twentieth century, presidents tasked their vice presidents with policy portfolios and other management duties.[164] As a 1964 Senate report concluded, "The office of the Vice President has become one of the most important positions in our country. . . . He has come to share and participate in the executive functioning of our Government, so that in the event of tragedy, there would be no break in the informed exercise of executive authority."[165]

Over the fourteen-month gap between November 1963 and the swearing in of a new vice president in January 1965, the man "a heartbeat away" from the presidency was Boston's John McCormack. News accounts described the seventy-one-year-old Speaker of the House as "a tall, gaunt, white-haired man" who "appears frail." Next in line after McCormack was Senator Carl Hayden, "a scrawny, stooped, 6-footer" from Arizona. Hayden, the Senate's president pro tempore, was portrayed as a "feeble" man "whose 86 years would suggest that Speaker McCormack is a mere boy."[166] Their places in the line of succession were determined by a 1947 law, passed under a provision of the Constitution authorizing Congress to decide who becomes president when the top two offices are vacant.[167] Between them, these "two congressional oldsters"[168] had nearly ninety years of Capitol Hill experience. One sharp-tongued commentator quipped that their place in line made "it necessary to pray nightly for the safekeeping of President Johnson" but, until the election, "sophisticated Americans will live in quiet terror."[169]

Days after Kennedy's assassination, the "two old timers" sat behind

President Johnson as he delivered an address to a joint session of Congress. "All I have I would have given gladly not to be standing here today," Johnson told a reeling nation. The new president vowed to turn his predecessor's "ideas and ideals . . . into effective action," starting with the "earliest possible passage" of civil rights legislation.[170]

Sitting in the audience, distracted by the optics, was Senator Birch Bayh. He'd been only ten months on job. When Estes Kefauver died unexpectedly that summer, the thirty-five-year-old "eager beaver from Indiana" lobbied James Eastland for the chairmanship of the subcommittee on constitutional amendments.[171] Described in a newspaper profile as "tall, handsome, rugged and dimpled," with a manner that evoked "a blend of 'Madison Avenue with the Midwestern outstretched hand and so glad to see you,'" the former high school debater and tomato growing champion from Terre Haute rose quickly in Hoosier State politics.[172] The Framers envisioned an "energetic" executive, Bayh thought.[173] Now more than ever, the country needed one. At fifty-five years old, Johnson may have fit the bill, but what about the two geriatric leaders sitting behind him? Were Johnson's presidency to be cut short, and McCormack or Hayden obliged to take the reins, either man would easily be the oldest to ever take the oath of office. And unlike Johnson, neither man was ever vetted for the role.

Two weeks after Johnson's address, Bayh introduced a comprehensive proposal to remedy the Constitution's gaps related to presidential succession and disability.[174] "Every reason and logic and sound organization calls upon us to deal simultaneously with the questions of death, resignation, removal, or inability," he declared. "Now is clearly the time to act—while the question of Presidential succession is uppermost in our minds."[175] To Bayh's relief, the response was positive. But first, lawmakers would have to sift through more than six dozen competing proposals. Although there was wide agreement on the need for an amendment, it would take a year and a half of legislative wrangling to hammer out the details. Throughout the process, the Indiana senator was "ever the driving force."[176]

From the outset, Bayh received crucial assistance from the American Bar Association. In January 1964, the nation's largest lawyers' organization established a Conference on Presidential Inability and Vice-Presidential Vacancy that convened experts to examine the many thorny problems and offer recommendations. Among its members was twenty-seven-year-old John Feerick, a recent graduate of Fordham Law School. As a student,

Feerick had written an article on presidential inability, which sufficed to make him one of the nation's leading authorities on the subject.[177] Apart from Bayh, no one would receive more credit for the amendment's realization.[178]

With significant input from many other lawmakers and experts, the two men led the effort to fashion a constitutional proposal. As finally adopted, the Twenty-Fifth Amendment is divided into four distinct sections addressing the interconnected topics of presidential succession, vice-presidential vacancies, and presidential inability.

Section 1 affirms the Tyler Precedent. Simply put, in the event of a presidential vacancy, the vice president becomes president. Since the amendment's adoption, this provision has been invoked only once. When Richard Nixon resigned in disgrace in August 1974, Vice President Gerald Ford unequivocally assumed the office of president.

Section 2 establishes a process for filling vice-presidential vacancies. Whenever that office is vacant, the president may nominate a replacement subject to confirmation by both houses of Congress. (Lawmakers rejected an alternative proposal to reconvene the Electoral College to make the decision.) This second provision has been invoked twice. After Vice President Spiro Agnew resigned in October 1973 under a cloud of fraud and corruption allegations, Richard Nixon nominated House Minority Leader Gerald Ford to take his place. Ten months later, when the office again became vacant, President Ford chose former New York governor Nelson Rockefeller for the number-two position. Had the amendment not been adopted, Nixon would have been succeeded by Democratic Speaker of the House Carl Albert.

Section 3 sets out an orderly way for a president to temporarily hand over power to the vice president, drawing on the informal arrangement devised by Dwight Eisenhower and Richard Nixon. Under this procedure, the president may submit a written declaration to congressional leaders notifying them of an inability to discharge the powers and duties of the office. Once submitted, the vice president becomes acting president until the president reclaims those powers through another written declaration. On three occasions, presidents have used this mechanism to transfer power for a few hours while undergoing planned surgery or medical tests.[179] Notably, it was not invoked in the aftermath of the 1981 shooting that nearly killed Ronald Reagan—the most serious episode of presidential inability since the amendment's adoption. Administration officials feared it would cause alarm.[180] Shortly after Reagan left office, the White House physician expressed regret for the failure to act: "If ever there was a time to use it, that was it."[181]

Section 4, by far the most complicated provision, sets forth a detailed process for high-stakes situations in which a chief executive cannot or will not acknowledge an inability to perform presidential duties. Lawmakers crafted this section for emergencies in which a president is unconscious, unavailable, or unable to make an appropriate judgment due to a serious impairment. In such circumstances, the vice president and Cabinet officers (or "such other body as Congress may by law provide") may declare the president incapacitated by a simple majority vote. Once they convey that judgment in writing to congressional leaders, the vice president assumes the role of acting president. The president can move to reclaim power through a separate written declaration. If there is a dispute between the two officials, Congress has twenty-one days to decide. It then takes a two-thirds majority vote in each chamber to keep the vice president in the role of acting president. Otherwise, the president resumes office.

To anticipate the full range of these scenarios, the text of the Twenty-Fifth Amendment required specificity more typical of statutes and regulations than constitutional amendments. Some lawmakers preferred a less prescriptive amendment authorizing Congress to address these questions through ordinary legislation, but Bayh was able to persuade his colleagues to adopt a more comprehensive approach.

The Senate moved quickly to approve an early iteration of the amendment in September 1964.[182] But given the media frenzy over Speaker McCormack's fitness for the presidency, Bayh knew the measure was unlikely to advance in the House of Representatives in the weeks before the election. As *Newsweek* reported, "Nobody in Congress or the Administration is willing to hurt McCormack's feelings."[183] So Bayh reintroduced his proposal in January 1965, after the election of a new vice president dislodged McCormack from his place as first in the line of succession. In a special message to Congress, President Johnson called for swift action. "While we are prepared for the possibility of a president's death," Johnson said, "we are all but defenseless against the probability of a president's incapacity by injury, illness, senility or other affliction."[184] To help build public support, the new ABA president (and future Supreme Court justice) Lewis Powell declared that the lawyers' association would "throw our full weight" behind the campaign.[185]

The debate in the Senate centered on an alternative proposal introduced by the Republican minority leader, Everett Dirksen. Like Bayh, Dirksen had an abiding interest in constitutional amendments. Over the years, in recurring bouts of what one scholar calls "erratic constitutionalism," the Illinois senator championed dozens of proposals—repealing the Sixteenth Amendment, overturning the Supreme Court's rulings on prayer in public schools, authorizing war by popular referendum—"to further his passion of the moment." [186] Dirksen's enduring anger over the Court's "one person, one vote" rulings, which invalidated legislative apportionment plans that unfairly favored rural voters, drove him to orchestrate a controversial campaign that very nearly summoned the first-ever Article V convention.[187]

Dirksen proposed a simpler amendment to give Congress the power to pass laws governing presidential disability. "This can be handled by a statute and rightly should be," Dirksen insisted. "It removes the fear that we may embed in the Constitution procedures which may not turn out to be workable." [188] Echoing that sentiment, Eugene McCarthy, a liberal Democrat representing Minnesota, argued that Constitution drew power from its "broad statement of powers and principles" and should not be "weighed down with detailed procedural provisions." [189] It was left to Sam Ervin, a conservative Democrat from North Carolina, to defend Bayh's approach. A Harvard-educated attorney who cultivated a folksy persona as "an ol' country lawyer," [190] Ervin was, according to one chronicler, "a bundle of paradoxes." He was "always in the forefront of Southern opposition to any civil rights bill" yet "easily the Senate's most outspoken champion of civil liberties." [191] Ervin argued that allowing a simple majority of legislators to establish procedures for declaring presidential disability "would place dangerous power in the hands of Congress." To illustrate his point, Ervin recalled the impeachment of President Andrew Johnson or, as he put it, "the tragic days" when the Radical Republicans sought "to take complete power in this nation" following the Civil War. The supermajority requirement for conviction "that saved Andrew Johnson" was also necessary for controversies over presidential inability. Otherwise, he said, "power-hungry men in Congress . . . could take charge of the presidency" by simply passing a statute.[192] In the end, Dirksen's proposal received only twelve votes.[193] Despite lingering questions from a handful of senators, the chamber voted unanimously to approve the Bayh resolution on February 19, 1965.[194]

After wading through nearly three dozen measures related to inability and succession, the House advanced its own version of the amendment on April 13, introducing three significant changes.[195] For clarity's sake, the House bill established Section 3 as a standalone provision. And to ensure that disputes over a president's fitness were adjudicated fairly, the lawmakers added two procedural safeguards to Section 4: requiring that the Cabinet or a congressionally created commission concur with the vice president's declaration of inability and imposing a ten-day time limit to resolve the matter.[196] A conference committee charged with ironing out the final details continued to grapple with the question of a time limit. Striking a balance between the need to gather all necessary facts and the need to move expeditiously, the conferees gave Congress twenty-one days to resolve disputes over any president's inability.[197] The *New York Times*'s editorial board warned it was "a dangerously long period for the nation to be leaderless."[198]

With these final tweaks, the House approved the resolution on June 30.[199] But as Bayh pressed for a final vote in the Senate, the measure encountered new snags that delayed the measure for another week. Albert Gore Sr., a Democrat from Tennessee, probed ambiguities relating to Congress's power to appoint a body to decide whether a president was unfit. And New York's Robert Kennedy, the martyred president's brother, worried about the prospect of two presidents and two cabinets vying for power.[200] Finally, Sam Ervin urged his colleagues to act. The proposal represented "an amalgamation of views . . . which may not satisfy any of its proponents entirely," he acknowledged,[201] but it was "the very best possible resolution on the subject obtainable."[202] After a few more objections were raised, the Senate approved it by a vote of 68–5.[203]

With the support of Congress secured at last, the proposal was sent to the states. Once again, the ABA played a crucial role. As Bayh recalled, state bar leaders "began to bombard the state legislators with information," mobilizing the support of opinion leaders in each state.[204] Bayh personally threw himself into the time-consuming task of lobbying state lawmakers.[205] Facing little opposition, the campaign convinced thirty legislatures to ratify the amendment within a year. Minnesota and Nevada put the measure over the top on February 10, 1967.[206] "It's a happy day," said Bayh. "A constitutional gap that has existed for almost two centuries has finally been filled."[207] By May of that year, forty-seven states ratified the amendment.[208]

The Twenty-Fifth Amendment stands out for its length and complexity: only the Twelfth and Fourteenth Amendments are longer. Like the Twelfth and Twentieth Amendments, it was adopted to fix flaws in the operation of the executive branch exposed through the experience of governance. As constitutional scholar Brian Kalt notes, the amendment "was not a response to a surging political movement," as so many others were. "It was just a good idea whose time had come."[209] Eisenhower's health scares and Kennedy's untimely death, coming in quick succession, created a rare consensus in favor of action.

The amendment is also a testament to the tenacity of Birch Bayh, whose extraordinary leadership was indispensable to its adoption. Bayh readily conceded that the amendment was "not perfect." For all its complexity, it does not address every imaginable what-if related to presidential succession and disability. In one glaring omission, the amendment fails to deal with vice-presidential inability. The amendment's drafters knew full well they were leaving gaps. They further understood that the amendment's operation depended on the good faith of key participants. However, the only alternative was to craft an even longer and more complicated amendment.[210] As Speaker John McCormack argued when he spoke out at last in favor of the measure, "We cannot legislate for every human consideration that might occur in the future."[211]

While the amendment's path to adoption was slowed by concerns that it could be abused to subvert the will of the people, the first big test of the Twenty-Fifth Amendment suggests that concerns over intrigue and self-dealing may have been overblown. When Vice President Agnew resigned to avoid criminal prosecution amid the cascading scandals of Watergate, the Democratic leadership in Congress resisted calls to "get control and keep control" by keeping the position vacant. Instead, lawmakers acted in a bipartisan fashion to confirm a replacement, placing a Republican vice president in the line of succession ahead of the Democratic Speaker of the House.[212]

More recently, the tumultuous presidency of Donald Trump inspired bouts of fevered speculation about the possibility of invoking the Twenty-Fifth Amendment to hasten the removal of an unfit president.[213] According to news reports, administration insiders were troubled enough by the behavior of the self-described "very stable genius" to seriously ponder this option near the start of his term.[214] Then, after Trump incited the January 2021 insurrection at the U.S. Capitol, the House of Representatives passed a resolution calling on the vice president to remove him due to his "absolute inability to discharge the most basic and fundamental powers and duties of his office."[215] But the inability provision in Section 4 was a poor fit. It was intended to provide a means of removing a president who becomes severely incapacitated, not of undoing the last election. To be sure, misconduct and maladministration are grave issues that raise important questions about a president's suitability for the nation's highest office. As we also learned during the Trump years, the constitutional remedy for that is impeachment.[216]

The Twenty-Sixth Amendment: Youth Voting

Until the middle of the twentieth century, Americans voted when they reached the age of twenty-one. Though the Constitution allows each state to set its own voter qualifications, the practice was remarkably uniform. Few people gave it much thought.[217] The Twenty-Sixth Amendment changed all that. Adopted *and* ratified in 1971, it set a nationwide minimum voting age of eighteen for federal and state elections. The third constitutional revision to expand voting rights in less than a dozen years, its story began nearly three decades earlier in the months following the attack on Pearl Harbor.

In November 1942, with the nation firmly on a war footing, Congress lowered the draft age from twenty years old to eighteen. The move prompted a flurry of proposals to reset the voting age by constitutional amendment.[218] For Congressman Jennings Randolph, a former newspaperman who came to Washington in 1933 as a New Deal Democrat, it was a matter of simple justice. Like his namesake, the populist icon William Jennings Bryan, the West Virginia Democrat excelled as "an old-style orator."[219] Introducing his proposal to members of a House subcommittee, Randolph delivered a set of sobering statistics: Americans between the ages of eighteen and twenty comprised one-quarter of the army, one-third of the navy, and fully one-half of the marine corps. Extolling the heroism of young soldiers who died fighting in the deserts of North Africa and "the agonizing fog-bound island of Attu," Randolph asked, "Who shall say: they were not old enough to have been voting citizens of the America for which they gave their lives?"[220]

Randolph's proposal sank without a ripple that year, but the congressman had found a cause. Over the next three decades, he promoted his pet amendment at every opportunity. It jostled for attention among more than 150 similar measures introduced in Congress between 1942 and 1970.[221] Randolph patterned his amendment after anti-discrimination language of the Fifteenth and Nineteenth Amendments: "The rights of citizens of the United States, who are eighteen years of age or older, to vote shall not be denied or abridged by the United States or by any state on account of age." Congress would adopt the amendment in that exact form twenty-nine years later.

For years, the push to lower the voting age remained a low-priority issue, bubbling to the surface from time to time. In his 1954 State of the Union Address, President Eisenhower prodded Congress to approve it. Like Randolph, the general-turned-politician viewed the youth voting issue through the lens of military service. "Our citizens between the ages of 18 and 21" had been regularly "summoned to fight for America," the president said. "They should participate in the political process that produces this fateful summons."[222] That May, in what the New York Times called a "rather mild and bungling drive," Senate Republicans brought the measure up for a vote. In a debate marked by "Southern bitterness," just four days after the Supreme Court's explosive ruling in Brown v. Board of Education, senators from the region assailed the measure as an intrusion on states' rights. After the measure went down to defeat, the editors of the Times questioned whether eighteen-year-olds have the "mature judgment" to vote. "Eighteen is not a hopeless age or condition," they sniffed. "If we live, as most of us do, we get over it all too soon."[223]

Southern resistance aside, it was Manny Celler who emerged as the amendment's most vocal opponent. The Brooklyn congressman dismissed the "old enough to fight, old enough to vote" rationale advanced by Randolph and Eisenhower as a "glib slogan." As Celler colorfully put it, "Voting is as different from fighting as chalk is from cheese." Teenagers, in his view, were fit for service on the battlefield because they were "easily molded" and "not likely to exercise critical judgment," qualities that made them unsuitable as voters.[224] From the time he retook the chairmanship of the House Judiciary Committee in 1955, after a two-year interlude of Republican control, Celler rebuffed any and all measures pertaining to youth voting.[225] Congress would not hold another vote on the issue until 1970.

In 1963, a presidential commission charged with examining America's low rates of voter registration and participation linked poor youth turnout to the voting age.[226] In its report, the commission found, "By the time they have turned 21 . . . many young people are so far removed from the stimulation of the educational process that their interest in public affairs has waned. Some may be lost as voters for the rest of their lives." The report recommended that states consider lowering the voting age to eighteen.[227] But just as woman suffragists learned decades earlier, changing state constitutions one at a time is not easy. While over thirty states had considered it, only two—Georgia in 1944 and Kentucky in 1955—had amended their charters to reduce the minimum voting age to eighteen.[228]

President Johnson embraced the issue in 1968, during his final months in office. "The hour has come to take the next great step in the march of democracy," he declared. "We should now extend the right to vote to more than ten million citizens unjustly denied that right." By this time, Johnson was deeply unpopular among young people due to the war in Vietnam. Notably, he redirected the conversation away from the military service rationale to a more inclusive appeal that emphasized social development and intellectual fitness. "Eighteen year old young Americans are prepared—by education, by experience, by exposure to public affairs of their own land and all the world—to assume and exercise the privilege of voting," he said.[229]

Johnson's call to action came at a moment of seismic generational change. Between 1960 and 1972, some 45 million Baby Boomers came of age, swelling the nation's college enrollment by more than 50 percent.[230] It was also a time of unprecedented political, social, and cultural rebellion, as young people embraced twin mantras: "Question authority" and "Don't trust anyone over 30." In 1966, Time took the unusual step of heralding people aged 25 and under as its Man of the Year.[231] Over the course of a decade, more than 2 million men from this cohort were conscripted to fight America's most unpopular war, comprising a disproportionate share of its casualties.[232]

Denied access to the ballot, young people turned to raucous activism. Student revolts rocked university campuses from coast to coast, as young people aired their grievances through antiwar rallies, teach-ins, and acts of civil disobedience. Most were peaceful. Some, like the wave of firebombing attacks targeting ROTC military recruitment centers on college grounds, were marred by violence and the senseless destruction of property.[233] "The world seems to be full today of embattled students," fretted one disconcerted member of the establishment. "Photographs of them may be seen daily: screaming, throwing stones, breaking windows, overturning cars, being beaten or dragged about by police."[234]

For some older Americans, the "moral energy in this generation" focused public attention on evils that had been too long neglected. But the insistent, unruly, inescapable demand for change also fueled a backlash, souring many on the idea of the youth vote.[235] In a May 1968 editorial, the *Chicago Tribune* opined that while "some outstanding young people" might have "the sense of responsibility and maturity of judgment" to vote, a "good many" others did not.

> Witness the antics of the Students for a Democratic Society; the campus riots and sit-ins; the irresponsible demands on school administrators and public leaders; the marchers and demonstrators, pot smokers, hippies, et al. Before Congress gives the vote to this sort it had better wait for some more conclusive evidence than is currently available that youths in this age bracket, by and large, have the wit to recognize the value of it.[236]

This growing "generation gap" helped tank state referendum campaigns aimed at lowering the voting age, including contests in Ohio and New Jersey in 1969.[237] But in Washington, the protests had the opposite effect, attracting lawmakers to the youth vote bandwagon.[238] Senator Jacob Javits was "convinced that self-styled student leaders who urge . . . acts of civil disobedience would find themselves with little or no support if students were given a more meaningful role in the electoral process."[239] In a similar vein, a presidential commission investigating an uptick in violence in society concluded that decreasing the voting age would offer younger Americans "a direct, constructive, and democratic channel for making their views felt and for giving them a responsible stake in the future of the nation."[240] Even Spiro Agnew, notorious for his harsh critiques of "the arrogant, reckless, inexperienced elements within our society," was on board.[241] He told a group of college students: "Once our young people can sound off at the polls, there will be less need to sound off in the streets."[242]

Capitalizing on this increased interest, Randolph re-introduced his youth vote amendment in August 1969.[243] Now representing West Virginia in the Senate, the "courtly and portly" elder statesman stood out for his "quiet southern sense of decorum."[244] In testimony before Bayh's subcommittee in March 1970, he reflected on his twenty-eight years of advocacy. "I have been patient," he said, with no small degree of understatement. "I have continued this effort because I believed that it was the right thing to do."[245] He encouraged his colleagues to welcome the perspective of young voters, likening them to "outside consultants" called upon "to take a fresh look." Young people, he said, offered "a clear view because it has not become clouded through time and involvement."[246]

The senator could be forgiven for believing that victory was finally at hand. He had sixty-seven co-sponsors, enough to advance the measure—*if* he could get it to the floor for a vote. But two key allies had other ideas. Inspired by a legal theory developed in the *Harvard Law Review*, Majority Leader Mike Mansfield and his whip Ted Kennedy concluded that the Fourteenth Amendment empowered Congress to establish a national voting age through ordinary legislation.[247] There was a ready vehicle to test this theory: a pending bill to re-authorize the Voting Rights Act, which was set to expire unless Congress renewed it. On March 4, before the hearings on Randolph's amendment proposal had even concluded, Mansfield announced that he would add a new section to the high-priority bill, instituting a national voting age of eighteen.[248]

Though he was careful not to criticize the majority leader, Randolph gamely insisted that the Senate was finally "ready to act" on his amendment proposal.[249] An irked Mansfield fired back: "The distinguished Senator from West Virginia . . . has been introducing resolutions since 1942, and where are they? Still in committee. Where are they when Congress adjourns? Dead."[250] With Randolph's acquiescence, the Mansfield rider passed handily.[251] But the *Congressional Quarterly* noted the "reluctant support from many Senators who said that such a change in suffrage should properly be made by constitutional amendment."[252]

The *Washington Post* predicted that the measure would face "formidable obstacles" in the House where Chairman Celler "promised to 'fight like hell'" to kill it.[253] Now in his forty-seventh year in Congress, Celler had adroitly rescued the District of Columbia and poll tax amendments from legislative quicksand. He'd also earned just acclaim for shepherding the Voting Rights Act to passage. But when it came to the youth vote, the eighty-one-year-old congressman was dug in, "a very powerful minority of one opposing the issue."[254] This time, however, Celler was in a bind. If he removed the Mansfield rider, the voting rights measure would go back to the Senate to face yet another filibuster by Southern Democrats.[255] Meanwhile, Mansfield was playing legislative hardball.[256] "There will either be an 18-year-old vote this year," he threatened, "or there won't be an extension of the voting rights bill."[257]

As Celler pondered his next move, a firestorm of student unrest upended his calculations. Amid a wave of campus protests following the

April 1970 invasion of Cambodia, soldiers from the Ohio National Guard fired into a crowd of students at Kent State University, killing four and wounding nine others.[258] The shocking event triggered a nationwide student strike. Less than two weeks later, in an incident that received far less coverage, police opened fire in front of a dormitory at Jackson State University, a historically Black college in Mississippi, killing two people while injuring twelve.[259] The unwarranted violence against these students only added pressure for Congress to bring young people into the political process. By June, Celler was ready to fold.[260] With his support, the House approved the extension of the Voting Rights Act with the Mansfield rider. It was estimated that the law would add as many as 11 million voters to the rolls.[261] In a signing statement, President Nixon expressed "misgivings" over the new law. Though he strongly supported setting the national voting age at eighteen, he believed it could only be accomplished by constitutional amendment. The president hoped a "swift court test" would resolve questions about the law's constitutionality.[262]

The Supreme Court heard the case of *Oregon v. Mitchell* on an expedited appeal, rendering its decision before Christmas, just days before the new national voting age was set to take effect. It was a ruling few expected: five opinions, totaling 184 pages, rendering a fractured verdict. On one side, four liberal justices voted to uphold the Mansfield rider as "a valid exercise of congressional power" under the Fourteenth Amendment.[263] On the other, four conservatives voted to invalidate it for intruding into an area reserved to the states.[264] In the middle was Justice Hugo Black, an eighty-four-year-old jurist appointed to the bench by President Franklin Roosevelt. Black agreed that Congress had power to set the voting age for federal elections, but maintained that, absent a showing of racial discrimination, it lacked the authority to override states' regulations of their own voter qualifications.[265]

"Vexed" election officials complained that the split decision would lead to confusion at the polls. "Congress has an obligation to rectify the imposition of an intolerable administrative burden upon the states," said one. "States will now have to hold separate elections for national officials and state and local officials."[266] Senator Kennedy expressed confidence that the states would fix the problem by modifying their laws.[267] But that was easier said than done. The change would require forty-seven states to amend their constitutions under procedures that could take years to complete. In most jurisdictions, a referendum would be required as well.[268] By one estimate, at least twenty states would not be able to lower their voting age before the 1972 election.[269]

As the *Hartford Courant* noted, lawmakers on Capitol Hill could no longer indulge in "the philosophical question of whether the 18-year-olds are qualified to vote," but rather "the pragmatic one of how a state is going to conduct a statewide election with two sets of election rolls without extraordinary confusion and expense resulting."[270] With no appetite in Congress to repeal the new law, there was only one way to synchronize federal and state election rules. Introducing his proposal for the *eleventh* time, with eighty-six senators backing him, Jennings Randolph's moment had finally arrived.[271] "We will bring our 18-, 19-, and 20-year-olds into the unique system of America," he promised.[272]

Lawmakers understood that time was of the essence, but in the sprint to organize a vote in the Senate, an unexpected hurdle emerged when Kennedy moved to attach a provision granting the District of Columbia full congressional representation.[273] Citing the Twenty-Third Amendment as "a striking precedent for our action today," Kennedy argued that the procedural move was the only way past the "gauntlet" of congressional committees determined to block it.[274] Mansfield broke with his ally to kill the proposal, unwilling to do anything that risked derailing the amendment.[275] Later that day, March 10, 1971, the Senate approved the measure by a unanimous vote.[276]

In the House, Manny Celler swallowed his deep distaste for "the teenage vote,"[277] managing the process with an outward show of cheer—and a chutzpah-laden dose of self-congratulation. "If this 26th amendment is ratified I will lay claim to sponsoring and cosponsoring four constitutional amendments," he boasted. "I say with all due modesty this is rather an achievement, and an achievement that I am extremely proud of."[278] The chamber's longest-serving member then tipped his hat to the mobilization that forced his hand. "This movement for voting by youths cannot be squashed," he said. "Any effort to stop the wave for the 18-year-old vote would be as useless as a telescope to a blind man."[279] When the roll was called on March 23, the House approved the resolution by a vote of 401–19.[280] The few dissenters, a mix of Southern Democrats and conservative Republicans, argued that Congress was buckling to pressure groups at the expense of states' rights.

Five states ratified the amendment that same day, two within an hour of the vote.[281] On July 1, 1971, precisely one hundred days after Congress lent its

approval, the Twenty-Sixth Amendment received the endorsement of the decisive thirty-eighth state, overtaking the Twelfth Amendment as the fastest
to be ratified.[282] Looking ahead to the 1972 election, most observers expected
the new crop of voters to benefit the Democrats.[283] But Republicans understood that the army of college students boosting the campaign of George Mc-
Govern, the Democrats' nominee for president, represented just a fraction
of the youth constituency.[284] Only one in five young people even attended
college in those days. To reach the "sons and daughters of the silent majority,"
the more conservative young people who steered clear of the campus rallies,
President Nixon's re-election campaign invested in an unprecedented voter
outreach effort.[285] Said one analysis: "The Republicans . . . are banking on the
belief that the political attitudes of most youth are . . . instilled by parents
and by the same kinds of social and economic pressures that bear on the
adult electorate."[286] Defying expectations, the under-twenty-one vote went
to Nixon on Election Day 52 percent to 46 percent.[287]

The Twenty-Sixth Amendment was the last successful amendment
proposed by Congress and the seventh adopted in response to a Supreme
Court ruling. It joins a noble line of constitutional amendments that eliminated barriers to the elective franchise, following the path blazed by African American and woman suffragists. And yet the story of the amendment
bears an important difference.

Unlike those earlier campaigns, there was no comparable youth suffrage
movement driving the effort. While the amendment's earliest champions
were inspired by the sacrifices of young men serving in the military, they
were not responding to the demands of young people themselves. Even
later, as a massive youth political movement flowered in the late 1960s, voting never seemed to register high on the list of demands. Small youth-led
pressure groups did begin to organize late in the game, investing energy
into state ballot-measure fights. Yet there were no visionary leaders following in the footsteps of Frederick Douglass, Susan B. Anthony, or Martin
Luther King Jr., challenging the older generation to "give us the ballot."

Another odd thing about the youth voting amendment is the way it
sped to adoption even as Americans were deeply split on the idea. From the
mid-1950s onwards, public opinion surveys revealed consistent majority
support for lowering the national voting age.[288] But as late as 1970—several
months *after* Congress had acted to lower the voting age—voters in eleven
states rejected ballot measures to make a corresponding change to their
own state constitutions.[289] The confounding ruling in *Oregon v. Mitchell*

quickly changed the dynamics, however, prompting federal and state lawmakers to fall into line. Many were proud to support a long-overdue expansion of voting rights. Others were simply looking for a way to avert chaos at the polls.

Most Americans soon came to terms with the Twenty-Sixth Amendment, but the prospect of a sizable student vote caused consternation in many college towns. "There is a fear that students might take over or unduly influence the city government," said one local official.[290] States responded by imposing strict residency requirements for voting.[291] Though courts have struck down most of these restrictions,[292] lawmakers continue to look for ways to curb the influence of student voters. In recent years, laws limiting registration drives and polling sites on campus, along with rules rejecting university ID cards as proof of identity, have been part of a new—and far more successful—wave of youth vote suppression efforts.[293]

During the debate in Congress, Birch Bayh sounded a note of optimism about this latest expansion of the electorate. "I predict that young people will vote, in large numbers," he said. "I believe that once these younger citizens have the right they have sought, they will use it."[294] Since the adoption of the Twenty-Sixth Amendment, however, youth turnout has consistently lagged behind that of other age groups. Years before his death in 1998, Jennings Randolph expressed dismay over youth apathy in politics.[295] Nevertheless, a new generation of lawmakers and advocates, encouraged by a resurgence of activism among today's high school students, argue that it's time once again to extend the franchise—this time to sixteen-year-olds.[296] "From gun violence, to immigration reform, to climate change, to the future of work—our young people are organizing, mobilizing, and calling us to action," says Representative Ayanna Pressley, the sponsor of a resolution to that effect with 124 co-sponsors. "They are at the forefront of social and legislative movements and have earned inclusion in our democracy."[297]

The Twenty-Sixth Amendment was the period's final amendment to surpass Article V's ratification threshold, coming amid the twilight of the Civil Rights revolution. But the reformist energy of the era was not yet spent. The successful adoption of four amendments in just over a decade had boosted confidence in the ability to resolve problems of national significance through the amendment process. Lawmakers in Congress soon came under immense pressure from activists backing longtime causes, resulting in the proposal of two additional constitutional amendments that failed to achieve ratification.

7

The 1970s—and the Rights Revolution That Wasn't

The reformist energy that produced three voting rights amendments to the Constitution between 1960 and 1971 was also manifest in the jurisprudence of the Warren Court—a "constitutional revolution" rivaling that of the New Deal era.[1] In a May 1964 profile, *Life* magazine observed that the Warren Court "has its finger in all kinds of juridical pies that previous Courts would never have thought of sampling."[2] While progressives welcomed the Court's engagement, others saw judicial overreach.[3] In frustration, conservatives in Congress introduced hundreds of constitutional amendment proposals to push back against rulings in cases ranging from desegregation to religion in the classroom.[4] Those efforts only accelerated after 1962, with the Court's "forays into the political thicket" of legislative apportionment.[5]

In the early twentieth century, most state legislative maps were drawn in a manner that overrepresented rural voters at the expense of city dwellers, and the disparity only grew over decades of rapid demographic change. In one of many egregious examples, 15,000 people living in one rural Alabama county had the same representation in the state senate as the 600,000 residents of Jefferson County, home to Birmingham, the state's largest city.[6] Invoking the principle of "one man, one vote," the justices put an end to this unfair and self-perpetuating practice, ruling that state legislative districts must be "substantially equal" in population to give each citizen's vote equal weight.[7] The rule was extended to apply to Congress as well.[8]

Today the principle of "one person, one vote" is widely embraced as a bedrock guarantee of electoral fairness. But the dwindling number of Americans living in farm country in the 1960s perceived it as a threat, portending a massive shift of political power toward the far more popu-lous, diverse, and liberal cities and suburbs.[9] In January 1965, after decry-ing the ruling as an intrusion into an area reserved to the states,[10] Senate minority leader Everett Dirksen introduced an amendment to modify the Court's mandate. His proposal would have permitted states to apportion one house of a legislature on a basis other than population.[11] But the mea-sure fell short.[12]

Undeterred, Dirksen quietly forged an alliance with the Council of State Governments, an interest group working without much success to obtain an amendment through the Article V convention process. Dirksen privately admitted he had no interest in summoning a convention, but he believed a credible threat of one would force Congress's hand.[13] Over many months, he ran a stealth operation to persuade state legislatures to submit petitions to Congress, hoping to make a "dramatic announcement" upon securing the thirty-four that were needed. And he very nearly succeeded. But when the *New York Times* reported in March 1967 that the campaign was just two states short of the number needed to trigger a constitutional convention, the effort attracted increased scrutiny.[14] Momentum stalled in the face of mounting concerns over the danger that a "runaway conven-tion" might propose far-ranging changes to the national charter. By 1969, states began withdrawing their applications. When Dirksen died later that year, the effort did as well.[15]

The "one person, one vote" principle also inspired a bold, almost suc-cessful effort to abolish the Electoral College. The issue loomed large for President Lyndon Johnson in the months after his landslide win in the 1964 election. Johnson worried that protest votes from "faithless elec-tors" unhappy with his civil rights agenda might hinder his re-election prospects in 1968. Impressed by Birch Bayh's success in shepherding the Twenty-Fifth Amendment through Congress, he asked the young subcom-mittee chair to propose a revision to the Electoral College system. Johnson imagined an amendment providing for the automatic casting of electoral votes, eliminating the need for electors themselves.[16] Bayh dutifully held hearings on the proposal in 1966. In the process, he came to see the need for a more transformative solution. Citing the nation's progress toward "universal suffrage," he called for "the next logical outgrowth of the per-sistent and inevitable movement toward the democratic ideal": an amend-ment providing for the direct popular election of the president.[17]

The effort gained traction after the 1968 presidential election. The

Republican candidate, Richard Nixon, edged Vice President Hubert Humphrey by just half a million votes. But in a close call, a third-party spoiler candidate, Alabama's segregationist governor George Wallace, won more than 13 percent of the popular vote and 46 electoral votes from five states in the deep South.[18] A switch of 53,000 votes in three states would have denied Nixon a majority in the Electoral College, forcing the first contingent run-off election in the House since 1824.[19] In such a scenario, Wallace might emerge as kingmaker, extracting concessions to reverse fragile progress on civil rights as the price of his support.[20]

The American Bar Association issued a report criticizing the Electoral College process as "archaic, undemocratic, complex, ambiguous, indirect and dangerous."[21] A Gallup poll taken in the weeks following the election found that 81 percent of Americans favored electing the president by a popular vote.[22] Buoyed by this momentum, the Democrat-controlled House of Representatives approved the Bayh amendment on September 18, 1969 by a decisive vote of 338–70.[23] Two weeks later, President Nixon issued a statement backing the proposal, calling for urgent action. "Unless the Senate follows the lead of the House, all opportunity for reform will be lost this year and possibly for years to come," he warned.[24]

Bayh hoped the measure would win swift approval in the Senate, but it faced resistance from a trio of Southern senators with a long record of opposing voting rights measures. Judiciary Chairman James Eastland kept the measure on the back burner for months as senators debated and rejected President Nixon's first two Supreme Court nominees, both Southern conservatives.[25] When Bayh finally managed to get the measure to the floor in September 1970, a full year after the House vote, it faced a filibuster led by Sam Ervin and Strom Thurmond.[26] In a minority report, the senators charged that the proposal was "a well-meant but dangerously naïve attempt to apply the logic of 'one-man, one-vote' to presidential elections, regardless of the consequences."[27] In fact, their defense of the status quo was inextricably tied to the Electoral College's long history of bolstering the power of white voters in the South—an outcome integral to its design and operation over more than two centuries.[28]

After two test votes, it became clear that Bayh and his allies lacked the votes to break the filibuster.[29] The campaign of obstruction had worked. The *Times* observed that after a year's delay the "heat of passion for electoral reform" had "cooled."[30] Decades later, Bayh recalled the near miss as the greatest disappointment of his political career.[31] But it was also a harbinger of stiffer headwinds ahead as Congress geared up to send two additional amendments to the states—the products of campaigns many years in the making.

The Equal Rights Amendment

Following the 1920 ratification of the Woman Suffrage Amendment after a half-century of campaigning, many suffragists considered the battle won, but a restive few saw it as just the first step toward full legal equality. Crystal Eastman, the pioneering labor lawyer, organizer, and "founding mother" of the American Civil Liberties Union, captured this sentiment in the December 1920 edition of *The Liberator*, a radical arts and politics magazine: "Men are saying perhaps 'Thank God, this everlasting woman's fight is over!' But women, if I know them, are saying, 'Now at last we can begin.'"[32]

To claim this bigger prize, Alice Paul's National Woman's Party launched another grand project: an amendment to guarantee equality of the sexes.[33] Paul collaborated with Eastman to craft the language: "Men and women shall have equal rights throughout the United States and every place subject to its jurisdiction." To commemorate the seventy-fifth anniversary of the Seneca Falls conference, they named the amendment after the feminist leader Lucretia Mott. By December 1923, they had convinced two Republican lawmakers from Kansas, a future vice president and the nephew of suffragist Susan B. Anthony, to introduce the measure in Congress.[34]

The proposal ran into opposition from the outset, as labor unions and some women's groups worried that mandating the equality of the sexes would eliminate workplace regulations intended to protect women.[35] Laws in more than forty states prevented women from working overtime and at night, exempted them from physically demanding tasks, and barred them from a wide range of occupations—from smelting to truck driving to bartending.[36] It was the height of the *Lochner* era, a time when the Supreme Court readily struck down laws protecting *male* workers. But the justices were content to uphold measures necessitated by a woman's "physical structure" and "maternal functions."[37] Supporters of the amendment argued that these laws were paternalistic and rooted in stereotypes, keeping women from securing better, high-paying jobs. Opponents saw the campaign for equal rights as a rich woman's crusade that would jeopardize hard-won gains. "The National Woman's Party does not know what it is to work ten or twelve hours a day in a factory," complained one union organizer.[38] For two decades, the protectionists' arguments shut down any possibility of progress.

The cause found a new audience during World War II, when women entered the workforce in unprecedented numbers. Encounters with pervasive discrimination on the job gave many women reason to consider their unequal status.[39] Looking to rekindle interest in the amendment, Paul revised its text in 1943 to conform to the style of the Fifteenth and Nineteenth Amendments: "Equality of rights under the law shall not be denied or abridged by the United States or any state on account of sex." Rebranded as the Equal Rights Amendment, the measure attracted new support from a respectable roster of women's organizations, from the General Federation of Women's Clubs to the National Association of Colored Women, as well as both major political parties, but organized labor and its allies in Congress remained unalterably opposed.[40] When the first legislative test came three years later, a narrow majority of senators voted in favor of the ERA, far short of the two-thirds majority needed.[41] The *New York Times* applauded the measure's defeat, citing the prevalent concern over legal protections for women. "Motherhood cannot be amended," the paper added, "and we are glad the Senate didn't try."[42]

When the Senate next took up the measure, in 1950, a veteran senator offered a compromise. "The proposed amendment," said Arizona Democrat Carl Hayden, "is based upon the fallacy that men and women are so much alike that they should, under all laws, be considered as equal. The truth is that they are not alike to any such degree."[43] Hayden's "common sense" solution was to add language clarifying that the amendment could not be construed to "impair any rights, benefits, or exemptions" conferred on women by law.[44] With this stipulation, senators approved the ERA in 1950 and again in 1953.[45] The "Hayden rider" allowed straddling lawmakers to cast a vote for women's rights without alienating supporters of protectionist laws. But for the measure's backers it was a deal breaker—"always, always a thorn in our flesh," Alice Paul recalled.[46] Prospects looked similarly bleak in the House of Representatives, where Judiciary Chairman Manny Celler, a staunch labor ally, made clear he would block any consideration of the measure.[47] Though supporters faithfully re-introduced the ERA in every Congress, progress came slowly in the male-dominated politics of the era.[48]

By the early 1960s, women's rights advocates started looking for other ways to make progress. In a 1963 report, a presidential commission chaired by Eleanor Roosevelt (a vocal protectionist opponent of the ERA) called for greater enforcement of women's rights under existing law.[49] At the time, no court had ever applied the Fourteenth Amendment's guarantee of equal protection to invalidate legal distinctions based on sex. Instead, such laws were presumed to be valid as long as they bore "some rational relationship to a legitimate state end," the most permissive legal standard.[50] But the commission's call inspired new thinking in the academy. In "Jane Crow and the Law," a landmark 1965 law review article, Pauli Murray and Mary Eastwood argued that despite the paucity of judicial precedent, the Fourteenth Amendment "may nevertheless be applicable to sex discrimination."[51] Their work impressed a brilliant legal newcomer. Over the next decade, ACLU litigator Ruth Bader Ginsburg drew on it to chart a strategy that persuaded the Supreme Court to adopt a new gender-equality jurisprudence, striking down a number of protectionist laws.[52]

Around this time, there were also promising developments on the legislative front. In 1963, Congress enacted the first equal-pay law.[53] Then, the following year, it made the decision to include "sex," alongside "race, color, religion, and national origin," as a protected category under Title VII, the fair employment provision of the Civil Rights Act of 1964.[54] The move is credited to Howard Smith, the segregationist chair of the House Rules Committee, who blindsided the measure's supporters.[55] Scholars have debated Smith's motives for engrafting the word "sex" into what he called a "nefarious bill" intended to remedy discrimination against African Americans. Some say he hoped his "mischievous contribution" would derail the measure.[56] As a reporter noted at the time, Smith would "joyfully disembowel the civil rights bill if he could."[57] Others contend that this longtime supporter of the ERA sincerely wanted to ensure that white women would have the same protections being extended to Black men and women.[58] Behind the scenes, he negotiated the change with his long-time friend Alice Paul.[59]

Years later, Smith said that he offered his proposal "as a joke."[60] And sure enough, the mostly male members of the House greeted it with laughter.[61] The patronizing banter only increased after Celler, the bill's floor manager, cracked that in forty-nine years of marriage, "I usually have the last two words, and those words are, 'Yes, dear.'"[62] This prompted a dry rebuke from Martha Griffiths, a Democratic congresswoman from Michigan:

"I presume that if there had been any necessity to have pointed out that women were a second-class sex, the laughter would have proved it."[63] The "prototype for many young activists of the 1970s," Griffiths worked her way up the political ladder as a state legislator and judge to become "one of the first career women elected to Congress."[64] As it happened, she was planning to introduce the measure herself because without it, she believed, "white women will be last at the hiring gate."[65] She gladly let Smith have the honor in the hope that he could swing Southern votes in favor of the proposal.

The inclusion of women in Title VII "proved highly significant in consolidating legal feminism as a force to be reckoned with," explains law professor Serena Mayeri.[66] But the agency created to enforce the law, the Equal Employment Opportunity Commission, was toothless at first, refusing to take most sex discrimination claims seriously.[67] Its executive director, a man, publicly quipped that "no man should be required to have a male secretary."[68] Recognizing the need for a pressure group that could serve as "an NAACP for women," over two dozen feminist leaders launched the National Organization for Women in June 1966.[69] By the end of the decade, NOW was seen as "the largest and least radical of the feminist groups," lobbying for new laws and engaging in public education to change attitudes toward women's role in society.[70] At its first national conference, the group endorsed the Equal Rights Amendment.[71]

"The feminist movement is gaining more recognition all the time," reported *Newsday* in December 1969, "although frequently it is from such headline catching tactics as bra burnings, protests against the Miss America Pageant, and marches for abortion repeal."[72] But even as a "second wave" of women's activism flowered, the ERA was going nowhere. In the House, Celler continued to ignore the measure, consigning it each time it was introduced to what one commentator called "burial without ceremony."[73] And while Birch Bayh liked to say that gender equality was "a driving force" in his public life, he never once bothered to hold a hearing on the ERA in eight years as the Senate's point person on constitutional amendments.[74] It would take an exercise in political theater to prod him into action.

In February 1970, as Bayh presided over hearings on Jennings Randolph's youth vote amendment, the proceedings were interrupted as fifteen members of NOW's Pittsburgh chapter, "all well dressed and mostly middle aged," staged a demonstration in the back of the room.[75] As Bayh remembered it, "a bunch of women held up signs—'ERA, ERA'—and started jumping up and down and yelling, just totally destroying the environment in the hearing." The senator instructed a staffer to "find out what those damn women want."[76] After a meeting, he agreed to hold hearings on the amendment. "This was the moment," writes Jane Mansbridge, author of *Why We Lost the ERA*. "Labor opposition was fading, and, because few radical claims had been made for the ERA, conservatives had little ammunition with which to oppose it."[77] True to his word, Bayh scheduled three days of testimony that May.

On the first day of the hearings, Representative Shirley Chisholm, the first Black woman elected to Congress, delivered memorable testimony. An early childhood educator–turned–politician, representing Brooklyn's Bedford-Stuyvesant neighborhood, she earned the moniker "Fighting Shirley Chisholm" for her fierce advocacy for working people.[78] The congresswoman was also known for her "Chisholmisms," pithy statements delivered in careful English that exposed the faint West Indian cadence of a dogged moral crusader. "The Black man must step forward," she would say, "but that doesn't mean that Black women have to step back."[79] Upon introducing her own ERA resolution the prior year, Chisholm, who was "no stranger to race prejudice," admitted, "In the political world I have been far oftener discriminated against because I am a woman than because I am Black."[80]

Black Americans "are not the only second class citizens in this country," Chisholm testified. "The largest single group of second class citizens is the majority of Americans, American women." In a classic Chisholmism, she told the mostly male panel, "It is not the intention of American women to become a nation of Amazons. We will no longer, however, be denied our rights as human beings, equal in all respects to males."[81] Over the next year, the freshman lawmaker from Brooklyn would be the ERA's most passionate advocate. Buoyed by the hearings, Bayh promised an "all-out effort" to pass the ERA.[82]

Emanuel Celler remained unmoved, however, even after the United Auto Workers, a key labor ally, endorsed the measure after decades of opposition. His continued refusal to consider the amendment marked him as a relic from a bygone era. As a reporter acidly noted, the veteran lawmaker "arrived in Congress the same year the amendment did."[83] To break through Celler's roadblock, Griffiths announced she would file a discharge petition, a rarely used procedural device that permits a majority to force legislation to the House floor. It was an ambitious goal: members had pulled off the feat only two dozen times in the chamber's history.[84] When Griffiths surprised her colleagues by collecting the requisite 218 signatures in just a month,[85] Celler quickly backtracked, promising to hold a hearing after nearly two decades of obstruction. Griffiths replied that she preferred to bring the measure to the floor,[86] enlisting the help of women's groups, which buried lawmakers in "an avalanche of letters."[87] On the eve of the August 10 debate, the New York Times reported there was "some doubt" whether supporters could muster the two-thirds vote needed for passage. Their "biggest advantage," said the paper, was "the known fervor of the supporters of the amendment."[88]

Deploying Celler's trademark legislative tactics against him, Griffiths managed a tightly controlled legislative process with only an hour set aside for debate. Celler cried foul, launching into a cringeworthy lecture. "Ever since Adam gave up his rib to make a woman," he said, "throughout the ages we have learned that physical, emotional, psychological and social differences exist and dare not be disregarded. Neither the National Woman's Party or the delightful, delectable and dedicated gentlelady from Michigan can change nature. They cannot do it."[89] But with the backing of a majority, the "gentlelady from Michigan" was now firmly in charge. After forty-seven years of inaction, the House of Representatives debated the Equal Rights Amendment for the very first time. "It is past time . . . that we begin the removal of any legal discrimination against women; as we are attempting to removal legal discriminations against all other minorities," said Griffiths.[90]

Opponents were allotted only fifteen minutes to raise their objections. Some criticized the rushed process. "We are being asked to forego our legislative responsibilities because it would be the gallant and gentlemanly thing to do," griped one congressman.[91] Most warned of "a pandora's box of legal complications." One dissenting lawmaker argued, "If there is to be absolute equality of the sexes, our selective service law would have to be revised to accommodate lady draftees. The entire structure of our family and domestic relations law as developed by the 50 states, especially those provisions giving preferential treatment to women, would be thrown into turmoil."[92]

In rapid succession, more than three dozen members of Congress stood up in support of the measure. Most agreed with the pithy sentiment expressed by Minority Leader Gerald Ford, who helped wrangle GOP votes:

The ERA was "an idea whose time has come."[93] But of all the measure's supporters, once again it was Congresswoman Chisholm who made the most lasting impression. The ERA "represents one of the most clear-cut opportunities . . . to declare our faith in the principles that shaped our Constitution," she declared, the chance to condemn prejudice "so widespread that it seems to many persons normal, natural and right." In a rousing call to action, Chisholm proclaimed:

> The time is clearly now to put this House on record for the fullest expression of that equality of opportunity which our Founding Fathers professed. They professed it, but they did not assure it to their daughters, as they tried to do for their sons. The Constitution they wrote was designed to protect the rights of white, male citizens. As there were no black Founding Fathers, there were no founding mothers—a great pity, on both counts. It is not too late to complete the work they left undone. Today, here, we should start to do so.[94]

When the roll was called, the result wasn't even close: 352 members voted in favor of the ERA, while just 15 opposed it.[95] "The one-sidedness of the vote surprised supporters of the amendment," said the *New York Times*.[96] In an editorial, however, the paper scolded "the henpecked House" for approving "a constitutional change of almost mischievous ambiguity" after only one hour of debate.[97]

With 81 senators on record supporting the measure, pro-ERA forces had reason to feel confident as the action moved to the upper chamber: but Senator Sam Ervin was prepared to do battle. The North Carolinian had already earned a reputation as "the Senate's most adamant opponent" of the amendment,[98] warning it would "rob millions of wives, homemakers, mothers and widows of rights they now enjoy."[99] Lacking the votes to sustain a filibuster, Ervin nonetheless persuaded his colleagues to add a proviso exempting women from the military draft—a concern of particular salience as the war in Vietnam dragged on. Muddying the waters further, another senator tacked on a provision to permit prayer in public schools.[100] In light of these developments, the amendment's backers had no choice but to shelve the measure.[101] Following the vote, a "beaming" Senator Ervin boasted, "'I'm trying to protect women from their fool friends and from themselves.'"[102]

Griffiths started the process anew when the next Congress convened in January 1971.[103] While Celler honored his promise to hold hearings, he used the opportunity to add yet another crippling provision. The so-called Wiggins amendment invoked the two most common criticisms of the ERA, stipulating that women would be exempted from the draft and that "reasonable" protective laws would remain in effect. For Griffiths, it was the return of "the old Hayden rider." Celler gloated, "This is the kiss of death."[104] But on October 12 the House stripped the Wiggins amendment and proceeded to approve the ERA by a vote of 354–24.[105]

The Senate took up the measure early the following year, setting aside four days for debate. This time, Senator Ervin launched a lengthy filibuster against "the unisex amendment,"[106] forcing a series of votes on "poison pill" amendments that prompted lengthy and often awkward discussions on inflammatory topics ranging from bathroom privacy to women in combat to gay rights.[107] Dismissing his objections, the Senate voted on March 22, 1972, to approve the ERA by an overwhelming bipartisan vote of 84–8.[108] But Ervin's actions were not in vain. As historian David Kyvig notes, the senator was deftly "sowing seeds of doubt that would germinate later," in the bruising ratification fight to come.[109]

According to reporting from inside the Senate chamber, "women of all ages and more than a few men, mostly young, applauded, cheered and let out a few cowboy yells."[110] Notably, Alice Paul did not join in the celebrations. At eighty-seven years of age, she had lived long enough to see the ERA make it out of Congress—the culmination of nearly five decades of advocacy. But she worried that the seven-year time limit for ratification would give opponents the opportunity to run out the clock. Griffiths and Bayh had agreed to the deadline as "customary," ignoring her warnings. A jubilant Griffiths predicted that the amendment would be ratified "as quickly as was the 18-year-old vote."[111] Bayh agreed that it would be adopted "with dispatch."[112] But though lawmakers in Hawaii raced to ratify the amendment that same day, and six other states ratified within a week, Paul's gloomy prediction proved prescient. "We lost," she sighed.[113]

For Chairman Celler, the fight over the ERA marked the end of a long political career. His efforts to defeat the amendment prompted a thirty-year-old community activist from Brooklyn to announce a long-shot challenge to his bid for a twenty-sixth term in office. In launching her campaign, Elizabeth Holtzman portrayed the incumbent as imperious and out of touch, citing his "high-handed opposition" to the ERA.[114] Celler dismissed his youthful challenger as a "nonentity," insisting that "any attempt to attack my record is as useless as trying to topple over the Washington Monument with a toothpick."[115] But in the June 1972 primary election, Holtzman bested Celler by 562 votes.[116]

At first, the ratification campaign proceeded apace: twenty-two states approved the ERA by the end of 1972. But by January 1973, the *New York Times* detected rising opposition. "Well organized and seemingly well financed opposition groups have appeared and they are making arguments against the amendment that many state legislators find persuasive," the paper reported. The "apparent leader" of the effort was Phyllis Schlafly, a self-described homemaker from Illinois.[117] An anti-Communist crusader who came late to the issue of women's rights,[118] Schlafly navigated her way in the world of GOP politics as a campaign staffer and twice-failed candidate for Congress. As her biographer notes, Schlafly "understood the nitty gritty of organizing." In annual conferences, she trained networks of conservative women in the fine points of waging an attention-getting pressure campaign in the age of television.[119]

Schlafly dedicated the February 1972 edition of the *Phyllis Schlafly Report*, a monthly newsletter reaching over six thousand subscribers throughout the country, to the supposed threat of the ERA.[120] "What's wrong with 'equal rights' for women?" she asked. "The truth is that American women never had it so good. Why should we lower ourselves to 'equal rights' when we already have the status of special privilege?"[121] The issue hit a nerve with Schlafly's subscribers, who distributed copies to friendly lawmakers in their state capitals. Weeks later, one called Schlafly to say, "We beat ERA in Oklahoma today and all we had was your *Report!*"[122]

Within a few months, Schlafly founded the STOP ERA campaign. ("STOP" was an acronym for Stop Taking Our Privileges, a nod to the protectionist arguments that clouded the amendment's prospects from the beginning.)[123] By early 1973, Schlafly boasted that the organization had several thousand members active in twenty-six states. Her messaging was lifted straight from the Ervin playbook. Feminists, she said, were "a bunch of anti-family radicals and lesbians and elitists."[124] The ERA would mean "coed everything—whether you like it or not."[125] Working with allies including the League of Housewives, National Council of Catholic Women, and Roman Catholic clergymen, Schlafly's group generated "floods of opposition mail" to stall ratification votes in key states.[126]

In response to the success of STOP ERA, the National Organization for Women vowed to step up its ratification campaign, promising "confrontation tactics" against recalcitrant lawmakers. But on the ground, pro-ERA forces were fatally slow to organize and woefully unprepared to counter the amendment's critics.[127] "The momentum for passage of the amendment has sort of worn out," said the chief of a pro-ERA group, attributing it to "a natural backlash setting in toward the gains that women are making."[128]

The turning point came in March 1973, when Nebraska's unicameral legislature voted to withdraw its support for the amendment.[129] The leading force behind the push to rescind was Richard Proud, the chamber's speaker. Though he had joined in the legislature's unanimous vote to ratify the ERA a year earlier, Proud later claimed, "I didn't know what I was voting for."[130] Vilifying the "extremists" and "women's libbers" who "led the members around by the nose,"[131] Proud called the push for equal rights "a covering for a far more sinister plan . . . to get all women, without regard for their own wishes, out of the home and into the work force."[132] Crucially, he tied the vote to abortion rights just weeks after the Supreme Court's controversial ruling in *Roe v. Wade*. ERA supporters were "the people who believe in abortion," he claimed, praising the ruling "with all their little heart and souls."[133] Though the state's action was of questionable legality—a Senate lawyer dismissed it as "null and void"—there was a growing sense that ratification was "now in question."[134] Within a year, seventeen state legislatures voted to reject the ERA, enough to sink it. Not one would reconsider its decision. Complicating matters further, lawmakers in four states followed Nebraska's lead by voting to revoke their prior support of the amendment.[135]

Amid these setbacks, ERA supporters persuaded four more states to approve the measure by 1977, raising the tally to thirty-five. They also persuaded Congress to extend the ratification period.[136] (In a bit of poetic justice, the proposal's champion was Elizabeth Holtzman, the congresswoman who replaced Emanuel Celler in the House.) Schlafly blasted the extension as "wrong, illegal, immoral, unprecedented, and unconstitutional."[137] But it made no difference. Despite the advocacy of ERA supporters, who organized rallies, boycotts, and letter-writing campaigns to prod recalcitrant lawmakers in targeted states, not a single additional ratification was secured by the new June 30, 1982, deadline.[138] That night, Schlafly threw a "gala goodbye" party, taking one last jab at the "vicious people" who supported the ERA. As women's groups vowed to continue the fight, Schlafly proclaimed the proposal "dead for now and forever in this century."[139]

"Schlafly has to be regarded as one of the two or three most important Americans of the last half of the twentieth century," says political scientist Alan Wolfe. "The ugliness of American politics today can be directly traced back to Schlafly's vituperative, apocalyptic, character-assassinating campaign against the ERA."[140] Her success helped accelerate the Republican Party's capture by the far right, a transformation personified by the rise of Ronald Reagan. As governor of California, Reagan enthusiastically backed the ERA, calling it "morally unassailable." But by 1980, when he ran as the Republican candidate for president, the party had retreated from forty years of support for the ERA to a squishy stance acknowledging "the legitimate efforts of those who support or oppose ratification."[141] Republicans won a convincing victory that year, capturing the White House and—for the first time since 1952—the Senate. Among the many Democrats swept away in the GOP tide was Birch Bayh.[142]

In the end, the ERA fell short in the same swath of Southern states that had rejected the Nineteenth Amendment half a century earlier.[143] Close-fought defeats on friendlier ground in Illinois and a trio of Western states sealed the measure's fate. And yet, even as the STOP ERA forces triumphed, a Gallup poll showed that 56 percent of Americans continued to favor the amendment.[144] In November 1983, backers hoped to start the process over, but a vote in the House of Representatives fell six votes short of the two-thirds needed to pass it.[145]

In the meantime, in the shadow of the amendment's defeat, the fight for gender equality made remarkable headway—in the courts, in the legislatures, and in the world of organizing and action. As state lawmakers argued over ratification, constitutional lawyers worked on a parallel track to win a remarkable series of cases, realizing the visionary legal theory expounded by Pauli Murray and Mary Eastwood in their seminal paper. Ruth Bader Ginsburg, founding director of the ACLU's women's rights project, drew on their reasoning to pioneer a litigation strategy that "began the dismantling of legally-codified gender stereotyping that had imprisoned women for centuries."[146]

In a result its opponents could scarcely foresee, many of the ERA's principal aims have been achieved in the courts through the adoption of what constitutional law professor Reva Siegel calls the "de facto ERA."[147] Siegel notes the irony: "No longer do professors write lengthy books analyzing why the ERA failed. Instead, in the legal academy, at least, the talk is about why the ERA prevailed."[148] Nevertheless, these gains cannot completely substitute for a clear constitutional mandate of women's equality. As Kathleen Sullivan, another constitutional law expert, reminds us, "What American women have gained in equality rests on a patchwork of both state and federal constitutional and statutory provisions, some even enacted by accident . . . and others created with limited ingredients."[149]

In time, the successes of the "de facto ERA" in the courts dampened interest in constitutional amendments as a tool for advancing progressive legal change. Before that energy was depleted, however, lawmakers in Washington approved one final change to the national charter—the last of the six amendments proposed by Congress but not ratified.

The District of Columbia Voting Representation Amendment

The story of the fourth and final wave of amendments, a remarkable surge of activity lasting two decades, begins and ends with the unique legal status of the District of Columbia. The 1961 ratification of the Twenty-Third Amendment represented an incremental victory in the fight to bring democracy to the District. As originally drafted, the measure provided for voting representation in the House of Representatives. But Emanuel Celler removed that part of Senator Kenneth Keating's plan, convinced that the measure could not win ratification otherwise. After the amendment glided to ratification in just nine months, advocates longing to rectify this wrong could only regret that Congress had settled on a half measure. Inspired by the era's broad expansion of the franchise, they were ready to fight for a more robust solution.

In a February 1967 message to Congress, President Lyndon Johnson proposed reforms "to bring new vitality and strength to the District's government." Among his recommendations was a constitutional amendment guaranteeing the District at least one voting member in the House.[150] The president's plan would have also given Congress the option to award additional representation in the House and Senate, up to the full complement the District would be entitled to as a state.[151] But when Celler's Judiciary Committee held hearings on the proposal that July, the measure failed to advance.

By the start of the next decade, as amendments on youth voting and equal rights for women moved to the top of Congress's agenda, Senator Ted Kennedy emerged as a leading champion for what he called "America's last colony."[152] Kennedy wanted Congress to propose a new amendment granting full voting rights to the District of Columbia, but when the issue failed to gain traction, he irritated allies by attempting to advance it as a rider to other amendment vehicles.[153] While those efforts were rebuffed, Kennedy's advocacy prodded Congress to adopt two important laws. The District of Columbia Delegate Act, a 1970 law, allowed Washingtonians to send a nonvoting delegate to the House of Representatives,[154] while the 1973 Home Rule Act empowered them to elect a mayor and city council.[155] While the two measures were important advances in the District's journey towards self-determination, Congress continued to wield significant control over its political affairs, retaining the power to approve budgets and nullify local ordinances.[156]

In March 1971, District residents chose Walter Fauntroy as their first elected delegate to Congress under the new law. A Baptist preacher and prominent civil rights activist, Fauntroy had served on President Johnson's Conference on Civil Rights. He also sat on the city council as a presidential appointee. In selecting a Democratic party insider, District voters were confident that they had chosen a politico who could lead an effective reform effort—something he pledged to do upon being sworn in. "The election of a congressman is but the first step toward full self-government for the District," Fauntroy declared. "The immediate next step is that of organizing the people for political action to make their congressman effective." [157]

Making good on that promise, Fauntroy introduced a bold plan for representation in June 1971. Under his proposal, the Constitution would be amended to give Washingtonians full voting representation in Congress as if the District were a state: a delegation comprising two senators and a number of representatives as fairly determined in the apportionment following each census. The Fauntroy plan would also have given the District a vote in the contingent presidential election held in the House of Representatives when the Electoral College fails to produce a winner. Curiously, Fauntroy's proposal left the Twenty-Third Amendment in place, along with its cap on the allotment of presidential electors.[158]

After his resolution died in committee that year, Fauntroy dedicated himself to marshaling support for the measure. His efforts focused on Black communities in the South, which were getting their first taste of political power in the decade following the enactment of the Voting Rights Act. In 1972, he mobilized Black voters in South Carolina to oust Representative John McMillan, a powerful committee chair who blocked democracy reforms for over two decades. A signer of the Southern Manifesto, McMillan once sent a truckload of watermelons to the city's African American mayor. *Ebony* magazine called McMillan's defeat "an ominous message to congressmen in other heavily Black congressional districts."[159] Following his loss, the chairmanship of the committee with jurisdiction over the District went to Charles Diggs Jr., an African American member and civil rights activist far more attuned to the needs of its residents.[160]

Mindful of what *Ebony* called the "arithmetic of political power in heavily Black congressional districts," Fauntroy "criss-crossed the nation" to build support for his constitutional amendment proposal.[161] By the time he reintroduced it in May 1975, he had the backing of over a hundred House colleagues.[162] Despite this show of strength, the resolution was pared back in the legislative process to resemble the measure that President Johnson had proposed a decade earlier.[163] In a March 1976 vote, the whittled-down proposal won a bare majority in the House but failed to advance.[164]

Out of that defeat, supporters launched a more aggressive advocacy campaign, coordinated by the coalition for Self-Determination for D.C.[165] Founded with the mission of organizing and mobilizing local residents for home rule and eventual statehood, the coalition grew into a national partnership of more than sixty civic organizations. Partners included the nation's largest civil rights and reform groups, including the Leadership Conference, NAACP, Common Cause, and League of Women Voters, as well as a diverse array of local associations and nonprofits, from the Washington Bar Association to the Roman Catholic archdiocese to Delta Sigma Theta, one of the nation's oldest Black sororities.[166] The coalition's initial goal was to flip the votes of twenty-one House members who opposed the measure in 1975.[167] Volunteers telephoned their constituents by the thousands, urging them to contact their representatives in support of the amendment. Some 3 million Americans enlisted in the "phone-athon" effort, blanketing more than one hundred congressional districts. Amplifying these voices from the grassroots, professional lobbyists from unions, churches, political groups, and corporations made the case directly to lawmakers and their staffs.[168]

With this intensified ground game, and an influential new sponsor, supporters were ready to make one final push. In July 1977, Don Edwards, a veteran California Democrat who chaired the House subcommittee with jurisdiction over amendments, re-introduced Fauntroy's proposal with two significant changes. First, where Fauntroy's proposal left the Twenty-Third Amendment in place, the Edwards version provided for its repeal.

Second, it gave the District the right to participate in the ratification of constitutional amendments, something overlooked in all previous versions of the amendment. However well intentioned, this latter provision left some perplexed. While Article V gives state legislatures the power to ratify constitutional amendments, the District had no comparable body. The Edwards proposal left the exercise of the power to "the people of the District constituting the seat of government, and as shall be provided by the Congress."[169]

Fauntroy embraced the plan, agreeing that it was "more logical and practical to include all necessary provisions in a single amendment."[170] Testifying before Edwards's committee, the delegate preached in the spirited tone of a Baptist minister:

> Are we to continue to say to District of Columbia Americans, like we said in the *Dred Scott* decision to another group of Americans, that you are less than whole persons in our eyes? Are we to continue to espouse the virtues of democracy to the world and halt that democracy at the borders of the District of Columbia? Are the gates to equality, freedom and independence to remain closed within view of the Washington Monument?[171]

While Fauntroy was optimistic that the amendment was "a reachable goal," a prominent civil rights attorney and strategist also testifying that day offered a more guarded assessment. "There are a lot of people who don't want two more liberal Senators such as we would get from the District of Columbia," said Joseph Rauh Jr. "Likely, there would be two Blacks. Likely, there would be two Democrats. Likely, there would be two liberals."[172]

Rauh had a point. When Congress had approved the Twenty-Third Amendment seventeen years earlier, Republicans had reason to believe they could be competitive in the District. By the 1970s, however, the political dynamics of the nation's capital were completely transformed. As white residents decamped to the suburbs and its African American population fled the party of Lincoln, the District took on a decidedly Democratic tilt.[173] Even so, some high-ranking Republicans continued to back the measure as a matter of principle. As lawmakers considered the Edwards plan, the chairman of the Republican National Committee joined a "unity letter" committing his support, citing the GOP platform.[174] A top campaign aide called this bipartisan support "a key to our success."[175]

As supporters pushed for another vote, President Jimmy Carter endorsed "full voting representation in Congress" in his January 1978 State of the Union message.[176] With the administration's help behind the scenes, the Democratic House leadership brought the proposal up for consideration in early March.[177] Fauntroy led off the debate, summoning the moral outrage of a population slighted for nearly two centuries. "We want no more and no less than that to which all Americans are entitled," he declared. "To have that, we must be represented in both the House and Senate."[178] Over the course of two days, the amendment's backers emphasized the injustice of taxation without representation and highlighted the District's contributions to the military—the primary arguments used to advance the Twenty-Third Amendment nearly two decades earlier. In a nod to the capital's changing demographics, they also framed voting representation as "the largest civil rights issue of the decade."[179]

Opponents argued that the amendment went too far. "It seems inconceivable to me that legislatures across the land will support the expansion of the United States Senate to include two entirely urban-oriented Members in that body," said Virginia Republican M. Caldwell Butler.[180] The congressman offered a substitute proposal limited to representation in the House, arguing that gradual reform offered a greater chance of success. "I subscribe to the principle that the time has come that the District of Columbia should have representation in Congress," he said, "but what I offer the members is a kite that will fly."[181] Edwards countered that it was unfair to limit representation to one chamber when Congress is composed of two houses, each with a set of unique powers.[182]

On March 2, the House adopted the Edwards plan by a vote of 289–127.[183] In a promising sign, there was significant Republican support for the measure as members from the party's moderate wing embraced the amendment as "a simple matter of justice"[184] and "the right thing for us to do."[185] With the unprecedented push to extend the ERA's ratification deadline in mind, the lawmakers also added a proviso making clear that the measure "shall be inoperative" if not ratified in seven years.[186]

The vote looked to be much closer in the Senate. When debate commenced on August 16, it was Ted Kennedy, the measure's indefatigable sponsor, who spoke first. At issue, he declared, was "an anachronism that defies justice and denies one of the basic and most cherished rights of representative government for the people of the nation's capital."[187] In a memorable sound bite, Kennedy put his finger on the "unstated concern" that threatened the amendment's prospects: "Opposition so far has seemed to arise from four 'toos' on the part of some Members of the Senate—the fear that Senators elected from the District of Columbia may be too liberal, too urban, too black or too Democratic."[188]

It was an inconvenient truth. But Orrin Hatch, a freshman Republican from Utah, was stung by Kennedy's bluntness. "Because a large number of District residents are Black, supporters of this measure have attempted to characterize the opposition as racist in nature," he said. "This is simply not true."[189] Hatch then zeroed in on the provisions added by Edwards, contending they were "poorly drafted." In the absence of a legislature, the California congressman's plan provided that the power to choose presidential electors and ratify constitutional amendments would be exercised by "the people of the District . . . *and* as provided by Congress." In Hatch's view, the arrangement gave special "privileges" to the citizens of the District not enjoyed by the citizens of any state.[190] Hatch also argued that awarding senators to a federal enclave was an unconstitutional infringement of Article V's guarantee that "no state, without its consent, shall be deprived of its equal suffrage in the Senate."[191] West Virginia's Robert Byrd was quick to shoot down Hatch's "very curious objection." In what reporters described as "a lecturing tone of voice," he retorted: "To state the obvious . . . by definition a constitutional amendment cannot be unconstitutional."[192]

Over three days of debate, the measure drew surprising support from Southern Democrats and conservative Republicans targeted by the advocacy campaign of the Self-Determination for D.C. Coalition. "We were besieged by telephone calls and telegrams from key Black leaders in the state," said one senate aide.[193] North Carolina senator Jesse Helms, a master of the "dog whistle" appeals to racism that supplanted the unfiltered fulminations of prior generations of Southern politicians, upbraided his colleagues for engaging in "a mad scramble for political advantage with a minority group." The chamber was "participating in a charade," he railed. "There is not one senator who believes it will be ratified."[194] One scholar suggests that some of these unlikely supporters did see the vote a "harmless, politically shrewd gesture" to Black constituents in their states.[195]

On August 22, 1978, after "frantic eleventh hour maneuvering" to defeat changes aimed at weakening the measure, the Senate voted to approve the District of Columbia Voting Representation Amendment by the barest of margins, 67–32. The outcome of "the breath-taking" vote was "in doubt to the end," said the *Washington Post*. In the gallery that day was "a who's who of the civil rights movement," including Coretta Scott King and Clarence Mitchell Jr. Supporters and opponents agreed that the victory was "due largely to its being linked successfully to the volatile civil rights issue." An ebullient Walter Fauntroy told reporters, "We put together a masterpiece of strategy and timing that made this day possible."[196]

The amendment got off to a slow start in the states. Only three voted to ratify in the first year. As early as March 1979, seven months after the vote in Congress, it was clear the amendment would face tougher than expected opposition. "The conservative causes are really coming out of the woodwork on this," said a ratification campaign spokesperson. Phyllis Schlafly even got into the act, arguing that ratification would be "just like giving the Federal bureaucracy two senators of their very own." Fauntroy conceded that supporters were "surprised by the intense opposition," given the Twenty-Third Amendment's relatively easy path to ratification. By the one-year mark, the chair of the Self-Determination for D.C. coalition offered a grim prognosis. "It's nowhere," he said. "History has shown that if constitutional amendments don't get passed in the first two years, they die a lingering death."[197]

With just nine states on board by 1980, pessimism set in. Activists that year unveiled a new strategy, launching a movement to admit the District as the fifty-first state.[198] In May 1985, with just a few months remaining before the ratification deadline, the Los Angeles Times predicted that "District of Columbia residents are destined to remain half-citizens, or less, . . . for some time to come."[199] The rise of a more conservative Republican party led to the erosion of bipartisan support. When the seven-year time for ratification expired that August, only sixteen state legislatures had endorsed the measure. All were controlled by Democrats.[200]

The District of Columbia Voting Rights Amendment, like the ERA before it, was the product of decades of political advocacy building on an earlier success. Though the amendment's proponents fell short of their goal, the campaign to bring a greater measure of democracy to the District resulted in incremental progress, including laws granting home rule and a nonvoting seat in the House. Those victories, in turn, helped prime lawmakers to support a far more comprehensive set of reforms via constitutional amendment. Washingtonians today agree that the most effective way to remedy the deficit of democracy is for lawmakers to approve its pending application for statehood. Until something is done, America will remain a global outlier for denying citizens of its capital representation in the national legislature.[201]

The demise of the two unratified amendment proposals marked the end of the fourth major period of amending activity. However, instead of a period of remission, like those that followed the end of the Reconstruction and Progressive Era surges, a flurry of new amendment activity was quietly building. America was about to enter an unprecedented era of conservative amendment politics.

8

The Era of Conservative
Amendment Politics

After the disheartening defeat of the last two amendments proposed by
Congress in the 1970s, progressives began to lose interest in pursuing constitutional change through the Article V process, repeating a pattern of
exhaustion and withdrawal seen in previous cycles. This time, however,
a new generation of constitutional warriors quickly filled the void. Since
the Anti-Federalist opposition to the Constitution melted away after the
adoption of the Bill of Rights, those rallying to the banner of states' rights
and limited government had rarely invested much energy in amendment
crusades.[1] But as legal historian Richard Bernstein observes, the successful
campaign to stop the Equal Rights Amendment "gave right-wing activists
a crash course in the workings of Article V." This "hands-on familiarity"
revealed the process's potential as means to realize their own constitutional
dreams.[2] This new interest in constitutional change on the right helped
propel a decades-long campaign to mandate a balanced federal budget.

The Balanced-Budget Amendment

At the Philadelphia Convention, the Framers gave Congress the power "to
borrow money on the credit of the United States."[3] They saw it as essential, allowing the government to invest in infrastructure and act quickly in
times of war or emergency.[4] But this expansive power proved controversial
from the start. In the first decade of governance under the Constitution,
Alexander Hamilton, the first Treasury secretary, argued that a well-
managed system of public debt would be a "national blessing," making the
economy more productive.[5] Hamilton's visionary policies successfully laid

the foundation of the modern American economy, but they were deeply opposed by two former allies, James Madison and Thomas Jefferson. "I go on the principle that a public debt is a public curse," Madison said.[6]

For most of American history, balanced federal budgets were the norm. Borrowing was limited to wars, recessions, and long-term investments in the form of territorial expansion and infrastructure.[7] Beginning with the New Deal, however, debt became a tool of fiscal policy wielded by an activist federal government to stimulate the economy and foster growth. Persistent deficits soon became a fact of American life. With the exception of a four-year stretch during the Clinton administration, the federal government has run a deficit every year since 1970.[8]

While the first proposal to amend the Constitution to require a balanced budget dates back to 1936, interest quickened in the 1970s as annual deficits started to mount.[9] The idea drew oxygen from a broader conservative push for smaller government and lower taxes that fueled California's Proposition 13 tax revolt and the rise of Ronald Reagan—an anti-government ideology that shaped American politics for a generation.[10] While there have been many versions of the balanced-budget proposal over the years, it was conceived as a simple requirement that federal budget outlays not exceed revenues in a given fiscal year, with a waiver permitted in case of an emergency (say, a war or recession).[11] Over the years, so-called fiscal conservatives piled on additional limitations to restrain taxes and spending.[12] "A Balanced Budget Amendment is not sound," says former attorney general Ed Meese, now a fellow at the conservative Heritage Foundation, "if it leads to balancing the budget by tax hikes instead of spending cuts."[13]

What would a "sound" amendment look like, you ask? Consider the version House Republicans brought to the floor in 2018 as a "symbolic move" after enacting a corporate tax cut projected to add nearly $2 trillion to the national debt over a decade.[14] In addition to its mandate of a balanced budget, the GOP proposal would have capped federal outlays at "one-fifth of economic output of the United States" (a threshold already exceeded many times over the past half-century). Additionally, a three-fifths vote of Congress would be required to raise taxes or increase the debt limit.[15] The exercise was aptly dismissed as "Republican budget theater."[16] Had these strictures been in effect, the 2018 tax cut would have forced $2 trillion in spending cuts unless supermajorities in each house voted to make up the revenue somewhere else. By making it difficult to raise taxes while keeping it easy to cut them, Meese's "sound amendment" would act as a one-way ratchet, shrinking the government through repeated cycles of tax and spending cuts. That was the point.

Proponents sell the amendment with a superficially appealing message: households and state governments have to balance their books, so why shouldn't the federal government do the same? (Families, of course, borrow money all the time to purchase homes and pay for education.) Backers also point out, fairly enough, that excessive government borrowing burdens future generations.[17] They argue that tough medicine is needed because Congress will never exercise fiscal responsibility without some external constraint. As one supporter put it, "This amendment is essential to force Congress to make the kind of difficult choices it has evaded for years."[18]

Critics counter that Congress already has the power to balance the budget, as evidenced by four straight years of budget surpluses during the Clinton administration. They say that the amendment's true purpose is to force drastic cuts to Social Security, Medicare, and other government programs that conservatives have opposed for years.[19] Opponents further argue that the amendment would lock fiscal austerity policies into the Constitution, limiting government's ability to stimulate the economy during a recession or to respond to unexpected emergencies like the 2020 coronavirus pandemic. As the nonpartisan Center on Budget and Policy Priorities explains, the amendment "would require the largest budget cuts or tax increases precisely when the economy is weakest."[20]

The long saga of the balanced-budget amendment began in 1975 when a pair of state lawmakers launched a quiet campaign to persuade states to petition Congress for an Article V convention.[21] The two men, both Democrats, had no particular interest in obtaining a convention. They simply viewed the effort as "a 'club' to get Congress's attention," just as an earlier generation of advocates forced a reluctant Senate to take up the Seventeenth Amendment, giving voters the power to choose their senators.[22] The men enlisted the aid of the National Taxpayers Union, a small-government advocacy group with a valuable mailing list of prospective donors. The collaboration launched the careers of two of the most prominent leaders on the right today: Grover Norquist, a man whose lifelong dedication to the anti-tax cause has earned him the moniker "Rasputin of the right," and David Keating, a crusader against campaign finance limits best known as "the mastermind behind the super PAC."[23]

Over four years, working largely under the radar, this small strike force of anti-taxers quietly racked up wins in the statehouses. "Nobody was paying any attention to what they were doing," said a Democratic Party insider.[24] It was only when Jerry Brown, California's iconoclastic Democratic governor, embraced the cause in 1979 that people started paying attention.[25] "Unless its new visibility slows it down, a campaign many people dismissed as farfetched could, very soon, force Congress to consider a balanced budget amendment to the Constitution," reported the *Washington Post*.[26] By the end of 1979, thirty states had submitted petitions to Congress. Only four more were needed to convene the first constitutional convention since 1787. But as state lawmakers faced closer scrutiny, the pace of the campaign slowed. "It was one thing when you could just pass the thing and send it off to Washington with nobody looking," said one Ohio legislator. "But now the newspapers are watching, you've got to have hearings. Everybody's more careful when this comes up in a legislature now."[27]

Leaders from across the political spectrum sounded the alarm. President Jimmy Carter characterized the call for a constitutional convention as "extremely dangerous," warning that "the Constitution could be amended *en masse*, with multitudes of amendments."[28] Senator Barry Goldwater, a leader of the Republican Party's right flank, also expressed his opposition. "If we hold a constitutional convention," Goldwater said, "every group in the country—majority, minority, middle-of-the-road, left, right, up, down—is going to get its two bits in and we are going to wind up with a Constitution that will be so far different from the one we have lived under for 200 years that I doubt that the Republic could continue."[29]

By 1983, the campaign reached a high-water mark of thirty-two state applications as the fear of gambling on a constitutional convention with no clear rules or precedent created a chilling effect. A defeat in Michigan proved pivotal. "I felt this resolution created a risk," said the lawmaker who cast the deciding vote to defeat the measure. "It is not a good political climate for a constitutional convention."[30] By 1988, states began to cancel their applications,[31] pushed by an unlikely left-right coalition that ranged from the liberal People for the American Way to Phyllis Schlafly's Eagle Forum.[32] Yet, even as the effort to force a constitutional convention went into remission, the push for a balanced-budget amendment lived on. Just as the campaign's instigators had hoped, the campaign caught the interest of Congress, as senators and representatives, fearful that the convention push might succeed, were finally roused to act.[33]

The timing was convenient enough. Fresh off a widely criticized vote to approve a budget with a record $100 billion shortfall, self-proclaimed "defi-cit hawks" in Washington were looking for a way to signal their fiscal vir-tue. When the Republican leadership in the Senate brought the "fig leaf"[34] measure up for a vote in August 1982, senators fell over themselves to pass the measure by a vote of 69–31, two more than the number needed.[35] Later, the measure fell short in the Democrat-controlled House.[36]

These first skirmishes revealed significant bipartisan support for the balanced-budget amendment. In the Senate, twenty-two Democrats—nearly half the caucus—endorsed the measure.[37] Nearly a third of House Democrats did the same.[38] It may seem surprising today, but many influ-ential Democrats, including Joe Biden, Dianne Feinstein, and Steny Hoyer, have supported a version of the balanced-budget amendment in the past.[39] Few do now, however. As Republicans moved the goalposts over the years, layering on further restrictions to force deep spending cuts, bipartisan support for a constitutional solution dried up.[40]

Over the next decade, however, pressure for the amendment contin-ued to build. The Senate took up the measure again in 1986, falling one vote short of the number needed to advance.[41] After Democrats retook the chamber that year, Republicans managed to force votes on the amendment in 1990 and 1992 over the objections of leadership. While neither effort was successful, the amendment's proponents seemed to have the wind at their backs.[42] After the 1992 vote, the *New York Times* reported a sense among Republicans that "while they had lost the vote, they had won a use-ful campaign issue."[43] Sure enough, in the 1994 midterm election, the issue featured prominently in the "Contract with America," the party's legisla-tive agenda for the first hundred days of the new Congress. Republicans claimed a sweeping victory that year, gaining fifty-two seats in the House and seven in the Senate.[44] The media described the end of four decades of Democratic control in the House of Representatives as a "Republican revolution."[45]

For the freshly minted GOP majority, the balanced-budget amend-ment was a top priority. The new Speaker of the House, Newt Gingrich, fast-tracked the measure, slating the debate for the final week in January. Leading the effort was Henry Hyde, a veteran lawmaker representing a ring of white-collar suburbs outside Chicago. Hyde was best known for his implacable opposition to abortion. His "stature and his ability to get things done" prompted Gingrich to award him the plum assignment of House Ju-diciary Committee chairman, pushing a more senior colleague aside. The

National Journal called Hyde "the ringmaster synchronizing a circus of legislative activities." But the seventy-year-old lawmaker, described as "a huge man" with "a voice that can fill the House chamber like a tuba in a closet," stuck out as a representative of the old guard in a leadership dominated by hot-headed revolutionaries. "If you were casting Newt's inner circle," said one colleague, "Henry Hyde would not be in the front row."[46]

In what the *New York Times* called "the express-train style of Speaker Newt Gingrich's new House," Hyde's committee approved the amendment resolution after a single day of hearings, cutting off debate as opponents cried foul.[47] True to the pledge in the Contract with America, the proposal had two parts: a mandate that the government operate on a balanced budget and a requirement that 60 percent of the House and Senate approve any tax increases. When the measure came to the floor, Hyde slammed the Democrats for their "fierce resistance" to the measure, mocking their "long-standing romance with big government." In response, Democrats blasted the new majority as heartless. Said one indignant lawmaker: "The truth is they are going to slash Social Security, they are going to slash Medicare, they are going to slash veterans' benefits, they are going to pick the pockets of our seniors."[48]

On the day of the vote, January 26, 1995, Republican lawmakers greeted the speaker with a chorus of "Newt! Newt! Newt!" The resolution passed easily that day, by a vote of 300–132. "It's a historic moment for the country," Gingrich crowed. "We kept our promise; we worked hard; we produced a real change."[49] But the promise of "real change" would prove elusive. When the Senate took up its own version of the amendment in March, the new Republican majority leader, Bob Dole, could muster only 66 votes—one less than the number needed. Six Democrats who had previously supported the measure defected, bolstered by polls revealing rising public concern over cuts to Social Security benefits. The *Los Angeles Times* called it "a severe blow to the Republican legislative agenda, killing the heart of the GOP's campaign platform."[50]

Senate backers of the balanced-budget amendment tried again in 1996 and 1997, losing narrowly each time.[51] The House Republican leadership, meanwhile, would not attempt another vote until 2011. Looking back, a member of the GOP class of 1994 still smarts over a history "full of frustrations, high-profile defections, reversals, and betrayals."[52] While the increased salience of the issue likely made it easier for Congress to cooperate with President Clinton to pass four balanced budgets in a row, this bipartisan accomplishment only undermined the argument that a drastic constitutional fix was needed. But the saga of the balanced-budget amendment was far from over.

Even as the push for the amendment stalled, conservative state lawmakers improbably breathed new life into another proposed addition to the Constitution—a measure left for dead two centuries earlier when the states ratified ten of twelve amendments in the original Bill of Rights. The story begins in the dorm room of a nineteen-year-old sophomore at the University of Texas at Austin.

The Twenty-Seventh Amendment: Madison's Final Revision

In 1982, Gregory Watson had a term paper to write. At first, he planned to explore whether Congress properly exercised its power when it extended the ratification deadline for the Equal Rights Amendment. But as he pored over books in the local public library, Watson stumbled upon a more intriguing topic.[53] "I'll never forget this as long as I live," he says. "I pull out a book that has within it a chapter of amendments that Congress has sent to the state legislatures, but which not enough state legislatures approved in order to become part of the Constitution. And this one jumped right out at me."[54]

The would-be addition to the Constitution that caught the young student's eye was adopted by the 1st Congress in 1789, transmitted to the states as the second of twelve amendments included in the original Bill of Rights. Intended as protection against legislative self-dealing, the measure provided that pay raises for members of Congress may take effect only after the next election. James Madison, the proposal's author, questioned its necessity, and only a few states ratified it at first. After ten of Congress's twelve amendments were adopted in 1791, the measure languished, all but forgotten.[55]

Because Congress never imposed an expiration date, Watson argued in his paper that the Congressional Pay Amendment could and should be ratified. To his dismay, his teacher gave him a C for his effort. "I was very disappointed given how much tender love and care I had put into the paper," Watson recalls. But the setback ignited a personal obsession: "I thought right then and there, 'I'm going to get that thing ratified.'"[56] Over many months, Watson sent letters to politicians of both parties, looking for legislative champions. Most ignored him until William Cohen, a

Republican senator from Maine, passed the idea along to lawmakers in his state. To Watson's delight, Maine ratified the amendment in April 1983. Encouraged by this first success, he redoubled his efforts. Apart from his studies, and a job as a legislative aide, Watson "would eat, drink, sleep, and breath[e] the ratification of the amendment all seven days of the week," painstakingly drafting appeals to lawmakers on his IBM Selectric typewriter.[57] He estimated he spent $5,000 of his own money on stationery and postage to advance the effort.[58]

Over the next nine years, Watson's one-man advocacy campaign secured a steady stream of additional ratifications. "I got a lot of help, interestingly enough, from Congress," he recalls.[59] Controversial pay raises and a succession of financial scandals stoked a grassroots desire to send Washington a message. By the turn of the decade, as the tally of ratifications neared the two-thirds threshold, a group of upstart GOP House freshmen muscled into the act. Led by their class president, the future Speaker of the House John Boehner, they introduced a resolution in Congress urging states to ratify the amendment as their "class project." Watson resented Boehner for "snatching undeserved credit" for his idea.[60] Nevertheless, on May 7, 1992, he was afforded the honor of listening in by phone as Michigan's legislature voted, lifting the amendment over Article V's ratification threshold.[61] He called it "the greatest thing in my thirty-year life."[62]

"The new amendment snuck up on the Hill with little fanfare or warning," reported the *Congressional Quarterly*.[63] Some lawmakers questioned the measure's validity.[64] Was it really possible to ratify a constitutional amendment more than two centuries after it was first proposed? Article V is silent on the timing of the ratification process. It simply provides that an amendment "shall be valid" when approved by three-fourths of the states. Complicating matters, a pair of Supreme Court decisions offered conflicting guidance. In *Dillon v. Gloss*, the 1921 case rejecting a challenge to the Prohibition Amendment, the Court declared that ratification by the states should be "sufficiently contemporaneous," not "scattered through a long series of years."[65] But then, in the 1939 case of *Coleman v. Miller*, the Court held that a legal dispute over the timeliness of the Child Labor Amendment—whether it "lost its vitality through lapse of time"—was a political question that Congress alone should decide.[66]

A week after the May 1992 vote in Michigan, members of Congress pressed for hearings to consider whether the amendment was duly ratified.[67] But a little-known bureaucrat named Don Wilson had other ideas. As archivist of the United States, Wilson had the responsibility under a 1984 law for managing the process of certifying constitutional amendments.[68] Though leaders in Congress warned him there would be "ramifications" if he acted before lawmakers had a chance to weigh in, Wilson maintained he had no choice but to certify the Twenty-Seventh Amendment as a valid addition to the Constitution.[69] Robert Byrd, the West Virginia Democrat long regarded as the Senate's leading institutionalist, reprimanded Wilson for disregarding "historic tradition."[70] But the Democratic Speaker of the House, Tom Foley, saw no point in resisting.[71] With an election approaching, Congress bowed to political reality, passing by overwhelming margins a resolution affirming the amendment as valid.[72]

The Twenty-Seventh Amendment's populist spirit fit the tenor of the times. This "sensible declaration,"[73] as the *New York Times* called it, was so benign that no substantial opposition ever emerged in response to it. But some scholars have expressed concerns about the precedent it set.[74] Shouldn't proposed amendments have a shelf life? In the years since its adoption, the improbable story of "the Madison Amendment" has inspired activists looking to restart the ratification process for the Equal Rights Amendment years after it, too, was presumed to be dead.[75]

A Case of "Constitutional Amendment Fever"

The 1992 adoption of the Twenty-Seventh Amendment coincided with rising interest in Article V as a means to advance right-wing causes. It was the dawn of the era of conservative amendment politics—a time when lawmakers casually invoked the constitutional amendment process as a powerful political wedge issue.[76] In the space of twelve years, the GOP-led Congress that came to Washington after the 1994 election brought no fewer than seven amendment proposals to the floor, seeking to constitutionalize a breathtaking array of policy goals. In addition to the balanced-budget amendment, some of the most notable measures were proposals to impose congressional term limits, criminalize flag desecration, and outlaw same-sex marriage.

Like the drive for a balanced-budget amendment, the campaign for legislative term limits was at the heart of the anti-government backlash that swept the Republicans back to power. The effort was inspired, at least in part, by frustration over decades of Democratic control of Congress, buoyed by the power of incumbency.[77] In the early 1990s, activists won laws in over twenty states to cap lawmakers' terms, most by ballot measure.[78] Building on this momentum, the Contract with America promised "a first-ever vote on term limits to replace career politicians with citizen legislators."[79] The issue was a visceral priority for many newly elected members, who made pious pledges to limit their own tenure in office. They pressed for a vote within the first hundred days of the new Congress. "Term limits would end congressional stagnation and careerism and bring a healthy infusion of new ideas and new people," argued Missouri congressman John Ashcroft, a member of the GOP freshman class. But the many career politicians in Congress were less enthused. Mitch McConnell of Kentucky, already a decade into what would be a long career in the Senate, insisted it was "absurd to contend that Congress is the only workplace in America where experience is inherently bad."[80]

While the Framers declined to impose term limits on federal officeholders, Anti-Federalists warned that lawmakers elected for long periods risk becoming "inattentive to the public good, callous, selfish, and the fountain of corruption."[81] After the adoption of the Twenty-Second Amendment in 1951, limiting presidents to two terms, the idea of imposing term limits on members of Congress gained new adherents. Over the next four decades, members of Congress introduced 141 amendment proposals to limit lawmakers' tenure.[82]

True to their word, GOP leaders in the House brought the term-limits amendment up for consideration in March 1995. The debate took place just three weeks after the Senate torpedoed the balanced-budget measure (and two months before the Supreme Court would rule that state-imposed congressional term limits were unconstitutional).[83] This time, however, there was division in the Republican ranks. Chafing at the demands of the freshmen in his caucus, Henry Hyde worked with Democrats to derail the measure. In a feisty oration that drew standing ovations from both sides of the aisle, the veteran congressman made the case for experienced leadership in government. "I will not concede to the angry, pessimistic populism that drives this movement, because it is just dead wrong," Hyde thundered. "America needs leaders. It needs statesmen. It needs giants, and you do not get them out of the phone book."[84]

The disappointing vote, falling sixty-one short of the threshold needed to advance, was a second black eye for the new Republican majority. "Most Republicans supported a term limits amendment," reported the *Congressional Quarterly*, "but the opposition of senior Republicans combined with

Democrats' distaste of the proposal contributed to its defeat."[85] Oklahoma congressman Tom Coburn, a true believer who would later step down after six years in Congress (one of only a few members of the class of 1994 to honor this pledge), blasted "the arrogance of career political elitism that we have heard today in this House."[86] The measure fared no better in the Senate, where opponents managed to block an up-or-down vote.[87]

The next amendment battle, over flag burning, arose in reaction to one of the most controversial Supreme Court decisions of the era. In *Texas v. Johnson*,[88] handed down in June 1989, the justices considered the case of Gregory Lee Johnson, a man convicted under a Texas law for burning an American flag to protest the policies of the Reagan administration. In an opinion that scrambled the Court's usual ideological divide, five justices (three liberals and two conservatives) concluded that Johnson's action was a form of symbolic speech protected by the First Amendment. "If there is a bedrock principle underlying the First Amendment," wrote Justice William Brennan Jr., "it is that the government may not prohibit the expression of an idea simply because society finds the idea itself offensive or disagreeable."[89] In a prickly dissent, Chief Justice William Rehnquist countered, "Surely one of the high purposes of a democratic society is to legislate against conduct that is regarded as evil and profoundly offensive to the majority of the people—whether it be murder, embezzlement, pollution or flag burning."[90]

The Court's ruling set off a political firestorm. Within a day, members of the House raced to introduce seventeen different amendment proposals to overturn it.[91] President George H. W. Bush, who had shamelessly exploited the Pledge of Allegiance in the 1988 campaign to depict his opponent as unpatriotic,[92] wasted no time in endorsing an amendment. "I believe that the flag of the United States should never be the object of desecration," he declared. "Protection of the flag, a unique national symbol, will in no way limit the opportunity nor the breadth of protest available in the exercise of free speech rights."[93] One grandstanding congressman called for a special Fourth of July session to approve the measure.[94]

Speaker Foley looked for a way to deflect the stampede to amend, which he considered little more than "a crass political maneuver" to portray Democrats as anti-American.[95] Rather than "rush in with an amendment to the First Amendment,"[96] the speaker persuaded Congress to pass a better tailored statute in the hope it could satisfy the Court. It was widely expected that the justices would invalidate the new law.[97] Protestors were ready, on cue, to burn flags for the television cameras as soon as it took effect. Within a year, the Court struck down the statute as skeptics predicted, reaffirming its holding that flag burning was a form of protected speech.[98] The clamor for an amendment resumed.

Foley's distaste for the measure had not abated, but he had prepared for this moment. Having bought some cooling-off time, he convened a task force to organize grassroots support against the amendment. New messaging helped to change the conversation. "Last year, the theme was that this is such a disgrace and that no one should be allowed to burn the flag," said a GOP legislative aide. "This year, they were saying, 'don't tamper with the Constitution.'"[99] The speaker moved quickly to schedule debate before the other side could fully mobilize.[100]

The amendment came to the floor of the House on June 21, 1990, ten days after the Court reaffirmed its earlier ruling. The measure's sponsor, the low-key Republican minority leader Bob Michel, laid out the case for a constitutional fix. "Any American, if he or she so chooses, can hate the flag with all the bitterness and rage the dark corners of the heart can generate," he said. "We say to them: Hate the flag if you must—but don't physically desecrate it."[101] Henry Hyde, who returned to the fold after defecting to kill the term-limits amendment, leaped in with a more emotional appeal. "Can we not get a symbol and elevate it and say that it unites us as a country?" he cried. "Too many people have paid for it with their blood."[102]

The measure's opponents, mostly Democrats, took pains to express their distaste for the vanishingly few flag burners in the country. "The physical desecration of the flag is a disgusting, offensive act," said Robert Kastenmeier, a Wisconsin Democrat who helped lead the opposition. "But, trying to protect the flag from a handful of flag burners does not warrant diminishing, for the first time in our history, the first amendment rights of 250 million Americans. If we pass this constitutional amendment, free speech and political expression will ultimately depend solely on what the Congress will permit."[103]

After an emotional five-hour debate, the House rejected the flag desecration amendment in a vote that fell thirty-four short of the two-thirds needed. The GOP caucus was largely united in favor of the measure, while the Democrats were split.[104] The *New York Times* called it a "vindication" for Foley, who "spent hours on the phone and in meetings, persuading wavering Democrats that it was possible to vote against the amendment without having their patriotism challenged or finding themselves the subject of negative campaign ads."[105] After a vote in the Senate fell short the following week,[106] Senator Strom Thurmond, a long-serving Republican from South Carolina, insisted the fight was not over. "I think you will see it come back again," he said. "I think you are going to see an aroused public because people believe in the flag."[107]

Thurmond was right. Republicans knew a potent electoral weapon when they saw one. Opinion polls showed that two-thirds of Americans supported an amendment to outlaw flag desecration.[108] Adding to the political pressure, legislatures in forty-nine states (all but Vermont) passed resolutions calling on Congress to act.[109] So it surprised no one when the new Republican majority revisited the topic of flag burning. Speaker Gingrich scheduled a vote for June 1995. It would be the chamber's *third* showdown over a constitutional amendment in six months, coming a week after the failed vote on the term-limits measure.

This time, the flag-desecration amendment passed handily by a vote of 312–120.[110] All but 12 Republicans supported the measure, while Democrats were again evenly split. "The overwhelming support," said the *Times*, "indicates that of all the Republican attempts to amend the Constitution this session, this may be the one that succeeds."[111] But when the measure came up for a Senate vote in December, supporters barely missed the two-thirds mark when three undecided Democrats voted no.[112] "We'll be back," promised the Citizens Flag Alliance, an umbrella coalition of civic and religious groups formed to back the measure.[113] Sure enough over the next decade, the GOP-led House passed the flag-desecration amendment five additional times.[114] In a familiar pattern, supporters could never quite muster the two-thirds support needed to advance the measure in the Senate.[115]

Why were House Republicans so tenacious in their pursuit of a largely symbolic fight over flag burning while losing interest in the balanced-budget and term-limit amendments that featured so prominently in their Contract with America? The answer can be found in the GOP's embrace of wedge-issue politics. By the 1990s, far-right advocacy groups figured out that sponsoring ballot measures on hot-button topics, ranging from gay rights to affirmative action to immigration, could excite social conservatives and bring them to the polls.[116] Working with allies in Congress, they perfected the art of forcing difficult votes on carefully crafted bills— from the ban on "partial birth abortion" to mandating the recital of the Pledge of Allegiance—as fodder for thirty-second attack ads. This cynical exploitation of the culture wars as an electoral strategy also explains the curious story of the campaign for a federal marriage amendment.

In November 2003, the Massachusetts high court ruled that excluding lesbian and gay couples from civil marriage was unlawful. "The Massachusetts Constitution affirms the dignity and equality of all individuals," declared the closely divided court.[117] It was a landmark victory for a scrappy, underfunded movement with a seemingly improbable goal: winning marriage equality in all fifty states.[118] The ruling hit America like a thunderbolt. Depending on one's point of view, the sight of joyous newlyweds of the same sex broadcast on the evening news was an inspiring breakthrough for human rights—or a troubling threat to a sacred institution.[119]

In our federal system, marriage laws are the responsibility of the states. Congress intruded into this sphere in 1996 when it passed the Defense of Marriage Act, preemptively barring any federal recognition of same-sex unions.[120] But for self-styled "defenders" of the institution, the law provided scant security. In an essay called "The 28th Amendment," written two years before the Massachusetts decision, Princeton professor Robert George warned that a "judicial assault on marriage," led by "socially liberal federal judges," could simply sweep the law aside. "The only sure safeguard against this assault," argued George, "is to use the ultimate democratic tool available to the American people: a constitutional amendment."[121] The day after the Massachusetts ruling, leaders of religious-right groups met to plot a strategy. "We must amend the Constitution if we are to stop a tyrannical judiciary from redefining marriage to the point of extinction," said Tony Perkins of the Family Research Council.[122] The New York Times noted that same-sex marriage was now "the most important battle in the nation's cultural wars," supplanting abortion.[123]

President George W. Bush endorsed a constitutional ban on February 24, 2004, 12 days after thousands of couples lined up to marry in San Francisco on Valentine's Day weekend.[124] "The amendment process has addressed many serious matters of national concern," he said, "and the preservation of marriage rises to this level of national importance."[125] While the chairman of a religious-right coalition predicted that "President Bush's leadership on this issue will make the difference," leaders of LGBT rights groups girded for a fight. "Not since the days of Jim Crow segregation has our nation faced the prospect of discrimination written into law in such a shameful way," said one activist.[126]

The Democrats' presumptive presidential candidate, John Kerry, dismissed the amendment push as "a wedge issue to divide the American people." [127] And he was right. At a time when few politicians had the courage to embrace marriage equality, Kerry included, Republicans gleefully pressed for a vote knowing the measure had little chance of passing. Their admitted goal, reported the *New York Times*, was to secure "a vote that puts every member of the Senate on record on an issue that both Republicans and Democrats see as a political wedge." [128] Senator John McCain, the Arizona Republican, argued that imposing a federal standard on an issue traditionally left to the states was "antithetical in every way to the core philosophy of Republicans." [129] Nevertheless, most of the usual champions of states' rights and the Tenth Amendment hypocritically backed the amendment.

Congresswoman Marilyn Musgrave, a stridently anti-gay Republican from Colorado, introduced the Federal Marriage Amendment in May 2004, just months before a hotly contested presidential election. The measure attracted 131 co-sponsors. [130] The congresswoman dismissed criticism that the amendment would enshrine discrimination in the Constitution. "Gays are not excluded from the benefits of marriage by others," she drily explained "They are excluded by their own choices." [131] Massachusetts representative Barney Frank, one of only three openly gay members of Congress at the time, appealed in starkly personal terms. "How is the fact that I or someone else wants to express love to another human being . . . how does that hurt you?" he asked. "Why is this considered an infringement?" [132]

The Senate took up the measure in July, delivering "a sound, and expected, defeat." [133] When the House voted in September, less than five weeks before the November election, the proposal fared no better. [134] "This is only the beginning," vowed the Republican whip, Tom DeLay. "This nation will protect marriage." [135] He was wrong, of course. Americans slowly came to accept marriage equality. Following another failed vote in 2006, Congress never returned to the topic. By 2015 marriage equality would be the law of the land. [136]

From 1995 to 2007, during twelve years of Republican control, Congress considered several other proposed changes to the Constitution that received far less attention. One proposal brought to the floor of the House of Representatives would have overturned Supreme Court cases enforcing the separation of church and state. [137] Another would have required a two-thirds vote in Congress to raise taxes. [138] Both measures were defeated soundly. During this period, Republican leaders in the Senate also took the unusual step of allowing a vote on a campaign finance proposal they actively opposed. The bipartisan measure would have empowered Congress and the states to "set reasonable limits" on campaign contributions and expenditures, overturning Supreme Court cases that have rolled back reforms to limit money in politics. It was a strategy pioneered by Nelson Aldrich and Spessard Holland, who pressed for constitutional amendments on the income tax and poll tax to take the steam out of efforts to advance those goals through ordinary legislation. For that reason, champions of campaign finance reform joined in the lopsided vote against the measure, insisting that "changing the Constitution was a cumbersome, unnecessary and unduly slow way to go about addressing the problem of campaign corruption." [139]

During this unusually active period, there was a surge of interest among conservative academics and activists in the history of constitutional amendments while some of their counterparts on the left retreated to a position of caution. Kathleen Sullivan, a prominent scholar, wrote an influential article criticizing Congress's outbreak of "constitutional amendment fever." The Constitution "should be amended sparingly," she cautioned, "not used as a chip in short-run political games." [140] In 1999, Sullivan joined "a bipartisan blue-ribbon" panel of prominent American scholars, thought leaders, and former government officials calling for more restraint. "It is not only wrong to trivialize the Constitution by cluttering it with measures embodying no more than ordinary policy; it is also a mistake to reopen basic questions of governance lightly," the panelists concluded. [141]

After losing control of Congress to the Democrats in 2006, the GOP's case of "constitutional amendmentitis" appeared to go into remission. But just four years later, when Republicans came storming back in the 2010 "Tea Party" election, they redoubled their efforts, bringing the fight back to Congress and, more consequentially, to the state legislatures.

"Look to the Past to Secure Our Future"

After Republicans gained control of half the nation's statehouses in 2010,[142] far-right activists revived their push for a balanced-budget convention. By that time, support for a convention had retreated dramatically from the peak reached in July 1983, when backers counted thirty-two Article V applications submitted to Congress—just two shy of the thirty-four needed to force a convention. Over the following three decades, sixteen states withdrew their applications. But in 2010, Florida filed the first new application in twenty-seven years. Alabama submitted one the following year. Their actions, steeped in Tea Party fervor, signaled a new round in this long and unresolved fight.

The Balanced Budget Amendment Task Force, a small Florida nonprofit launched in 2010, is the nominal leader of this rebooted campaign. Operating with an annual budget of just over $50,000,[143] the group claims to be "the national organization coordinating the effort to convene a convention for proposing a balanced budget amendment."[144] But the real driver of this enterprise is the American Legislative Exchange Council. ALEC, as the organization is known, describes itself as "America's largest nonpartisan, voluntary membership organization of state legislators dedicated to the principles of limited government, free markets and federalism," claiming nearly a quarter of all state lawmakers as members.[145] The liberal watchdog group Common Cause calls it "a corporate lobbying group masquerading as a charity."[146]

Business interests fund almost all of ALEC's operations. In return, the group's lobbyists work with friendly state lawmakers to craft "model bills" advancing a deregulatory, pro-business agenda in state capitals across the country.[147] Over the past decade, ALEC has embraced the right's Article V campaigns with gusto.[148] To coordinate those efforts, it set up a State Legislators Article V Caucus, whose stated mission is "to re-establish federalism as our Founders intended, and limit the runaway growth of the Federal Government."[149] To make things easy for receptive lawmakers, ALEC has developed model state petitions (lawmakers just need to fill in a few blanks) and a handbook of talking points and legal arguments.[150]

By 2017, the renewed push for a balanced-budget convention yielded nineteen new state applications. When added to stale petitions dating back to 1957, supporters now claim to have secured twenty-eight of the thirty-four states needed to obtain a constitutional convention.[151] Experts say it's an open question whether Congress would consider this jumble of petitions as sufficiently consistent and timely to be counted together.[152] Nevertheless, the *New York Times* concluded that "what was once a pet project of the party's fringe has become a proposal with a plausible chance of success."[153]

The balanced-budget campaign is not the only Article V convention game in town. A new and more sophisticated effort, launched in 2014, has more far-reaching aims. The Convention of States project seeks a convention under Article V to devise a package of revisions to the Constitution covering three broad topics: restraints on federal spending, term limits for members of Congress, and—most ambitiously—curbs on the power and jurisdiction of the federal government. Unlike the balanced-budget campaign, which purports to focus on a single topic, the vague and sweeping language in the Convention of States model application anticipates multiple amendments. Its grandiose focus on limiting "the power, size, and spending of the federal government" puts much of the national charter in play. Critics say it's nothing less than an *invitation* to a runaway convention.[154]

The Convention of States was conceived by Michael Farris, an influential leader of the religious right who founded the Home School Legal Defense Association and Patrick Henry College, an evangelical school with the ambition to be "God's Harvard."[155] Farris sees the convention as a means to revise our entire system of government. "We're going back to the original balance of power between the states and the federal government," he vows.[156] The Convention of States project is organized by Citizens for Self-Governance (CSG), a Texas nonprofit founded in 2010 with the mission of coordinating "a nationwide network of self-governing citizen activists, committed to bringing government back to the people."[157] The group's leaders are Mark Meckler, a co-founder of Tea Party Patriots who helped lead the opposition to Obamacare, and Eric O'Keefe, a term-limits campaigner–turned–"Koch-tied dark money man"—a reference to billionaire brothers Charles and David Koch, major funders of anti-progressive causes.[158] To advance the project, CSG deploys paid lobbyists and field volunteers—"the largest grassroots army in the history of the United States," it is claimed—to pressure state legislators to submit Article V convention applications to Congress.[159] ALEC has also adopted the Convention of States as a top legislative priority.[160]

In March 2014, Georgia sent the first Convention of States resolution to Congress. Since then, the tally has risen to fifteen applications, primarily from Republican-led states in the South and West.[161] With the project's success has come endorsements from a who's who of the far right: senators Marco Rubio and Rand Paul, governors Greg Abbott and Mike Huckabee, and media personalities Mark Levin and Sean Hannity. While Meckler and O'Keefe refuse to identify the group's donors, tax filings reveal a dark-money trail back to the Koch brothers and other conservative megadonors. O'Keefe sits on the boards of nonprofits funded by the Kochs, including charities that can raise unlimited sums without having to reveal the sources of their income. With this shadowy support, CSG has grown to an organization with a $5 million annual budget. What's the return on this investment? As one investigative report put it, "Right-wing billionaires are buying themselves a new Constitution." [162]

The project's backers claim to be simply restoring the constitutional balance of power the Framers intended, but their case is based on a skewed version of history. Consider the argument put forth by former senator Tom Coburn, the Oklahoma Tea Party Republican who served the campaign as senior advisor from 2017 until his death in 2020. In *Smashing the DC Monopoly*, a book-length manifesto for the Article V movement, Coburn maintains that the Constitution was devised as a blueprint for limited government. "Gaining independence from a distant and oppressive . . . monarchy," he writes, "the Founders had a well-earned fear of power concentrated in a strong central authority. So they focused on limiting the power of the new federal government and containing the natural drive for power in the country's leaders." [163]

Is this true? It depends on which founders Coburn is referring to. To be sure, a mistrust of central authority inspired thirteen sovereign states to enter into their "firm league of friendship" under the Articles of Confederation, maintaining a jealous regard for their independence and sovereignty. But the Confederation government's inadequacy changed a lot of minds. By 1787, the men who drafted the Constitution and prevailed in the fight to ratify it were animated mainly by the desire to craft a plan of government that could meet the needs of a vast nation. As Gordon Wood, a leading historian of the period, explains, "In place of the impotent confederation of separate states that had existed in the 1780s, the Federalists aimed to build a strong, consolidated, and prosperous 'fiscal-military' state in emulation of eighteenth-century England, united 'for the accomplishment of great purposes' by an energetic government composed of the best men in society." [164] Richard Morris, a Federalist leader in New York, embodied this can-do spirit at the 1788 New York ratifying convention when he declared, "An energetic, federal government is essential to the preservation of our union." [165]

Of course, during the great national debate that preceded the Constitution's adoption many Americans did worry about putting too much power in the hands of the new national government. The pseudonymous Anti-Federalist essayist Brutus expected that the new federal government "is to possess absolute and uncontrollable power . . . with respect to every object to which it extends." He further insisted that the Constitution would "annihilate all the state governments, and reduce this country to one single government,"[166] just as Patrick Henry, leader of the Anti-Federalist forces in Virginia, inveighed against a "great consolidated government."[167] But they lost. And they were wrong. Over more than 230 years of governance under the Constitution, the federal system crafted by the Framers has proved to be resilient.

In his misleading meander through the history of America's founding, Coburn makes a telling admission. His affinity, he confesses, lies with "the generation of wary Rhode Islanders in 1790" who "guardedly assented to the Constitution and the new national government."[168] Where James Madison saw only "wickedness and folly," Coburn sees a "sober presence of mind."[169] Coburn laments the failure of Rhode Island's leaders to secure an amendment to the Constitution reserving to the states all powers not "expressly delegated" to the federal government.[170] Of course, that was the same stingy delegation of power that hopelessly hobbled the Confederation government, rendering it inadequate to meet the nation's needs.

Today, self-anointed "constitutionalists"[171] like Coburn claim to seek a restoration of the Framers' design, but an honest look at history puts these constitutional combatants squarely on the side of the Anti-Federalists. They champion a vision of governance with deep roots in American political thought, to be sure, but it is misleading to suggest that they are faithful to the Framers' intent. Should it ever come to pass, their Convention of States would fulfill the dreams of George Mason, Patrick Henry, and New York's Anti-Federalists, who demanded a second constitutional convention to undo the Framers' great accomplishment.

So what does the Convention of States crowd really hope to achieve? We don't have to speculate about their ambitions. In 2016 they staged a revealing trial run. The slogan in a promotional video proclaimed: "Look to the past to secure our future." As if to emphasize their affinity with the Anti-Federalist cause, the participants in this "simulated convention" met in Colonial Williamsburg, with a keynote speech by a Patrick Henry impersonator. "We felt the essence of the founders there," an Arizona lawmaker gushed.[172] No doubt Henry, who relentlessly plotted a second constitutional convention from this very state, would have approved.

Attending this staged exercise were some 120 state lawmakers— predominantly white, male, middle-aged, and Christian. Over three days, they debated and approved six proposed amendments to the Constitution.[173] Their desired revisions would:

- Repeal the Sixteenth Amendment to eliminate Congress's power to tax incomes, gifts, or estates.
- Require a two-thirds vote of each house before Congress can raise the debt limit or increase taxes.
- Limit the tenure of members of Congress to twelve years.
- Narrowly redefine Congress's power to regulate interstate commerce, which serves as the constitutional basis for key federal programs and initiatives, from Social Security and Medicare to environmental laws.
- Allow Congress to void regulations by independent federal agencies by a majority vote in each house.
- Allow three-fifths of the states to "abrogate" any federal law, regulation, or executive order.[174]

Simply put, these proposals would radically change the nature of American government. As their backers readily concede, that's the point. In an interview during a break in the proceedings, Farris didn't mince words. "We can really curtail the federal government," he promised.[175] At times, there was a conspiratorial air to the discussion. Setting aside any notion of local government's greater connection to the people, Farris explained how a small minority could easily foist a constitutional revolution on an unwitting country. "In state legislative matters," he intimated, "less than one percent of the people ever participate, so with one percent of the American public—that's about three million people. I guarantee you, this gets done."[176]

As simulations go, the three-day gathering in Colonial Williamsburg had all the authenticity of a fantasy football league. The participants reveled in minor period details, addressing each other as "commissioner" and fussily parsing *Robert's Rules of Order*. The self-congratulation was laid on thick as attendees ironed out minor drafting disputes over amendments they largely agreed on. Conspicuously absent was anyone contesting their reactionary premise—as if no state in this diverse and polarized nation would send delegates to oppose their radical plan. Missing, too, were the lobbyists and interest groups who would surely swarm an actual constitutional convention, eager to press their private agendas. But perhaps the most amusing conceit of the enterprise was the shared belief among this group of Article V enthusiasts that *they* would actually get to run such a convening.

The two leading "Con-Con" efforts, balanced budget and Convention of States, have reignited concerns over a runaway convention. Proponents bristle at the very mention of the phrase, knowing that the fear of unleashing a constitutional convention unbounded in scope and authority has, more than anything, foiled their efforts over the past four decades. An Article V convention is not dangerous, these activists insist.[177] And even if a convention did exceed its mandate, the high bar of winning ratification by three-fourths of the states provides a reassuring check. "All it takes is thirteen judiciary chairmen, in thirteen states, to stop anything stupid that might come out of that," says Coburn.[178] But America's most recent experience with a constitutional convention, back in the summer of 1787, offers a cautionary tale. The Philadelphia Convention was tasked with the limited mandate of crafting amendments to the Articles of Confederation. Behind closed doors, however, the delegates completely rewrote the national charter *and* eased the ratification procedure to boot.

To allay fears of a runaway convention, a third Article V convention vehicle—the "Compact for America"—has put forth a novel, if convoluted, plan to propose and ratify a balanced-budget amendment in a preprogrammed procedure. Under the proposal, state legislatures would agree to define every step of the process in advance: choosing the delegates, setting the rules, approving the amendment, and ratifying it.[179] Proponents claim that constraining the process in this way would eliminate any possibility of a runaway convention. But skeptics say its protections are illusory because states would have no way to bind delegates once they are selected.[180] Still, five states have subscribed to this unlikeliest of vehicles.[181] ALEC supports it too.[182]

The truth is, no one knows how an Article V convention would play out. It's conceivable that the delegates would act with restraint.[183] Or not. James Madison understood as much when he worried that "difficulties might arise" should a convention ever be summoned.[184] Simply put, there are no rules, no referees, and no sure answers to the many questions raised. What *is* clear is that any call for a constitutional convention in the twenty-first century would raise profound questions of democratic legitimacy and fairness. For a start, no one can say for certain how delegates would be selected. Most Article V convention aficionados simply assume that a convention would follow the process used in 1787.[185] That would give state legislators in gerrymandered districts the power to appoint delegates in a manner that distorts the preferences of people in their state.

As an alternative, states might decide to send delegates chosen by popular election. It's the method the Framers prescribed for the state ratifying conventions to realize their promise that "We the People" would establish and ordain the new national charter. But in today's polarized politics, these contests would surely degenerate into donnybrooks influenced by special interests and dark money. "Supporters of an Article V convention conjure a fairytale process with citizens from across the country coming together with openness and good will to seek the common good," says legal scholar David Super. "The reality of today's bare-knuckle politics suggests otherwise. Big-money interests that already spend heavily to influence Congress would redouble their efforts in pursuit of permanent protection for their interests through a constitutional amendment."[186]

Also not clear is the question of representation. Coburn blithely assumes "the long-standing convention precedent of 'one state, one vote'" would apply.[187] That would grant red Wyoming, a state with just over half a million people, as much power to craft amendments as California, with its nearly 40 million people. Viewed through a different partisan lens, blue Vermont's 623,000 people would have as much say as 29 million Texans. Nothing in the Constitution requires or forbids such an unfair result, but the unfair "one state, one vote" rule would be reason enough to reject the convention approach.

In what Common Cause president Karen Hobert Flynn calls a coast-to-coast "game of Whac-A-Mole," a coalition of progressive groups has urged states to withdraw their calls for a convention, with some success.[188] Since 2016, four states—Delaware, Maryland, New Mexico, and Nevada—have canceled their applications for the balanced-budget convention.[189] The increased visibility of the issue has made some lawmakers skittish about supporting an Article V convention, even in legislatures controlled by Republicans. In 2014, when the campaign for the Convention of States came to the Virginia legislature—once the base for Patrick Henry's schemes to defeat the Constitution—cooler heads prevailed. "This is something very fundamental that may alter the structure of government," said one GOP lawmaker. "There is no clear understanding how this would proceed."[190]

Lately, some progressives have begun to pursue Article V convention dreams of their own. Take Wolf-PAC, a left-leaning nonprofit founded in

2011 to promote a constitutional amendment to restore the integrity of our elections. Its amendment would overturn Supreme Court campaign finance rulings, like *Citizens United*, that have thwarted meaningful reform. Inspired by the history of the Seventeenth Amendment, the group maintains that "pressure from the states is an important check against the federal government and an effective way to get Congress to act."[191] Pursuing this strategy, Wolf-PAC has convinced five blue state legislatures to submit applications for "a limited convention under Article V."[192] Legal scholar Lawrence Lessig III also sees the Article V convention route as a promising avenue for reform.[193] Lessig has forged an unlikely alliance with some of the right's Article V warriors to make the case that the Article V convention is a safe vehicle "open to reformers from all sides."[194] But these efforts continue to be opposed by a wide array of progressive allies who share their commitment to reform but consider the Article V approach too risky.[195]

Meanwhile, some of the most vocal and energetic opponents of an Article V convention can be found on the far right. "Some conservatives assume that a constitutional convention would propose only conservative ideas like a balanced budget," said Phyllis Schlafly, who remained adamantly opposed to the idea until her death in 2016. "It never occurs to them that Bernie Sanders supporters would show up to demand constitutional amendments requiring the taxpayers to pay for free college and other free stuff for everyone."[196] Similarly, the far-right John Birch Society regularly warns its members about the danger of "a 'runaway' convention that could completely change the Constitution."[197] Still, the energy—and the most receptive audience—for a new constitutional convention can be found mainly on the right. "This is the battle of our generation, literally," says Meckler.[198] Americans of every political stripe should be wary.

Changing the Constitution by Other Means

After four decades of effort, the conservatives' Article V dreams have yet to produce a single successful revision to the national charter apart from the resurrection of James Madison's Congressional Pay Amendment. Then again, they have not needed to rely on constitutional amendments to advance their vision of the law. Over the same period, an ascendant conservative legal movement has mobilized to change the Constitution by other means. Their goal: rolling back decades of liberal dominance in American constitutional thought to move the law decisively to the right. To achieve this aim, a network of far-right donors has developed and nurtured an infrastructure of influential conservative legal groups organized around five interlocking strategies.

First, they invested in a new generation of legal scholarship to reframe the debate over contested constitutional principles. To advance this goal, they endowed centers, professorships, and academic chairs, giving conservatives a foothold in the nation's top law schools. Many of these scholars rely on a methodology known as "originalism," which claims authority by divining "the framers' original intent or the original understanding of the members of the ratifying generation."[199] But this method of constitutional interpretation is a "smokescreen," argues Berkeley Law dean Erwin Chemerinsky, invented to allow conservatives "to portray themselves as untainted by value choices and adherents of the 'true' meaning of the Constitution," while trapping us in the worldview of a bygone era.[200] The right's resulting scholarship—focusing on a wide array of issues ranging from gun rights to religious freedom to the constitutional underpinnings of the administrative state—has helped encourage a rethinking of long-settled legal precedents and established political traditions.[201]

Second, they organized a vibrant community of conservative activists, academics, legal practitioners, students, politicians, and judges around a shared set of principles and values finished with an originalist gloss. At the center of this galaxy is the Federalist Society, a national network comprised of law-school and practicing-lawyer chapters. Founded in the 1982 as a "lonely hearts club" for conservatives outnumbered and marginalized on law-school campuses, the organization has grown into a force.[202] Today, it boasts a membership of over seventy-five thousand students and professionals.[203] Through convenings and law school debates, the Federalist Society nurtures the development and dissemination of conservative legal ideas. For students and lawyers active in the network, membership provides an opportunity to develop intellectually and professionally, fostering self-confidence and leadership skills. For the conservative movement, it has built a pipeline of future lawyers, judges, politicians, and academics who aim to take its ideas from marginalized to mainstream to dominant.[204]

Third, they supported the creation of conservative legal foundations to advance their pet causes with new jurisprudential strategies in the courts. Founded to counter the influence of the American Civil Liberties Union and other liberal public interest organizations, groups like the Center for

Individual Freedom and the Institute for Justice have successfully copied their model. In the process, a new cohort of public interest lawyers has helped to change the constitutional order by advancing the aims of a broad coalition of conservative interest groups and constituencies, from the religious right to free-market libertarians to corporate America.[205]

Fourth, they launched a network of policy centers and think tanks that help shape public discourse on the law and judicial decision making. These organizations provide a platform for the movement's public intellectuals, publishing their books and positioning them in the media as experts. In an array of conservative media outlets, commentators frame and perpetuate a narrative of "liberal judicial activism" at war with "conservative judicial restraint," masterfully stoking decades of anger over Supreme Court decisions on racial integration, school prayer, abortion, and other controversial issues. Although much of this rhetoric is deceptive and self-serving, it has mobilized a powerful grassroots constituency.[206]

Fifth, and perhaps most consequentially, conservatives have invested heavily over many years in an effort to populate the courts with ideologically reliable judges. This focus on judicial appointments began during Ed Meese's stewardship of the Justice Department during the Reagan administration. By the presidency of George W. Bush, the Federalist Society was vetting judicial nominees to ensure ideological purity. As the writer David Margolick presciently observed in 2003, the society operated as "a sort of judicial hatchery, spawning and cultivating reliably conservative judges and their reliably conservative law clerks the way state-of-the-art fish farms produce salmon, leaving little to the maddening caprices of nature."[207] The three newest Supreme Court justices, Neil Gorsuch, Brett Kavanaugh, and Amy Coney Barrett, are all products of this farm team system for the high court.[208] The effort to capture the federal judiciary accelerated during the presidency of Donald Trump, as a Republican Senate rubber-stamped a list of nominees outsourced to the Federalist Society, confirming them to lifetime seats on the federal bench with unprecedented speed.[209] While it is too soon to know for sure, these ideologically driven appointments suggest that we may be on the cusp of the most conservative Court since the Lochner era: a court protective of property, wealth, and racial privilege but hostile to democracy.[210] Should there be a jurisprudential lurch to the right, history suggests that a new surge of interest in constitutional amendments is likely to follow.

9

The People's Constitution

The historical pattern of constitutional change is fairly clear. In recurring cycles, long stretches of quiescence give way to short-lived periods of ferment, animated by the concerns of the day. In time, however, popular interest in the work of amending the Constitution begins to wane. The fight over the document's meaning and purpose returns to the judicial arena and scholarly debate, where the latest additions to the national charter are cemented (or ignored). But this scouring and parsing the Constitution's text and principles and values can take us only so far. Eventually, when our national charter proves unable to adapt to changing times, political pressure builds until the nation is ready for a new wave of constitutional change.

This final chapter explores some of the factors that have inspired the American people to amend the Constitution in the past—and considers their relevance for us today. While Americans may have various motivations for desiring constitutional change, certain indicators have historically coincided with increased interest in the Article V amending process. These factors include discontent over Supreme Court decisions, transformational social change, the upheavals of war and other crises, policy experimentation in the states, and extreme political polarization. Far from being confined to history, these indicators have uncanny resonance today. They offer a glimpse at how this generation may make its own imprint on the national charter. That is, of course, if we're willing to take up the challenge.

Misguided Supreme Court Decisions

Discontent over Supreme Court rulings has been among the most predictable galvanizers of popular interest in constitutional amendments. Today, the term "judicial activism" is glibly used by conservatives to disparage rulings they don't like, but for a century and a half, until President Franklin Roosevelt faced down the "nine old men" of the *Lochner* Court, it was progressives who chafed under the heavy-handed jurisprudence of a reactionary federal judiciary. Time and again, when stifled by the courts, social movements and reformers came to conclude that the only way forward was to fix the text of the Constitution itself. By invoking Article V to push back against misguided judicial rulings, they left a legacy. They made the Constitution a more progressive document.

During the ratification contest, the great Federalist champion James Wilson offered an expansive view of the courts' role in the new plan of government. When a law is "incompatible with the superior power of the Constitution," Wilson argued, "it is their duty to pronounce it void."[1] This broad power led Elbridge Gerry, a leading skeptic, to warn that "the judicial department will be oppressive."[2] Indeed, it didn't take long before the exercise of the judicial power stoked white-hot controversy. In 1793 the Supreme Court ruled that Georgia could be sued in federal court by a litigant from another state. Anticipating a negative reaction from state officials, one justice helpfully remarked that "a regular mode is pointed out for amendment" in Article V.[3] In short order, Congress responded to pressure from the states by crafting the Eleventh Amendment.[4] While the measure addressed a relatively narrow issue relating to state sovereignty and the courts' jurisdiction, this resort to Article V to correct a ruling by the Court set an important precedent.

The extent of the judiciary's power arose again in the 1803 case of *Marbury v. Madison*, in which Chief Justice John Marshall proclaimed, "It is emphatically the province and duty of the judicial department to say what the law is."[5] Americans have come to accept that it is the Supreme Court's responsibility to construe the meaning of the Constitution. But that has not been the end of the matter. Sometimes, after the Court issues a misguided ruling, sustained public criticism or the development of new legal thinking can persuade the justices to reverse course. The most famous example of this approach to constitutional change occurred in the case of

Brown v. Board of Education, when the Court repudiated the "separate but equal" doctrine that sanctioned racial segregation. At other times, when the prospect of relief from the courts has seemed dim, Americans have turned to the amendment process to vindicate their own view of the Constitution's meaning and promise.

The *Dred Scott* decision, handed down in 1857, was the most notorious judicial ruling to inspire a resort to Article V. It would ultimately take *two* constitutional amendments to repudiate the high court's decree that African Americans "had no rights which the white man was bound to respect."[6] The Thirteenth Amendment rid the Constitution of its most grievous flaw by prohibiting slavery, while the Fourteenth Amendment guaranteed the equal citizenship of Black Americans. Not long after, a setback at the Supreme Court set the woman suffrage movement on the long path of achieving its objective by constitutional amendment. In the 1875 case of *Minor v. Happersett*, the justices rejected a claim that the Fourteenth Amendment's prohibition on abridging the "privileges or immunities of citizens of the United States" conferred the right to vote on women.[7] As Susan B. Anthony and Elizabeth Cady Stanton would later recall, the Court's dismissive response "made all agitation in that direction hopeless." Concluding that "the time had come for some clearly-defined recognition of their citizenship," they drafted the measure that would be adopted four decades later as the Nineteenth Amendment.[8]

Widespread disapproval of the *Lochner*-era rulings set the stage for two of the Progressive Era amendments. The Sixteenth Amendment overruled *Pollock v. Farmers' Loan & Trust Company*, the controversial 1895 decision that curbed Congress's power to impose an income tax.[9] The deeply unpopular ruling damaged the Court's reputation for decades, leaving a future chief justice to lament that it "aroused a criticism of the court which has never been entirely stilled."[10] Likewise, the Child Labor Amendment, though never ratified, took aim at the 1918 ruling in *Hammer v. Dagenhart*, a decision denounced as "practically infamous" for striking down a law that "freed many thousands of children from virtual slavery."[11] With no other option left, Congress turned to Article V, delivering an extraordinary bipartisan rebuke to the justices' narrow vision of the nation's power to address a grievous social ill.

The brief Warren Court era, from 1953 to 1969, flipped the longstanding partisan divide over the proper role of the courts. While rulings in hot-button cases relating to desegregation, redistricting, and school prayer gladdened liberals, they stoked a sense of grievance on the right that smolders to this day. Though Republican presidential appointees have dominated the high court since the Nixon era, eroding many Warren Court precedents, the demonization of "activist judges" remains a mainstay of GOP politics. So far, the right's efforts to overturn progressive judicial rulings by constitutional amendment have all fallen short. Senator Everett Dirksen so despised the "one person, one vote" mandate of *Reynolds v. Sims*[12] that he campaigned for—and nearly triggered—an Article V convention. During the period of Republican control following the 1994 wave election, proposals to criminalize flag burning and prohibit same-sex marriage also failed to advance. These later attempts to overrule the courts were primarily exercises in wedge politics, designed to excite a conservative base but lacking the broad appeal needed to win supermajority support.

In recent years, the Court's hard right turn has sparked renewed frustration on the left. Of all the rulings issued by the Roberts Court, few have been more damaging than *Citizens United v. Federal Election Commission*,[13] the 2010 decision that struck down a sixty-year-old ban on corporation and union spending in elections. *Citizens United* was just one in a series of cases dating back to 1976 that have eviscerated laws regulating money in politics under the theory that they violate First Amendment speech rights of campaign spenders. With a heavy-handedness reminiscent of the *Lochner* era, this intrusive line of cases has second-guessed lawmakers and voters alike, taking away their power to enact commonsense regulations to safeguard the integrity of our elections.

The ruling in *Citizens United* heralded the age of dark money and billionaire-funded super PACs, an era in which corporations, well-funded special interest groups, and the wealthiest Americans have been free to spend staggering sums to influence elections, steadily moving the nation towards plutocracy.[14] "In a time of historic wealth inequality, the decision has helped reinforce the growing sense that our democracy primarily serves the interests of the wealthy few, and that democratic participation for the vast majority of citizens is of relatively little value," explains the Brennan Center for Justice.[15] In response, a handful of reform groups, including the Brennan Center, have worked to mitigate the ruling's harmful effects through improved transparency and small-donor public financing reforms while building a legal strategy to persuade a future Supreme Court to reverse course.[16] For other reform groups, though, the path toward fixing our elections starts with Article V.

American Promise is one such group. Founded in 2016, the organization is committed to building support for an amendment that would permit Congress and the states to set reasonable limits on campaign spending. Jeff Clements is the organization's founder. "It is not true that the Supreme Court has the last word on what the Constitution means," says Clements. "When the Supreme Court gets it catastrophically wrong, as it has done before, the amendment process is the correction; it is the rudder that Americans reach for to bring us back on course."[17] This approach has broad bipartisan appeal. A 2018 poll found that 85 percent of Democrats and 66 percent of Republicans favor a constitutional amendment to reduce the influence of large campaign donors.[18] Aided by a small volunteer army, American Promise has launched a campaign to turn that support into a "winnable, realistic strategy" on Capitol Hill.[19] For now, building the cross-party coalition essential to success remains an uphill climb. A 2019 proposal introduced by Representative Ted Deutch counted 221 members of the House and 47 senators as supporters, but only 1 was a Republican.[20] To increase the pressure, American Promise has expanded its outreach in the states, persuading twenty state legislatures to pass resolutions calling on Congress to act.[21]

Move to Amend, a coalition of progressive grassroots organizations, is taking a different tack. Its advocates promote a "We the People" amendment, a measure to establish that "human beings, not corporations, are persons entitled to constitutional rights."[22] Sponsored by Representative Pramila Jayapal, a progressive Democrat from Washington, the proposal has over seventy congressional supporters.[23] Finally, as noted in chapter 8, the reform group Wolf-PAC has taken the fight to the state legislatures, lobbying lawmakers to petition Congress for an Article V convention. Allies express concern about the risk of a runaway convention. In response, Wolf-PAC points out that the prospect of a convention has spurred Congress to propose amendments in the past, going back to the adoption of the Bill of Rights. "There's a really strong case to be made," says the group's executive director, "that the reason that Washington is so out of whack is because we haven't used the one and only constitutional check that we have."[24]

Controversial rulings scaling back voting rights have rekindled interest in yet another measure: an amendment guaranteeing the fundamental right to vote to every adult American. The idea dates back to the years after the Civil War, when woman suffragists championed a universal suffrage amendment. It was the road not taken in the 1960s, when Congress passed the Poll Tax Amendment over the objections of those who preferred a measure outlawing *all* obstructions to the right to vote. Rather than seek a robust constitutional fix, Congress adopted a super statute, the Voting Rights Act of 1965. For decades, the law was an effective weapon against barriers to voting in the states, thanks mainly to a provision requiring jurisdictions with a history of discrimination to obtain federal government approval before changing their election laws and practices. Unfortunately, in 2013, the Supreme Court gutted that part of the Act in the case of *Shelby County v. Holder*,[25] leaving it to Congress to enact a new law that "speaks to current conditions."

States freed from preclearance requirements wasted little time in adopting a spate of voter suppression laws and polling place closures, including restrictions previously rejected for their disproportionate impact on people of color and the poor. Civil rights activist Reverend William Barber II has called the rash of legislation passed in the wake of *Shelby County* "the worst attack on voting rights we've seen since Jim Crow."[26]

While a coalition of civil rights groups has urged Congress to update the Voting Rights Act, a hardy few say that it's time to address one of the Constitution's great anomalies: the lack of an affirmative textual guarantee. "Enshrining an explicit right to vote in the Constitution would guarantee the voting rights of every citizen of voting age, ensure that every vote is counted correctly, and defend against attempts to effectively disenfranchise eligible voters," says FairVote, a democracy reform group.[27] One such proposal, sponsored by Representative Mark Pocan, would recognize "the fundamental right to vote" and give Congress power to enforce it.[28] Some question whether the campaign is worth the time and effort.[29] Proponents respond that the effort could have "tremendous movement-building value"—just as the campaign for the Equal Rights Amendment lifted efforts to win change in legislatures and the courts. "A Right to Vote Amendment," says progressive philanthropist Jonathan Soros, "would be a 'Yes We Can' Amendment."[30]

Of course, it is still up to judges to construe the meaning of any new amendment to the Constitution. Whether they would do so faithfully is anyone's guess. In the decades after Reconstruction, the Supreme Court distorted the Fourteenth Amendment beyond recognition, routinely invoking it to shield corporations from regulation while declining to protect African Americans as its drafters intended. To take a more recent example, the Court recast the Second Amendment as protecting a right to keep guns for self-defense, displacing the long-settled understanding that the right applied only to service in a militia.

Given the vast power of the judiciary—which James Madison imagined would be "the least dangerous branch"—reformers have also suggested amending the Constitution to make the courts more accountable. Some advocates, mainly on the right, have proposed amendments giving Congress the power to override judicial decisions. Others, conservative *and* progressive, have called for limiting the terms of Supreme Court justices.[31] "An appointment system designed for a Court that was originally characterized as 'feeble' does not fit a Court that has become immensely powerful," argues the Brennan Center's Fritz Schwarz Jr.[32] His proposal would establish eighteen-year terms, giving presidents the opportunity to appoint a justice every two years. Such a reform, Schwarz contends, would reduce the gamesmanship around judicial nominations and retirements, and produce a Court that more closely resembles the will of the voters.[33]

Transformational Social Change

Over more than two centuries, successive generations of Americans have shaped and reshaped the nation in ways the Framers could scarcely have imagined. In a highly dynamic process—marked by changing demographics, technological innovation, an ever transforming economy, and a relentless push for democracy and social progress—America has repeatedly reinvented itself. So it is no surprise that, at critical junctures, a Constitution drawn up by men in an era of powdered wigs and horse-drawn carriages has tended to show its age. During these periods of disruption and flux, support grows for updates to the national charter to better meet the needs and values of a changing country.

Such was the case in the decades leading up to the Civil War, a period of unprecedented social and economic change. By 1860, a nation originally comprising thirteen states along the eastern seaboard had grown to thirty-three states stretching to the Pacific Ocean. Advances in technology, from the steam engine to the sewing machine, brought new vibrance to the economy, profoundly altering the way people lived and worked. A "transportation revolution" facilitated the movement of people and goods, and sped the dissemination of news.[34] In the South, Eli Whitney's cotton gin resuscitated the prospects of a languishing agricultural staple, increasing the demand for slave hands.[35] Meanwhile, in the North a surge of immigrant labor powered the region's bustling mills and manufacturing plants, an early sign of a great demographic shift. These divergent paths of change deepened a vast sectional rift. As industrialization and emancipation spread across the North, the Slave Power only dug in deeper in the South.

New forms of popular mobilization emerged during this period, thanks to the era's advances in transportation and communications. Anti-slavery societies sprang up throughout the North, linked to a global abolitionist movement. Tapping into "moral outrage and religious conviction,"[36] abolitionist orators traveled by steamboat and train to cities and towns all over the country, delivering fiery speeches and recruiting disciples. By engaging thousands of Americans, this new kind of mass movement helped shape public sentiment, paving the way for Lincoln's "new birth of freedom" and the adoption of the three Reconstruction Amendments. The abolitionist crusade also lent strength to two other important social movements. Though they would achieve their aims many decades later, temperance activists and suffragists learned the skills of organizing, public speaking, and lobbying from the abolitionists' successful playbook.

Toward the end of the nineteenth century, the social and political transformations of the Gilded Age spurred new demands for constitutional renewal. It was the era of the Second Industrial Revolution, a time of breakneck innovation in manufacturing, communications, and transportation that accelerated the nation's transition from an agrarian economy to one driven by industry and trade. Advances in the production of steel, chemicals, energy, and consumer goods brought tremendous changes to people's lives. The telegraph, telephone, typewriter, and radio greatly expanded the dissemination of news and information, while trains, automobiles, and bicycles made it easier to travel and transport goods. Taken together, these changes fueled the growth of cities, as immigrants and farmers competed for jobs on the assembly line. By 1900, about 40 percent of Americans lived in cities, up from just 6 percent a century earlier.[37] But with urbanization came a proliferation of social ills. The conditions in poorly regulated factories and mines threatened the health and safety of workers. At the same time, the extravagant wealth of a new capitalist aristocracy helped foster a culture of public corruption and graft, as robber barons, speculators, and industry titans lavished largesse on public officials to advance their narrow interests.

Taking advantage of advances in communications, a new generation of reformers spotlighted the era's glaring inequities. In his 1904 book, *Poverty*, the first statistical survey of the nation's poor, Robert Hunter revealed that 10 million Americans, one in seven, were "underfed, underclothed, and poorly housed."[38] In "The Treason of the Senate," the muckraking journalist David Graham Phillips exposed the "public plunderers" who corruptly served the interests of Wall Street in Washington.[39] In 1906, Upton Sinclair's sensational novel, *The Jungle*, dramatized "the inferno of exploitation" endured by meatpacking industry workers.[40] These publications and many others like them helped shape public sentiment, inspiring Americans to demand a more just society. Coupled with the advocacy of a new generation of modern pressure groups in the model of the Anti-Saloon League and the National Child Labor Committee, which used cutting-edge tools of research and public persuasion to quicken "the public consciousness,"[41] these efforts created the tailwind that propelled the addition of four modernizing amendments to the Constitution.

The most recent wave of amendments arose amid the social upheavals of the mid-twentieth century, which peaked in the turbulent decade of the 1960s. Faced with civil rights activists' peaceful sit-ins and marches, and the televised violence unleashed on them, lawmakers felt pressure to extend the franchise to African Americans. Raucous demonstrations on college campuses, led by a generation impatient with the status quo, prompted calls to channel youth energy toward the ballot box. And the rise of a "second wave" women's liberation movement helped awaken the nation's conscience to the pervasiveness of sex discrimination. These social movements revealed a rapidly changing America and the injustices that its most marginalized members were forced to endure. Together, they triggered an era of constitutional reform that added three amendments to the Constitution to expand voting rights, along with two unsuccessful measures that sparked progress on women's rights and on political representation for residents of the nation's capital. The spirit of these amendments represents the Constitution's fullest embrace of the people to date.

In these first decades of the twenty-first century, America finds itself once again in a time of transformational social change. The nation's demographic makeup is changing, fueled by immigration, globalization, and declining birth rates. Experts predict that by 2045 a majority of Americans will be nonwhite.[42] In six states, white people are already in the minority.[43] All too predictably, these changes have incited a reaction, as evidenced by the rise of domestic hate groups and white supremacist activity.[44] Recent spikes in attacks on Latinos, Asian Americans, Muslims, Jews, and other vulnerable communities show that marginalized groups are once again being scapegoated for some of society's nagging structural problems.[45]

Likewise, we find ourselves in an era of cutting-edge technological advances. The internet has revolutionized the exchange of information, transforming every field from commerce to healthcare to the media. And yet, for all its benefits, this revolution has come with its share of difficulties. The tech boom has contributed to the extreme stratification of wealth that is the hallmark of today's Second Gilded Age, generating vast riches for a few while relegating more and more workers to low-paying jobs and the vagaries of the "gig economy."[46] Furthermore, today's technologies have brought new concerns to the fore, disrupting previous understandings of speech and privacy and even democracy.

As in prior eras of transformational social change, energetic popular movements have sprung up to highlight the negative externalities of these developments—harnessing new technologies to advance structural reform. In 2011, the Occupy Wall Street movement emerged from the ashes of the 2008 financial meltdown, reframing the public discussion around wealth and class. Its rallying cry, "We are the 99%," emphasizes the injustice of a system that increasingly burdens the many while the economic elite reaps unprecedented gains. When seventeen-year-old Trayvon Martin was murdered with impunity the following year, the event set the stage for a robust campaign for racial justice. Black Lives Matter, a decentralized, multiracial movement born of a hashtag gone viral, was organized "to build local power and to intervene in violence inflicted on Black communities by the state and vigilantes."[47] The movement has steadily gained in influence, igniting protests all over the globe in the wake of the 2020 slayings of Ahmaud Arbery, Breonna Taylor, and George Floyd.

While these two twenty-first-century movements have not yet chosen to advance their aims through the Article V process, a new generation of women's rights activists has set its sights on a constitutional prize a century in the making. From the Time's Up movement that fights for fair treatment in the workplace to the historic Women's Marches that inspired record numbers of women to run for political office and win, an upwelling of activism has brought renewed scrutiny to the inequities that affect women's lives. For some in this reinvigorated movement, finishing the business of ratifying the Equal Rights Amendment has emerged as a top priority. In a surprise move, Nevada's majority-female legislature ratified the amendment in 2017, the first state to do so in four decades. "It's never too late to support equality," says Pat Spearman, the state senator who led the effort.[48] After similar action by Illinois and Virginia, pro-ERA forces celebrated the long-delayed milestone of securing ratifications by thirty-eight state legislatures. Opponents counter that the deadline expired in 1982,[49] but it will be up to Congress and the courts to determine whether the measure proposed in 1972 has been duly ratified as the Twenty-Eighth Amendment.[50] Should this effort fall short, there are lawmakers prepared to start the process anew. A "new ERA" proposal championed by Representative Carolyn Maloney has already gained the support of 180 members.[51]

Leading this campaign to enshrine gender equality in the Constitution is the ERA Coalition, a New York–based network of about a hundred partner organizations dedicated to getting the amendment across the finish line. Operating on a small budget, the coalition works closely with lawmakers in Washington and key state capitals to build support for the measure. Jessica Neuwirth, the coalition's founder, argues that it is "the perfect moment" to pass the ERA. Indeed, a 2020 poll found that 89 percent of Democrats and 61 percent of Republicans favor it.[52] "Virtually no one today argues against the ERA as a matter of principle," says Neuwirth. "The challenge is rather the misbelief that equal rights for women must already be in the Constitution."[53] As the movement draws more young people to the cause, Neuwirth sees reason for hope. "This new generation, skilled in using social media tools that were previously unimaginable, is capable of mobilizing action on an unprecedented scale."[54]

War and Insecurity

Americans in every generation have faced times of insecurity and peril. Our Union was forged in the crucible of revolutionary conflict. Since then, the nation has waged eleven major wars and prosecuted countless lesser military engagements. It has experienced seasons of protest, social unrest, and rebellion. It has endured recurrent financial panics, recessions, and depressions. Time and again, these periods of war and insecurity have exposed our collective vulnerability and with it the limits of the Constitution. But they have also summoned a spirit of solidarity and shared sacrifice as Americans demonstrate their commitment to the nation's most cherished ideals. In such times, the country has proved especially receptive to constitutional reform—and to expanding our conception of who truly counts as an American.

On the eve of the Civil War, politicians in Washington looked to Article V as the last best chance to avert disunion. Abolition was a political non-starter at the time, and Black civil and political rights seemed, at best, a fantasy. To preserve the nation, President Abraham Lincoln imprudently lent his support to a measure that would have forever prohibited interference with the "domestic institutions" of the slave states. In the hours before Lincoln took the oath of office, lawmakers in the Capitol frantically approved the pro-slavery Corwin Amendment, the first constitutional amendment approved by Congress since the Titles of Nobility Amendment of 1810 (itself a product of public anxiety over war).

As the conflict exacted its heavy toll, Lincoln's ambition grew. Like many Americans, the wartime president gradually came to see that the Framers' Constitution, which sanctioned "property in men," was no longer "adequate to the exigencies of the union."[55] As a tentative step, he first urged Congress to approve an amendment requiring the gradual emancipation of slaves. "The dogmas of the quiet past are inadequate to the stormy present," Lincoln declared. "As our case is new, so we must think anew, and act anew."[56] By the war's end, however, the political environment was conducive to a bolder set of solutions. The wartime service of Black soldiers who fought valiantly for the Union gave crucial impetus to the adoption of the three Reconstruction amendments. As Maine congressman Sidney Perham saw it, "The men who will peril their lives on the field of battle in defense of our Constitution will vote for it if you will give them an opportunity."[57]

The patriotic fervor that accompanied America's entry into World War I also provided a boost to amendment campaigns. Emergency wartime measures to limit the production of alcoholic beverages, coupled with a heightened public disdain for all things German, provided the momentum needed to propel the Eighteenth Amendment to ratification in 1919. Meanwhile, the contributions of women in the struggle to "save the world for democracy" provided a powerful new argument in the campaign to win votes for women, winning over a reluctant President Wilson. It paved the way for the adoption of the Nineteenth Amendment a year later.

While the postwar "return to normalcy" sapped interest in the Progressives' reform efforts during the 1920s, interest in Article V solutions revived as the nation sank into the Great Depression. After sweeping Democratic gains in the election of 1930, lawmakers adopted the Twentieth Amendment to shorten the lame-duck period. Then, after the ranks of "wet" lawmakers were decimated in Franklin Roosevelt's 1932 electoral landslide, Congress approved the Twenty-First Amendment to repeal Prohibition. As the new president confronted the Supreme Court over the constitutionality of his New Deal programs, it appeared that the nation might be primed for a new wave of amendments to modernize our founding charter. But Roosevelt worried that the economic crisis was too urgent to entrust to the time-consuming process of Article V. Instead, he fought to vindicate the Framers' vision of an energetic government adequate to meet the nation's needs.

The economic emergency that prompted the New Deal was soon overshadowed by World War II and the Cold War. Over three decades, the sacrifice of American servicemembers in conflicts spanning the globe, from Normandy to Inchon to Khe Sanh, influenced no fewer than three Civil Rights Era amendments. From the time Jennings Randolph first proposed lowering the national voting age in 1943 until the adoption of the Twenty-Sixth Amendment almost three decades later, proponents lifted up the wartime service of young soldiers with the slogan "Old enough to fight, old enough to vote." The contributions of Black servicemembers similarly forced lawmakers to confront the hypocrisy of sending troops to fight for democracy abroad while denying them its benefits at home. This moral claim to full participation in the nation's political life lent undeniable new force to the Civil Rights Movement.[58] It reverberated throughout the 1960s as Congress debated amendments to abolish the poll tax and expand voting rights for residents of the nation's capital. Political scientist Ronald Krebs calls it "the politics of postwar gratitude." The contributions of marginalized groups in wartime, says Krebs, can "provide crucial evidence of the population's worthiness for first-class citizenship."[59]

Finally, as Cold War fears deepened their hold on the American psyche, the specter of a third world war fought with atomic bombs revealed a Constitution poorly equipped to respond to new and frightening contingencies. President Dwight Eisenhower's incapacitation following a heart attack and stroke highlighted the need to have an able and alert commander in chief at the helm at all times. The Twenty-Fifth Amendment, adopted after the assassination of President John F. Kennedy, established an orderly plan of succession to the nation's highest office. Senator Estes Kefauver also sought to fix a constitutional gap that would leave the House of Representatives unable to function in the aftermath of a nuclear attack. His proposed continuity of government amendment, allowing governors to make temporary appointments in the wake of a mass casualty event, won the support of the Senate in 1960 but failed to advance in the House.

Though the fear of nuclear war is less salient today, Congress's failure to act on Kefauver's proposal still haunts policymakers in an era of terrorist attacks and mass shooting events. There was renewed interest in a continuity-of-government amendment after al-Qaeda operatives attempted to fly an airplane into the Capitol on September 11, 2001, and following the anthrax attacks in the subsequent weeks.[60] Interest spiked again in 2017 after a gunman opened fire on federal lawmakers practicing for a charity baseball game.[61] It did so again after January 6, 2021, when a mob incited by President Donald Trump stormed the Capitol in a failed insurrection. As memories of these troubling episodes fade, however, many members of the House remain philosophically attached to the Constitution's requirement of election "by the people" in all circumstances. Until that sentiment gives way, addressing this constitutional flaw will remain an elusive goal.

Constitutional Experimentation in the States

From its inception, our Constitution has been shaped by experimentation in the states. When the Framers met in 1787 to devise a new plan of government, they looked to the various state constitutions for inspiration. Because many of the delegates had participated in the creation of these state charters, they possessed strong opinions born of practical experience. Thus the Constitution's form and substance was derived from a "skillful synthesis" of practices taken from two decades of governance in the states.[62] The Senate, for instance, was modeled on Maryland's upper house.[63] Our system of judicial appointments was borrowed from the practice in Massachusetts.[64] In the years since, reform and innovation in the states have continued to play a significant role in shaping the Constitution through the amendment process.

There is no better example of this phenomenon than the first set of amendments. In the waning days of the Philadelphia Convention, George Mason urged that the Constitution be prefaced with a bill of rights to be drawn up "with the aid of the state declarations."[65] Two years later, when James Madison presented the 1st Congress with the set of proposals that would become the Bill of Rights, he borrowed liberally from provisions in state constitutions. The First Amendment's guarantee of the free exercise of religion was inspired by the Virginia Declaration of Rights.[66] The Sixth Amendment's guarantee of trial by jury was lifted from Georgia's constitution.[67] Had there been no early state charters to draw from, the style and substance of the first ten amendments might have been markedly different.

Congress likewise followed the lead of many states when it approved a constitutional ban on slavery. In 1780, Pennsylvania passed the nation's first abolition law, a measure providing for gradual emancipation through 1847.[68] That same year, enslaved persons in Massachusetts were manumitted when the state's highest court ruled that slavery was incompatible with its newly adopted constitution.[69] By the first decade of the nineteenth century, each of the seven original states north of the Mason-Dixon Line acted to phase out slavery or abolish it outright. As new states entered the Union, more than half did so under free constitutions. By the time the Thirteenth Amendment took effect in 1865, twenty of the thirty-six states had already acted to end slavery.

In the twentieth century, states served as incubators of political innovation, pioneering democracy reforms that would later be embraced nationally. In a noteworthy example, states in the West led the push for the direct election of senators to bring greater accountability to an institution widely viewed as tarnished by corruption and cronyism.[70] When the Senate stood in the way of a constitutional amendment, states responded with creative workarounds. The most influential of these was the Oregon Plan, which allowed voters to express their preference in a popular referendum. This surge of democratic experimentation in the states helped to force the Senate's hand. By 1912, when Congress finally approved the Seventeenth Amendment, a majority of senators were already being chosen in a de facto system of popular election.[71] The campaign to enforce nationwide Prohibition gained strength from a series of successful campaigns to enact state and local liquor bans. In the span of a single decade, between 1907 and 1917, temperance activists won dry laws in twenty-six states, lending crucial momentum to the push for the Eighteenth Amendment.[72] Similarly, when Congress approved the Twenty-Fourth Amendment's ban on poll taxes in federal elections, it also followed the lead of states that had ended the practice.

On the other hand, a failure to gain traction in the states has not necessarily impeded the adoption of constitutional amendments. The suffragists, for example, spent over four decades waging campaigns to gain the franchise through state referendums, claiming just four wins during that period. Their fortunes changed only when they traded the failed state-by-state strategy for one focused on advancing the Nineteenth Amendment. By the same token, state campaigns to lower the voting age had mixed results even as a quick consensus formed in support of a constitutional amendment. As late as 1970, just months before Congress sent the Twenty-Sixth Amendment to the states for ratification, voters in eleven states rejected ballot measures to lower the voting age in state constitutions.[73]

Today states continue to embrace their role as "laboratories" of democratic and constitutional experimentation, as Justice Louis Brandeis famously called them.[74] The country saw this in the striking progression of marriage equality from a controversial Massachusetts court ruling in 2003 to the law of the land just a dozen years later. It is also the hallmark of a state-led initiative to reimagine the role of the Electoral College in our presidential elections, a plan called the National Popular Vote Interstate Compact. If enacted, the compact would establish a de facto popular vote system without the need for a constitutional amendment.

The idea was born after the 2000 presidential election when, for the first time since 1888, the Electoral College delivered the presidency to a candidate who lost the popular vote. In response, legal scholars and reformers devised an innovative plan that would award the presidency to the winner of the national popular vote within our existing system.[75] The plan draws on a provision of the Constitution that gives each state's legislature the authority to determine how its presidential electors are chosen. Member states enter into a binding agreement to abandon their current practice of awarding electoral votes to the candidate who receives the most votes in their state, pledging instead to award them to the winner of the most votes nationally. Once states controlling 270 electoral votes join the compact, the number needed to win the presidency, the plan will take effect.

After years of organizing, supporters say their ambitious goal may be finally within reach. As of 2021, fifteen states and the District of Columbia have signed on, controlling 196 electoral votes. When the plan is finally implemented, presidential election contests would be transformed. Candidates would no longer have an incentive to focus their resources and energy on a handful of "battleground" states. Instead, to win the most votes nationally they would have to compete for support in every part of the country. By transforming the current system, the compact might also have the salutary effect of neutralizing resistance to the adoption of a more enduring reform by constitutional amendment—just as innovation in the states helped pave the way for the popular election of senators through the Seventeenth Amendment.[76]

Efforts in the states to summon an Article V convention highlight another way that states have influenced constitutional change. When interest in amending the Constitution begins to build, there tends to be a corresponding surge in convention applications submitted to Congress. Though no convention push has succeeded to date, history demonstrates that the credible threat of one can have a prodding effect on Congress, making way for changes demanded by the states.[77] The Anti-Federalists' push for a second convention lent urgency to the adoption of the Bill of Rights. The submission of Article V petitions in the early twentieth century helped break years of Senate obstruction, forcing a vote on the Seventeenth Amendment. And the looming threat of a balanced-budget convention in the early 1980s prompted lawmakers to take action to reduce deficit spending, if only for a time. This history has inspired today's Article V warriors to envision a twenty-first-century convention as their best opportunity to relitigate the Framers' plan for a government capable of meeting the nation's challenges.

Whichever way this contest over competing constitutional visions is resolved in the coming years, it is clear that experimentation in the states has helped to shape the scope of our democracy, our liberties, and our shared values. This innovation is not easily contained within a single state's borders. When new ideas inspire change in a critical mass of states, the Constitution can change too. This rich history reveals that amending the Constitution is not the top-down endeavor that the Anti-Federalists feared. States are very much partners in the process.

Extreme Political Polarization

Finally, history shows that periods of deep political division and gridlock tend to spark interest in amending the Constitution. When the country is polarized along partisan or regional divides, blocking the normal channels of legal change, reformers are pushed to consider extraordinary means to achieve their aims. Once the fever of polarization breaks, usually following an election that provides an unmistakable mandate to a party or a cross-party coalition, the country may suddenly reach a new consensus on the need for constitutional change.

The adoption of the Bill of Rights followed the fight over the ratification of the Constitution, a contest that exposed a deep philosophical fault line in the country. The Federalists welcomed a new national charter that would bring "firmness and vigor" to the government, while the Anti-Federalists deemed it a threat to liberty. The fight could have gone either way. The Anti-Federalist critique of the Constitution was shared by many Americans. But the Federalists reassured skeptics with a vow to make improvements through the Article V process. When they won a surprisingly broad mandate in the elections for the 1st Congress, the Federalists made good on that promise by crafting amendments to address popular concern over the protection of rights even as they deflected other changes that would have weakened the new central government.

The next bundle of amendments, adopted in the Reconstruction Era, was preceded by a division so great that it pulled the nation into the abyss of civil conflict. It was the nation's first great sectional rift, what James Madison called the "great division of interests" between the North and South over slavery.[78] The two regions clashed for decades in repeated cycles of brinkmanship and compromise, preserving a tenuous balance of power between slave states and free states at the cost of appeasing the South. Though the nation's polarized politics made war inevitable, the conflict cemented an historic political realignment that provided an opening for fundamental change. President Lincoln's convincing re-election victory in 1864 rendered a "popular verdict" in favor of the Thirteenth Amendment, which had languished in Congress for nearly a year.[79] Republicans also made sweeping gains in Congress that year, ushering in a six-year stretch of supermajority control.[80] Buoyed by commanding majorities, lawmakers laid the groundwork for a series of reforms that included two new amendments to the Constitution. In 1866, Congress approved the Fourteenth Amendment to safeguard the civil rights of the newly freed. And then, in the lame-duck session following the 1868 election, as the Republicans' power ebbed, Congress proposed the Fifteenth Amendment to guarantee the franchise to all American men.

The spate of Progressive Era amendments had its origins in the polarization that characterized the politics of the late nineteenth century's Gilded Age. In the decades after Reconstruction, a new sectional divide pitted the agrarian South and frontier West against the rapidly urbanizing East and Midwest. National elections were closely fought, resulting in frequent swings in party control. Amid the fractious politics of the time, social inequality and corruption flourished as elected officials catered to the interests of the emergent millionaire class. Out of this crucible arose vibrant political movements demanding change. First came the Populists, the exponents of a reform agenda that included the direct election of senators, the income tax, and votes for women. When Democrats briefly won unified control of the presidency and Congress after the election of 1892, they embraced much of the Populists' policy agenda, though it would take decades to realize their constitutional aims. Over time, the current of populism merged with the modernizing force of progressivism to win adherents in both political parties. These disorienting ideological crosscurrents divided Republicans in the first decade of the new century, propelling Democrats to victory in the twin wave elections of 1910 and 1912. This remarkable swing permitted the formation of a left-leaning, cross-party coalition that lifted the Sixteenth and Seventeenth Amendments to ratification after years of fruitless advocacy. The Eighteenth and Nineteenth Amendments, adopted later in the decade, also received a boost from the era's reformist energy.

Today we find ourselves in a new era of political polarization that rivals the Gilded Age. A 2017 survey by the Pew Research Center reported that Republicans and Democrats were "further apart ideologically than at any point in more than two decades," as growing majorities in both parties held very unfavorable views of the other.[81] The familiar red-state–blue-state map reveals stark differences in outlook between residents of the coastal states and those in the heartland, a divergence that has only deepened as our increasingly mobile population sorts itself by region. This latest sectional split has defined the dynamics of our modern political contests. Since 2000, control of Congress has swung back and forth in three wave elections. In four of the past six presidential contests, the popular vote margin has been 4 percent or less.[82] And the Electoral College has produced two presidents who failed to win the support of a national majority.

It is eerily reminiscent of the closely fought politics of the Gilded Age, when the yawning chasm between that era's 1 percent and the nation's struggling farmers and exploited laborers produced a dramatic leftward swing in public opinion. That sense of urgency, especially from the aggrieved, gave new energy to social and political movements seeking to advance enduring change through constitutional reform. It is reasonable to anticipate that this time of partisan gridlock will someday give way to a new governing consensus. Only time will tell whether the American people will be inspired, as previous generations have been, to form the political coalitions needed to foster the next wave of constitutional change.

On September 17, 1787, whose anniversary we commemorate as Constitution Day, George Washington wrote a letter to the president of the Confederation Congress transmitting the product of four months of painstaking negotiation and frustrating compromise. "The Constitution which we now present is the result of a spirit of amity and of that mutual deference and concession which the peculiarity of our political situation rendered indispensable," Washington explained. It was unlikely to "meet the full and entire approbation of every state," he admitted, yet it was "liable to as few exceptions as could reasonably have been expected."[83]

This "mutual deference and concession" produced a beta version of the Constitution that was profoundly visionary but fundamentally flawed. Fortunately, it was only the first chapter in a much longer story. From the debate between Federalists and Anti-Federalists over starkly different conceptions of the republic, to the Reconstruction Amendments' promise of a "second founding," to today's renewed push to adopt an Equal Rights Amendment after a century of campaigning, the real history of the Constitution is the story of how "We the People" have reshaped and updated our founding document over more than two centuries amid some of the most colorful, contested, and controversial struggles in American political life. By invoking the admittedly cumbersome process of Article V, generations of Americans have moved the Constitution ever closer toward its promise of "a more perfect Union."

Perhaps no one has ever captured this process more powerfully than Thurgood Marshall, the grandson of a slave who championed civil rights and then, in his later years, earned the distinction of becoming the first African American justice of the United States Supreme Court. In 1987, as the nation marked the Constitution's bicentennial, Marshall criticized the degree to which the celebration invited "a complacent belief that the vision of those who debated and compromised in Philadelphia yielded the 'more perfect Union' it is said we now enjoy."[84] In a speech intended as a counterpoint to the gauzy festivities organized in honor of the Framers' accomplishment, the justice offered a dissenting view:

I do not believe that the meaning of the Constitution was forever "fixed" at the Philadelphia Convention. Nor do I find the wisdom, foresight, and sense of justice exhibited by the Framers particularly profound. To the contrary, the government they devised was defective from the start, requiring several amendments, a civil war, and momentous social transformation to attain the system of constitutional government, and its respect for the individual freedoms and human rights, that we hold as fundamental today. When contemporary Americans cite "The Constitution," they invoke a concept that is vastly different from what the Framers barely began to construct two centuries ago.[85]

The *New York Times* reported that Marshall's speech "struck perhaps the most negative note yet sounded in this bicentennial year by so prominent a public official," a stark contrast to "the lavish praise of the Framers' wisdom and devotion to liberty and justice by figures including President Reagan and Warren E. Burger," the former chief justice.[86] But this criticism surely missed the point. Marshall was merely saving his praise for the many framers who came after, the men and women who fought to expand a narrow conception of "We the People" to produce a Constitution that is more democratic, more inclusive, and more just. As Justice Marshall noted:

> The men who gathered in Philadelphia in 1787 could not have envisioned these changes. They could not have imagined, nor would they have accepted, that the document they were drafting would one day be construed by a Supreme Court to which had been appointed a woman and the descendant of an African slave. "We the People" no longer enslave, but the credit does not belong to the Framers. It belongs to those who refused to acquiesce in outdated notions of "liberty," "justice," and "equality," and who strived to better them.[87]

Rather than encourage "a blind pilgrimage to the shrine of the original document now stored in a vault in the National Archives," Marshall urged Americans to "seek, instead, a sensitive understanding of the Constitution's inherent defects, and its promising evolution through 200 years of history."[88] In doing so, Marshall promised, "We will see that the true miracle was not the birth of the Constitution, but its life, a life nurtured through two turbulent centuries of our own making."[89]

It was in this way, through periodic infusions of democratic energy channeled through the Article V amendment process, that the Framer's Constitution became the People's Constitution.

Acknowledgments

The idea for a book on the history of constitutional change germinated in the weeks following the 2016 presidential election. For the second time in sixteen years, America's intentionally undemocratic system of presidential selection delivered victory to a candidate who failed to secure the most votes. We, like millions of Americans, support changing this system to let the people decide who should wield the awesome powers of that office. And yet, to most Americans concerned about the vitality of our democracy, the idea of fixing the Constitution's flaws seems impractical if not impossible. This sense of defeatism raised two intriguing questions: How did earlier generations find a way to make their imprint on our national charter? And can our generation do the same?

This germ of an idea would have remained that way if it were not for the enthusiasm of Diane Wachtell, executive director of The New Press, and Carl Bromley, then a member of her editorial team. They immediately saw the potential for a popular history of the amendments to the Constitution and urged us to take this project on. As first-time authors, we benefited greatly from their guidance and encouragement. We would also like to thank other members of the New Press team: Marc Favreau, our insightful and supportive editor, who took over the editorial responsibility for the project and patiently helped us get it past the finish line; production editor Emily Albarillo and copy editor Gary Stimeling; and everyone at the organization who helped to make this dream a reality.

We are also extremely grateful for the mentoring and support of Michael Waldman, president of the Brennan Center for Justice, who is an enthusiastic believer in books as a means to advance new and pathbreaking ideas. His two most recent volumes, *The Second Amendment: A Biography* and *The Fight to Vote*, exemplify a rigorous, accessible, and lively style of writing we could only hope to emulate. Michael has been our biggest booster and for that we are deeply appreciative.

Another special thank-you is due to our immensely talented and resourceful researcher, Alex Cohen. He has been a dedicated and invaluable member of the team, going above and beyond the call of duty to aid in the book's production. From the day he joined this collaboration, Alex exhibited a rare combination of intellect, creativity, curiosity, efficiency, and affability that helped maintain the momentum for this four-year project.

We also benefited from the wisdom and insights of many Brennan Center colleagues, starting with Dan Okrent, the acclaimed author of six books, whose early read of the manuscript helped make it immeasurably better. Much gratitude to Jeanine Chirlin, Fritz Schwarz, and Walter Shapiro for their keen eye and feedback on drafts. Thanks also to Ethan Herenstein, Douglas Keith, Annie Lo, Eric Ruben, and Tom Wolf, who read parts of the manuscript and offered many helpful suggestions. We were also fortunate to have the help of an impressive group of Brennan Center interns, who assisted with research and related tasks: Brandon Faske, Garrett Fisher, Aesetou Hydara, Kalli Jackson, and Magdalene Zier. Amanda Grooms did extraordinary work on fact checking. And, finally, we want to express our thanks to a cohort of recently published Brennan Center authors—L.B. Eisen, Michael German, Ted Johnson, Ciara Torres-Spelliscy, and Jennifer Weiss-Wolf—who offered moral support and their hard-earned insights into the writing process. We are truly delighted to join the club.

We are indebted to the historians and legal scholars who very generously invested their time to review chapters, offering thoughtful insights and probing questions from their vast store of knowledge. They include Marcia Chatelain, Ellen Chesler, Gregory Downs, Paul Finkelman, Richard Labunski, Sophia Lee, Nancy MacLean, Kate Masur, Wendy Schiller, and Jeff Shesol. In addition to their invaluable expertise, we appreciate their many expressions of kindness and support along the way. We are particularly indebted to John R. Vile, one of the nation's leading scholars of the Article V amending process, who very generously reviewed the manuscript.

Thanks also to our lay readers, who served as our test audience of non–subject matter experts, including Jessica Harding, Roophy Roy, and Lisa Zhu.

Finally, we would like to express our deepest appreciation to our partners, Vladimir Lenskiy and Felipe Serrano, as well as to our families and friends for their endless support, patience, and understanding. They have put up with a lot throughout this process—long and late hours of research, writing, and all-too-frequent digressions on the topic of constitutional amendments. Without their love and encouragement, this book would not be possible.

Appendix A

The Text of the Constitution of the United States as Amended, and the Text of the Unratified Amendments

Preamble

We the People of the United States, in Order to form a more perfect Union, establish Justice, insure domestic Tranquility, provide for the common defence, promote the general Welfare, and secure the Blessings of Liberty to ourselves and our Posterity, do ordain and establish this Constitution for the United States of America.

Article I

Section 1

All legislative Powers herein granted shall be vested in a Congress of the United States, which shall consist of a Senate and House of Representatives.

Section 2

The House of Representatives shall be composed of Members chosen every second Year by the People of the several States, and the Electors in each State shall have the Qualifications requisite for Electors of the most numerous Branch of the State Legislature.

No Person shall be a Representative who shall not have attained to the Age of twenty five Years, and been seven Years a Citizen of the United States, and who shall not, when elected, be an Inhabitant of that State in which he shall be chosen.

Representatives and direct Taxes shall be apportioned among the several States which may be included within this Union, according to their respective Numbers, which shall be determined by adding to the whole Number of free Persons, including those bound to Service for a Term of Years, and excluding Indians not taxed, three fifths of all other Persons. The actual Enumeration shall be made within three Years after the first Meeting of the Congress of the United States, and within every subsequent Term of ten Years, in such Manner as they shall by Law direct. The number of Representatives shall not exceed one for every thirty Thousand, but each State shall have at Least one Representative; and until such enumeration shall be made, the State of New Hampshire shall be entitled to chuse three, Massachusetts eight, Rhode-Island and Providence Plantations one, Connecticut five, New-York six, New Jersey four, Pennsylvania eight, Delaware one, Maryland six, Virginia ten, North Carolina five, South Carolina five, and Georgia three.

When vacancies happen in the Representation from any State, the Executive Authority thereof shall issue Writs of Election to fill such Vacancies.

The House of Representatives shall chuse their Speaker and other Officers; and shall have the sole Power of Impeachment.

Section 3
The Senate of the United States shall be composed of two Senators from each State, chosen by the Legislature thereof, for six Years; and each Senator shall have one Vote.

Immediately after they shall be assembled in Consequence of the first Election, they shall be divided as equally as may be into three Classes. The Seats of the Senators of the first Class shall be vacated at the Expiration of the second Year, of the second Class at the Expiration of the fourth Year, and of the third Class at the Expiration of the sixth Year, so that one third may be chosen every second Year; and if Vacancies happen by Resignation, or otherwise, during the Recess of the Legislature of any State, the Executive thereof may make temporary Appointments until the next Meeting of the Legislature, which shall then fill such Vacancies.

No Person shall be a Senator who shall not have attained to the Age of thirty Years, and been nine Years a Citizen of the United States, and who shall not, when elected, be an Inhabitant of that State for which he shall be chosen.

The Vice President of the United States shall be President of the Senate, but shall have no Vote, unless they be equally divided.

The Senate shall chuse their other Officers, and also a President pro tempore, in the Absence of the Vice President, or when he shall exercise the Office of President of the United States.

The Senate shall have the sole Power to try all Impeachments. When sitting for that Purpose, they shall be on Oath or Affirmation. When the President of the United States is tried, the Chief Justice shall preside: And no Person shall be convicted without the Concurrence of two thirds of the Members present.

Judgment in Cases of Impeachment shall not extend further than to removal from Office, and disqualification to hold and enjoy any Office of honor, Trust or Profit under the United States: but the Party convicted shall nevertheless be liable and subject to Indictment, Trial, Judgment and Punishment, according to Law.

Section 4

The Times, Places and Manner of holding Elections for Senators and Representatives, shall be prescribed in each State by the Legislature thereof; but the Congress may at any time by Law make or alter such Regulations, except as to the Places of chusing Senators.

The Congress shall assemble at least once in every Year, and such Meeting shall be on the first Monday in December, unless they shall by Law appoint a different Day.

Section 5

Each House shall be the Judge of the Elections, Returns and Qualifications of its own Members, and a Majority of each shall constitute a Quorum to do Business; but a smaller Number may adjourn from day to day, and may be authorized to compel the Attendance of absent Members, in such Manner, and under such Penalties as each House may provide.

Each House may determine the Rules of its Proceedings, punish its Members for disorderly Behaviour, and, with the Concurrence of two thirds, expel a Member.

Each House shall keep a Journal of its Proceedings, and from time to time publish the same, excepting such Parts as may in their Judgment require Secrecy; and the Yeas and Nays of the Members of either House on any question shall, at the Desire of one fifth of those Present, be entered on the Journal.

Neither House, during the Session of Congress, shall, without the Consent of the other, adjourn for more than three days, nor to any other Place than that in which the two Houses shall be sitting.

Section 6

The Senators and Representatives shall receive a Compensation for their Services, to be ascertained by Law, and paid out of the Treasury of the United States. They shall in all Cases, except Treason, Felony and Breach of the Peace, be privileged from Arrest during their Attendance at the Session of their respective Houses, and in going to and returning from the same; and for any Speech or Debate in either House, they shall not be questioned in any other Place.

No Senator or Representative shall, during the Time for which he was elected, be appointed to any civil Office under the Authority of the United States, which shall have been created, or the Emoluments whereof shall have been encreased during such time; and no Person holding any Office under the United States, shall be a Member of either House during his Continuance in Office.

Section 7

All Bills for raising Revenue shall originate in the House of Representatives; but the Senate may propose or concur with Amendments as on other Bills.

Every Bill which shall have passed the House of Representatives and the Senate, shall, before it become a Law, be presented to the President of the United States; If he approve he shall sign it, but if not he shall return it, with his Objections to that House in which it shall have originated, who shall enter the Objections at large on their Journal, and proceed to reconsider it. If after such Reconsideration two thirds of that House shall agree to pass the Bill, it shall be sent, together with the Objections, to the other House, by which it shall likewise be reconsidered, and if approved by two thirds of that House, it shall become a Law. But in all such Cases the Votes of both Houses shall be determined by Yeas and Nays, and the Names of the Persons voting for and against the Bill shall be entered on the Journal of each House respectively. If any Bill shall not be returned by the President within ten Days (Sundays excepted) after it shall have been presented to him, the Same shall be a Law, in like Manner as if he had signed it, unless the Congress by their Adjournment prevent its Return, in which Case it shall not be a Law.

Every Order, Resolution, or Vote to which the Concurrence of the Senate and House of Representatives may be necessary (except on a question of Adjournment) shall be presented to the President of the United States; and before the

Same shall take Effect, shall be approved by him, or being disapproved by him, shall be repassed by two thirds of the Senate and House of Representatives, according to the Rules and Limitations prescribed in the Case of a Bill.

Section 8

The Congress shall have Power To lay and collect Taxes, Duties, Imposts and Excises, to pay the Debts and provide for the common Defence and general Welfare of the United States; but all Duties, Imposts and Excises shall be uniform throughout the United States;

To borrow Money on the credit of the United States;

To regulate Commerce with foreign Nations, and among the several States, and with the Indian Tribes;

To establish a uniform Rule of Naturalization, and uniform Laws on the subject of Bankruptcies throughout the United States;

To coin Money, regulate the Value thereof, and of foreign Coin, and fix the Standard of Weights and Measures;

To provide for the Punishment of counterfeiting the Securities and current Coin of the United States;

To establish Post Offices and post Roads;

To promote the Progress of Science and useful Arts, by securing for limited Times to Authors and Inventors the exclusive Right to their respective Writings and Discoveries;

To constitute Tribunals inferior to the supreme Court;

To define and punish Piracies and Felonies committed on the high Seas, and Offenses against the Law of Nations;

To declare War, grant Letters of Marque and Reprisal, and make Rules concerning Captures on Land and Water;

To raise and support Armies, but no Appropriation of Money to that Use shall be for a longer Term than two Years;

To provide and maintain a Navy;

To make Rules for the Government and Regulation of the land and naval Forces;

To provide for calling forth the Militia to execute the Laws of the Union, suppress Insurrections and repel Invasions;

To provide for organizing, arming, and disciplining, the Militia, and for governing such Part of them as may be employed in the Service of the United States, reserving to the States respectively, the Appointment of the Officers, and the Authority of training the Militia according to the discipline prescribed by Congress;

To exercise exclusive Legislation in all Cases whatsoever, over such District (not exceeding ten Miles square) as may, by Cession of particular States, and the Acceptance of Congress, become the Seat of the Government of the United States, and to exercise like Authority over all Places purchased by the Consent of the Legislature of the State in which the Same shall be, for the Erection of Forts, Magazines, Arsenals, dock-Yards and other needful Buildings;—And

To make all Laws which shall be necessary and proper for carrying into Execution the foregoing Powers, and all other Powers vested by this Constitution in the Government of the United States, or in any Department or Officer thereof.

Section 9

The Migration or Importation of such Persons as any of the States now existing shall think proper to admit, shall not be prohibited by the Congress prior to the Year one thousand eight hundred and eight, but a Tax or duty may be imposed on such Importation, not exceeding ten dollars for each Person.

The Privilege of the Writ of Habeas Corpus shall not be suspended, unless when in Cases of Rebellion or Invasion the public Safety may require it.

No Bill of Attainder or ex post facto Law shall be passed.

No Capitation, or other direct, Tax shall be laid, unless in Proportion to the Census or Enumeration herein before directed to be taken.

No Tax or Duty shall be laid on Articles exported from any State.

No Preference shall be given by any Regulation of Commerce or Revenue to the Ports of one State over those of another: nor shall Vessels bound to, or from, one State, be obliged to enter, clear, or pay Duties in another.

No Money shall be drawn from the Treasury, but in Consequence of Appropriations made by Law; and a regular Statement and Account of the Receipts and Expenditures of all public Money shall be published from time to time.

No Title of Nobility shall be granted by the United States: And no Person holding any Office of Profit or Trust under them, shall, without the Consent of the Congress, accept of any present, Emolument, Office, or Title, of any kind whatever, from any King, Prince, or foreign State.

Section 10
No State shall enter into any Treaty, Alliance, or Confederation; grant Letters of Marque and Reprisal; coin Money; emit Bills of Credit; make any Thing but gold and silver Coin a Tender in Payment of Debts; pass any Bill of Attainder, ex post facto Law, or Law impairing the Obligation of Contracts, or grant any Title of Nobility.

No State shall, without the Consent of the Congress, lay any Imposts or Duties on Imports or Exports, except what may be absolutely necessary for executing it's inspection Laws: and the net Produce of all Duties and Imposts, laid by any State on Imports or Exports, shall be for the Use of the Treasury of the United States; and all such Laws shall be subject to the Revision and Controul of the Congress.

No State shall, without the Consent of Congress, lay any Duty of Tonnage, keep Troops, or Ships of War in time of Peace, enter into any Agreement or Compact with another State, or with a foreign Power, or engage in War, unless actually invaded, or in such imminent Danger as will not admit of delay.

Article II

Section 1
The executive Power shall be vested in a President of the United States of America.

He shall hold his Office during the Term of four Years, and, together with the Vice President, chosen for the same Term, be elected, as follows:

Each State shall appoint, in such Manner as the Legislature thereof may direct, a Number of Electors, equal to the whole Number of Senators and Representatives to which the State may be entitled in the Congress: but no Senator or Representative, or Person holding an Office of Trust or Profit under the United States, shall be appointed an Elector.

The Electors shall meet in their respective States, and vote by Ballot for two Persons, of whom one at least shall not be an Inhabitant of the same State with themselves. And they shall make a List of all the Persons voted for, and of the Number of Votes for each; which List they shall sign and certify, and transmit sealed to the Seat of the Government of the United States, directed to the President of the Senate. The President of the Senate shall, in the Presence of the Senate and House of Representatives, open all the Certificates, and the Votes shall then be counted. The Person having the greatest Number of Votes shall be the President, if such Number be a Majority of the whole Number of Electors appointed; and if there be more than one who have such Majority, and have an equal Number of Votes, then the House of Representatives shall immediately chuse by Ballot one of them for President; and if no Person have a Majority, then from the five highest on the List the said House shall in like Manner chuse the President. But in chusing the President, the Votes shall be taken by States, the Representation from each State having one Vote; A quorum for this Purpose shall consist of a Member or Members from two thirds of the States, and a Majority of all the States shall be necessary to a Choice. In every Case, after the Choice of the President, the Person having the greatest Number of Votes of the Electors shall be the Vice President. But if there should remain two or more who have equal Votes, the Senate shall chuse from them by Ballot the Vice President.

The Congress may determine the Time of chusing the Electors, and the Day on which they shall give their Votes; which Day shall be the same throughout the United States.

No Person except a natural born Citizen, or a Citizen of the United States, at the time of the Adoption of this Constitution, shall be eligible to the Office of President; neither shall any person be eligible to that Office who shall not have attained to the Age of thirty five Years, and been fourteen Years a Resident within the United States.

In Case of the Removal of the President from Office, or of his Death, Resignation, or Inability to discharge the Powers and Duties of the said Office, the Same shall devolve on the Vice President, and the Congress may by Law provide for the Case of Removal, Death, Resignation or Inability, both of the President and Vice President, declaring what Officer shall then act as President, and such Officer shall act accordingly, until the Disability be removed, or a President shall be elected.

The President shall, at stated Times, receive for his Services, a Compensation, which shall neither be increased nor diminished during the Period for which he shall have been elected, and he shall not receive within that Period any other Emolument from the United States, or any of them.

Before he enter on the Execution of his Office, he shall take the following Oath or Affirmation:—"I do solemnly swear (or affirm) that I will faithfully execute the Office of President of the United States, and will to the best of my Ability, preserve, protect and defend the Constitution of the United States."

Section 2

The President shall be Commander in Chief of the Army and Navy of the United States, and of the Militia of the several States, when called into the actual Service of the United States; he may require the Opinion, in writing, of the principal Officer in each of the executive Departments, upon any Subject relating to the Duties of their respective Offices, and he shall have Power to grant Reprieves and Pardons for Offenses against the United States, except in Cases of Impeachment.

He shall have Power, by and with the Advice and Consent of the Senate, to make Treaties, provided two thirds of the Senators present concur; and he shall nominate, and by and with the Advice and Consent of the Senate, shall appoint Ambassadors, other public Ministers and Consuls, Judges of the supreme Court, and all other Officers of the United States, whose Appointments are not herein otherwise provided for, and which shall be established by Law: but the Congress may by Law vest the Appointment of such inferior Officers, as they think proper, in the President alone, in the Courts of Law, or in the Heads of Departments.

The President shall have Power to fill up all Vacancies that may happen during the Recess of the Senate, by granting Commissions which shall expire at the End of their next Session.

Section 3

He shall from time to time give to the Congress Information of the State of the Union, and recommend to their Consideration such Measures as he shall judge necessary and expedient; he may, on extraordinary Occasions, convene both Houses, or either of them, and in Case of Disagreement between them, with Respect to the Time of Adjournment, he may adjourn them to such Time as he shall think proper; he shall receive Ambassadors and other public Ministers; he shall take Care that the Laws be faithfully executed, and shall Commission all the Officers of the United States.

Section 4

The President, Vice President and all civil Officers of the United States, shall be removed from Office on Impeachment for, and Conviction of, Treason, Bribery, or other high Crimes and Misdemeanors.

Article III

Section 1

The judicial Power of the United States, shall be vested in one supreme Court, and in such inferior Courts as the Congress may from time to time ordain and establish. The Judges, both of the supreme and inferior Courts, shall hold their Offices during good Behaviour, and shall, at stated Times, receive for their Services, a Compensation, which shall not be diminished during their Continuance in Office.

Section 2

The judicial Power shall extend to all Cases, in Law and Equity, arising under this Constitution, the Laws of the United States, and Treaties made, or which shall be made, under their Authority;—to all Cases affecting Ambassadors, other public Ministers and Consuls;—to all Cases of admiralty and maritime Jurisdiction;—to Controversies to which the United States shall be a Party;—to Controversies between two or more States;—between a State and Citizens of another State;—between Citizens of different States;—between Citizens of the same State claiming Lands under Grants of different States, and between a State, or the Citizens thereof, and foreign States, Citizens or Subjects.

In all Cases affecting Ambassadors, other public Ministers and Consuls, and those in which a State shall be Party, the supreme Court shall have original Jurisdiction. In all the other Cases before mentioned, the supreme Court shall have appellate Jurisdiction, both as to Law and Fact, with such Exceptions, and under such Regulations as the Congress shall make.

The Trial of all Crimes, except in Cases of Impeachment; shall be by Jury; and such Trial shall be held in the State where the said Crimes shall have been committed; but when not committed within any State, the Trial shall be at such Place or Places as the Congress may by Law have directed.

Section 3

Treason against the United States, shall consist only in levying War against them, or in adhering to their Enemies, giving them Aid and Comfort. No

Person shall be convicted of Treason unless on the Testimony of two Witnesses to the same overt Act, or on Confession in open Court.

The Congress shall have Power to declare the Punishment of Treason, but no Attainder of Treason shall work Corruption of Blood, or Forfeiture except during the Life of the Person attainted.

Article IV

Section 1
Full Faith and Credit shall be given in each State to the public Acts, Records, and judicial Proceedings of every other State. And the Congress may by general Laws prescribe the Manner in which such Acts, Records and Proceedings shall be proved, and the Effect thereof.

Section 2
The Citizens of each State shall be entitled to all Privileges and Immunities of Citizens in the several States.

A Person charged in any State with Treason, Felony, or other Crime, who shall flee from Justice, and be found in another State, shall on Demand of the executive Authority of the State from which he fled, be delivered up, to be removed to the State having Jurisdiction of the Crime.

No Person held to Service or Labour in one State, under the Laws thereof, escaping into another, shall, in Consequence of any Law or Regulation therein, be discharged from such Service or Labour, but shall be delivered up on Claim of the Party to whom such Service or Labour may be due.

Section 3
New States may be admitted by the Congress into this Union; but no new State shall be formed or erected within the Jurisdiction of any other State; nor any State be formed by the Junction of two or more States, or Parts of States, without the Consent of the Legislatures of the States concerned as well as of the Congress.

The Congress shall have Power to dispose of and make all needful Rules and Regulations respecting the Territory or other Property belonging to the United States; and nothing in this Constitution shall be so construed as to Prejudice any Claims of the United States, or of any particular State.

Section 4

The United States shall guarantee to every State in this Union a Republican Form of Government, and shall protect each of them against Invasion; and on Application of the Legislature, or of the Executive (when the Legislature cannot be convened) against domestic Violence.

Article V

The Congress, whenever two thirds of both Houses shall deem it necessary, shall propose Amendments to this Constitution, or, on the Application of the Legislatures of two thirds of the several States, shall call a Convention for proposing Amendments, which, in either Case, shall be valid to all Intents and Purposes, as Part of this Constitution, when ratified by the Legislatures of three fourths of the several States, or by Conventions in three fourths thereof, as the one or the other Mode of Ratification may be proposed by the Congress; Provided that no Amendment which may be made prior to the Year One thousand eight hundred and eight shall in any Manner affect the first and fourth Clauses in the Ninth Section of the first Article; and that no State, without its Consent, shall be deprived of its equal Suffrage in the Senate.

Article VI

All Debts contracted and Engagements entered into, before the Adoption of this Constitution, shall be as valid against the United States under this Constitution, as under the Confederation.

This Constitution, and the Laws of the United States which shall be made in Pursuance thereof; and all Treaties made, or which shall be made, under the Authority of the United States, shall be the supreme Law of the Land; and the Judges in every State shall be bound thereby, any Thing in the Constitution or Laws of any State to the Contrary notwithstanding.

The Senators and Representatives before mentioned, and the Members of the several State Legislatures, and all executive and judicial Officers, both of the United States and of the several States, shall be bound by Oath or Affirmation, to support this Constitution; but no religious Test shall ever be required as a Qualification to any Office or public Trust under the United States.

Article VII

The Ratification of the Conventions of nine States, shall be sufficient for the Establishment of this Constitution between the States so ratifying the Same.

First Amendment

Congress shall make no law respecting an establishment of religion, or prohibiting the free exercise thereof; or abridging the freedom of speech, or of the press; or the right of the people peaceably to assemble, and to petition the Government for a redress of grievances.

Second Amendment

A well regulated Militia, being necessary to the security of a free State, the right of the people to keep and bear Arms, shall not be infringed.

Third Amendment

No Soldier shall, in time of peace be quartered in any house, without the consent of the Owner, nor in time of war, but in a manner to be prescribed by law.

Fourth Amendment

The right of the people to be secure in their persons, houses, papers, and effects, against unreasonable searches and seizures, shall not be violated, and no Warrants shall issue, but upon probable cause, supported by Oath or affirmation, and particularly describing the place to be searched, and the persons or things to be seized.

Fifth Amendment

No person shall be held to answer for a capital, or otherwise infamous crime, unless on a presentment or indictment of a Grand Jury, except in cases arising in the land or naval forces, or in the Militia, when in actual service in time of War or public danger; nor shall any person be subject for the same offence to be twice put in jeopardy of life or limb; nor shall be compelled in any criminal case to be a witness against himself, nor be deprived of life, liberty, or property, without due process of law; nor shall private property be taken for public use, without just compensation.

Sixth Amendment

In all criminal prosecutions, the accused shall enjoy the right to a speedy and public trial, by an impartial jury of the State and district wherein the crime shall have been committed, which district shall have been previously ascertained by law, and to be informed of the nature and cause of the accusation; to be confronted with the witnesses against him; to have compulsory process for obtaining witnesses in his favor, and to have the Assistance of Counsel for his defence.

Seventh Amendment

In Suits at common law, where the value in controversy shall exceed twenty dollars, the right of trial by jury shall be preserved, and no fact tried by a jury, shall be otherwise reexamined in any Court of the United States, than according to the rules of the common law.

Eighth Amendment

Excessive bail shall not be required, nor excessive fines imposed, nor cruel and unusual punishments inflicted.

Ninth Amendment

The enumeration in the Constitution, of certain rights, shall not be construed to deny or disparage others retained by the people.

Tenth Amendment

The powers not delegated to the United States by the Constitution, nor prohibited by it to the States, are reserved to the States respectively, or to the people.

Eleventh Amendment

The Judicial power of the United States shall not be construed to extend to any suit in law or equity, commenced or prosecuted against one of the United States by Citizens of another State, or by Citizens or Subjects of any Foreign State.

Twelfth Amendment

The Electors shall meet in their respective states and vote by ballot for President and Vice-President, one of whom, at least, shall not be an inhabitant of the same state with themselves; they shall name in their ballots the person voted for as President, and in distinct ballots the person voted for as Vice-President, and they shall make distinct lists of all persons voted for as President, and of all persons voted for as Vice-President, and of the number of votes for each, which lists they shall sign and certify, and transmit sealed to the seat of the government of the United States, directed to the President of the Senate; — The President of the Senate shall, in the presence of the Senate and House of Representatives, open all the certificates and the votes shall then be counted; — The person having the greatest number of votes for President, shall be the President, if such number be a majority of the whole number of Electors appointed; and if no person have such majority, then from the persons having the highest numbers not exceeding three on the list of those voted for as President, the House of Representatives shall choose immediately, by ballot, the President. But in choosing the President, the votes shall be taken by states, the representation from each state having one vote; a quorum for this purpose shall consist of a member or members from two-thirds of the states, and a majority of all the states shall be necessary to a choice. And if the House of Representatives shall not choose a President whenever the right of choice shall devolve upon them, before the fourth day of March next following, then the Vice-President shall act as President, as in case of the death or other constitutional disability of the President.— The person having the greatest number of votes as Vice-President, shall be the Vice-President, if such number be a majority of the whole number of Electors appointed, and if no person have a majority, then from the two highest numbers on the list, the Senate shall choose the Vice-President; a quorum for the purpose shall consist of two-thirds of the whole number of Senators, and a majority of the whole number shall be necessary to a choice. But no person constitutionally ineligible to the office of President shall be eligible to that of Vice-President of the United States.

Thirteenth Amendment

Section 1
Neither slavery nor involuntary servitude, except as a punishment for crime whereof the party shall have been duly convicted, shall exist within the United States, or any place subject to their jurisdiction.

Section 2
Congress shall have power to enforce this article by appropriate legislation.

Fourteenth Amendment

Section 1
All persons born or naturalized in the United States, and subject to the jurisdiction thereof, are citizens of the United States and of the State wherein they reside. No State shall make or enforce any law which shall abridge the privileges or immunities of citizens of the United States; nor shall any State deprive any person of life, liberty, or property, without due process of law; nor deny to any person within its jurisdiction the equal protection of the laws.

Section 2
Representatives shall be apportioned among the several States according to their respective numbers, counting the whole number of persons in each State, excluding Indians not taxed. But when the right to vote at any election for the choice of electors for President and Vice-President of the United States, Representatives in Congress, the Executive and Judicial officers of a State, or the members of the Legislature thereof, is denied to any of the male inhabitants of such State, being twenty-one years of age, and citizens of the United States, or in any way abridged, except for participation in rebellion, or other crime, the basis of representation therein shall be reduced in the proportion which the number of such male citizens shall bear to the whole number of male citizens twenty-one years of age in such State.

Section 3
No person shall be a Senator or Representative in Congress, or elector of President and Vice-President, or hold any office, civil or military, under the United States, or under any State, who, having previously taken an oath, as a member of Congress, or as an officer of the United States, or as a member of any State legislature, or as an executive or judicial officer of any State, to support the Constitution of the United States, shall have engaged in insurrection or rebellion against the same, or given aid or comfort to the enemies

thereof. But Congress may by a vote of two-thirds of each House, remove such disability.

Section 4
The validity of the public debt of the United States, authorized by law, including debts incurred for payment of pensions and bounties for services in suppressing insurrection or rebellion, shall not be questioned. But neither the United States nor any State shall assume or pay any debt or obligation incurred in aid of insurrection or rebellion against the United States, or any claim for the loss or emancipation of any slave; but all such debts, obligations and claims shall be held illegal and void.

Section 5
The Congress shall have the power to enforce, by appropriate legislation, the provisions of this article.

Fifteenth Amendment

Section 1
The right of citizens of the United States to vote shall not be denied or abridged by the United States or by any State on account of race, color, or previous condition of servitude.

Section 2
The Congress shall have the power to enforce this article by appropriate legislation.

Sixteenth Amendment

The Congress shall have power to lay and collect taxes on incomes, from whatever source derived, without apportionment among the several States, and without regard to any census or enumeration.

Seventeenth Amendment

The Senate of the United States shall be composed of two Senators from each State, elected by the people thereof, for six years; and each Senator shall have one vote. The electors in each State shall have the qualifications requisite for electors of the most numerous branch of the State legislatures.

When vacancies happen in the representation of any State in the Senate, the executive authority of such State shall issue writs of election to fill such vacancies: Provided, That the legislature of any State may empower the executive thereof to make temporary appointments until the people fill the vacancies by election as the legislature may direct.

This amendment shall not be so construed as to affect the election or term of any Senator chosen before it becomes valid as part of the Constitution.

Eighteenth Amendment

Section 1
After one year from the ratification of this article the manufacture, sale, or transportation of intoxicating liquors within, the importation thereof into, or the exportation thereof from the United States and all territory subject to the jurisdiction thereof for beverage purposes is hereby prohibited.

Section 2
The Congress and the several States shall have concurrent power to enforce this article by appropriate legislation.

Section 3
This article shall be inoperative unless it shall have been ratified as an amendment to the Constitution by the legislatures of the several States, as provided in the Constitution, within seven years from the date of the submission hereof to the States by the Congress.

Nineteenth Amendment

The right of citizens of the United States to vote shall not be denied or abridged by the United States or by any State on account of sex.

Congress shall have power to enforce this article by appropriate legislation.

Twentieth Amendment

Section 1
The terms of the President and the Vice President shall end at noon on the 20th day of January, and the terms of Senators and Representatives at noon on

the 3d day of January, of the years in which such terms would have ended if this article had not been ratified; and the terms of their successors shall then begin.

Section 2
The Congress shall assemble at least once in every year, and such meeting shall begin at noon on the 3d day of January, unless they shall by law appoint a different day.

Section 3
If, at the time fixed for the beginning of the term of the President, the President elect shall have died, the Vice President elect shall become President. If a President shall not have been chosen before the time fixed for the beginning of his term, or if the President elect shall have failed to qualify, then the Vice President elect shall act as President until a President shall have qualified; and the Congress may by law provide for the case wherein neither a President elect nor a Vice President shall have qualified, declaring who shall then act as President, or the manner in which one who is to act shall be selected, and such person shall act accordingly until a President or Vice President shall have qualified.

Section 4
The Congress may by law provide for the case of the death of any of the persons from whom the House of Representatives may choose a President whenever the right of choice shall have devolved upon them, and for the case of the death of any of the persons from whom the Senate may choose a Vice President whenever the right of choice shall have devolved upon them.

Section 5
Sections 1 and 2 shall take effect on the 15th day of October following the ratification of this article.

Section 6
This article shall be inoperative unless it shall have been ratified as an amendment to the Constitution by the legislatures of three-fourths of the several States within seven years from the date of its submission.

Twenty-First Amendment

Section 1
The eighteenth article of amendment to the Constitution of the United States is hereby repealed.

Section 2
The transportation or importation into any State, Territory, or Possession of the United States for delivery or use therein of intoxicating liquors, in violation of the laws thereof, is hereby prohibited.

Section 3
This article shall be inoperative unless it shall have been ratified as an amendment to the Constitution by conventions in the several States, as provided in the Constitution, within seven years from the date of the submission hereof to the States by the Congress.

Twenty-Second Amendment

Section 1
No person shall be elected to the office of the President more than twice, and no person who has held the office of President, or acted as President, for more than two years of a term to which some other person was elected President shall be elected to the office of President more than once. But this Article shall not apply to any person holding the office of President when this Article was proposed by Congress, and shall not prevent any person who may be holding the office of President, or acting as President, during the term within which this Article becomes operative from holding the office of President or acting as President during the remainder of such term.

Section 2
This article shall be inoperative unless it shall have been ratified as an amendment to the Constitution by the legislatures of three-fourths of the several States within seven years from the date of its submission to the States by the Congress.

Twenty-Third Amendment

Section 1
The District constituting the seat of Government of the United States shall appoint in such manner as Congress may direct:

A number of electors of President and Vice President equal to the whole number of Senators and Representatives in Congress to which the District would be entitled if it were a State, but in no event more than the least populous State; they shall be in addition to those appointed by the States, but they shall be considered, for the purposes of the election of President and Vice President, to be electors appointed by a State; and they shall meet in the District and perform such duties as provided by the twelfth article of amendment.

Section 2
The Congress shall have power to enforce this article by appropriate legislation.

Twenty-Fourth Amendment

Section 1
The right of citizens of the United States to vote in any primary or other election for President or Vice President, for electors for President or Vice President, or for Senator or Representative in Congress, shall not be denied or abridged by the United States or any State by reason of failure to pay poll tax or other tax.

Section 2
The Congress shall have power to enforce this article by appropriate legislation.

Twenty-Fifth Amendment

Section 1
In case of the removal of the President from office or of his death or resignation, the Vice President shall become President.

Section 2
Whenever there is a vacancy in the office of the Vice President, the President shall nominate a Vice President who shall take office upon confirmation by a majority vote of both Houses of Congress.

Section 3

Whenever the President transmits to the President pro tempore of the Senate and the Speaker of the House of Representatives his written declaration that he is unable to discharge the powers and duties of his office, and until he transmits to them a written declaration to the contrary, such powers and duties shall be discharged by the Vice President as Acting President.

Section 4

Whenever the Vice President and a majority of either the principal officers of the executive departments or of such other body as Congress may by law provide, transmit to the President pro tempore of the Senate and the Speaker of the House of Representatives their written declaration that the President is unable to discharge the powers and duties of his office, the Vice President shall immediately assume the powers and duties of the office as Acting President.

Thereafter, when the President transmits to the President pro tempore of the Senate and the Speaker of the House of Representatives his written declaration that no inability exists, he shall resume the powers and duties of his office unless the Vice President and a majority of either the principal officers of the executive department or of such other body as Congress may by law provide, transmit within four days to the President pro tempore of the Senate and the Speaker of the House of Representatives their written declaration that the President is unable to discharge the powers and duties of his office. Thereupon Congress shall decide the issue, assembling within forty-eight hours for that purpose if not in session. If the Congress, within twenty-one days after receipt of the latter written declaration, or, if Congress is not in session, within twenty-one days after Congress is required to assemble, determines by two-thirds vote of both Houses that the President is unable to discharge the powers and duties of his office, the Vice President shall continue to discharge the same as Acting President; otherwise, the President shall resume the powers and duties of his office.

Twenty-Sixth Amendment

Section 1

The right of citizens of the United States, who are eighteen years of age or older, to vote shall not be denied or abridged by the United States or by any State on account of age.

Section 2
The Congress shall have power to enforce this article by appropriate legislation.

Twenty-Seventh Amendment

No law, varying the compensation for the services of the Senators and Representatives, shall take effect, until an election of representatives shall have intervened.

UNRATIFIED AMENDMENTS
Representation Amendment

After the first enumeration required by the first article of the Constitution, there shall be one Representative for every thirty thousand, until the number shall amount to one hundred, after which the proportion shall be so regulated by Congress, that there shall be not less than one hundred Representatives, nor less than one Representative for every forty thousand persons, until the number of Representatives shall amount to two hundred; after which the proportion shall be so regulated by Congress, that there shall not be less than two hundred Representatives, nor more than one Representative for every fifty thousand persons.

Titles of Nobility Amendment

If any citizen of the United States shall accept, claim, receive or retain any title of nobility or honour, or shall, without the consent of Congress, accept and retain any present, pension, office or emolument of any kind whatever, from any emperor, king, prince or foreign power, such person shall cease to be a citizen of the United States, and shall be incapable of holding any office of trust or profit under them, or either of them.

Corwin Amendment

No amendment shall be made to the Constitution which will authorize or give to Congress the power to abolish or interfere, within any State, with the domestic institutions thereof, including that of persons held to labor or service by the laws of said State.

Child Labor Amendment

Section 1
The Congress shall have power to limit, regulate, and prohibit the labor of persons under 18 years of age.

Section 2
The power of the several States is unimpaired by this article except that the operation of State laws shall be suspended to the extent necessary to give effect to legislation enacted by the Congress.

Equal Rights Amendment

Section 1
Equality of rights under the law shall not be denied or abridged by the United States or by any State on account of sex.

Section 2
The Congress shall have the power to enforce, by appropriate legislation, the provisions of this article.

Section 3
This amendment shall take effect two years after the date of ratification.

District of Columbia Voting Representation Amendment

Section 1
For purposes of representation in the Congress, election of the President and Vice President, and article V of this Constitution, the District constituting the seat of government of the United States shall be treated as though it were a State.

Section 2
The exercise of the rights and powers conferred under this article shall be by the people of the District constituting the seat of government, and as shall be provided by the Congress.

Section 3

The twenty-third article of amendment to the Constitution of the United States is hereby repealed.

Section 4

This article shall be inoperative, unless it shall have been ratified as an amendment to the Constitution by the legislatures of three-fourths of the several States within seven years from the date of its submission.

Appendix B

Passage and Ratifications of the Amendments to the Constitution

First Through Tenth Amendments

PASSED

House: Sep. 24, 1789 (37 yea, 14 nay) [1 Annals of Cong. 948 (Joseph Gales, ed., 1834)]
Senate: Sep. 25, 1789 (unrecorded vote) [Senate Journal, 1st. Cong, 1st. Sess. 1789, 77]

RATIFIED

1. New Jersey, Nov. 20, 1789
2. Maryland, Dec. 19, 1789
3. North Carolina, Dec. 22, 1789
4. South Carolina, Jan. 19, 1790
5. New Hampshire, Jan. 25, 1790
6. Delaware, Jan. 28, 1790
7. New York, Feb. 27, 1790
8. Pennsylvania, Mar. 10, 1790
9. Rhode Island, Jun. 7, 1790
10. Vermont, Nov. 3, 1791
11. **Virginia, Dec. 15, 1791**
12. Massachusetts, Mar. 2, 1939
13. Georgia, Mar. 24, 1939
14. Connecticut, Apr. 24, 1939

Eleventh Amendment

PASSED

Senate: Jan. 14, 1794 (23 yea, 2 nay) [4 Annals of Cong. 30-31 (1794)]
House: Mar. 4, 1794 (81 yea, 9 nay) [4 Annals of Cong. 477-478 (1794)]

RATIFIED

1. New York, Mar. 27, 1794
2. Rhode Island, Mar. 31, 1794
3. Connecticut, May 8, 1794
4. New Hampshire, Jun. 16, 1794
5. Massachusetts, Jun. 26, 1794
6. Vermont, Oct. 28, 1794
7. Virginia, Nov. 18, 1794
8. Georgia, Nov. 29, 1794

9. Kentucky, Dec. 7, 1794

10. Maryland, Dec. 26, 1794

11. Delaware, Jan. 23, 1795

12. North Carolina, Feb. 7, 1795

13. South Carolina, Dec. 4, 1797

NO ACTION

1. New Jersey

2. Pennsylvania

Twelfth Amendment

PASSED

Senate: Dec. 2, 1803 (22 yea, 10 nay) [13 Annals of Cong. 209 (1803)]

House: Dec. 9, 1803 (32 yea, 42 nay) [13 Annals of Cong. 775-776 (1803)]

RATIFIED

1. North Carolina, Dec. 21, 1803

2. Maryland, Dec. 24, 1803

3. Kentucky, Dec. 27, 1803

4. Ohio, Dec. 30, 1803

5. Pennsylvania, Jan. 5, 1804

6. Vermont, Jan. 30, 1804

7. Virginia, Feb. 3, 1804

8. New York, Feb. 10, 1804

9. New Jersey, Feb. 22, 1804

10. Rhode Island, Mar. 12, 1804

11. South Carolina, May 15, 1804

12. Georgia, May 19, 1804

13. New Hampshire, Jun. 15, 1804

14. Tennessee, Jul. 27, 1804

15. Massachusetts, 1961 (previously rejected Feb. 3, 1804)

REJECTED

1. Delaware, Jan. 18, 1804

2. Connecticut, during its May 10, 1804 session

Thirteenth Amendment

PASSED

Senate: Apr. 8, 1864 (38 yea, 6 nay) [Cong. Globe, 38th Cong., 1st Sess. 1490 (1864)]

House: Jan. 31, 1865 (119 yea, 56 nay) [Cong. Globe, 38th Cong., 2nd Sess. 531 (1865)]

RATIFIED

1. Illinois, Feb. 1, 1865

2. Rhode Island, Feb. 2, 1865

3. Michigan, Feb. 2, 1865

4. Maryland, Feb. 3, 1865

5. New York, Feb. 3, 1865

6. Pennsylvania, Feb. 3, 1865

7. West Virginia, Feb. 3, 1865

8. Missouri, Feb. 6, 1865

9. Maine, Feb. 7, 1865

10. Kansas, Feb. 7, 1865

11. Massachusetts, Feb. 7, 1865

12. Virginia, Feb. 9, 1865

13. Ohio, Feb. 10, 1865

14. Indiana, Feb. 13, 1865

15. Nevada, Feb. 16, 1865

16. Louisiana, Feb. 17, 1865

17. Minnesota, Feb. 23, 1865

18. Wisconsin, Feb. 24, 1865

19. Vermont, Mar. 9, 1865
20. Tennessee, Apr. 7, 1865
21. Arkansas, Apr. 14, 1865
22. Connecticut, May 4, 1865
23. New Hampshire, Jul. 1, 1865
24. South Carolina, Nov. 13, 1865
25. Alabama, Dec. 2, 1865
26. North Carolina, Dec. 4, 1865
27. Georgia, Dec. 6, 1865
28. Oregon, Dec. 8, 1865
29. California, Dec. 19, 1865

30. Florida, Dec. 28, 1865
    and Jun. 9, 1868
31. Iowa, Jan. 15, 1866
32. New Jersey, Jan. 23, 1866 (previously
    rejected Mar. 16, 1865)
33. Texas, Feb. 18, 1870
34. Delaware, Feb. 12, 1901 (previously
    rejected Feb. 8, 1865)
35. Kentucky, Mar. 18, 1976 (previously
    rejected Feb. 24, 1865)
36. Mississippi, Mar. 16, 1995
    (previously rejected Dec. 4, 1865)

Fourteenth Amendment

PASSED

Senate: Jun. 8, 1866 (33 yea, 11 nay) [Cong. Globe, 39th Cong., 1st Sess. 3042 (1866)]
House: Jun. 13, 1866 (120 yea, 32 nay) [Cong. Globe, 39th Cong., 1st Sess. 3149 (1866)]

RATIFIED

1. Connecticut, Jun. 27, 1866
2. New Hampshire, Jul. 6, 1866
3. Tennessee, Jul. 19, 1866
4. New Jersey, Sep. 11, 1866
   (rescinded Mar. 24, 1868, re-
   ratified Apr. 23, 2003)
5. Oregon, Sep. 19, 1866
   (rescinded Oct. 15, 1868, re-
   ratified Apr. 25, 1973)
6. Vermont, Oct. 30, 1866
7. Ohio, Jan. 4, 1867 (rescinded Jan.
   15, 1868, re-ratified Mar. 12, 2003)
8. New York, Jan. 10, 1867
9. Kansas, Jan. 11, 1867
10. Illinois, Jan. 15, 1867
11. West Virginia, Jan. 16, 1867
12. Michigan, Jan. 16, 1867
13. Minnesota, Jan. 16, 1867
14. Maine, Jan. 19, 1867
15. Nevada, Jan. 22, 1867
16. Indiana, Jan. 23, 1867
17. Missouri, Jan. 25, 1867
18. Pennsylvania, Feb. 6, 1867
19. Rhode Island, Feb. 7, 1867
20. Wisconsin, Feb. 13, 1867

21. Massachusetts, Mar. 20, 1867
22. Nebraska, Jun. 15, 1867
23. Iowa, Mar. 16, 1868
24. Arkansas, Apr. 6, 1868 (previously
    rejected Dec. 17, 1866)
25. Florida, Jun. 9, 1868 (previously
    rejected Dec. 6, 1866)
26. North Carolina, Jul. 4, 1868
    (previously rejected Dec. 14, 1866)
27. Louisiana, Jul. 9, 1868 (previously
    rejected Feb. 6, 1867)
**28. South Carolina, Jul. 9, 1868
    (previously rejected Dec. 20, 1866)**
29. Alabama, Jul. 13, 1868 (previously
    rejected Dec. 7, 1866)
30. Georgia, Jul. 21, 1868 (previously
    rejected Nov. 9, 1866)
31. Virginia, Oct. 8, 1869 (previously
    rejected Jan. 9, 1867)
32. Mississippi, Jan. 17, 1870
    (previously rejected Jan. 29, 1867)
33. Texas, Feb. 18, 1870 (previously
    rejected Oct. 27, 1866)
34. Delaware, Feb. 12, 1901 (previously
    rejected Feb. 8, 1867)

35. Maryland, Apr. 4, 1959 (previously rejected Mar. 23, 1867)
36. California, May 6, 1959
37. Kentucky, Mar. 18, 1976 (previously rejected Jan. 8, 1867)

Fifteenth Amendment

PASSED

House: Feb. 25, 1869 (144 yea, 44 nay) [Cong. Globe, 40th Cong., 3rd Sess. 1563-1564 (1869)]

Senate: Feb. 26, 1869 (39 yea, 13 nay) [Cong. Globe, 40th Cong., 3rd Sess. 1641 (1869)]

RATIFIED

1. Nevada, Mar. 1, 1869
2. West Virginia, Mar. 3, 1869
3. Illinois, Mar. 5, 1869
4. Louisiana, Mar. 5, 1869
5. North Carolina, Mar. 5, 1869
6. Michigan, Mar. 8, 1869
7. Wisconsin, Mar. 9, 1869
8. Maine, Mar. 11, 1869
9. Massachusetts, Mar. 12, 1869
10. Arkansas, Mar. 15, 1869
11. South Carolina, Mar. 15, 1869
12. Pennsylvania, Mar. 25, 1869
13. New York, Apr. 14, 1869 (rescinded Jan. 5, 1870, re-ratified Mar. 30, 1970)
14. Indiana, May 14, 1869
15. Connecticut, May 19, 1869
16. Florida, Jun. 14, 1869
17. New Hampshire, Jul. 1, 1869
18. Virginia, Oct. 8, 1869
19. Vermont, Oct. 20, 1869
20. Alabama, Nov. 16, 1869
21. Missouri, Jan. 7, 1870
22. Minnesota, Jan. 13, 1870
23. Mississippi, Jan. 17, 1870
24. Rhode Island, Jan. 18, 1870
25. Kansas, Jan. 19, 1870
26. Ohio, Jan. 27, 1870 (previously rejected Apr. 30, 1869)
27. Georgia, Feb. 2, 1870
28. Iowa, Feb. 3, 1870
29. Nebraska, Feb. 17, 1870
30. Texas, Feb. 18, 1870
31. New Jersey, Feb. 15, 1871 (previously rejected Feb. 7, 1870)
32. Delaware, Feb. 12, 1901 (previously rejected Mar. 18, 1869)
33. Oregon, Feb. 24, 1959
34. California, Apr. 3, 1962 (previously rejected Jan. 28, 1870)
35. Kentucky, Mar. 18, 1976 (previously rejected Mar. 12, 1869)
36. Maryland, May 7, 1973 (previously rejected Feb. 26, 1870)
37. Tennessee, Apr. 8, 1997 (previously rejected Nov. 16, 1868)

Sixteenth Amendment

PASSED

Senate: Jul. 5, 1909 (77 yea) [44 Cong. Rec. 4121 (1909)]

House: Jul. 12, 1909 (318 yea, 14 nay) [44 Cong. Rec. 4440 (1909)]

RATIFIED

1. Alabama, Aug. 10, 1909
2. Kentucky, Feb. 8, 1910
3. South Carolina, Feb. 19, 1910
4. Illinois, Mar. 1, 1910

5. Mississippi, Mar. 7, 1910
6. Oklahoma, Mar. 10, 1910
7. Maryland, Apr. 8, 1910
8. Georgia, Aug. 3, 1910
9. Texas, Aug. 16, 1910
10. Ohio, Jan. 19, 1911
11. Idaho, Jan. 20, 1911
12. Oregon, Jan. 23, 1911
13. Washington, Jan. 26, 1911
14. Montana, Jan. 30, 1911
15. Indiana, Jan. 30, 1911
16. California, Jan. 31, 1911
17. Nevada, Jan. 31, 1911
18. South Dakota, Feb. 3, 1911
19. Nebraska, Feb. 9, 1911
20. North Carolina, Feb. 11, 1911
21. Colorado, Feb. 15, 1911
22. North Dakota, Feb. 17, 1911
23. Kansas, Feb. 18, 1911
24. Michigan, Feb. 23, 1911

25. Iowa, Feb. 24, 1911
26. Kansas, Mar. 2, 1911
27. Missouri, Mar. 16, 1911
28. Maine, Mar. 31, 1911
29. Tennessee, Apr. 7, 1911
30. Arkansas, Apr. 22, 1911 (previously rejected at the Jan. 9, 1911 session)
31. Wisconsin, May 26, 1911
32. New York, Jul. 12, 1911
33. Arizona, Apr. 6, 1912
34. Minnesota, Jun. 11, 1912
35. Louisiana, Jun. 28, 1912
36. **West Virginia, Jan. 31, 1913**
37. Delaware, Feb. 3, 1913
38. New Mexico, Feb. 3, 1913
39. Wyoming, Feb. 3, 1913
40. Vermont, Feb. 19, 1913
41. Massachusetts, Mar. 4, 1913
42. New Hampshire, Mar. 7, 1913 (previously rejected Mar. 2, 1911

REJECTED

1. Rhode Island, Apr. 29, 1910
2. Utah, Mar. 9, 1911

3. Connecticut, Jun. 28, 1911
4. Florida, May 31, 1913

NO ACTION

1. Pennsylvania

2. Virginia

Seventeenth Amendment

PASSED

Senate: Jun. 12, 1911 (64 yea, 24 nay) [47 Cong. Rec. 1924-1925 (1911)]
House: May 13, 1912 (238 yea, 39 nay) [47 Cong. Rec. 6369 (1912)]

RATIFIED

1. Massachusetts, May 22, 1912
2. Arizona, Jun. 3, 1912
3. Minnesota, Jun. 10, 1912
4. New York, Jan. 15, 1913
5. Kansas, Jan. 17, 1913
6. Oregon, Jan. 23, 1913
7. North Carolina, Jan. 25, 1913
8. California, Jan. 28, 1913
9. Michigan, Jan. 28, 1913
10. Iowa, Jan. 30, 1913

11. Montana, Jan. 30, 1913
12. Idaho, Jan. 31, 1913
13. West Virginia, Feb. 4, 1913
14. Colorado, Feb. 5, 1913
15. Nevada, Feb. 6, 1913
16. Texas, Feb. 7, 1913
17. Washington, Feb. 7, 1913
18. Wyoming, Feb. 8, 1913
19. Arkansas, Feb. 11, 1913
20. Maine, Feb. 11, 1913

21. Illinois, Feb. 13, 1913
22. North Dakota, Feb. 14, 1913
23. Wisconsin, Feb. 18, 1913
24. Indiana, Feb. 19, 1913
25. New Hampshire, Feb. 19, 1913
26. Vermont, Feb. 19, 1913
27. South Dakota, Feb. 19, 1913
28. Oklahoma, Feb. 24, 1913
29. Ohio, Feb. 25, 1913
30. Missouri, Mar. 7, 1913
31. New Mexico, Mar. 13, 1913

32. Nebraska, Mar. 14, 1913
33. New Jersey, Mar. 17, 1913
34. Tennessee, Apr. 1, 1913
35. Pennsylvania, Apr. 2, 1913
36. **Connecticut, Apr. 8, 1913**
37. Louisiana, Jun. 11, 1914
38. Alabama, Apr. 11, 2002
39. Delaware, Jul. 1, 2010
40. Maryland, Apr. 1, 2012
41. Rhode Island, Jun. 20, 2014

REJECTED
1. Utah, Feb. 26, 1913

NO ACTION
1. Florida
2. Georgia
3. Kentucky

4. Mississippi
5. South Carolina
6. Virginia

Eighteenth Amendment

PASSED

Senate: Aug. 1, 1917 (65 yea, 20 nay), Dec. 18, 1917 (voice vote) [55 Cong. Rec. 5666 (1917); 56 Cong. Rec. 478 (1918)]

House: Dec. 17, 1917 (282 yea, 128 nay) [56 Cong. Rec. 469-470 (1918)]

RATIFIED

1. Mississippi, Jan. 8, 1918
2. Virginia, Jan. 11, 1918
3. Kentucky, Jan. 14, 1918
4. North Dakota, Jan. 25, 1918
5. South Carolina, Jan. 29, 1918
6. Maryland, Feb. 13, 1918
7. Montana, Feb. 19, 1918
8. Texas, Mar. 4, 1918
9. Delaware, Mar. 18, 1918
10. South Dakota, Mar. 20, 1918
11. Massachusetts, Apr. 2, 1918
12. Arizona, May 24, 1918
13. Georgia, Jun. 26, 1918
14. Louisiana, Aug. 3, 1918
15. Florida, Nov. 27, 1918
16. Michigan, Jan. 2, 1919
17. Ohio, Jan. 7, 1919

18. Oklahoma, Jan. 7, 1919
19. Idaho, Jan. 8, 1919
20. Maine, Jan. 8, 1919
21. West Virginia, Jan. 9, 1919
22. California, Jan. 13, 1919
23. Tennessee, Jan. 13, 1919
24. Washington, Jan. 13, 1919
25. Indiana, Jan. 14, 1919
26. Illinois, Jan. 14, 1919
27. Arkansas, Jan. 14, 1919
28. Kansas, Jan. 14, 1919
29. Alabama, Jan. 15, 1919
30. Colorado, Jan. 15, 1919
31. Iowa, Jan. 15, 1919
32. New Hampshire, Jan. 15, 1919
33. Oregon, Jan. 15, 1919
34. North Carolina, Jan. 16, 1919

35. Utah, Jan. 16, 1919
36. Nebraska, Jan. 16, 1919
37. Missouri, Jan. 16, 1919
38. Wyoming, Jan. 16, 1919
39. Minnesota, Jan. 17, 1919
40. Wisconsin, Jan. 17, 1919

41. New Mexico, Jan. 20, 1919
42. Nevada, Jan. 21, 1919
43. New York, Jan. 29, 1919
44. Vermont, Jan. 29, 1919
45. Pennsylvania, Feb. 25, 1919
46. New Jersey, Mar. 9, 1922

REJECTED
1. Rhode Island, Feb. 6, 1919

2. Connecticut, May 6, 1919

Nineteenth Amendment

PASSED
House: May 21, 1919 (304 yea, 90 nay) [58 Cong. Rec. 94 (1919)]
Senate: Jun. 4, 1919 (56 yea, 24 nay) [58 Cong. Rec. 635 (1919)]

RATIFIED
1. Illinois, Jun. 10, 1919
   and Jun. 17, 1919
2. Michigan, Jun. 10, 1919
3. Wisconsin, Jun. 10, 1919
4. Kansas, Jun. 16, 1919
5. New York, Jun. 16, 1919
6. Ohio, Jun. 16, 1919
7. Pennsylvania, Jun. 24, 1919
8. Massachusetts, Jun. 25, 1919
9. Texas, Jun. 28, 1919
10. Iowa, Jul. 2, 1919
11. Missouri, Jul. 3, 1919
12. Arkansas, Jul. 28, 1919
13. Montana, Aug. 2, 1919
14. Nebraska, Aug. 2, 1919
15. Minnesota, Sep. 8, 1919
16. New Hampshire, Sep. 10, 1919
17. Utah, Oct. 2, 1919
18. California, Nov. 1, 1919
19. Maine, Nov. 5, 1919
20. North Dakota, Dec. 1, 1919
21. South Dakota, Dec. 4, 1919
22. Colorado, Dec. 15, 1919
23. Kentucky, Jan. 6, 1920
24. Rhode Island, Jan. 6, 1920
25. Oregon, Jan. 13, 1920
26. Indiana, Jan. 16, 1920
27. Wyoming, Jan. 27, 1920

28. Nevada, Feb. 7, 1920
29. New Jersey, Feb. 9, 1920
30. Idaho, Feb. 11, 1920
31. Arizona, Feb. 12, 1920
32. 21, 1920
33. Oklahoma, Feb. 28, 1920
34. West Virginia, Mar. 10, 1920
35. Washington, Mar. 22, 1920
36. Tennessee, Aug. 18, 1920
37. Connecticut, Sep. 21, 1920
38. Vermont, Feb. 8, 1921
39. Delaware, Mar. 6, 1923 (previously
   rejected Jun. 2, 1920)
40. Maryland, Mar. 29, 1941
   (previously rejected Feb. 24,
   1920, certified Feb. 25, 1958)
41. Virginia, Feb. 21, 1952 (previously
   rejected Feb. 12, 1920)
42. Alabama, Sep. 8, 1953 (previously
   rejected Sep. 22, 1919)
43. Florida, May 13, 1969
44. South Carolina, Jul. 1, 1969
   (previously rejected Jan. 28,
   1920, certified Aug. 22, 1973)
45. Georgia, Feb. 20, 1970 (previously
   rejected Jul. 24, 1919)
46. Louisiana, Jun. 11, 1970
   (previously rejected Jul. 1, 1920)

47. North Carolina, May 6, 1971

48. Mississippi, Mar. 22, 1984
(previously rejected Mar. 29, 1920)

Twentieth Amendment

PASSED

House: Feb. 16, 1932 (336 yea, 56 nay), Mar. 1, 1932 (voice vote) [75 Cong. Rec. 4060, 5027 (1932)]

Senate: Mar. 2, 1932 (74 yea, 3 nay) [75 Cong. Rec. 5086 (1932)]

RATIFIED

1. Virginia, Mar. 4, 1932
2. New York, Mar. 11, 1932
3. Mississippi, Mar. 16, 1932
4. Arkansas, Mar. 17, 1932
5. Kentucky, Mar. 17, 1932
6. New Jersey, Mar. 21, 1932
7. South Carolina, Mar. 25, 1932
8. Michigan, Mar. 31, 1932
9. Maine, Apr. 1, 1932
10. Rhode Island, Apr. 14, 1932
11. Illinois, Apr. 21, 1932
12. Louisiana, Jun. 22, 1932
13. West Virginia, Jul. 30, 1932
14. Pennsylvania, Aug. 11, 1932
15. Indiana, Aug. 15, 1932
16. Texas, Sep. 7, 1932
17. Alabama, Sep. 13, 1932
18. California, Jan. 4, 1933
19. North Carolina, Jan. 5, 1933
20. North Dakota, Jan. 9, 1933
21. Minnesota, Jan. 12, 1933
22. Arizona, Jan. 13, 1933
23. Montana, Jan. 13, 1933
24. Nebraska, Jan. 13, 1933
25. Oklahoma, Jan. 13, 1933
26. Kansas, Jan. 16, 1933
27. Oregon, Jan. 16, 1933
28. Delaware, Jan. 19, 1933
29. Washington, Jan. 19, 1933
30. Wyoming, Jan. 19, 1933
31. Iowa, Jan. 20, 1933
32. South Dakota, Jan. 20, 1933
33. Tennessee, Jan. 20, 1933
34. Idaho, Jan. 21, 1933
35. New Mexico, Jan. 21, 1933
36. Georgia, Jan. 23, 1933
37. Ohio, Jan. 23, 1933
38. **Missouri, Jan. 23, 1933**
39. Utah, Jan. 23, 1933
40. Massachusetts, Jan. 24, 1933
41. Wisconsin, Jan. 24, 1933
42. Colorado, Jan. 24, 1933
43. Nevada, Jan. 26, 1933
44. Connecticut, Jan. 27, 1933
45. New Hampshire, Jan. 31, 1933
46. Vermont, Feb. 2, 1933
47. Maryland, Mar. 24, 1933
48. Florida, Apr. 26, 1933

Twenty-First Amendment

Senate: Feb. 16, 1933 (63 yea, 23 nay) [76 Cong. Rec. 4231 (1933)]

House: Feb. 20, 1933 (289 yea, 121 nay) [76 Cong. Rec. 4516 (1933)]

RATIFIED

1. Michigan, Apr. 10, 1933
2. Wisconsin, Apr. 25, 1933
3. Rhode Island, May 8, 1933
4. Wyoming, May 25, 1933

5. New Jersey, Jun. 1, 1933
6. Delaware, Jun. 24, 1933
7. Massachusetts, Jun. 26, 1933
8. Indiana, Jun. 26, 1933
9. New York, Jun. 27, 1933
10. Illinois, Jul. 10, 1933
11. Iowa, Jul. 10, 1933
12. Connecticut, Jul. 11, 1933
13. New Hampshire, Jul. 11, 1933
14. California, Jul. 24, 1933
15. West Virginia, Jul. 25, 1933
16. Arkansas, Aug. 1, 1933
17. Oregon, Aug. 7, 1933
18. Alabama, Aug. 8, 1933
19. Tennessee, Aug. 11, 1933
20. Missouri, Aug. 29, 1933
21. Nevada, Sep. 5, 1933

22. Arizona, Sep. 5, 1933
23. Vermont, Sep. 23, 1933
24. Colorado, Sep. 26, 1933
25. Washington, Oct. 3, 1933
26. Minnesota, Oct. 10, 1933
27. Idaho, Oct. 17, 1933
28. Maryland, Oct. 18, 1933
29. Virginia, Oct. 25, 1933
30. New Mexico, Nov. 2, 1933
31. Florida, Nov. 14, 1933
32. Texas, Nov. 24, 1933
33. Kentucky, Nov. 27, 1933
34. Pennsylvania, Dec. 5, 1933
35. Ohio, Dec. 5, 1933
36. Utah, Dec. 5, 1933
37. Maine, Dec. 6, 1933
38. Montana, Aug. 6, 1934

REJECTED
1. South Carolina, Dec. 4, 1933

NO ACTION
1. Georgia
2. Kansas
3. Louisiana
4. Mississippi
5. Nebraska

6. North Dakota
7. North Carolina*
8. Oklahoma
9. South Dakota

*North Carolina voted against holding a ratifying convention on Nov. 7, 1933.

Twenty-Second Amendment

PASSAGE
House: Feb. 6, 1947 (285 yea, 121 nay), Mar. 21, 1947 (81 yea, 29 nay) [93 Cong. Rec. 872, 2392 (1947)]
Senate: Mar. 12, 1947 (59 yea, 23 nay) [93 Cong. Rec. 1978 (1947)]

RATIFIED
1. Maine, Mar. 31, 1947
2. Michigan, Mar. 31, 1947
3. New Hampshire, Apr. 1, 1947
4. Iowa, Apr. 1, 1947
5. Kansas, Apr. 1, 1947
6. Delaware, Apr. 2, 1947
7. Illinois, Apr. 3, 1947

8. Oregon, Apr. 3, 1947
9. Colorado, Apr. 12, 1947
10. New Jersey, Apr. 15, 1947
11. Vermont, Apr. 15, 1947
12. California, Apr. 15, 1947
13. Ohio, Apr. 16, 1947
14. Wisconsin, Apr. 16, 1947

15. Pennsylvania, Apr. 29, 1947
16. Connecticut, May 21, 1947
17. Missouri, May 22, 1947
18. Nebraska, May 23, 1947
19. Virginia, Jan. 1, 1948
20. Mississippi, Feb. 12, 1948
21. New York, Mar. 9, 1948
22. South Dakota, Jan. 21, 1949
23. North Dakota, Feb. 25, 1949
24. Louisiana, May 17, 1950
25. Montana, Jan. 25, 1951
26. Indiana, Jan. 29, 1951
27. Idaho, Jan. 30, 1951
28. Wyoming, Feb. 12, 1951

29. New Mexico, Feb. 12, 1951
30. Arkansas, Feb. 15, 1951
31. Georgia, Feb. 17, 1951
32. Tennessee, Feb. 20, 1951
33. Texas, Feb. 22, 1951
34. Nevada, Feb. 26, 1951
35. Utah, Feb. 26, 1951
36. Minnesota, Feb. 27, 1951
37. North Carolina, Feb. 28, 1951
38. South Carolina, Mar. 13, 1951
39. Maryland, Mar. 14, 1951
40. Florida, Apr. 16, 1951
41. Alabama, May 5, 1951

REJECTED

1. Oklahoma, Jun. 1947

2. Massachusetts, Jun. 6, 1949

NO ACTION

1. Arizona
2. Kentucky
3. Rhode Island

4. Washington
5. West Virginia

Twenty-Third Amendment

PASSAGE

Senate: Feb. 2, 1960 (70 yea, 12 nay), Jun. 16, 1960 (voice vote) [106 Cong. Rec. 1765, 12858 (1960)]
House: Jun. 14, 1960 (voice vote) [106 Cong. Rec. 12571]

RATIFIED

1. Hawaii, Jun. 23, 1960
2. Massachusetts, Aug. 22, 1960
3. New Jersey, Dec. 19, 1960
4. New York, Jan. 17, 1961
5. California, Jan. 19, 1961
6. Oregon, Jan. 27, 1961
7. Maryland, Jan. 30, 1961
8. Maine, Jan. 31, 1961
9. Minnesota, Jan. 31, 1961
10. Idaho, Jan. 31, 1961
11. New Mexico, Feb. 1, 1961
12. Nevada, Feb. 2, 1961
13. Montana, Feb. 6, 1961
14. Colorado, Feb. 8, 1961

15. Washington, Feb. 9, 1961
16. West Virginia, Feb. 9, 1961
17. Alaska, Feb. 10, 1961
18. Wyoming, Feb. 13, 1961
19. South Dakota, Feb. 14, 1961
20. Delaware, Feb. 20, 1961
21. Utah, Feb. 21, 1961
22. Wisconsin, Feb. 21, 1961
23. Pennsylvania, Feb. 28, 1961
24. Indiana, Mar. 3, 1961
25. North Dakota, Mar. 3, 1961
26. Tennessee, Mar. 6, 1961
27. Michigan, Mar. 8, 1961
28. Connecticut, Mar. 9, 1961

29. Arizona, Mar. 10, 1961
30. Illinois, Mar. 14, 1961
31. Nebraska, Mar. 15, 1961
32. Vermont, Mar. 15, 1961
33. Iowa, Mar. 16, 1961
34. Missouri, Mar. 20, 1961

35. Oklahoma, Mar. 21, 1961
36. Rhode Island, Mar. 22, 1961
37. Kansas, Mar. 29, 1961
38. **Ohio, Mar. 29, 1961**
39. New Hampshire, Mar. 30, 1961
40. Alabama, Apr. 11, 2002

REJECTED
1. Arkansas, Jan. 24, 1961

NO ACTION
1. Florida
2. Georgia
3. Kentucky
4. Louisiana
5. Mississippi

6. North Carolina
7. South Carolina
8. Texas
9. Virginia

Twenty-Fourth Amendment

PASSAGE
Senate: Mar. 27, 1962 (77 yea, 16 nay) [108 Cong. Rec. 5105 (1962)]
House: Aug. 27, 1962 (294 yea, 86 nay) [108 Cong. Rec. 17670 (1962)]

RATIFIED
1. Illinois, Nov. 14, 1962
2. New Jersey, Dec. 3, 1962
3. Oregon, Jan. 25, 1963
4. Montana, Jan. 28, 1963
5. West Virginia, Feb. 1, 1963
6. New York, Feb. 4, 1963
7. Maryland, Feb. 6, 1963
8. California, Feb. 7, 1963
9. Alaska, Feb. 11, 1963
10. Rhode Island, Feb. 14, 1963
11. Indiana, Feb. 19, 1963
12. Utah, Feb. 20, 1963
13. Michigan, Feb. 20, 1963
14. Colorado, Feb. 21, 1963
15. Ohio, Feb. 27, 1963
16. Minnesota, Feb. 27, 1963
17. New Mexico, Mar. 5, 1963
18. Hawaii, Mar. 6, 1963
19. North Dakota, Mar. 7, 1963
20. Idaho, Mar. 8, 1963
21. Washington, Mar. 14, 1963

22. Vermont, Mar. 15, 1963
23. Nevada, Mar. 19, 1963
24. Connecticut, Mar. 20, 1963
25. Tennessee, Mar. 21, 1963
26. Pennsylvania, Mar. 25, 1963
27. Wisconsin, Mar. 26, 1963
28. Kansas, Mar. 28, 1963
29. Massachusetts, Mar. 28, 1963
30. Nebraska, Apr. 4, 1963
31. Florida, Apr. 18, 1963
32. Iowa, Apr. 24, 1963
33. Delaware, May 1, 1963
34. Missouri, May 13, 1963
35. New Hampshire, Jun. 12, 1963
36. Kentucky, Jun. 27, 1963
37. Maine, Jan. 16, 1964
38. **South Dakota, Jan. 23, 1964**
39. Virginia, Feb. 25, 1977
40. North Carolina, May 3, 1989
41. Alabama, Apr. 11, 2002
42. Texas, May 22, 2009

REJECTED
1. Mississippi, Dec. 20, 1962

NO ACTION
1. Arizona
2. Arkansas
3. Georgia
4. Louisiana

5. Oklahoma
6. South Carolina
7. Wyoming

Twenty-Fifth Amendment

PASSAGE
Senate: Feb. 19, 1965 (72 yea), Jul. 6, 1965 (68 yea, 5 nay) [111 Cong. Rec. 3286, 15596 (1965)]
House: Apr. 13, 1965 (368 yea, 29 nay), Jun. 30, 1965 (voice vote) [111 Cong. Rec. 7969, 15216 (1965)]

RATIFIED
1. Nebraska, Jul. 12, 1965
2. Wisconsin, Jul. 13, 1965
3. Oklahoma, Jul. 16, 1965
4. Massachusetts, Aug. 9, 1965
5. Pennsylvania, Aug. 18, 1965
6. Kentucky, Sep. 15, 1965
7. Arizona, Sep. 22, 1965
8. Michigan, Oct. 5, 1965
9. Indiana, Oct. 20, 1965
10. California, Oct. 21, 1965
11. Arkansas, Nov. 4, 1965
12. New Jersey, Nov. 29, 1965
13. Delaware, Dec. 7, 1965
14. Utah, Jan. 17, 1966
15. West Virginia, Jan. 20, 1966
16. Maine, Jan. 24, 1966
17. Rhode Island, Jan. 28, 1966
18. Colorado, Feb. 3, 1966
19. New Mexico, Feb. 3, 1966
20. Kansas, Feb. 8, 1966
21. Vermont, Feb. 10, 1966
22. Alaska, Feb. 18, 1966
23. Idaho, Mar. 2, 1966
24. Hawaii, Mar. 3, 1966

25. Virginia, Mar. 8, 1966
26. Mississippi, Mar. 10, 1966
27. New York, Mar. 14, 1966
28. Maryland, Mar. 23, 1966
29. Missouri, Mar. 30, 1966
30. New Hampshire, Jun. 13, 1966
31. Louisiana, Jul. 5, 1966
32. Tennessee, Jan. 12, 1967
33. Wyoming, Jan. 25, 1967
34. Washington, Jan. 26, 1967
35. Iowa, Jan. 26, 1967
36. Oregon, Feb. 2, 1967
37. Minnesota, Feb. 10, 1967
38. Nevada, Feb. 10, 1967
39. Connecticut, Feb. 14, 1967
40. Montana, Feb. 15, 1967
41. South Dakota, Mar. 6, 1967
42. Ohio, Mar. 7, 1967
43. Alabama, Mar. 14, 1967
44. North Carolina, Mar. 22, 1967
45. Illinois, Mar. 22, 1967
46. Texas, Apr. 25, 1967
47. Florida, May 25, 1967

NO ACTION
1. Georgia
2. North Dakota

3. South Carolina

Twenty-Sixth Amendment

PASSAGE

Senate: Mar. 10, 1971 (94 yea) [117 Cong. Rec. 5830 (1971)]
House: Mar. 23, 1971 (401 yea, 19 nay) [117 Cong. Rec. 7569-70 (1971)]

RATIFIED

1. Minnesota, Mar. 23, 1971
2. Delaware, Mar. 23, 1971
3. Connecticut, Mar. 23, 1971
4. Tennessee, Mar. 23, 1971
5. Washington, Mar. 23, 1971
6. Hawaii, Mar. 24, 1971
7. Massachusetts, Mar. 24, 1971
8. Montana, Mar. 29, 1971
9. Arkansas, Mar. 30, 1971
10. Idaho, Mar. 30, 1971
11. Iowa, Mar. 30, 1971
12. Nebraska, Apr. 2, 1971
13. New Jersey, Apr. 3, 1971
14. Kansas, Apr. 7, 1971
15. Michigan, Apr. 7, 1971
16. Alaska, Apr. 8, 1971
17. Maryland, Apr. 8, 1971
18. Indiana, Apr. 8, 1971
19. Maine, Apr. 9, 1971
20. Vermont, Apr. 16, 1971
21. Louisiana, Apr. 17, 1971
22. California, Apr. 19, 1971

23. Colorado, Apr. 27, 1971
24. Pennsylvania, Apr. 27, 1971
25. Texas, Apr. 27, 1971
26. South Carolina, Apr. 28, 1971
27. West Virginia, Apr. 28, 1971
28. New Hampshire, May 13, 1971
29. Arizona, May 14, 1971
30. Rhode Island, May 27, 1971
31. New York, Jun. 2, 1971
32. Oregon, Jun. 4, 1971
33. Missouri, Jun. 14, 1971
34. Wisconsin, Jun. 22, 1971
35. Illinois, Jun. 29, 1971
36. Alabama, Jun. 30, 1971
37. Ohio, Jun. 30, 1971
38. **North Carolina, Jul. 1, 1971**
39. Oklahoma, Jul. 1, 1971
40. Virginia, Jul. 8, 1971
41. Wyoming, Jul. 8, 1971
42. Georgia, Oct. 4, 1971
43. South Dakota, Mar. 4, 2014

NO ACTION

1. Florida
2. Kentucky
3. Mississippi
4. Nevada

5. New Mexico
6. North Dakota
7. Utah

Twenty-Seventh Amendment

PASSAGE

House: Sep. 24, 1789 (37 yea, 14 nay) [1 Annals of Cong. 948 (Joseph Gales, ed., 1834)]
Senate: Sep. 25, 1789 (unrecorded vote) [Senate Journal, 1st. Cong, 1st. Sess. 1789, 77]

RATIFIED

1. Maryland, Dec. 19, 1789
2. North Carolina, Dec. 22, 1789 and Jul. 4, 1989
3. South Carolina, Jan. 19, 1790
4. Delaware, Jan. 28, 1790
5. Vermont, Nov. 3, 1791
6. Virginia, Dec. 15, 1791
7. Kentucky, Jun. 27, 1792 and Mar. 21, 1996
8. Ohio, May 6, 1873
9. Wyoming, Mar. 6, 1978
10. Maine, Apr. 27, 1983
11. Colorado, Apr. 22, 1984
12. South Dakota, Feb. 21, 1985
13. New Hampshire, Mar. 7, 1985 (previously rejected Jan. 26, 1790)
14. Arizona, Apr. 3, 1985
15. Tennessee, May 28, 1985
16. Oklahoma, Jul. 1, 1985
17. New Mexico, Feb. 14, 1986
18. Indiana, Feb. 24, 1986
19. Utah, Feb. 25, 1986
20. Arkansas, Mar. 13, 1987
21. Montana, Mar. 17, 1987
22. Connecticut, May 13, 1987
23. Wisconsin, Jul. 15, 1987
24. Georgia, Feb. 2, 1988
25. West Virginia, Mar. 10, 1988
26. Louisiana, Jul. 7, 1988
27. Iowa, Feb. 9, 1989
28. Idaho, Mar. 23, 1989
29. Nevada, Apr. 26, 1989
30. Alaska, May 6, 1989
31. Oregon, May 19, 1989
32. Minnesota, May 22, 1989
33. Texas, May 25, 1989
34. Kansas, Apr. 5, 1990
35. Florida, May 31, 1990
36. North Dakota, Mar. 25, 1991
37. Missouri, May 5, 1992
38. **Alabama, May 5, 1992**
39. Michigan, May 7, 1992
40. New Jersey, May 7, 1992 (previously rejected Nov. 20, 1789)
41. Illinois, May 12, 1992
42. California, Jun. 26, 1992
43. Rhode Island, Jun. 10, 1993 (previously rejected Jun. 7, 1790)
44. Hawaii, Apr. 29, 1994
45. Washington, Apr. 6, 1995
46. Nebraska, Apr. 1, 2016

NO ACTION

1. Massachusetts
2. Mississippi
3. New York
4. Pennsylvania

Appendix C

Passage and Ratifications of the Unratified Amendments to the Constitution

Representation Amendment

PASSED

House: Sep. 24, 1789 (37 yea, 14 nay) [1 Annals of Cong. 948 (Joseph Gales, ed., 1834)]
Senate: Sep. 25, 1789 (unrecorded vote) [Senate Journal, 1st. Cong, 1st. Sess. 1789, 77]

RATIFIED

1. New Jersey, Nov. 20, 1789
2. Maryland, Dec. 19, 1789
3. North Carolina, Dec. 22, 1789
4. South Carolina, Jan. 19, 1790
5. New Hampshire, Jan. 25, 1790
6. New York, Feb. 10, 1790
7. Rhode Island, Jun. 7, 1790
8. Pennsylvania, Sep. 21, 1791
   (previously rejected Mar. 10, 1790)
9. Vermont, Nov. 3, 1791
10. Virginia, Dec. 15, 1791
11. Kentucky, Jun. 27, 1792

NO ACTION

1. Delaware
2. Georgia
3. Massachusetts
4. Connecticut

Titles of Nobility Amendment

PASSED

Senate: Apr. 27, 1810 (19 yea, 5 nay) [21 Annals of Cong. 672 (1810)]
House: May 1, 1810 (87 yea, 3 nay) [21 Annals of Cong. 2050-2051 (1810)]

RATIFIED

1. Maryland, Dec. 25, 1810
2. Kentucky, Jan. 31, 1811
3. Ohio, Jan. 31, 1811
4. Delaware, Feb. 2, 1811

5. Pennsylvania, Feb. 6, 1811
6. New Jersey, Feb. 13, 1811
7. Vermont, Oct. 24, 1811
8. Tennessee, Nov. 21, 1811

9. North Carolina, Dec. 23, 1811
10. Georgia, Dec. 31, 1811
11. Massachusetts, Feb. 27, 1812
12. New Hampshire, Dec. 9, 1812

REJECTED
1. Virginia, Feb. 14, 1811
2. New York, Mar. 12, 1812
3. Connecticut, May 13, 1813

4. Rhode Island, Sep. 15, 1814
5. South Carolina, Dec. 21, 1814

NO ACTION
1. Louisiana

Corwin Amendment

PASSED
House: Feb. 28, 1861 (133 yea, 65 nay) [Cong. Globe, 36th Cong., 2nd Sess. 1285 (1861)]
Senate: Mar. 4, 1861 (24 yea, 12 nay) [Cong. Globe, 36th Cong., 2nd Sess. 1403 (1861)]

RATIFIED
1. Kentucky, Apr. 4, 1861
2. Ohio, May 13, 1861
   (rescinded Mar. 31, 1864)
3. Rhode Island, May 31, 1861
4. Maryland, Jan. 10, 1862
   (rescinded Apr. 7, 2014)

5. Virginia, Feb. 13, 1862 (by the
   Restored Government of Virginia)
6. Illinois, Jun. 2, 1863 (preceded by
   irregular ratification on Feb. 14,
   1862 by constitutional convention)

NO ACTION
1. Alabama
2. Arkansas
3. California
4. Connecticut
5. Delaware
6. Florida
7. Georgia
8. Indiana
9. Iowa
10. Kansas
11. Louisiana
12. Maine
13. Massachusetts
14. Michigan
15. Minnesota
16. Mississippi
17. Missouri

18. New Hampshire
19. New Jersey
20. New York
21. North Carolina
22. Oregon
23. Pennsylvania
24. South Carolina
25. Tennessee
26. Texas
27. Vermont
28. Wisconsin

Child Labor Amendment

PASSED

House: Apr. 26, 1924 (297 yea, 69 nay) [65 Cong. Rec. 7295 (1924)]
Senate: Jun. 2, 1924 (61 yea, 23, nay) [65 Cong. Rec. 10142)]

RATIFIED

1. Arkansas, Jun. 28, 1924
2. California, Jan. 8, 1925
3. Arizona, Jan. 29, 1925
4. Wisconsin, Feb. 25, 1925
5. Montana, Feb. 11, 1927
6. Colorado, Apr. 28, 1931
7. Oregon, Jan. 31, 1933
8. Washington, Feb. 3, 1933
9. North Dakota, Mar. 4, 1933 (previously rejected Jan. 28, 1925)
10. Ohio, Mar. 22, 1933
11. Michigan, May 10, 1933
12. New Hampshire, May 17, 1933 (previously rejected Mar. 18, 1925)
13. New Jersey, Jun. 12, 1933
14. Illinois, Jun. 30, 1933
15. Oklahoma, Jul. 5, 1933
16. Iowa, Dec. 5, 1933 (previously rejected Mar. 11, 1925)
17. West Virginia, Dec. 12, 1933
18. Minnesota, Dec. 14, 1933 (previously rejected Apr. 14, 1925)
19. Maine, Dec. 16, 1933 (previously rejected Apr. 10, 1925)
20. Pennsylvania, Dec. 21, 1933 (previously rejected Apr. 16, 1925)
21. Wyoming, Jan. 31, 1935
22. Utah, Feb. 5, 1935 (previously rejected Feb. 4, 1925)
23. Idaho, Feb. 7, 1935 (previously rejected Feb. 7, 1925)
24. Indiana, Feb. 8, 1935 (previously rejected Mar. 5, 1925)
25. Kentucky, Jan. 13, 1937 (previously rejected Mar. 24, 1926)
26. Nevada, Jan. 29, 1937
27. New Mexico, Feb. 12, 1937 (previously rejected 1935)
28. Kansas, Feb. 25, 1937 (previously rejected Jan. 30, 1925)

REJECTED

1. Louisiana, Jun. 27, 1924
2. Georgia, Aug. 6, 1924
3. North Carolina, Aug. 23, 1924
4. Missouri, Jan. 13, 1925
5. South Carolina, Jan. 14, 1925
6. Delaware, Jan. 23, 1925
7. Texas, Jan. 27, 1925
8. Connecticut, Feb. 3, 1925
9. Tennessee, Feb. 4, 1925
10. Massachusetts, Feb. 19, 1925
11. South Dakota, Feb. 24, 1925
12. Vermont, Feb. 26, 1925
13. Maryland, Mar. 10, 1927
14. Florida, May 7, 1925
15. Virginia, Jan. 26, 1926

NO ACTION

1. Alabama
2. Mississippi
3. Nebraska
4. New York
5. Rhode Island

Equal Rights Amendment

PASSED
House: Oct. 12, 1971 (354 yea, 24 nay) [117 Cong. Rec. 35815 (1971)]
Senate: Mar. 22, 1972 (84 yea, 8 nay) [118 Cong. Rec. 9598 (1972)]

Ratified

1. Hawaii, Mar. 22, 1972
2. New Hampshire, Mar. 23, 1972
3. Delaware, Mar. 23, 1972
4. Iowa, Mar. 24, 1972
5. Idaho, Mar. 24, 1972
   (rescinded Feb. 8, 1977)
6. Kansas, Mar. 28, 1972
7. Nebraska, Mar. 29, 1972
   (rescinded Mar. 15, 1973)
8. Texas, Mar. 30, 1972
9. Tennessee, Apr. 4, 1972
   (rescinded Apr. 23, 1974)
10. Alaska, Apr. 5, 1972
11. Rhode Island, Apr. 14, 1972
12. New Jersey, Apr. 17, 1972
13. Colorado, Apr. 21, 1972
14. West Virginia, Apr. 22, 1972
15. Wisconsin, Apr. 26, 1972
16. New York, May 18, 1972
17. Michigan, May 22, 1972
18. Maryland, May 26, 1972
19. Massachusetts, Jun. 21, 1972
20. Kentucky, Jun. 27, 1972
    (rescinded Mar. 17, 1978)
21. Pennsylvania, Sep. 26, 1972

22. California, Nov. 13, 1972
23. Wyoming, Jan. 26, 1973
24. South Dakota, Feb. 5, 1973
    (rescinded Mar. 5, 1979)
25. Oregon, Feb. 8, 1973
26. Minnesota, Feb. 8, 1973
27. New Mexico, Feb. 28, 1973
28. Vermont, Mar. 1, 1973
29. Connecticut, Mar. 15, 1973
    (previously rejected Apr. 7, 1972)
30. Washington, Mar. 22, 1973
31. Maine, Jan. 18, 1974
32. Montana, Jan. 25, 1974 (previously
    rejected Feb. 2, 1973)
33. Ohio, Feb. 7, 1974
34. North Dakota, Feb. 3, 1975
35. Indiana, Jan. 18, 1977 (previously
    rejected Mar. 10, 1975)
36. Nevada, Mar. 22, 2017 (previous
    rejected Feb. 11, 1977)
37. Illinois, May 30, 2018 (previously
    rejected Jun. 7, 1978)
38. **Virginia, Jan. 15, 2020 (previously
    rejected Jan. 27, 1977)**

REJECTED
1. Louisiana, Jul. 3, 1972
2. Arkansas, Feb. 1, 1973
3. Oklahoma, Jan. 22, 1975
4. Georgia, Feb. 17, 1975
5. Mississippi, Jan. 28, 1977
6. North Carolina, Mar. 1, 1977

7. Missouri, Mar. 15, 1977
8. Arizona, May 12, 1977
9. Alabama, Jan. 31, 1978
10. South Carolina, Feb. 7, 1978
11. Utah, Jan. 23, 1979
12. Florida, May 25, 1979

*The status of the Equal Rights Amendment is currently pending before Congress and the courts. While several states rejected the ERA on multiple occasions, only the most recent historical rejection is listed per state.

District of Columbia Voting Representation Amendment

PASSED

House: Mar. 2, 1978 (289 yea, 127 nay) [124 Cong. Rec. 5273 (1978)]
Senate: Aug. 22, 1978 (67 yea, 32 nay) [124 Cong. Rec. 27260 (1978)]

RATIFIED

1. New Jersey, Sep. 11, 1978
2. Michigan, Dec. 13, 1978
3. Ohio, Dec. 21, 1978
4. Minnesota, Mar. 19, 1979
5. Massachusetts, Mar. 19, 1979
6. Connecticut, Apr. 11, 1979
7. Wisconsin, Nov. 1, 1979
8. Maryland, Mar. 19, 1980
   (previously rejected Feb. 27, 1979)
9. Hawaii, Apr. 17, 1980
10. Oregon, Jul. 6, 1981
11. Maine, Feb. 16, 1983 (previously rejected Apr. 28, 1981)
12. West Virginia, Feb. 23, 1983 (previously rejected Apr. 11, 1979)
13. Rhode Island, May 13, 1983
14. Iowa, Jan. 19, 1984
15. Louisiana, Jun. 24, 1984 (previously rejected Jul. 1980)
16. Delaware, Jun. 28, 1984 (previously rejected Aug. 31, 1978)

REJECTED

1. Pennsylvania, Nov. 14, 1978
2. North Dakota, Jan. 17, 1979
3. Wyoming, Jan. 19, 1979
4. South Carolina, Jan. 31, 1979
5. Idaho, Feb. 26, 1979
6. Missouri, Feb. 28, 1979
7. Arizona, Mar. 1, 1979
8. New Mexico, Mar. 14, 1979
9. Washington, Apr. 2, 1979
10. New Hampshire, Apr. 27, 1979
11. South Dakota, Feb. 5, 1980
12. Nebraska, Feb. 11, 1980
13. California, Nov. 30, 1980

NO ACTION

1. Alabama
2. Alaska
3. Arkansas
4. Colorado
5. Florida
6. Georgia
7. Illinois
8. Indiana
9. Kansas
10. Kentucky
11. Mississippi
12. Montana
13. Nevada
14. New York
15. North Carolina
16. Oklahoma
17. Tennessee
18. Texas
19. Utah
20. Vermont
21. Virginia

Notes

Introduction

1. Lexi Krock, "Case Closed," Saving the National Treasures, NOVA Science Programming on Air and Online, February 2005, www.pbs.org/wgbh/nova/charters/case.html; Mary Lynn Ritzenthaler and Catherine Nicholson, "A New Era Begins for the Charters of Freedom," *Prologue Magazine* 35, no. 3 (Fall 2003), www.archives.gov/publications/prologue/2003/fall/charters -new-era.html.

2. Rhode Island was the only state not represented at the convention. "Meet the Framers of the Constitution," National Archives, March 16, 2020, www.archives.gov/founding-docs /founding-fathers.

3. William Pierce, Character Sketches of Delegates to the Federal Convention, in Max Farrand, ed., *The Records of the Federal Convention of 1787*, vol. 3 (New Haven, CT: Yale University Press, 1911), 90, 97 (hereafter Farrand, *Records*).

4. February 21, 1787, *Journals of the Continental Congress, 1774–1789*, ed. Worthingon C. Ford et al. (Washington, DC, 1904–37), 32: 73–74.

5. James Madison, *Federalist* no. 51, Avalon Project, avalon.law.yale.edu/18th_century/fed51 .asp; Matthew E. Glassman, *Separation of Powers: An Overview* (Washington, DC: Congressional Research Service R44334, 2016).

6. Madison, *Federalist* 51.

7. Thomas Jefferson to John Adams, Paris, August 30, 1787, Founders Online, National Archives, founders.archives.gov/documents/Jefferson/01-12-02-0075. Original source: *The Papers of Thomas Jefferson*, vol. 12, *7 August 1787–31 March 1788*, ed. Julian P. Boyd (Princeton, NJ: Princeton University Press, 1955), 66–69.

8. Robert A. Dahl, *How Democratic Is the American Constitution?* (New Haven, CT: Yale University Press, 2002).

9. Farrand, *Records*, vol. 1, 202–3.

10. "Amending America: Proposed Amendments to the United States Constitution, 1787 to 2014," National Archives, www.archives.gov/open/dataset-amendments.html. In tracking every amendment introduced in Congress from 2014–2021, the authors have determined that the total number has surpassed twelve thousand.

11. "Not a Democracy," *Washington Post*, March 11, 1888.

12. Franklin D. Roosevelt, Letter on the Court Reform Recommendation, July 5, 1937, American Presidency Project, www.presidency.ucsb.edu/node/208605.

13. Richard Albert, "America's Unamendable Constitution," *Cato Unbound: A Journal of Debate*, December 11, 2015, www.cato-unbound.org/2015/12/11/richard-albert/americas -unamendable-constitution.

14. Sanford Levinson, *Our Undemocratic Constitution: Where the Constitution Goes Wrong (and How We the People Can Correct It)* (New York: Oxford University Press, 2006), 21.

15. James Madison, *Federalist* 43, Avalon Project, avalon.law.yale.edu/18th_century/fed43 .asp.

16. Eric Posner, "The U.S. Constitution Is Impossible to Amend," *Slate*, May 5, 2014, slate. com/news-and-politics/2014/05/amending-the-constitution-is-much-too-hard-blame-the -founders.html.

17. See, e.g., Sanford Levinson, "The Constitution Needs a Reboot," *Politico*, September 9, 2018, www.politico.com/magazine/story/2018/09/05/new-constitution-change-amendment-law -219586; Dan Roberts, "Amending the US Constitution: The Political Rarity That's Suddenly in Vogue," *The Guardian*, May 6, 2015, www.theguardian.com/us-news/2015/may/06/amending -consitution-politics-trend; Albert, "America's Unamendable Constitution"; Posner, "The U.S. Constitution Is Impossible to Amend."

18. Vicki C. Jackson, "The (Myth of un)Amendability of the US Constitution and the Democratic Component of Constitutionalism," *International Journal of Constitutional Law* 13, no. 3 (July 2015): 576–77, 602.

19. Jeff Broadwater, *George Mason: Forgotten Founder* (Chapel Hill: University of North Carolina Press, 2006); Stephan A. Schwartz, "George Mason: Forgotten Founder, He Conceived the Bill of Rights," *Smithsonian Magazine*, April 30, 2000.

20. Gerard N. Magliocca, "The Father of the 14th Amendment," *New York Times*, September 17, 2013.

21. "Miss Susan B. Anthony Died This Morning," *New York Times*, March 13, 1906.

22. Jesse Wegman, "The Man Who Changed the Constitution, Twice," *New York Times*, March 14, 2019.

23. Sanford Levinson, "The Political Implications of Amending Clauses," *Constitutional Commentary* 13, no. 1 (Spring 1996): 117. "Amendatory change is often masked as 'constitutional interpretation,' at immense costs in intellectual cogency or candor. This also gives to judges both responsibility and power that one might well think they are unsuited for, yet another political implication of such a rigorous amending clause. Even worse, perhaps, is that highly desirable change is stifled because one cannot in fact figure out an alternative to use of the formal procedures."

Chapter 1: An Imperfect Constitution

1. Catherine Drinker Bowen, *Miracle at Philadelphia: The Story of the Constitutional Convention May to September 1787* (New York: Little, Brown, 1966).

2. "Dissent of the Minority of the Convention," December 18, 1787, in *The Documentary History of the Ratification of the Constitution*, digital edition, ed. John P. Kaminski, Gaspare J. Saladino, Richard Leffler, Charles H. Schoenleber, and Margaret A. Hogan (Charlottesville: University of Virginia Press, 2009) (hereafter *DHRC* digital edition).

3. Debates of the Virginia Ratifying Convention, June 4, 1788, *DHRC* digital edition.

4. Articles of Confederation, Art. III (U.S. 1781). See also Akhil Amar, *America's Constitution: A Biography* (New York: Random House, 2005), 25; Richard Beeman, *Plain, Honest Men: The Making of the American Constitution* (New York: Random House, 2009), 8–9.

5. Articles of Confederation, Art. V (U.S. 1781).

6. Articles of Confederation, Art. XIII.

7. Declaration of Independence (U.S. 1776).

8. Thomas Jefferson, *Autobiography of Thomas Jefferson* (New York: G. P. Putnam's Sons, 1914), 52–53.

9. Jefferson, *Autobiography*, 52, 51.

10. Max Farrand, *The Records of the Federal Convention of 1787*, vol. 1, ed. Max Farrand (New Haven, CT: Yale University Press, 1911), 467 (hereafter Farrand, *Records*).

11. Three small states—Delaware, New Jersey, and Maryland—were not satisfied with their big victory on the question of representation. They refused to consent to the Articles in a dispute over other states' claims to Western territories. See 1780 Md. Laws xvi–xx.

12. Articles of Confederation, Art. II (U.S. 1781).

13. Articles of Confederation, Art. VIII.

14. Articles of Confederation, Art. II.

15. Articles of Confederation, Art. XIII.

16. Jack N. Rakove, *Original Meanings: Politics and Ideas in the Making of the Constitution* (New York: Vintage Books, 1997), 28.

17. *Journals of the Continental Congress, 1774–1789*, ed. Worthingon C. Ford et al. (Washington, DC, 1904–37), 19:105, February 1, 1781. See also Beeman, *Plain, Honest Men*, 11–12.

18. Edmund Pendleton to James Madison, Virginia, December 9, 1782, Founders Online, National Archives, founders.archives.gov/documents/Madison/01-05-02-0161. Original source: *The Papers of James Madison*, vol. 5, *1 August 1782–31 December 1782*, ed. William T. Hutchinson and William M. E. Rachal (Chicago: University of Chicago Press, 1967), 382–86.

19. Beeman, *Plain, Honest Men*, 15–16; Klarman, *Framers' Coup*, 30–31.

20. Ron Chernow, *Alexander Hamilton* (New York: Penguin Press, 2004), 175.

21. Edward Coles to Hugh Blair Grigsby, December 23, 1854, Grigsby Papers, Virginia Historical Society, cited in Richard Labunski, *James Madison and the Struggle for the Bill of Rights* (New York: Oxford University Press, 2006), 89.

22. Richard Brookhiser, *James Madison* (New York: Basic Books, 2011), 18; Jeff Broadwater, *James Madison: A Son of Virginia and a Founder of the Nation* (Chapel Hill: University of North Carolina Press, 2012), 8.

23. James Madison to George Washington, Richmond, December 9, 1785, Founders Online, National Archives, founders.archives.gov/documents/Washington/04-03-02-0375. Original source: *The Papers of George Washington*, Confederation Series, vol. 3, *19 May 1785–31 March 1786*, ed. W. W. Abbot (Charlottesville: University Press of Virginia, 1994), 439–42.

24. George Washington to Benjamin Harrison, Mount Vernon, January 18, 1784, Founders Online, National Archives, founders.archives.gov/documents/Washington/04-01-02-0039. Original source: *The Papers of George Washington*, Confederation Series, vol. 1, *1 January 1784–17 July 1784*, ed. W. W. Abbot (Charlottesville: University Press of Virginia, 1992), 56–57.

25. Jonathan Elliot, *The Debates in the Several State Conventions on the Adoption of the Federal Constitution as Recommended by the General Convention at Philadelphia in 1787*, vol. 1, ed. Jonathan Elliot (Washington, 1836), 115 (hereafter Elliot, *Debates*).

26. Alexander Hamilton et al. "Address of the Annapolis Convention," September 14, 1786, Founders Online, National Archives, founders.archives.gov/documents/Hamilton/01-03-02-0556. Original source: *The Papers of Alexander Hamilton*, vol. 3, *1782–1786*, ed. Harold C. Syrett (New York: Columbia University Press, 1962), 686–90. The five states that sent delegates to Annapolis were Delaware, New Jersey, New York, Pennsylvania, and Virginia.

27. Beeman, *Plain, Honest Men*, 18–19; Klarman, *Framers' Coup*, 108–9.

28. Hamilton et al., "Address of the Annapolis Convention."

29. Klarman, *Framers' Coup*, 111–25.

30. Thomas Jefferson to James Madison, Paris, September 1, 1785, Founders Online, National Archives, founders.archives.gov/documents/Jefferson/01-08-02-0360. Original source: *The Papers of Thomas Jefferson*, vol. 8, *25 February–31 October 1785*, ed. Julian P. Boyd (Princeton, NJ: Princeton University Press, 1953), 460–64.

31. Beeman, *Plain, Honest Men*, 59.

32. James Madison to Edmund Randolph, New York, April 2, 1787, Founders Online, National Archives, founders.archives.gov/documents/Madison/01-09-02-0190. Original source: *The Papers of James Madison*, vol. 9, *9 April 1786–24 May 1787 and Supplement 1781–1784*, ed. Robert A. Rutland and William M. E. Rachal (Chicago: University of Chicago Press, 1975), 361–62.

33. James Madison to James Monroe, Philadelphia, June 10, 1787, Founders Online, National Archives, founders.archives.gov/documents/Madison/01-10-02-0026. Original source: *The Papers of James Madison*, vol. 10, *27 May 1787–3 March 1788*, ed. Robert A. Rutland, Charles F. Hobson, William M. E. Rachal, and Frederika J. Teute (Chicago: University of Chicago Press, 1977), 43.

34. Henry Knox to George Washington, New York, January 14, 1787, Founders Online, National Archives, founders.archives.gov/documents/Washington/04-04-02-0444. Original source: *The Papers of George Washington*, Confederation Series, vol. 4, *2 April 1786–31 January 1787*, ed. W. W. Abbot (Charlottesville: University Press of Virginia, 1995), 518–23. See also Klarman, *Framers' Coup*, 114.

35. Articles of Confederation, Art. XIII (U.S. 1781).

36. February 21, 1787, *Journals of the Continental Congress, 1774–1789*, 32:73–74. See also Beeman, *Plain, Honest Men*, 20–21; Klarman, *Framers' Coup*, 119.

37. James Madison to George Washington, New York, February 21, 1787, Founders Online, National Archives, founders.archives.gov/documents/Madison/01-09-02-0146. Original source: *The Papers of James Madison*, vol. 9, 285–86.

38. George Washington to James Madison, Mount Vernon, March 31, 1787, Founders Online, National Archives, founders.archives.gov/GEWN-04-05-02-0111. Original source: *The Papers of George Washington*, Confederation Series, vol. 5, *1 February 1787–31 December 1787*, ed. W. W. Abbot (Charlottesville: University Press of Virginia, 1997), 114–17.

39. Broadwater, *James Madison*, 44.

40. The average age of delegates at the Convention was forty-three. Jeff Broadwater, *George Mason: Forgotten Founder* (Chapel Hill: University of North Carolina Press, 2006), 137, 162.

41. Broadwater, *George Mason*, 91.

42. Broadwater, *George Mason*, 9, 57, 81, 156.

43. George Mason to George Mason Jr., Philadelphia, May 20, 1787, Farrand, *Records*, vol. 3, 22–24.

44. Farrand, *Records*, vol. 1, 20–22.

45. Beeman, *Plain, Honest Men*, 87–88; Klarman, *Framers' Coup*, 137.

46. Beeman, *Plain, Honest Men*, 86–90.

47. Farrand, *Records*, vol. 1, 20–22.

48. The Virginia Plan provided an alternative means of determining the right of suffrage, "proportioned to the Quotas of contribution" (i.e., the share of taxes paid by each state). Farrand, *Records*, vol. 1, 20.

49. Farrand, *Records*, vol. 1, 34.

50. U.S. Census Bureau, Census 1790, "Return of the Whole Number of Persons within the Several Districts of the United States," www.census.gov/library/publications/1793/dec/number-of-persons.html. Note that current census data lists Virginia's 1790 population as 691,737. The discrepancy is the result of extracting the 55,873 people who lived in the counties that today comprise West Virginia from Virginia's total population. West Virginia did not become a separate state until 1863.

51. See *Baker v. Carr*, 369 U.S. 186 (1962) and *Reynolds v. Sims*, 377 U.S. 533 (1964).

52. Farrand, *Records*, vol. 1, 182–83.

53. Farrand, *Records*, vol. 1, 4, 37.

54. Farrand, *Records*, vol. 1, 527–28.

55. David O. Stewart, *The Summer of 1787* (New York: Simon & Schuster, 2007), 65.

56. Farrand, *Records*, vol. 1, 242–45.

57. Farrand, *Records*, vol. 1, 20. The Framers envisioned that the federal government would raise revenue in two ways: through the imposition of tariffs and through the levying of "direct taxes" on the states. "Direct taxes and Representatives are to be apportioned according to population." *Congressional Globe*, 42nd Congress, 2nd Sess. 1790 (1872).

58. Beeman, *Plain, Honest Men*, 152–55.

59. Farrand, *Records*, vol. 1, 196.

60. Farrand, *Records*, vol. 1, 193. The three-fifths formulation was not invented at the Philadelphia Convention. In 1783, the Continental Congress considered using the formula to calculate the states' direct tax quotas, which had been based on population. Paul Finkelman, *Slavery and the Founders: Race and Liberty in the Age of Jefferson* (New York: Routledge, 2014), 11–12; Stewart, *Summer of 1787*, 79.

61. Constitution of Massachusetts, Art. I (1780).

62. Beeman, *Plain, Honest Men*, 102, 112.

63. Farrand, *Records*, vol. 1, 201.

64. Farrand, *Records*, vol. 1, 201.

65. Amar, *America's Constitution*, 97.

66. Farrand, *Records*, vol. 1, 196.

67. Farrand, *Records*, vol. 2, 13.

68. Farrand, *Records*, vol. 3, 333. See also Stewart, *Summer of 1787*, 125.

69. Sanford Levinson, *Our Undemocratic Constitution: Where the Constitution Goes Wrong (And How We the People Can Correct It)* (New York: Oxford University Press, 2006), 50–51.

70. Philip Bump, "In about 20 years, half the population will live in eight states," *Washington Post*, July 12, 2018; Shonei Sen, "National Population Projections: 2020, 2030, 2040," Stat Chat, Weldon Cooper Center for Public Service, University of Virginia, February 11, 2019, statchatva .org/2019/02/11/national-population-projections-2020-2030-2040.

71. Levinson, *Our Undemocratic Constitution*, 60.

72. Farrand, *Records*, vol. 1, 296–97.

73. Beeman, *Plain, Honest Men*, 169.

74. Farrand, *Records*, vol. 1, 322–23 (statement of James Wilson).

75. Stewart, *Summer of 1787*, 89.

76. James Madison to George Washington, New York, April 16, 1787, Founders Online, National Archives, founders.archives.gov/documents/Madison/01-09-02-0208. Original source: *The Papers of James Madison*, vol. 9, 382–87.

77. Klarman, *Framers' Coup*, 253–54.

78. Farrand, *Records*, vol. 2, 390.

79. Beeman, *Plain, Honest Men*, 146, 228–29.

80. Farrand, *Records*, vol. 2, 26.

81. Stewart, *Summer of 1787*, 171.

82. U.S. Constitution, Art. I, Sec. 8.

83. Amar, *America's Constitution*, 57.

84. Beeman, *Plain, Honest Men*, 288–90.

85. George William Van Cleve, *We Have Not a Government: The Articles of Confederation and the Road to the Constitution* (Chicago: University of Chicago Press, 2017), 189–213.

86. Klarman, *Framers' Coup*, 77–80; George Van Cleve, "The Anti-Federalists' Toughest Challenge: Paper Money, Debt Relief, and the Ratification of the Constitution," *Journal of the Early Republic* 34 (Winter 2014): 543–44.

87. Beeman, *Plain, Honest Men*, 67.

88. Klarman, *Framers' Coup*, 86.

89. Farrand, *Records*, vol. 1, 48–50.

90. Farrand, *Records*, vol. 1, 48, 50.

91. Beeman, *Plain, Honest Men*, 89–90.

92. U.S. Constitution, Art. 1, Sec. 2, cl. 1.

93. Farrand, *Records*, vol. 1, 49–50.

94. Alexander Keyssar, *The Right to Vote: The Contested History of Democracy in the United States* (New York: Basic Books, 2000), table A1. In the original thirteen colonies, free Black people were barred from voting only in Virginia, South Carolina, and Georgia. However, between 1792 and 1835, Black suffrage was made illegal in every state except Massachusetts, New Hampshire, Vermont, and Maine. See Eric Ledell Smith, "The End of Black Voting Rights in Pennsylvania: African Americans and the Pennsylvania Constitutional Convention of 1837–1838," *Pennsylvania History: A Journal of Mid-Atlantic Studies* 65, no. 3 (Summer 1998): 279–99; Brainerd Dyer, "One Hundred Years of Negro Suffrage," *Pacific Historical Review* 37, no. 1 (February 1968): 1–20; Paul Finkelman, "Who Counted, Who Voted, and Who Could They Vote For," *Saint Louis University Law Journal* 58, no. 4 (2014): 1088. In New Jersey, some women with property were enfranchised between 1776 and 1807. See Jan Ellen Lewis, "Rethinking Women's Suffrage in New Jersey, 1776–1807," *Rutgers Law Review* 63, no. 3 (Spring 2011): 1017–35.

95. Michael Waldman, *The Fight to Vote* (New York: Simon & Schuster, 2017), 12–15.

96. Amar, *America's Constitution*, 64–65.

97. Farrand, *Records*, vol. 2, 202.

98. Farrand, *Records*, vol. 2, 202.

99. Farrand, *Records*, vol. 2, 201.

100. Farrand, *Records*, vol. 2, 201; Amar, *America's Constitution*, 67.

101. The convention rejected a motion by Gouverneur Morris to add a provision that would "restrain the right of suffrage to freeholders" by a vote of seven state delegations to one. One state abstained and one was not present. Farrand, *Records*, vol. 2, 206.

102. U.S. Constitution, Art. I, Sec. 2 ("the Electors in each State shall have the Qualifications requisite for Electors of the most numerous Branch of the State Legislature," typically the lower house).

103. Keyssar, *Right to Vote*, 24.

104. Farrand, *Records*, vol. 1, 50.

105. Farrand, *Records*, vol. 1, 156.

106. Alexander Keyssar, *Why Do We Still Have the Electoral College?* (Cambridge, MA: Harvard University Press, 2020), 17–27.

107. Farrand, *Records*, vol. 1, 21.

108. Klarman, *Framers' Coup*, 226.

109. Farrand, *Records*, vol. 2, 56.

110. Farrand, *Records*, vol. 1, 80.

111. Farrand, *Records*, vol. 2, 56.

112. Farrand, *Records*, vol. 2, 57.

113. Farrand, *Records*, vol. 2, 32, 402.

114. Thomas H. Neale, *The Electoral College: How It Works in Contemporary Presidential Elections* (Washington, DC: Congressional Research Service, RL32611, 2017), 3–4: See also Amar, *America's Constitution*, 21 ("Article II likewise handed slave states extra seats in the electoral college, giving the South a sizeable head start in presidential elections."); Wilfred U. Codrington III, "The Electoral College's Racist Origins," *The Atlantic*, November 19, 2019, www.theatlantic.com/ideas/archive/2019/11/electoral-college-racist-origins/601918.

115. Beeman, *Plain, Honest Men*, 67.

116. Gary B. Nash, "Franklin and Slavery," *Proceedings of the American Philosophical Society* 150, no. 4 (December 2006): 618–35; Gary B. Nash, "Slavery's Foe, at Last," *Time*, July 7, 2003; "Benjamin Franklin Anti-Slavery Petitions Congress," Center for Legislative Archives, National Archives, December 17, 2018, www.archives.gov/legislative/features/franklin.

117. Ralph Ketcham, *James Madison: A Biography* (Newtown, CT: American Political Biography Press, 1971), 428; Callie Hopkins, "The Enslaved Household of President James

Madison," White House Historical Association, www.whitehousehistory.org/slavery-in-the -james-madison-white-house.

118. Farrand, *Records*, vol. 1, 486.

119. Farrand, *Records*, vol. 2, 95.

120. Farrand, *Records*, vol. 2, 373.

121. Farrand, *Records*, vol. 2, 221.

122. Luther Martin, Genuine Information VII, *Baltimore Maryland Gazette*, January 18, 1788, *DHRC* digital edition.

123. Farrand, *Records*, vol. 2, 417.

124. U.S. Constitution, Art. 1, Sec. 2, cl. 3.

125. U.S. Census Bureau, Census 1790, "Return of the Whole Number of Persons Within the Several Districts of the United States," www.census.gov/library/publications/1793/dec/number -of-persons.html.

126. U.S. Constitution, Art. 1, Sec. 9.

127. Farrand, *Records*, vol. 2, 370–71.

128. Farrand, *Records*, vol. 2, 415.

129. Farrand, *Records*, vol. 2, 371.

130. See Steven Deyle, "An 'Abominable' New Trade: The Closing of the African Slave Trade and the Changing Patterns of U.S. Political Power, 1808–1860," *William and Mary Quarterly* 66, no. 4 (October 2009): 833–50; Jack Trammell, *The Richmond Slave Trade: The Economic Backbone of the Old Dominion* (Charleston, SC: History Press, 2012).

131. See Deyle, "An 'Abominable' New Trade"; Karl Rhodes, "Economic History: Mother of the Domestic Slave Trade," *Econ Focus (Federal Reserve Bank of Richmond)* 17, no. 2 (Second Quarter 2013): 37–40; "Slavery," *The Story of Virginia*, Virginia Museum of History and Culture, www.virginiahistory.org/what-you-can-see/story-virginia/explore-story-virginia/1825-1861 /slavery.

132. U.S. Constitution, Art. IV, Sec. 2, cl. 3.

133. Charles Cotesworth Pinckney, Speech in the South Carolina House of Representatives, January 17, 1788, University of Wisconsin–Madison, Center for the Study of the American Constitution, archive.csac.history.wisc.edu/sc_cotesworth_pinckney.pdf.

134. Farrand, *Records*, vol. 2, 371.

135. U.S. Constitution, Art. I, Sec. 4, cl. 2. This provision was modified by the Twentieth Amendment, which provides that Congress shall convene on January 3.

136. U.S. Constitution, Art. I, Sec. 8.

137. Farrand, *Records*, vol. 2, 587–88. See also Alan P. Grimes, *Democracy and the Amendments to the Constitution* (Lanham, MD: Lexington Books, 1978), 6.

138. Farrand, *Records*, vol. 2, 587–88. See also Grimes, *Democracy and the Amendments to the Constitution*, 6–7.

139. George Mason to Thomas Jefferson, Gunston Hall, Virginia, May 26, 1788, Founders Online, National Archives, founders.archives.gov/documents/Jefferson/01-13-02-0117. Original source: *The Papers of Thomas Jefferson*, vol. 13, *March–7 October 1788*, ed. Julian P. Boyd (Princeton, NJ: Princeton University Press, 1956), 204–7.

140. Farrand, *Records*, vol. 2, 479; Broadwater, *George Mason*, 198.

141. Paul Finkelman, "James Madison and the Bill of Rights: A Reluctant Paternity," *Supreme Court Review* 9, no. 301 (1990): 308.

142. Jack N. Rakove, *Original Meanings: Politics and Ideas in the Making of the Constitution* (New York: Vintage Books, 1997), 288.

143. Farrand, *Records*, vol. 1, 122.

144. Farrand, *Records*, vol. 1, 22.

145. Farrand, *Records*, vol. 1, 22.

146. Farrand, *Records*, vol. 1, 202–3.

147. Farrand, *Records*, vol. 1, 202. See Richard Labunski, *James Madison and the Struggle for the Bill of Rights* (New York: Oxford University Press, 2006), 127.

148. Farrand, *Records*, vol. 1, 203.

149. Farrand, *Records*, vol. 2, 188.

150. By way of comparison, Article XXI of the Committee of Detail's August 6 draft provided that "The ratification of the Conventions of States shall be sufficient for organizing this Constitution."

151. Farrand, *Records*, vol. 2, 467–68.

152. Farrand, *Records*, vol. 2, 557–58.

153. Farrand, *Records*, vol. 2, 558.

154. Farrand, *Records*, vol. 2, 558.

155. Farrand, *Records*, vol. 2, 559, 578. James Wilson moved to lower the ratification threshold to two-thirds of the states. It was narrowly rejected by a vote of six states to five.

156. Farrand, *Records*, vol. 2, 559.

157. Farrand, *Records*, vol. 2, 559, 578.

158. Farrand, *Records*, vol. 2, 559.

159. Kevin R. C. Gutzman, *James Madison and the Making of America* (New York: St. Martin's Press, 2012), 125.

160. Another provision, as we will see, places a different sort of limit on the people's ability to amend the Constitution to undo the equal representation of states in the Senate.

161. Ketcham, *James Madison*, 225.

162. Farrand, *Records*, vol. 2, 629.

163. Farrand, *Records*, vol. 2, 631.

164. Farrand, *Records*, vol. 2, 629 and n8. In the margin of his copy of the draft Constitution, Mason further laid out his objections: "By this article only Congress have [sic] the power of proposing amendments at any future time to this constitution and should it prove ever so oppressive, the whole people of America can't make, or even propose alterations to it; a doctrine utterly subversive of the fundamental principles of the rights and liberties of the people."

165. Farrand, *Records*, vol. 2, 629.

166. Farrand, *Records*, vol. 2, 558.

167. Farrand, *Records*, vol. 2, 629–30.

168. Farrand, *Records*, vol. 2, 630.

169. Farrand, *Records*, vol. 1, 533. See also Broadwater, *George Mason*, 174; Klarman, *Framers' Coup*, 199.

170. Farrand, *Records*, vol. 2, 632.

171. Ketcham, *James Madison*, 225.

172. Farrand, *Records*, vol. 2, 633.

173. U.S. Constitution, Preamble.

174. Joseph J. Ellis, *The Quartet: Orchestrating the Second American Revolution, 1783–1789* (New York: Knopf, 2015), 151.

175. Amar, *America's Constitution*, 29.

176. Farrand, *Records*, vol. 1, 123.

177. Rakove, *Original Meanings*, 101–04.

178. Farrand, *Records*, vol. 2, 641–42.

179. James Madison to William Cogswell, Montpelier, March 10, 1834, Founders Online, National Archives, founders.archives.gov/documents/Madison/99-02-02-2952. This is an Early Access Document from *The Papers of James Madison*. It is not an authoritative final version.

180. James Madison to Thomas Jefferson, Philadelphia, September 6, 1787, Founders Online, National Archives, founders.archives.gov/documents/Madison/01-10-02-0115. Original source: *The Papers of James Madison*, vol. 10, *27 May 1787–3 March 1788*, ed. Robert A. Rutland,

Charles F. Hobson, William M. E. Rachal, and Frederika J. Teute (Chicago: University of Chicago Press, 1977), 163–65.

181. Pauline Maier, *Ratification: The People Debate the Constitution, 1787–1788* (New York: Simon & Schuster, 2011), ix; Klarman, *Framers' Coup*, 399.

182. James Madison to Thomas Jefferson, New York, December 9, 1787, Founders Online, National Archives, founders.archives.gov/documents/Jefferson/01-12-02-0418. Original source: *The Papers of Thomas Jefferson*, vol. 12, *7 August 1787–31 March 1788*, ed. Julian P. Boyd (Princeton, NJ: Princeton University Press, 1955), 408–13.

183. *Worcester Magazine*, November 8, 1787, *DHRC* digital edition.

184. "Definitions," *American Herald*, December 10, 1878, *DHRC* digital edition.

185. Maier, *Ratification*, 92–93.

186. *Centinel*, Letter I, in Herbert J. Storing and Murray Dry, eds., *The Anti-Federalist: Writings by the Opponents of the Constitution* (Chicago: University of Chicago Press, 1985), 18; "Brutus," Essay I, in Storing, *Anti-Federalist*, 116. See also Herbert J. Storing, *What the Anti-Federalists Were For: The Political Thought of the Opponents of the Constitution* (Chicago: University of Chicago Press, 1981), 15–23.

187. Alexander Hamilton's Speech to the New York Ratifying Convention, Convention Debates, June 24, 1788, *DHRC* digital edition.

188. George Washington to Sir Edward Newenham, Mount Vernon, December 25, 1787, Founders Online, National Archives, founders.archives.gov/documents/Washington/04-05-02-0455. Original Source: *The Papers of George Washington*, Confederation Series, vol. 5, *1 February 1787–31 December 1787*, ed. W. W. Abbot (Charlottesville: University Press of Virginia, 1997), 508–9.

189. Saul Cornell, *The Other Founders: Anti-Federalism and the Dissenting Tradition in America, 1788–1828* (Chapel Hill: University of North Carolina Press, 1999), 22.

190. Gordon S. Wood, *Empire of Liberty: A History of the Early Republic, 1789–1915* (New York: Oxford University Press, 2009), 35–36.

191. "Brutus," Essay I, in Storing, *Anti-Federalist*, 109.

192. Elbridge Gerry to the Massachusetts General Court, October 18, 1787, *DHRC* digital edition.

193. Richard Henry Lee to Samuel Adams, New York, October 5, 1787, *DHRC* digital edition.

194. Farrand, *Records*, vol. 2, 632.

195. Rakove, *Original Meanings*, 96.

196. Cornell, *Other Founders*, 20–21.

197. Maier, *Ratification*, 69–70.

198. Publius Valerius Poplicola co-founded the Roman Republic. As consul he is credited with saving the early republic from tyranny and military subjugation. James Madison to James K. Paulding, Montpelier, July 23, 1818, Founders Online, National Archives, founders.archives.gov/documents/Madison/04-01-02-0273. Original source: *The Papers of James Madison*, Retirement Series, vol. 1, *4 March 1817–31 January 1820*, ed. David B. Mattern, J.C.A. Stagg, Mary Parke Johnson, and Anne Mandeville Colony (Charlottesville: University of Virginia Press, 2009), 309–11.

199. "Brutus," Essay I in Storing, *Anti-Federalist*, 110.

200. Mercy Otis Warren, *Observations on the New Constitution, and on the Federal and State Conventions, by a Columbian Patriot* (Boston: 1788), hdl.handle.net/2027/uc1.31175035150849. Warren never received any credit for the influential tract while she was alive, as it was written under a pseudonym and most assumed that Elbridge Gerry wrote it. See Cheryl Z. Oreovicz, "Mercy Otis Warren," *Legacy* 13, no. 1 (1996): 59.

201. Convention Debates, February 5, 1788, a.m., *DHRC* digital edition. See Rakove, *Original Meanings*, 120.

202. "Introductory Note: New York Ratifying Convention [17 June–26 July 1788]," Founders Online, National Archives, founders.archives.gov/documents/Hamilton/01-05-02-0012-0001. Original source: *The Papers of Alexander Hamilton*, vol. 5, *June 1788–November 1789*, ed. Harold C. Syrett (New York: Columbia University Press, 1962), 11–13.

203. The vote at the convention was 30–0. The Delaware Form of Ratification, December 7, 1787, *DHRC* digital edition.

204. See "The New Jersey Convention," December 11–20, 1787, *DHRC* digital edition; Mary R. Murrin, "New Jersey and the Two Constitutions," in *The Constitution and the States: The Role of the Original Thirteen in the Framing and Adoption of the Federal Constitution*, ed. Patrick T. Conley and John P. Kaminski (Madison, WI: Madison House, 1988), 71; "The Georgia Convention," December 25, 1787–January 5, 1788, *DHRC* digital edition; "The Connecticut Convention," January 3–9, 1788, *DHRC* digital edition; Christopher Collier, "Sovereignty Finessed," in Conley and Kaminski, *Constitution and the States*, 109. See also Rakove, *Original Meanings*, 115.

205. "Proceedings of the Pennsylvania Ratifying Convention," November 26, 1787, *DHRC* digital edition.

206. "Debates of the Pennsylvania Ratifying Convention," November 28, 1787, *DHRC* digital edition.

207. "Debates of the Pennsylvania Ratifying Convention," November 28, 1787, *DHRC* digital edition.

208. James Wilson, Pennsylvania Convention Debates, November 28, 1787, *DHRC* digital edition. See also Leonard W. Levy, *Origins of the Bill of Rights* (New Haven, CT: Yale University Press, 2001), 13.

209. "Proceedings of the Pennsylvania Ratifying Convention," November 26, 1787, *DHRC* digital edition; Klarman, *Framers' Coup*, 429–30.

210. Samuel Powel to George Washington, Philadelphia, December 12, 1787, *DHRC* digital edition.

211. "Dissent of the Minority of the Convention," December 18, 1787, *DHRC* digital edition; Maier, *Ratification*, 120.

212. "Dissent of the Minority of the Convention," December 18, 1787, *DHRC* digital edition.

213. Convention Debates, January 23, 1788, a.m., *DHRC* digital edition.

214. Nathaniel Gorham to James Madison, Charlestown, MA, January 27, 1788, Founders Online, National Archives, founders.archives.gov/documents/Madison/01-10-02-0258. Original source: *The Papers of James Madison*, vol. 10, 411. Also: Rufus King to James Madison, Boston, January 23, 1788, Founders Online, National Archives, founders.archives.gov/documents /Madison/01-10-02-0247. Original source: *The Papers of James Madison*, vol. 10, 411. See also Klarman, *Framers' Coup*, 438.

215. See, e.g., Rufus King to George Thatcher, Boston, January 20, 1788, *DHRC* digital edition. "Hancock is still confined, or rather he has not yet taken his Seat; as soon as the majority is exhibited on either side I think his Health will suffer him to be abroad."

216. Convention Debates, January 31, 1788, p.m., *DHRC* digital edition.

217. Convention Debates, January 31, 1788, p.m., *DHRC* digital edition.

218. Convention Debates, January 31, 1788, p.m., *DHRC* digital edition.

219. Convention Debates, January 31, 1788, p.m., *DHRC* digital edition.

220. In Maryland, the convention formed a committee to recommend amendments to the Constitution, which later adjourned without agreement. In response, a leader of the Anti-Federalists published a set of thirteen proposed amendments in a separate minority report. *Annapolis Maryland Gazette*, May 1, 1788, *DHRC* digital edition.

221. South Carolina Form of Ratification, May 23, 1788, *DHRC* digital edition; Robert M. Weir, "South Carolinians and the Adoption of the United States Constitution," *South Carolina Historical Magazine* 89, no. 2 (April 1988): 73–89; Maier, *Ratification*, 251–52; Rakove, *Original Meanings*, 116.

222. New Hampshire Form of Ratification, June 21, 1788, *DHRC* digital edition.

223. Samuel Parker to Samuel Peters, Boston, June 21, 1788, *DHRC* digital edition.

224. Debates of the Virginia Ratifying Convention, June 24, 1788, *DHRC* digital edition.

225. See Maier, *Ratification*, 310; Alan V. Briceland, "The Cement of the Union in the Constitution and the States" in Conley and Kaminski, *Constitution and the States*, 211.

226. Edmund Randolph to James Madison, Richmond, April 17, 1788, *DHRC* digital edition ("under their cover, a higher game might be played").

227. Debates of the Virginia Ratifying Convention, June 24, 1788, *DHRC* digital edition (statement of George Wythe). See Rakove, *Original Meanings*, 124.

228. Ratification of the Constitution by the State of Virginia, June 25, 1788, *DHRC* digital edition.

229. James Madison to Alexander Hamilton, Richmond, June 27, 1788, Founders Online, National Archives, founders.archives.gov/documents/Hamilton/01-05-02-0012-0032. Original source: *Papers of Alexander Hamilton*, vol. 5, 91–92. See also Maier, *Ratification*, 309.

230. James Madison to George Washington, Richmond, June 27, 1788, Founders Online, National Archives, https://founders.archives.gov/documents/Madison/01-11-02-0119. Original source: *The Papers of James Madison, vol. 11, 7 March 1788–1 March 1789*, ed. Robert A. Rutland and Charles F. Hobson (Charlottesville: University Press of Virginia, 1977), 182–83.

231. Convention Debates, June 25, 1788, *DHRC* digital edition.

232. Ratification of the Constitution by the State of New York, July 26, 1788, *DHRC* digital edition.

233. Convention Debates and Proceedings, July 23, 1788, *DHRC* digital edition. See Rakove, *Original Meanings*, 125–27.

234. James Madison to George Washington, New York, August 24, 1788, Founders Online, National Archives, founders.archives.gov/documents/Washington/04-06-02-0423. Original source: *The Papers of George Washington*, Confederation Series, vol. 6, *1 January 1788–23 September 1788*, ed. W. W. Abbot (Charlottesville: University Press of Virginia, 1997), 468–71.

235. James Madison to Edmund Randolph, New York, 22 August 1788, Founders Online, National Archives, founders.archives.gov/documents/Madison/01-11-02-0170. Original source: *The Papers of James Madison*, vol. 11, 237–38.

236. Maier, *Ratification*, 422. On August 1, 1788, the North Carolina ratifying convention voted down a motion to adopt the Constitution with a set of recommended amendments for consideration by Congress. The next day, the delegates approved a set of recommended amendments to the Constitution, based on the proposals published by the Virginia convention.

237. James Madison, Debates of the Virginia Ratifying Convention, June 6, 1788, *DHRC* digital edition.

238. Circular Letter to State Executives, July 26, 1788, as printed in the *Poughkeepsie Country Journal*, August 5, 1788, *DHRC* digital edition.

239. New York Legislature Recommends the Calling of a Second Constitutional Convention, 4 February–5 May 1789, *DHRC* digital edition.

240. George Lee Turberville to James Madison, Richmond, November 10, 1788, Founders Online, National Archives, founders.archives.gov/documents/Madison/01-11-02-0249. Original source: *The Papers of James Madison*, vol. 11, 350.

241. Proceedings of the New York Antifederalist Society, October 30, 1788, *DHRC* digital edition.

242. Proceedings of the New York Antifederalist Society, October 30, 1788.

Chapter 2: The Founding Era Amendments (1789–1804)

1. This number was calculated by the authors in a thorough review of the 166 amendments proposed by the following six states during the ratification contests: Massachusetts, South Carolina, New Hampshire, Virginia, New York, and North Carolina (submitted by its convention

after it initially voted down the Constitution in August 1788). Also included in this analysis were the fourteen proposed amendments listed in the Dissent of the Minority in Pennsylvania, and the thirteen drafted but unpublished amendment recommendations from the Maryland Convention. Not included are the thirty-nine amendments recommended by the Rhode Island convention on May 19, 1790, after Congress sent twelve proposed amendments to the states for ratification. Amendment proposals with similar substantive effects or intents were grouped together in categories.

2. Restrictions on taxation were proposed by the conventions in Massachusetts, South Carolina, New Hampshire, Virginia, New York, and North Carolina. They were additionally proposed by the Pennsylvania Minority. Debates of the Virginia Ratifying Convention, June 11, 1788, in *The Documentary History of the Ratification of the Constitution* digital edition, ed. John P. Kaminski, Gaspare J. Saladino, Richard Leffler, Charles H. Schoenleber and Margaret A. Hogan (Charlottesville: University of Virginia Press, 2009) (hereafter *DHRC* digital edition).

3. James Madison to George Washington, New York, February 15, 1788, Founders Online, National Archives, founders.archives.gov/documents/Washington/04-06-02-0094. Original source: *The Papers of George Washington*, Confederation Series, vol. 6, *1 January 1788–23 September 1788*, ed. W. W. Abbot (Charlottesville: University Press of Virginia, 1997), 115. Also: James Madison to Richard Peters, New York, August 19, 1789, Founders Online, National Archives, founders.archives.gov/documents/Madison/01-12-02-0230. Original source: *The Papers of James Madison*, vol. 12, *2 March 1789–20 January 1790 and Supplement 24 October 1775–24 January 1789*, ed. Charles F. Hobson and Robert A. Rutland (Charlottesville: University Press of Virginia, 1979), 346–48.

4. James Madison to Alexander Hamilton, Richmond, June 27, 1788, Founders Online, National Archives, founders.archives.gov/documents/Hamilton/01-05-02-0012-0032. Original source: *The Papers of Alexander Hamilton*, vol. 5, *June 1788–November 1789*, ed. Harold C. Syrett (New York: Columbia University Press, 1962), 91–92. See also Pauline Maier, *Ratification: The People Debate the Constitution, 1787–1788* (New York: Simon & Schuster, 2011), 309; Richard Beeman, *Plain, Honest Men: The Making of the American Constitution* (New York: Random House, 2009), 399–400.

5. James Madison to George Washington, New York, August 11, 1788, Founders Online, National Archives, https://founders.archives.gov/documents/Washington/04-06-02-0399. Original source: *The Papers of George Washington*, Confederation Series, vol. 6, 437–39.

6. Kenneth R. Bowling, "'A Tub to the Whale': The Founding Fathers and Adoption of the Federal Bill of Rights," *Journal of the Early Republic* 8 (Fall 1988): 230.

7. George Washington to James Madison, Mount Vernon, September 23, 1788, Founders Online, National Archives, founders.archives.gov/documents/Washington/04-06-02-0471. Original source: *The Papers of George Washington*, Confederation Series, vol. 6, 533–34.

8. George Washington to James Madison, Mount Vernon, September 23, 1788, Founders Online, National Archives, founders.archives.gov/documents/Washington/04-06-02-0471. Original source: *The Papers of George Washington*, Confederation Series, vol. 6, 533–34.

9. Virginia Declaration of Rights, sec. 1, 2, 15 (1776), Avalon Project, avalon.law.yale .edu/18th_century/virginia.asp.

10. Virginia Declaration of Rights, sec. 6, 8, 11, 16. The Declaration also recognized other important rights, including protections for criminal defendants, a restriction on excessive bails and fines and cruel and unusual punishments, a ban on general warrants, and freedom of the press (sec. 8, 9, 10, and 12).

11. Virginia Declaration of Rights; Leonard W. Levy, *Origins of the Bill of Rights* (New Haven, CT: Yale University Press, 2001), 9, 22.

12. Alan P. Grimes, *Democracy and the Amendments to the Constitution* (Lanham, MD: Lexington Books, 1978), 3.

13. U.S. Constitution, Art. I, Secs. 9 and 10.

14. U.S. Constitution, Art. I, Sec. 9. See Levy, *Origins of the Bill of Rights*, 44.

15. U.S. Constitution, Art. III, Sec. 2. See also Grimes, *Democracy and the Amendments to the Constitution*, 2–3.

16. Michael J. Klarman, *The Framers' Coup* (New York: Oxford University Press, 2016), 549–50; Bowling, "'A Tub to the Whale,'" 226.

17. James Madison to Thomas Jefferson, New York, October 17, 1788, Founders Online, National Archives, founders.archives.gov/documents/Madison/01-11-02-0218. Original source: *The Papers of James Madison*, vol. 11, *7 March 1788–1 March 1789*, ed. Robert A. Rutland and Charles F. Hobson (Charlottesville: University Press of Virginia, 1977), 295–300, cited in Klarman, *Framers' Coup*, 562; Levy, *Origins of the Bill of Rights*, 22.

18. Benjamin Rush, Pennsylvania Convention Debates, November 30, 1787, *DHRC* digital edition; Klarman, *Framers' Coup*, 549, 552; Bowling, "'A Tub to the Whale,'" 226.

19. Levy, *Origins of the Bill of Rights*, 30.

20. Patrick Henry, Virginia Convention Debates, June 16, 1788, *DHRC* digital edition, cited in Levy, *Origins of the Bill of Rights*, 28.

21. George Mason, Virginia Convention Debates, June 16, 1788, *DHRC* digital edition.

22. James Madison to Thomas Jefferson, Philadelphia, December 8, 1788, Founders Online, National Archives, founders.archives.gov/documents/Jefferson/01-14-02-0119. Original source: *The Papers of Thomas Jefferson*, vol. 14, *8 October 1788–26 March 1789*, ed. Julian P. Boyd (Princeton, NJ: Princeton University Press, 1958), 339–42. See also Klarman, *Framers' Coup*, 563.

23. Richard Labunski, *James Madison and the Struggle for the Bill of Rights* (New York: Oxford University Press, 2006), 136. Also: Charles Lee to George Washington, Richmond, October 29, 1788, Founders Online, National Archives, founders.archives.gov/documents/Washington/05-01-02-0062. Original source: *The Papers of George Washington*, Presidential Series, vol. 1, *24 September 1788–31 March 1789*, ed. Dorothy Twohig (Charlottesville: University Press of Virginia, 1987), 82–84.

24. Labunski, *James Madison and the Struggle for the Bill of Rights*, 158.

25. James Madison to George Eve, January 2, 1789, Founders Online, National Archives, founders.archives.gov/documents/Madison/01-11-02-0297. Original source: *The Papers of James Madison*, vol. 11, 404–6. See Labunski, *James Madison and the Struggle for the Bill of Rights*, 164–65.

26. Bowling, "'A Tub to the Whale,'" 230–31; Paul Finkelman, "The Nefarious Intentions of the Framers," *University of Chicago Law Review*, no. 84 (2017): 2157.

27. Robert Morris to Mary Morris, New York, March 4, 1789, in Charles Henry Hart, "Mary White—Mrs. Robert Morris," *Pennsylvania Magazine of History and Biography* 2 (1878): 171–72, books.google.com/books?id=bWASut7SGtsC. Original Source: *Documentary History of the First Federal Congress of the United States of America*, vol. 15, *Correspondence: First Session, March–May 1789*, ed. Charles Bangs Bickford, Kenneth R. Bowling, Helen E. Veit, and William C. diGiacomantonio (Baltimore: Johns Hopkins University Press, 2004), 17, cited in Fergus M. Bordewich, *The First Congress: How James Madison, George Washington, and a Group of Extraordinary Men Invented the Government* (New York: Simon & Schuster, 2016), 26.

28. Bordewich, *First Congress*, 27.

29. Bordewich, *First Congress*, 30–31.

30. Klarman, *Framers' Coup*, 568–69.

31. Abraham Baldwin to Joel Barlow, March 1, 1789, cited in Klarman, *Framers' Coup*, 568–69.

32. Klarman, *Framers' Coup*, 572; George Washington, Inaugural Address, New York, April 30, 1789, American Presidency Project, www.presidency.ucsb.edu/node/200393.

33. 1 *Annals of Congress*, ed. Joseph Gales (1834), 440–41. See also Grimes, *Democracy and the Amendments to the Constitution*, 9–11; Klarman, *Framers' Coup*, 572.

34. 1 *Annals of Congress*, 441. See also Grimes, *Democracy and the Amendments to the Constitution*, 9–10.

35. 1 *Annals of Congress*, 444, 449.

36. 1 *Annals of Congress*, 449.

37. 1 *Annals of Congress*, 449.

38. Levy, *Origins of the Bill of Rights*, 11.

39. 1 *Annals of Congress*, 452.

40. 1 *Annals of Congress*, 735; Labunski, *James Madison and the Struggle for the Bill of Rights*, 200–201.

41. 1 *Annals of Congress*, 734; Scott D. Gerber, "Roger Sherman and the Bill of Rights," *Polity* 28 (Summer 1996): 525–26.

42. 1 *Annals of Congress*, 451–53.

43. 1 *Annals of Congress*, 451–53. See Bowling, "'A Tub to the Whale,'" 236.

44. 1 *Annals of Congress*, 452.

45. 1 *Annals of Congress*, 458.

46. 1 *Annals of Congress*, 784; Labunski, *James Madison and the Struggle for the Bill of Rights*, 226–27.

47. 1 *Annals of Congress*, 459.

48. 1 *Annals of Congress*, 463.

49. 1 *Annals of Congress*, 468. See Levy, *Origins of the Bill of Rights*, 37; Burt Neuborne, *Madison's Music: On Reading the First Amendment* (New York: New Press, 2015), 206.

50. 1 *Annals of Congress*, 685.

51. 1 *Annals of Congress*, 690. See also Bowling, "'A Tub to the Whale,'" 239.

52. They were Abraham Baldwin (Georgia), George Clymer (Pennsylvania), Nicholas Gilman (New Hampshire), James Madison (Virginia), and Roger Sherman (Connecticut). See Neuborne, *Madison's Music*, 207.

53. Statement of Rep. Aedanus Burke, 1 *Annals of Congress*, 774.

54. Neuborne, *Madison's Music*, 216.

55. Bowling, "'A Tub to the Whale,'" 241–42.

56. Levy, *Origins of the Bill of Rights*, 38.

57. 1 *Annals of Congress*, 735–44.

58. 1 *Annals of Congress*, 735.

59. Klarman, *Framers' Coup*, 583; Bowling, "'A Tub to the Whale,'" 243.

60. 1 *Annals of Congress* 804; Bowling, "'A Tub to the Whale,'" 243–44.

61. Klarman, *The Framers' Coup*, 583; Bowling, "'A Tub to the Whale,'" 243.

62. 1 *Annals of Congress*, 765; Labunski, *James Madison and the Struggle for the Bill of Rights*, 224–25.

63. 1 *Annals of Congress*, 774–75.

64. 1 *Annals of Congress*, 775, cited in Bowling, "'A Tub to the Whale,'" 241.

65. 1 *Annals of Congress*, 774. See also Klarman, *Framers' Coup*, 583.

66. Bowling, "'A Tub to the Whale,'" 242–44.

67. *The Documentary History of the First Federal Congress*, vol. 9, *The Diary of William Maclay and Other Notes on Senate Debates*, ed. Kenneth R. Bowling and Helen E. Veit (Baltimore: Johns Hopkins University Press, 1988), 133, cited in Bowling, "'A Tub to the Whale,'" 245.

68. Bowling, "'A Tub to the Whale,'" 245–46.

69. Akhil Amar, *The Bill of Rights: Creation and Reconstruction* (New Haven, CT: Yale University Press, 2000), 9.

70. U.S. Constitution, Art. I, Sec. 2, cl. 3. During the debate in Philadelphia, the Framers originally decided to cap the number of House seats at one representative for every forty thousand constituents, but after an extraordinary last-minute objection—raised at the signing ceremony, no less—the cap was reduced to one member for every thirty thousand constituents. Max Farrand, ed., *The Records of the Federal Convention of 1787*, vol. 2 (New Haven, CT: Yale University Press, 1911), 643–44 (hereafter Farrand, *Records*).

71. Amar, *Bill of Rights*, 11–12.

72. Debates of the Virginia Ratifying Convention, June 5, 1788, *DHRC*.

73. Amar, *Bill of Rights*, 14. See Ratification of the Constitution by the State of Massachusetts, February 6, 1788; Ratification of the Constitution by the State of New Hampshire, June 21, 1788; Ratification of the Constitution by the State of Virginia, June 25, 1788; Ratification of the Constitution by the State of New York, July 26, 1788, Ratification of the Constitution by the State of North Carolina, November 21, 1789: all *DHRC* digital edition.

74. Neuborne, *Madison's Music*, 221–22.

75. The threshold of 3 million people was surpassed in the first census in 1790. Of course, counting the number of Americans for purposes of representation was further complicated by the requirement that slaves be counted as three-fifths of a person. See U.S. Constitution, Art. I, Sec. 2. The first census counted 3,199,355 free people and 694,280 slaves for a total population of 3,893,635. But because slaves were counted as three-fifths of a person for purposes of representation, the total population for purposes of legislative apportionment was 3,615,925. U.S. Census Bureau, Census 1790, "Return of the Whole Number of Persons within the Several Districts of the United States," www.census.gov/library/publications/1793/dec/number-of-persons.html. Note that current census data lists the 1790 population at 3,929,214, correcting for slight mathematical errors and including the 35,691 people living in the Southwest Territory that would later become the state of Tennessee.

76. 1 *Annals of Congress*, 451; Amar, *Bill of Rights*, 15.

77. Delaware, Massachusetts, Connecticut, and Georgia all failed to ratify the measure. Grimes, *Democracy and the Amendments to the Constitution*, 13; Amar, *Bill of Rights*, 16–17.

78. The 1820 census counted 8,100,431 free people and 1,538,022 slaves for a total population of 9,638,453. Through operation of the three-fifths formula, the total population for legislative apportionment purposes, was 9,023,044. Dividing this figure by 50,000 would have resulted in 180 legislative seats, lower than the 200 minimum under the terms of the amendment. U.S. Census Bureau, *Census for 1820*, "Aggregate amount of each description of persons in the United States and their Territories, according to the Census taken in virtue of the act of Congress of the 14th of March, 1820, and the act of 3d of March, 1821; compiled from returns received at the Department of State," www.census.gov/library/publications/1821/dec/1820a.html.

79. Paul Finkelman, "Who Counted, Who Voted, and Who Could They Vote For," *Saint Louis University Law Journal* 58, no. 4 (2014): 1082.

80. Drew DeSilver, "U.S. Population Keeps Growing, but House of Representatives Is Same Size as in Taft Era," Fact Tank, Pew Research Center, May 31, 2018, www.pewresearch.org/fact-tank/2018/05/31/u-s-population-keeps-growing-but-house-of-representatives-is-same-size-as-in-taft-era. Based on 2019 population estimates, the ratio is now around one representative for every 754,000 Americans. See U.S. Census Bureau, "Population, Population Change, and Estimated Components of Population Change: April 1, 2010 to July 1, 2019 (NST-EST2019-alldata)," Table 1. Annual Estimates of the Resident Population for the United States, Regions, States, and Puerto Rico: April 1, 2010 to July 1, 2019, census.gov/data/tables/time-series/demo/popest/2010s-state-total.html.

81. U.S. Constitution, Art. I, Sec. 6.

82. Broadsheet, "Congress of the United States, begun and held at the city of New-York, on Wednesday, the fourth of March, one thousand seven hundred eighty-nine . . . Articles in Addition to, and Amendment of, the Constitution of the United States of America, proposed by Congress, and ratified by the Legislatures of the Several States, pursuant to the Fifth Article of the original Constitution," Documents from the Continental Congress and the Constitutional Convention, 1774–89, Library of Congress, lccn.loc.gov/90898145.

83. Labunski, *James Madison and the Struggle for the Bill of Rights*, 222–23.

84. Amar, *Bill of Rights*, 18.

85. The three states were Virginia, New York, and North Carolina. Amar, *Bill of Rights*, 18; Richard B. Bernstein, "The Sleeper Wakes: The History and Legacy of the Twenty-Seventh

Amendment," *Fordham Law Review* 61, no. 3 (1992): 514. See also Labunski, *James Madison and the Struggle for the Bill of Rights*, 223, citing *Documentary History of the First Federal Congress*, vol. 11, *Debates in the House of Representatives, First Session, June–September, 1789*, ed. Charlene Bangs Bickford, Kenneth R. Bowling, and Helen E. Veit (Baltimore: Johns Hopkins University Press, 1992), 1253.

86. 1 *Annals of Congress*, 457–58. See Bernstein, "Sleeper Wakes," 522.

87. The six states that voted to ratify the amendment were Delaware, Maryland, North Carolina, South Carolina, Virginia, and Vermont. It was later discovered that Kentucky also ratified the amendment in 1792.

88. Amar, *Bill of Rights*, 19.

89. Scholars commonly separate the Bill of Rights amendments into categories similar to these. See generally, Amar, *Bill of Rights*.

90. Neuborne, *Madison's Music*, 11–12.

91. Amendments passed by the House of Representatives, August 24, 1789, Art. 3 and 4. "First Draft of the Bill of Rights: 17 Amendments Approved by the House (SOLD)," Seth Kaller, Inc., Historic Documents & Legacy Collection, www.sethkaller.com/item/182-First-Draft-of-the -Bill-of-Rights:-17-Amendments-Approved-by-the-House. Original Source: *Connecticut Gazette*, September 4, 1789.

92. Amar, *Bill of Rights*, 38–39. Later, in a series of cases interpreting the Fourteenth Amendment, adopted in 1868, courts have held that most of the limits on government contained in the Bill of Rights apply to state and local government agencies and officials through a process called "incorporation."

93. U.S. Constitution, Amend. I. When adopted, these prohibitions did not apply to the states, which remained free to favor religious sects and impose religious tests for officers. In a 1940 case, the U.S. Supreme Court held that the Free Exercise Clause applies to states through the Fourteenth Amendment's guarantee that no state shall deny liberty without due process of law. *Cantwell v. Connecticut*, 310 U.S. 296 (1940). In 1947, the Court similarly applied the Establishment Clause as limiting state and local governments. *Everson v. Board of Education*, 330 U.S. 1 (1947). See Amar, *Bill of Rights*, 32–33.

94. Neuborne, *Madison's Music*, 18.

95. 1 *Annals of Congress*, 451, cited in Levy, *Origins of the Bill of Rights*, 55.

96. Neuborne, *Madison's Music*, 19. See *United States v. Seeger*, 380 U.S. 163 (1965); *Welsh v. United States*, 398 U.S. 333 (1970).

97. See, e.g., Kenneth Klukowski, "Reclaiming Religious Liberty by Restoring the Original Meaning of the Establishment Clause" (Washington, DC: Heritage Foundation, 2018), www .heritage.org/courts/report/reclaiming-religious-liberty-restoring-the-original-meaning -the-establishment-clause.

98. Thomas Jefferson, "Reply to the Danbury Baptist Association, Washington, DC, January 1, 1802, *Papers of Thomas Jefferson*, Princeton University, jeffersonpapers.princeton.edu/selected -documents/reply-danbury-baptist-association. Original source: *The Papers of Thomas Jefferson*, vol. 36, *1 December 1801 to 3 March 1802* (Princeton, NJ: Princeton University Press, 2009), 253–58.

99. E.g. *Engel v. Vitale*, 370 U.S. 421 (1962).

100. See generally John R. Vile, *Encyclopedia of Constitutional Amendments, Proposed Amendments, and Amending Issues 1789–2010*, vol. 2, 3rd ed. (Santa Barbara, CA: ABC-CLIO, 2010), 371–73 (hereafter Vile, *Encyclopedia of Constitutional Amendments*). See, e.g., Proposal to Permit the Offering of Prayers in Public Schools, S. J. Res. 207, 87th Congress (1962); A Joint Resolution Proposing an Amendment to the Constitution of the United States Relative to the Free Exercise of Religion, S. J. Res. 199, 104th Congress (1995); Proposing an Amendment to the Constitution of the United States to Further Protect Religious Freedom, Including the Right of Students in Public Schools to Pray Without Government Sponsorship or Compulsion, by

Clarifying the Proper Construction of Any Prohibition on Laws Respecting an Establishment of Religion, H. J. Res. 184, 104th Congress (1996).

101. See Vile, *Encyclopedia of Constitutional Amendments*, vol. 1, 200–201. See, e.g., *Van Orden v. Perry*, 545 U.S. 677 (2005).

102. *West Virginia State Board of Education v. Barnette*, 319 U.S. 624 (1943).

103. *Employment Division v. Smith*, 494 U.S. 872 (1990). For more on the proposed Religious Equality Amendment, H. J. Res. 121 (1995), see Vile, *Encyclopedia of Constitutional Amendments*, vol. 2, 402–4.

104. E.g., *Masterpiece Cakeshop v. Colorado Civil Rights Commission*, 584 U.S. ___ (2018).

105. Neuborne, *Madison's Music*, 18.

106. *New York Times Co. v. Sullivan*, 376 U.S. 254 (1964), finding that press reports about public officials cannot be libelous without proof of actual malice; *Tinker v. Des Moines Independent Community School District*, 393 U.S. 503 (1969), protecting the wearing of an armband as symbolic speech; *Texas v. Johnson*, 491 U.S. 397 (1989) and *U.S. v. Eichman*, 496 U.S. 310 (1990), invalidating laws banning flag desecration.

107. Vile, *Encyclopedia of Constitutional Amendments*, vol. 1, 207.

108. See generally, Vile, *Encyclopedia of Constitutional Amendments*, vol. 1, 202; *Brandenburg v. Ohio*, 395 U.S. 444 (1969).

109. Neuborne, *Madison's Music*, 6.

110. *Masterpiece Cakeshop v. Colorado Civil Rights Commission*, 584 U.S. ___ (2018). See Dorothy Samuels, "A Baker's Toxic Recipe for Discrimination," *American Prospect*, October 18, 2017, prospect.org/article/baker's-toxic-recipe-discrimination.

111. E.g., *Buckley v. Valeo*, 424 U.S. 1 (1976), holding that the Free Speech Clause prohibits campaign expenditure limits; *Citizens United v. Federal Elections Commission*, 558 U.S. 310 (2010), holding that the Free Speech Clause prohibits the government from restricting independent campaign expenditures by corporations and unions.

112. Levy, *Origins of the Bill of Rights*, 117.

113. Leonard W. Levy, *Emergence of a Free Press* (New York: Oxford University Press, 1985), 272.

114. State conventions from Virginia, New York, and North Carolina recommended an amendment to protect freedom of the press. In addition, the Pennsylvania Minority Dissent and Maryland Draft Amendments included it in their list of recommended amendments. See Levy, *Origins of the Bill of Rights*, 115–16.

115. Levy, *Emergence of a Free Press*, 266.

116. Levy, *Origins of the Bill of Rights*, 120–21. As Leonard Levy points out, after independence no American state repudiated the common law doctrine of seditious libel. Levy, *Emergence of a Free Press*, 219.

117. E.g., *New York Times Co. v. Sullivan*, 376 U.S. 254 (1964), holding that to sustain a claim for defamation or libel, the First Amendment requires showing of actual malice; *New York Times Co. v. U.S.*, 403 U.S. 713 (1971), upholding the right to publish the Pentagon Papers over attempted prior restraint.

118. See Vile, *Encyclopedia of Constitutional Amendments*, vol. 1, 200.

119. Vile, *Encyclopedia of Constitutional Amendments*, vol. 1, 203.

120. U.S. Constitution, Amend. II.

121. Michael Waldman, *The Second Amendment: A Biography* (New York: Simon & Schuster, 2014), 23.

122. Ratification of the Constitution by the State of New York, July 26, 1788, *DHRC* digital edition, cited in *The Complete Bill of Rights: The Drafts, Debates, Sources & Origins*, ed. Neil H. Cogan (New York: Oxford University Press, 1997), 181–82.

123. Ratification of the Constitution by the State of New Hampshire, June 21, 1788; Ratification of the Constitution by the State of Virginia, June 25, 1788; Ratification of the Constitution by the State of North Carolina, November 21, 1789, all in *DHRC* digital edition.

124. Waldman, *Second Amendment*, 65–67.

125. Paul Finkelman, "'A Well Regulated Militia': The Second Amendment in Historical Perspective," *Chicago-Kent Law Review* 76, no. 1 (2000): 226–27.

126. Waldman, *Second Amendment*, 97.

127. Warren Burger, Interview on *PBS NewsHour* by Charlayne Hunter-Gault, December 16, 1991 (cited in Waldman, *Second Amendment*, 84).

128. Waldman, *Second Amendment*, 174–75.

129. *District of Columbia v. Heller*, 554 U.S. 570 (2008).

130. Richard Posner, "In Defense of Looseness," *The New Republic*, August 27, 2008, newrepublic.com/article/62124/defense-looseness.

131. Joseph Blocker and Eric Ruben, "The Second Amendment Allows for More Gun Control Than You Think," *Vox*, June 14, 2018, www.vox.com/the-big-idea/2018/5/23/17383644/second-2nd-amendment-gun-control-debate-santa-fe-parkland-heller-anniversary-constitution.

132. Quartering Act of 1765, Avalon Project, avalon.law.yale.edu/18th_century/quartering_act_165.asp. Original source: Danby Pickering, *The Statutes at Large . . .* [from 1225 to 1867] (Cambridge, UK: Printed by Benthem, for C. Bathhurst, London, 1762–1869); Quartering Act of 1774, Avalon Project, avalon.law.yale.edu/18th_century/quartering_act_1774.asp. Original source: Pickering, *Statutes at Large*.

133. Declaration of Independence (U.S. 1776).

134. Patrick Henry, Debates of the Virginia Ratifying Convention, June 16, 1788, *DHRC* digital edition, cited in Amar, *Bill of Rights*, 60–61.

135. See Ratification of the Constitution by the State of New Hampshire, June 21, 1788; Ratification of the Constitution by the State of Virginia, June 25, 1788; Ratification of the Constitution by the State of New York, July 26, 1788; Ratification of the Constitution by the State of North Carolina, November 21, 1789, all in *DHRC* digital edition.

136. *Griswold v. Connecticut*, 381 U.S. 479, 484 (1965).

137. Neuborne, *Madison's Music*, 25.

138. "A Farmer and a Planter," April 1, 1788, *Maryland Journal*, in *The Complete Anti-Federalist*, vol. 5, *Maryland and Virginia and the South*, ed. Herbert Storing and Murray Dry (Chicago: University of Chicago Press, 1981), 75, cited in Cogan, *Complete Bill of Rights*, 241–42.

139. See Ratification of the Constitution by the State of Virginia, June 25, 1788; Ratification of the Constitution by the State of New York, July 26, 1788; Ratification of the Constitution by the State of North Carolina, November 21, 1789, all *DHRC* digital edition. Three state convention minority reports also proposed amendments related to searches and seizures: Pennsylvania, December 12, 1787; Massachusetts, February 6, 1788; Maryland, April 26, 1788, in Cogan, *Complete Bill of Rights*, 232–33.

140. U.S. Constitution, Amend. IV.

141. Neuborne, *Madison's Music*, 26. See Levy, *Origins of the Bill of Rights*, 175–79.

142. Vile, *Encyclopedia of Constitutional Amendments*, vol. 1, 213. See *Terry v. Ohio*, 392 U.S. 1 (1968), holding that police may stop and frisk suspects incident to an arrest; *Horton v. California*, 496 U.S. 128 1990; *Illinois v. McArthur*, 531 U.S. 326 (2001).

143. Christopher Dunn, *Stop and Frisk in the DeBlasio Era* (New York: New York Civil Liberties Union, March 2019), www.nyclu.org/sites/default/files/field_documents/20190314_nyclu_stopfrisk_singles.pdf; *Stop-And-Frisk 2011*, NYCLU Briefing, May 9, 2012, www.nyclu.org/sites/default/files/publications/NYCLU_2011_Stop-and-Frisk_Report.pdf. Notably, the exclusionary rule, a judicially created tool, seeks to incentivize compliance with the law by excluding most illegally obtained evidence from use at trial. *Mapp v. Ohio*, 367 U.S. 643 (1961). See Vile, *Encyclopedia of Constitutional Amendments*, vol. 1, 214.

144. Grand juries in the colonial era famously refused to indict the publisher John Peter Zenger and leaders of protests against the Stamp Act. Amar, *Bill of Rights*, 84–85.

145. Vile, *Encyclopedia of Constitutional Amendments*, vol. 1, 197. See also Neuborne, *Madison's Music*, 26.

146. Vile, *Encyclopedia of Constitutional Amendments*, vol. 1, 197. This protection only applies to federal courts. State prosecutors are free to indict defendants acquitted in a federal proceeding for the same act. Similarly, federal prosecutors can indict individuals following acquittal in a state proceeding.

147. *Miranda v. Arizona*, 384 U.S. 436 (1966).

148. More controversially, courts have invoked the due process guarantee as a powerful tool to vindicate rights not explicitly mentioned in the Constitution. (Legal scholars call this "substantive due process.") See Nathan Chapman and Kenji Yoshino, "The Fourteenth Amendment Due Process Clause," National Constitution Center, Interactive Constitution, constitutioncenter.org /interactive-constitution/interpretation/amendment-xiv/clauses/701.

149. Amar, *Bill of Rights*, 79–80.

150. Pennsylvania Constitution, Art. VIII (1776); Massachusetts Constitution, Part I Art. X; Vermont Constitution, Sec. 2 (1777). See William Michael Treanor, "The Original Understanding of the Takings Clause and the Political Process," *Columbia Law Review* 95, no. 4 (May 1995): 789–91; Bowling, "'A Tub to the Whale,'" 236.

151. James Madison, "Property," *National Gazette*, March 27, 1792, cited in Treanor, "Original Understanding of the Takings Clause and the Political Process," 838.

152. *Kelo v. City of New London*, 545 U.S. 469 (2005).

153. Declaration of Independence (U.S. 1776).

154. Amar, *Bill of Rights*, 83.

155. New York, North Carolina, and Virginia called for amendments to guarantee jury trials in both civil and criminal cases. Massachusetts and New Hampshire called for the guarantee only in civil cases. See Cogan, *Complete Bill of Rights*, 401–2, 506–8.

156. U.S. Constitution, Art. III, Sec. 2.

157. Amar, *Bill of Rights*, 105–106.

158. *Powell v. Alabama*, 287 U.S. 45 (1932); *Gideon v. Wainwright*, 372 U.S. 335 (1963). See Vile, *Encyclopedia of Constitutional Amendments*, vol. 2, 438.

159. Thomas Giovanni and Roopal Patel, "*Gideon* at 50: Three Reforms to Revive the Right to Counsel," Brennan Center for Justice, April 9, 2013, www.brennancenter.org/sites/default /files/2019-08/Report_Gideon-at-50.pdf.

160. Farrand, *Records*, vol. 2, 587–88.

161. Preston, The Election of Convention Delegates, November 26, 1787, *DHRC* digital edition.

162. See Ratification of the Constitution by the State of Massachusetts, February 6, 1788; Ratification of the Constitution by the State of New Hampshire, June 21, 1788; Ratification of the Constitution by the State of Virginia, June 25, 1788; Ratification of the Constitution by the State of New York, July 26, 1788; Ratification of the Constitution by the State of North Carolina, November 21, 1789, all *DHRC* digital edition.

163. In the Judiciary Act of 1789, passed one day before Congress approved the Bill of Rights, Congress set an even higher jurisdictional minimum of $500.

164. See Andrew C. Cook, *Tort Reform Update: Recently Enacted Legislative Reforms and State Court Challenges* (Washington, DC: Federalist Society, 2012), fedsoc.org/commentary/publica tions/tort-reform-update-recently-enacted-legislative-reforms-and-state-court-challenges.

165. Levy, *Origins of the Bill of Rights*, 231.

166. Virginia Declaration of Rights, Chapter 2, Sec. IX (1776); Delaware Declaration of Rights, Sec. 16 (1776); Maryland Declaration of Rights, Art. XXII (1776); North Carolina Declaration of Rights, Sec. X (1776); Pennsylvania Constitution, Sec. 29 (1776); Massachusetts Constitution, Part I, Art. XXVI (1780); New Hampshire Bill of Rights, Part I, Art. XXXIII (1783); New York Bill of Rights, Sec. 8 (1787); South Carolina Constitution, Art. IX, Sec. 4 (1790). In addition, the Georgia and Vermont constitutions barred excessive bails and fines

but did not expressly prohibit cruel and unusual punishment. Georgia Constitution, Art. LIX (1777); Vermont Constitution, Sec. XXVI (1777).

167. Levy, *Origins of the Bill of Rights*, 237–38.

168. Massachusetts Convention Debates, January 30, 1788, a.m., *DHRC* digital edition.

169. Ratification of the Constitution by the State of Virginia, June 25, 1788; Ratification of the Constitution by the State of New York, July 26, 1788; Ratification of the Constitution by the State of North Carolina, November 21, 1789, all *DHRC* digital edition. The minority report from the Pennsylvania convention also proposed the amendment. "The Address and Reasons of Dissent of the Minority of the Convention of the State of Pennsylvania to their Constituents," December 12, 1788, *DHRC* digital edition.

170. 1 *Annals of Congress*, 782.

171. 1 *Annals of Congress*, 782–83.

172. *Trop v. Dulles*, 356 U.S. 86 (1958).

173. *Atkins v. Virginia*, 536 U.S. 304 (2002), holding that execution of mentally handicapped persons is prohibited; *Roper v. Simmons*, 543 U.S. 551 (2005), holding that capital punishment for crimes committed while a minor is prohibited; *Graham v. Florida*, 560 U.S. 48 (2010), holding that execution of juvenile offenders is prohibited for non-homicide offenses.

174. James Madison, Debates of the Virginia Ratifying Convention, June 24, 1788, *DHRC* digital edition.

175. 1 *Annals of Congress*, 456.

176. Most famously, the Supreme Court invoked the Ninth Amendment in the case of *Griswold v. Connecticut*, a challenge to Connecticut's ban on contraception. The opinion of the Court cited the Ninth Amendment among other provisions to find a right to marital privacy. *Griswold v. Connecticut*, 381 U.S. 479 (1965).

177. Robert H. Jackson, *The Supreme Court in the American System of Government* (Cambridge, MA: Harvard University Press, 1955), 74–75.

178. *Nomination of Robert H. Bork to be Associate Justice of the Supreme Court of the United States*, before the Senate Committee on the Judiciary, 100th Congress 249 (1987), statement of Robert H. Bork, circuit judge, United States Court of Appeals for the District of Columbia Circuit, www.loc.gov/law/find/nominations/bork/hearing-pt1.pdf. See also Ramesh Ponnuru, "Judge Bork's Ink Blot," *National Review*, December 20, 2012, www.nationalreview.com/2012/12/judge-borks-ink-blot-ramesh-ponnuru.

179. Randy Barnett, "The Ninth Amendment: It Means What It Says," *Texas Law Review* 85, no. 1 (2016): 2.

180. Russell Caplan, "The History and Meaning of the Ninth Amendment," *Virginia Law Review* 69, no. 2 (March 1983): 223.

181. Neuborne, *Madison's Music*, 29–34.

182. U.S. Constitution, Art. I, Sec. 8.

183. Articles of Confederation, Art. 2 (U.S. 1781).

184. Ratification of the Constitution by the State of Massachusetts, February 6, 1788; Ratification of the Constitution by the State of South Carolina, May 23, 1788; Ratification of the Constitution by the State of New Hampshire, June 21, 1788; Ratification of the Constitution by the State of Virginia, June 25, 1788; Ratification of the Constitution by the State of New York, July 26, 1788; Ratification of the Constitution by the State of North Carolina, November 21, 1789: *DHRC* digital edition.

185. 1 *Annals of Congress*, 459.

186. 1 *Annals of Congress*, 790.

187. 1 *Annals of Congress*, 790.

188. 1 *Annals of Congress*, 790. See Labunski, *James Madison and the Struggle for the Bill of Rights*, 230.

189. Amar, *Bill of Rights*, 124.

190. E.g., *Printz v. United States*, 521 U.S. 898 (1997), holding that a federal law requiring state and local law enforcement officials to conduct background checks for handgun purchasers violated the Tenth Amendment; *Murphy v. National College Athletic Association*, 584 U.S. ___ (2018), holding that a federal ban on state-sponsored sports gambling violated the amendment's "anti-commandeering" rule; *National Collegiate Federation of Independent Business v. Sebelius*, 567 U.S. 519 (2012), upholding the Affordable Care Act but finding its Medicaid expansion to be unconstitutional.

191. See Garrett Epps, "Constitutional Myth #7: The 10th Amendment Protects 'States' Rights,'" *The Atlantic*, July 11, 2011, www.theatlantic.com/national/archive/2011/07/constitutional-myth -7-the-10th-amendment-protects-states-rights/241671.

192. In a circular letter dated October 2, 1789, President George Washington submitted Congress's twelve proposed amendments to the governors of the eleven states then in the Union and "like copies to the executives of the states of Rhode Island and North Carolina." George Washington, Circular to the Governors of the States, October 2, 1789, Founders Online, National Archives, founders.archives.gov/documents/Washington/05-04-02-0087. Original source: *The Papers of George Washington*, Presidential Series, vol. 4, *8 September 1789–15 January 1790*, ed. Dorothy Twohig (Charlottesville: University Press of Virginia, 1993), 125–27.

193. The North Carolina ratifying convention approved the Constitution on November 21, 1789. The following month, on December 22, its legislature ratified all twelve amendments. Rhode Island's ratifying convention adopted the Constitution on May 17, 1790. Less than two weeks later, on June 7, its legislature ratified eleven amendments, rejecting only the congressional pay amendment.

194. Grimes, *Democracy and the Amendments to the Constitution*, 28–29 n40. A lawsuit filed by Eugene LaVergne alleged that the Connecticut Legislature had actually ratified the amendments—including the failed Representation Amendment, which then should have been added to the Constitution in 1792. LaVergne sought for the United States District Court for the District of Columbia to "order that Congress is constitutionally required to add at least 5,795 seats to the House of Representatives and apportion them among the states, and to invalidate legislation Congress enacted without the requisite 3,116-member quorum." The Court dismissed the case as a political question on June 11, 2019. *Eugene Martin LaVergne, et al., v. United States House of Representatives, et al.*, Civil Action No. 1:17-cv-00793-CKK-CP-RDM (D.D.C. 2018), 2.

195. Levy, *Origins of the Bill of Rights*, 41. See also Grimes, *Democracy and the Amendments to the Constitution*, 28 n40.

196. Levy, *Origins of the Bill of Rights*, 40; Klarman, *Framers' Coup*, 587–88.

197. Levy, *Origins of the Bill of Rights*, 41.

198. Convention Proceedings, June 17, 1788, *DHRC* digital edition.

199. Patrick Henry to Richard Henry Lee, August 28, 1789, *ConSource*, www.consource.org /document/patrick-henry-to-richard-henry-lee-1789-8-28. Original Source: *Creating the Bill of Rights*, ed. Kenneth R. Bowling and Helen E. Veit (Baltimore: Johns Hopkins University Press, 1991), 289–90, cited in Labunski, *James Madison and the Struggle for the Bill of Rights*, 242.

200. This number includes the minority and draft amendments from Pennsylvania and Maryland. Labunski, *James Madison and the Struggle for the Bill of Rights*, 246.

201. J. Gordon Hylton, "Virginia and the Ratification of the Bill of Rights, 1789–1791," *University of Richmond Law Review* 25, no. 3 (1991): 460–62.

202. Levy, *Origins of the Bill of Rights*, 42–43.

203. See Michael J. Douma, "How the First Ten Amendments Became the Bill of Rights," *Georgetown Journal of Law and Public Policy* 15, no. 2 (2017): 593–614.

204. Labunski, *James Madison and the Struggle for the Bill of Rights*, 256–57, 263.

205. Thomas Jefferson, Circular to the Governors of the States, Philadelphia, March 1, 1792, Founders Online, National Archives, founders.archives.gov/documents/Jefferson/01 -27-02-0774. Original source: *The Papers of Thomas Jefferson*, vol. 27, *1 September–31*

December 1793, ed. John Catanzariti (Princeton, NJ: Princeton University Press, 1997), 815. See also Levy, *Origins of the Bill of Rights*, 12.

206. Farrand, *Records*, vol. 1, 123.

207. Grimes, *Democracy and the Amendments to the Constitution*, 17–18.

208. Women in New Jersey could vote between 1776 and 1807, and many early state constitutions did not explicitly bar free Black people from the franchise. The vast majorities of these populations, however, remained entirely disenfranchised until the ratifications of the Fifteenth and Nineteenth Amendments, and later, the passage of the Voting Rights Act of 1965. See chapters 3, 5.

209. Farrand, *Records*, vol. 2, 587–88. See also Grimes, *Democracy and the Amendments to the Constitution*, 6.

210. James Madison to Richard Peters, New York, August 19, 1789, Founders Online, National Archives, founders.archives.gov/documents/Madison/01-12-02-0230. Original source: *Papers of James Madison*, vol. 12, 346–48.

211. Thomas Jefferson to the Marquis de Lafayette, New York, April 2, 1790, Founders Online, National Archives, founders.archives.gov/documents/Jefferson/01-16-02-0163. Original source: *The Papers of Thomas Jefferson*, vol. 16, *30 November 1789–4 July 1790*, ed. Julian P. Boyd (Princeton, NJ: Princeton University Press, 1961), 292–93.

212. Gordon S. Wood, *The American Revolution* (New York: Modern Library, 2003), 164–65.

213. *Gideon v. Wainwright*, 372 U.S. 335, 341 (1963).

214. See Suja A. Thomas, "Nonincorporation: The Bill of Rights after *McDonald v. Chicago*," *Notre Dame Law Review* 88, no. 1 (2012): 162–64, briefly describing the history of incorporation doctrine.

215. Alexander Hamilton, *Federalist* no. 78, Avalon Project, avalon.law.yale.edu/18th_century /fed78.asp.

216. "Brutus" XV, *New York Journal*, March 20, 1788, *DHRC* digital edition.

217. U.S. Constitution, Art. III, Sec. 2.

218. See, e.g., Bradford R. Clark, "The Eleventh Amendment and the Nature of the Union," *Harvard Law Review* 123, no. 8 (June 2010): 1863.

219. Bradford R. Clark, "The Eleventh Amendment and the Nature of the Union," *Harvard Law Review* 123, no. 8 (June 2010): 1862–63.

220. Debates of the Virginia Ratifying Convention, June 20, 1788, *DHRC* digital edition.

221. See Ratification of the Constitution by the State of New York, July 26, 1788, stating that "Judicial Power of the United States in cases in which a State may be a party, does not extend to criminal Prosecutions, or to authorize any Suit by any Person against a State." Rhode Island's ratifying convention, which occurred after the twelve original amendment proposals were sent to the states, proposed a similar amendment. Ratification of the Constitution by the State of Rhode Island, May 29, 1790, in which "It is declared by the Convention, that the judicial power of the United States, in cases in which a state may be a party, does not extend to criminal prosecutions, or to authorize any suit by any person against a State . . .": *DHRC* digital edition.

222. Kurt T. Lash, "Leaving the *Chisholm* Trail: The Eleventh Amendment and the Background Principle of Strict Construction," *William & Mary Law Review* 50, no. 5 (2009): 1585.

223. *Chisholm v. Georgia*, 2 U.S. 419, 466 (1793).

224. *Chisholm v. Georgia*, 419. Justice James Iredell, the lone dissenter, presided over the case while riding the circuit. *The Documentary History of the Supreme Court of the United States, 1789–1800*, vol. 5, ed. Maeva Marcus (New York: Columbia University Press, 1994), 148–55 (hereafter *DHSCOTUS*). At the Supreme Court, he contended that the states remained "sovereign as to all the powers reserved," which included immunity from citizens suits. *Chisholm v. Georgia*, 2 U.S. 419, 435 (1793).

225. Martha A. Field, "The Eleventh Amendment and Other Sovereign Immunity Doctrines: Part One," *University of Pennsylvania Law Review* 126, no. 3 (1978): 536 n78.

226. Proclamation by Governor John Hancock, *Independent Chronicle*, July 9, 1793, in *DH-SCOTUS*, vol. 5, 387–89; Address from Governor John Hancock to the Massachusetts General Court, *Independent Chronicle*, September 18, 1793, in *DHSCOTUS*, vol. 5, 416.

227. Resolution of the Massachusetts General Court, September 27, 1793, in *DHSCOTUS*, vol. 5, 440.

228. Proceedings of the U.S. House of Representatives, *Gazette of the United States*, February 19, 1793, in *DHSCOTUS*, vol. 5, 605–6.

229. Resolution in the U.S. Senate, February 20, 1793, in *DHSCOTUS*, vol. 5, 607–8. See Clark, "The Eleventh Amendment and the Nature of the Union," 1885–86, 1891–92.

230. 4 *Annals of Congress*, 30–31, 477–78 (1794).

231. John Adams, Special Message, January 8, 1798, American Presidency Project, www .presidency.ucsb.edu/documents/special-message-3304. The ambiguity over the amendment's status stemmed from the failure of some states to inform Congress of their actions. To ascertain whether the requisite number of states had ratified the Eleventh Amendment, Congress asked President John Adams to obtain proof of ratification from the states. See William D. Guthrie, "The Eleventh Article of Amendment to the Constitution of the United States," *Columbia Law Review* 8, no. 3 (March 1908): 185–86; Clark, "The Eleventh Amendment and the Nature of the Union," 1893–94.

232. Lash, "Leaving the *Chisholm* Trail," 1585; Bradford, "The Eleventh Amendment and the Nature of the Union," 1875.

233. "Brutus" XV, *New York Journal*, March 20, 1788, *DHRC* digital edition.

234. See Lash, "Leaving the *Chisholm* Trail," 1586, arguing that "Despite Madison's successful effort to produce a bill of rights, the broad generalities of the Ninth and Tenth Amendments were not enough." And see pp. 1609–13.

235. Vile, *Encyclopedia of Constitutional Amendments*, vol. 1, 166–68.

236. E.g., *Alden v. Maine*, 527 U.S. 706 (1999); *Kimel v. Florida Board of Regents*, 528 U.S. 62 (2000). See generally John T. Noonan Jr., *Narrowing the Nation's Power* (Berkeley: University of California Press, 2002).

237. Noonan, *Narrowing the Nation's Power*, 152, 156.

238. Alexander Hamilton, *Federalist* no. 68, Avalon Project, avalon.law.yale.edu/18th_century /fed68.asp.

239. Farrand, *Records*, vol. 1, 69; Klarman, *Framers' Coup*, 226.

240. Farrand, *Records*, vol. 1, 80.

241. Farrand, *Records*, vol. 1, 80.

242. Farrand, *Records*, vol. 2, 32, 402.

243. Farrand, *Records*, vol. 2, 31.

244. Farrand, *Records*, vol. 2, 32.

245. Farrand, *Records*, vol. 2, 57.

246. Farrand, *Records*, vol. 1, 175–76.

247. Farrand, *Records*, vol. 2, 501.

248. Donald Lutz, Philip Abbott, Barbara Allen, and Russell Hanson, "The Electoral College in Historical and Philosophical Perspective," in *Choosing a President: The Electoral College and Beyond*, ed. Paul D. Schumaker and Burdett Loomis (New York: Seven Bridges Press, 2002), 33.

249. Alexander Keyssar argues that the Electoral College "was, in effect, a consensus second choice, made acceptable, in part, by the remarkably complex details of the electoral process, details that themselves constituted compromises among, or gestures toward, particular constituencies and convictions." Keyssar, *Why Do We Still Have the Electoral College?*, 24.

250. According to 2019 population estimates, the ten smallest states by population (New Hampshire, Maine, Montana, Rhode Island, Delaware, South Dakota, North Dakota, Alaska, Vermont, and Wyoming) had a total population of 9,386,840, about 2.9 percent of the total estimated U.S. population of 328,239,523. Those same states had 33 electoral votes in the post-2010

census apportionment, 6.1 percent of the 538 total. U.S. Census Bureau, "Population, Population Change, and Estimated Components of Population Change: April 1, 2010 to July 1, 2019 (NST-EST2019-alldata)," Table 1. Annual Estimates of the Resident Population for the United States, Regions, States, and Puerto Rico: April 1, 2010 to July 1, 2019, census.gov/data/tables/time-series/demo/popest/2010s-state-total.html.

251. Thomas H. Neale, *The Electoral College: How It Works in Contemporary Presidential Elections* (Washington, DC: Congressional Research Service, RL32611, 2017), 3–4. See also Akhil Amar, *America's Constitution: A Biography* (New York: Random House, 2005), 21: "Article II likewise handed slave states extra seats in the electoral college, giving the South a sizeable head start in presidential elections."

252. U.S. Census Bureau, Census 1790, "Return of the Whole Number of Persons Within the Several Districts of the United States," census.gov/library/publications/1793/dec/number-of-persons.html.

253. U.S. Constitution, Art. II, Sec. 1.

254. Lisa Thomason, "Jacksonian Democracy and the Electoral College: Politics and Reform in the Method of Selecting Presidential Electors, 1824–1833," Doctor of Philosophy (History) Dissertation, University of North Texas, 2001, 153–64, digital.library.unt.edu/ark:/67531/metadc2775/m2/1/high_res_d/dissertation.pdf.

255. *Bush v. Gore*, 531 U.S. 98, 104 (2000).

256. Lawrence Lessig and Jason Harrow, "State Legislatures Can't Ignore the Popular Vote in Appointing Electors," *Lawfare*, Nov. 6, 2020, www.lawfareblog.com/state-legislatures-cant-ignore-popular-vote-appointing-electors.

257. Alexander Hamilton, *Federalist* no. 68, Avalon Project, avalon.law.yale.edu/18th_century/fed68.asp. See Klarman, *Framers' Coup*, 231. Requiring electors to meet in their respective states would also be less costly. Beeman, *Plain, Honest Men*, 300.

258. The provision specified that the winning candidate needed to win "a Majority of the whole Number of Electors," and not a majority of the ballots cast (which was double the total number of electors). That means a candidate could win the presidency with only 25 percent of the total ballots cast.

259. U.S. Constitution, Art. II, Sec. 1.

260. *The Documentary History of the First Federal Elections, 1788–1790*, vol. 3, ed. Merrill Jensen, Lucy Trumbull Brown, Robert A. Becker, Gordon DenBoer, and Charles D. Hagermann (Madison: University of Wisconsin Press, 1986), 217.

261. John Ferling, *Adams vs. Jefferson: The Tumultuous Election of 1800* (New York: Oxford University Press, 2004), 183. In his "initial pronouncement," Burr "seemed to accept Jefferson's presidency." But he took that position "prior to the final disclosure of the electoral college balloting," when "he believed the Virginian had won the election."

262. See, e.g., David W. Abbott and James P. Levine, *Wrong Winner: The Coming Debacle in the Electoral College* (Westport, CT: Praeger, 1991), 11; "Rethinking the Electoral College Debate: The Framers, Federalism, and One Person, One Vote," *Harvard Law Review* 114, no. 8 (June, 2001): 2528.

263. See Department of State, *Documentary History of the Constitution of the United States of America*, vol. 5 (1905), 256. The book mistakenly indicates that Hamilton addressed the letter to New York senator Gouvernor Morris. In fact, it was addressed to Delaware congressman James A. Bayard. See Alexander Hamilton to James A. Bayard, Washington, DC, April 6, 1802, Founders Online, National Archives, founders.archives.gov/documents/Hamilton/01-25-02-0315. Original source: *The Papers of Alexander Hamilton*, vol. 25, *July 1800–April 1802*, ed. Harold C. Syrett (New York: Columbia University Press, 1977), 600–601. See Draft of a Resolution for the Legislature of New York for the Amendment of the Constitution of the United States, January 29, 1802, Founders Online, National Archives, founders.archives.gov/documents/Hamilton/01-25-02-0289. Original source: *The Papers of Alexander Hamilton*, vol. 25, 512–13.

264. See Donald Lutz, Philip Abbott, Barbara Allen, and Russell Hansen, "The Electoral College in Historical and Philosophical Perspective," in *Choosing a President: The Electoral College and Beyond*, ed. Paul D. Schumaker and Burdett Loomis (New York: Seven Bridges Press, 2002), 37.

265. 13 *Annals of Congress*, 209, 775–76 (1803). The vote was 22–10 in the Senate, and 83–42 in the House.

266. The Senate retains the power to select the vice president in the event of a tie for that race, deciding between the top two candidates.

267. The Twentieth Amendment adjusted this last provision, changing it from the outgoing vice president to the incoming one. U.S. Constitution, Amend. XX.

268. The Democratic-Republican candidates won every electoral vote in fourteen states. In another, Maryland, they won 9 of 11. "Electoral Votes for President and Vice President 1789–1821," *Historical Election Results*, National Archives, www.archives.gov/federal-register/electoral-college/votes/1789_1821.html.

269. "Electoral Votes for President and Vice President 1789–1821."

270. See Victor Williams and Alison M. MacDonald, "Rethinking Article II, Section 1 and its Twelfth Amendment Restatement: Challenging our Nation's Malapportioned Undemocratic Presidential Election Systems," *Marquette Law Review* 77, no. 2 (Winter 1994): 217–19.

271. See chapter 3.

272. See Spencer Overton, *Stealing Democracy: The New Politics of Voter Suppression* (New York: Norton, 2007), 28–32.

273. Gideon M. Hart, "The 'Original' Thirteenth Amendment: The Misunderstood Titles of Nobility Amendment," *Marquette Law Review* 94 (October 2010): 316. "Responding to this great foreign pressure, individuals on both sides of the political spectrum became increasingly suspicious of each other's loyalties, as both parties regularly accused the other of secret collusion and cooperation with foreign states." See also Hart, pp. 336–37, 343–46.

274. Notably, the proposed Titles of Nobility Amendment—unlike the Emoluments Clause—contains the word *emperor*. This lends support to the theory that the Congress was concerned about Napoléon when drafting the proposal. Curt E. Conklin, "The Case of the Phantom Thirteenth Amendment: A Historical and Bibliographic Nightmare," *Law Library Journal* 88, no. 1 (Winter 1996): 124; Jol A. Silversmith, "The 'Missing Thirteenth Amendment': Constitutional Nonsense and Titles of Nobility," *Southern California Interdisciplinary Law Journal* 8, no. 2 (1999): 584 n44; Hart, "The 'Original' Thirteenth Amendment," 338–39, 346–47.

275. Norman L. Eisen, Richard Painter and Lawrence Tribe, *The Emoluments Clause: Its Text, Meaning and Application to Donald J. Trump* (Washington, DC: Governance Studies at Brookings Institution, December 16, 2016), www.brookings.edu/wp-content/uploads/2016/12/gs_121616_emoluments-clause1.pdf.

276. U.S. Constitution, Art. I, Sec. 9.

277. Silversmith, "The 'Missing Thirteenth Amendment,'" 578.

278. The Senate approved the amendment on April 27, 1810, by a vote of 19–5. See 21 *Annals of Congress*, 672 (1810). The House followed suit on May 1, 1810, by a vote of 87–3. *Annals*, 2050–51.

279. While it provides no further insight, there was a notable voting pattern in Congress. In the House, three members voted against the Titles of Nobility Amendment, two from Tennessee and one from New York. 21 *Annals of Congress*, 2051 (1810). Likewise, New York and Tennessee's senators accounted for three of five votes casted against the proposal in the upper chamber. *Senate Journal*, 11th Congress, 2nd Sess. 506 (1810).

280. See generally Hart, "The 'Original' Thirteenth Amendment," 311–71; Silversmith, "The 'Missing Thirteenth Amendment,'" 577–612; Conklin, "The Case of the Phantom Thirteenth Amendment," 121–27.

281. See, e.g., Articles of Confederation, Art. VI, para. 1 (U.S. 1781): "[N]or shall any person holding any office of profit or trust under the United States, or any of them, accept any

present, emolument, office or title of any kind whatever from any King, Prince or foreign State; nor shall the United States in Congress assembled, or any of them, grant any title of nobility." Also: John Jay to George Washington, New York, July 25, 1787, Founders Online, National Archives, founders.archives.gov/documents/Washington/04-05-02-0251. Original source: *The Papers of George Washington*, Confederation Series, vol. 5, *1 February 1787-31 December 1787*, ed. W. W. Abbot (Charlottesville: University Press of Virginia, 1997), 271-72: "Permit me to hint, whether it would not be wise & seasonable to provide a strong check to the admission of Foreigners into the administration of our national Government, and to declare expressly that the Command in chief of the [A]merican army shall not be given to, nor devolved on, any but a natural born Citizen." Also: Alexander Hamilton, *Federalist* no. 84, Avalon Project, avalon. law.yale.edu/18th_century/fed84.asp: "Nothing need be said to illustrate the importance of the prohibition of titles of nobility. This may truly be denominated the corner-stone of republican government; for so long as they are excluded, there can never be serious danger that the government will be any other than that of the people." State ratifying conventions raised similar concerns, as reflected in their ratifying instruments. See, e.g., Ratification of the Constitution by the State of Massachusetts, February 6, 1788: "The Convention do therefore recommend that . . . Congress shall at no time consent that any person holding an office of trust or profit under the United States shall accept of a title of Nobility or any other title or office from any King, prince or Foreign State." Also: Ratification of the Constitution by the State of New York, July 26, 1788, recommending "[t]hat the words without the Consent of the Congress in the seventh Clause of the ninth Section of the first Article of the Constitution, be expunged." *DHRC* digital edition. New Hampshire and Rhode Island made similar recommendations. See also U.S. Constitution, Art. I, Sec. 9, cl. 8, the Emoluments Clause; U.S. Constitution, Art. I, Sec. 10, cl. 1, prohibiting states from "grant[ing] any title of nobility." See, e.g., *Senate Journal*, 1st Congress, 1st Sess. 73, 96-97 (1789), for Congress considering such a provision during its first session.

282. Hart, "The 'Original' Thirteenth Amendment," 315-16.

283. Silversmith, "The 'Missing Thirteenth Amendment,'" 584.

284. The editor noted that "[t]here ha[d] been some difficulty in ascertaining whether the amendment proposed, which is stated as the thirteenth . . . has, or has not, been adopted by a sufficient number of state legislatures. . . ." He therefore made a judgment call "to publish the proposed amendment in its proper place, as if it had been adopted, with this explanation to prevent misconception." Hart, "The 'Original' Thirteenth Amendment," 363, citing *Laws of the United States of America, 1789-1815*, vol. 1, ed. John Bioren and W. John Duane (Philadelphia, 1815), ix.

285. See Silversmith, "The 'Missing Thirteenth Amendment,'" 590-91; Vile, *Encyclopedia of Constitutional Amendments*, vol. 2, 483-84.

286. Jerry Adler, "The Move to 'Restore' the 13th Amendment," *Newsweek*, July 26, 2010; Erik Hayden, "Iowa Republicans' Bizarre Plan to Strip Obama's Nobel Prize," *The Atlantic*, July 28, 2010.

287. *Marbury v. Madison*, 5 U.S. 137 (1803).

288. Act of February 13, 1801, An Act to Provide for the More Convenient Organization of the Courts of the United States, ch. 4, 2 Stat. 89; Act of February 27, 1801, An Act Concerning the District of Columbia, ch. 15, sec. 11, 2 Stat. 107.

289. In that same lame-duck session, Adams and his Federalist allies in Congress also passed the Judiciary Act of 1801, which allowed the outgoing president to appoint sixteen new circuit judges. See Kathryn Turner, "The Midnight Judges," *University of Pennsylvania Law Review* 109, no. 4 (1961): 494.

290. Jean Edward Smith, *John Marshall: Definer of a Nation* (New York: Henry Holt, 1996), 300.

291. Smith, *John Marshall*, 279-80.

292. *Marbury v. Madison*, 5 U.S. 137, 177 (1803).

293. See Smith, *John Marshall*, 323–24.

294. The Supreme Court first exercised judicial review of a statute in 1796 in the case of *Hylton v. United States*, upholding a federal tax on carriages. 3 U.S. 171 (1796).

295. See Smith, *John Marshall*, 323.

296. Alexander Hamilton, *Federalist* no. 78, Avalon Project, avalon.law.yale.edu/18th_century /fed78.asp.

297. *McCulloch v. Maryland*, 17 U.S. 316 (1819).

298. 2 *Annals of Congress*, 1944–51.

299. James Madison, *Federalist* no. 44, Avalon Project, avalon.law.yale.edu/18th_century /fed44.asp. See Ron Chernow, *Alexander Hamilton* (New York: Penguin Press, 2004), 350.

300. Chernow, *Alexander Hamilton*, 350.

301. 2 *Annals of Congress*, 1945–46.

302. Chernow, *Alexander Hamilton*, 352–54.

303. Daniel A. Farber, "The Story of *McCulloch*: Banking on National Power," *Constitutional Commentary* 20, no. 3 (Winter 2003): 682–89.

304. *McCulloch v. Maryland*, 17 U.S. 316 (1819); Farber, "Story of *McCulloch*," 682–89.

305. Farber, "Story of *McCulloch*," 682–89; Jennifer Mason McAward, "*McCulloch* and the Thirteenth Amendment," *Columbia Law Review* 112, no. 7 (November 2012): 1775. Opinion of Alexander Hamilton, Final Version of an Opinion on the Constitutionality of an Act to Establish a Bank, February 23, 1791, Founders Online, National Archives, founders.archives.gov/ documents/Hamilton/01-08-02-0060-0003. Original source: *The Papers of Alexander Hamilton*, vol. 8, *February 1791–July 1791*, ed. Harold C. Syrett (New York: Columbia University Press, 1965), 97–134. "Th[e] restrictive interpretation of the word *necessary* is also contrary to this sound maxim of construction namely, that the powers contained in a constitution of government, especially those which concern the general administration of the affairs of a country, its finances, trade, defence &c ought to be construed liberally, in advancement of the public good." Compare with Thomas Jefferson, Opinion on the Constitutionality of the Bill for Establishing a National Bank, February 15, 1791, Founders Online, National Archives, founders.archives.gov /documents/Jefferson/01-19-02-0051. Original source: *The Papers of Thomas Jefferson*, vol. 19, *24 January–31 March 1791*, ed. Julian P. Boyd (Princeton, NJ: Princeton University Press, 1974), 275–82. "Perhaps indeed bank bills may be a more *convenient* vehicle than treasury orders. But a little *difference* in the degree of *convenience*, cannot constitute the necessity which the constitution makes the ground for assuming any non-enumerated power." And with: James Madison to George Washington, February 21, 1791, Founders Online, National Archives, founders.archives .gov/documents/Washington/05-07-02-0232. Original source: *The Papers of George Washington*, Presidential Series, vol. 7, *1 December 1790–21 March 1791*, ed. Jack D. Warren Jr. (Charlottesville: University Press of Virginia, 1998), 395–97. Washington objects to the Bank of the United States "because it is an essential principle of the Government that powers not delegated by the Constitution cannot be rightfully exercised," and "the power" to establish the Bank "is not expressly delegated" to Congress.

306. *McCulloch v. Maryland*, 17 U.S. 316, 406 (1819).

307. *McCulloch*, 406–8.

308. *McCulloch*, 421.

Chapter 3: The Reconstruction Era Amendments (1865–1870)

1. Max Farrand, ed., *The Records of the Federal Convention of 1787*, vol. 2, (New Haven, CT: Yale University Press, 1911), 417 (hereafter Farrand, *Records*).

2. Frederick Douglass, "The Constitution and Slavery," *North Star*, March 16, 1849.

3. See Annette Gordon-Reed, "America's Original Sin: Slavery and the Legacy of White Supremacy," *Foreign Affairs*, January–February 2018.

4. U.S. Constitution, Art. I, Sec. 2, cl. 3.

5. See, e.g., Russel B. Nye, "The Slave Power Conspiracy: 1830–1860," *Science & Society* 10, no. 3 (Summer 1946): 262–74; Akhil Amar, "Did the Fourteenth Amendment Incorporate the Bill of Rights Against States?" *Harvard Journal of Law and Public Policy* 19 (1996): 443, discussing the Fourteenth Amendment as incorporating the Bill of Rights, the principles of which were ignored for decades in the promotion of slavery, the Slave Power, and the Slaveocracy; Akhil Amar, "The Inaugural Abraham Lincoln Lecture on Constitutional Law: Electoral College Reform, Lincoln Style," *Northwestern University Law Review* 112 (2017): 63–72, arguing that "the Electoral College had been intentionally engineered in 1787–88 and purposefully redesigned in 1803–04 to bolster the slaveholding South. . . ."

6. U.S. Constitution, Art. I, Sec. 9.

7. U.S. Constitution, Art. V. In a related provision, no amendment was permitted to the fourth paragraph of Article I, Section 9, which set out the rule that capitation or other direct taxes (which included taxes on slaves) are to be apportioned among the states according to the census.

8. Farrand, *Records*, vol. 2, 373.

9. "Trans-Atlantic Slave Trade Database," Slave Voyages, www.slavevoyages.org/voyage /database.

10. U.S. Constitution, Art. IV, Sec. 2, cl. 3.

11. Thomas D. Morris, *Free Men All: The Personal Liberty Laws of the North, 1780—1861* (Clark, NJ: Lawbook Exchange, 2001), 219–22.

12. An Act to Amend, and Supplementary to, the Act Entitled "An Act Respecting Fugitives from Justice, and Persons Escaping from the Service of Their Masters," Approved February Twelfth, One Thousand Seven Hundred and Ninety Three (commonly known as the Fugitive Slave Act of 1850), 9 Stat. 462 (1850).

13. Farrand, *Records*, vol. 2, 371.

14. See Victor Rabinowitz, "Is Stability an Unmitigated Good? The Constitution and Radical Change," in *A Less than Perfect Union: Alternative Perspectives on the U.S. Constitution*, ed. Jules Lobel (New York: Monthly Review Press, 1988), 27, estimating between $1.4 and $2.8 billion; Roger Ransom and Richard Sutch, "Capitalists Without Capital: The Burden of Slavery and the Impact of Emancipation," *Agricultural History* 62, no. 3, *Quantitative Studies in Agrarian History* (Summer 1988): 133–60, estimating around $3 billion); Economic History Association, "Slavery in the United States," eh.net/encyclopedia/slavery-in-the-united-states, estimating between $3.1 and $3.6 billion. A different monetary estimate by Samuel H. Williamson and Louis P. Cain looks at the total wealth held in slaves from 1806 to 1865. They find that "while it varies with the price of slaves . . . it is never less than six trillion 2016 dollars, and, at the time of Emancipation, was close to thirteen trillion 2016 dollars." This is approximately equivalent to $420 billion in 1860, far higher than the total market value of the industry. Dr. Samuel H. Williamson & Dr. Louis P. Cain, "Measuring Slavery in 2016 Dollars," Measuring Worth, www .measuringworth.com/slavery.php.

15. Farrand, *Records*, vol. 1, 486.

16. An Act to Authorize the People of the Missouri Territory to Form a Constitution and State Government, and for the Admission of Such State into the Union on an Equal Footing with the Original States, and to Prohibit Slavery in Certain Territories ("the Missouri Compromise"), 3 Stat. 545 (1820).

17. *Congressional Globe*, 29th Congress, 1st Sess. 1217 (1846).

18. Eric Foner, "The Wilmot Proviso Revisited," *Journal of American History* 56, no. 2 (September 1969): 262.

19. Vermont, Massachusetts, and New Hampshire provided for immediate abolition through their state constitutions, while Pennsylvania, Connecticut, Rhode Island, New York, and New Jersey provided only for a gradual end to the practice through laws passed by their state legislatures. Vermont Constitution of 1777, Ch. 1, Sec. 1; An Act for the Gradual Abolition of Slavery, 1780 Pa. Laws 282; *Commonwealth v. Jennison* (Massachusetts, 1783, unreported), in which the

Court interpreted the Massachusetts Declaration of Rights as a basis for outlawing slavery; New Hampshire Constitution of 1783, Art. 1; An Act Concerning Indian, Molatto, and Negro Servants and Slaves, 1784 Conn. Pub. Acts. 233; An Act Authorizing the Manumission of Negroes Mulattoes and Others, and for the Gradual Abolition of Slavery, 1784 R.I. Pub. Laws 6; An Act for the gradual abolition of slavery, 1799 N.Y. Laws 388; An Act for the Gradual Abolition of Slavery, 1804 N.J. Laws 251.

20. Adam Chamberlain, "From Pressure Group to Political Party: The Case of the American Anti-Slavery Society and the Liberty Party," *Social Sciences Quarterly* 99, no. 1 (March 2018): 246–61.

21. Edward L. Rubin, "Passing Through the Door; Social Movement Literature and Legal Scholarship," *University of Pennsylvania Law Review* 150, no. 1 (November 2001): 66.

22. Constitution of the American Anti-Slavery Society, December 1833.

23. George A. Levesque, "Black Abolitionists in the Age of Jackson: Catalysts in the Radicalization of American Abolitionism," *Journal of Black Studies* 1, no. 2 (December 1970): 188–89.

24. Levesque, "Black Abolitionists," 191.

25. Levesque, "Black Abolitionists," 197–98.

26. David Herbert Donald, *Charles Sumner and the Coming of the Civil War* (Naperville, IL: Sourcebooks, 2009), 162.

27. Daniel W. Crofts, *Lincoln and the Politics of Slavery: The Other Thirteenth Amendment and the Struggle to Save the Union* (Chapel Hill: University of North Carolina Press, 2016), 30.

28. Douglass, "Constitution and Slavery," *North Star*, March 16, 1849.

29. *Congressional Globe*, 31st Congress, 1st Sess. App. 115–27 (1850).

30. James D. Richardson, ed., *A Compilation of the Messages and Papers of the Presidents, 1789–1902*, vol. 5, (New York: GPO, 1907), 93.

31. An Act to Organize the Territories of Nebraska and Kansas ("Kansas-Nebraska Act"), 10 Stat. 277 (1854).

32. Crofts, *Lincoln and the Politics of Slavery*, 49.

33. Kansas-Nebraska Act, 10 Stat. 277 (1854), 283, 289.

34. Kansas entered the Union as a free state on January 29, 1861, shortly before the onset of war.

35. Charles Sumner, *The Crime Against Kansas. The Apologies for the Crime. The True Remedy. Speech of Hon. Charles Sumner in the Senate of the United States* (Boston: John P. Jewett, 1856), 5, 9; Isaac Bassett, "Caning of Sumner," A Senate Memoir, United States Senate Art and History, https://web.archive.org/web/20200823132122/www.senate.gov/artandhistory/art/special/Bassett/tdetail.cfm?id=17.

36. Douglass, "Constitution and Slavery," *North Star*, March 16, 1849.

37. *The Liberator*, July 7, 1854.

38. *Dred Scott v. Sandford*, 60 U.S. 393, 406 (1857).

39. *Dred Scott*, 404, 407.

40. *Dred Scott*, 525.

41. *Congressional Globe*, 38th Congress, 2nd Sess. 1013 (1865).

42. U.S. Census Bureau, "Immigration," *1860 Census* (1860), Introduction, xxviii.

43. U.S. Census Bureau, "Principal Cities and Towns; Native and Foreign Population," *1860 Census* (1860), Introduction, xxxi.

44. U.S. Census Bureau, "Occupation of Passengers Arriving in the United States from Foreign Countries During the Forty-One Years, Ending with 1860," *1860 Census* (1860), Introduction, xxi–xxii.

45. U.S. Census Bureau, *1860 Census* (1860), Introduction, vii.

46. See Eric H. Walther, "The Fire-Eaters and ~~Seward~~ Lincoln," *Journal of the Abraham Lincoln Association* 32, no. 1 (Winter 2011): 18–32; Jeff Wallenfeldt, "How the *Dred Scott* Decision Affected the U.S. Election of 1860," *Encyclopedia Britannica*, Demystified, www.britannica.com/story/how-the-dred-scott-decision-affected-the-us-election-of-1860.

47. David E. Kyvig, *Explicit and Authentic Acts: Amending the U.S. Constitution, 1776–1995* (Lawrence: University Press of Kansas, 1996), 146.

48. *Congressional Globe*, 36th Congress, 2nd Sess. 112–14 (1860). See also Allan Nevins, *The Emergence of Lincoln: Prologue to Civil War 1859–1861* (New York: Scribner's, 1950), 391. The Crittenden Compromise also included resolutions related to enforcement of the Fugitive Slave Act and repeal of state personal liberty laws.

49. "The Crittenden Compromise," United States Senate Art and History, www.senate.gov /artandhistory/history/minute/Crittenden_Compromise.htm.

50. Nevins, *Emergence of Lincoln*, 405–10; Crofts, *Lincoln and the Politics of Slavery*, 130.

51. Nevins, *Emergence of Lincoln*, 406–7.

52. *Congressional Globe*, 36th Congress, 2nd Sess. 378 (1861).

53. Frederic Bancroft, "The Final Efforts at Compromise, 1860–61," *Political Science Quarterly* 6, no. 3 (September 1891): 410–11; Crofts, *Lincoln and the Politics of Slavery*, 139.

54. Crofts, *Lincoln and the Politics of Slavery*, 139–40.

55. Nevins, *Emergence of Lincoln*, 411; Adam Goodheart, "The Ashen Ruin," *New York Times*, February 15, 2011, opinionator.blogs.nytimes.com/2011/02/15/the-ashen-ruin.

56. Those not present were the seven Southern states that had already seceded, along with Arkansas, Michigan, Minnesota, Wisconsin, Oregon, and California. Robert G. Gunderson, "The Washington Peace Conference of 1861: Selection of Delegates," *Journal of Southern History* 24, no. 3 (August 1958): 359; Peace Conference Resolution of the Virginia General Assembly, 1861 Va. Acts 24–27, 337–39.

57. "Proceedings of the Peace Conference.; Speech of Ex-President Tyler," *New York Times*, February 6, 1861.

58. "The Compromise Convention," *New-York Tribune*, February 6, 1861, citing the *New York Herald*; Goodheart, "Ashen Ruin."

59. "Money-Changers' Threats: Gov. Chase and Mr. Collamer on a National Convention— Position of Republicans at Washington," *New-York Tribune*, February 12, 1861.

60. Harold Holzer, *Lincoln President-Elect: Abraham Lincoln and the Great Secession Winter 1860–1861* (New York: Simon & Schuster, 2008), 321 (statement of Amos Tuck, friend of Abraham Lincoln).

61. "The Peace Conference," *Macon Daily Telegraph*, February 28, 1861.

62. "Amendments Proposed by the Peace Conference, February 8–27, 1861," Avalon Project, avalon.law.yale.edu/19th_century/peace.asp.

63. The plan was rejected by a vote of 28–7. *Congressional Globe*, 36th Congress, 2nd Sess. 1404–5 (1861).

64. Goodheart, "Ashen Ruin."

65. While Texas had already seceded, it was not represented at the convention. Nevins, *Emergence of Lincoln*, 433.

66. Nevins, *Emergence of Lincoln*, 434.

67. Nevins, *Emergence of Lincoln*, 434–35.

68. "Constitution of the Confederate States; March 11, 1861," Avalon Project, avalon.law.yale .edu/19th_century/csa_csa.asp.

69. "Constitution of the Confederate States; March 11, 1861."

70. Nevins, *Emergence of Lincoln*, 435.

71. *Congressional Globe*, 36th Congress, 2nd Sess. 1333 (1861).

72. *Congressional Globe*, 36th Congress, 2nd Sess. 1333 (1861). See Bancroft, "Final Efforts at Compromise, 1860–1861," 417.

73. Horatio Bateman, *Biographies of Two Hundred and Fifty Distinguished National Men* (New York: John T. Giles, 1871), 80.

74. Crofts, *Lincoln and the Politics of Slavery*, 213.

75. Crofts, *Lincoln and the Politics of Slavery*, 139.

76. Crofts, *Lincoln and the Politics of Slavery*, 212–13, 230, 232.

77. Crofts, *Lincoln and the Politics of Slavery*, 120, 213.

78. *Congressional Globe*, 36th Congress, 2nd Sess. 1236 (1861).

79. Crofts, *Lincoln and the Politics of Slavery*, 230.

80. *Congressional Globe*, 36th Congress, 2nd Sess. 1234 (1861).

81. Crofts, *Lincoln and the Politics of Slavery*, 214.

82. *Congressional Globe*, 36th Congress, 2nd Sess. 1285 (1861); Crofts, *Lincoln and the Politics of Slavery*, 215–16, 219.

83. Crofts, *Lincoln and the Politics of Slavery*, 224.

84. "Two Nights in the Senate," *Harper's Weekly*, March 16, 1861.

85. "Two Nights in the Senate."

86. *Congressional Globe*, 36th Congress, 2nd Sess. 1403 (1861). The *Congressional Globe* does not indicate the correct date during the later part of these debates. Despite the fact that the Corwin Amendment was passed the morning of Lincoln's Inauguration (March 4, 1860), the Globe lists the vote as having taken place two days prior (March 2, 1860).

87. Crofts, *Lincoln and the Politics of Slavery*, 231.

88. Abraham Lincoln, Inaugural Address, Washington, DC, March 4, 1861, American Presidency Project, www.presidency.ucsb.edu/node/202167.

89. Frederick Douglass, "The Inaugural Address," *Douglass' Monthly*, April 1861.

90. "The Border States in the Present Crisis, Dark Clouds over the Future," *New York Herald*, March 2, 1861.

91. "The Proposed Amendment to the Constitution," *New York Times*, March 16, 1861.

92. Kentucky ratified the Corwin Amendment in April 1861, followed by Ohio and Rhode Island in May. Maryland ratified it in January 1862. In addition, there were two irregular "ratifications." In February 1862, the provisional government of West Virginia voted to ratify. That same month, a constitutional convention in Illinois also purported to do so. The Illinois legislature appears to have later ratified the amendment in June 1863. Crofts, *Lincoln and the Politics of Slavery*, 246–52.

93. Abraham Lincoln to Horace Greeley, Washington, DC, August 22, 1862, in *The Collected Works of Abraham Lincoln*, vol. 5, ed. Roy P. Basler (New Brunswick, NJ: Rutgers University Press, 1953), 389.

94. *Congressional Globe*, 37th Congress, 2nd Sess. 1142 (1862).

95. An Act for the Release of Certain Persons Held to Service or Labor in the District of Columbia ("District of Columbia Compensated Emancipation Act"), 12 Stat. 376 (1862); An Act to Secure Freedom to All Persons Within the Territories of the United States, 12 Stat. 432 (1862). See also *Congressional Globe*, 38th Congress, 1st Sess. 1313 (1864), statement of Senator Trumbull on Lincoln's wartime measures.

96. Abraham Lincoln, "Declaring the Objectives of the War Including Emancipation of Slaves in Rebellious States on January 1, 1863," proclamation, September 22, 1862, American Presidency Project, www.presidency.ucsb.edu/node/202404.

97. Abraham Lincoln, "Regarding the Status of Slaves in States Engaged in Rebellion Against the United States," Emancipation Proclamation, January 1, 1863, American Presidency Project, www.presidency.ucsb.edu/node/203073.

98. Abraham Lincoln, Second Annual Message, December 1, 1861, American Presidency Project, www.presidency.ucsb.edu/node/202180.

99. Eric Foner, *The Fiery Trial: Abraham Lincoln and American Slavery* (New York: Norton, 2010), 167.

100. Thavolia Glymph, "Noncombatant Military Laborers in the Civil War," Organization of American Historians, *OAH Magazine of History* 26, no. 2 (April 2012): 25–29.

101. Rick Beard, "When Douglass Met Lincoln," *New York Times*, August 9, 2013, opinionator.blogs.nytimes.com/2013/08/09/when-douglass-met-lincoln. Months later, alongside their

discussions in earnest about abolition, Congress was also debating pay equalization. See, e.g., *Congressional Globe*, 38th Congress, 1st Sess. 466 (1864).

102. Foner, *Fiery Trial*, 253; "Lincoln's Evolving Thoughts on Slavery, and Freedom," National Public Radio, October 11, 2010, www.npr.org/2010/10/11/130489804/lincolns-evolving -thoughts-on-slavery-and-freedom.

103. Frederick Douglass, Introduction, *Duplicate Copy of the Souvenir from the Afro-American League of Tennessee to Hon. James M. Ashley of Ohio*, ed. Benjamin Arnett, African Methodist Episcopal Church (Philadelphia: Publishing House of the AME Church, 1894), 3.

104. *Congressional Globe*, 38th Congress, 1st Sess. 19 (1863). Arthur Livermore (in 1818) and John Quincy Adams (in 1839) had proposed measures of partial abolition (e.g., disallowing slavery in new states and territories). 32 *Annals of Congress*, 1675 (1818); *Congressional Globe*, 25th Congress, 3rd Sess. 205 (1839). Iowa's James F. Wilson, the House Judiciary Committee chair, introduced an abolition proposal shortly after Ashley, which also influenced the Thirteenth Amendment. *Congressional Globe*, 38th Congress, 1st Sess. 21 (1863).

105. *Congressional Globe*, 38th Congress, 1st Sess. 145 (1864).

106. Ava DuVernay, director, *13th* (Los Gatos, CA: Netflix, 2016). See also Taja-Nia Henderson, "The Ironic Promise of the Thirteenth Amendment for Offender Anti-Discrimination Law," *Lewis & Clark Law Review* 17, no. 4 (2013): 1141–89.

107. Jamal Greene, "The Thirteenth Amendment and the Constitutional Imagination," National Constitution Center, Interpretive Constitution, www.constitutioncenter.org/interactive-constitution/interpretation/amendment-xiii/interps/137; U.S. Constitution, Art. I, Sec. 8.

108. This enabling language is found in the Fourteenth, Fifteenth, Eighteenth, Nineteenth, Twenty-Third, Twenty-Fourth, and Twenty-Sixth Amendments. See Akhil Amar, *America's Constitution: A Biography* (New York: Random House, 2005), 361.

109. *Congressional Globe*, 38th Congress, 1st Sess. 1313 (1864).

110. *Congressional Globe*, 38th Congress, 1st Sess. 1313 (1864).

111. *Congressional Globe*, 38th Congress, 1st Sess. 1314 (1864).

112. *Congressional Globe*, 38th Congress, 1st Sess. 1319 (1864).

113. *Congressional Globe*, 38th Congress, 1st Sess. 1323 (1864)

114. *Congressional Globe*, 38th Congress, 1st Sess. 1439 (1864).

115. *Congressional Globe*, 38th Congress, 1st Sess. 1440 (1864).

116. Ben C. Truman, "In the Convivial Days of Old," in *Overland Monthly*, vol. 55 (San Francisco: Overland Monthly, 1910), 318; Daniel Rolph, "The Real Conflicts in Government: Canes, Guns, and Fisticuffs in the Halls of Congress," Historical Society of Pennsylvania, February 6, 2013, hsp.org/blogs/hidden-histories/the-real-conflicts-in-government-canes-guns -and-fisticuffs-in-the-halls-of-congress.

117. *Congressional Globe*, 38th Congress, 1st Sess. 1364–65 (1864).

118. *Congressional Globe*, 38th Congress, 1st Sess. 1365 (1864).

119. *Congressional Globe*, 38th Congress, 1st Sess. 1366–67 (1864).

120. *Congressional Globe*, 38th Congress, 1st Sess. 1365 (1864).

121. *Congressional Globe*, 38th Congress, 1st Sess. 1367–68 (1864).

122. *Congressional Globe*, 38th Congress, 1st Sess. 1367 (1864).

123. *Congressional Globe*, 38th Congress, 1st Sess. 1457 (1864).

124. *Congressional Globe*, 38th Congress, 1st Sess. 1484 (1864).

125. *Congressional Globe*, 38th Congress, 1st Sess. 1370, 1424 (1864).

126. *Congressional Globe*, 38th Congress, 1st Sess. 1425 (1864).

127. *Congressional Globe*, 38th Congress, 1st Sess. 1480 (1864).

128. *Congressional Globe*, 38th Congress, 1st Sess. 521 (1864).

129. *Congressional Globe*, 38th Congress, 1st Sess. 1490 (1864).

130. *Congressional Globe*, 38th Congress, 1st Sess. 1490 (1864).

131. *Congressional Globe*, 38th Congress, 1st Sess. 1199 (1864).

132. *Congressional Globe*, 38th Congress, 1st Sess. 2995 (1864).

133. Rebecca E. Zietlow, *The Forgotten Emancipator* (New York: Cambridge University Press, 2018), 117.

134. *Congressional Globe*, 38th Congress, 1st Sess. 2992 (1864).

135. *Congressional Globe*, 38th Congress, 1st Sess. 2992 (1864).

136. *Congressional Globe*, 38th Congress, 1st Sess. 2993 (1864).

137. "Republican Party Platform of 1864," June 7, 1864, American Presidency Project, www.presidency.ucsb.edu/node/273298.

138. Biographical Directory of the United States Congress 1774–Present, U.S. Congress, bioguide.congress.gov/biosearch/biosearch.asp.

139. *Congressional Globe*, 38th Congress, 1st Sess. 2995 (1864).

140. Zietlow, *Forgotten Emancipator*, 120–22.

141. *Congressional Globe*, 38th Congress, 2nd Sess. 141 (1865).

142. *Congressional Globe*, 38th Congress, 2nd Sess. 531 (1865).

143. *Congressional Globe*, 38th Congress, 2nd Sess. 530 (1865).

144. *Congressional Globe*, 38th Congress, 2nd Sess. 531 (1865).

145. *Congressional Globe*, 38th Congress, 2nd Sess. 531 (1865).

146. "The Dawning of Jubilee. The Day of Doom to Man Selling," *Chicago Tribune*, February 1, 1865.

147. "The Consummation: Slavery Forever Dead in the United States," *New York Times*, December 19, 1865.

148. "The Work Accomplished," *New York Times*, December 19, 1865.

149. "Death of Gov. Corwin," *New York Times*, December 19, 1865.

150. See Alan P. Grimes, *Democracy and the Amendments to the Constitution* (Lanham, MD: Lexington Books, 1978), 41.

151. Jennifer Mason McAward, "The Thirteenth Amendment: A Constitutional Success Story," National Constitution Center Interpretive Constitution, www.constitutioncenter.org/interactive-constitution/interpretation/amendment-xiii/interps/137.

152. See Tiya Miles, "The South Doesn't Own Slavery," *New York Times*, September 11, 2017.

153. Frederick Douglass, "The Constitution of the United States: Is It Pro-Slavery or Antislavery," Speech, Glasgow, Scotland, March 26, 1860, in *Frederick Douglass: Selected Speeches and Writings*, ed. Phillip S. Foner and Yuval Taylor (Chicago: Chicago Review Press, 2000), 379–90.

154. Julie Roy Jeffrey, "The Dissolution of the Antislavery Societies," in *Abolitionists Remember: Antislavery Autobiographies and the Unfinished Work of Emancipation* (Chapel Hill: University of North Carolina Press, 2008), 11–12.

155. Eric Foner, *The Second Founding* (New York: Norton, 2019), 52–53.

156. William D. Forten, "An Address and Resolutions," in *Proceedings of the First Annual Meeting of the National Equal Rights League Held in Cleveland Ohio, October 19th, 20th and 21st, 1865* (Philadelphia: E. C. Markley & Son, 1865), 42, coloredconventions.org/items/show/562.

157. Forten, "An Address and Resolutions," 39.

158. "Another Black Code that existed in Alabama that was established in 1866 was known as 'The Act to define the relative duties of master and apprentice.' . . . [T]he act stated that if the apprentice was to leave the employment of their master without the consent of the master then the master had the right to capture the apprentice, and bring them back. If the apprentice refuses to return to their place of employment then the apprentice would be given a trial, and if found guilty would be subject to the penalties established under the vagrant laws." *Changes in Law and Society During the Civil War and Reconstruction*, ed. Christian G. Samito (Carbondale: Southern Illinois University Press, 2009): 189–92; An Act to Define the Relative Duties of Master and Apprentice, 1865–1866 Ala. Laws 128–31. See also *Congressional Globe*, 39th Congress, 1st Sess. 474 (1866): Senator Trumbull discussing a Mississippi statute that punished Black people who

entered the state "for the purposes of residing there" with slavery, and those traveling within the state between counties "without having a pass or certificate" with imprisonment.

159. An Act Concerning Negroes and Persons of Color or of Mixed Blood, Sec. 7, 1866 N.C. Sess. Laws 101.

160. An Act to Amend an Act entitled an Act to Establish a Code of Criminal Procedure for the State of Texas, Approved August 26th, 1866, and to Repeal Certain Portions Thereof, Sec. 1, 1866 Tex. Gen. Laws 59.

161. An Act to Punish Vagrants and Vagabonds, 1865 Fla. Laws 28.

162. W.E.B. Du Bois, "Reconstruction and its Benefits," *American Historical Review* 15, no. 4 (July 1910): 784. In drafting the state's labor laws, South Carolina's legislature did not even feign compliance with the Thirteenth Amendment, referring to "All persons of color who make contracts for service or labor . . . as servants, and those with whom they contract, . . . masters." An Act to Establish and Regulate the Domestic Relations of Persons of Colour, and to Amend the Law in Relation to Paupers and Vagrancy, Sec. 35, 1864–1865 S.C. Acts 291–304, 295.

163. *Congressional Globe*, 39th Congress, 1st Sess. 322–23 (1866), statement of Senator Trumbull. See Barry Sullivan, "Historical Reconstruction, Reconstruction History, and the Proper Scope of Section 1981," *Yale Law Journal* 98, no. 3 (1989): 549.

164. *Congressional Globe*, 39th Congress, 1st Sess. 322–23 (1866), statement of Senator Trumbull.

165. James F. Wilson, also known as "Jefferson Jim," is not to be confused with James "Tama Jim" Wilson, referenced previously in this chapter. Both were prominent Iowa Republicans serving in Congress during Reconstruction. Their nicknames refer to the counties they represented.

166. *Congressional Globe*, 39th Congress, 1st Sess. 1118 (1866).

167. An Act to Protect All Persons in the United States in their Civil Rights, and Furnish the Means of their Vindication (hereafter Civil Rights Act of 1866), Sec. 1, 14 Stat. 27 (1866).

168. See also Taja-Nia Henderson, "Dignity Contradictions: Reconstruction as Restoration," *Chicago-Kent Law Review* 92, no. 3 (March 2018): 1135–54.

169. Compare Fugitive Slave Act of 1850, Sec. 7, 9 Stat. 462 (1850) with Civil Rights Act of 1866, Sec. 6, 14 Stat. 27 (1866).

170. *Congressional Globe*, 39th Congress, 1st Sess. 475 (1866).

171. *Congressional Globe*, 39th Congress, 1st Sess. 476 (1866).

172. Andrew Johnson, "Veto Message," An Act to Protect All Persons in the United States in Their Civil Rights and Furnish the Means of Their Vindication, March 27, 1866, American Presidency Project, www.presidency.ucsb.edu/node/202450.

173. *United States v. Rhodes*, 27 F. Cas. 785, 794 (1866).

174. *United States v. Rhodes*, 27 F. Cas. 785, 794 (1866). See also *In re Turner*, 24 F. Cas. 337, 339 (1867).

175. *Report of the Joint Committee on Reconstruction* (Washington, DC: Government Printing Office, 1866), archive.org/details/jointreconstruct00congrich.

176. *Report of the Joint Committee on Reconstruction.*

177. Robert J. Kaczorowski, "To Begin the Nation Anew: Congress, Citizenship, and Civil Rights After the Civil War," *American Historical Review* 92, no. 1 (February 1987): 52.

178. Hans Louis Trefousse, *Thaddeus Stevens: Nineteenth-Century Egalitarian* (Chapel Hill: University of North Carolina Press, 2013), 16; Ralph Korngold, *Thaddeus Stevens: A Being Darkly Wise and Rudely Great* (New York: Harcourt, Brace, 1955), 125.

179. Eric Foner, "Thaddeus Stevens, Confiscation, and Reconstruction," in Eric Foner, *Politics and Ideology in the Age of the Civil War* (New York: Oxford University Press, 1980), 128; originally published in *The Hofstadter Aegis: A Memorial*, ed. Stanley Elkins and Eric McKitrick (New York: Knopf, 1974), 154–83.

180. Foner, "Thaddeus Stevens," 128.

181. Korngold, *Thaddeus Stevens*, 332.

182. Gerard N. Magliocca, *American Founding Son: John Bingham and the Invention of the Fourteenth Amendment* (New York: New York University Press, 2013), 23.

183. Magliocca, *American Founding Son*, 68, quoting *New York Times*, January 16, 1860.

184. Magliocca, *American Founding Son*, 2. In addition to his illegal firing of Secretary of War Edwin Stanton, Andrew Johnson was also impeached for bringing "disgrace, ridicule, hatred, contempt, and reproach" toward Congress through his frustration of their Reconstruction goals. He avoided conviction and removal in the Senate by one vote. See "The Impeachment of Andrew Johnson (1868) President of the United States," United States Senate Art and History, www .senate.gov/artandhistory/history/common/briefing/Impeachment_Johnson.htm; Michael Les Benedict, *The Impeachment and Trial of Andrew Johnson* (New York: Norton, 1999).

185. Magliocca, *American Founding Son*, 128.

186. *Congressional Globe*, 39th Congress, 1st Sess. 10 (1865).

187. Foner, *Second Founding*, 59–60.

188. U.S. Census Bureau, "Apportionment of Membership of the House of Representatives: 1789 to 1990," *United States Summary: 2010 Population and Housing Unit Counts*, table 3.

189. *Congressional Globe*, 39th Congress, 1st Sess. 1307 (1866), statement of Representative Orth.

190. H.R. No. 51; *Congressional Globe*, 39th Congress, 1st Sess. 535 (1866).

191. The vote was 120 members in favor, 46 opposed, and 16 not voting. *Congressional Globe*, 39th Congress, 1st Sess. 538 (1866).

192. *Congressional Globe*, 39th Congress, 1st Sess. 1288 (1866).

193. "Special Meeting of the American Anti-Slavery Society," *National Anti-Slavery Standard*, February 3, 1866.

194. The vote was 25 senators in favor, 22 opposed. *Congressional Globe*, 39th Congress, 1st Sess. 1289 (1866). See Foner, *Second Founding*, 62–63.

195. *Congressional Globe*, 39th Congress, 1st Sess. 1033–34 (1866).

196. "Washington News: Debate in the Senate on the Concurrent Resolutions," *New York Times*, February 28, 1866.

197. *Congressional Globe*, 39th Congress, 1st Sess. 1095 (1866).

198. Earl M. Maltz, "Moving Beyond Race: The Joint Committee on Reconstruction and the Drafting of the Fourteenth Amendment," *Hastings Constitutional Law Quarterly* 42, no. 2 (Winter 2015): 307. "From the time that Thaddeus Stevens introduced the Owen proposal on April 21st, the Republicans on the Joint Committee remained committed to the idea of using a multifaceted constitutional amendment as the vehicle for defining the official position of the party on Reconstruction." Also see Foner, *Second Founding*, 70.

199. "The Debate on Reconstruction," *New York Times*, May 21, 1866.

200. *Congressional Globe*, 39th Congress, 1st Sess. 2890 (1866).

201. *Dred Scott v. Sandford*, 60 U.S. 393, 407 (1857).

202. Akhil Amar, "America's Equal Citizenship Clause," National Constitution Center Interactive Constitution, constitutioncenter.org/interactive-constitution/interpretation/amendment -xiv/clauses/700#americas-equal-citizenship-clause-by-akhil-reed-amar.

203. See *Congressional Globe*, 39th Congress, 1st Sess. 1290–92 (1866), speech of Representative Bingham.

204. *Congressional Globe*, 39th Congress, 1st Sess. 2498 (1866). Future President James Garfield, then in Congress, lamented "the sad moment" when the Democrats took power. He likewise supported including the Citizenship Clause in the Fourteenth Amendment to place citizenship rights "beyond the reach of the plots and machinations of any party." *Globe*, 2462.

205. Amar, "America's Equal Citizenship Clause."

206. *United States v. Wong Kim Ark*, 169 U.S. 649, 704 (1898). "The fact [ ] that acts of Congress or treaties have" prevented Chinese persons born abroad from becoming naturalized citizens "cannot exclude Chinese persons born in this country from the operation of the broad and clear

words of the Constitution, 'All persons born in the United States, and subject to the jurisdiction thereof, are citizens of the United States.'" See Marie A. Failinger, "*Yick Wo* at 125: Four Simple Lessons for the Contemporary Supreme Court," *Michigan Journal of Race & Law* 17, no. 2 (Spring 2012): 238. The author notes that in the late 1800s, the Justices could not avoid "popular references to 'the Yellow Peril,' the hysterical view that Chinese and other Asian immigrants would overwhelm Caucasian civilization."

207. Julie Hirschfeld Davis, "President Wants to Use Executive Order to End Birthright Citizenship," *New York Times*, October 30, 2018; Edward J. Erler, "Trump's Critics Are Wrong About the 14th Amendment and Birthright Citizenship," *National Review*, August 19, 2015. Erler claims, erroneously, that *Wong Kim Ark* "was a 5–4 opinion." In fact, the Supreme Court decided the case 6–2. Associate Justice Joseph McKenna took no part in the decision, as he was sworn in just two months before it issued.

208. Akhil Amar, "The Privileges or Immunities Clause: America's Lost Clause," National Constitution Center Interactive Constitution, constitutioncenter.org/interactive-constitution /interpretation/amendment-xiv/clauses/704#the-privileges-or-immunities-clause-americas -lost-clause-by-akhil-reed-amar.

209. U.S. Constitution, Amend. XIV.

210. *Congressional Globe*, 39th Congress, 1st Sess. 2765 (1866).

211. *Congressional Globe*, 39th Congress, 1st Sess. 1090 (1866).

212. Nathan S. Chapman and Kenji Yoshino, "The Fourteenth Amendment Due Process Clause," National Constitution Center Interpretive Constitution, constitutioncenter.org /interactive-constitution/interpretation/amendment-xiv/clauses/701.

213. *Congressional Globe*, 39th Congress, 1st Sess. 1090 (1866).

214. Chapman and Yoshino, "Fourteenth Amendment Due Process Clause."

215. *Lochner v. New York*, 198 U.S. 45 (1905).

216. *Griswold v. Connecticut*, 381 U.S. 479 (1965); *Roe v. Wade*, 410 U.S. 113 (1973).

217. Chapman and Yoshino, "Fourteenth Amendment Due Process Clause."

218. *Korematsu v. United States*, 323 U.S. 214, 216, 223 (1944).

219. *Trump v. Hawaii*, 585 U.S. ___ (2018).

220. *Congressional Globe*, 39th Congress, 1st Sess. 2768 (1866). See Erwin Chemerinsky and Earl M. Maltz, "The Fourteenth Amendment Enforcement Clause," National Constitution Center Interpretive Constitution, constitutioncenter.org/interactive-constitution/interpretation /amendment-xiv/clauses/703.

221. *Katzenbach v. Morgan*, 384 U.S. 641, 650 (1966), citing *McCulloch v. Maryland*, 17 U.S. 316, 421 (1819).

222. Foner, *Second Founding*, 85; Erwin Chemerinsky, "Congress's Broad Powers Under Section 5 of the Fourteenth Amendment," National Constitution Center Interpretive Constitution, constitutioncenter.org/interactive-constitution/interpretation/amendment-xiv/clauses/703 #congresss-broad-powers-under-section-5-of-the-fourteenth-amendment.

223. U.S. Constitution, Amend. XIV, Sec. 2. As in the original Constitution, this rule excludes "Indians not taxed," a reference to Indigenous people living under the jurisdiction of a tribe. That distinction is no longer relevant today.

224. *Congressional Globe*, 39th Congress, 1st Sess. 2542 (1866).

225. *Report of the Joint Committee on Reconstruction* (Washington, DC: Government Printing Office, 1866), xx, archive.org/details/jointreconstruct00congrich.

226. *Congressional Globe*, 39th Congress, 1st Sess. App. 228 (1866).

227. An Act to Remove Political Disabilities by the Fourteenth Article of the Amendments to the Constitution of the United States ("General Amnesty Act of 1872"), 17 Stat. 142 (1872); An Act to Remove the Disability Imposed by Section Three of the Fourteenth Amendment to the Constitution of the United States ("Amnesty Act of 1898"), 30 Stat. 432 (1898); James A. Rawley,

"The General Amnesty Act of 1872: A Note," *Mississippi Valley Historical Review* 47, no. 3 (December 1960): 480–84.

228. Francis MacDonnell, "Reconstruction in the Wake of Vietnam: The Pardoning of Robert E. Lee and Jefferson Davis," *Civil War History* 40, no. 2 (June 1994): 119–33; Olivia B. Waxman, "Why Jefferson Davis Got His U.S. Citizenship Back," *Time*, June 5, 2017, time.com/4802270/jefferson-davis-day-2017.

229. See James Wagstaffe, "Time to Reconsider the 14th Amendment for Trump's Role in Insurrection," Just Security, February 11, 2021, justsecurity.org/74657/time-to-reconsider-the-14th-amendment-for-trumps-role-in-the-insurrection; Lyle Denniston, "Is 14th Amendment Sec. 3 a Dead Letter?," *Lyle Denniston Law News*, January 10, 2021, lyldenlawnews.com/2021/01/10/is-14th-amendment-sec-3-a-dead-letter; Deepak Gupta and Brian Beutler, "Impeachment Isn't the Only Option Against Trump," *New York Times*, January 12, 2021.

230. U.S. Constitution, Amend. XIV, Sec. 4. See Abraham Lincoln, "Message to Congress Recommending Compensated Emancipation," March 6, 1862, American Presidency Project, www.presidency.ucsb.edu/node/203215.

231. *Congressional Globe*, 39th Congress, 1st Sess. 3034–36 (1866).

232. *Congressional Globe*, 39th Congress, 1st Sess. 2771 (1866).

233. *Congressional Globe*, 39th Congress, 1st Sess. 3042 (1866).

234. *Congressional Globe*, 39th Congress, 1st Sess. 3149 (1866).

235. *Congressional Globe*, 39th Congress, 1st Sess. 2538, 2939 (1866).

236. *Congressional Globe*, 39th Congress, 1st Sess. 2459 (1866).

237. Eric Foner, *Reconstruction: America's Unfinished Revolution 1863–1877* (New York: Harper & Row, 1988), 255. See Foner, *Second Founding*, 86–88.

238. Andrew Johnson, "Special Message," June 22, 1866, American Presidency Project, www.presidency.ucsb.edu/node/202310.

239. Foner, *Second Founding*, 89.

240. Foner, *Second Founding*, 89.

241. *Texas House Journal 1866*, 577–84; *Texas Senate Journal 1866*, 471; *Georgia House Journal 1866*, 61–69; *Georgia Senate Journal 1866*, 65–72; *Alabama House Journal 1866*, 208–13; *Alabama Senate Journal 1866*, 182–83; *North Carolina House Journal 1866–1867*, 182–85; *North Carolina Senate Journal 1866–1867*, 91–139; *Arkansas House Journal 1866*, 288–91; *Arkansas Senate Journal 1866*, 262; *South Carolina House Journal 1866*, 284; *South Carolina Senate Journal 1866*, 230; *Kentucky House Journal 1867*, 60–65; *Kentucky Senate Journal 1867*; 62–65; *Virginia House Journal 1866–1867*, 108; *Virginia Senate Journal 1866–1867*, 101–3; 1867 La. Acts. 9. While Tennessee voted in favor earlier on, the state police had to force some of its lawmakers to the capital for the vote. Kyvig, *Explicit and Authentic Acts*, 170. Alan P. Grimes claims the vote was irregular. See Grimes, *Democracy and the Amendments to the Constitution*, 50.

242. *Maryland House Journal 1867*, 1139–41; *Maryland Senate Journal 1867*, 808; *Delaware House Journal 1867*, 223–26; *Delaware Senate Journal 1867*, 169, 175–76, 208.

243. See Abraham Lincoln, "Special Session Message to Congress," Washington, DC, July 4, 1861, American Presidency Project, www.presidency.ucsb.edu/node/202522: "The States have their status in the Union, and they have no other legal status. If they break from this, they can only do so against law and by revolution."

244. An Act to Provide for the More Efficient Government of the Rebel States, 14 Stat. 428–30 (1867).

245. *Congressional Globe*, 40th Congress, 2nd Sess. 4295–96 (1866).

246. 15 Stat. 706–8 (1868).

247. 347 U.S. 483 (1954).

248. 377 U.S. 533 (1964).

249. 372 U.S. 335 (1963); 476 U.S. 79 (1986).

250. *Loving v. Virginia*, 388 U.S. 1, 12 (1967); *Obergefell v. Hodges*, 576 U.S. 644 (2015).

251. "Episode 102: The Fourteenth Amendment," *Civics 101: A Podcast*, transcript, www.civics 101podcast.org/civics-101-episodes/ep102. The quote is from Professor Theodore Shaw, former president of the NAACP Legal Defense Fund. See also William D. Araiza, "The Enforcement Power in Crisis," *University of Pennsylvania Journal of Constitutional Law* 18, JCL Online (2015): 1, referring to the Voting Rights Act, which Congress adopted pursuant to the Fourteenth and Fifteenth Amendments, as "one of the crown jewels of the modern civil rights movement."

252. *Congressional Globe*, 39th Congress, 1st Sess. 1287 (1866).

253. *Congressional Globe*, 39th Congress, 1st Sess. 2766 (1866).

254. "The Late President Lincoln on Negro Suffrage: A Letter from Him to Gov. Hahn of Louisiana," *New York Times*, June 23, 1865.

255. Johnson urged Governor William L. Sharkey of Mississippi to "extend the elective franchise to all persons of color who can read the Constitution . . . and write their names, and to all persons of color who own real estate . . . and pay taxes thereon. . . ." Doing so, he suggested, would not only allow Mississippi to "completely disarm the adversary and set an example the other States will follow," but it would also "place the southern States, in reference to free persons of color, upon the same basis with the free States." Du Bois, "Reconstruction and Its Benefits," 781, 783.

256. *Congressional Globe*, 39th Congress, 1st Sess. 476 (1866).

257. The House of Representatives and Senate overrode the veto by a vote of 113–38 and 29–10, respectively. Andrew Johnson, "Veto Message for 'An Act to Regulate the Elective Franchise in the District of Columbia,' January 5, 1867, American Presidency Project, www.presidency.ucsb .edu/node/203025; *Congressional Globe*, 39th Congress, 2nd Sess. 313, 344 (1867).

258. An Act to Regulate the Elective Franchise in the Territories of the United States, 14 Stat. 379 (1867); *Congressional Globe*, 39th Congress, 2nd Sess. 399, 456 (1867).

259. An Act for the Admission of the State of Nebraska into the Union, 14 Stat. 391 (1867); *Congressional Globe*, 39th Congress, 2nd Sess. 1096, 1117 (1867).

260. U.S. Commission on Civil Rights, *Political Participation* (Washington, DC: Government Printing Office, 1968), 1.

261. U.S. Commission on Civil Rights, *Political Participation*, 1–2.

262. Florida and Alabama were the only two Southern states with majority-Black electorates that did not have majority-Black populations. Minion K. C. Morrison, *African Americans and Political Participation: A Reference Handbook* (Santa Barbara, CA: ABC-CLIO, 2003), 200; Pamela S. Karlan, "Unduly Partial: The Supreme Court and the Fourteenth Amendment in *Bush v. Gore*," *Florida State University Law Review* 29, no. 2 (Winter 2001): 592 n30; "Voter Registration Rolls, 1867–68," Florida Memory State Library & Archives of Florida, www.floridamemory.com /discover/historical_records/election1867/county; "Alabama 1867 Voter Registration Records Database," Alabama Department of Archives and History, www.archives.alabama.gov/voterreg /search.cfm; U.S. Census Bureau, "Population of the United States (by States and Territories) in the Aggregate, and as White, Colored, Free Colored, Slave, Chinese, and Indian, at Each Census," *1870 Census*, table 1 (1870).

263. Prior to 1800, upwards of 80 percent of the states permitted Black men to vote. There was a fairly consistent decline—alongside the rise of Jacksonian liberalization of democracy for white men—as new states were admitted and others changed their laws. After 1836 and until the Reconstruction Era, that figure would remain under 20 percent. Brainerd Dyer, "One Hundred Years of Negro Suffrage," *Pacific Historical Review* 37, no. 1 (February 1968): 1; Eric Ledell Smith, "The End of Black Voting Rights in Pennsylvania: African Americans and the Pennsylvania Constitutional Convention of 1837–1838," *Pennsylvania History: A Journal of Mid-Atlantic Studies* 65, no. 3 (Summer 1998): 279; Chilton Williamson, *American Suffrage: From Property to Democracy 1760–1860* (Princeton, NJ: Princeton University Press, 1960); "'No Negro Shall Have the Right'—The Black Struggle for the Vote Across the North and South," *This Cruel War*, March 10, 2016, thiscruelwar.wordpress.com/2016/03/10/no-negro-shall-have-the-right-the

-black-struggle-for-the-vote-across-the-north-and-south. One scholar referred to the era of Jacksonian Democracy as the "the extension of white supremacy across the American continent." See David R. Mayhew, *The Imprint of Congress* (New Haven, CT: Yale University Press, 2017), 27, citing Daniel Walker Howe, *What Hath God Wrought: The Transformation of America, 1815–1848* (New York: Oxford University Press, 2009), 356–57.

264. *Memphis Avalanche*, July 9, 1867.

265. LaWanda Cox and John Cox, "Negro Suffrage and Republican Politics: The Problem of Motivation in Reconstruction Historiography," *Journal of Southern History* 33, no. 3 (August 1967): 303 n1.

266. Cox and Cox, "Negro Suffrage and Republican Politics," 318–19: "In short, Republican sponsorship of Negro suffrage meant flirtation with disaster, particularly in any one or all of the seven pivotal states where both the prejudice of race and the Democratic opposition were strong."

267. Cox and Cox, "Negro Suffrage and Republican Politics," 318–19. Voters in Connecticut, Kansas, Michigan, New York, Ohio, and Wisconsin voted to reject state constitutional amendments to end the prohibition on voting by nonwhites.

268. "General Summary," *California China Mail and Flying Dragon* (San Francisco), January 1, 1867.

269. Foner, *Second Founding*, 96.

270. Democratic Party Platform of 1868, July 4, 1868, Democratic Party Platforms, American Presidency Project, presidency.ucsb.edu/node/273175.

271. Republican Party Platform of 1868, May 20, 1868, Republican Party Platforms, American Presidency Project, www.presidency.ucsb.edu/node/273300. See Foner, *Second Founding*, 97.

272. Resolutions of the New England Anti-Slavery Society, *National Anti-Slavery Standard*, June 6, 1868; James McPherson, *The Struggle for Equality* (Princeton, NJ: Princeton University Press, 1967), 421.

273. McPherson, *Struggle for Equality*, 421; Thaddeus Stevens to Samuel Shoch[?], Washington DC, June 24, 1868, rough draft, in *The Selected Papers of Thaddeus Stevens*, vol. 2, *April 1865–August 1868*, ed. Beverly Wilson Palmer and Holly Byers Ochoa (Pittsburgh, PA: University of Pittsburgh Press, 1998).

274. Grimes, *Democracy and the Amendments to the Constitution*, 53–54.

275. Grimes, *Democracy and the Amendments to the Constitution*, 54–55.

276. Kyvig, *Explicit and Authentic Acts*, 179.

277. *Congressional Globe*, 40th Congress, 3rd Sess. App. 102 (1869). In the House, Pennsylvania Congressman John Broomall argued for the right of anyone "not under [another's] legal control" to an "equal voice." For him, a fully universal suffrage was the ideal, one that "make[s] no distinction of wealth, intelligence, race, family, or sex."

278. *Congressional Globe*, 40th Congress, 3rd Sess. 560 (1869).

279. *Congressional Globe*, 40th Congress, 3rd Sess. 1641 (1869).

280. Foner, *Second Founding*, 101.

281. Lani Guinier, "No Affirmative Right to Vote," *New York Times*, June 22, 2009, in "The Battle, Not the War, on Voting Rights," *New York Times*, June 22, 2009.

282. Lani Guinier and Penda D. Hair, "A Voting Rights Amendment Would End Voting Suppression," *New York Times*, November 3, 2014.

283. *Congressional Globe*, 40th Congress, 3rd Sess. 901 (1869).

284. *Congressional Globe*, 40th Congress, 3rd Sess. 1037 (1869).

285. *Congressional Globe*, 40th Congress, 3rd Sess. 1307 (1869).

286. *Congressional Globe*, 40th Congress, 3rd Sess. 668 (1869).

287. *Congressional Globe*, 40th Congress, 3rd Sess. 1298 (1869); Grimes, *Democracy and the Amendments to the Constitution*, 55.

288. Foner, *Second Founding*, 103.

289. *Congressional Globe*, 40th Congress, 3rd Sess. 1426 (1869).

290. *Congressional Globe*, 40th Congress, 3rd Sess. App. 152 (1869).

291. *Congressional Globe*, 40th Congress, 3rd Sess. 1639 (1869).

292. *Congressional Globe*, 40th Congress, 3rd Sess. 1303-4 (1869).

293. *Congressional Globe*, 40th Congress, 3rd Sess. 904 (1869).

294. S.R. 8, 40th Congress; *Congressional Globe*, 40th Congress, 3rd Sess. 1300, 1318 (1869).

295. *Congressional Globe*, 40th Congress, 3rd Sess. 1426-28 (1869).

296. Foner, *Second Founding*, 104.

297. The vote was 144-44. No Democrats voted in support. *Congressional Globe*, 40th Congress, 3rd Sess. 1563-64 (1869).

298. *Congressional Globe*, 40th Congress, 3rd Sess. 1639-40.

299. *Congressional Globe*, 40th Congress, 3rd Sess. 1641.

300. *Congressional Globe*, 40th Congress, 3rd Sess. 1641.

301. Foner, *Second Founding*, 105.

302. Foner, *Second Founding*, 105.

303. "The Fifteenth Amendment: Jubilee in Brooklyn," *New-York Tribune*, April 12, 1870.

304. Thirty-Sixth Annual Report of the Philadelphia Female Anti-Slavery Society, *National Anti-Slavery Standard*, April 2, 1870.

305. Foner, *Second Founding*, 112.

306. Julie Roy Jeffrey, The Dissolution of the Antislavery Societies," in *Abolitionists Remember: Antislavery Autobiographies and the Unfinished Work of Emancipation* (Chapel Hill: University of North Carolina Press, 2008), 17.

307. Cox and Cox, "Negro Suffrage and Republican Politics," 315, quoting James M. McPherson, *The Struggle for Equality: Abolitionists and the Negro in the Civil War and Reconstruction* (Princeton, NJ: Princeton University Press, 1964), viii.

308. Cox and Cox, "Negro Suffrage and Republican Politics," 314, quoting Kenneth M. Stampp, *Era of Reconstruction, 1865-1877* (New York: Random House, 1965), 101.

309. *Congressional Globe*, 40th Congress, 3rd Sess. 904 (1869). In addition, the quote is out of context. Sumner's morality is revealed in the rest of the quote, which continued, "But in standing by them you stand by all which is most dear in the Republic."

310. Glenn M. Linden, "A Note on Negro Suffrage and Republican Politics," *Journal of Southern History* 36, no. 3 (August 1970): 419.

311. Cox and Cox, "Negro Suffrage and Republican Politics," 318.

312. See Michael Les Benedict, "Preserving the Constitution: The Conservative Basis of Radical Reconstruction," *Journal of American History* 61, no. 1 (June 1974): 65-90.

313. Benedict, "Preserving the Constitution."

314. Arthur W. Machen Jr., "Is the Fifteenth Amendment Void?" *Harvard Law Review* 23, no. 3 (January 1910): 182. The author argues not only against the Fifteenth Amendment's validity, but also its goal of investing "these negro slaves, these strangers to the social compact . . . with the highest political right." M. F. Morris, "The Fifteenth Amendment to the Federal Constitution," *North American Review* 189, no. 638 (January 1909): 82-92. The author makes several arguments to the effect that the "the so-called Fifteenth Amendment" has been a failure and "should be regarded as a nullity." John R. Dos Passos, "The Negro Question," *Yale Law Journal* 12, no. 8 (June 1903): 476. Proclaiming himself to be among "[t]he best friends of the negro," the author felt "forced to admit, nearly forty years after the War, that negro suffrage in the South was a monumental error."

315. *Shelby County v. Holder*, 570 U.S. 529 (2013); *Mobile v. Bolden*, 446 U.S. 55 (1980); *James v. Bowman*, 190 U.S. 127 (1903); *United States v. Reese*, 92 U.S. 214 (1875). In *South Carolina v. Katzenbach*, 383 U.S. 301 (1966), the Supreme Court upheld the first challenge to the Voting Rights Act of 1965. That same year, a lawyer who argued that the law was unconstitutional wrote a widely cited article concluding that "it is [ ] abundantly clear that [literacy] tests cannot

be suspended merely because their practical effect is to deny suffrage to more Negroes than whites. . . ." Alfred Avins, "The Fifteenth Amendment and Literacy Tests: The Original Intent," *Stanford Law Review* 18, no. 5 (April 1966): 821–22. See also *Husted v. Randolph Institute*, No. 16-980, 584 U.S. ___ (2018).

316. 4 *Congressional Record* 2101–14 (1876).

317. Xi Wang, "Appendix Seven: Criminal Prosecutions Under Enforcement Acts, 1870–1894, by Section and Year," in *The Trial of Democracy: Black Suffrage and Northern Republicans, 1860–1910* (Atlanta: University of Georgia Press, 1997), 300.

318. Joan Waugh, *U.S. Grant, American Hero, American Myth* (Chapel Hill: University of North Carolina Press, 2009), 144–48; Joan Waugh, "Ulysses S. Grant: Domestic Affairs," UVA Miller Center on the Presidency, millercenter.org/president/grant/domestic-affairs.

319. Albert T. Morgan, *Yazoo: On the Picket Line of Freedom in the South: A Personal Narrative* (Washington, DC: 1884), 487.

320. Du Bois, "Reconstruction and its Benefits," 789.

321. Everette Swinney, "Enforcing the Fifteenth Amendment, 1870–1877," *Journal of Southern History* 28, no. 2 (May 1962): 218.

322. *The Butcher's Benevolent Association of New Orleans v. The Crescent City Live-Stock Landing and Slaughter-House Company* (the *Slaughterhouse Cases*), 83 U.S. 36, 60, 67 (1873).

323. *Slaughterhouse Cases*, 71–72.

324. *Slaughterhouse Cases*, 78.

325. *Slaughterhouse Cases*, 78.

326. *Slaughterhouse Cases*, 78.

327. *Slaughterhouse Cases*, 96.

328. Foner, *Second Founding*, 136.

329. Henry Louis Gates Jr., "What Was the Colfax Massacre?" *The Root*, July 29, 2013, www.theroot.com/what-was-the-colfax-massacre-1790897517; Danny Lewis, "The 1873 Colfax Massacre Crippled the Reconstruction Era," *Smithsonian Magazine*, April 13, 2016, www.smithsonianmag.com/smart-news/1873-colfax-massacre-crippled-reconstruction -180958746/#5EWdiq58C4HSaKCM.99.

330. Some sources say that ninety-eight men were indicted. See Christopher Waldrep, *Racial Violence on Trial: A Handbook with Cases, Laws, and Documents* (Santa Barbara, CA: ABC-CLIO, 2001), 113.

331. *United States v. Cruikshank*, 92 U.S. 542, 554 (1876).

332. "A Peaceful Election Farce in Kentucky," *New-York Tribune*, January 31, 1873.

333. *Cincinnati Commercial*, January 30, 1873.

334. *United States v. Reese*, 92 U.S. 214, 217 (1875).

335. A single electoral vote was contested in Oregon as well. While Hayes won the popular vote, the state's Democratic governor replaced a Hayes elector with one committed to Tilden.

336. Malvina Shanklin Harlan, "Some Memories of a Long Life, 1854–1911," *Journal of Supreme Court History* 26, no. 2 (July 2001): 113.

337. Loren P. Beth, *John Marshall Harlan: The Last Whig Justice* (Lexington: University Press of Kentucky, 1992), 75.

338. Beth, *John Marshall Harlan*, 89.

339. *United States v. Stanley* (the *Civil Rights Cases*), 109 U.S. 3, 5 (1883).

340. *Civil Rights Cases*, 4.

341. *Civil Rights Cases*, 8–9.

342. Shanklin Harlan, "Some Memories of a Long Life," 167.

343. *Civil Rights Cases*, 109 U.S. 3, 57 (1883).

344. *Civil Rights Cases*, 25.

345. *Civil Rights Cases*, 25. See also Darren Lenard Hutchinson, "Racial Exhaustion," *Washington University Law Review* 86, no. 4 (2009): 942.

346. *Brown County World* (Hiawatha, Kansas), October 25, 1883.

347. Christopher Waldrep and Lynne Curry, *The Constitution and the Nation: The Civil War & American Constitutionalism 1830–1890* (New York: Peter Lang International Academic Publishers, 2003), 207, citing *New York Globe*, January 19, 1884.

348. "Black and tan" was a pejorative reference to the large African American delegation at Reconstruction-era state constitutional conventions in the South. See Richard L. Hume, "The Arkansas Constitutional Convention of 1868: A Case Study in the Politics of Reconstruction," *Journal of Southern History* 39, no. 2 (May 1973): 183–206.

349. The new constitutions of Florida, Mississippi, South Carolina, Louisiana, Alabama, and Mississippi were drafted by state constitutional conventions. Florida Constitution of 1885; Mississippi Constitution of 1890; South Carolina Constitution of 1895; Louisiana Constitution of 1898; Alabama Constitution of 1901; Virginia Constitution of 1902.

350. Tennessee, Arkansas, North Carolina, Texas, and Georgia amended their existing constitutions. See 1889 Tenn. Pub. Acts 168, 364–71, 414–20, 437–38; Arkansas Constitution of 1874, Amend. 8 (1892), and 1891 Ark. Acts 32–53; North Carolina Constitution of 1868, Amend. 1900; Texas Constitution of 1876, Amend. 1902, as well as 1903 Tex. Gen. Laws 133–57, and 1905 Tex. Gen. Laws 520–65; Georgia Constitution of 1877, Amend. 1908.

351. U. S. Commission on Civil Rights, *Voting in Mississippi* (Washington, DC: Government Printing Office, 1965), 3.

352. Russell Brooker, *The American Civil Rights Movement 1865–1950: Black Agency and People of Good Will* (Lanham, MD: Lexington Books, 2017), 63–64.

353. *Williams v. Mississippi*, 170 U.S. 213, 222 (1898).

354. In 1876, there were 52,705 registered Black voters in Mississippi. In 1898, there were 3,573. John Lewis and Archie E. Allen, "Black Voter Registration Efforts in the South," *Notre Dame Law Review* 48, no. 1 (October 1972): 107.

355. *Report of the Proceedings and Debates of the Constitutional Convention: State of Virginia*, ed. James H. Lindsay (Richmond: Hermitage Press, 1906), 3076–77, statement of Carter Glass.

356. *Plessy v. Ferguson*, 163 U.S. 537, 541 (1896).

357. *Plessy v. Ferguson*, 552–53.

358. *Plessy v. Ferguson*, 555–56.

359. *Plessy v. Ferguson*, 559.

360. *Brown v. Board of Education of Topeka*, 347 U.S. 483 (1954).

361. Booker T. Washington, *The Booker T. Washington Papers*, vol. 3, ed. Louis Harlan (Urbana: University of Illinois Press, 1974), 583–87.

362. 38 *Congressional Record* 1275 (1904); Liette Gidlow, "The Sequel: The Fifteenth Amendment, the Nineteenth Amendment, and Southern Black Women's Struggle to Vote," *Journal of the Gilded Age and Progressive Era* 17, no. 3 (July 2018): 436.

363. "An Important Question Before the United States Supreme Court," *Boston Daily Journal*, October 9, 1883.

364. *Santa Clara County v. Southern Pacific Railroad Co.*, 118 U.S. 394 (1886).

365. Adam Winkler, "'Corporations Are People' Is Built on an Incredible 19th-Century Lie," *The Atlantic*, March 5, 2018, www.theatlantic.com/business/archive/2018/03/corporations -people-adam-winkler/554852.

366. *Santa Clara County v. Southern Pacific Railroad Co.*, 118 U.S. 394, 396, 397 (1886). The court reporter included two statements on this point. "Before argument, Mr. Chief Justice Waite said: The court does not wish to hear argument on the question whether the provision in the Fourteenth Amendment to the Constitution which forbids a State to deny to any person within its jurisdiction the equal protection of the laws applies to these corporations. We are all of opinion that it does." Then, there is Headnote 4, which reads, "The provision of the Fourteenth Amendment to the Constitution of the United States, which forbids a State to deny to any person within its jurisdiction the equal protection of the law, applies to corporations." See

Adam Winkler, *We the Corporations: How American Business Won Their Civil Rights* (New York: Liveright, 2018), 401.

367. Winkler, *We the Corporations*, xv.

368. W.E.B. Du Bois, *Black Reconstruction in America 1860–1880* (New York: Russell & Russell, 1935), 691.

Chapter 4: The Progressive Era Amendments (1909–1920)

1. "Constitutional Revision," *Washington Post*, October 4, 1899.

2. E.g., Paul Krugman, "Why We're in a New Gilded Age," review of *Capital in the Twenty-First Century*, by Thomas Piketty, *New York Review of Books*, May 8, 2014, www.nybooks.com/articles/2014/05/08/thomas-piketty-new-gilded-age; Larry Elliott, "In Second Gilded Age, Trump Shows No Sign of Taking On Rigged System," *The Guardian*, November 12, 2017, www.theguardian.com/inequality/economics-blog/2017/nov/12/second-gilded-age-trump-no-sign-of-taking-on-rigged-system-concentrated-wealth-robber-barons-superrich.

3. In the 47th Congress (1881–83), the Senate was evenly divided between thirty-seven Republicans and thirty-seven Democrats. Alan P. Grimes, *Democracy and the Amendments to the Constitution* (Lanham, MD: Lexington Books, 1978), 66.

4. Richard White, *The Republic for Which It Stands* (New York: Oxford University Press, 2017), 748–49.

5. Populist Party Platform of 1892, Minor/Third Party Platforms, American Presidency Project, www.presidency.ucsb.edu/node/273285. See Richard Hofstadter, *The Age of Reform* (New York: Knopf, 1955), 66–67.

6. Hofstadter, *Age of Reform*, 60.

7. Hofstadter, *Age of Reform*, 61.

8. Michael Kammen, *A Machine That Would Go of Itself: The Constitution in American Culture* (New York: Knopf, 1986), 190.

9. Erwin Chemerinsky, *We the People: A Progressive Reading of the Constitution for the Twenty-First Century* (New York: Picador, 2018), 108.

10. 198 U.S. 45 (1905).

11. Ian Millhiser, *Injustices: The Supreme Court's History of Comforting the Comfortable and Afflicting the Afflicted* (New York: Nation Books, 2015), 97.

12. An Act to Regulate the Manufacture of Flour and Meal Food Products (the New York Bakeshop Act of 1895), 1895 N.Y. Laws 305.

13. *Lochner v. New York*, 198 U.S. 45, 59 (1905).

14. Thomas Gaskell Shearman, "The Owners of the United States," *The Forum* 8 (November 1889), 269.

15. Shearman, "Owners of the United States," 271–72.

16. Shearman, "Owners of the United States," 273. See Steven R. Weisman, *The Great Tax Wars: Lincoln to Wilson—the Fierce Battles over Money and Power That Transformed the Nation* (New York: Simon & Schuster, 2002), 123.

17. U.S. Constitution, Art. I, Sec. 8.

18. Alexander Hamilton, "Final Version of the Report on Manufactures," December 5, 1791, Founders Online, National Archives, founders.archives.gov/documents/Hamilton/01-10-02-0001-0007. Original source: *The Papers of Alexander Hamilton*, vol. 10, *December 1791–January 1792*, ed. Harold C. Syrett (New York: Columbia University Press, 1966), 230–340.

19. U.S. Constitution, Art. I, Sec. 9. See Grimes, *Democracy and the Amendments*, 67.

20. Michael J. Klarman, *The Framers' Coup* (New York: Oxford University Press, 2016), 275; Akhil Amar, *America's Constitution: A Biography* (New York: Random House, 2005), 406–7.

21. Max Farrand, ed. *The Records of the Federal Convention of 1787*, vol. 2 (New Haven, CT: Yale University Press, 1911), 350 (hereafter Farrand, *Records*).

22. Alexander Hamilton, *The Works of Alexander Hamilton* (Federal Edition), vol. 8, ed. Henry Cabot Lodge (1904), 378–79, cited in *Springer v. U.S.*, 102 U.S. 586, 598 (1880).

23. *Cleveland Plain Dealer*, May 6, 1888, statement of Senator D. W. Voorhees: "With the treasury filled to overflowing with money not needed for the expenses of the government, with millions and tens of millions still pouring in, and all drawn from the weary hands of labor . . ." See, e.g., *Indianapolis Freeman*, October 13, 1888: "The chief producer, the greatest taxpayer, the workingman, without whom no individual interest would have the means of existence, is as poor in the pocket and as helpless at soul as he ever was. . . ."

24. *Springer v. United States*, 102 U.S. 586, 599–600 (1880); An Act to Lay and Collect a Direct Tax Within the United States, 1 Stat. 597; An Act for the Assessment and Collection of Direct Taxes and Internal Duties, 3 Stat. 22. See Charles J. Bullock, "The Origin, Purpose and Effect of the Direct-Tax Clause of the Federal Constitution," part 2, *Political Science Quarterly* 15, no. 3 (September 1900): 452–81.

25. Weisman, *Great Tax Wars*, 31.

26. Weisman, *Great Tax Wars*, 32; Grimes, *Democracy and the Amendments*, 67.

27. *Congressional Globe*, 37th Congress, 1st Sess. 283 (1861), statement of Representative Thomas Edwards.

28. Act of August 5, 1861 (Revenue Act of 1861), 12 Stat. 292 (1861).

29. Weisman, *Great Tax Wars*, 41–42.

30. Weisman, *Great Tax Wars*, 98–99.

31. Weisman, Great Tax Wars, 101–2.

32. Populist Party Platform of 1892, Minor/Third Party Platforms, American Presidency Project, www.presidency.ucsb.edu/node/273285. See Grimes, *Democracy and the Amendments*, 69.

33. An Act to Reduce Taxation, to Provide Revenue for the Government, and for Other Purposes (Wilson-Gorman Tariff), Pub. L. 53-349, 28 Stat. 509 (1894).

34. 26 *Congressional Record* App. 464 (1894).

35. 26 *Congressional Record* App. 467 (1894).

36. 26 *Congressional Record* 7136, 7189, 8505 (1894).

37. *Springer v. United States*, 102 U.S. 586, 602 (1880).

38. *Pollock v. Farmers' Loan & Trust Company*, 157 U.S. 429, affirmed on rehearing, 158 U.S. 601 (1895).

39. *Pollock v. Farmers' Loan & Trust Company*, 158 U.S. 601, 695 (1895).

40. Weisman, *Great Tax Wars*, 148.

41. "Death of the Income Tax," *Literary Digest* 11, no. 5 (1895), 6.

42. John R. Vile, *Encyclopedia of Constitutional Amendments, Proposed Amendments, and Amending Issues 1789–2010*, 3rd ed., vol. 2 (Santa Barbara, CA: ABC-CLIO, 2010), 436 (hereafter Vile, *Encyclopedia of Constitutional Amendments*).

43. 1908 Democratic Party Platform, Democratic Party Platforms, American Presidency Project, www.presidency.ucsb.edu/node/273198.

44. Weisman, *Great Tax Wars*, 211–12.

45. 44 *Congressional Record* 1352 (1909); Sidney Ratner, *American Taxation: Its History as a Social Force in Democracy* (New York: Norton, 1942), 280–82; Grimes, *Democracy and the Amendments to the Constitution*, 73.

46. Nathaniel W. Stephenson, *Nelson W. Aldrich: A Leader in American Politics* (New York: Scribner, 1930), 354.

47. Claude Bowers, *Beveridge and the Progressive Era* (New York: Literary Guild, 1932), 312.

48. Bowers, *Beveridge and the Progressive Era*, 312.

49. See Stephenson, *Nelson W. Aldrich*.

50. Bowers, *Beveridge and the Progressive Era*, 318.

51. Jerome L. Sternstein, "Corruption in the Gilded Age Senate: Nelson W. Aldrich and the Sugar Trust," *Capitol Studies: A Journal of the Capitol and Congress* 6, no. 1 (Spring 1978).

52. Lincoln Steffens, "Rhode Island: A State for Sale," *McClure's Magazine*, February 1905.

53. Ratner, *American Taxation*, 285; "Income Tax May Win," *New York Times*, May 26, 1909.

54. Roy G. Blakey and Gladys C. Blakey, *The Federal Income Tax* (New York: Longmans, Green, 1940), 45 n101, citing Archibald Butt, *Taft and Roosevelt: The Intimate Letters of Archie Butt*, vol. 1 (New York: Doubleday, Doran, 1930), 134.

55. Blakey and Blakey, *Federal Income Tax*, 28.

56. "Aldrich Sees Taft About Tariff Bill," *New York Times*, June 9, 1909.

57. Blakey and Blakey, *Federal Income Tax*, 42–43; Stephenson, *Nelson W. Aldrich*, 355–56; "Taft Tax Message Fails to Unite Party," *New York Times*, June 17, 1909.

58. 44 *Congressional Record* 3929 (1909); John D. Buenker, "The Ratification of the Federal Income Tax Amendment," *Cato Journal* 1, no. 1 (1981): 189–90.

59. Blakey and Blakey, *Federal Income Tax*, 60.

60. U.S. Constitution, Amend. XVI.

61. The Senate approved the proposal by a vote of 77–0, with 15 senators not voting. 44 *Congressional Record* 4121 (1909); Blakey and Blakey, *Federal Income Tax*, 61–62; Grimes, *Democracy and the Amendments to the Constitution*, 74.

62. The House of Representatives approved the proposal by a vote of 318–14, with 55 members not voting. 44 *Congressional Record* 4440 (1909); Blakey and Blakey, *Federal Income Tax*, 62; "House for Income Tax Plan," *New York Times*, July 13, 1909.

63. 44 *Congressional Record* 4400–4404 (1909).

64. See Blakey and Blakey, *Federal Income Tax*, 68.

65. Grimes, *Democracy and the Amendments to the Constitution*, 74.

66. Debates of the Virginia Ratifying Convention, June 5, 1788, statement of Patrick Henry, in *The Documentary History of the Ratification of the Constitution* digital edition, ed. John P. Kaminski, Gaspare J. Saladino, Richard Leffler, Charles H. Schoenleber, and Margaret A. Hogan (Charlottesville: University of Virginia Press, 2009) (hereafter *DHRC* digital edition).

67. *Richmond Times-Dispatch*, March 3, 1910, cited in Blakey and Blakey, *Federal Income Tax*, 70.

68. CQ Press Staff, ed., "1912 Presidential Election," *Presidential Elections 1789–2008*, 10th ed. (Washington, DC: CQ Press, 2009).

69. "Income Tax Ratified by Delaware's Vote," *New York Times*, February 4, 1913.

70. Four states (Connecticut, Utah, Florida, and Aldrich's Rhode Island) rejected the Sixteenth Amendment, while two others (Pennsylvania and Virginia) failed to act on it. Weisman, *Great Tax Wars*, 264.

71. "Change in the Constitution," *Washington Post*, February 6, 1913.

72. "Evading Easier Than Amendment," *Washington Post*, December 22, 1904.

73. Stephenson, *Nelson W. Aldrich*, 354; "David S. Barry, Sergeant at Arms, 1919–1933," U.S. Senate, www.senate.gov/about/officers-staff/sergeant-at-arms/SAA-David-S-Barry.htm.

74. "Senator Aldrich to Give Up Power," *New York Times*, April 16, 1910.

75. Weisman, *Great Tax Wars*, 281.

76. Revenue from income taxes (both individual and corporate) has been a majority of Federal revenue since 1942. See Erica York, "The Composition of Federal Revenue Has Changed Over Time," Tax Foundation, February 28, 2019, taxfoundation.org/composition-of-federal-revenue -over-time; "Federal Revenue: Where Does the Money Come From," Federal Budget 101, National Priorities Project, www.nationalpriorities.org/budget-basics/federal-budget-101/revenues.

77. Joseph R. Fishkin, William E. Forbath, and Erik M. Jensen, "The Sixteenth Amendment," National Constitution Center, constitutioncenter.org/interactive-constitution/interpretation /amendment-xvi/interps/139.

78. Proposing an Amendment to the Constitution of the United States to Repeal the Sixteenth Article of Amendment, H. J. Res. 104, 113th Congress, November 15, 2013. See also "Bridenstine Moves to Repeal Federal Income Tax," *Tulsa World*, November 18, 2013.

79. The Eleventh Amendment overruled *Chisolm v. Georgia* (1793), and the Thirteenth and Fourteenth Amendments repudiated *Dred Scott v. Sandford* (1857). See Grimes, *Democracy and the Amendments to the Constitution*, 67.

80. Joseph R. Long, "Tinkering with the Constitution," *Yale Law Journal* 24, no. 7 (May 1915): 577.

81. Farrand, *Records*, vol. 1, 151. See also p. 154, statement of Roger Sherman.

82. See James Madison, *Federalist* no. 62, Avalon Project, avalon.law.yale.edu/18th_century /fed62.asp. The appointment of senators by state legislatures would give states "such agency in the formation of the federal government as must secure the authority of the former, and form a convenient link between the two systems.

83. 2 *Register of Debates* 1348–49 (1826); George Haynes, *The Senate of the United States: Its History and Practice*, vol. 1 (Boston: Houghton Mifflin, 1938), 96; Vile, *Encyclopedia of Constitutional Amendments*, vol. 2, 431.

84. Grimes, *Democracy and the Amendments to the Constitution*, 75.

85. David Graham Phillips, "The Treason of the Senate," *Cosmopolitan* 40, no. 5 (March 1906): 488.

86. David Graham Phillips, "The Treason of the Senate: Aldrich, the Head of It All," *Cosmopolitan* 40, no. 6 (April 1906): 632.

87. Wendy J. Schiller and Charles Stewart III, *Electing the Senate: Indirect Democracy Before the Seventeenth Amendment* (Princeton, NJ: Princeton University Press, 2014), 10.

88. 34 *Congressional Record* 3422 (1901).

89. A lieutenant in the scheme, Fred Whiteside, testified to a Montana House Select Committee about the use of money to buy votes, claiming that "the amounts which they paid or put up for each member was from five to ten thousand dollars." *Montana House Journal 1899*, 31, cited in Schiller and Stewart, *Electing the Senate*, 47. See also Haynes, *Senate of the United States*, vol. 1, 130–31; "The Election Case of William A. Clark of Montana," U.S. Senate Historical Office, www.cop.senate.gov/artandhistory/history/common/contested_elections/089William_Clark.htm.

90. Roy Swanstrom, "The United States Senate 1787–1801: A Dissertation of the First Fourteen Years of the Upper Legislative Body," S. Doc. No. 87-64, at 29 (1961); Haynes, *Senate of the United States*, vol. 1, 86.

91. George Haynes, *The Election of Senators* (New York: Henry Holt, 1906), 38–39.

92. Jay S. Bybee, "Ulysses at the Mast: Democracy, Federalism and the Sirens' Song of the Seventeenth Amendment," *Northwestern University Law Review* 91, no. 2 (1997): 542.

93. Haynes, *Senate of the United States*, vol. 1, 92; Bybee, "Ulysses at the Mast," 542.

94. 26 *Congressional Record* 7775 (1894).

95. 24 *Congressional Record* 618 (1893).

96. 26 *Congressional Record* 7782 (1894); 31 *Congressional Record* 4825 (1898); 33 *Congressional Record* 4128 (1900); 35 *Congressional Record* 1722 (1902).

97. Grimes, *Democracy and the Amendments to the Constitution*, 76; Vile, *Encyclopedia of Constitutional Amendments*, vol. 2, 431.

98. Grimes, *Democracy and the Amendments to the Constitution*, 76.

99. Nebraska Constitution of 1875, Propositions Separately Submitted, Election, babel.hathitrust.org/cgi/pt?id=uiug.30112071755190&view=1up&seq=37.

100. 1888 S.C. Acts 10; Sara Brandes Crook, "The Consequences of the Seventeenth Amendment: The Twentieth Century Senate," Doctor of Philosophy (Political Science) Dissertation, University of Nebraska, May 1992, 27.

101. The first version of the "Oregon System" was passed in 1901 but proved ineffective in practice. In 1904, voters approved an initiated statute that instituted nonbinding pledges for state legislative candidates. And in a 1908 referendum, voters amended the state's constitution to make the voters' primary preferences binding. 1901 Or. Laws 143; 1905 Or. Laws 7; 1909 Or.

Laws 15; Vile, *Encyclopedia of Constitutional Amendments*, vol. 2, 431; Bybee, "Ulysses at the Mast," 537.

102. In 1912, twenty-nine states implemented a form of direct election for their primary or general elections. Direct Election of Senators, U.S. Senate Art and History, www.senate.gov /artandhistory/history/common/briefing/Direct_Election_Senators.htm. See Schiller and Stewart, *Electing the Senate*, 111–14; David N. Schleicher and Todd J. Zywicki, "The Seventeenth Amendment," National Constitution Center, constitutioncenter.org/interactive-constitution /interpretation/amendment-xvii/interps/147.

103. Thomas H. Neale, *The Article V Convention for Proposing Constitutional Amendments: Historical Perspectives for Congress* (Washington, DC: Congressional Research Service, R42592, 2012), 9; Haynes, *Election of Senators*, 275; Russell L. Caplan, *Constitutional Brinkmanship: Amending the Constitution by National Convention* (New York: Oxford University Press, 1988), 63.

104. Haynes, *Election of Senators*, 275; Caplan, *Constitutional Brinkmanship*, 63.

105. The 31 states that applied for an Article V Convention for the direct election of senators were: Nebraska (1893); Arkansas, Colorado, Idaho, Michigan, Minnesota, Missouri, Montana, Nevada, North Carolina, Oregon, Pennsylvania, South Dakota, Tennessee, Texas, and Utah (1901); Kentucky (1902); California, Illinois, North Dakota, Washington, and Wisconsin (1903); Iowa (1904); Indiana, Kansas, Louisiana, and New Jersey (1907); Ohio and Oklahoma (1908); Alabama (1909); and Maine (1911). Several states applied multiple times. See 1893 Neb. Laws 466–67; 1901 Ark. Acts 406–7; 1901 Colo. Sess. Laws 115–16; 1901 Idaho Sess. Laws 60–61; 1901 Mich. Pub. Acts 387; 1901 Minn. Laws 676–77; 1901 Mo. Laws 268; 1901 Mont. Laws 212; 1901 Nev. Stat. 141–42; 1901 N.C. Sess. Laws 1039; 1901 Or. Laws 493; 1901 Pa. Laws 860–61; 1901 S.D. Sess. Laws 262–63; 1901 Tenn. Pub. Acts 1262; 1901 Tex. Gen. Laws 1210–11; *Senate Journal, Fourth Session of the Legislature of Utah* (1901), 129; 1902 Ky. Acts 394–95; 1903 Cal. Stat. 682–83; 1903 Ill. Laws 361; *State of North Dakota, Journal of the House of the Eighth Session of the Legislative Assembly* (1903), 554; 1903 Wash. Sess. Laws 79; 1903 Wis. Sess. Laws 774; 1904 Iowa Acts 209; 1907 Ind. Acts 696; 1907 Kan. Sess. Laws 640–41; 1907 La. Acts 5–6; 1907 N.J. Laws 736–37; 1908 Ohio Laws 641–42; 1908 Okla. Sess. Laws 776–78; 1909 Ala. Laws 1; *Legislative Record of the 75th Legislature of the State of Maine* (1911), 299. Alabama's 1909 application is of questionable validity—the text refers to the application for a constitutional convention, but then only asks Congress to submit the amendment to the states. Contemporary newspaper accounts interpreted this as an application. *Richmond* [VA] *Times Dispatch*, August 15, 1909.

106. U.S. Constitution, Art V.

107. Newspaper accounts indicate confusion over the number of states that applied. Two articles from 1909 indicate twenty-eight and thirty-one states, respectively, while an article from 1910 indicates twenty-seven states. The *Times Dispatch* wrote that "because of the various forms in which such demands are phrased, some constitutional in their effect, others mere expressions of opinion, and because of the frequency with which some States repeat votes of this kind, it is hard to keep track of the exact number of demands that have been made for the calling of a convention. . . ." *Richmond Times Dispatch*, August 15, 1909; *Rockford* [IL] *Daily Register-Gazette*, October 8, 1909; *Dallas Morning News*, December 13, 1910. Even today experts disagree over the number of petitions submitted by states at the time.

108. Henry Litchfield West, "Proposed Amendments to the Constitution," *Forum* 33 (1902), 215; Henry Litchfield West, "American Politics," *Forum* 37 (1905), 160; Henry Litchfield West, "Shall United States Senators Be Elected by the People?" *Forum* 42 (1909), 298, cited in Caplan, *Constitutional Brinkmanship*, 64.

109. Bybee, "Ulysses at the Mast," 537–38.

110. 46 *Congressional Record* 2241 (1911).

111. 46 *Congressional Record*, 2242–43 (1911).

112. 47 *Congressional Record* 203 (1911); Richard B. Bernstein and Jerome Agel, *Amending America* (New York: Times Books, 1993), 127.

113. 47 *Congressional Record* 219 (1911).

114. 47 *Congressional Record* 219 (1911).

115. 47 *Congressional Record* 228 (1911), statement of Representative Morgan.

116. 47 *Congressional Record* 241–43 (1911). See Grimes, *Democracy and the Amendments to the Constitution*, 81.

117. 47 *Congressional Record* 1889 (1911).

118. 47 *Congressional Record* 1889 (1911).

119. Haynes, *Senate of the United States*, vol. 1, 110–11; 47 *Congressional Record* 1923 (1911).

120. 47 *Congressional Record* 1924–25 (1911); Haynes, *Senate of the United States*, vol. 1, 114. Opposing the measure were sixteen Republicans, mainly from the Northeast, and eight Southern Democrats.

121. 48 *Congressional Record* 6367 (1912); Grimes, *Democracy and the Amendments to the Constitution*, 82.

122. "Senators by Direct Vote Passes House," *New York Times*, May 14, 1912.

123. 48 *Congressional Record* 6369 (1912); "Direct Election of U.S. Senators Goes to States," *Atlanta Constitution*, May 14, 1912; "House OK Makes Direct Vote Sure on U.S. Senators," *St. Louis Post-Dispatch*, May 14, 1912; "Direct Election Wins," *Washington Post*, May 14, 1912.

124. "Direct Election of Senators in Sight," *New York Sun*, May 14, 1912.

125. Vile, *Encyclopedia of Constitutional Amendments*, vol. 2, 432; Caplan, *Constitutional Brinkmanship*, 65.

126. Schiller and Stewart, *Electing the Senate*, 12, 195–96.

127. Schiller and Stewart, *Electing the Senate*, 194.

128. 47 *Congressional Record* 208 (1911).

129. Schiller and Stewart, *Electing the Senate*, 200, 216.

130. Bernstein and Agel, *Amending America*, 122.

131. See Todd J. Zywicki, "The Original Senate and the Seventeenth Amendment," National Constitution Center, constitutioncenter.org/interactive-constitution/interpretation/amendment-xvii/interps/147#the-original-senate-and-the-seventeenth-amendment-by-todd-zywicki.

132. Bybee, "Ulysses at the Mast," 505.

133. Alan Greenblatt, "Rethinking the 17th Amendment: An Old Idea Gets Fresh Opposition," National Public Radio, February 5, 2014, www.npr.org/sections/itsallpolitics/2014/02/05/271937304/rethinking-the-17th-amendment-an-old-idea-gets-fresh-opposition, citing Ted Cruz's speech to the ALEC States and Nation Policy Summit, December 5, 2013.

134. See Schiller and Stewart, *Electing the Senate*, 10. See, e.g., Bybee, "Ulysses at the Mast," 539: "Whatever the general impressions, members of Congress cited very few specifics in support of their claims of bribery and corruption."

135. See Schiller and Stewart, *Electing the Senate*, 13.

136. Poll Results: Senators, You Gov Poll, November 6, 2013, today.yougov.com/topics/politics/articles-reports/2013/11/06/poll-results-senators.

137. David E. Kyvig, "Sober Thoughts: Myths and Realities of National Prohibition After Fifty Years," in *Law, Alcohol, and Order: Perspectives on National Prohibition*, ed. David E. Kyvig (Santa Barbara, CA: Praeger, 1985), 7 (hereafter Kyvig, "Sober Thoughts"). See Emma Green, "Colonial Americans Drank Roughly Three Times as Much as Americans Do Now," *The Atlantic*, June 29, 2015, www.theatlantic.com/health/archive/2015/06/benjamin-rush-booze-morality-democracy/396818.

138. Kyvig, "Sober Thoughts," 8.

139. Kyvig, "Sober Thoughts," 8; David E. Kyvig, *Repealing National Prohibition* (Chicago: University of Chicago Press, 1979), 6.

140. Daniel Okrent, *Last Call: The Rise and Fall of Prohibition* (New York: Scribner's, 2010), 42.

141. Grimes, *Democracy and the Amendments to the Constitution*, 83–84; Okrent, *Last Call*, 26; David A. J. Richards, "The Dark Side of the Noble Experiment," National Constitution Center, con-

stitutioncenter.org/interactive-constitution/interpretation/amendment-xviii/interps/169#the
-eighteenth-amendment-by-david-richards.

142. See, e.g., Thomas R. Pegram, *Battling Demon Rum: The Struggle for a Dry America 1800–1933* (New York: Ivan R. Dee, 1999).

143. The law went into effect in 1851 and was repealed in 1856. 1846 Me. Laws 189; Grimes, *Democracy and the Amendments to the Constitution*, 83. See Henry S. Club, *The Maine Liquor Law: Its Origin, History and Results, Including a Life of Hon. Neal Dow* (New York: Fowler & Wells, 1856).

144. K. Austin Kerr, "Organizing for Reform: The Anti-Saloon League and Innovation in Politics," *American Quarterly* 32, no. 1 (Spring 1980): 40.

145. Daniel Okrent, "Wayne B. Wheeler: The Man Who Turned Off the Taps," *Smithsonian Magazine* (May 2010).

146. Kerr, "Organizing for Reform," 48; Ernest Cherrington, *History of the Anti-Saloon League* (Westerville, OH: American Issue Publishing, 1913), 61.

147. Cherrington, *History of the Anti-Saloon League*, 37–38; Daniel Okrent, "Wayne B. Wheeler," *Smithsonian Magazine* (May 2010).

148. Kyvig, *Repealing National Prohibition*, 7; Okrent, *Last Call*, 35–41.

149. Cherrington, *History of the Anti-Saloon League*, 37–38.

150. Kyvig, *Repealing National Prohibition*, 7.

151. Grimes, *Democracy and the Amendments to the Constitution*, 83.

152. Gaines M. Foster, *Moral Reconstruction: Christian Lobbyists and the Federal Legislation of Morality, 1865–1920* (Chapel Hill: University of North Carolina Press, 2002), 194.

153. Kyvig, *Repealing National Prohibition*, 5; Okrent, "Wayne B. Wheeler."

154. "Anti-Rum Army at Capitol," *New York Times*, December 11, 1913.

155. See Audrey Redford and Benjamin Powell, "Dynamics of Intervention in the War on Drugs: The Buildup to the Harrison Act of 1914," *Independent Review* 20, no. 4 (Spring 2016): 509–30.

156. 52 *Congressional Record* 336 (1914); Vile, *Encyclopedia of Constitutional Amendments*, vol. 1, 157.

157. The vote was 197 members in favor, 190 against. 52 *Congressional Record* 616 (1914). See "Prohibition Is Beaten in House," *New York Times*, December 23, 1914; Grimes, *Democracy and the Amendments to the Constitution*, 85.

158. Grimes, *Democracy and the Amendments to the Constitution*, 85; Kyvig, "Sober Thoughts," 10; Kyvig, *Repealing National Prohibition*, 11.

159. "Pabst Charge Is Filed," *Milwaukee Journal*, February 13, 1918, cited in Okrent, "Wayne B. Wheeler."

160. 55 *Congressional Record* 197 (1917).

161. "Sheppard Gave 13 Years to Shakespearean Index," *New York Times*, April 12, 1941.

162. Nancy Beck Young, "Morris Sheppard," *American National Biography* (1999), doi.org/10.1093/anb/9780198606697.article.0600594.

163. "Prohibition: The 21st Amendment," *Time*, February 27, 1933; Richard Bailey, "Sheppard, John Morris," *Handbook of Texas Online*, Texas State Historical Association, tshaonline.org/handbook/online/articles/fsh24.

164. 55 *Congressional Record* 5549 (1917).

165. 55 *Congressional Record* 5642 (1917).

166. 55 *Congressional Record* 5637 (1917).

167. 55 *Congressional Record* 5637 (1917).

168. 55 *Congressional Record* 5661 (1917), statement of Senator Stone on compensation, and 5636, statement of Senator Calder on the amendment's effects on immigrant communities.

169. On August 1, 1917 the Senate approved the Prohibition Amendment by a vote of 65–20, with 11 senators not voting. 55 *Congressional Record* 5666 (1917). On December 17, 1917, the

House approved it by a vote of 282–128. 56 *Congressional Record* 469–70 (1918). Because the House made some changes to the text, senators adopted the final version of the amendment with a voice vote. 56 *Congressional Record* 478 (1918). See Kyvig, *Repealing National Prohibition*, 11.

170. Kyvig, *Repealing National Prohibition*, 98.

171. Okrent, *Last Call*, 86–92, 193–200.

172. U. S. Constitution, Amend. XVIII.

173. 55 *Congressional Record* 5648 (1917).

174. "The Great Dry Mystery," *New-York Tribune*, January 16, 1919.

175. *Brewing and Liquor Interests and German and Bolshevik Propaganda*, Report and Hearings before the Senate Committee on the Judiciary, 65th Congress (1918); Okrent, "Wayne B. Wheeler."

176. New Jersey ratified the amendment in 1922. Grimes, *Democracy and the Amendments to the Constitution*, 89. Some sources mistakenly claim that Connecticut ratified the amendment. See Henry S. Cohn and Ethan Davis, "Stopping the Wind That Blows and the Rivers That Run: Connecticut and Rhode Island Reject the Prohibition Amendment," *Quinnipiac Law Review* 27, no. 2 (2009).

177. Kyvig, *Repealing National Prohibition*, 13; Vile, *Encyclopedia of Constitutional Amendments*, vol. 1, 158; National Prohibition Act (Volstead Act), 41 Stat. 305, Pub. L. 66-66 (1919).

178. Kyvig, *Repealing National Prohibition*, 13.

179. Clement E. Vose, "Repeal as a Political Achievement," in *Law, Alcohol, and Order: Perspectives on National Prohibition*, ed. David E. Kyvig (Santa Barbara, CA: Praeger, 1985), 100.

180. 253 U.S. 350 (1920).

181. Root "was undoubtedly conscious of his own feeling about entering into a campaign." Philip C. Jessup, *Elihu Root*, vol. 2 (New York: Dodd, Mead, 1938), 242.

182. Nicholas Murray Butler, *Across the Busy Years*, vol. 2 (New York: Scribner, 1939–1940), 333–34, cited in Kyvig, *Repealing National Prohibition*, 17–18.

183. See *National Prohibition Cases*, 253 U.S. 350 (1920).

184. Kyvig, "Sober Thoughts," 12–13.

185. Kyvig, *Repealing National Prohibition*, 24.

186. Kyvig, *Repealing National Prohibition*, 25.

187. The state's 1776 constitution provided "that all Inhabitants of this Colony, of full age, who are worth fifty pounds proclamation money, clear estate in the same, and have resided within the county in which they claim a vote for twelve months immediately preceding the election, shall be entitled to vote for Representatives in Council and Assembly; and also for all other public officers, that shall be elected by the people of the county at large." N.J. Constitution of 1776, Art. IV. See Irwin N. Gertzog, "Female Suffrage in New Jersey, 1790–1807," *Women & Politics* 10, no. 2 (October 2008): 47; Judith Apter Klinghoffer and Lois Elkis, "'The Petticoat Electors': Women's Suffrage in New Jersey, 1776–1807," *Journal of the Early Republic* 12, no. 2 (Summer 1992): 159–93.

188. 1790 N.J. Laws 673.

189. Gertzog, "Female Suffrage in New Jersey," 53.

190. 1807 N.J. Laws 14; Eleanor Flexner and Ellen Fitzpatrick, *Century of Struggle: The Woman's Rights Movement in the United States*, enlarged ed. (Cambridge, MA: Belknap Press, 1996), 157; Edward Raymond Turner, "Women's Suffrage in New Jersey, 1790–1807," *Smith College Studies in History* 1, no. 4 (July 1916); Vile, *Encyclopedia of Constitutional Amendments*, vol. 2, 338.

191. Gertzog, "Female Suffrage in New Jersey," 56; Klinghoffer and Elkis, "'The Petticoat Electors,'" 163–64. See chapter 3, note 263.

192. Flexner and Fitzpatrick, *Century of Struggle*, 38.

193. Flexner and Fitzpatrick, *Century of Struggle*, 68–69. Historian Lisa Tetrault argues that the narrative of Seneca Falls as the "beginning" of the movement was constructed by Anthony and Stanton in their *History of Women's Suffrage* as a way to cement their place in the movement.

Tetrault characterizes it as "the most enduring and long-standing myth ever produced by a U.S. social movement." Lisa Tetrault, *The Myth of Seneca Falls: Memory and the Women's Suffrage Movement, 1848–1898* (Chapel Hill: University of North Carolina Press, 2014), 21.

194. Margaret Hope Bacon, *Valiant Friend: The Life of Lucretia Mott* (New York: Walker, 1980), 25–26; Carol Faulkner, *Lucretia Mott's Heresy: Abolition and Women's Rights in Nineteenth-Century America* (Philadelphia: University of Pennsylvania Press, 2012), 4.

195. Lori D. Ginzberg, *Elizabeth Cady Stanton: An American Life* (New York: Hill & Wang, 2009), 25.

196. Ginzberg, *Elizabeth Cady Stanton*, 46–47.

197. Seneca Falls Conference, The Declaration of Sentiments (1848), from *A History of Woman Suffrage*, vol. 1, ed. Elizabeth Cady Stanton, Susan B. Anthony, and Matilda Joslyn Gage, 2nd ed. (Rochester, NY: Fowler & Wells, 1889), 72.

198. *Elizabeth Cady Stanton as Revealed in Her Letters, Diary, and Reminiscences*, vol. 1, ed. Theodore Stanton and Harriot Stanton Blatch (New York: Harper & Brothers, 1922), 146.

199. Flexner and Fitzpatrick, *Century of Struggle*, 70; Harriot Stanton Blatch, *Challenging Years: The Memoirs of Harriot Stanton Blatch* (New York: Putnam's, 1940), 106; Stanton and Stanton Blatch, *Elizabeth Cady Stanton as Revealed in Her Letters, Diary, and Reminiscences*, vol. 1, 146.

200. Vile, *Encyclopedia of Constitutional Amendments*, vol. 2, 338.

201. See Ellen Carol DuBois, *Feminism and Suffrage: The Emergence of an Independent Women's Movement in America, 1848–1869* (Ithaca, NY: Cornell University Press, 1978), 46, cited in Alison M. Parker, "The Case for Reform: Antecedents for the Woman's Rights Movement," in *Votes for Women: The Struggle for Suffrage Revisited*, ed. Jean H. Baker (New York: Oxford University Press, 2002), 35.

202. Flexner and Fitzpatrick, *Century of Struggle*, 77–78; Jean H. Baker, Introduction, in *Votes for Women: The Struggle for Suffrage Revisited*, ed. Jean H. Baker (New York: Oxford University Press, 2002), 3; Parker, "Case for Reform," in Baker, *Votes for Women*, 22.

203. Rheta-Childe Dorr, *Susan B. Anthony: The Woman Who Changed the Mind of a Nation* (Frederick A. Stokes, New York, 1928; repr. New York: AMS Press, 1970), 12.

204. Nancy Hewitt, Introduction, *Susan B. Anthony and the Struggle for Equal Rights*, ed. Christine L. Ridarsky and Mary M. Huth (Rochester, NY: University of Rochester Press, 2012), 1.

205. Ginzberg, *Elizabeth Cady Stanton*, 78.

206. Nancie Caraway, *Segregated Sisterhood: Racism and the Politics of Feminism* (Knoxville: University of Tennessee Press, 1991), 138–39.

207. "A Petition for Universal Suffrage," January 29, 1866, www.visitthecapitol.gov /exhibitions/artifact/petition-universal-suffrage-january-29-1866.

208. *Congressional Globe*, 39th Congress, 1st Sess. 951 (1866), statement of Senator Henderson.

209. Doris Weatherford, *A History of the American Suffragist Movement* (Santa Barbara, CA: ABC-CLIO, 1998), 91.

210. Flexner and Fitzpatrick, *Century of Struggle*, 137.

211. Nell Irvin Painter, "Sojourner Truth, Francis Watkins Harper, and the Struggle for Woman Suffrage," in *Votes for Women: The Struggle for Suffrage Revisited*, ed. Jean H. Baker (New York: Oxford University Press, 2002), 45.

212. *A History of Woman Suffrage*, vol. 2, ed. Elizabeth Cady Stanton, Susan B. Anthony, and Matilda Joslyn Gage (Rochester, NY: Charles Mann, 1881), 384.

213. The original source for this often cited quote is Ida Husted Harper's biography of Anthony. The relevant passage says: "Miss Anthony . . . was highly indignant and declared that she would sooner cut off her right hand than ask the ballot for the black man and not the woman." Ida Husted Harper, *The Life and Work of Susan B. Anthony*, vol. 1 (Indianapolis and Kansas City: Bowen-Merrill, 1899), 261. See also Flexner and Fitzpatrick, Century of Struggle, 137–38.

214. Elizabeth Cady Stanton to the *National Anti-Slavery Standard*, December 26, 1865, in Donna L. Dickerson, *The Reconstruction Era: Primary Documents on Events from 1865–1877*

(Westport, CT: Greenwood Press, 2003), 228; Stanton, Anthony, and Gage, *A History of Woman Suffrage*, vol. 2, 333; Weatherford, *History of the American Suffragist Movement*, 107.

215. Ginzberg, *Elizabeth Cady Stanton*, 121.

216. Rosalyn Terborg-Penn, *African American Women in the Struggle for the Vote, 1850–1920* (Bloomington: Indiana University Press, 1998), 14.

217. Frances Ellen Watkins Harper, "We Are All Bound Up Together," Speech, New York, May 1, 1866, in *Proceedings of the Eleventh Women's Rights Convention* (New York: Robert J. Johnston, 1866), 90.

218. Caraway, *Segregated Sisterhood*, 139.

219. Flexner and Fitzpatrick, *Century of Struggle*, 145; Baker, "Introduction," in Baker, *Votes for Women*, 6.

220. Terborg-Penn, *African American Women*, 47.

221. Flexner and Fitzpatrick, *Century of Struggle*, 158–61; Ann D. Gordon, *The Trial of Susan B. Anthony*, Federal Trials and Great Debates in United States History, Federal Judicial Center, Federal Judicial History Office, 2005, www.fjc.gov/sites/default/files/trials/susanban thony.pdf.

222. *Minor v. Happersett*, 88 U.S. 162 (1875).

223. *Minor v. Happersett*, 178. See Allison Sneider, "Woman Suffrage in Congress: American Expansion and the Politics of Federalism, 1870–1890," in *Votes for Women: The Struggle for Suffrage Revisited*, ed. Jean H. Baker (New York: Oxford University Press, 2002), 79–80.

224. Gloria G. Harris and Hannah S. Cohen, *Women Trailblazers of California: Pioneers to the Present* (Charleston, SC: History Press, 2012), 49–52; Flexner and Fitzpatrick, *Century of Struggle*, 165.

225. 7 *Congressional Record* 252 (1878). In 1868, as Congress considered the Fifteenth Amendment, Senator Samuel Pomeroy proposed a universal suffrage amendment that would have enfranchised women. *Congressional Globe*, 40th Congress, 3rd Sess. 6 (1868).

226. U.S. Constitution, Amend. XIX.

227. Amar, *America's Constitution*, 421.

228. 18 *Congressional Record* 984 (1887).

229. 18 *Congressional Record* 981, 983 (1887).

230. 18 *Congressional Record* 981 (1887).

231. Flexner and Fitzpatrick, *Century of Struggle*, 167.

232. 1869 Wyo. Sess. Laws 371.

233. 1870 Utah Laws 8. Women in Utah were subsequently disenfranchised in 1887 by the Edmund-Tucker Act, passed by Congress to restrict polygamy in the territory. Anti-Plural Marriage Act of 1887 (Edmund-Tucker Act), Pub. L. 49-397, 24 Stat. 635 (1887). Women in Utah regained full suffrage in 1896, upon Utah's entrance into the union.

234. Weatherford, *A History of the American Suffragist Movement*, 99–100, 103–5; Rebecca Edwards, "Pioneers at the Polls: Woman Suffrage in the West," in *Votes for Women: The Struggle for Suffrage Revisited*, ed. Jean H. Baker (New York: Oxford University Press, 2002), 91–93.

235. Suffragists won referendums in Colorado and Idaho. Flexner and Fitzpatrick, *Century of Struggle*, 213–14.

236. Amar, *America's Constitution*, 419.

237. Okrent, *Last Call*, 62–66.

238. Flexner and Fitzpatrick, *Century of Struggle*, 241.

239. 1910 Wash. Sess. Laws. 26; 1911 Cal. Stat. 1548–49.

240. In 1912, voters in Arizona, Kansas, and Oregon approved woman suffrage while their counterparts in Michigan, Ohio, and Wisconsin voted to reject it. In 1914, suffragists prevailed in two referendum contests while losing five. In 1915, they lost all four ballot measures. Flexner and Fitzpatrick, *Century of Struggle*, 252, 260, 262–63.

241. J. D. Zahniser and Amelia R. Fry, *Alice Paul: Claiming Power* (New York: Oxford University Press, 2014), 1, 4.

242. Tina Cassidy, *Mr. President, How Long Must We Wait?* (New York: 37 INK/Atria, 2019), 6.

243. Ida Husted Harper, "Capital Mobs Made Converts to Suffrage," *New-York Tribune*, March 8, 1913.

244. Zahniser and Fry, *Alice Paul*, 138–39; Cassidy, *Mr. President, How Long Must We Wait?*, 54-55.

245. Marjorie Julian Spruill, "Race, Reform, and Reaction at the Turn of the Century: Southern Strategists, the NAWSA, and the 'Southern Strategy' in Context," in *Votes for Women: The Struggle for Suffrage Revisited*, ed. Jean H. Baker (New York: Oxford University Press, 2002), 113; Mary Walton, "The Day the Deltas Marched into History," *Washington Post*, March 1, 2013.

246. Cassidy, *Mr. President, How Long Must We Wait?*, 73–74.

247. Flexner and Fitzpatrick, *Century of Struggle*, 258.

248. Flexner and Fitzpatrick, *Century of Struggle*, 261.

249. The vote was 35 in favor to 34 against. 51 *Congressional Record* 5108 (1914).

250. The January 12 vote in the House of Representatives was 174 votes in favor, 204 against, with 46 not voting. 52 *Congressional Record* 1483–84 (1915); Grimes, *Democracy and the Amendments to the Constitution*, 90; Flexner and Fitzpatrick, *Century of Struggle*, 262–63.

251. 52 *Congressional Record* 1413–14 (1915).

252. 51 *Congressional Record* 5091 (1914), statement of Senator Lee.

253. Grimes, *Democracy and the Amendments to the Constitution*, 91; Amar, *America's Constitution*, 425; Kimberly A. Hamlin, "How Racism Almost Killed Women's Right to Vote," *Washington Post*, June 4, 2019.

254. Grimes, *Democracy and the Amendments to the Constitution*, 90; Flexner and Fitzpatrick, *Century of Struggle*, 296–97.

255. Robert Booth Fowler and Spencer Jones, "Carrie Chapman Catt and the Last Years of the Struggle for Woman Suffrage: 'The Winning Plan,'" in *Votes for Women: The Struggle for Suffrage Revisited*, ed. Jean H. Baker (New York: Oxford University Press, 2002), 135–37; Aileen S. Kraditor, *The Ideas of the Woman Suffrage Movement* (New York: Columbia University Press, 1965), 9–10.

256. U.S. Senate Historical Office, "Woman Suffrage Centennial: The Senate and Women's Fight for the Vote," 10–11, www.senate.gov/artandhistory/history/resources/pdf/Woman SuffrageFullEssaysCitation.pdf.

257. Cassidy, *Mr. President, How Long Must We Wait?*, 223.

258. Bethanee Bemis, "'Mr. President, How Long Must Women Wait For Liberty?'" *Smithsonian Magazine*, January 12, 2017; Vile, *Encyclopedia of Constitutional Amendments*, vol. 2, 339; Flexner and Fitzpatrick, *Century of Struggle*, 275.

259. Flexner and Fitzpatrick, *Century of Struggle*, 275–80; Cassidy, *Mr. President, How Long Must We Wait?*, 137–42.

260. Grimes, *Democracy and the Amendments to the Constitution*, 92; Flexner and Fitzpatrick, *Century of Struggle*, 280–81.

261. Maud Wood Park, *Front Door Lobby*, ed. Edna Lamprey Stantial (Boston: Beacon Press, 1960), 137.

262. 56 *Congressional Record* 810 (1918).

263. Flexner and Fitzpatrick, *Century of Struggle*, 276.

264. On October 1, 1918, the Senate vote was 53–31. 56 *Congressional Record* 10987–88 (1918). In a second vote taken on February 10, 1919, the vote was 55–29. 57 *Congressional Record* 3062 (1919). See also Flexner and Fitzpatrick, *Century of Struggle*, 302–3; "Wilson Makes Suffrage Appeal, but Senate Waits," *New York Times*, October 1, 1918.

265. The vote was 304–90. 58 *Congressional Record* 94 (1919).

266. "Senate Filibuster Holds Up Suffrage," *New York Times*, May 27, 1919.

267. "Curtains for Cotton Ed," *Time*, August 7, 1944.

268. 58 *Congressional Record* 618–19 (1919).

269. The vote was 56–25 with 15 senators not voting. 58 *Congressional Record* 635 (1919). "Suffrage Victory Today Predicted," *New York Times*, June 4, 1919; "Suffrage Wins in Senate," *New York Times*, June 5, 1919.

270. Flexner and Fitzpatrick, *Century of Struggle*, 309–10.

271. Rebecca L. Price, "The True Story of Tennessee Suffragettes," *Nashville Lifestyles*, December 26, 2015, nashvillelifestyles.com/living/community/the-true-story-of-tennessee-suffragettes.

272. Febb E. Burn to Harry T. Burn, August 17, 1920, Harry T. Burn Papers, C. M. McClung Historical Collection, Knox County Public Library, cmdc.knoxlib.org/cdm/compoundobject /collection/p265301coll8/id/699/rec/1; Flexner and Fitzpatrick, *Century of Struggle*, 315–17.

273. "1916 Presidential Election," *Presidential Elections 1789–2008*, ed. CQ Press Staff, 10th ed., 2009; "1920 Presidential Election," *Presidential Elections 1789–2008*, ed. CQ Press Staff, 10th ed., 2009.

274. Holly Jackson, "The 19th Amendment Was a Crucial Achievement, but It Wasn't Enough to Liberate Women," *Washington Post*, October 17, 2019.

275. See Sara Alpern and Dale Baum, "Female Ballots: The Impact of the Nineteenth Amendment," *Journal of Interdisciplinary History* 16, no. 1 (Summer 1985): 43–67.

276. "Coulter Culture," *New York Observer*, October 2, 2007, observer.com/2007/10/coulter -culture.

277. Amar, *America's Constitution*, 419.

278. Carrie Chapman Catt and Nettie Shuler, *Woman Suffrage and Politics: The Inner Story of the Suffrage Movement* (New York: Scribner, 1923), 107.

279. Martha S. Jones, *Vanguard: How Black Women Broke Barriers, Won the Vote, and Insisted on Equality for All* (New York: Basic Books, 2020), 1–3. See also Martha S. Jones, "What the 19th Amendment Meant for Black Women," *Politico Magazine*, August 26, 2020, politico.com/news /magazine/2020/08/26/19th-amendment-meant-for-black-women-400995.

280. *Women Suffrage by Federal Constitutional Amendment*, ed. Carrie Chapman Catt (New York: National Women Suffrage Publishing, 1917), 74; "Suffragette's Racial Remark Haunts College," *New York Times*, May 5, 1996.

281. See Cathleen D. Cahill, *Recasting the Vote: How Women of Color Transformed the Suffrage Movement* (Chapel Hill: University of North Carolina Press, 2020). Cahill highlights six women in her book, including Yankton Sioux author Zitkála-Šá, New Mexican Hispana educator Nina Otero-Warren and Chinese immigrant activist Mabel Ping-Hua Lee.

282. Walter I. Trattner, *Crusade for the Children: A History of the National Child Labor Committee and Child Labor Reform in America* (Chicago: Quadrangle Books, 1970), 10.

283. Trattner, *Crusade for the Children*, 41; Stephen B. Wood, *Constitutional Politics in the Progressive Era: Child Labor and the Law* (Chicago: University of Chicago Press, 1968), 3.

284. "A National Child-Labor Committee: The Announcement of Its Organization," *Charities: A Weekly Review of Local and General Philanthropy* 12, no. 16 (April 23, 1904): 411; Trattner, *Crusade for the Children*, 58–60; Grimes, *Democracy and the Amendments to the Constitution*, 101.

285. Trattner, *Crusade for the Children*, 114–15.

286. Trattner, *Crusade for the Children*, 40.

287. Trattner, *Crusade for the Children*, 189.

288. Trattner, *Crusade for the Children*, 116.

289. The Act of September 1, 1916 (Keating-Owen Act), 39 Stat. 675 (1916).

290. Woodrow Wilson, Address at Sea Girt, New Jersey, Accepting the Democratic Nomination for President, September 2, 1916, American Presidency Project, www.presidency.ucsb.edu /node/206580.

291. *Hammer v. Dagenhart*, 247 U.S. 251, 276 (1918).

NOTES TO PAGES 155–159

292. *Hammer v. Dagenhart.*

293. *Gibbons v. Ogden,* 22 U.S. 1, 196 (1824).

294. See Millhiser, *Injustices,* 79–80; Chemerinsky, *We the People.*

295. "A Disheartening Decision," *Washington Herald,* June 9, 1918.

296. *Bailey v. Drexel Furniture Co.,* 259 U.S. 20 (1922). See Trattner, *Crusade for the Children,* 139–42.

297. 43 Stat. 670 (1924).

298. 65 *Congressional Record* 10119, 10122 (1924). See Grimes, *Democracy and the Amendments to the Constitution,* 103.

299. Richard B. Sherman, "The Rejection of the Child Labor Amendment," *Mid-America,* January 1963, 8–9.

300. 65 *Congressional Record* 7295 (1924).

301. 65 *Congressional Record* 10142 (1924).

302. Grimes, *Democracy and the Amendments to the Constitution,* 103.

303. Trattner, *Crusade for the Children,* 169.

304. "News Notes," *American Child* 7 (April 1925): 6, cited in Trattner, *Crusade for the Children,* 171); and Vile, *Encyclopedia of Constitutional Amendments,* vol. 1, 65.

305. Trattner, *Crusade for the Children,* 172–78; Sherman, "Rejection of the Child Labor Amendment," 10.

306. 65 *Congressional Record* 9963 (1924).

307. Trattner, *Crusade for the Children,* 176.

308. *American Power Farmer* 24 (February 1925): 7, cited in Trattner, *Crusade for the Children,* 284 n32.

309. Grimes, *Democracy and the Amendments to the Constitution,* 103.

310. Sherman, "Rejection of the Child Labor Amendment," 14.

311. Trattner, *Crusade for the Children,* 189.

312. Trattner, *Crusade for the Children,* 189–90.

313. William F. Swindler, "A Dubious Constitutional Experiment" in *Law, Alcohol, and Order: Perspectives on National Prohibition,* ed. David E. Kyvig (Santa Barbara, CA: Praeger, 1985), 53.

314. Jane J. Mansbridge, *Why We Lost the ERA* (Chicago: University of Chicago Press, 1986), 31–32.

Chapter 5: The New Deal—and the Amending Wave That Wasn't

1. "Republicans Lose Grip on Congress," *New York Times,* November 6, 1930; "Nip and Tuck for the House," *New York Times,* November 6, 1930. Republicans actually retained control of Congress by two seats after the November 1930 election. However, over the thirteen months before the next session, fourteen Republican members died, and Democrats won many of the subsequent special elections. By the time Congress met in 1931, the Democrats were in the majority. Alan P. Grimes, *Democracy and the Amendments to the Constitution* (Lanham, MD: Lexington Books, 1978), 107–8. See "A Look Back at the Midterm Election of 1930," *All Things Considered,* NPR, November 3, 2010, www.npr.org/templates/story/story.php?storyId=131048598.

2. Andrew E. Busch, "1930 Midterms Heralded New Deal," Ashbrook Center, April 2006, ashbrook.org/publications/oped-busch-06-1930.

3. See John Copeland Nagle, "A Twentieth Amendment Parable," *New York University Law Review* 72 (1997): 484; Grimes, *Democracy and the Amendments to the Constitution,* 104.

4. Grimes, *Democracy and the Amendments to the Constitution,* 105.

5. After his election victory in 1860, a frustrated Abraham Lincoln said he would shorten his life by "a period of years" if it would shorten the delay before his inauguration. Jeff Shesol, "'One President at a Time': Tightening the Presidential Transition," National Constitution Center, constitutioncenter.org/interactive-constitution/interpretation/amendment-xx/interps/153#one-president-at-a-time-tightening-the-presidential-transition-by-jeff-shes.

6. G.A.C. Jr., "The Proposed Twentieth Constitutional Amendment," *Georgetown Law Journal* 21 (1932): 64.

7. U.S. Constitution, Art. I, Sec. 4.

8. Nagle, "Twentieth Amendment Parable," 483.

9. John R. Vile, *Encyclopedia of Constitutional Amendments, Proposed Amendments, and Amending Issues 1789–2010*, vol. 2, 3rd ed. (Santa Barbara, CA: ABC-CLIO, 2010), 495 (hereafter Vile, *Encyclopedia of Constitutional Amendments*).

10. U.S. Constitution, Art. I, Sec. 3. See Senate Historical Office, Extraordinary Sessions of Congress: A Brief History, web.archive.org/web/20190802182526/www.senate.gov/artandhistory/history/resources/pdf/ExtraSessions.pdf.

11. Grimes, *Democracy and the Amendments to the Constitution*, 105; Edward J. Larson and Jeff Shesol, "The Twentieth Amendment," National Constitutional Center, www.constitutioncenter.org/interactive-constitution/interpretation/amendment-xx/interps/153.

12. Jeff Shesol and Edward Larson point out that "one of the Amendment's more consequential effects—shortening the transition period between presidential administrations by six weeks—was not among the [Judiciary] Committee's principal reasons [for the change]; the prospect of a lame-duck presidency elicited less concern than that of a lame-duck Congress." Larson and Shesol, "The Twentieth Amendment."

13. 75 *Congressional Record* 3828 (1932).

14. U.S. Constitution, Amend. XII.

15. In 1800 and 1824, no candidate for president received a majority of the electoral votes, thus resulting in a contingent election in the House. In 1876, the House ratified the decision of the Electoral Commission to resolve the disputes over electoral votes in several Southern states.

16. Nagle, "Twentieth Amendment Parable," 481; 75 *Congressional Record* 3857 (1932), statement of Representative McKeown.

17. Norman L. Zucker, *George Norris: Gentle Knight of American Democracy* (Urbana: University of Illinois Press, 1966), 11.

18. Zucker, *George Norris*, 29.

19. Richard L. Neuberger and Stephen B. Kahn, *Integrity: The Life of George W. Norris* (New York: Vanguard Press, 1937), 272.

20. 75 *Congressional Record* 1372 (1932).

21. Grimes, *Democracy and the Amendments to the Constitution*, 106–7.

22. 75 *Congressional Record* 4246 (1932).

23. 75 *Congressional Record* 3853 (1932), statement of Representative Tilson.

24. 75 *Congressional Record* 1374 (1932).

25. Grimes, *Democracy and the Amendments to the Constitution*, 108.

26. 75 *Congressional Record* 4060, 5027, 5086 (1932).

27. U.S. Constitution, Amend. XX, Sec. 3.

28. U.S. Constitution, Amend. XX, Sec. 4.

29. CQ Press Staff, ed., "1936 Presidential Election," *Presidential Elections 1789–2008*, 10th ed. (Washington, DC: CQ Press, 2009).

30. Sanford Levinson, "Presidential Elections and Constitutional Stupidities," *Constitutional Commentary* 12 (1995): 184–85.

31. Akhil Amar, *America's Constitution: A Biography* (New York: Random House, 2005), 429.

32. "Lansing Mother Gets Life Term as Liquor Felon," *Battle Creek Enquirer*, December 31, 1928; "Fight in Legislature Looms Over Life Term for Woman Dry Violator," *Minneapolis Star*, December 22, 1928; "Liquor Life Sentence Reversed in Michigan," *New York Times*, March 8, 1930.

33. "Prohibition: From and After," *Time*, January 14, 1929. See also Daniel Okrent, *Last Call: The Rise and Fall of Prohibition* (New York: Scribner, 2010), 319. Note that another news report listed the number of Miller's living children as four. "Green Attacks New Life Term Law," *Detroit News*, December 14, 1928.

34. 55 *Congressional Record* 5642 (1917), statement of Senator Myers.

35. "Hoover States Dry Laws Views: Tells Borah He Is Not in Favor of Repealing Eighteenth Amendment," *Detroit News*, February 23, 1928, citing Herbert Hoover to William Borah, Washington, DC, February 23, 1928.

36. David E. Kyvig, "Sober Thoughts: Myths and Realities of National Prohibition After Fifty Years," in *Law, Alcohol, and Order: Perspectives on National Prohibition*, ed. David E. Kyvig (Santa Barbara, CA: Praeger, 1985), 13 (hereafter Kyvig, "Sober Thoughts").

37. David E. Kyvig, *Repealing National Prohibition* (Chicago: University of Chicago Press, 1979), 107.

38. Thomas R. Pegram, "Hoodwinked: The Anti-Saloon League and the Ku Klux Klan in 1920s Prohibition Enforcement," *Journal of the Gilded Age and Progressive Era* 7, no. 1 (January 2008): 89-119; Okrent, *Last Call*, 86.

39. Pegram, "Hoodwinked," 114.

40. Kyvig, *Repealing National Prohibition*, 128, citing Volunteer Committee of Lawyers incorporation statement.

41. Walter Davenport, "Bartender's Guide to Washington," *Collier's* 83, no. 7 (February 16, 1929): 8.

42. Herbert Hoover, Inaugural Address, Washington, DC, March 4, 1929, American Presidency Project, www.presidency.ucsb.edu/node/207571.

43. National Commission on Law Observance and Enforcement, *Report on the Enforcement of the Prohibition Laws of the United States* (Washington, DC: Department of Justice, 1931).

44. *Report on the Enforcement of the Prohibition Laws*, 146. See also Kyvig, *Repealing National Prohibition*, 113.

45. "Drys Hail Report as Helping Cause," *New York Times*, January 21, 1931.

46. "Capitol Appraises Report," *New York Times*, January 21, 1931.

47. Kyvig, *Repealing National Prohibition*, 2.

48. "Senator Sheppard Says Country Will Stay Dry," *Washington Post*, September 25, 1930.

49. Vile, *Encyclopedia of Constitutional Amendments*, vol. 2, 500.

50. Peter Odegard, *Pressure Politics: The Story of the Anti-Saloon League* (New York: Oxford University Press, 1928), 173.

51. Okrent, *Last Call*, 239.

52. Grimes, *Democracy and the Amendments to the Constitution*, 109.

53. Kyvig, "Sober Thoughts," 15.

54. Kyvig, *Repealing National Prohibition*, 46.

55. Kyvig, *Repealing National Prohibition*, 95–97.

56. Kyvig, "Sober Thoughts," 15.

57. Kyvig, *Repealing National Prohibition*, 108, citing Association Against the Prohibition Amendment, *Prohibition Enforcement: Its Effect on Courts and Prisons* (Washington, DC: 1930).

58. Kyvig, *Repealing National Prohibition*, 131, citing Association Against the Prohibition Amendment, *Prohibition and the Deficit* (Washington, DC: January 1932).

59. Mark Edward Lender, "The Historian and Repeal: A Survey of the Literature and Research Opportunities," in *Law, Alcohol, and Order: Perspectives on National Prohibition*, ed. David E. Kyvig (Santa Barbara, CA: Praeger, 1985), 184.

60. Okrent, *Last Call*, 300–301; Daniel Okrent, "Wayne B. Wheeler: The Man Who Turned Off the Taps," *Smithsonian Magazine* (May 2010).

61. "Wets Gain In House," *New York Times*, November 5. 1930.

62. Kyvig, *Repealing National Prohibition*, 98.

63. Arthur Krock, "Democrats Pledge Party to Repeal of the Dry Law and Quick Modification to Legalize Beer," *New York Times*, June 30, 1932.

64. Franklin Delano Roosevelt, Campaign Address on Prohibition in Sea Girt, New Jersey, August 27, 1932, American Presidency Project, www.presidency.ucsb.edu/node/289317.

65. Republican Party Platform of 1932, Republican Party Platforms, American Presidency Project, www.presidency.ucsb.edu/node/273383.

66. Kyvig, *Repealing National Prohibition*, 160.

67. Voters abolished state prohibition laws in nine states: Arizona, California, Colorado, Louisiana, Michigan, New Jersey, North Dakota, Oregon, and Washington. Voters in Connecticut and Wyoming passed measures calling on Congress to repeal the amendment. Kyvig, *Repealing National Prohibition*, 168.

68. "Wets Clinch Margin for Repeal in House," *New York Times*, November 10, 1932. See Kyvig, *Repealing National Prohibition*, 168.

69. U.S. Constitution, Amend. XXI; U.S. Constitution, Amend. XVIII.

70. Robert P. George and David A. J. Richards, "The Twenty-First Amendment," National Constitution Center, www.constitutioncenter.org/interactive-constitution/interpretation /amendment-xxi/interps/151.

71. U.S. Constitution, Amend. XVIII.

72. Clement E. Vose, "Repeal as a Political Achievement," in *Law, Alcohol, and Order: Perspectives on National Prohibition*, ed. David E. Kyvig (Santa Barbara, CA: Praeger, 1985), 107, 100–101.

73. Vose, "Repeal as a Political Achievement," in Kyvig, *Law, Alcohol, and Order*, 107, 111–12.

74. 75 *Congressional Record* 2108 (1932).

75. See 76 *Congressional Record* 4008–61 (1933).

76. "Prohibition: The 21st Amendment," *Time*, February 27, 1933.

77. "Prohibition: The 21st Amendment." See Okrent, *Last Call*, 352.

78. 76 *Congressional Record* 4216–17 (1933).

79. In support of the measure were 63 senators; 23 were opposed, and 10 did not vote. 76 *Congressional Record* 4231 (1933).

80. The fifteen senators who voted yea on both the Eighteenth and Twenty-First Amendments were: Ashurst (D-AZ), Fletcher (D-FL), Hale (R-ME), Johnson (R-CA), Kendrick (D-WY), King (D-UT), McKellar (D-TN), McNary (R-OR), Pittman (D-NV), Robinson (D-AR), Smith (D-SC), Swanson (D-VA), Trammell (D-FL), Walsh (D-MT), and Watson (R-IN). The five consistently dry senators who supported Prohibition and opposed repeal were Borah (R-ID), Gore (D-OK), Norris (R-NE), Sheppard (D-TX), and Smoot (R-UT). The only senator to oppose Prohibition and support repeal was Lewis (D-IL).

81. In support were 289 representatives; 121 were opposed, and 16 did not vote. 76 *Congressional Record* 4516 (1933); Okrent, *Last Call*, 352.

82. Grimes, *Democracy and the Amendments to the Constitution*, 109.

83. 76 *Congressional Record* 4513 (1933).

84. 76 *Congressional Record* 4512 (1933).

85. South Carolina's was the only elected convention to reject the Twenty-First Amendment. "South Carolina Votes First 'No,'" *New York Times*, December 5, 1933.

86. Vose, "Repeal as a Political Achievement," in Kyvig, *Law, Alcohol, and Order*, 113–14; Kyvig, *Repealing National Prohibition*, 178–79.

87. Vose, "Repeal as a Political Achievement," in Kyvig, *Law, Alcohol, and Order*, 115.

88. Grimes, *Democracy and the Amendments to the Constitution*, 109.

89. See 78 *Congressional Record* 11603 (1934); 79 *Congressional Record* 868 (1935); 81 *Congressional Record* 178 (1937); 84 *Congressional Record* 89 (1939); 87 *Congressional Record* 145 (1941).

90. Richard Hofstadter, *The Age of Reform: From Bryan to F.D.R.* (New York: Knopf, 1955), 289–90, 292.

91. Kyvig, "Sober Thoughts," 14; Kyvig, *Repealing National Prohibition*, 128; Lisa McGirr, "How Prohibition Fueled the Klan," *New York Times*, January 16, 2019.

92. *"Great and Extraordinary Occasions": Developing Guidelines for Constitutional Change* (New York: Century Foundation Press, 1999), 2–4; Kyvig, *Repealing National Prohibition*, 200.

93. New York Ratifying Convention Debates, June 24, 1788, statement of Richard Morris, in *The Documentary History of the Ratification of the Constitution* digital edition, ed. John P. Kaminski, Gaspare J. Saladino, Richard Leffler, Charles H. Schoenleber and Margaret A. Hogan (Charlottesville: University of Virginia Press, 2009) (hereafter *DHRC* digital edition).

94. Goodwin Liu, Pamela S. Karlan, and Christopher H. Schroeder, *Keeping Faith with the Constitution* (Washington, DC: American Constitution Society for Law and Policy, 2009), 65–67; Erwin Chemerinsky, *We the People: A Progressive Reading of the Constitution for the Twenty-First Century* (New York: Picador, 2018), 109–17.

95. Franklin Delano Roosevelt, Address Accepting the Presidential Nomination at the Democratic National Convention in Chicago, July 2, 1932, American Presidency Project, www.presidency.ucsb.edu/node/275484.

96. James MacGregor Burns, *Packing the Court: The Rise of Judicial Power and the Coming Crisis of the Supreme Court* (New York: Penguin Press, 2009), 139.

97. 295 U.S. 495 (1935).

98. Jeff Shesol, *Supreme Power: Franklin Roosevelt vs. the Supreme Court* (New York: Norton, 2010), 43–44; Burns, *Packing the Court*, 140.

99. The Court also invalidated the statute on the ground that Congress improperly delegated its legislative powers to the executive. 295 U.S. at 542.

100. 295 U.S. at 548.

101. Franklin Delano Roosevelt, "Press Conference," May 31, 1935, American Presidency Project, www.presidency.ucsb.edu/node/208710.

102. Shesol, *Supreme Power*, 151.

103. "Washington Studies Plan for a Quick Amendment of Federal Constitution," *New York Times*, June 2, 1935.

104. George Creel, "Looking Ahead with Roosevelt," *Collier's Weekly*, September 7, 1935.

105. Shesol, *Supreme Power*, 154; Burns, *Packing the Court*, 144–45.

106. Liu, Karlan, and Schroeder, *Keeping Faith with the Constitution*, 69.

107. Bruce Ackerman, *We the People*, vol. 2, *Transformations* (Cambridge, MA: Harvard University Press, 2000), 24, 314; Burns, *Packing the Court*, 145–46.

108. Franklin Delano Roosevelt, Annual Message to Congress, Washington, DC, January 6, 1937, American Presidency Project, www.presidency.ucsb.edu/node/209043.

109. Franklin Delano Roosevelt, Second Inaugural Address, Washington, DC, January 20, 1937, American Presidency Project, www.presidency.ucsb.edu/node/209135.

110. Roosevelt, Second Inaugural Address.

111. Arthur Krock, "Roosevelt Asks Power to Reform Courts," *New York Times*, February 6, 1937.

112. Franklin Delano Roosevelt, Excerpts from Press Conference, October 18, 1940, American Presidency Project, www.presidency.ucsb.edu/node/20963; Liu, Karlan, and Schroeder, *Keeping Faith with the Constitution*, 69; Burns, *Packing the Court*, 145–46.

113. Turner Catledge, "Bill Is Introduced," *New York Times*, February 6, 1937.

114. "Comment by Members of Congress on Court Proposal," *New York Times*, February 6, 1937.

115. *West Coast Hotel Co. v. Parrish*, 300 U.S. 379 (1937). The swing justice in the case, Owen Roberts, revealed his change of heart in a private conference among the justices in December 1936, after Roosevelt's commanding win but before the release of the bill. Burns, *Packing the Court*, 148–49.

116. *NLRB v. Jones & Laughlin Steel Corp.*, 301 U.S. 1 (1937); *Steward Machine Co. v. Davis*, 301 U.S. 548 (1937). See Liu, Karlan, and Schroeder, *Keeping Faith with the Constitution*, 69–70.

117. After the justices' change of heart, support for the bill eroded. After hearings, a majority of the Senate Judiciary Committee issued a report in June 1937 urging rejection of the bill. The measure died after that. "Court Bill Nears Floor After 4-Month Conflict," *New York Times*, June 11, 1937; Burns, *Packing the Court*, 151–52.

118. Ackerman, *We the People*, vol. 2, 26.

119. Ackerman, *We the People*, vol. 2, 26.

120. Judge Douglas Ginsburg coined the term. Douglas H. Ginsburg, "Delegation Run Riot," review of *Power Without Responsibility: How Congress Abuses the People Through Delegation*, by David Schoenbrod, *Regulation* 1 (1995): 84.

121. Jeffrey Rosen, "The Unregulated Offensive," *New York Times*, April 17, 2005.

122. "The Third Term," *New York Times*, November 4, 1940.

123. Richard Moe, *Roosevelt's Second Act: The Election of 1940 and the Politics of War* (New York: Oxford University Press, 2013), 98.

124. Moe, *Roosevelt's Second Act*, 191–93.

125. Turner Catledge, "By 'Acclamation,'" *New York Times*, July 18, 1940.

126. James A. Hagerty, "Third Term a Peril, Willkie Declares," *New York Times*, September 12, 1940.

127. "Text of the Ohio Address by Herbert Hoover Assailing 'Drifts' of the New Deal," *New York Times*, October 25, 1940.

128. James C. Hagerty, "Pledge by Willkie: Would Ask Congress to Initiate Amendment Limiting Tenure," *New York Times*, November 4, 1940.

129. Warren Moscow, "Dewey Ridicules Roosevelt Pledge; Gives Own Program," *New York Times*, October 31, 1944.

130. Delaware Constitution of 1776, Art. 7; Georgia Constitution of 1777, Art. XXIII; Maryland Constitution of 1776, Art. XXXI; North Carolina Constitution of 1777, Art. XV; South Carolina Constitution of 1778, Art. VI; Virginia Constitution of 1776. The Articles of Confederation also limited the tenure of the president of the Confederation Congress, to one year during any three-year period. Articles of Confederation, Art. IX, Sec. 5 (U.S. 1781).

131. Maryland Constitution of 1776, Declaration of Rights, Sec. XXXI. See also Michael J. Klarman, *The Framers' Coup: The Making of the United States Constitution* (New York: Oxford University Press, 2016), 234.

132. Max Farrand, ed. *The Records of the Federal Convention of 1787*, vol. 2, (New Haven, CT: Yale University Press, 1911), 119–20 (hereafter Farrand, *Records*).

133. James Wilson and Roger Sherman advocated for short terms, three years in length, with re-election eligibility. Charles Pinkney and James Madison preferred a single seven-year term. When the convention proposed the idea of service "during good behavior," George Mason said that he "considered an Executive during good behavior as a softer name only for an Executive for life." Farrand, *Records*, vol. 1, 64, 68; vol. 2, 2, 35. See F. H. Buckley and Gilliam Metzger, "Twenty-Second Amendment," National Constitution Center Interactive Constitution, constitutioncenter.org/interactive-constitution/interpretation/amendment-xxii/interps/149.

134. George Washington to Marquis de Lafayette, Mount Vernon, April 28, 1788, Founders Online, National Archives, founders.archives.gov/documents/Washington/04-06-02-0211. Original source: *The Papers of George Washington*, Confederation Series, vol. 6, *1 January 1788–23 September 1788*, ed. W. W. Abbot (Charlottesville: University Press of Virginia, 1997), 242–46.

135. Thomas Jefferson to Alexander Donald, Paris, February 7, 1788, Founders Online, National Archives, founders.archives.gov/documents/Jefferson/01-12-02-0602. Original source: *The Papers of Thomas Jefferson*, vol. 12, *7 August 1787–31 March 1788*, ed. Julian P. Boyd (Princeton, NJ: Princeton University Press, 1955), 570–72.

136. Thomas Jefferson to the New Jersey Legislature, December 10, 1807, Founders Online, National Archives, founders.archives.gov/documents/Jefferson/99-01-02-6955. This is an Early Access document from *The Papers of Thomas Jefferson*. It is not an authoritative final version.

137. Charles W. Stein, *The Third-Term Tradition: Its Rise and Collapse in American Politics* (New York: Columbia University Press, 1943), 72–76.

138. "President Grant's Purpose," *New York Daily Tribune*, May 19, 1875.

139. Stein, *Third-Term Tradition*, 76–78; Kat Eschner, "The Third-Term Controversy That Gave the Republican Party Its Symbol," *Smithsonian Magazine*, November 7, 2017.

140. 4 *Congressional Record* 228 (1875). See Stephen W. Stathis, "The Twenty Second Amendment: A Practical Remedy or Partisan Maneuver?" *Constitutional Commentary* 7 (1990): 64.

141. Stein, *Third-Term Tradition*, 84–89; "The Revival of the Grant Boom," *The Nation*, October 9, 1879.

142. 93 *Congressional Record* 1776 (1947), statement of Senator Hill; Bruce G. Peabody, "George Washington, Presidential Term Limits, and the Problem of Reluctant Political Leadership," *Presidential Studies Quarterly* 31, no. 3 (September 2001): 447; Stein, *Third-Term Tradition*, 104–11.

143. *Harper's Weekly*, June 26, 1880; Stein, *Third-Term Tradition*, 112–13.

144. "Roosevelt Sweeps North and West and Is Elected President," *New York Times*, November 9, 1904.

145. Stein, *Third-Term Tradition*, 185.

146. Stein, *Third-Term Tradition*, 191, citing *Current Literature* 52 (March 1912), 251.

147. Stein, *Third-Term Tradition*, 204–5.

148. Stathis, "Twenty Second Amendment," 62–63.

149. Paul G. Willis and George L. Willis, "The Politics of the Twenty-Second Amendment," *Western Political Quarterly* 5, no. 3 (September 1952): 469.

150. Andrew E. Busch, "1946 Midterm Gives GOP First Majority Since 1928 Elections," Ashbrook Center, June 2006, ashbrook.org/publications/oped-busch-06-1946.

151. "'2-Term President' Bill to Be Voted, Says Martin," *New York Times*, January 9, 1947; 93 *Congressional Record* 48 (1947).

152. 93 *Congressional Record* 841 (1947).

153. 93 *Congressional Record* 841–42 (1947).

154. 93 *Congressional Record* 842–43 (1947).

155. 93 *Congressional Record* 843–44 (1947).

156. John D. Morris, "Limit of Two Terms for Any President Approved by House," *New York Times*, February 7, 1947.

157. 93 *Congressional Record* 857–58 (1947).

158. 93 *Congressional Record* 858 (1947).

159. 93 *Congressional Record* 872 (1947).

160. 93 *Congressional Record* 2392 (1947); David E. Kyvig, "Everett Dirksen's Constitutional Crusades," *Journal of the Illinois State Historical Society* 95, no. 1 (Spring 2002): 71.

161. 93 *Congressional Record* 1945 (1947).

162. 93 *Congressional Record* 1777 (1947).

163. 93 *Congressional Record* 1978 (1947).

164. 80 *Congressional Record* 2807 (1936).

165. 93 *Congressional Record* 1938 (1947).

166. 93 *Congressional Record* 2392 (1947).

167. 93 *Congressional Record* 2482 (1947).

168. U.S. Constitution, Amend. XXII.

169. See "Ban on Third Term Lags Among States," *New York Times*, July 16, 1950. "It is now considered possible that the amendment could fail to win ratification by the required thirty-six states."

170. Arthur Krock, "In the Nation: Proving That the Constitution Is Flexible," *New York Times*, March 1, 1951.

171. Kyvig, "Everett Dirksen's Constitutional Crusades," 71.

172. Krock, "In the Nation."

173. See S. J. Res. 37, H. J. Res. 9, H. J. Res 31, H. J. Res. 178, H. J. Res. 182, 85th Congress (1957); 103 *Congressional Record* 89, 822, 860 (1957); Stephen W. Stathis, *Presidential Tenure: A History*

and Analysis of the President's Term of Office (Washington, DC: Congressional Research Service, R81-129, 1981), 44–46.

174. Dwight D. Eisenhower, The President's News Conference on October 5, 1956, *Public Papers of the Presidents of the United States: Dwight D. Eisenhower: January 1 to December 31, 1956,* ed. David C. Eberhart (Washington, DC: Government Printing Office, 1962), 862. See Kyvig, "Everett Dirksen's Constitutional Crusades," 73.

175. "The New Amendment," *Wall Street Journal,* February 28, 1951.

176. 97 *Congressional Record* 1602 (1951).

177. 97 *Congressional Record* 1606-7 (1951); Willard Edwards, "Limit on Tenure Hailed as Blow to Dictatorship," *Chicago Daily Tribune,* February 28, 1951.

178. A conservative Republican Congress also proposed the Sixteenth Amendment in 1909. As explained in chapter 4, the support was tactical, offered in the expectation that the measure would fail to achieve ratification in the states.

Chapter 6: The Civil Rights Era Amendments (1960–1971)

1. Edward Zuckerman, *The Day After World War III* (New York: Viking Press, 1984), 85–86.

2. Proposing an Amendment to the Constitution Relating to the Nomination and Election of Candidates for President and Vice President, and to Succession to the Office of President in the Event of the Death or Inability of the President, S. J. Res. 4, 86th Congress (1959); 105 *Congressional Record* 231 (1959).

3. Proposing an Amendment to the Constitution to Provide That the People of the District of Columbia Shall Be Entitled to Vote in Presidential Elections and for Delegates to the House of Representatives, S. J. Res. 134, 86th Congress (1959); 105 *Congressional Record* 16111 (1959). It was one of three competing proposals. See Proposing an Amendment to the Constitution of the United States Granting Representation in the House of Representatives and in the Electoral College to the District of Columbia, S. J. Res. 60, 86th Congress (1959); 105 *Congressional Record* 2978 (1959); Proposing an Amendment to the Constitution to Provide That the People of the District of Columbia Shall Be Entitled to Vote in Presidential Elections, S. J. Res. 71, 86th Congress (1959); 105 *Congressional Record* 3529 (1959).

4. Proposing an Amendment to the Constitution of the United States Granting to Citizens of the United States Who Have Attained the Age of 18 the Right to Vote, S. J. Res. 81, 86th Congress (1959); 105 *Congressional Record* 5024 (1959).

5. Proposing an Amendment to the Constitution of the United States Relative to the Equal Rights for Men and Women, S. J. Res. 69, 86th Congress (1959); 105 *Congressional Record* 3529 (1959).

6. Proposing an Amendment to the Constitution of the United States Relating to the Qualifications of Electors, S. J. Res. 126, 86th Congress (1959); 105 *Congressional Record* 15215 (1959).

7. Leigh McWhite, "Mr. Chairman: U.S. Senator James O. Eastland and the Judiciary Committee, 1956–1978," *Mississippi Law Journal* 86 (2017): 956.

8. John H. Averill, "Sen. Eastland Is Top Paradox in the Senate," *Los Angeles Times,* September 15, 1965; McWhite, "Mr. Chairman," 953.

9. Averill, "Sen. Eastland Is Top Paradox," *Los Angeles Times,* September 15, 1965.

10. "Angry Young Man of 71," *New York Times,* March 19, 1960.

11. "Angry Young Man of 71," *New York Times,* March 19, 1960.

12. Appointment of Representatives, Senate Report no. 86-561, at 4 (1959).

13. An Act to Provide for the Performance of the Duties of the Office of President in Case of the Removal, Resignation, Death, or Inability Both of the President and Vice President (Presidential Succession Act of 1947), Pub. L. 80-199, 61 Stat. 380.

14. Appointment of Representatives, Senate Report no. 86-561 (1959), at 2.

15. Appointment of Representatives, Senate Report no. 86-561 (1959), at 4.

16. "Constitutional Amendment on D.C. Suffrage," *CQ Almanac 1960*, 16th ed., 09-284-9-287 (Washington, DC: Congressional Quarterly, 1960), library.cqpress.com/cqalmanac/document .php?id=cqal60-1330390.

17. Max Farrand, ed. *The Records of the Federal Convention of 1787*, vol. 2, (New Haven, CT: Yale University Press, 1911), 261 (hereafter Farrand, *Records*).

18. U.S. Constitution, Art. I, Sec. 8, cl. 17.

19. *Adams v. Clinton*, 90 F. Supp. 2d 35, 77 (D.D.C. 2000).

20. Jonathan Elliot, *The Debates in the Several State Conventions on the Adoption of the Federal Constitution as Recommended by the General Convention at Philadelphia in 1787* (hereafter Elliot's *Debates*), vol. 2, ed. Jonathan Elliot (Washington, 1836), 402, statement of Thomas Tredwell.

21. An Act for Establishing the Temporary and Permanent Seat of the Government of the United States (Residence Act), 1 Stat. 130 (1790).

22. 10 *Annals of Congress*, 997 (1801).

23. U.S. Constitution, Art. I, Sec. 8.

24. James Madison, *Federalist* no. 43, Avalon Project, avalon.law.yale.edu/18th_century /fed43.asp.

25. See W. V. Thomas, Washington, D.C., Voting Representation, *Editorial Research Reports 1979*, vol. 1, (Washington, DC: CQ Press, 1979), library.cqpress.com/cqresearcher/cqresrrel 979010500.

26. This change was formalized in 1878. District of Columbia Organic Act (Organic Act of 1878), 20 Stat. 102 (1878).

27. Clement E. Vose, "When District of Columbia Representation Collides with the Constitutional Amendment Institution," *Publius: The Journal of American Federalism* 9, no. 1 (Winter 1979): 107; "D.C. Home Rule," Council of the District of Columbia, dccouncil.us/dc-home-rule.

28. Proposing an Amendment of the Constitution to Confer Representation to the District of Columbia in the Two Houses of Congress, S. Res. 82, 50th Congress (1888); 19 *Congressional Record* 4144 (1888).

29. Vose, "When District of Columbia Representation Collides with the Constitutional Amendment Institution," 114–15.

30. 106 *Congressional Record* 1748 (1960).

31. 106 *Congressional Record* 1759 (1960).

32. 106 *Congressional Record* 1759 (1960).

33. Senator Keating listed the following states: New Hampshire, Vermont, North Dakota, South Dakota, Delaware, Montana, Idaho, Wyoming, Nevada, New Mexico, Alaska, and Hawaii. 106 *Congressional Record* 1759 (1960).

34. 106 *Congressional Record* 1759 (1960).

35. 106 *Congressional Record* 1765 (1960).

36. 106 *Congressional Record* 12554 (1960), statement of Representative Smith, Virginia.

37. 106 *Congressional Record* 12556 (1960), statement of Representative Udall.

38. U.S. Constitution, Art. II, Sec. 1; 106 *Congressional Record* 12558 (1960), statement of Representative McCulloch.

39. 106 *Congressional Record* 12563 (1960).

40. In the 1960 census, which formed the basis for apportionment in 1961, the District of Columbia's population (763,956) was larger than the population of six states that received four electoral votes: New Hampshire, North Dakota, Hawaii, Idaho, Montana, and South Dakota. U.S. Census Bureau, "Rank of States According to Population: 1910 to 1960," *1960 Census*, vol. 1, part 1, table 15.

41. 106 *Congressional Record* 12551 (1960).

42. 106 *Congressional Record* 12555 (1960).

43. 103 *Congressional Record* 8658 (1957). Whitener's quote continued, "This has been their record. This pending legislation, if enacted, would tie the hands of the law-enforcement officers throughout the country, and would place law-abiding men, women, and children at the mercy of brutal, merciless, hardened criminals." 103 *Congressional Record* 8658 (1957).

44. 106 *Congressional Record* 12561 (1960).

45. 106 *Congressional Record* 12558 (1960).

46. Jay G. Hayden, "Jay G. Hayden of Our Washington Bureau," *Detroit News*, June 16, 1960.

47. 106 *Congressional Record* 12853 (1960).

48. 106 *Congressional Record* 12858 (1960).

49. Morton Mintz, "23rd Amendment Adopted 9 Months After 'Hill' Action," *Washington Post*, March 30, 1961.

50. U.S. Census Bureau, "Comparison of Complete Count and Sample Data for Selected Characteristics, for the State [Hawaii], Urban and Rural: 1960," *1960 Census*, vol. 1, part 13, table A. See also Akhil Amar, *America's Constitution: A Biography* (New York: Random House, 2005), 441.

51. "States Fuss Over Which Was 38th to Give D.C. Vote," *Tulsa Daily World*, March 31, 1961.

52. Mintz, "23rd Amendment Adopted," *Washington Post*, March 30, 1961.

53. Georgia, Florida, Kentucky, Louisiana, Mississippi, North Carolina, South Carolina, Virginia, and Texas never ratified or voted on the amendment. Arkansas rejected the amendment on January 24, 1961, and Alabama ratified it more than forty years later, on April 11, 2002.

54. Russell Baker, "District of Columbia Wins Vote by 23d Amendment," *New York Times*, March 30, 1961.

55. John F. Kennedy, "Statement by the President Following Ratification of the 23d Amendment to the Constitution," March 29, 1961, American Presidency Project, www.presidency.ucsb.edu/node/234488.

56. Vose, "When District of Columbia Representation Collides with the Constitutional Amendment Institution," 119.

57. Elsie Carper, "Johnson Captures D.C. with 5 to 1 Margin over Sen. Goldwater," *Washington Post*, November 4, 1961; "Big Capital Vote Goes to Johnson," *New York Times*, November 4, 1964; "The 1964 Election," *CQ Almanac 1964*, 20th ed., 1021–68 (Washington, DC: *Congressional Quarterly*, 1965), library.cqpress.com/cqalmanac/cqal64-1302939. Indeed, no GOP presidential candidate has ever won more than 22 percent of the vote in the nation's capital.

58. In 1972, Richard Nixon won 21.6 percent of the vote in the 1972 election. "1972 Presidential Election," *Presidential Elections 1789–2008*, ed. CQ Press Staff, 10th ed., 2009.

59. In 1956 elections for national party convention delegates, approximately 24,000 voters in the District cast ballots in the Democratic contest, compared to 22,000 in the Republican contest. Vose, "When District of Columbia Representation Collides with the Constitutional Amendment Institution," 116.

60. Republican Party Platform of 1956, Republican Party Platforms, American Presidency Project, www.presidency.ucsb.edu/node/273398.

61. U.S. Census Bureau, "Race by Sex for the District of Columbia: 1880 to 1950," *1950 Census*, vol. 2, part 9, table 14.

62. U.S. Census Bureau, "Age by Color and Sex for the District of Columbia: 1940 and 1950," *1950 Census*, vol. 2, part 9, table 15.

63. U.S. Census Bureau, "Race by Sex for the District of Columbia: 1890 to 1960," *1960 Census*, vol. 1, part 9, table 15.

64. Garry Young, "The District of Columbia and Its Lack of Representation in Congress: What Difference Does It Make?" (Washington, DC: Center for Washington Area Studies, 2009), 61, gwipp.gwu.edu/sites/g/files/zaxdzs2181/f/downloads/DC%20Representation%20Main%20Report%20Final.pdf. "1) The United States is the only democracy that does not provide full

representation for its capital city; 2) The United States is the only democratic nation that restricts the legislative authority of its capital representatives. . . ."

65. "The Vote at Last," *Washington Post*, March 30, 1961.

66. See Michelle Norris, "The Woolworth Sit-In That Launched a Movement," NPR, February 1, 2008, www.npr.org/templates/story/story.php?storyId=18615556.

67. See Debra Michals, "Ruby Bridges," National Women's History Museum, 2015, www .womenshistory.org/education-resources/biographies/ruby-bridges.

68. See Marian Smith Holmes, "The Freedom Riders, Then and Now," *Smithsonian Magazine*, February 2009, www.smithsonianmag.com/history/the-freedom-riders-then-and-now-45351758.

69. 108 *Congressional Record* 17656 (1962), statement of Representative Celler.

70. Farrand, *Records*, vol. 2, 202.

71. These states were Delaware, Pennsylvania, and Rhode Island. "Disenfranchisement by Means of the Poll Tax," *Harvard Law Review* 53, no. 4 (February 1940): 646–47.

72. *Journal of the Proceedings of the Constitutional Convention of the State of Alabama, Held in the City of Montgomery, Commencing May 21st, 1901* (Montgomery, AL: Brown Printing, 1901), 9.

73. 108 *Congressional Record* 5095 (1962), statement of Senator Douglas. "One of the two major devices which they used was to impose literacy tests together with property and poll taxes. Mississippi had instituted this system earlier, in 1890, probably as a reaction to the Lodge bill. Other States began to follow suit, such as South Carolina in 1895, Louisiana in 1898, North Carolina in 1900, Alabama in 1901, Virginia in 1902, in the celebrated Virginia constitutional convention, Georgia in 1908, and Oklahoma in 1910. Other States which adopted the poll tax were Florida, Tennessee, Arkansas, and Texas. In a relatively short time the whole South was covered with poll tax provisions, as well as with a web of other provisions."

74. CPI Inflation Calculator, Official Data Foundation, www.in2013dollars.com/1889-dollars -in-2021?amount=2.

75. 1889 Fla. Laws 13. See Russell Brooker, *The American Civil Rights Movement 1865–1950: Black Agency and People of Good Will* (Lanham, MD: Lexington Books, 2017), 62. Typical poll tax ranged from one to three dollars, paid at least a month in advance of the election, receipts to be retained for two years, and voters had to pay anything in arrears. Jerrold G. Rusk and John T. Stucker, "The Effect of the Southern System of Election Laws on Voting," in *The History of American Electoral Behavior*, ed. Joel H. Silbey, Allan G. Bogue, and William H. Flanigan (Princeton, NJ: Princeton University Press, 1978), 224. See also Charles D. Farris, "The Re-enfranchisement of Negroes in Florida," *Journal of Negro History* 39, no. 4 (October 1954): 261.

76. *Guinn v. United States*, 238 U.S. 347, 365 (1915). See 108 *Congressional Record* 5095 (1962), statement of Senator Douglas. "A web of other restrictions, such as property, literacy, ability to pass so-called citizenship tests, the 'white primary' and so forth, was also woven and still further restricted Negro suffrage; but it was made somewhat easier for the whites to penetrate these measures." Also: *Smith v. Allwright*, 321 U.S. 649 (1944), overruling *Grovey v. Townsend*, 295 U.S. 45 (1935). See also *Nixon v. Herndon*, 273 U.S. 536 (1927); *Nixon v. Condon*, 286 U.S. 73 (1932).

77. *Breedlove v. Suttles*, 302 U.S. 277 (1937).

78. *Breedlove v. Suttles*, 302 U.S. 277 (1937), at 282–83.

79. President's Committee on Civil Rights, *To Secure These Rights: The Report of the President's Committee on Civil Rights* (Washington, DC: Government Printing Office, 1947), 39.

80. President's Committee on Civil Rights, *To Secure These Rights*, 39, 160. Note that the Committee also recommended that Congress extend self-government rights to the District of Columbia, as well as for its representation in Congress and suffrage in federal elections, at 161.

81. President's Committee on Civil Rights, *To Secure These Rights*, 160.

82. "Spessard L. Holland Dies at 79: Former Senator From Florida," *New York Times*, November 7, 1971; John R. Nemmers, "A Guide to the Spessard L. Holland Papers," University of Florida Smathers Libraries, Special and Area Studies Collections, January 2005, www.uflib.ufl.edu

/spec/pkyonge/holland.htm. The law firm that bears his name, Holland & Knight, thrives today, a global giant with 1,400 attorneys in four countries. Holland & Knight, www.hklaw.com/en.

83. In 1940, the average rate of participation among voting-age residents in poll-tax states was 3 percent, compared to 25 percent in non-poll-tax states. The figure for non-poll-tax states includes Florida, Louisiana, and North Carolina, which had just recently eliminated their poll tax and had participation rates of 5, 4, and 9 percent, respectively. William M. Brewer, "The Poll Tax and Poll Taxers," *Journal of Negro History* 29 (July 1944): 266. Furthermore, in 1942, eight Congressmen from poll-tax states were elected with only 1% support from the voting-age population in their districts. Brewer, "Poll Tax and Poll Taxers," 272.

84. Brewer, "Poll Tax and Poll Taxers," 272–75, 278–81.

85. "Anti–Poll Tax Amendment Ratified by the States," *CQ Almanac 1964*, 20th ed., 381–82 (Washington, DC: Congressional Quarterly, 1965), library.cqpress.com/cqalmanac /cqal64-1304646.

86. Bruce Ackerman and Jennifer Nou, "Canonizing the Civil Rights Revolution: The People and the Poll Tax," *Northwestern University Law Review* 103 (2009): 70; 111 *Congressional Record* 9797 (1965).

87. See Ackerman and Nou, "Canonizing the Civil Rights Revolution," 72 n39, 76 n67.

88. *Poll Tax and Enfranchisement of District of Columbia*, before the Subcommittee on Constitutional Amendments of the Senate Committee on the Judiciary, 86th Congress 7 (1959).

89. 108 *Congressional Record* 5075 (1962), statement of Senator Holland.

90. Holland explained that in his home state, repeal led to "a great surge forward in participation by the poor white people" with "gradually increased participation by the colored people of the State." 106 *Congressional Record* 12854 (1960).

91. Brewer, "Poll Tax and Poll Taxers," 264–65, 264 n15.

92. "Anti–Poll Tax Amendment Ratified by the States," *CQ Almanac 1964*, 20th ed., 381–82 (Washington, DC: *Congressional Quarterly*, 1965), library.cqpress.com/cqalmanac /cqal64-1304646.

93. U.S. Constitution, Art. I, Sec. 2; U.S. Constitution, Amend. XVII.

94. U.S. Constitution, Art. I, Sec. 4.

95. *Poll Tax and Enfranchisement of District of Columbia*, 86th Congress 6 (1959).

96. *Poll Tax and Enfranchisement of District of Columbia*, 86th Congress 48 (1959).

97. *Poll Tax and Enfranchisement of District of Columbia*, 86th Congress 71 (1959), statement of Clarence Mitchell, director of the Washington Bureau of the NAACP; *Abolition of Poll Tax in Federal Elections*, before Subcommittee No. 5 of the House Committee on the Judiciary, 87th Congress 28 (1962), statement of Clarence Mitchell.

98. The six other organizations were the American Jewish Congress, the American Veterans Committee, Americans for Democratic Action, the Anti-Defamation League, the International Union of Electrical Workers, and the United Automobile Workers of America. "NAACP, Six Other Groups Oppose Poll Tax Amendment," *Atlanta Daily World*, March 25, 1962.

99. Chris Myers Asch, *The Senator and the Sharecropper: The Freedom Struggles of James O. Eastland and Fannie Lou Hamer* (Chapel Hill: University of North Carolina Press, 2008), 97.

100. 106 *Congressional Record* 1765 (1960).

101. 106 *Congressional Record* 1745 (1960).

102. 106 *Congressional Record* 12856 (1960).

103. 108 *Congressional Record* 5074 (1962). At Celler's suggestion, the earlier versions' ban on property requirements was removed, at 5074–75.

104. 108 *Congressional Record* 5097 (1962).

105. 108 *Congressional Record* 5078 (1962). Just two decades earlier, Stennis's immediate predecessor predicted a parade of horribles that would result from a repeal of the poll tax. Theodore Bilbo, the self-anointed "real friend to the Negro," explained, "If that is done, we will have no way of preventing the Negro from voting," adding that "as the Negroes get their political power,

they will demand social rights, economic rights, and other rights." 88 *Congressional Record* 8957–58 (1942).

106. Providing for the establishing of the former dwelling house of Alexander Hamilton as a national memorial, S. J. Res. 171, 87th Congress (1962), sponsored by senators Javits and Keating); 108 *Congressional Record* 4150, 4174, 5075 (1962).

107. 108 *Congressional Record* 4151 (1962).

108. 108 *Congressional Record* 4151 (1962).

109. 108 *Congressional Record* 4209 (1962).

110. The following senators participated in the March 1962 filibuster of the poll-tax amendment: Richard Russell Jr. (D-GA), Harry F. Byrd Sr. (D-VA), Allen J. Ellender (D-LA), Joseph Hill (D-AL), James Eastland (D-MS), John Little McClellan (D-AR), J. William Fulbright (D-AR), Olin D. Johnston (D-SC), A. Willis Robertson (D-VA), John Sparkman (D-AL), John C. Stennis (D-MS), Sam Ervin (D-NC), Strom Thurmond (D-SC), Herman Talmadge (D-GA), and John Tower (R-TX).

111. "Question of Democracy," *Washington Post*, March 20, 1960; Gregory Koger, *Filibustering: A Political History of Obstruction in the House and Senate* (Chicago: University of Chicago Press, 2010), 168.

112. Anthony Lewis, "Rights Filibuster Keeps Droning On," *New York Times*, March 24, 1962.

113. Russell also claimed that anytime "a man from one of the minority groups says, 'Put it through,' we find a way to put it through without regard to the rules." 108 *Congressional Record* 5084 (1962).

114. John F. Kennedy to Spessard Holland, Washington, DC, March 6, 1962, read by Senator Holland on 108 *Congressional Record* 4368 (1962).

115. 108 *Congressional Record* 5088–89 (1962).

116. 108 *Congressional Record* 5101 (1962).

117. 108 *Congressional Record* 5105 (1962).

118. E. W. Kenworthy, "Quips Mark Start of Rights Hearing," *New York Times*, January 10, 1964.

119. Don Oberdorfer, " 'Judge' Smith Moves with Deliberate Drag," *New York Times Magazine*, January 12, 1964.

120. 108 *Congressional Record* 17656 (1962).

121. 108 *Congressional Record* 17660–61 (1962), statement of Representative Forrester.

122. 108 *Congressional Record* 17656 (1962), statement of Representative Celler.

123. 108 *Congressional Record* 17660 (1962).

124. 108 *Congressional Record* 17659–60 (1962).

125. 108 *Congressional Record* 17659 (1962).

126. 108 *Congressional Record* 17670 (1962).

127. Lyndon Johnson, Remarks upon Witnessing the Certification of the 24th Amendment to the Constitution, Washington, DC, February 4, 1964, American Presidency Project, www .presidency.ucsb.edu/node/240004.

128. "24th Amendment, Banning Poll Tax, Has Been Ratified," *New York Times*, January 24, 1964.

129. 110 *Congressional Record* 14319 (1964).

130. Ackerman and Nou, "Canonizing the Civil Rights Revolution," 87–88.

131. Ackerman and Nou, "Canonizing the Civil Rights Revolution," 91–93.

132. President Lyndon B. Johnson, Remarks in the Capitol Rotunda at the Signing of the Voting Rights Act, Washington, DC, August 6, 1965, American Presidency Project, www .presidency.ucsb.edu/node/241195.

133. Ackerman and Nou, "Canonizing the Civil Rights Revolution," 88–89.

134. 111 *Congressional Record* 10028 (1965).

135. 111 *Congressional Record* 9797 (1965).

136. *Harper v. Virginia State Board of Elections*, 383 U.S. 663, at 666, 668 (1966).

137. *Jones v. Desantis*, 4:19-cv-00300-MW-MJF (N.D. Fla. 2019). See also *Harvey v. Brewer*, 605 F.3d 1067 (9th Cir. 2010), holding that an Arizona law requiring those convicted of felonies to pay any required fines or restitution before their voting rights are restored does not impose a poll tax; *Johnson v. Bredesen*, 624 F.3d 742 (6th Cir. 2010), holding that a Tennessee statute conditioning re-enfranchisement of convicted felons on payment of restitution and child support obligations does not violate the Twenty-Fourth Amendment because convicted felons possess no right to vote and child support and restitution payments do not qualify as poll taxes.

138. Deborah N. Archer, "The Role of the Twenty-Fourth Amendment in Challenging Financial Burdens on the Right to Vote," National Constitution Center, constitution-center.org/interactive-constitution/interpretation/amendment-xxiv/interps/157#the-role-of-twenty-fourth-amendment-in-challenging-financial-burdens-on-the.

139. U.S. Constitution, Art. II, Sec. 1, cl. 6.

140. See Edward J. Larson, "A Constitutional Afterthought: The Origins of the Vice Presidency, 1787 to 1804," *Pepperdine Law Review* 44, no. 3, *Symposium: The United States Vice Presidency: In History, Practice, and the Future* (March 2017): 516. "In its 1787 origins, the creation of an office of Vice President was an afterthought at the Constitutional Convention and reflected spectacularly little forethought." And: Richard B. Cheney, Edwin Meese III, and Douglas W. Kmiec, "The Vice President—More than an Afterthought?" *Pepperdine Law Review* 44, no. 3, *Symposium: The United States Vice Presidency: In History, Practice, and the Future* (March 2017): 536. Former vice president Dick Cheney remarked, "I think it was an afterthought," explaining that the position of vice president was created to make some of the Framers more comfortable with the Constitution. He added, "I think it was a band aid, an effort to deal with the short-term problem; and the rationale behind it, at the time, was pretty much uninformed."

141. Jared Cohen, *Accidental Presidents: Eight Men Who Changed America* (New York: Simon & Schuster, 2019), 9. According to scholar Ruth C. Silva, "Legend tells us that the precedent was established merely because Tyler claimed presidential status." However, there was a bill in each chamber of Congress to explicitly substitute "President" with "Vice President now acting as President," both of which failed (in the Senate by a 38–8 vote). See Ruth C. Silva, *Presidential Succession* (Ann Arbor: University of Michigan Press, 1951), 14; Robert S. Rankin, "Presidential Succession in the United States," *Journal of Politics* 8, no. 1 (February 1946): 45.

142. See Amar, *America's Constitution*, 448, discussing the perks of being president, not just vice president, including a salary increase and constitutional protection from Congress "tinkering" therewith; Cohen, *Accidental Presidents*, 9; Callie Hopkins, "John Tyler and Presidential Succession," White House Historical Association, March 22, 2019, www.whitehousehistory.org/john-tyler-and-presidential-succession.

143. John Tyler, Address upon Assuming the Office of President of the United States, April 9, 1841, American Presidency Project, www.presidency.ucsb.edu/node/267861.

144. John Q. Adams, *Memoirs of John Quincy Adams*, vol. 10, ed. Charles Francis Adams (Philadelphia: J. B. Lippincott, 1876) 463–64. See John D. Feerick, "The Twenty-Fifth Amendment: An Explanation and Defense," *Wake Forest Law Review* 30, no. 3 (1995): 481, 484.

145. Cohen, *Accidental Presidents*, 11, 25.

146. "Death of Ex-President Tyler," *New York Times*, January 22, 1862.

147. U.S. Constitution, Art. II, Sec. 1, cl. 6.

148. Cohen, *Accidental Presidents*, 137; Stephen W. Stathis, "Presidential Disability Agreements Prior to the 25th Amendment," *Presidential Studies Quarterly* 12, no. 2 (Spring 1982): 208.

149. Zachary Karabell, *Chester Alan Arthur* (New York: Times Books, 2004), 59; Cohen, *Accidental Presidents*, 162.

150. Jules Witcover, *The American Vice Presidency: From Irrelevance to Power* (Washington, DC: Smithsonian Books, 2014), 193–94.

151. Feerick, "Twenty-Fifth Amendment," 486–87; Jacob M. Appel, "Meet the First Woman to Wield Presidential Power: Edith Wilson," *The Hill*, December 29, 2018.

152. Appel, "Meet the First Woman to Wield Presidential Power."

153. Manuel Roig-Franzia, "Did We Once Have an Unelected Madam President?" *Washington Post*, November 18, 2016.

154. Feerick, "Twenty-Fifth Amendment," 487; Witcover, *American Vice Presidency*, 263–64.

155. Witcover, *American Vice Presidency*, 265; "Thomas R. Marshall, 28th Vice President (1913–1921)," U.S. Senate Historical Office, www.senate.gov/about/officers-staff/vice-president /VP_Thomas_Marshall.htm.

156. See Adam Kucharski, "Medical Management of Political Patients: The Case of Dwight D. Eisenhower," *Perspectives in Biology and Medicine* 22, no. 1 (1978): 115–26; Robert E. Gilbert, "Eisenhower's 1955 Heart Attack: Medical Treatment, Political Effects, and the 'Behind the Scenes' Leadership Style," *Politics and Life Sciences* 27, no. 1 (March 2008): 2–21.

157. Stathis, "Presidential Disability Agreements," 209–10; see Dwight D. Eisenhower, "Agreement Between the President and the Vice President as to Procedures in the Event of Presidential Disability," March 3, 1958, American Presidency Project, www.presidency.ucsb.edu /node/234514, establishing rules "in accord with the purposes and provisions of Article 2, Section I, of the Constitution," to ensure seamless governance upon presidential inability and a return of power upon the president's determination that the inability has ceased.

158. Roy E. Brownell II, "What to Do If Simultaneous Presidential and Vice Presidential Inability Struck Today," *Fordham Law Review* 86, no. 3 (2017): 1039.

159. 111 *Congressional Record* 3250 (1965).

160. The next in line was of the opposite party or political allegiance during all or part of the following vice-presidential vacancies: John Tyler (1841–45), Millard Fillmore (1850–53), Andrew Johnson (1865–69), Chester Arthur (1881–85), Grover Cleveland (1885–89), and Harry Truman (1945–49).

161. John Adams to Abigail Adams, Philadelphia, December 19, 1793, Founders Online, National Archives, founders.archives.gov/documents/Adams/04-09-02-0278. Original source: *The Adams Papers*, Adams Family Correspondence, vol. 9, *January 1790–December 1793*, ed. C. James Taylor, Margaret A. Hogan, Karen N. Barzilay, Gregg L. Lint, Hobson Woodward, Mary T. Claffey, Robert F. Karachuk, and Sara B. Sikes (Cambridge, MA: Harvard University Press, 2009), 476–77.

162. See Carl M. Cannon, "How to Pick a Veep: Eight Historical Criteria," *Real Clear Politics*, May 30, 2012, www.realclearpolitics.com/articles/2012/05/30/how_to_pick_a_veep_eight_his torical_criteria_114311.html; Hendrik Hertzberg, "Vice Squads," *The New Yorker*, March 14, 2004, www.newyorker.com/magazine/2004/03/22/vice-squads.

163. See Larson, "Constitutional Afterthought," 516.

164. Nicholas deB. Katzenbach "Participation of the Vice President in the Affairs of the Executive Branch," in *Supplemental Opinions of the Office of Legal Counsel of the U.S. Department of Justice*, ed. Nathan A. Forrester (Washington, DC: 2013).

165. Presidential Inability and Vacancies in the Office of the Vice President, Senate Report no. 88-1382 (1964), at 13.

166. Geoffrey Gould, "It's Who Comes Next After the Vice President and the Disability Issue That Cause Controversy," *Lexington Sunday Herald Leader*, December 15, 1963; "Speaker Got Early Start; It's Silent Sen. Hayden," *Washington Post*, November 24, 1963; "The Succession," *Chicago Tribune*, December 10, 1963.

167. An Act to Provide for the Performance of the Duties of the Office of President in Case of the Removal, Resignation, Death, or Inability Both of the President and Vice President (Presidential Succession Act of 1947), Pub. L. 80-199, 61 Stat. 380; U.S. Constitution, Art. II, Sec. 1, cl. 6.

168. "Two Old Timers Next in Line for Presidency of U.S.," *Chicago Tribune*, December 1, 1963.

169. Birch Bayh, *One Heartbeat Away* (Indianapolis: Bobbs-Merrill, 1968), 41.

170. Lyndon B. Johnson, Address Before a Joint Session of the Congress, Washington, DC, November 27, 1963, www.presidency.ucsb.edu/node/238734; Tom Wicker, "Johnson Bids

Congress Enact Civil Rights Bill with Speed; Asks End of Hate and Violence," *New York Times*, November 28, 1963; Layhmond Robinson Jr., "Negroes Praise Johnson Speech," *New York Times*, November 28, 1963.

171. "Amendment Sponsor Birch Evan Bayh Jr.," *New York Times*, February 11, 1967; "How a national tragedy led to the 25th Amendment," *National Constitution Center Blog*, February 10, 2020, constitutioncenter.org/interactive-constitution/blog/how-jfks-assassination-led-to-a-constitutional-amendment-2.

172. "Amendment Sponsor Birch Evan Bayh Jr.," *New York Times*, February 11, 1967.

173. Alexander Hamilton, *Federalist* no. 70, Avalon Project, avalon.law.yale.edu/18th_century/fed70.asp.

174. 109 *Congressional Record* 24330 (1963).

175. 109 *Congressional Record* 24420 (1963).

176. David E. Kyvig, *Explicit and Authentic Acts: Amending the U.S. Constitution 1776–1995* (Lawrence: University of Kansas Press, 1996), 359.

177. John D. Feerick, "The Problem of Presidential Inability—Will Congress Ever Solve It?" *Fordham Law Review* 32 (1963): 73; *Presidential Inability and Vacancies in the Office of Vice President*, before the Subcommittee on Constitutional Amendments of the Senate Committee on the Judiciary, 88th Congress 150 (1964), statement of John D. Feerick, attorney, American Bar Association.

178. Bayh later wrote that Feerick "did his part, as we knew he would, to help us in writing a solid legislative record." Bayh, *One Heartbeat Away*, 68–69.

179. In July 1985, Ronald Reagan temporarily transferred power to George H. W. Bush as he underwent surgery to remove a benign polyp from his colon. Twice, in June 2002 and July 2007, George W. Bush invoked section 3 in connection with routine colonoscopy exams. John D. Feerick, *The Twenty-Fifth Amendment: Its Complete History and Applications*, 3rd ed. (New York: Fordham University Press, 2014), 196–99, 202–3.

180. Feerick, *Twenty-Fifth Amendment*, 190–96.

181. Lawrence K. Altman, "Presidential Power: Reagan Doctor Says He Erred," *New York Times*, February 20, 1989.

182. C. P. Trussell, "Plan for Replacing an Ailing President Is Voted by Senate," *New York Times*, September 29, 1964; C. P. Trussell, "Senate Repasses Succession Bill," *New York Times*, September 30, 1964.

183. Kenneth Crawford, "Calling All Worriers: McCormack's Fitness," *Newsweek*, April 27, 1964.

184. Lyndon B. Johnson, Special Message to the Congress on Presidential Disability and Related Matters, January 28, 1965, American Presidency Project, www.presidency.ucsb.edu/node/241639; Kyvig, *Explicit and Authentic Acts*, 361.

185. Felix Belair Jr., "Capitol Hearings Set on Succession," *New York Times*, January 26, 1965; Alan P. Grimes, *Democracy and the Amendments to the Constitution* (Lanham, MD: Lexington Books, 1978), 137.

186. Dirksen's "ill-considered, if hard-fought, campaigns for various amendments . . . with potentially serious negative consequences for the conduct of government, suggest that Dirksen was not always the 'senatorial statesman' that at least some of his biographers have proclaimed." David E. Kyvig, "Everett Dirksen's Constitutional Crusades," *Journal of the Illinois State Historical Society* 95, no. 1 (Spring 2002): 70–82, 83.

187. Kyvig, "Everett Dirksen's Constitutional Crusades," 76–82.

188. "Presidential Inability and Vacancies in the Office of the Vice President," Senate Report no. 89-66, at 17, 19 (1965). See also 111 *Congressional Record* 3257, 3265 (1962).

189. C. P. Trussell, "M'Carthy Fights Disability Plan," *New York Times*, February 16, 1965.

190. "Sam Ervin: A Featured Biography," Senators, U.S. Senate, www.senate.gov/senators/FeaturedBios/Featured_Bio_ErvinSam.htm.

191. "Former Sen. Sam Ervin, 88, Watergate Folk Hero, Dies," *Los Angeles Times*, April 24, 1985.

192. 111 *Congressional Record* 3269 (1965); Tom Wicker, "Senate Votes Amendment on Presidential Disability," *New York Times*, February 20, 1965.

193. 111 *Congressional Record* 3265, 3272 (1965); Wicker, "Senate Votes Amendment."

194. 111 *Congressional Record* 3286 (1965); Wicker, "Senate Votes Amendment."

195. Tom Wicker, "Disability Plan Voted by House," *New York Times*, April 14, 1965.

196. "The Disability Amendment," *New York Times*, April 18, 1965.

197. E. W. Kenworthy, "Conferees Back Succession Plan," *New York Times*, June 25, 1965.

198. "Only a Partial Solution," *New York Times*, February 12, 1967.

199. 111 *Congressional Record* 15216 (1965); John D. Morris "Disability Plan Hits Senate Snag," *New York Times*, July 1, 1965.

200. Morris, "Disability Plan Hits Senate Snag"; Bayh, *One Heartbeat Away*, 306–18.

201. 111 *Congressional Record* 15590 (1965).

202. 111 *Congressional Record* 15594–95 (1965).

203. 111 *Congressional Record* 15596 (1965).

204. Bayh, *One Heartbeat Away*, 336.

205. Robert Blaemire, *Birch Bayh: Making a Difference* (Bloomington: Indiana University Press, 2019), 79.

206. Feerick, *Twenty-Fifth Amendment*, 107.

207. John Herbers, "25th Amendment, Presidency Plan, Has Been Ratified," *New York Times*, February 11, 1967.

208. No state rejected it, but Georgia, North Dakota, and South Carolina failed to act on it. In North Dakota, the Amendment did pass the Senate but was held up in the House by a lone representative who called it a "poor piece of legislation" and successfully requested indefinite postponement of the matter. Sydney Mook, "North Dakota Never Ratified the 25th Amendment. Why?" *Grand Forks Herald*, September 16, 2018.

209. Brian C. Kalt, "The Unusual, Imperfect, Excellent Twenty-Fifth Amendment," National Constitution Center Interactive Constitution, constitutioncenter.org/interactive -constitution/interpretation/amendment-xxv/interps/159#the-unusual-imperfect-excellent -twenty-fifth-amendment-by-brian-kalt.

210. Kalt, "Unusual, Imperfect, Excellent Twenty-Fifth Amendment."

211. 111 *Congressional Record* 7698 (1965). See Feerick, *Twenty-Fifth Amendment*, 100.

212. Gerald R. Ford, "The Path Back to Dignity," *New York Times*, October 4, 1998.

213. See., e.g., Richard Cohen, "How to Remove Trump from Office," *Washington Post*, January 9, 2017; Ross Douthat, "The 25th Amendment Solution for Removing Trump," *New York Times*, May 16, 2017; Julian Zelizer, "Is It Time to Talk About the 25th Amendment?" CNN, October 16, 2017; Robert Dallek, "Is Trump Unfit for Office? The Constitution Says Yes," *Newsweek*, December 16, 2017; Paul Campos, "Pence Should Remove Trump from Office on Sunday," *New York Magazine*, December 23, 2020; Calling on Vice President Michael R. Pence to Convene and Mobilize the Principal Officers of the Executive Departments of the Cabinet to Activate Section 4 of the 25th Amendment to Declare President Donald J. Trump Incapable of Executing the Duties of His Office and to Immediately Exercise Powers as Acting President, H. Res. 21, 117th Congress (2021), passed in the House on January 12, 2021.

214. Miles Taylor, "I Am Part of the Resistance Inside the Trump Administration," *New York Times*, September 5, 2018: "Given the instability many witnessed, there were early whispers within the cabinet of invoking the 25th Amendment, which would start a complex process for removing the president. But no one wanted to precipitate a constitutional crisis." Also: Rebecca Harrington and Lauren Frias, "Some of Trump's Top-Most Advisers Have Reportedly Discussed Invoking the 25th Amendment, Which Lets 14 People Remove a Sitting President from Office. Here's How It Works," *Business Insider*, February 14, 2019, updated October 2, 2020; Tim Wyatt,

"Top US Officials Considered Removing Trump Using 25th Amendment, FBI Lawyers Confirm," *Independent*, February 17, 2019.

215. Nicholas Wu and Christal Hayes, "House Passes Measure Calling on Pence to Invoke 25th Amendment and Remove Trump from Office," *USA Today*, January 12, 2021.

216. See Alexander Hamilton, *Federalist* no. 65, Avalon Project, avalon.law.yale.edu/18th _century/fed65.asp, explaining that impeachment is for "those offenses which proceed from the misconduct of public men, or, in other words, from the abuse or violation of some public trust"; Corey Brettschneider, *The Oath and the Office: A Guide to the Constitution for Future Presidents* (New York: Norton, 2018), 207-22, describing impeachment as "a severe and rarely used check on a president who continually disregards the oath and imperils the nation," and discussing its historical use; Harrington and Frias, "Some of Trump's Top-Most Advisers Have Reportedly Discussed Invoking the 25th Amendment," quoting John D. Feerick as saying, "If you read the debates, it's also clear that policy and political differences are not included, unpopularity is not included, poor judgment, incompetence, laziness, or impeachable conduct—none of that, you'll find in the debates in the congressional record, is intended to be covered by Section IV."

217. Joshua A. Douglas, "In Defense of Lowering the Voting Age," *University of Pennsylvania Law Review Online* 165, no. 1 (2017): 3-4.

218. Jenny Diamond Cheng, "Uncovering the Twenty-Sixth Amendment," Doctor of Philosophy (Political Science) Dissertation, University of Michigan, May 2008, 15, deepblue.lib.umich. edu/bitstream/handle/2027.42/58431/jdiamond_1.pdf. "The first proposal to amend the federal constitution to provide for eighteen-year-old voting came in October 1942, when Representative Victor Wickersham (D-OK) offered such an amendment on the same day that the House voted to lower the minimum draft age from twenty to eighteen." Also: Joint Resolution Proposing an Amendment to the Constitution of the United States to Permit Persons 18 Years of Age to Vote in All Elections for Federal Officers, H. J. Res. 352, 77th Congress (1942); 88 *Congressional Record* 8312 (1942). See also Proposing an Amendment to the Constitution of the United States Extending the Right to Vote to Citizens 18 Years of Age or Older, S. J. Res. 166, 77th Congress (1942); 88 *Congressional Record* 8316 (1942); Joint Resolution Proposing an Amendment to the Constitution of the United States Extending the Right to Vote to Citizens 18 Years of Age or Older, H. J. Res. 354, 77th Congress (1942); 88 *Congressional Record* 8507 (1942). Notably, Wickersham's measure proposed lowering the voting age to eighteen in federal elections only, while Vandenberg's and Randolph's also applied to state elections.

219. David Stout, "Senator Jennings Randolph of West Virginia Dies at 96," *New York Times*, May 9, 1998; Michael Barone, "Jennings Randolph," e-WV: The West Virginia Encyclopedia, December 8, 2015, www.wvencyclopedia.org/articles/10.

220. *Constitutional Amendment to Reduce Voting Age to Eighteen*, before Subcommittee No. 1 of the House Committee on the Judiciary, 78th Congress 4 (1943).

221. Eric S. Fish, "The Twenty-Sixth Amendment Enforcement Power," *Yale Law Journal* 121, no. 4 (March 2012): 1184. "Constitutional amendments to lower the voting age were proposed over 150 times in Congress between 1942 and 1970, and all but one of them died in committee."

222. Dwight D. Eisenhower, Annual Message to the Congress on the State of the Union, Washington, DC, January 7, 1954, American Presidency Project, www.presidency.ucsb.edu /node/232936.

223. The Senate vote was 34 in favor versus 24 against, with 37 not voting. 100 *Congressional Record* 6979-80 (1954); C. P. Trussell, "Senate Defeats President's Plan for Voting at 18," *New York Times*, May 22, 1954; "Eighteen Is Too Young," *New York Times*, May 23, 1954.

224. 100 *Congressional Record* 3050 (1954).

225. Jenny Diamond Cheng, *How Eighteen-Year-Olds Got the Vote* (August 4, 2016), 21-22, Social Science Research Network, ssrn.com/abstract=2818730.

226. Executive Order 11100, Establishing the President's Commission on Registration and Voting Participation, 28 FR 3149 (March 30, 1963).

227. Report of the President's Commission on Registration and Voter Participation (Washington, DC: Government Printing Office, 1963), 43.

228. Cheng, *How Eighteen-Year-Olds Got the Vote*, 10, 20. Upon gaining statehood in 1959, Alaska and Hawaii had minimum voting ages of nineteen and twenty respectively.

229. Lyndon B. Johnson, Special Message to the Congress: "To Vote at Eighteen—Democracy Fulfilled and Enriched," Washington, DC, June 27, 1968, American Presidency Project, www.presidency.ucsb.edu/node/236909.

230. Joseph A. Fry, "Unpopular Messengers: Student Opposition to the Vietnam War," in *The War That Never Ends: New Perspectives on the Vietnam War*, ed. David L. Anderson and John Ernst (Lexington: University of Kentucky Press, 2007), 221. "Between 1960 and 1972, 45 million Americans turned eighteen; and, during the 1960s, the number of college students ballooned from 16 to 25 million."

231. "Man of the Year: The Inheritor," *Time*, January 6, 1967.

232. Amar, *America's Constitution*, 446.

233. Fry, "Unpopular Messengers," in Anderson and Ernst, *War That Never Ends*, 228-29.

234. George F. Kennan, "Rebels Without a Program," *New York Times Magazine*, January 21, 1968.

235. "Opposition to Lowering Voting Age Laid to TV Coverage of College Unrest," *New York Times*, February 17, 1970; Lyndon B. Johnson, Commencement Address at Texas Christian University, Fort Worth, TX, May 29, 1968, www.presidency.ucsb.edu/node/237233.

236. "Too Young to Vote," *Chicago Tribune*, May 14, 1968.

237. Ohio Amendment 1, General Election Overview, Official Tabulation: November 4, 1969, www.sos.state.oh.us/elections/election-results-and-data/1960-1969-official-election-results/general-election-overview, rejected proposed amendment to Ohio constitution to reduce the voting age from twenty-one to nineteen); New Jersey Public Question No. 2, November 4, 1969, rejected proposed amendment to New Jersey constitution to reduce the voting age from twenty-one to eighteen; Maggie Astor, "16-Year-Olds Want a Vote: Fifty Years Ago, So Did 18-Year-Olds," *New York Times*, May 19, 2019, www.nytimes.com/2019/05/19/us/politics/voting-age.html, www.njelections.org/assets/pdf/election-results/1920-1970//1969-general-election.pdf.

238. Jenny Diamond Cheng, "Voting Rights for Millennials: Breathing New Life into the Twenty-Sixth Amendment," *Syracuse Law Review* 67 (2017): 670; Michael Waldman, *The Fight to Vote* (New York: Simon & Schuster, 2016), 163.

239. *Lowering the Voting Age to 18*, before the Subcommittee on Constitutional Amendments of the Senate Committee on the Judiciary, 90th Congress 12 (1968).

240. *To Establish Justice, to Insure Domestic Tranquility*, Final Report of the National Commission on the Causes and Prevention of Violence, xix, 225 (1969).

241. Spiro Agnew, "Impudence in the Streets," Address at Pennsylvania Republican Dinner, Harrisburg, PA, October 30, 1969, in *A History of Our Time*, 3rd ed., ed. William H. Chafe and Harvard Sitkoff (New York: Oxford University Press, 1991), 397.

242. "Vote Act Endorsed by Agnew," *Boston Globe*, June 18, 1970.

243. 115 *Congressional Record* 23522-24 (1969).

244. Tom Lewis, *Divided Highways: Building the Interstate Highways, Transforming America* (Ithaca, NY: Cornell University Press, 2013), 222-23.

245. *Lowering the Voting Age to 18*, 91st Congress 4 (1970).

246. *Lowering the Voting Age to 18*, 91st Congress 10 (1970).

247. Archibald Cox, "Foreword: Constitutional Adjudication and the Promotion of Human Rights," *Harvard Law Review* 80, no. 1 (November 1966): 107, arguing that according to the Court's logic in *Katzenbach v. Morgan*, federal lawmakers could enact legislation to reduce the age for voting after making findings about "state laws denying the franchise to eighteen-, nineteen-, and twenty-year-olds [who] . . . work, pay taxes, raise families, and are subject to military service."

248. 116 *Congressional Record* 5950 (1970).

249. 116 *Congressional Record* 6943 (1970).

250. 116 *Congressional Record* 6944 (1970).

251. The vote was 64–17. 116 *Congressional Record* 7093, 7095 (1970).

252. "Congress Lowers Voting Age, Extends Voting Rights Act," in *CQ Almanac 1970*, 26th ed., 05-192-05-199 (Washington, DC: Congressional Quarterly, 1971), library.cqpress.com /cqalmanac/cqal70-1292888.

253. Spencer Rich, "Senate Approves Vote at 18 in All Elections," *Washington Post*, March 13, 1970.

254. *Bloomington-Bedford Herald Times*, January 8, 1967, entered into 113 *Congressional Record* 533 (1967) by Senator Bayh.

255. 116 *Congressional Record* 20160 (1970).

256. "A Filibuster Threat over Voting Act," *San Francisco Chronicle*, May 11, 1970.

257. "Filibuster Threat over Voting Act."

258. Thomas M. Grace, *Kent State: Death and Dissent in the Long Sixties* (Boston: University of Massachusetts Press, 2016), 224–30. See also Waldman, *Fight to Vote*.

259. Fry, "Unpopular Messengers," in Anderson and Ernst, *War That Never Ends*, 236.

260. 116 *Congressional Record* 20162 (1970).

261. "Congress Lowers Voting Age, Extends Voting Rights Act," in *CQ Almanac 1970*, 26th ed., 05-192-05-199 (Washington, DC: *Congressional Quarterly*, 1971), library.cqpress.com /cqalmanac/cqal70-1292888.

262. Richard Nixon, Statement on Signing of the Voting Rights Act Amendments of 1970, June 22, 1970, American Presidency Project, www.presidency.ucsb.edu/node/239895.

263. *Oregon v. Mitchell*, 400 U.S. 112, 240 (1970): Douglas, Brennan, White, and Marshall.

264. *Oregon v. Mitchell*, 212, Harlan.

265. *Oregon v. Mitchell*, 124–25.

266. Richard Reeves, "Officials Vexed," *New York Times*, December 22, 1970.

267. Fred P. Graham, "A 5-to-4 Decision," *New York Times*, December 22, 1970.

268. 117 *Congressional Record* 5334 (1971), statement of Representative Celler. "A revision of the State voting age qualification apparently requires an amendment to the State constitution in every State. Processing such a constitutional amendment differs from jurisdiction to juris-diction. In at least 16 States the adoption of an amendment requires approval by two separate sessions of the State legislature to be followed by a referendum. Because not all State legislatures meet annually and a number of States require approval by two sessions of the legislature and be-cause every State except Delaware requires a referendum to be held on a proposed amendment, it appears that more than 20 States will be unable to lower the voting age prior to November 1972."

269. 117 *Congressional Record* 5334 (1971), statement of Representative Celler, as above.

270. "The Pragmatic 26th Amendment," *Hartford Courant*, March 9, 1971.

271. 117 *Congressional Record* 5516 (1971).

272. 117 *Congressional Record* 5516 (1971).

273. 117 *Congressional Record* 5802 (1971). See Grimes, *Democracy and the Amendments*, 144.

274. 117 *Congressional Record* 5810 (1971).

275. The vote was 68–23. 117 *Congressional Record* 5815–16 (1971); Irna Moore, "District Rep-resentation Rider Killed," *Washington Post*, March 11, 1971.

276. The vote was 94–0. 117 *Congressional Record* 5830 (1971); Steve Gerstel, "Senate O.K.'s Lowering of Voting Age," *Atlanta Daily World*, March 14, 1971.

277. Marjorie Hunter, "Vote at 18 Nears Full House Test," *New York Times*, March 17, 1970.

278. 117 *Congressional Record* 7532 (1971).

279. 117 *Congressional Record* 7533 (1971).

280. Twelve members did not vote on the resolution. 117 *Congressional Record* 7569–70 (1971).

281. Minnesota and Delaware were the first two states to ratify. The other states to lend their assent on the day of the House vote were Connecticut, Tennessee, and Washington. "Delaware Ratifies Bill," *The Review* (University of Delaware), April 5, 1971: "Minnesota ratified [the amendment] 21 minutes before" it was passed by the House; "Vote-at-18 Amendment Gets Final OK in House," *Los Angeles Times*, March 24, 1971.

282. In all, forty-three states ratified the measure, South Dakota becoming the latest to do so, in 2014—forty-three years after its ratification. 2014 S.D. Sess. Laws. ch. 1, 19. Seven states—Florida, Kentucky, Mississippi, Nevada, New Mexico, North Dakota, and Utah—failed to ratify it.

283. "The Youth Vote," *New York Times*, August 21, 1972.

284. "First-Time Voters," *New York Times*, August 27, 1972.

285. Seth E. Blumenthal, "Children of the 'Silent Majority': Richard Nixon's Young Voters for the President, 1972," *Journal of Policy History* 27, no. 2 (2015), 337–38.

286. "First-Time Voters."

287. "National Exit Poll Tables," *New York Times*, November 5, 2008, https://www.nytimes.com/elections/2008/results/president/national-exit-polls.html; "Delaware Ratifies Bill," *The Review* (University of Delaware), April 5, 1971: "Republican strategists have conceded privately that they have something to worry about: the possibility that the vocal opposition of college students, in particular to President Nixon and Vice President Spiro T. Agnew, might be translated into votes. Only a small switch might endanger their chances. The immediate reaction of the Democratic National Committee was to set in motion a massive registration drive for young people. But how will they vote? For the most part, studies have suggested that young voters vote the way their parents do."

288. Hazel Erskine, "The Polls: The Politics of Age," *Public Opinion Quarterly* 35, no. 3 (Autumn 1971): 485–86.

289. Oregon failed to lower to nineteen via constitutional amendment on the ballot on May 26, 1970. Colorado, Connecticut, Florida, Hawaii, and Michigan failed to lower to eighteen via constitutional amendment on the ballot, and Illinois failed to lower to eighteen via a constitutional convention referral, on November 3, 1970. New Jersey, South Dakota, Washington, and Wyoming failed to lower to nineteen via constitutional amendment on the ballot on November 3, 1970. Oregon Voting Age of 19, Measure 5 (May 26, 1970); Colorado Voting Age and Residency Requirements Reduction, Measure 4 (November 3, 1970); Connecticut Qualifications of Electors, Question 3 (November 3, 1970); Florida 18-Year-Old Voting, Amendment 1 (November 3, 1970); Hawaii Voting Age, Proposition 3 (November 3, 1970); Michigan Voting Age Amendment, Proposal B (November 3, 1970); New Jersey Public Question No. 1 (November 3, 1970); Illinois Voting Age Amendment (December 15, 1970); Washington Voting Age of 19 Amendment, H. J. Res. 6 (November 3, 1970); South Dakota Voting Age, Amendment F (November 3, 1970); Wyoming Qualifications of Electors, Amendment 2 (November 3, 1970).

290. "College-Town Worry: Will 18-to-21 Voters Take Over?" *US News and World Report*, September 6, 1971.

291. R. W. Apple Jr., "The States Ratify Full Vote at 18," *New York Times*, July 1, 1971: "Most states have forbidden students to register at school, and experience indicates that they will not vote heavily if forced to resort to the absentee ballot."

292. E.g., *Symm v. U.S.*, 439 U.S. 1105 (1979).

293. See, e.g., Michael Wines, "The Student Vote Is Surging. So Are Efforts to Suppress It," *New York Times*, October 24, 2019; Zachary Roth, "Wisconsin Throws Up Major Voter Registration Hurdle," MSNBC, March 25, 2016, www.msnbc.com/msnbc/wisconsin-throws-major-voter-registration-hurdle; Bertrand M. Gutierrez, "Access to Boone Voting Site Raised as Major Concern," *Winston-Salem Journal*, August 18, 2013, www.journalnow.com/news/state_region/article_9a0bc822-07a6-11e3-ab6f-001a4bcf6878.html; Paul J. Weber, "Court Upholds

Texas' Law in Another Big Voter ID Ruling," *Associated Press*, April 27, 2018, www.apnews .com/7f712e26f0df4e339318d143a6badd03.

294. 117 *Congressional Record* 5830 (1971).

295. Senator Robert C. Byrd and James E. Casto, "Remembering Senator Jennings Randolph," *Appalachia Magazine*, May–August 1998.

296. See, e.g., John Nichols, "Let the 16 Year Olds Who Are Marching for the Planet Vote to Save It," *The Nation*, March 15, 2019, www.thenation.com/article/voting-age-16-climate-strike -green-new-deal-ayanna-pressley; Maggie Astor, "16-Year-Olds Want a Vote: Fifty Years Ago, So Did 18-Year-Olds," *New York Times*, May 19, 2019, www.nytimes.com/2019/05/19/us/politics /voting-age.html.

297. John Nichols, "Let the 16 Year Olds Who Are Marching for the Planet Vote to Save It," *The Nation*, March 15, 2019, www.thenation.com/article/voting-age-16-climate-strike -green-new-deal-ayanna-pressley.

Chapter 7: The 1970s—and the Rights Revolution That Wasn't

1. Morton J. Horwitz, "The Warren Court and the Pursuit of Justice," *Washington and Lee Law Review* 50, no. 5 (1993): 5.

2. Ernest Havemann, "Storm Center of Justice," *Life*, May 22, 1964.

3. William H. Stringer, "State of the Nations: The 'Actionist' Supreme Court of the U.S.," *Christian Science Monitor*, July 10, 1964.

4. David E. Kyvig, *Explicit & Authentic Acts: Amending the Constitution 1776–1995* (Lawrence: University Press of Kansas, 1996), 370, 379–85; John R. Vile, *Encyclopedia of Constitutional Amendments, Proposed Amendments, and Amending Issues 1789–2010*, vol. 1 (Santa Barbara, CA: ABC-CLIO, 2010), 54–55; "The Warren Court: Fateful Decade," *Newsweek*, May 11, 1964.

5. Guy-Uriel Charles, "Judging the Law of Politics," *Michigan Law Review* 103, no. 6 (2005): 1139.

6. Jesse Wegman, *Let the People Pick the President: The Case for Abolishing the Electoral College* (New York: St. Martin's Press, 2020), 137.

7. *Reynolds v. Sims*, 377 U.S. 533 (1964).

8. *Wesberry v. Sanders*, 376 U.S. 1 (1964).

9. Kyvig, *Explicit & Authentic Acts*, 374–75.

10. Russell Caplan, *Constitutional Brinkmanship: Amending the Constitution by National Convention* (New York: Oxford University Press, 1988), 78.

11. Kyvig, *Explicit & Authentic Acts*, 375; Russell Caplan, "Everett Dirksen's Constitutional Crusades," *Journal of the Illinois State Historical Society* 95, no. 1 (2002): 77.

12. 111 Cong. Rec. 19355 (1965).

13. Caplan, *Constitutional Brinkmanship*, 74; Caplan, "Everett Dirksen's Constitutional Crusades," 79.

14. Fred P. Graham, "Efforts to Amend the Constitution on Districts Gain," *New York Times*, March 18, 1967. See also Arthur Earl Bonfield, "The Dirksen Amendment and the Article V Convention Process," *Michigan Law Review* 66, no. 5 (1968): 949.

15. Caplan, *Constitutional Brinkmanship*, 76.

16. Alexander Keyssar, *Why Do We Still Have the Electoral College?* (Cambridge, MA: Harvard University Press, 2020), 213–14.

17. 112 Cong. Rec. 10998 (1966).

18. "1968 Presidential Election," *Presidential Elections 1789–2008*, ed. CQ Press Staff, 10th ed., 2009.

19. Keyssar, *Why Do We Still Have the Electoral College?*, 217.

20. Wegman, *Let the People Pick the President*, 148–51.

21. American Bar Association, Commission on Electoral College Reform, *Electing the President: A Report of the Commission on Electoral College Reform* (Chicago: American Bar

Association, 1967), 220. See "Last Call for Electoral Reform," *New York Times*, September 29, 1970.

22. Gallup News Service, "Americans Have Long Questioned Electoral College," November 16, 2000, https://news.gallup.com/poll/2305/americans-long-questioned-electoral-college .aspx. See Keyssar, *Why Do We Still Have the Electoral College?*, 383.

23. 115 Cong. Rec. 26007–08 (1969).

24. Richard M. Nixon, Statement on Congressional Action on Electoral Reform, September 30, 1969, American Presidency Project, https://www.presidency.ucsb.edu/node/239728.

25. Keyssar, *Why Do We Still Have the Electoral College?*, 229–32.

26. Alexander Keyssar, "Peculiar Institution," *Boston Globe*, October 17, 2004.

27. Direct Popular Election of the President: Report, Together with Individual, Separate and Minority Views, to Accompany S.J. Res. 1, S. Rep. No. 91-1123 at 50 (August 14, 1970).

28. Wilfred U. Codrington III, "The Electoral College's Racist Origins," *The Atlantic*, November 17, 2019.

29. Warren Weaver Jr., "Senate Puts Off Direct Vote Plan," *New York Times*, September 30, 1970.

30. "Possibly Fatal Setback for Electoral Reform," *New York Times*, September 20, 1970.

31. Robert Blaemire, *Birch Bayh: Making a Difference* (Bloomington: Indiana University Press, 2019), 413.

32. Crystal Eastman, "Now We Can Begin" *The Liberator* 3, no. 12 (December 1920), reprinted from speech delivered in 1920; Melissa Murray, "The Equal Rights Amendment: A Century in the Making," symposium, foreword, *NYU Review of Law and Social Change Harbinger* 43 (2019): 91.

33. Herma Hill Kay, "Ruth Bader Ginsburg, Professor of Law," *Columbia Law Review* 104 (2004): 17; David E. Kyvig, "Historical Misunderstandings and the Defeat of the Equal Rights Amendment," *Public Historian* 18, no. 1 (Winter 1996): 49.

34. Joint Resolution Proposing an Amendment to the Constitution of the United States Relative to Equal Rights for Men and Women, S. J. Res. 21, 68th Congress (1923); 65 *Congressional Record* 150 (1923); Joint Resolution Proposing an Amendment to the Constitution of the United States, H. J. Res. 75, 68th Congress (1923), 65 *Congressional Record* 285 (1923); Thomas H. Neale, *The Proposed Equal Rights Amendment: Contemporary Ratification Issues* (Washington, DC: Congressional Research Service, R42979, 2018), 9.

35. "2 Organizations of Women Differ on 'Rights' Bill," *Atlanta Constitution*, November 12, 1922; "Women See Coolidge on 'Blanket Equality,'" *New York Times*, December 13, 1923.

36. Helen B. Schaffer, "Woman's Place in the Economy," CQ Researcher, *Editorial Research Reports 1957*, vol. 1 (February 13, 1957); Susan Lehrer, *Origins of Protective Labor Legislation for Women, 1905–1925* (Albany: State University of New York Press, 1987), 61; Pauli Murray and Mary O. Eastwood, "Jane Crow and the Law: Sex Discrimination and Title VII," *George Washington Law Review* 34, no. 2 (December 1965): 248.

37. *Muller v. Oregon*, 208 U.S. 412, 422 (1908).

38. *The Textile Worker* 11, no. 1 (April 1923), 684. See also Fabiola Cineas, "The Equal Rights Amendment May Have Found Its Moment," *The New Republic*, January 16, 2020.

39. Kyvig, *Explicit and Authentic Acts*, 398.

40. Bess Furman, "Senate to Vote on Equal Rights," *New York Times*, July 19, 1946.

41. The vote was 38 senators in favor, 35 against. See "Equal Rights Amendment," *CQ Almanac 1946*, 2nd ed., 08-540-08-541 (Washington, DC: *Congressional Quarterly*, 1947), library.cqpress .com/cqalmanac/cqal46-1411328.

42. "'Equal Rights' Amendment,'" *New York Times*, July 20, 1946.

43. 96 *Congressional Record* 868 (1950).

44. "Equal Rights Amendment," in *CQ Almanac 1950*, 6th ed., 419–22 (Washington, DC: *Congressional Quarterly*, 1951), library.cqpress.com/cqalmanac/cqal50-1378264; "Equal Rights," in

CQ Almanac 1953, 9th ed., 08-333 (Washington, DC: *Congressional Quarterly*, 1954), library .cqpress.com/cqalmanac/cqal53-1369074.

45. In 1950 the Senate endorsed the ERA by a vote of 63–19. 96 *Congressional Record* 872–73 (1950). In 1953 the vote was 73–11. 99 *Congressional Record* 8973–74 (1953). See Kyvig, *Explicit and Authentic Acts*, 400.

46. Amelia R. Fry, "Conversations with Alice Paul: Woman Suffrage and the Equal Rights Amendment," ERA and the Hayden Rider 1950–1971, at 518, Suffragists Oral History Project, University of California, accessed at content.cdlib.org/view?docId=kt6f59n89c&doc .view=entire_text.

47. Neale, *Proposed Equal Rights Amendment*, 11–12.

48. Wilfred Codrington and Alex Cohen, "Continuing the Fight for Constitutional Equality," *Ms.* magazine, January 25, 2019, msmagazine.com/2019/01/25/continuing-fight-constitutional -equality: "Proponents introduced resolutions proposing an ERA, but made little headway in a Congress that, from 1917 to 1970, had a grand total of 67 female members, with no more than 22 serving at any given time." Also: "Equal Rights Amendment," *CQ Almanac 1950*, 6th ed., 419–22 (Washington, DC: *Congressional Quarterly*, 1951), library.cqpress.com/cqalmanac /cqal50-1378264. See Murray, "Equal Rights Amendment," 92–93.

49. *American Women*, Report of the President's Commission on the Status of Women (Washington, DC: U.S. Department of Labor, 1963), 45.

50. *McDonald v. Board of Election Commissioners*, 394 U.S. 802, at 809 (1969).

51. Murray and Eastwood, "Jane Crow and the Law," 237.

52. Lenora M. Lapidus, "Ruth Bader Ginsburg and the Development of Gender Equality Jurisprudence Under the Fourteenth Amendment," *NYU Review of Law and Social Change* and *The Harbinger* (online) 43 (2019): 149; Burt Neuborne, "Introduction of Justice Ruth Bader Ginsburg," *California Law Review* 95, no. 6 (December 2007): 2213–15.

53. An Act to Prohibit Discrimination on Account of Sex in the Payment of Wages by Employers Engaged in Commerce or in the Production of Goods for Commerce and to Provide for the Restitution of Wages Lost by Employees by Reason of Any Such Discrimination (Equal Pay Act of 1963), Pub. L. 88-38, 77 Stat. 56 (1963).

54. 110 *Congressional Record* 2577 (1964).

55. Clay Risen, *The Bill of the Century: The Epic Battle for the Civil Rights Act* (New York: Bloomsbury Press, 2014), 150–52.

56. Kyvig, *Explicit and Authentic Acts*, 402–03.

57. Don Oberdorfer, "'Judge' Smith Moves with Deliberate Drag," *New York Times*, January 12, 1964.

58. Risen, *Bill of the Century*, 160–61; Louis Menand, "How Women Got In on the Civil Rights Act: Uncovering the Alternative History of Women's Rights," *The New Yorker*, July 14, 2014; Caroline Fredrickson, "How the Most Important U.S. Civil Rights Law Came to Include Women," *NYU Review of Law and Social Change* and *The Harbinger* (online) 43 (2019): 123–25.

59. Risen, *Bill of the Century*, 160–61; Menand, "How Women Got In on the Civil Rights Act"; Fredrickson, "How the Most Important U.S. Civil Rights Law Came to Include Women," 123–25.

60. Women in Congress, 1917–2017, A Changing of the Guard: Traditionalists, Feminists, and the New Face of Women in Congress, 1955–1976, H.R. Doc. 108-223, at 330–31, accessed at www.govinfo.gov/content/pkg/GPO-CDOC-108hdoc223/pdf/GPO-CDOC-108hdoc223-2-3 .pdf.

61. 110 *Congressional Record* 2577–84 (1964); Menand, "How Women Got In on the Civil Rights Act," *The New Yorker*, July 14, 2014.

62. 110 *Congressional Record* 2577 (1964).

63. 110 *Congressional Record* 2578 (1964).

64. *Women in Congress, 1917–2017, a Changing of the Guard: Traditionalists, Feminists, and the New Face of Women in Congress, 1955–1976*, H. R. Doc. 108-223, at 330.

65. "Mr. Chairman, I rise in support of the amendment primarily because I feel as a White woman when this bill has passed this House and the Senate and has been signed by the President that white women will be last at the hiring gate." 110 *Congressional Record* 2578 (1964), statement of Representative Griffiths. See Cynthia Harrison, *On Account of Sex: The Politics of Women's Issues, 1945-1968* (Berkeley: University of California Press, 1988), 178-79.

66. Serena Mayeri, "Constitutional Choices: Legal Feminism and the Historical Dynamics of Change," *California Law Review* 92, no. 3 (May 2004): 770.

67. An Act to Enforce the Constitutional Right to Vote, to Confer Jurisdiction upon the District Courts of the United States of America to Provide Injunctive Relief Against Discrimination in Public Accommodations, to Authorize the Attorney General to Institute Suits to Protect Constitutional Rights in Public Facilities and Public Education, to Extend the Commission on Civil Rights, to Prevent Discrimination in Federally Assisted Programs, to Establish a Commission on Equal Employment Opportunity, and for Other Purposes (Civil Rights Act of 1964), Title VII, sec. 705, Pub. L. 88-352, 78 Stat. 241 (1964); Sonia Pressman Fuentes, "Representing Women," *Frontiers: A Journal of Women Studies* 18, no. 3 (1997): 97; Barry Friedman, *The Will of the People: How Public Opinion Has Influenced the Supreme Court and Shaped the Meaning of the Constitution* (New York: Farrar, Straus & Giroux, 2009), 290; Mayeri, "Constitutional Choices," 769-70.

68. Hugh Davis Graham, *The Civil Rights Era: Origins and Development of National Policy, 1960-1972* (New York: Oxford University Press, 1990), 217.

69. Jo Freeman, "The Origins of the Women's Liberation Movement," *American Journal of Sociology* 78, no. 4 (January 1973): 797-98. "The forces which led to NOW's formation were first set in motion in 1961 when President Kennedy established the President's Commission on the Status of Women at the behest of Esther Petersen, to be chaired by Eleanor Roosevelt." And: Fredrickson, "How the Most Important U.S. Civil Rights Law Came to Include Women," 125.

70. Marilyn Goldstein, "The Feminist Mystique I: Making Waves for Equality," *Newsday*, December 1, 1969.

71. Kyvig, *Explicit and Authentic Acts*, 403.

72. Goldstein, "The Feminist Mystique I," *Newsday*, December 1, 1969.

73. Robert Sherrill, "That Equal-Rights Amendment: What, Exactly, Does It Mean?" *New York Times Magazine*, September 20, 1970.

74. "A Modern Father of Our Constitution: An Interview with Former Senator Birch Bayh," *Fordham Law Review* 79, no. 3 (2010): 818.

75. "Support Is Voiced for Lower Voting Age," *Baton Rouge Morning Advocate*, February 18, 1970.

76. "Modern Father of Our Constitution," 818; Blaemire, *Birch Bayh*, 188.

77. Jane Mansbridge, *Why We Lost the ERA* (Chicago: University of Chicago Press, 1986), 10.

78. Susan Brownmiller, "This Is Fighting Shirley Chisholm," *New York Times*, April 13, 1969.

79. Brownmiller, "This Is Fighting Shirley Chisholm."

80. 115 *Congressional Record* 13380 (1969).

81. *The "Equal Rights" Amendment*, before the Subcommittee on Constitutional Amendments of the Senate Committee on the Judiciary, 92nd Congress 32, 35 (1970).

82. *The "Equal Rights" Amendment*, 92nd Congress 1 (1970).

83. Eileen Shanahan, "Equal Rights Plan for Women Voted by House," *New York Times*, August 11, 1970.

84. Neale, *Proposed Equal Rights Amendment*, 13.

85. "Equal Rights for Women Amendment Dropped in Senate," in *CQ Almanac 1970*, 26th ed., 03-706-03-709 (Washington, DC: *Congressional Quarterly*, 1971), library.cqpress.com/cqalmanac/cqal70-1294725.

86. 116 *Congressional Record* 27999-28000, 28006 (1970).

87. Sherill, "Equal-Rights Amendment: What, Exactly, Does It Mean?"

88. Eileen Shanahan, "House Vote Expected Tomorrow on Amendment for Equal Rights for Women," *New York Times*, August 9, 1970.

89. 116 *Congressional Record* 28000–28001 (1970).

90. 116 *Congressional Record* 28005 (1970).

91. 116 *Congressional Record* 28006 (1970), statement of Representative Wiggins.

92. "Mischief in Rights Amendment," *Durham Morning Herald*, August 14, 1970; 116 *Congressional Record* 28006 (1970), statement of Representative McCulloch.

93. 116 *Congressional Record* 28016 (1970).

94. 116 *Congressional Record* 28029 (1970).

95. 116 *Congressional Record* 28036–37 (1970).

96. Shanahan, "Equal Rights Plan for Women Voted by House, 350–15," *New York Times*, August 11, 1970.

97. "The Henpecked House," *New York Times*, August 12, 1970.

98. "Mrs. Ervin Says the Senator Is Right," *Washington Post*, September 19, 1970.

99. "Equal Rights for Women Amendment Dropped in Senate," in *CQ Almanac 1970*, 26th ed., 03-706-03-709 (Washington, DC: Congressional Quarterly, 1971), library.cqpress.com /cqalmanac/cqal70-1294725.

100. 116 *Congressional Record* 36450–51, 36505 (1970); Neale, *Proposed Equal Rights Amendment*, 13.

101. "Equal Rights for Women Amendment Dropped in Senate."

102. Eileen Shanahan, "Senators Amend Equal Rights Bill; It May Die for '70," *New York Times*, October 14, 1970.

103. The measure was reintroduced as H. J. Res. 208. "House Passes Equal Rights Constitutional Amendment," in *CQ Almanac 1971*, 27th ed., 05-656-05-658 (Washington, DC: Congressional Quarterly, 1972), library.cqpress.com/cqalmanac/cqal71-1254111.

104. 117 *Congressional Record* 35796 (1971); "Deals Blow to Women's Rights Bill," *Chicago Tribune*, June 23, 1971.

105. 117 *Congressional Record* 35813, 35815 (1971); "House Passes Rights Resolution for Women," *Los Angeles Times*, October 13, 1971.

106. 118 *Congressional Record* 9080, 9084, 9091, 9517, 9519 (1972); Grimes, *Democracy and the Amendments to the Constitution*, 151.

107. Amendment No. 1070, 118 *Congressional Record* 9529–31 (1972); Amendment No. 1044, 118 *Congressional Record* 9538–40 (1972); Amendment No. 1071, 118 *Congressional Record* 9531–37 (1972).

108. 118 *Congressional Record* 9598 (1972); Donald T. Critchlow, *Phyllis Schlafly and Grassroots Conservatism: A Woman's Crusade* (Princeton, NJ: Princeton University Press, 2005), 215–16; Kyvig, "Historical Misunderstandings and the Defeat of the Equal Rights Amendment," 50–51.

109. Kyvig, *Explicit and Authentic Acts*, 407.

110. Eileen Shanahan, "Equal Rights Amendment Is Approved by Congress," *New York Times*, March 23, 1972.

111. 117 *Congressional Record* 35814–15 (1971), statement of Representative Griffiths.

112. Shanahan, "Equal Rights Amendment Is Approved by Congress."

113. Amelia Fry, "Alice Paul and the ERA," in *Rights of Passage: The Past and Future of the ERA*, Joan Hoff-Wilson, ed. (Bloomington: Indiana University Press, 1986), 8, 21.

114. Thomas P. Ronan, "A Woman Leader in Brooklyn to Challenge Celler in Primary," *New York Times*, March 29, 1972.

115. Linda Charlton, "Celler Defends Record as Challenger Assails It," *New York Times*, June 13, 1972; "Celler's Label for Liz: 'A Nonentity,'" *Newsday*, June 28, 1972; Laura Peimer, "The Toothpick and the Washington Monument," Radcliffe Institute for Advanced Study, Harvard University, January 28, 2016, www.radcliffe.harvard.edu/schlesinger-library/blog /toothpick-and-washington-monument.

116. "They Came a Long Way, Tuesday," *New York Times*, June 25, 1972.

117. Eileen Shanahan, "Opposition Rises to Amendment on Equal Rights," *New York Times*, January 15, 1973.

118. Critchlow, *Phyllis Schlafly and Grassroots Conservatism*, 23–26, 28, 217; Susan E. Marshall, "Who Speaks for American Women? The Future of Antifeminism," *Annals of the American Academy of Political and Social Science* 515 (May 1991): 56–57.

119. Carol Felsenthal, *The Sweetheart of the Silent Majority: The Biography of Phyllis Schlafly* (New York: Doubleday, 1981), 266–67.

120. Felsenthal, *Sweetheart of the Silent Majority*, 81–82.

121. Eric C. Miller, "Phyllis Schlafly's 'Positive' Freedom: Liberty, Liberation, and the Equal Rights Amendment," *Rhetoric & Public Affairs* 18, no. 2 (2015): 286, quoting Phyllis Schlafly, "What's Wrong with 'Equal Rights' for Women?" *Phyllis Schlafly Report*, February 1972; Felsenthal, *Sweetheart of the Silent Majority*, 268–69.

122. Felsenthal, *Sweetheart of the Silent Majority*, 269–70.

123. Critchlow, *Phyllis Schlafly and Grassroots Conservatism*, 220.

124. Felsenthal, *Sweetheart of the Silent Majority*, 289.

125. Judy Klemesrud, "Opponent of E.R.A. Confident of Its Defeat," *New York Times*, December 15, 1975; "Women Lobby Against 'Rights,'" *New York Times*, April 15, 1973.

126. Shanahan, "Opposition Rises to Amendment on Equal Rights."

127. Kyvig, *Explicit and Authentic Acts*, 411–12.

128. Shanahan, "Opposition Rises to Amendment on Equal Rights."

129. Nebraska ratified the Equal Rights Amendment on March 29, 1972, one week after Congress proposed it.

130. "Equal Rights Amendment: Pros and Cons," *Omaha World-Herald*, March 11, 1973.

131. Don Pieper, "Verdict Delayed on Equal Rights," *Omaha World-Herald*, February 23, 1973.

132. Senator Richard F. Proud, "Equal Rights a Covering to Get All Women Out of the Home," *Omaha World-Herald*, February 18, 1973.

133. Pieper, "Verdict Delayed on Equal Rights."

134. Warren Weaver Jr., "Equal Rights Vote Now in Question," *New York Times*, March 17, 1973.

135. In addition to Nebraska, legislatures in Tennessee, Idaho, Kentucky, and South Dakota voted to rescind previous votes to ratify the Equal Rights Amendment.

136. 124 *Congressional Record* 26264–65, 34314–15 (1978).

137. "Battle over ERA Heads to Courts," *Wisconsin State Journal*, March 23, 1979.

138. Kyvig, "Historical Misunderstandings and the Defeat of the Equal Rights Amendment," 45–46.

139. Elizabeth Bumiller, "Schlafly's Gala Goodbye to ERA," *Washington Post*, July 1, 1982; Sandra R. Gregg and Bill Peterson, "Backers, Foes Mark End of ERA Battle: Both Sides Agree Fight Will Continue," *Washington Post*, July 1, 1982.

140. Alan Wolfe, "Mrs. America," *The New Republic*, October 2, 2005, newrepublic.com /article/63477/mrs-america.

141. Republican Party Platform of 1980, July 15, 1980, Republican Party Platforms, American Presidency Project, www.presidency.ucsb.edu/node/273420.

142. Blaemire, *Birch Bayh*, 397–98.

143. Grimes, *Democracy and the Amendments to the Constitution*, 153.

144. Adam Clymer, "Time Runs Out for Proposed Rights Amendment," *New York Times*, July 1, 1982.

145. Kyvig, *Explicit and Authentic Acts*, 419; 129 *Congressional Record* 32684–85 (1983).

146. Burt Neuborne, "Introduction of Justice Ruth Bader Ginsburg," *California Law Review* 95, no. 6 (December 2007): 2213–14. See Lapidus, "Ruth Bader Ginsburg and the Development of Gender Equality Jurisprudence Under the Fourteenth Amendment," 149–54.

147. Reva B. Siegel, "Constitutional Culture, Social Movement Conflict, and Constitutional Change: The Case of the de Facto ERA," *California Law Review* 94, no. 5 (October 2006): 1368. Siegel argues that those leading the movement for gender equality in the U.S. "acted with a sophisticated grasp of constitutional culture, making constitutional arguments in multiple arenas and employing practices of norm contestation to capture official sites of constitutional norm articulation." See Cary Franklin, "The ERA, the Military, and the Making of Constitutional Meaning," *NYU Review of Law and Social Change: The Harbinger* 43 (2019): 119–20: "But what the history of the ERA actually shows is a striking degree of responsiveness on the part of courts to social movement activism—at first in a progressive direction, but then overwhelmingly in a conservative direction as the New Right came to power, oversaw the appointment of conservative judges to the federal bench, and convinced large numbers of Americans that the ERA threatened deeply held values and treasured ways of life."

148. Siegel, "Constitutional Culture, Social Movement Conflict and Constitutional Change," 1333.

149. Kathleen M. Sullivan, "Constitutionalizing Women's Equality," *California Law Review* 90, no. 3 (May 2002): 763.

150. Lyndon B. Johnson, Special Message to the Congress: The Nation's Capital, February 27, 1967, American Presidency Project, www.presidency.ucsb.edu/node/237696.

151. H. J. Res. 396, 90th Congress (1967).

152. *Voting Representation for the District of Columbia*, before the Subcommittee on Constitutional Amendments of the Senate Committee on the Judiciary, 91st Congress 2 (1970).

153. On March 10, 1971, Kennedy sought to append his proposal as a rider to the Twenty-Sixth Amendment. 117 *Congressional Record* 5802 (1971); Grimes, *Democracy and the Amendments to the Constitution*, 144. On March 10, 1972, he tried and failed to add it to the proposed Equal Rights Amendment. 117 *Congressional Record* 5815–16 (1971).

154. 116 *Congressional Record* 31040 (1970); An Act to Establish a Commission on the Organization of the Government of the District of Columbia and to Provide for a Delegate to the House of Representatives from the District of Columbia (District of Columbia Delegate Act), Pub. L. No. 91-405, 84 Stat. 848 (1970), codified at 2 U.S.C. § 25a (1988), also codified at D.C. Code Ann. § 1-401 (1987). Delegates to Congress lack the right to vote for measures under consideration on the House floor, whether they are being amended in the Committee of the Whole or when up for final passage. In recent times, when Democrats have had the majority in the House of Representatives, their rules have provided delegates with the right to vote in the Committee of the Whole. Notably, delegates possess the other rights granted to members of Congress, including to introduce and sponsor legislation, and to hold leadership positions on committees and in the party.

155. District of Columbia Self-Government and Governmental Reorganization Act (District of Columbia Home Rule Act), Pub. L. No. 93-198; 87 Stat. 774 (1973).

156. The law further prevents the local government from imposing a commuter tax to raise money on those coming from the suburbs to work in the city, and from changing zoning laws regarding the height of buildings. Since 2016, a budget autonomy amendment to the District's charter changed the process. Now, instead of requiring Congress's active approval, the District's budget is considered passed if Congress does not act on it within thirty days. Local Budget Autonomy Amendment Act of 2012, D.C. Law 19-321, 60 DCR 1724, approved by voters in a special election held April 23, 2013; sustained by *Council of the District of Columbia v. Dewitt*, no. 2014-CA-2371-B, D.C. Super. Ct. March 18, 2016.

157. Walter Edward Fauntroy, History, Art & Archives, U.S. House of Representatives, history .house.gov/People/detail/13023.

158. H. J. Res. 684, 92nd Congress, introduced June 4, 1971.

159. Alex Poinsett, "How Blacks Can Gain Two Senators," *Ebony*, June 1978.

160. Herb Boyd, "An Undaunted Civil and Human Rights Advocate, Rep. Charles Diggs Jr.," *New York Amsterdam News*, December 13, 2017.

161. Poinsett, "How Blacks Can Gain Two Senators."

162. To Amend the Constitution to Provide for Representation of the District of Columbia in the Congress, H. J. Res. 431, 94th Congress (1975); 121 *Congressional Record* 13129 (1975).

163. Joint Resolution to Amend the Constitution to Provide for Representation of the District of Columbia in the Congress, H. J. Res. 280, 94th Congress (1975); 121 *Congressional Record* 5242 (1975).

164. Eugene Boyd, *District of Columbia Voting Representation in Congress: An Analysis of Legislative Proposals* (Washington, DC: Congressional Research Service, RL33830, 2010), 5.

165. Donald P. Baker, "Coalition Strategy: How to Win Votes for D.C. Voice in Congress," *Washington Post*, March 5, 1978.

166. A Simple Case of Democracy Denied, A Booklet Used to Recruit Co-sponsors for the DC Voting Rights Amendment in Congress, DC Vote, www.dcvote.org/simple-case-democracy-denied-booklet-used-recruit-co-sponsors-dc-voting-rights-amendment-congress.

167. *Representation for the District of Columbia*, before the Subcommittee on Civil and Constitutional Rights Amendments of the House Committee on the Judiciary, 95th Congress 5 (1977), statement of Walter Fauntroy, U.S. Delegate from the District of Columbia, U.S. House of Representatives.

168. Baker, "Coalition Strategy," *Washington Post*, March 5, 1978.

169. H. J. Res. 554, 95th Congress (1977); 123 *Congressional Record* 24795 (1977) introduced July 25, 1977; William Donlon Edwards, District of Columbia Representation in Congress, H.R. Rep. 95-886, at 7 (1978), Report on H. J. Res. 554 from the House Committee on the Judiciary.

170. *Representation for the District of Columbia*, before the Subcommittee on Civil and Constitutional Rights Amendments of the House Committee on the Judiciary, 95th Congress 7 (1977), statement of Walter Fauntroy, U.S. delegate from the District of Columbia, U.S. House of Representatives.

171. *Representation for the District of Columbia*.

172. *Representation for the District of Columbia*, 81, statement of Joseph Rauh Jr., general counsel of the Leadership Conference on Civil Rights.

173. The District has always voted for the Democrat in presidential contests and in elections for delegate to Congress. See Election Statistics, American Presidency Project, www.presidency.ucsb.edu/statistics/elections. As of 2020, every elected mayor of the District—Walter Washington, Marion Barry, Sharon Pratt, Anthony Williams, Adrian Fenty, Vincent Gray, and Muriel Bowser—has also been a Democrat.

174. Republican Party Platform of 1976, August 18, 1976, Republican Party Platforms, American Presidency Project, www.presidency.ucsb.edu/node/273415.

175. Donald P. Baker, "Bipartisan Push Given D.C. Bill," *Washington Post*, May 24, 1978.

176. Notably, President Carter did not mention the representation for the District in his spoken address, only in the written missive to Congress. Jimmy Carter, "The State of the Union Annual Message to Congress," Washington, DC, January 19, 1978, American Presidency Project, www.presidency.ucsb.edu/node/245130.

177. Baker, "Coalition Strategy," March 5, 1978.

178. 124 *Congressional Record* 5098 (1978).

179. 124 *Congressional Record* 5103 (1978). See Donald P. Baker, "Full D.C. Representation Debated; House Vote Today," *Washington Post*, March 2, 1978.

180. 124 *Congressional Record* 5105 (1978).

181. 124 *Congressional Record* 5263–64 (1978).

182. 124 *Congressional Record* 5266 (1978).

183. 124 *Congressional Record* 5273 (1978).

184. 124 *Congressional Record* 5100 (1978).

185. 124 *Congressional Record* 5266 (1978).

186. Edwards, District of Columbia Representation in Congress, H. R. Rep. 95-886 (1978), Report on H. J. Res. 554 from the House Committee on the Judiciary, at 7–8. See Orrin Hatch,

"Should the Capital Vote in Congress: A Critical Analysis of the Proposed D.C. Representation Amendment," *Fordham University Law Journal* 7, no. 3 (1979): 483.

187. 124 *Congressional Record* 26344 (1978).

188. 124 *Congressional Record* 26345 (1978). Senator Kennedy first used the line in an op-ed penned with the conservative South Carolina Democrat, Ernest Hollings. Edward M. Kennedy and Ernest Hollings, "Representation for the District," *Washington Post*, May 19, 1978.

189. 124 *Congressional Record* 26370 (1978).

190. 124 *Congressional Record* 26370 (1978).

191. 124 *Congressional Record* 27249, 27259 (1978).

192. 124 *Congressional Record* 27258 (1978); Donald P. Baker and Karlyn Barker, "67–32 Roll Call Sends Measure to the States," *Washington Post*, August 23, 1978.

193. Donnel Nunes and LaBarbara Bowman, "Dole, Robert Byrd Join Backers of D.C. Voting Bill," *Washington Post*, August 20, 1978; Baker and Barker, "67–32 Roll Call Sends Measure to the States," *Washington Post*, August 23, 1978; Kenneth Bredemier and LaBarbara Bowman, "Fauntroy Mans Command Post: Intensive Lobbying Keyed Victory," *Washington Post*, August 23, 1978.

194. Donald P. Baker, "Senate Sets Decision on D.C. Voting: 1 or 2 Senators Seen Decisive in Vote Today," *Washington Post*, August 22, 1978.

195. Kyvig, *Explicit and Authentic Acts*, 422.

196. 124 *Congressional Record* 27260 (1978); Baker, "Senate Sets Decision on D.C. Voting," *Washington Post*, August 22, 1978; Nunes and Bowman, "Dole, Robert Byrd Join Backers"; Baker and Barker, "67-to-32 Roll Call Sends Measure to the States."

197. "Capital Voting Rights Amendment Runs into Trouble," *New York Times*, March 27, 1979; "States Lagging in Drive to Ratify Amendment on Voting in Capital," *New York Times*, September 12, 1979.

198. District of Columbia Statehood Constitutional Convention of 1979, D.C. Law 3-171, 27 DCR 4732 (approved by voters on November 4, 1980).

199. "D.C. Is Too Too Too Too," *Los Angeles Times*, May 14, 1985.

200. Those sixteen states were New Jersey (1978), Michigan (1978), Ohio (1978), Minnesota (1979), Massachusetts (1979), Connecticut (1979), Wisconsin (1979), Maryland (1980), Hawaii (1980), Oregon (1981), Maine (1983), West Virginia (1983), Rhode Island (1983), Iowa (1984), Louisiana (1984), and Delaware (1984).

201. "The last holdout was Brazil, which granted full representation to the citizens of Brasília in 1986." Garry Young, "The District of Columbia and Its Lack of Representation in Congress: What Difference Does It Make?" (Washington, DC: Center for Washington Area Studies, 2009), 7, gwipp.gwu.edu/sites/g/files/zaxdzs2181/f/downloads/DC%20Representation%20Main%20Report%20Final.pdf.

Chapter 8: The Era of Conservative Amendment Politics

1. Conservative interest in constitutional amendments was kindled in the 1960s by rulings of the liberal Warren Court relating to school prayer and "one person, one vote." David E. Kyvig, *Explicit & Authentic Acts: Amending the Constitution 1776–1995* (Lawrence: University Press of Kansas, 1996), 370–85. After the Supreme Court's January 1973 ruling in *Roe v. Wade*, which recognized a woman's right to an abortion, pro-life activists and politicians proposed a variety of amendments to the Constitution to recognize a right to life for unborn persons or to give Congress and the states the power to restrict or ban abortion. The push for an amendment stalled by 1975 after the Senate Judiciary Committee defeated eight amendment proposals championed by pro-life activists. Mary Ziegler, *After Roe: The Lost History of the Abortion Debate* (Cambridge, MA: Harvard University Press, 2015), 41–42, 53. In 1981, Senator Orrin Hatch, a Republican from Utah, introduced a Human Life Federalism Amendment giving states and Congress concurrent power to restrict or ban abortion. After reaching the floor in 1982, the measure was

defeated in the Senate by a vote of 49–50. S.J. Res. 110, 97th Cong., 1st Sess. (1981). See Kyvig, *Explicit & Authentic Acts*, 450–51; 370, 379–85; John R. Vile, *Encyclopedia of Constitutional Amendments, Proposed Amendments, and Amending Issues 1789–2010*, vol. 2 (Santa Barbara, CA: ABC-CLIO, 2010), 409–412 (hereafter Vile, *Encyclopedia*).

2. See Richard B. Bernstein, "The Sleeper Wakes: The History and Legacy of the Twenty-Seventh Amendment," *Fordham Law Review* 61, no. 3 (1992): 553.

3. U.S. Constitution, Art. I, Sec 8.

4. Akhil Amar, *America's Constitution: A Biography* (New York: Random House, 2005), 107.

5. Alexander Hamilton, "Report Relative to a Provision for the Support of Public Credit," January 9, 1790, Founders Online, National Archives, founders.archives.gov/documents /Hamilton/01-06-02-0076-0002-0001. Original Source: *The Papers of Alexander Hamilton*, vol. 6, *December 1789–August 1790*, ed. Harold C. Syrett (New York: Columbia University Press, 1962), 65–110.

6. James Madison to Henry Lee, New York, April 13, 1790, Founders Online, National Archives, founders.archives.gov/documents/Madison/01-13-02-0106. Original source: *The Papers of James Madison*, vol. 13, *20 January 1790–31 March 1791*, ed. Charles F. Hobson and Robert A. Rutland (Charlottesville: University Press of Virginia, 1981): 147–48.

7. James V. Saturno and Megan S. Lynch, *A Balanced Budget Constitutional Amendment: Background and Congressional Options* (Washington, DC: Congressional Research Service, R41907, 2019), 1.

8. U.S. Office of Management and Budget, Federal Surplus or Deficit—FYFSD, FRED, Federal Reserve Bank of St. Louis, fred.stlouisfed.org/series/FYFSD, October 23, 2019.

9. An Amendment to the Constitution of the United States, H. J. Res. 579, 74th Congress (1936); 80 *Congressional Record* 6667, 6677 (1936); David E. Kyvig, "Reforming or Resisting Modern Government? The Balanced Budget Amendment to the U.S. Constitution," *Akron Law Review* 28, no. 2 (Fall–Winter 1995): 102–3.

10. Russell L. Caplan, *Constitutional Brinkmanship: Amending the Constitution by National Convention* (New York: Oxford University Press, 1988), 79. For more on Proposition 13 and the rise of anti-tax politics in the late 1970s, see Laura Kalman, *Right Star Rising: A New Politics* (New York: W.W. Norton and Company, 2010), 232–48.

11. James V. Saturno and Megan S. Lynch, CRS Insight, IN10884, Balanced Budget Amendments (April 10, 2018).

12. See Ernest J. Istook Jr., *Considering a Balanced Budget Amendment: Lessons from History*, Heritage Foundation Backgrounder, no. 2581 (Washington, DC: Heritage Foundation, July 14, 2011), 5.

13. Edwin Meese III, *Balanced Budget Amendment: Instrument to Force Spending Cuts, Not Tax Hikes*, Heritage Foundation Report, No. 3323 (Washington, DC: Heritage Foundation, July 21, 2011), 1.

14. Thomas Kaplan, "As Deficits Mount, Amendment to Require Balanced Budget Fails in House," *New York Times*, April 12, 2018.

15. Proposing a Balanced Budget Amendment to the Constitution of the United States, H. J. Res. 2, 115th Congress (2017).

16. Tara Golshan, "House Republicans Are Voting to Make Deficits Unconstitutional After Their $1.5 Trillion Tax Cuts," *Vox*, April 12, 2018, www.vox.com/policy-and -politics/2018/4/12/17216828/balanced-budget-amendment-trump-ryan-tax.

17. See, e.g., 164 *Congressional Record* H3162–H3163 (April 12, 2018), statement of Representative Goodlatte, republicans-judiciary.house.gov/press-release/goodlatte-floor-statement-in-support-of-h-j-res-2; William H. Fruth, *Debts, Deficits & the Balanced Budget Amendment* (Palm City, FL: Balanced Budget Amendment Task Force, 2018), bba4usa.org/wp-content/up loads/2018/02/DDBBA-2018.pdf.

18. 141 *Congressional Record* 2383 (1995).

19. E.g., Richard Kogan, "Balanced Budget Amendment Could Lead to Extreme Budget Cuts," Center on Budget and Policy Priorities Research Report, April 11, 2018, www.cbpp.org/research /federal-budget/balanced-budget-amendment-could-lead-to-extreme-budget-cuts; Kyvig, "Reforming or Resisting Modern Government?" 100.

20. *The Perils of Constitutionalizing the Budget Debate*, before the Subcommittee on the Constitution, Civil Rights and Human Rights of the Senate Committee on the Judiciary, 112th Congress 4 (2011), statement of Robert Greenstein, president, Center on Budget and Policy Priorities, www.cbpp.org/sites/default/files/atoms/files/11-30-11bud-test.pdf.

21. The lawmakers were James Clark of Maryland and David Halbrook of Mississippi. Caplan, *Constitutional Brinkmanship*, 79.

22. "How a Small Crusade Grew," *Washington Post*, February 14, 1979; Adam Clymer, "Proposed Convention on Balancing Budget," *New York Times*, February 16, 1979.

23. Chris Suellentrop, "Grover Norquist: The Republican Party's Prophet of Permanence," *Slate*, July 7, 2003, slate.com/news-and-politics/2003/07/grover-norquist-gop-prophet-of -permanence.html; Alex Altman, "Meet the Man Who Invented the Super PAC," *Time*, May 13, 2015.

24. Charles Mohr, "Tax Union Playing Chief Role in Drive," *New York Times*, May 15, 1979.

25. Kyvig, "Reforming or Resisting Modern Government?," 107.

26. "How a Small Crusade Grew," *Washington Post*, February 14, 1979.

27. "Balanced-Budget Amendment Campaign Falters," *Washington Post*, May 29, 1979.

28. Jimmy Carter, News Conference, January 17, 1979, American Presidency Project, www .presidency.ucsb.edu/node/249229.

29. Caplan, *Constitutional Brinkmanship*, 81.

30. Kevin Klose, "Michigan Lawmaker Stalls Budget-Amendment Drive," *Washington Post*, September 14, 1984, cited in Tom A. Coburn, *Smashing the DC Monopoly* (Washington, DC: WND Books, 2017), 174.

31. In 1983, Maryland was the first state to vote on rescission. See "Effort to Amend Constitution Lags," *New York Times*, August 21, 1983. Between 1988 and 2010, sixteen states rescinded all of their active Balanced Budget convention applications, and Nevada repealed one of its two. 1988 Ala. Laws 571, 759; S.M. 302, *Journal of the House of Representatives of Florida* (1988), 545; 1989 Nev. Stat. 2338–39; H. C. Res. 218, Regular Session of the Legislature of La., 1990; S.J.M. 9, 70th Or. Legislative Assembly (1999); 1999 Idaho Sess. Laws 1108–1109; S.C. Res. 4028, *Journal of the House of Representatives of North Dakota* (2001), 500; 2001 Utah Laws 2737–38; 2003 Ariz. Sess. Laws 1443–44; 2004 Ga. Laws 1081–84; H. 3400, *Journal of the House of Representatives of South Carolina* (January 22, 2003); 2004 Va. Acts 2179; 2009 Okla. Sess. Laws 2433–34; 2009 Wyo. Sess. Laws 513–14; H.C. Res. 28, *Journal of the House of Representatives of New Hampshire* (May 5, 2010); 2010 Tenn. Pub. Acts Resolutions Index 1; 2010 S.D. Sess. Laws 18–19.

32. Martha M. Hamilton, "Blow to Balanced-Budget Amendment," *Washington Post*, May 9, 1988. See also Caplan, *Constitutional Brinkmanship*, 87.

33. "Balanced Budget Amendment Fails in House," *CQ Almanac, 1982*, 38th ed., 391–94 (Washington, DC: *Congressional Quarterly*, 1983), library.cqpress.com/cqalmanac/cqal82-1164709.

34. 128 *Congressional Record* 15966 (1982).

35. A Joint Resolution Proposing an Amendment to the Constitution Altering Federal Fiscal Decision-Making Procedures, S. J. Res. 58, 97th Congress (1982). See "Balanced Budget Amendment Fails in House"; Steven V. Roberts, "Plan to Require Budget Balance Voted in Senate," *New York Times*, August 5, 1982.

36. The vote was 236 in favor, 187 against. A Joint Resolution Proposing an Amendment to the Constitution Altering Federal Budget Procedures, H. J. Res. 350, 97th Congress (1982). See "Balanced Budget Amendment Fails in House."

37. 128 *Congressional Record* 19229 (1982).

38. 128 *Congressional Record* 27255 (1982). See Steven V. Roberts, "House, by 46 Votes, Rejects Proposal on a Budget Limit," *New York Times*, October 2, 1982.

39. "2 Senate Liberals Back Balanced-Budget Rule," *Los Angeles Times*, February 24, 1995: Senator Biden announced, "I have concluded that there is nothing left to try except the balanced-budget amendment." Edwin Chen and Michael Ross, "Balanced-Budget Amendment Falls Short in Tight Senate Vote," *Los Angeles Times*, March 3, 1995: In casting a vote against the amendment, Senator Feinstein said, "I want to see a balanced-budget amendment pass Congress." Also: "How the House Voted on the Balanced-Budget Amendment," *New York Times*, January 27, 1995: Representative Steny Hoyer voted yes.

40. Jake Sherman and Marin Cogan, "GOP's Balanced Budget Right Turn," *Politico*, July 1, 2011, www.politico.com/story/2011/07/gops-balanced-budget-right-turn-058164; Alana Goodman, "20 Senate Dems Support Balanced Budget Amendment?," *Commentary*, July 21, 2011, www .commentarymagazine.com/politics-ideas/liberals-democrats/20-senate-dems-support -balanced-budget-amendment; Istook, *Considering a Balanced Budget Amendment*, 2.

41. An Original Joint Resolution Proposing an Amendment to the Constitution Relating to a Federal Balanced Budget, S. J. Res. 225, 99th Congress (1986). The resolution failed 66–34.

42. Proposing an Amendment to the Constitution to Provide for a Balanced Budget for the United States Government and for Greater Accountability in the Enactment of Tax Legislation, H. J. Res. 268, 101st Congress (1990). The resolution failed 279–150. Also: Proposing an Amendment to the Constitution to Provide for a Balanced Budget for the United States Government and for Greater Accountability in the Enactment of Tax Legislation, H. J. Res. 290, 102nd Congress (1992). The resolution failed 280–153.

43. Adam Clymer, "Balanced-Budget Amendment Fails to Gain House Approval," *New York Times*, June 12, 1992.

44. "After 40 Years, GOP Wins House," in *CQ Almanac 1994,* 50th ed., 570–78 (Washington, DC: *Congressional Quarterly,* 1995), library.cqpress.com/cqalmanac/cqal94-1102790; "Republicans Capture Senate," in *CQ Almanac 1994,* 50th ed., 565–70 (Washington, DC: *Congressional Quarterly,* 1995), library.cqpress.com/cqalmanac/cqal94-1102780.

45. Andrew Glass, "Congress Runs into 'Republican Revolution' Nov. 8, 1994," *Politico*, November 8, 2007, www.politico.com/story/2007/11/congress-runs-into-republican-revolution-nov-8-1994-006757. See Nancy MacLean, *Democracy in Chains: The Deep History of the Radical Right's Stealth Plan for America* (New York: Viking, 2017), 190–92.

46. W. John Moore, "The Big Man," *National Journal* 27, no. 5 (February 4, 1995); Kevin Merida, "The Judiciary Chairman's Trying Times," *Washington Post*, December 11, 1998. See Also "Rep. Henry Hyde Is Waiting for History's Verdict," *Washington Post*, December 11, 1998.

47. Michael Wines, "House Committee Advances Balanced-Budget Measure," *New York Times*, January 12, 1995.

48. "Balanced Budget Plan Stumbles on 1st Vote," *Omaha World Herald*, January 26, 1995.

49. Michael Wines, "House Approves Bill to Mandate a Balanced Budget," *New York Times*, January 27, 1995.

50. The six Democrats who switched were Feinstein (CA), Daschle (SD), Bingaman (NM), Dorgan (ND), Ford (KY), and Hollings (SC). Immediately after the vote, Bob Dole switched his vote to a no, making the final total 65–35. This was "a parliamentary maneuver" to "enable him to call up the amendment for debate and another vote at any time." Edward Chen and Michael Ross, "Balanced-Budget Amendment Falls Short in Tight Senate Vote," *Los Angeles Times*, March 3, 1995.

51. See Joint Resolution Proposing a Balanced Budget Amendment to the Constitution of the United States, H. J. Res. 1, 104th Congress (1996), which failed 64–35, 142 *Congressional Record* 13330 (1996); A Joint Resolution Proposing an Amendment to the Constitution of the United States to Require a Balanced Budget, S. J. Res. 1, 105th Congress (1997), which failed 66–34, 143 *Congressional Record* 3080 (1997).

52. Istook, *Considering a Balanced Budget Amendment*, 1.

53. "Q&A with Gregory Watson," C-SPAN, June 22, 2018, www.c-span.org/video/?447078-1 /qa-gregory-watson.

54. Matt Largey, "The Bad Grade That Changed the U.S. Constitution," *NPR*, May 5, 2017, www.npr.org/2017/05/05/526900818/the-bad-grade-that-changed-the-u-s-constitution.

55. Watson believed, based on available information, that six states had ratified by 1792, followed by Ohio in 1873 and Wyoming in 1978. It was uncovered later that Kentucky also had ratified the amendment in 1792.

56. "Q&A with Gregory Watson," C-SPAN, June 22, 2018. See also Largey, "Bad Grade That Changed the U.S. Constitution"; Barry Brownstein, "Gregory Watson: The C Student Who Amended the Constitution," *Intellectual Takeout*, March 22, 2017, www.intellectualtakeout.org /blog/gregory-watson-c-student-who-amended-constitution.

57. Largey, "Bad Grade That Changed the U.S. Constitution"; John Heltman, "27th Amendment or Bust," *American Prospect*, May 30, 2012, prospect.org/justice/27th-amendment-bust.

58. Don Phillips, "Proposed Amendment, Age 200, Showing Life," *Washington Post*, March 29, 1989.

59. "Q&A with Gregory Watson," C-SPAN, June 22, 2018.

60. "Madison Amendment Surprises Lawmakers," *CQ Almanac 1992*, 48th ed., 58–59 (Washington, DC: *Congressional Quarterly*, 1993), library.cqpress.com/cqalmanac/cqal92-1106979; Heltman, "27th Amendment or Bust."

61. Largey, "Bad Grade That Changed the U.S. Constitution."

62. Richard B. Bernstein, "The Sleeper Wakes: The History and Legacy of the Twenty-Seventh Amendment," *Fordham Law Review* 61, no. 3 (1992): 542.

63. "Madison Amendment Surprises Lawmakers."

64. Bill McAllister, "Across Two Centuries, a Founder Updates the Constitution," *Washington Post*, May 14, 1992; Richard L. Berke, "1789 Amendment Is Ratified but Now the Debate Begins," *New York Times*, May 8, 1992.

65. *Dillon v. Gloss*, 256 U.S. 368, 375 (1921). In dictum, at 375, the justices said it was "quite untenable" that an amendment proposed in 1789 could still be pending.

66. *Coleman v. Miller*, 307 U.S. 433, 451, 456 (1939).

67. McAllister, "Across Two Centuries"; Heltman, "27th Amendment or Bust," *American Prospect*, May 30, 2012.

68. An Act to Establish the National Archives and Records Administration, and for other purposes ("National Archives and Records Administration Act of 1984"), Pub. L. No. 98-497, 98 Stat. 2280 (1984).

69. Heltman, "27th Amendment or Bust," *American Prospect*, May 30, 2012; Jessie Kratz, "The National Archives' Role in Amending the Constitution," *Prologue Magazine* 49, no. 1 (Spring 2017), www.archives.gov/publications/prologue/2017/spring/historian-27-amendment.

70. "Madison Amendment Surprises Lawmakers," *CQ Almanac 1992*, 48th ed. (Washington, DC: *Congressional Quarterly*, 1993) 58–59, library.cqpress.com/cqalmanac/cqal92-1106 979.

71. "Madison Amendment Surprises Lawmakers."

72. The resolution passed in the House by a vote of 414–3 while the Senate passed it 99–0. See Richard Berke, "Congress Backs 27th Amendment," *New York Times*, May 21, 1992.

73. "The Ageless 27th Amendment," *New York Times*, May 16, 1992.

74. E.g., Brannon P. Denning and John R. Vile, "Necromancing the Equal Rights Amendment," *Constitutional Commentary* 85 (2000); Willam W. Van Alstyne, "What Do You Think About the Twenty-Seventh Amendment?" *Constitutional Commentary* 1139 (1993); Michael Stokes Paulsen, "A General Theory of Article V: The Constitutional Lessons of the Twenty-Seventh Amendment," *Yale Law Journal* 103 (1993); Richard L. Berke, "1789 Amendment Is Ratified but Now the Debate Begins," *New York Times*, May 8, 1992.

75. See, e.g., Allison L. Held, Sheryl L. Herndon, and Danielle M. Stager, "The Equal Rights Amendment: Why the ERA Remains Legally Viable and Properly Before the States," *William & Mary Journal of Women & the Law* 3, no. 1 (1997): 113.

76. See Bernstein, "Sleeper Wakes," 551–54.

77. Kyvig, *Explicit & Authentic Acts*, 454. Democrats maintained continuous control of the House of Representatives from 1955 to 1995. Similarly, they controlled the Senate from 1955 to 1981.

78. "Term Limits Amendment Falls Short," *CQ Almanac 1995*, 51st ed., 1-35–1-38 (Washington, DC: *Congressional Quarterly*, 1996), library.cqpress.com/cqalmanac/cqal95-1099494. While the Supreme Court later struck down state limits on members of Congress in *U.S. Term Limits, Inc. v. Thornton*, 514 U.S. 779 (1995) on the ground that states can't add new qualifications beyond those enumerated in Article I, fifteen states continue to limit the tenure of state lawmakers. "State legislatures with term limits," Ballotpedia, ballotpedia.org /State_legislatures_with_term_limits.

79. "Republican Contract with America," September 27, 1994, web.archive.org/web/1999 0427174200/www.house.gov/house/Contract/CONTRACT.html.

80. "Term Limits Amendment Falls Short."

81. "Federal Farmer," Letter 11, January 10, 1788, in *The Documentary History of the Ratification of the Constitution* digital edition, ed. John P. Kaminski, Gaspare J. Saladino, Richard Leffler, Charles H. Schoenleber, and Margaret A. Hogan (Charlottesville: University of Virginia Press, 2009), hereafter *DHRC* digital edition.

82. Barbara Silberdick Feinberg, *Term Limits for Congress?* (New York: Twenty-First Century Books, 1996), 25.

83. See *U.S. Term Limits, Inc. v. Thornton*, 514 U.S. 779 (1995).

84. 141 *Congressional Record* 9685 (1995); Katharine Q. Seelye, "House Turns Back Measures to Limit Terms in Congress," *New York Times*, March 30, 1995.

85. "Term Limits Amendment Falls Short," *CQ Almanac 1995*, 51st ed., 1-35–1-38 (Washington, DC: *Congressional Quarterly*, 1996), library.cqpress.com/cqalmanac/cqal95-1099494.

86. 141 *Congressional Record* 9727 (1995).

87. "Term Limits Measure Fails in Senate," *CQ Almanac 1996*, 52nd ed., 1-25–1-26 (Washington, DC: *Congressional Quarterly*, 1997), library.cqpress.com/cqalmanac/cqal96-841-24595-1091401.

88. 491 U.S. 397 (1989).

89. 491 U.S. 414 (1989).

90. 491 U.S. 419 (1989).

91. "Court Sets Off Furor on Flag Burning," *CQ Almanac 1989*, 45th ed., 307–14 (Washington, DC: *Congressional Quarterly*, 1990), library.cqpress.com/cqalmanac/cqal89-1138866.

92. Walter Shapiro, "George HW Bush's Presidential Campaign Was Nothing to Be Proud Of," *The Guardian*, December 3, 2018.

93. George H. W. Bush, News Conference, June 27, 1989, American Presidency Project, www .presidency.ucsb.edu/node/263500.

94. James Gerstenzang, "Bush Asks Ban on Flag Desecration: Backs Constitutional Amendment in Wake of Supreme Court Ruling," *Los Angeles Times*, June 28, 1989.

95. Steven A. Holmes, "Amendment to Bar Flag Desecration Fails in the House," *New York Times*, June 22, 1990.

96. Gerstenzang, "Bush Asks Ban on Flag Desecration."

97. An Act to Amend Section 700 of title 18, United States Code, to Protect the Physical Integrity of the Flag (Flag Protection Act of 1989), Pub. L. No. 101-31, 103 Stat. 777 (1989); Roger C. Hartley, *How Failed Attempts to Amend the Constitution Mobilize Political Change* (Nashville: Vanderbilt University Press, 2017), 77.

98. *United States v. Eichman*, 496 U.S. 310 (1990).

99. "Amendment to Ban Flag Burning Fails," *CQ Almanac 1990*, 46th ed., 524–28 (Washington, DC: *Congressional Quarterly*, 1991), library.cqpress.com/cqalmanac/cqal90-1113240.

100. "Amendment to Ban Flag Burning Fails."

101. 136 *Congressional Record* 15242 (1990).

102. 136 *Congressional Record* 15316 (1990).

103. 136 *Congressional Record* 15246 (1990).

104. The vote in the House was 254–177. 136 *Congressional Record* 15318 (1990). See Holmes, "Amendment to Bar Flag Desecration Fails in the House," *New York Times*, June 22, 1990.

105. Susan F. Rasky, "Foley Vindicated by Vote on Flag," *New York Times*, June 22, 1990.

106. The vote on June 26, 1990, was 58 in favor and 42 against. 136 *Congressional Record* 15588 (1990); "Senate Rejects New Move to Outlaw Flag Burning," *New York Times*, June 27, 1990.

107. "Amendment to Ban Flag Burning Fails," *CQ Almanac 1990*, 46th ed., 524–28 (Washington, DC: *Congressional Quarterly*, 1991), library.cqpress.com/cqalmanac/cqal90-1113240.

108. "Amendment to Ban Flag Burning Fails."

109. "Flag Burning Amendment Rejected," *CQ Almanac 1995*, 51st ed., 6-22–6-24 (Washington, DC: *Congressional Quarterly*, 1996), library.cqpress.com/cqalmanac/cqal95-1100498.

110. 141 *Congressional Record* 17601-2 (1995); Kenneth J. Cooper, "House Approves Amendment on Flag Desecration," *Washington Post*, June 29, 1995; "Flag Burning Amendment Rejected," *CQ Almanac 1995*, 51st ed., 6-22–6-24 (Washington, DC: *Congressional Quarterly*, 1996), library.cqpress.com/cqalmanac/cqal95-1100498.

111. Katharine Q. Seelye, "House Easily Passes Amendment to Ban Desecration of Flag," *New York Times*, June 29, 1995.

112. 141 *Congressional Record* 36097 (1995); "Flag Burning Amendment Rejected," *CQ Almanac 1995*, 51st ed., 6-22–6-24 (Washington, DC: *Congressional Quarterly*, 1996), library.cqpress.com/cqalmanac/cqal95-1100498; Robin Toner, "Flag-Burning Amendment Fails in Senate, but Margin Narrows," *New York Times*, December 13, 1995.

113. Toner, "Flag-Burning Amendment Fails in Senate, but Margin Narrows."

114. Proposing an Amendment to the Constitution of the United States Authorizing the Congress to Prohibit the Physical Desecration of the Flag of the United States, H. J. Res. 54, 105th Congress (1997), passed 310–114; Proposing an Amendment to the Constitution of the United States Authorizing the Congress to Prohibit the Physical Desecration of the Flag of the United States, H. J. Res. 33, 106th Congress (1999), passed 305–124; Proposing an Amendment to the Constitution of the United States Authorizing the Congress to Prohibit the Physical Desecration of the Flag of the United States, H. J. Res. 36, 107th Congress (2001), passed 298–125; Proposing an Amendment to the Constitution of the United States Authorizing the Congress to Prohibit the Physical Desecration of the Flag of the United States, H. J. Res. 4, 108th Congress (2003), passed 300–125; Proposing an Amendment to the Constitution of the United States Authorizing the Congress to Prohibit the Physical Desecration of the Flag of the United States, H. J. Res. 10, 109th Congress (2005), passed 286–130.

115. A Joint Resolution Proposing an Amendment to the Constitution of the United States Authorizing Congress to Prohibit the Physical Desecration of the Flag of the United States, S. J. Res. 14, 106th Congress (1999), failed by a vote of 63–37; A Joint Resolution Proposing an Amendment to the Constitution of the United States Authorizing Congress to Prohibit the Physical Desecration of the Flag of the United States, S. J. Res. 12, 109th Congress (2006), failed by a vote of 66–34.

116. Notable examples include Amendment 2, the 1992 Colorado ballot measure to prohibit the adoption of antidiscrimination protections based on sexual orientation, and California's Proposition 187, a 1994 ballot initiative to deny public services to undocumented immigrants. For an insightful analysis of the rise of conservative wedge-issue campaigns in the 1980s and 1990, see Jean Stefancic and Richard Delgado, *No Mercy: How Conservative Think Tanks and Foundations Changed America's Social Agenda* (Philadelphia: Temple University Press, 1996).

117. *Goodridge v. Department of Public Health*, 440 Mass. 309, 312 (2003).

118. The litigation victory in Massachusetts was preceded by a short-lived breakthrough in Hawaii. In 1993, the Hawaii Supreme Court ruled that the denial of marriage licenses to

same-sex couples violated the equal protection clause of the Hawaii Constitution absent a compelling state interest. After a 1996 trial, the case was rendered moot after the state's voters approved an amendment to the Hawaii Constitution giving the legislature the power to define marriage as limited to a man and a woman. John F. Kowal, "The Improbable Victory of Marriage Equality" in *Legal Change: Lessons from America's Social Movements*, ed. Jennifer Weiss-Wolf and Jeanine Plant-Chirlin (New York: Brennan Center for Justice, 2015), 27–29.

119. See *Obergefell v. Hodges*, 576 U.S. 644 (2015); Kowal, "The Improbable Victory of Marriage Equality," in Weiss-Wolf and Plant-Chirlin, *Legal Change*.

120. An Act to Define and Protect the Institution of Marriage (Defense of Marriage Act), Pub. L. 104-199, 110 Stat. 2419 (1996).

121. Robert P. George, "The 28th Amendment," *National Review*, July 23, 2001, www.national review.com/2004/07/28th-amendment-robert-p-george.

122. Pam Belluck, "Same Sex Marriage: The Overview" *New York Times*, November 19, 2003.

123. Katharine Q. Seelye, "Conservatives Mobilize Against Ruling on Gay Marriage," *New York Times*, November 20, 2003.

124. David Stout, "San Francisco City Officials Perform Gay Marriages," *New York Times*, February 14, 2004.

125. David Stout, "Bush Backs Ban in Constitution on Gay Marriage," *New York Times*, February 24, 2004.

126. Stout, "Bush Backs Ban."

127. Stout, "Bush Backs Ban."

128. Carl Hulse and David D. Kirkpatrick, "The 2004 Campaign: The Marriage Issue," *New York Times*, July 9, 2004.

129. Carl Hulse, "Senators Block Initiative to Ban Same-Sex Unions," *New York Times*, July 15, 2004.

130. Proposing an Amendment to the Constitution Relating to Marriage, H. J. Res. 56, 108th Congress (2004); Vile, *Encyclopedia*, vol. 1, 191.

131. *Federal Marriage Amendment (The Musgrave Amendment)*, before the Subcommittee on the Constitution of the House Committee on the Judiciary, 108th Congress (2004), 5–6.

132. Mary Curtius, "Experts, Lawmakers Clash over Impact of Gay Marriage," *Los Angeles Times*, March 24, 2004.

133. Federal Marriage Amendment, S. J. Res. 40, 108th Congress (2004), failed by a vote of 48–50); Hulse, "Senators Block Initiative to Ban Same-Sex Unions," *New York Times*, July 15, 2004.

134. Proposing an Amendment to the Constitution of the United States Relating to Marriage, H. J. Res. 106, 108th Congress (2004), failed by a vote of 227–186.

135. 150 *Congressional Record* 20103 (2004).

136. *Obergefell v. Hodges*, 576 U.S. 644 (2015). See Kowal, "Improbable Victory of Marriage Equality," in Weiss-Wolf and Plant-Chirlin, *Legal Change*.

137. Proposing an Amendment to the Constitution of the United States Restoring Religious Freedom, H. J. Res. 78, 105th Congress (1997). See David M. Ackerman and James Sayler, Congressional Research Service, 98-504A, The Religious Freedom Amendment: H. J. Res. 78 (1998).

138. Proposing an Amendment to the Constitution of the United States with Respect to Tax Limitations, H. J. Res. 62, 105th Congress (1997).

139. Proposing an Amendment to the Constitution of the United States Relating to Contributions and Expenditures Intended to Affect Elections, S. J. Res. 18, 105th Congress (1997), defeated March 18, 1997, by a vote of 61–38. See also Proposing an Amendment to the Constitution of the United States to Limit Campaign Spending, H. J. Res. 47, 105th Congress (1997); "Senate Rejects Fund-Raising Change," *Hartford Courant*, March 19, 1997.

140. Kathleen M. Sullivan, "What's Wrong with Constitutional Amendments," in Alan Brinkley, Nelson W. Polsby, and Kathleen M. Sullivan, *New Federalist Papers: Essays in Defense of the Constitution* (New York: Norton, 1997), 61. See also Kathleen Sullivan,

"Constitutional Amendmentitis," *American Prospect*, December 19, 2001, prospect.org/power /constitutional-amendmentitis.

141. *Great and Extraordinary Occasions: Developing Guidelines for Constitutional Change* (New York: Century Foundation, 1999), constitutionproject.org/wp-content/uploads/2012/09/32.pdf.

142. 2011 State and Legislative Partisan Composition, National Conference of State Legislatures, January 31, 2011, www.ncsl.org/documents/statevote/2010_Legis_and_State_post.pdf.

143. "Balanced Budget Amendment Inc.," Nonprofit Explorer, ProPublica, projects.pro publica.org/nonprofits/organizations/271351108.

144. See William H. Fruth, *Debts, Deficits & the Balanced Budget Amendment* (Palm City, FL: Balanced Budget Amendment Task Force, 2018), bba4usa.org/wp-content/uploads/2018/02 /DDBBA-2018.pdf. See also Tom A. Coburn, *Smashing the DC Monopoly* (Washington, DC: WND Books, 2017), 87–89.

145. "About ALEC," American Legislative Exchange Council, www.alec.org/about.

146. Jay Riestenberg, "U.S. Constitution Threatened as Article V Convention Movement Nears Success," Common Cause Background Memo, March 2019, www.commoncause.org /resource/u-s-constitution-threatened-as-article-v-convention-movement-nears-success.

147. Jay Riestenberg and Dale Eisen, *The Dangerous Path: Big Money's Plan to Shred the Constitution* (Washington, DC: Common Cause, 2016), www.commoncause.org/wp-content /uploads/2018/03/dangerous-path-report-1.pdf; "ALEC Exposed," Center for Media and Democracy, www.alecexposed.org/wiki/ALEC_Exposed.

148. Karla Jones, "ALEC Reaffirms Support for Article V Initiatives," American Legislative Exchange Council, February 11, 2016, www.alec.org/article/alec-reaffirms-support-for -article-v-initiatives.

149. Coburn, *Smashing the DC Monopoly*, 98–99.

150. "Resolution Calling for a Federal Balanced Budget Amendment," American Legislative Exchange Council, finalized December 3, 2015, amended January 16, 2016, www.alec.org /model-policy/a-resolution-calling-for-a-federal-balanced-budget-amendment; Rob Natelson, *Proposing Constitutional Amendments by a Convention of the States: A Handbook for State Lawmakers* (Arlington, VA: American Legislative Exchange Council, 2016), www.alec.org /publication/article-v-a-handbook-for-state-lawmakers.

151. See Balanced Budget Amendment Task Force, home page, bba4usa.org.

152. E.g., Jeffrey A. Kimble, "Acknowledging the Elephant in the Room: The Congressional Obstacle to the Balanced Budget Amendment Task Force's Effort to Achieve a Convention Call," Compact with America Policy Brief no. 5, January 25, 2016, docs.wixstatic.com /ugd/e48202_f127027c82734a108bbfbe6520100812.pdf; Wilfred Codrington "A Campaign to Rewrite the Constitution Is Underway," *The Hill*, September 13, 2018, thehill.com/opinion /judiciary/406581-a-campaign-to-rewrite-the-constitution-is-underway.

153. Michael Wines, "Inside the Conservative Push for States to Amend the Constitution," *New York Times*, August 22, 2016.

154. "Model Convention of States Application/Resolution," Convention of States Action, conventionofstates.com/files/model-convention-of-states-application; "Citizen's Pocket Guide 2018 Edition," Convention of States Action, Convention of States Project Wiki, wiki .conventionofstates.com/doku.php?id=documents:cosproject:pocket_guide. For criticisms see Brendan O'Connor, "Right-Wing Billionaires Are Buying Themselves a New Constitution," *Splinter*, April 4, 2017, splinternews.com/right-wing-billionaires-are-buying-themselves-a -new-con-1793960357: "Under the Convention of States proposal, literally anything could be brought up." Also: John Austin, "Convention of States: Too Close for Comfort?" *Jacksonville Progress*, June 22, 2017: "They could more or less create a new constitution: change our system of government, and not for the better."

155. O'Connor, "Right-Wing Billionaires Are Buying Themselves a New Constitution," *Splinter*, April 4, 2017; Nina Easton, "Political Fundamentals," *New York Times*, September 9, 2007.

156. "Full-Length Convention of States Simulation (official)," YouTube video, 5:54:25, "Convention of States Project," September 23, 2017, 2:55:45, youtu.be/lVJ6xkA-LrI?t=10547, statement of Michael Farris.

157. Home page, Citizens for Self-Governance.

158. Sanya Mansoor, "A Tea Party Movement to Overhaul the Constitution Is Quietly Gaining Steam," *Time*, August 2, 2018, time.com/5356045/constitutional-convention-tea-party; "Citizens for Self-Governance," SourceWatch, Center for Media and Democracy, www.source watch.org/index.php?title=Citizens_for_Self-Governance; Arn Pearson, "Koch Convention to Rewrite Constitution Runs into Roadblocks," *Exposed by CMD*, Center for Media and Democracy, June 12, 2017, www.exposedbycmd.org/2017/06/12/koch-convention-rewrite-constitution -roadblocks; Bruce Murphy, "Dark Money's Front Man," *The Progressive*, January 22, 2016, progressive.org/magazine/dark-money-s-front-man.

159. Riestenberg and Eisen, *Dangerous Path*; Simon Davis-Cohen, "Corporate America Is Inching Even Closer to a Constitutional Convention," *In These Times*, January 13, 2017, inthesetimes.com /article/19811/constitutional-convention-of-states-alec-balanced-budget-corporate-america.

160. Davis-Cohen, "Corporate America Is Inching Even Closer." See "Application for a Convention of the States Under Article V of the Constitution of the United States," American Legislative Exchange Council Model Policy, finalized July 24, 2015, amended September 4, 2015, www.alec.org/model-policy/article-v-convention-of-the-states.

161. As of November 2020, the states are Georgia, Alaska, Florida, Alabama, Indiana, Louisiana, Tennessee, Oklahoma, Arizona, North Dakota, Texas, Missouri, Arkansas, Utah, and Mississippi. 2014 Ga. Laws 894–96; 2014 Alaska Sess. Laws Leg. Resolve 68; 2014 Fla. Laws 3118–20; 2015 Ala. Laws 655–56; 2016 Ind. Acts 3201–02; S.C. Res. 52, Regular Session of the La. Legislature (2016); S. J. Res. 67, 109th Gen. Assembly of Tenn. (2016); 2016 Okla. Sess. Laws 1675–77; 2017 Ariz. Sess. Laws 2454–55; 2017 N.D. Laws 1868–69; 2017 Tex. Gen. Laws 4474–75; 2017 Mo. Laws 691–92; S. J. Res. 3, 92nd Gen. Assembly of Ark. (2019); S.C. Res. 596, Regular Sess. of the Miss. Legislature (2019); S. J. Res. 9, General Sess. of the Utah Legislature (2019).

162. "Citizens for Self-Governance," SourceWatch, Center for Media and Democracy, www .sourcewatch.org/index.php?title=Citizens_for_Self-Governance; Pearson, "Koch Convention to Rewrite Constitution Runs into Roadblocks," *Exposed by CMD*, Center for Media and Democracy, June 12, 2017; Fredreka Schouten, "Exclusive: In Latest Job, Jim DeMint Wants to Give Tea Party 'a New Mission,'" *USA Today*, June 12, 2017, www.usatoday.com/story /news/politics/2017/06/12/jim-demint-joins-group-that-wants-to-amend-constitution-tea -party/102748540; O'Connor, "Right-Wing Billionaires Are Buying Themselves a New Constitution," *Splinter*, April 4, 2017.

163. Coburn, *Smashing the DC Monopoly*, 6–7.

164. Gordon S. Wood, *The Radicalism of the American Revolution* (New York: Knopf, 1992), 262.

165. Convention Debates, June 24, 1788, *DHRC* digital edition.

166. "Brutus" 1, *New York Journal*, October 18, 1787, *DHRC* digital edition.

167. Debates of the Virginia Ratifying Convention, June 4, 1788, *DHRC* digital edition. See also Michael Klarman, *The Framers' Coup* (New York: Oxford University Press, 2016), 314.

168. Coburn, *Smashing the DC Monopoly*, 111.

169. James Madison to Edmund Randolph, New York, April 2, 1787, Founders Online, National Archives, founders.archives.gov/documents/Madison/01-09-02-0190. Original source: *The Papers of James Madison*, vol. 9, *9 April 1786–24 May 1787 and supplement 1781–1784*, ed. Robert A. Rutland and William M. E. Rachal (Chicago: University of Chicago Press, 1975), 361–62.

170. Coburn, *Smashing the DC Monopoly*, 109–10.

171. See, e.g., Eli Y. Adashi and Senator Tom Coburn, "The Sustainable Growth Rate— What Happens Now?" Medscape, June 30, 2011, www.medscape.com/viewarticle/745412.

In an interview, Senator Coburn referred to himself as "a fiscal conservative and also . . . a constitutionalist.

172. Mansoor, "Tea Party Movement to Overhaul the Constitution Is Quietly Gaining Steam," *Time*, August 1, 2018.

173. Mansoor, "Tea Party Movement"; Davis-Cohen, "Corporate America Is Inching Even Closer to a Constitutional Convention," *In These Times*, January 13, 2017; O'Connor, "Right-Wing Billionaires Are Buying Themselves a New Constitution," *Splinter*, April 4, 2017.

174. "Official Proposals of the Simulated Convention of States," adopted September 23, 2016 in Williamsburg, VA, Convention of States Historic Simulation, www.foavc.org/reference /COS_Proposals.pdf; "COS Simulation," Convention of States Historic Simulation, convention ofstates.com/cos-simulation.

175. "Full-Length Convention of States Simulation (official)," YouTube video, 5:54:25, "Convention of States Project," September 23, 2017, 2:54:21, youtu.be/lVJ6xkA-LrI?t=10461 (statement of Michael Farris).

176. "Full-Length Convention of States Simulation," 3:10:20, youtu.be/lVJ6xkA-LrI?t=11417, statement of Michael Farris.

177. E.g., Coburn, *Smashing the DC Monopoly*, xv.

178. Jamiles Lartey, "Conservatives Call for Constitutional Convention Last Seen 230 Years Ago," *The Guardian*, August 11, 2018, www.theguardian.com/us-news/2018/aug/11 /conservatives-call-for-constitutional-convention-alec.

179. Coburn, *Smashing the DC Monopoly*, 93–95; "Compact for America: Balanced Budget Amendment," American Legislative Exchange Council Model Policy, amended January 28, 2013, www.alec.org/model-policy/resolution-to-effectuate-the-compact-for-america.

180. Rob Natelson, "A New Theory Supporting the Use of the Tenth Amendment to Control the Article V Process—and Why the Theory Doesn't Work," Article V Information Center, Independence Institute, March 6, 2016, articlevinfocenter.com/a-new-theory -supporting-the-use-of-the-tenth-amendment-to-control-the-article-v-process-and -why-the-theory-doesnt-work; David A. Super, "A 'Convention of States' Is the Last Thing America Needs Right Now," *The Hill*, March 27, 2018, thehill.com/opinion/campaign /380467-a-convention-of-states-is-the-last-thing-america-needs-right-now.

181. The five states, as of November 2020, are Alaska, Arizona, Georgia, Mississippi, and North Dakota. "Compact for America," Compact for America, www.compactforamerica.org /solution.

182. Karla Jones, "ALEC Reaffirms Support for Article V Initiatives," American Legislative Exchange Council, February 11, 2016, www.alec.org/article/alec-reaffirms-support -for-article-v-initiatives.

183. John R. Vile, a respected expert on Article V, argues that the weight of historical and scholarly evidence indicates that the states and Congress have the legal right to limit the scope of an Article V convention to a single subject and that political conditions would make a runaway convention unlikely. See John R. Vile, *Conventional Wisdom: The Alternate Article V Mechanism for Proposing Amendments to the U.S. Constitution* (Athens: University of Georgia Press, 2020).

184. Max Farrand, ed., *The Records of the Federal Convention of 1787*, vol. 2, (New Haven, CT: Yale University Press, 1911), 630.

185. Coburn, *Smashing the DC Monopoly*, 61–65.

186. David A. Super, "The Hidden Threat to Our Constitution," Expert Forum, American Constitution Society, June 19, 2019, www.acslaw.org/expertforum/the-hidden-threat-to -our-constitution.

187. Coburn, *Smashing the DC Monopoly*, 61–62, 64.

188. Matt Sedensky, "Conservatives Want to Bypass the Usual Way to Amend Constitution," Associated Press, November 3, 2018, www.apnews.com/e84cdca5b568402398e abfcd2b6ada07. See also Wilfred U. Codrington III, "Amending the Constitution: A

Civics Test Americans Need to Pass," *American Prospect*, August 28, 2017, prospect.org/justice /amending-constitution-civics-test-americans-need-pass.

189. Riestenberg, "U.S. Constitution Threatened."

190. Markus Schmidt, "House Defeats Bid for Convention of the States," *Richmond Times Dispatch*, February 7, 2014.

191. "Wolf-PAC Cover Letter," Resources, Wolf-PAC, wolf-pac.com/about/resources.

192. As of November 2019, Vermont, California, Illinois, New Jersey, and Rhode Island have approved the Wolf-PAC resolution for an Article V convention. 2014 Vt. Acts & Resolves 1531; A.J. Res. 1, Regular Session of the Ca. Legislature (2013–2014); 2014 Ill. Laws 6544–46; S.C. Res. 132, 216th Legislature of N.J. (2014); 2016 R.I. Pub. Laws 206–7. See Riestenberg, "U.S. Constitution Threatened."

193. See Lawrence Lessig, "Calling for a Convention," *American Prospect*, January 4, 2012, prospect.org/justice/calling-convention.

194. Nick Dranias and Lawrence Lessig, "So What Are D.C. Insiders Really Afraid Of?" *Constitution Daily*, National Constitution Center, November 2, 2014, web.archive.org/web/2017050903 4709/constitutioncenter.org/blog/so-what-are-the-d-c-insiders-really-afraid-of.

195. See, e.g., "More than 200 Organizations Oppose Calls for New Constitutional Convention, Warn of Dangers," press release, Common Cause, April 14, 2017, www.commoncause.org /media/articlevcoalitionletterrelease.

196. Douglas Martin, "Phyllis Schlafly, 'First Lady' of a Political March to the Right, Dies at 92," *New York Times*, September 5, 2016; Phyllis Schlafly, "Opinion: Failed Republicans Want to Rewrite the Constitution," *The Telegraph*, May 24, 2016, updated February 10, 2018, www .thetelegraph.com/opinion/article/Opinion-Failed-Republicans-want-to-rewrite-the-12597 416.php.

197. "A Convention Threatens Our Rights," Stop A Con-Con, John Birch Society, www.jbs .org/con-con.

198. Craig Millward, "Mark Meckler with Levin on Convention of States: 'This Is the Battle of Our Generation, Literally,'" CNS News, www.cnsnews.com/blog/craig-millward /mark-meckler-levin-convention-states-battle-our-generation-literally.

199. Jamal Greene, "Originalism's Race Problem," *Denver University Law Review* 88, no. 3 (2011): 517.

200. Erwin Chemerinsky, *We the People: A Progressive Reading of the Constitution for the Twenty-First Century* (New York: Picador, 2018), 31, 46.

201. Steven M. Teles, *The Rise of the Conservative Legal Movement: The Battle for Control of the Law* (Princeton, NJ: Princeton University Press, 2008); Jefferson Decker, *The Other Rights Revolution: Conservative Lawyers and the Remaking of American Government* (New York: Oxford University Press, 2016); Michael Waldman, *The Second Amendment: A Biography* (New York: Simon & Schuster, 2014).

202. Teles, *Rise of the Conservative Legal Movement*, 135–80.

203. "Leonard A. Leo," Federalist Society, web.archive.org/web/20190815224144/fedsoc.org /staff/leonard-leo.

204. Teles, *Rise of the Conservative Legal Movement*, 143. See also Amanda Hollis-Brusky, *Ideas with Consequences: The Federalist Society and the Conservative Counterrevolution* (New York: Oxford University Press), 152–53.

205. See Teles, *Rise of the Conservative Legal Movement*; Decker, *The Other Rights Revolution*; Waldman, *The Second Amendment*.

206. See Teles, *The Rise of the Conservative Legal Movement*; Decker, *Other Rights Revolution*; Waldman, *Second Amendment*.

207. David Margolick, "Bush's Court Advantage," *Vanity Fair*, December 2003, 150.

208. See Michael Avery and Danielle McLaughlin, *The Federalist Society: How Conservatives Took the Law Back from Liberals* (Nashville: Vanderbilt University Press, 2013), 32, noting that

Brett Kavanaugh was one of "the two most important staff lawyers for judicial selection" during the first few years of the George W. Bush presidency.

209. In his four-year term, President Trump appointed 54 appeals court judges and 174 district court judges. John Gramlich, "How Trump Compares with Other Presidents in Appointing Federal Judges," FactTank News in the Numbers, Pew Research Center, pewresearch.org/fact-tank/2021/01/13/how-trump-compares-with-other-recent-presidents-in-appointing-federal-judges.

210. For a compelling look at the right's focus on the courts as a means of reshaping our understanding of the Constitution, see MacLean, *Democracy in Chains*, 222–30.

Chapter 9: The People's Constitution

1. Pennsylvania Convention Debates, December 1, 1787, in *The Documentary History of the Ratification of the Constitution* digital edition, ed. John P. Kaminski, Gaspare J. Saladino, Richard Leffler, Charles H. Schoenleber, and Margaret A. Hogan (Charlottesville: University of Virginia Press, 2009), hereafter *DHRC* digital edition.

2. Elbridge Gerry to the Massachusetts General Court, New York, October 18, 1787, *DHRC* digital edition.

3. *Chisholm v. Georgia*, 2 U.S. 419, 468 (1793).

4. The Eleventh Amendment's prohibition extends to "Citizens of another State, or . . . Citizens or Subjects of any Foreign State." U.S. Constitution, Amend. XI.

5. *Marbury v. Madison*, 5 U.S. 137, 177 (1803).

6. *Dred Scott v. Sandford*, 60 U.S. 393, 407 (1857).

7. *A History of Woman Suffrage*, vol. 2, ed. Elizabeth Cady Stanton, Susan B. Anthony, and Matilda Joslyn Gage (Rochester, NY: Charles Mann, 1881), 586; U.S. Constitution, Amend. XIV, Sec. 1.

8. *A History of Woman Suffrage*, vol. 3, ed. Elizabeth Cady Stanton, Susan B. Anthony, and Matilda Joslyn Gage (Rochester, NY: Fowler & Wells, 1889), 58.

9. *Pollock v. Farmers' Loan & Trust Company*, 157 U.S. 429, affirmed on rehearing, 158 U.S. 601 (1895).

10. Charles Evans Hughes, *The Supreme Court of the United States, Its Foundations, Methods and Achievements: An Interpretation* (Garden City, NY: Garden City Publishing, 1936), 54.

11. "Child Labor Decision a Long Step Backward," *Sacramento Bee*, June 27, 1918.

12. *Reynolds v. Sims*, 377 U.S. 533 (1964).

13. 558 U.S. 310 (2010).

14. See Richard L. Hasen, *Plutocrats United: Campaign Money, the Supreme Court, and the Distortion of American Elections* (New Haven, CT: Yale University Press, 2000).

15. Daniel I. Wiener, *Citizens United Five Years Later*, Report (New York: Brennan Center for Justice, 2015), www.brennancenter.org/sites/default/files/analysis/Citizens_United_%20Five_Years_Later.pdf.

16. See Adam Skaggs and Fred Wertheimer, *Empowering Small Donors in Federal Elections* (New York: Brennan Center for Justice, 2012), www.brennancenter.org/sites/default/files/2019-08/Report_Empowering_Small_Donors_Federal_Elections.pdf.

17. Jeffrey D. Clements, *Corporations Are Not People: Reclaiming Democracy from Big Money and Global Corporations* (San Francisco: Berrett-Koehler, 2014), 154.

18. "Very Large Majorities Support Congressional Bills to Reduce Influence of Big Campaign Donors," Program for Public Consultation, School of Public Policy, University of Maryland, May 10, 2018, www.publicconsultation.org/redblue/very-large-majorities-support-congressional-bills-to-reduce-influence-of-big-campaign-donors.

19. Email interview with Jeff Clements, June 17, 2020.

20. The group supports a proposed amendment sponsored by Representative Theodore Deutch, a Democrat from Florida, but is open to other proposals as well. H. J. Res. 2, Proposing

an Amendment to the Constitution of the United States Relating to Contributions and Expenditures Intended to Affect Elections, 116th Congress (2019).

21. Ryan Liston, "Citizens Win in New Hampshire!" *American Promise Blog*, June 6, 2019, americanpromise.net/blog/2019/06/06/citizens-win-in-new-hampshire.

22. Move to Amend, homepage, www.movetoamend.org.

23. "Move to Amend's Proposed 28th Amendment to the Constitution," www.movetoamend.org/amendment; Proposing an Amendment to the Constitution of the United States Providing That the Rights Extended by the Constitution Are the Rights of Natural Persons Only, H. J. Res. 48, 116th Congress (2019).

24. Bryan Bowman, "The Case for a Constitutional Amendment to Overturn *Citizens United*," *The Globe Post*, February 6, 2019, theglobepost.com/2019/02/06/wolf-pac-interview.

25. 570 U.S. 529 (2013).

26. Melissa Boughton, "Barber, Other NC Panelists at Congressional Hearing: Restore the Voting Rights Act," *NC Policy Watch*, April 22, 2019, www.ncpolicywatch.com/2019/04/22/barber-other-nc-panelists-at-congressional-hearing-restore-the-voting-rights-act.

27. "Right to Vote Amendment," FairVote, www.fairvote.org/right_to_vote_amendment.

28. Proposing an Amendment to the Constitution of the United States Regarding the Right to Vote, H. J. Res. 93, 116th Congress (2020).

29. See Heather K. Gerken, "The Right to Vote: Is the Amendment Game Worth the Candle?," *William and Mary Bill of Rights Journal* 23 (2014): 11–25.

30. Jonathan Soros, "The Missing Right: A Constitutional Right to Vote," *Democracy: A Journal of Ideas*, no. 28 (Spring 2013).

31. John Fund, "It's Time for Term Limits on the Supreme Court," *National Review*, November 24, 2019, www.nationalreview.com/2019/11/supreme-court-term-limits-have-bipartisan-support; Frederick A. O. "Fritz" Schwarz Jr., "Saving the Supreme Court," *Democracy: A Journal of Ideas*, no. 54 (Fall 2019).

32. Schwarz, "Saving the Supreme Court."

33. Schwarz, "Saving the Supreme Court."

34. John J. Binder, "The Transportation Revolution and Antebellum Sectional Disagreement," *Social Science History* 35, no. 1 (Spring 2011): 19–57.

35. Ronald Bailey, "The Other Side of Slavery: Black Labor, Cotton, and Textile Industrialization in Great Britain and the United States," *Agricultural History* 68, no. 2 (Spring 1994): 35–36: "For each decade between 1790 and 1860, the slave population increased between 25 percent and 33 percent, averaging 28.7 percent over the period. The more rapid increase in the percentage of cotton produced—which was 1500 percent over the same period—undoubtedly speaks to the more intense exploitation of slave labor, and the greater fertility of the soil as cotton production shifted and expanded into the black belt of the lower South."

36. Edward L. Rubin, "Passing Through the Door; Social Movement Literature and Legal Scholarship," *University of Pennsylvania Law Review* 150, no. 1 (November 2001): 66.

37. Census of U.S. Population, 1790–1990, Table 4, Population: 1790 to 1990, United States Urban and Rural. In 1800, 6.1% of the population, or 322,371 out of 5,308,483 Americans, lived in cities. By 1900, that number was 39.5%, or 30,214,832 out of 76,212,168.

38. Robert Hunter, *Poverty* (New York: Macmillan, 1904), vi.

39. David Graham Phillips, "The Treason of the Senate," *Cosmopolitan* 40, no. 5 (March 1906).

40. Upton Sinclair, *The Jungle* (New York: Doubleday, Page, 1906); Dan Rather, ed., *Our Times: America at the Birth of the Twentieth Century* (New York: Scribner, 1996), 222.

41. "A National Child-Labor Committee: The Announcement of Its Organization," *Charities: A Weekly Review of Local and General Philanthropy* 12, no. 16 (April 23, 1904): 411.

42. Sandra L. Colby and Jennifer M. Ortman, "Projections of the Size and Composition of the U.S. Population: 2014 to 2060," U.S. Census Bureau Current Population Reports, P25-1143,

March 2015, www.census.gov/content/dam/Census/library/publications/2015/demo/p25-1143. pdf: "By 2044, more than half of all Americans are projected to belong to a minority group (any group other than non-Hispanic White alone)."

43. Jenée Desmond-Harris, "Here's When You Can Expect Racial Minorities to Be the Majority in Each State," *Vox*, February 26, 2015, www.vox.com/2015/2/26/8109947/minority-majority -states-race. As of 2019, with a white population of 50.0 percent, Maryland, is likely to become the next minority-majority state. U.S. Census Bureau, "QuickFacts Maryland," www.census .gov/quickfacts/MD.

44. Liam Stack, "Over 1,000 Hate Groups Are Now Active in United States, Civil Rights Group Says," *New York Times*, February 20, 2019, www.nytimes.com/2019/02/20/us/hate-groups-rise.html.

45. Adeel Hassan, "Hate-Crime Violence Hit8/10s 16-Year High, F.B.I. Report," *New York Times*, November 12, 2019, www.nytimes.com/2019/11/12/us/hate-crimes-fbi-report.html; "FBI Data Shows Sharp Rise in US Hate Crimes," *The Guardian*, November 13, 2018, www.theguardian .com/us-news/2018/nov/13/fbi-data-hate-crimes-rise-us-report.

46. Zia Qureshi, "Globalization, Technology, and Inequality: It's the Policies, Stupid," *Brookings Institution Blog*, February 16, 2018, www.brookings.edu/blog/up-front/2018/02/16 /globalization-technology-and-inequality-its-the-policies-stupid: "Most dynamic economic change inevitably creates winners and losers. Globalization and technology are no exceptions. They are key forces that drive innovation, productivity, and economic growth. But they also have been important factors behind the rise in inequalities we have witnessed—with technological change playing a stronger role."

47. Leah Fessler, "How the Leader of Black Lives Matter Defines 'Power,'" *Quartz*, September 16, 2018, qz.com/1391762/black-lives-matter-co-founder-alicia-garzas-definition-of-power.

48. David Montero, "Thirty-Five Years Past a Deadline Set by Congress, Nevada Ratifies the Equal Rights Amendment," *Los Angeles Times*, March 20, 2017.

49. Darlene Ricker, "What Does Equal Rights Amendment Ratification in Virginia Mean for Its Chances?" *ABA Journal*, January 16, 2020, www.abajournal.com/web/article /era-ratification-in-virginia-doesnt-seal-its-fate-timing-is-everything.

50. John Kowal, "The Equal Rights Amendment's Revival: Questions for Congress, the Courts and the American People," *NYU Review of Law and Social Change Harbinger* 43 (2019): 141–48.

51. Proposing an Amendment to the Constitution of the United States Relative to Equal Rights for Men and Women, H. J. Res. 35, 116th Congress (2019).

52. Maryclaire Dale and Jocelyn Noveck, "AP-NORC Poll: Most Americans Support Equal Rights Amendment," Associated Press, February 24, 2020, apnews.com/article /42b93fd7386089110543f4e1827ded67.

53. Jessica Neuwirth, "Time for the Equal Rights Amendment," *NYU Review of Law and Social Change Harbinger* 43 (2019): 161.

54. Neuwirth, "Time for the Equal Rights Amendment," 162.

55. "Annapolis Convention. Address of the Annapolis Convention," September 14, 1786, Founders Online, National Archives, founders.archives.gov/documents/Hamilton/01-03 -02-0556. Original source: *The Papers of Alexander Hamilton*, vol. 3, *1782–1786*, ed. Harold C. Syrett (New York: Columbia University Press, 1962), 686–90.

56. Abraham Lincoln, Second Annual Message, December 1, 1862, American Presidency Project, www.presidency.ucsb.edu/node/202180. See Mark Tushnet, "Emergencies and the Idea of Constitutionalism," in *Constitution in Wartime: Beyond Alarmism and Complacency*, ed. Mark Tushnet (Durham, NC: Duke University Press, 2005), 40.

57. *Congressional Globe*, 39th Congress, 1st Sess. 2085 (1866), statement of Representative Perham.

58. Mark E. Brandon, "History of American Military Conflict," in *Constitution in Wartime: Beyond Alarmism and Complacency*, ed. Mark Tushnet (Durham, NC: Duke University Press, 2005), 20: "Lucas Powe notes that the United States' brief *amicus curiae* in *Brown* explicitly

invoked the relation between civil rights for blacks at home and the struggle against communism abroad." In deciding the recent affirmative-action cases, the justices emphasized a point made in the brief of defense officials, which noted the importance of racial and ethnic diversity for national security. Brief for Lt. Gen. Julius W. Becton Jr. et al. as Amici Curiae, Supporting Respondents, *Fisher v. University of Texas at Austin*, 579 U.S. ___ (2016), no. 14-981.

59. Ronald R. Krebs, "In the Shadow of War: The Effects of Conflict on Liberal Democracy," *International Organization* 63, no. 1 (2009): 191.

60. E.g., Proposing an Amendment to the Constitution of the United States Regarding the Appointment of Individuals to Serve as Members of the House of Representatives in the Event a Significant Number of Members Are Unable to Serve at Any Time Because of a National Emergency, H. J. Res. 67, 107th Congress (2001), Representative Baird; Continuity of Government Commission, *Preserving Our Institutions: The Continuity of Congress* (Washington, DC: American Enterprise Institute and Brookings Institution, May 2003), www.brookings.edu/wp-content/uploads/2016/06/continuityofgovernment.pdf.

61. Garrett M. Graff, "How Congress Failed to Plan for Doomsday," *Politico*, June 15, 2017, www.politico.com/magazine/story/2017/06/15/how-congress-failed-to-plan-for-doomsday-215266; Norman J. Ornstein, "The Constitutional Crisis That Almost Was," *Washington Post*, June 19, 2017, www.washingtonpost.com/opinions/the-constitutional-crisis-that-almost-was/2017/06/19/889cc6f2-5524-11e7-ba90-f5875b7d1876_story.html.

62. James Harvey Robinson, "The Original and Derived Features of the Constitution," *Annals of the American Academy of Political and Social Science* 1 (October 1890): 242.

63. See "The Senate and the United States Constitution," United States Senate Art and History, senate.gov/artandhistory/history/common/briefing/Constitution_Senate.htm.

64. See "Constitutional Origins of the Federal Judiciary: Talking Points," Federal Judicial Center, fjc.gov/history/talking/teaching-and-civic-outreach-resources-constitutional-origins-federal-judiciary-3.

65. Max Farrand, *The Records of the Federal Convention of 1787*, vol. 2, ed. Max Farrand (New Haven, CT: Yale University Press, 1911), 587–88, hereafter Farrand, *Records*).

66. See Vincent Phillip Muñoz, "The Original Meaning of the Free Exercise Clause: The Evidence from the First Congress," *Harvard Journal of Law & Public Policy* 31 (June 2008): 1083–1120.

67. See Georgia Constitution of 1777, Art. LXI.

68. An Act for the Gradual Abolition of Slavery, 1780 Pa. Acts. 282; A. Leon Higginbotham Jr., *In the Matter of Color: Race & the American Legal Process* (New York: Oxford University Press, 1978), 310.

69. Higginbotham, *In the Matter of Color*, 91.

70. Marvin Krislov and Daniel M. Katz, "Taking State Constitutions Seriously," *Cornell Journal of Law and Public Policy* 17, no. 2 (Spring 2008): 300. "Driven by the perception the political marketplace was captured by powerful entrenched interests, progressives working in the early twentieth century sought mechanisms to combat both legislative capture and the shirking of politicians."

71. David E. Kyvig, *Explicit & Authentic Acts: Amending the Constitution 1776–1995* (Lawrence: University Press of Kansas, 1996), 210.

72. Roger C. Hartley, *How Failed Attempts to Amend the Constitution Mobilize Political Change* (Nashville: Vanderbilt University Press, 2017), 31.

73. In 1970, voters in Colorado, Connecticut, Florida, Hawaii, Illinois, Michigan, New Jersey, Oregon, South Dakota, Washington, and Wyoming voted to reject ballot measures to lower the voting age in those states. In the following five states, voters approved such measures: Alaska, Maine, Massachusetts, Montana, and Nebraska.

74. See *New State Ice Co. v. Liebmann*, 285 U.S. 262, at 311 (1932): "It is one of the happy incidents of the federal system that a single courageous State may, if its citizens choose, serve

as a laboratory; and try novel social and economic experiments without risk to the rest of the country."

75. Robert W. Bennett, "Popular Election of the President Without a Constitutional Amendment," *Green Bag* 4, no. 3 (2001): 241; Akhil Reed Amar and Vikram David Amar, "How to Achieve Direct National Election of the President Without Amending the Constitution," *FindLaw*, December 28, 2001; Matthew Yi, "Stanford Professor Stumps for Electoral Alternative," *San Francisco Chronicle*, July 24, 2006.

76. Wilfred U. Codrington III, "So Goes the Nation: The Constitution, the Compact, and What the American West Can Tell Us About How We'll Choose the President in 2020 and Beyond," *Columbia University Law Review Forum* 120, no. 2 (March 2020): 43–66.

77. Hartley, *How Failed Attempts to Amend the Constitution Mobilize Political Change*, 87–108, describing various failed campaigns to secure an Article V convention that resulted in some accommodation by lawmakers and even courts.

78. Farrand, *Records*, vol. 1, 486.

79. Michael Vorenberg, *Final Freedom: The Civil War, the Abolition of Slavery, and the Thirteenth Amendment* (New York: Cambridge University Press, 2004), 187.

80. When the new class of lawmakers were gaveled into session in December 1865, they controlled 132 of 183 seats in the House of Representatives and 37 of 50 seats in the Senate.

81. "The Partisan Divide on Political Values Grows Even Wider," Pew Research Center, October 5, 2017, www.pewresearch.org/politics/2017/10/05/1-partisan-divides-over-political-values-widen.

82. In 2000, the margin between the popular vote winner Al Gore and George W. Bush was 0.51 percent. In 2004, George W. Bush defeated John Kerry by a margin of 2.46 percent. In 2012, Barack Obama defeated John McCain by 3.86 percent. And in 2016, Hillary Clinton edged Donald Trump in the national popular vote by 2.09 percent. Federal Elections 2000: Election Results for the U.S. President, the U.S. Senate and the U.S. House of Representatives, Federal Election Commission, June 2001; Federal Elections 2004: Election Results for the U.S. President, the U.S. Senate and the U.S. House of Representatives, Federal Election Commission, May 2005; Federal Elections 2012: Election Results for the U.S. President, the U.S. Senate and the U.S. House of Representatives, Federal Election Commission, July 2013; Federal Elections 2016: Federal Elections 2016: Election Results for the U.S. President, the U.S. Senate and the U.S. House of Representatives, Federal Election Commission, December 2017; David Wasserman, "2020 National Popular Vote Tracker," Cook Political Report, cookpolitical.com/2020-national-popular-vote-tracker.

83. "From George Washington to the President of Congress, 17 September 1787," Founders Online, National Archives, founders.archives.gov/documents/Washington/04-05-02-0306. Original source: *The Papers of George Washington, Confederation Series*, vol. 5, *1 February 1787–31 December 1787*, ed. W. W. Abbot (Charlottesville: University Press of Virginia, 1997) 330–33.

84. Thurgood Marshall, "The Constitution's Bicentennial: Commemorating the Wrong Document," *Vanderbilt Law Review* 40, no. 6 (November 1987): 1338.

85. Marshall, "Constitution's Bicentennial."

86. Stuart Taylor Jr., "Marshall Sounds Critical Note on Bicentennial," *New York Times*, May 7, 1987.

87. Marshall, "Constitution's Bicentennial," 1341.

88. Marshall, "Constitution's Bicentennial," 1341.

89. Marshall, "Constitution's Bicentennial," 1341.

Image Credits

1. Image 2 of John C. Payne's Copy of James Madison's Original Notes
   on Debates in the Federal Convention of 1787
   Library of Congress, Manuscript Division, James Madison Papers
   Microfilm Reel 28, Subseries 5F
   Library of Congress Digital ID: hdl.loc.gov/loc.mss/
   mjm.28_0270_1617
2. Elbridge Gerry
   New York Public Library, Miriam and Ira D. Wallach Division of
   Art, Prints and Photographs: Print Collection
   Wood engraving, c. 1860
   New York Public Library Image ID: 1253390
   New York Public Library Reference #: EM2678
3. George Mason
   New York Public Library, Miriam and Ira D. Wallach Division of
   Art, Prints and Photographs: Print Collection
   Etching, c. 1850–1890 (approximate)
   Albert Rosenthal
   New York Public Library Image ID: 420360
   New York Public Library Reference #: EM1113
4. The Federal Pillars
   Library of Congress, Serial and Government Publications Division
   Woodcut, *Massachusetts Centinel*, August 2, 1788
   Library of Congress Reproduction #: LC-USZ62-45591 (b&w film
   copy neg. of August 2, 1788)
5. James Madison
   Library of Congress, Popular and Applied Graphic Arts
   Etching, 92 × 122 cm

Jacques Reich, 1911
Library of Congress Reproduction #: LC-DIG-ppmsca-46744
 (digital file from original item)

6. Patrick Henry
New York Public Library, Miriam and Ira D. Wallach Division of
 Art, Prints and Photographs: Print Collection
Portrait, c. 1776–1890 (approximate)
New York Public Library Image ID: 421225
New York Public Library Reference #: EM10153

7. Senate Revisions to House Proposed Amendments to the U.S.
 Constitution
United States National Archives and Records Administration
United States Senate, September 9, 1789
National Archives Identifier: 3535588
Local Identifier: Sen 1A-C2

8. Dred Scott
Wikimedia Commons
Photograph, uncredited, c. 1857

9. Southern Chivalry—Argument versus Clubs
Digital Commonwealth Massachusetts Collections Online
Boston Public Library, Arts Department, Americana Collection
Lithograph, 14¼ × 22 in.
John L. Magee, 1856
Accession #: 11_03_000157

10. Thomas Corwin by Wilcox
Wikimedia Commons
Boston engraving
J.A.J. Wilcox, 1882, in Addison Peale Russell, *Thomas Corwin: A
 Sketch* (Cincinnati: Robert Clarke)

11. Hon. James Mitchell Ashley of Ohio, Editor of [*Columbus*]
 Dispatch & Gov. of Territory of Montana, Born 1824, Died 1896
Brady-Handy Photograph Collection, Library of Congress, Prints
 and Photographs Division
Negative: glass, wet collodion
Library of Congress Reproduction Number: LC-DIG-cwpbh-03557
 (digital file from original neg.)

12. Exciting Scene in the House of Representatives
Frank Leslie's Illustrated Newspaper via Internet Archive
Frank Leslie, February 18, 1865
Digitized by the Indiana State Library and Lincoln Financial
 Foundation Collection

13. Hon. Thaddeus Stevens of Penn.

Brady-Handy Photograph Collection, Library of Congress, Prints
    and Photographs Division
Negative: glass, wet collodion
Library of Congress Reproduction Number: LC-DIG-cwpbh-00460
    (digital file from original neg.)

14. Hon. John Armor Bingham of Ohio
Brady-Handy Photograph Collection, Library of Congress, Prints
    and Photographs Division
Negative: glass, wet collodion
Library of Congress Reproduction Number: LC-DIG-cwpbh-03570
    (digital file from original neg.)

15. The First Colored Senator and Representatives—in the 41st and
    42nd Congress of the United States
Library of Congress, Popular Graphic Art Print Filing Series
Lithograph, 28.6 × 37.7 cm
Currier & Ives, 1872
Library of Congress Reproduction Number: LC-DIG-ppmsca-17564
    (digital file from original print)

16. Nelson Wilmarth Aldrich
National Portrait Gallery, Smithsonian Institution; gift of Stephanie
    Edgell in memory of Elsie Aldrich Campbell
Painting, oil on canvas, 130.8 × 97.8 cm
Anders Leonard Zorn (1860–1920), 1913
National Portrait Gallery Object #: NPG.69.85

17. The Issue—1900. Liberty. Justice. Humanity. W. J. Bryan
Library of Congress, Prints and Photographs Division
Print
Strobridge & Co., 1900
Library of Congress Reproduction #: LC-DIG-pga-02808 (digital file
    from original print)

18. "Will You Back Me—or back Booze?" advertisement
Ohio History Connection Archives
Ohio Dry Federation, 1918
Source #: OVS 7473

19. Wayne Bidwell Wheeler
Library of Congress, Prints and Photographs Division
Photographic print
Harris & Ewing, January 5, 1920
Library of Congress Reproduction #: LC-DIG-ds-00046 (digital file
    from original photograph)

20. Elizabeth Cady Stanton and Susan B. Anthony
Library of Congress, Prints and Photographs Division

Photographic print, c. 1880–1902

Library of Congress Reproduction #: LC-USZ61-791 (b&w film copy neg.)

21. Alice Paul, full-length portrait, standing, facing left, raising glass with right hand

Library of Congress, Prints and Photographs Division

Photograph: gelatin silver print, mounted on gray board, 18 × 12.8 cm

Harris & Ewing, September 3, 1920

Library of Congress Reproduction #: LC-DIG-ds-00180 (digital file from original item)

22. The spirit from Occoquon/Allender. We shall fight for Democracy at home.

Library of Congress, Prints and Photographs Division

Drawing: charcoal, 41 × 39 cm

Nina Allender, October 6, 1917

Library of Congress Reproduction #: LC-DIG-ppmsca-69099 (digital file from original)

Library of Congress Digital ID: hdl.loc.gov/loc.pnp/ppmsca.69099

23. Ida B. Wells at the 1913 Suffrage Parade

Chicago Daily Tribune, March 5, 1913, via Wikimedia Commons

24. Emanuel Celler, three-quarter length portrait, seated, facing front

Library of Congress, *New York World-Telegram* and *The Sun* Newspaper Photograph Collection

Photographic print

New York World-Telegram and *The Sun* staff photograph, 1951

Library of Congress Reproduction #: LC-USZ62-127299 (b&w film copy neg.)

25. James O. Eastland

Associated Press

Uncredited, March 2, 1956

AP ID: 168211540761

Transmission Reference: APHS443481

26. Senator Birch Bayh Addresses a Group of Students

Senatorial Papers of Birch Bayh, Indiana University, via Wikimedia Commons

Birch Bayh Senate Office, c. 1970s

27. LBJ, McCormack, Hayden

Wikimedia Commons

Uncredited, November 27, 1963

28. African American demonstrators outside the White House, with signs "We demand the right to vote, everywhere" and signs

protesting police brutality against civil rights demonstrators in
Selma, Alabama
Library of Congress, Prints and Photographs Division
U.S. News & World Report Magazine Photograph Collection
Negative: film; 35mm
Warren K. Leffler, March 12, 1965
Library of Congress Reproduction #: LC-DIG-ds-05267 (digital file
from original)

29. Walter Fauntroy and a woman with voting rights bumper stickers
District of Columbia Public Library, Special Collections
Washington Star Photo Collection
January 1, 1975
Handle: http://hdl.handle.net/1961/dcplislandora:118015

30. U.S. Representative Martha Griffiths
Associated Press
John Rous, August 23, 1963
AP ID: 6308230264
Transmission Reference: APHS433081

31. House Black Caucus, Shirley Chisholm
Library of Congress, Prints and Photographs Division
U.S. News & World Report Magazine Photograph Collection
Photograph: safety negative; film width 35mm (roll format)
Warren K. Leffler, January 31, 1973
Library of Congress Reproduction #: LC-DIG-ppmsca-55931 (digital
file from original)

32. Activist Phyllis Schlafly wearing a "Stop ERA" badge,
demonstrating with other women against the Equal Rights
Amendment in front of the White House, Washington, DC
Library of Congress, Prints and Photographs Division
U.S. News & World Report Magazine Photograph Collection
Negative: film
Warren K. Leffler, February 4, 1977
Library of Congress Reproduction #: LC-DIG-ds-00757 (digital file
from original negative)

Index

About the Authors

John F. Kowal, a former director of grantmaking initiatives at the Ford Foundation and Open Society Foundations, is vice president for programs at the Brennan Center for Justice at NYU School of Law, where he is responsible for coordinating and guiding the organization's programs on democracy, justice, and liberty and national security. Kowal writes on issues of constitutional law and democracy reform. A graduate of New York University and Harvard Law School, he lives in New York City.

Wilfred U. Codrington III is an assistant professor of law at Brooklyn Law School and a fellow at the Brennan Center for Justice at NYU School of Law. His teaching and scholarship focus on constitutional law, election law, race, and antidiscrimination. Prior to joining Brooklyn Law School, Codrington was an adjunct assistant professor of public service at New York University's Wagner Graduate School of Public Service, an associate at DLA Piper, LLP, and a law clerk for Hon. Deborah A. Batts, U.S.D.J. A graduate of Brown University, the University of Pennsylvania's Fels Institute of Government, and Stanford Law School, he lives in New York City.

Publishing in the Public Interest

Thank you for reading this book published by The New Press. The New Press is a nonprofit, public interest publisher. New Press books and authors play a crucial role in sparking conversations about the key political and social issues of our day.

We hope you enjoyed this book and that you will stay in touch with The New Press. Here are a few ways to stay up to date with our books, events, and the issues we cover:

- Sign up at www.thenewpress.com/subscribe to receive updates on New Press authors and issues and to be notified about local events.
- Like us on Facebook: www.facebook.com/newpressbooks.
- Follow us on Twitter: www.twitter.com/thenewpress.
- Follow us on Instagram: www.instagram.com/thenewpress.

Please consider buying New Press books for yourself; for friends and family; or to donate to schools, libraries, community centers, prison libraries, and other organizations involved with the issues our authors write about.

The New Press is a 501(c)(3) nonprofit organization. You can also support our work with a tax-deductible gift by visiting www.thenew press.com/donate.